The Complete Book of Child Health

The Complete Book of Child Health

FOREWORD BY DR S. LINGAM, MD (HONS)
FRCP DCH DRCOG
EDITED BY HEATHER WELFORD

MARSHALL CAVENDISH

CONTENTS

The Complete Book of Child Health

FOREWORD

*M*y work as a paediatrician involves me in many areas of child care, from practical involvement on the clinical level to the rather more theoretical demands of academic and teaching posts and related research. Both as Consultant Paediatrician in Community Child Health and Clinical Tutor at St Ann's Hospital, London, and as Consultant Paediatrician in General Paediatrics at North Middlesex Hospital, London, I am in constant contact with a wide variety of individuals, professional or otherwise, all responsible in their different capacities for the well-being of children.

Outside the medical and nursing expertise of the hospitals and community exists a large number of people which looks after children on a day-to-day basis – specialists, such as teachers, social workers, nursery staff and play therapists, and most important of all, parents.

Everyone, especially parents who have no formal training in child care, needs to be equipped to recognise problems, of whatever severity, relating to a child's health and to determine the appropriate course of action. In the course of my work, I have had many occasions to witness how suitable action taken at the outset of an illness or accident can have a beneficial effect on the final outcome.

Illness and injury are traumatic enough in themselves, but when they happen to a young child in your care the emotional pressures to ease their suffering and 'make it better' are intense. *The Complete Book of Child Health* provides the first practical step. Detailing over 275 of the most common childhood illnesses and complaints, it addresses those problems with which we are all familiar, such as nappy rash and grazed knees, as well as the more uncommon and, therefore, potentially more worrying ones of vomiting and fever.

Importantly, not only are the medical symptoms and treatments addressed, but also the social and educational issues involved. It is as necessary to be able to cope with a child's emotional needs as with its asthma attacks, for example, and the reader will find advice on how to deal with the physical manifestations of deeper emotional problems.

One of the key concerns of parents involves the general question of what to expect as their child develops: what's normal and what's not? *The Complete Book of Child Health* is an instant reference source which highlights the key stages of development and points parents in the right direction when things go wrong, be it to apply antiseptic and a plaster, or to seek further medical attention.

In a career which has spanned over 20 years I have been witness to the many and varied medical advances made in the field of paediatrics. All the information contained in this book is compatible with the latest findings and treatments, and I am sure that as the fruits of research continue to evolve, future developments will show yet more new solutions for old problems.

As the author or editor of and contributor to a number of books and journals, and primarily as a parent of two young children, I also endorse the clear presentation of the information. Question-and-answer panels clarifying parents' most frequent worries, and helpful photographs and diagrams, complement the more detailed explanation in the main text to convey an impressive amount of information in the most accessible way. This invaluable book should fill a large gap on every family and schoolroom bookshelf.

Dr S. Lingam, MD (Hons), FRCP, DCH, DRCOG

About the Author

Dr S. Lingam MD (Hons) FRCP DCH DRCOG is a well-known paediatrician. He holds several academic and teaching posts, including that of Consultant Paediatrician in Community Child Health and Clinical Tutor at St Ann's Hospital, London, as well as that of Consultant Paediatrician in General Paediatrics at North Middlesex Hospital, London. He has written and contributed to a wide range of medical books and journals, including a child health and development diary called *It's Your Life*.

About the Editor

Heather Welford is a freelance journalist and author who contributes regularly to the health and parents' pages of a number of national newspapers. She has written several books on pregnancy, birth and childcare, including the *Illustrated Dictionary of Pregnancy and Birth* and *The Complete Mothercare Manual*. She regularly appears on television and radio and has fronted Proctor and Gamble's Pampers Trainers launch.

The Complete Book of Child Health

A comprehensive guide to childhood illnesses and medical problems – and how to cope with them

■ ABDOMINAL PAIN

See also TUMMY ACHE, APPENDICITIS

Tummy ache is a common complaint in children and can be a symptom of both physical and emotional problems – in times of stress the body automatically increases the squeezing action of the intestine.

Some emotional causes will be easy to identify – for example, going to playgroup may bring on tummy ache for a shy child. Often, however, it is difficult to tell whether the tummy ache has a physical or emotional source and you may need to enlist the help of your childminder, health visitor or doctor.

SYMPTOMS

The tummy ache will differ in location, timing, type and severity, from mild discomfort to severe colic, depending on what is wrong. Check for any related symptoms such as un-usual bowel motions, problems with urination, vomiting, rashes or signs of infection. They often give a clue as to the cause of the tummy ache.

CAUSES

A number of illnesses can cause abdominal pain – measles and

Severe 'tummy ache' can be most distressing for a young child.

mumps for example – but it can also be caused by food allergies, a swallowed object, asthma, worms, reaction to medication and indigestion among others. In children especially, seemingly unrelated infections and complaints such as tonsillitis or middle-ear infection, can also be the cause of great pain in the abdomen.

If the pain is accompanied by vomiting or diarrhoea it may be caused by an infection of the bowel or, if severe, by appendicitis.

WHAT IS THE ABDOMEN?

The abdomen is often called the 'tummy'. It contains a great number of organs:

- stomach
- liver
- pancreas
- spleen
- a huge network of blood vessels
- kidneys
- ureters
- bladder
- nearly all the sex organs in girls (in boys the testicles descend to a position outside the body before birth)
- approximately 10m of intestines
- peritoneum (abdominal lining)

TREATMENT

Tummy pains often go away by not eating, because food is hard to digest when the abdomen is tight. A hot drink may give comfort and relief.

Don't assume, however, that the strength of the pain matches its seriousness. A severe pain could be nothing more than wind, while a mild pain with no obvious cause might be something more serious.

It is always better to be safe than sorry. If the pain seems serious, is recurrent, continues for a long period or simply worries you, you must consult your doctor.

CONSULT YOUR DOCTOR IF

- you suspect the problem is emotional but cannot easily identify it
- there are related symptoms such as vomiting, the tummy is swollen and tender to the touch, motions contain blood or tar-like substances
- the pain lasts for more than 6 hours, or is recurrent
- you are at all worried about your child's health in general

■ ABRASIONS

An abrasion is an area of skin that has been torn away by force. Light scuffing of the skin is called a graze, but sometimes a large, deep area of skin is affected and the abrasion is more like a burn.

Abrasions sound less dramatic than cuts, but can be much more painful as millions of tiny nerve endings are exposed. They can become full of dirt or grit, so the main problem in dealing with them is to get rid of dirt and prevent infection.

Small cuts can be caused by anything sharp; glass, razors, kitchen knives or even paper. Even small cuts tend to gape slightly, so to help them heal faster they should be taped up in some way.

HOW THE BODY COPES

The body is very efficient at dealing with wounds, at staunching the bleeding, fighting infection and healing the skin, but it often needs help. Whenever the skin is broken, blood vessels may be torn and germs can enter the body, so all wounds need to be cleaned.

When the bleeding has stopped and the wound is clear of infection, a fibrous scab begins to form. The scab shrinks over the next few days and forms an extremely strong bond between the cut surfaces.

TREATMENT

How to stop bleeding You can staunch the flow of blood from a small wound quite quickly by pressing on it with a clean pad – a folded bandage or clean handkerchief. Hold it there without lifting it off or changing it for about five minutes, until the bleeding stops.

Cleaning the wound It is essential to clean every last bit of dirt out of any contaminated wound, as dirt causes infection. Antiseptics can reduce the risk of infection but are no substitute for thorough cleaning.

A small cut or graze will quickly heal with a plaster and a cuddle.

Wounds can be cleaned with a variety of liquids, from mild antiseptics to soap and water. Tap water is quite clean, so you don't have to boil water in a kettle before using it to clean the wound.

If you use any antiseptic other than hydrogen peroxide BP, which is safe to use straight from the bottle, make sure you dilute it as instructed. By using too strong a solution you may damage the tissues and make the wound even worse.

Removing grit If there is any grit in the wound, a quick scrub with a clean brush under running water will get it out, but it will no doubt hurt. If you cannot remove all the grit, seek medical advice. Larger pieces of grit can be picked out carefully with tweezers.

Brush any last bits of dirt from the wound with small swabs of gauze or cotton wool soaked in antiseptic. Use separate swabs for each stroke, and always work from the centre of the wound outwards.

Applying a dressing A small, clean cut can be covered with a plaster. A larger cut will need a non-stick dressing held in place with a cotton or crêpe bandage.

Never use cotton wool or the woolly side of lint against the wound, as it will stick to it and harm the scab when removed.

ACTIONPLAN

- As a rule, wet weepy wounds should be covered, while dry wounds should be left uncovered in clean conditions.
- Never pull a dressing off quickly. If it has stuck to the scab, soak it off in a mild antiseptic solution.
- Don't make too much fuss of your child if it is just a small cut or graze; a calm manner and a 'kiss to make it better' is sufficient.

ANTHEA SIEVEKING NETWORK

■ ABSCESSES

An abscess is a gathering of pus around a local infection. It can range from a simple stye, pimple or boil, to a serious tooth abscess or an internal abscess.

The pus shows that the body has been fighting the infection, and there are bacteria in it as well as the infection-fighting white blood cells.

SYMPTOMS

The earliest sign of a skin abscess is a red, hot, painful swelling which becomes filled with pus. Nearby glands may become swollen and tender.

Internal abscesses are often accompanied by fever and a feeling of being generally unwell.

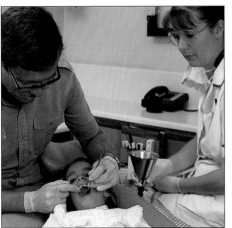

A gumboil needs to be treated by a dentist if the trouble persists.

TREATMENT

Sometimes abscesses clear by themselves, without any discharge. A hard, painless lump remains which will disappear after a few months.

A small, superficial abscess may either discharge pus on its own accord, or may be 'lanced', that is safely drained with a sterile needle, heated to red-hot and then allowed to cool.

An abscess can be drawn using a dry dressing covered with magnesium sulphate paste, which is available from any chemist. Larger abscesses need medical attention and may require a small incision made under local or general anaesthetic. Antibiotics are often given to ensure there is no danger of the infection spreading.

YOUR QUESTIONS

Q What is a gumboil, and how can I treat it?

A A gumboil is a relatively harmless abscess caused when infection gets between the tooth and gum. A mouthwash of hot, salty water will relieve discomfort and help to rupture the abscess so that the pus can drain away. In all cases, see your dentist.

■ ACCIDENTS

see also FIRST AID and SHOCK

Every child will suffer bumps, grazes and other non-serious injuries. Your reactions to these minor accidents are important, for your child will learn from your example. Too much sympathy for a small cut will suggest that trivial injuries are more serious than they really are, or a good way of getting attention.

Similarly, if you can remain calm and unruffled in the event of a more serious injury, pain and fear will hopefully be controlled as the child follows your example. A serious accident can be anything from a broken bone to loss of consciousness. See under Checklist and separate headings for further explanations.

CHECKLIST

HOW SERIOUS IS IT?

HEAVY BLEEDING Wipe the blood away gently. Fold a clean cloth into a pad and use it to press as hard as you can on the wound until the bleeding stops. Do not remove the pad unless you have to change it. Bandage firmly in place. A wound which bleeds heavily may need stitches. Take your child to the Accident and Emergency department of the hospital.

SCREAMING This is often due to panic. Examine the child for signs of injury. If nothing is obviously wrong — an arm or leg twisted, for example — move each limb to test for pain.

If the child will not let you touch a particular part of her body, something may be sprained or broken. If you suspect a break (limb cannot be used and is badly swollen), take the child to hospital.

UNCONSCIOUS CHILD Check for breathing and heartbeat. If either is absent, tell the emergency operator, when telephoning for help (see ARTIFICIAL RESPIRATION).

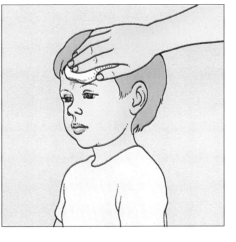

1. *With a clean pad, apply pressure to the cut to stop bleeding.*

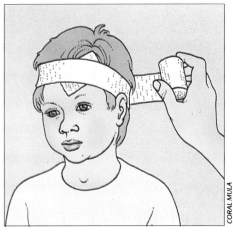

2. *Cover the wound with a dressing and bandage in place.*

MINOR INJURIES

Small cuts do not need antiseptics. Use only clean water to bathe wounds and don't overdress the wound – a plain adhesive dressing is adequate, if a dressing is needed at all. Make sure it is not air tight, so the wound can 'breathe'.

SERIOUS ACCIDENTS

Remember always to remain calm and try to reduce your child's fear. Keep first aid to the minimum, and call for the experts. Look after the child until medical help arrives.

Watch the child carefully in case she develops shock symptoms (see SHOCK). A child in shock will turn very pale and the skin will be cold and clammy to the touch. Do not attempt to give her anything by mouth. Keep her warm and quiet, and make sure she can breathe freely.

When help arrives, if your child needs treatment, stay with her while it is given. This will show that you approve of what is happening, as well as providing reassurance for your child in a strange and potentially frightening situation.

■ ADENOIDS

These are lymph glands and therefore part of the body's defence system, like the tonsils. Also like the tonsils, they sometimes become swollen and infected themselves.

Adenoids are situated at the back of the nose, just where the air passages join those of the back of the mouth. Their purpose is to trap bacteria in air on its way to the lungs.

Adenoids are present from birth, are most obvious from the age of one to four, then generally reduce in size before puberty.

SYMPTOMS

If the adenoids become swollen from infection, they can interfere with the flow of air through the nose so that the child has to breathe through the mouth. This may cause heavy snoring when the child is sleeping. The child's speech may sound nasal and he may

Swollen adenoids cause breathing problems and make a child listless.

become very thirsty, because breathing through the mouth makes it very dry.

A yellowish discharge – quite different from a normal runny nose – may be seen. The child will sniff to try and clear it, but the discharge tends to run down the back of the throat and make the child cough. The cough is particularly obvious at night and is a typical sign of infected adenoids.

The child may seem listless and slow simply because breathing is such a chore.

EAR INFECTIONS

Enlarged adenoids may also obstruct the Eustachian tubes, which connect the passages of the nose to the inner ear. Fluid cannot drain from the ear into the throat, ear infections can occur and hearing may be impaired.

TREATMENT

Gargling is of no use. Take your child to the doctor, who may prescribe a decongestant, antihistamine or antibiotic to clear the infection.

If these prove ineffective, the adenoids may be removed in a simple operation under general anaesthetic. (The tonsils are sometimes removed at the same time.) Symptoms often go away of their own accord, however, when the child is about six.

■ AIDS

AIDS is acquired immune-deficiency syndrome caused by the HIV virus. At present, scientific consensus is that AIDS is inevitably fatal – it supposedly lowers the body's immunity to a range of diseases, as a result of a progressive weakening of the immune system by the HIV virus.

HOW AIDS IS CONTRACTED

HIV is transmitted in one of three ways: unprotected sexual intercourse with an infected person; through transfusion of infected blood or injection with an infected needle; or from mother to child. It appears possible for an HIV-positive mother to transmit the virus to her baby via her breast milk, though some research has indicated that breastfeeding may help build up the defences of a baby born to a mother with HIV/AIDS. Mothers who may be HIV-positive need to seek advice from an HIV counsellor when deciding on which feeding method to use.

PRECAUTIONS

In the UK and all Western countries, blood intended for transfusion is routinely screened, so the risk of you or your child contracting the HIV virus this way is virtually non-existent. If you and your family travel outside Europe, and you need an injection, make sure a clean, sterile needle and syringe are used. It's possible to buy special travel packs for this purpose.

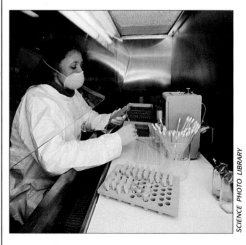

A technician prepares blood samples for an AIDS test.

■ ALLERGIES

see also ASTHMA, ECZEMA, FOOD ALLERGY, HAY FEVER, RASHES

An allergy is a sensitivity to a substance which does not normally cause people any discomfort or harm.

Allergies can affect almost any part of the body and be caused by a vast range of natural and artificial substances from pollen to nail varnish.

An allergic reaction is seldom life-threatening, though symptoms can be dangerous and are at the very least very uncomfortable for the person who suffers them.

CAUSES

There are many things that may cause allergic reactions. These are known as allergens and include certain foods and food additives, dust, pollen, feathers, fur and insect bites.

Allergies do tend to run in families so, if you are a sufferer, it is possible your child may inherit the condition.

SYMPTOMS

As a rule, the symptoms of an allergy tend to show up in those parts of the body which are exposed to the allergy-causing substance, or allergen.

For example, an airborne allergen such as pollen has its severest impact on the eyes, nose and air passages, causing a runny nose, sneezing and breathing difficulties.

Food allergies can reveal themselves through swollen lips, stomach upsets or diarrhoea.

An allergy to metal will usually affect the skin and an allergy to rubber could result in a rash where, for example, elastic in underwear

ANTHEA SIEVEKING NETWORK

Pollen, the allergen that causes hay fever, affects the eyes, nose and air passages.

COMMON ALLERGIES

Condition	Allergen	Symptoms	Treatment	Prevention
Asthma	Dust mites Animal hair Pollen Some foods and food additives	Difficulty in breathing Severe cough Shortness of breath on minimal exercise	Relievers – bronchodilator Preventers – anti-inflammatory agents (steroids, Intal)	Keep house dust-free Avoid pollen, keep clear of allergic foods
Contact dermatitis	Contact with allergen, eg. jewellery, chemicals in washing powder	Itchy, blistery inflammation	Steroid creams given on doctor's prescription	Avoid contact with allergens
Eczema	Some foods, especially cow's milk, flour, eggs, possibly some seafoods	Rash on hands, face, neck, arms and legs; looks like scaly skin	Antihistamine tablets and creams given for skin condition	Take diet precautions to avoid allergen
Food allergy	Could be caused by almost any food – more commonly milk, flour, eggs; also strawberries, shellfish, nuts, some food additives	Upset stomach and general nausea, acute reaction produces swollen tongue and lip, as well as diarrhoea. If food is absorbed into bloodstream, it can cause eczema and migraine	Antigen avoidance diet – avoiding causative foods. Dietician's help required to prevent malnutrition	Breastfeeding reduces the tendency for allergy
Hay fever	Pollen; may react to just one pollen or to several different types	Sore, itchy eyes, runny or stuffy nose, prolonged sneezing	Prick test to confirm allergy. Course of injections and antihistamine tablets to relieve symptoms	Keep windows shut Listen to pollen count on weather report Avoid open air Wear sun glasses
Migraine	Sometimes caused by cheese, red wine, yeast extract, but not only caused by an allergy	Blinding headache	Elimination diet test if complaint due to food allergy	Avoid allergen foods
Urticaria	Foods Handling certain plants Hot and cold water	Red, irritating swelling with white in centre	Skin condition treated with antihistamine pills, if necessary	Avoid the allergens

came into contact with a child's skin.

If an allergen gets into the bloodstream, however, it can cause reactions almost anywhere. This is particularly true of food allergens, which can cause rashes, eczema, asthma, hyperactivity or migraine.

TREATMENT

Allergies are difficult to cure, yet they can appear and disappear without warning.

It is often difficult to identify the exact cause of an allergic reaction. If it is very obvious what is causing the problem, your child is lucky: you can just try to eliminate the allergen. For example, strawberries can be avoided, cat hairs cleaned up, a washing powder changed.

Your doctor will advise you on the best way to find out which allergen is affecting your child, and may recommend medication to soothe the symptoms. There are many brands of antihistamines, whether given as cream, drops, drugs or lotions, which may be prescribed for the child.

YOUR QUESTIONS

Q My son of four is allergic to cats and touching them brings him out in a nasty rash. Will he grow out of this problem or will it remain with him for life?

A Either is possible. Children who suffer from allergic rashes or eczema often do grow out of those problems though they may suffer from other forms of allergy (asthma for example) when they are older because they have a basic tendency to be allergic.

Q My daughter's little friend sometimes has bad eczema. I can't help wondering if it is infectious?

A Eczema is an allergy and, like all allergies, is not catching nor can you pick up any of the symptoms.

■ ANAEMIA

This is a disorder of the blood affecting the red blood cells which carry oxygen from the lungs around the body, where it is needed for energy. It occurs when the haemoglobin (red pigment) level in the blood cells falls.

CAUSES

Anaemia can be caused by blood loss or by certain rare diseases affecting the bone marrow, but it is most commonly caused by lack of iron in the diet. Children who are fussy about their food, pregnant women and the elderly are particularly prone to anaemia of this type.

SYMPTOMS

The classic symptoms of anaemia are pallor of the skin, especially at the fingertips and around the eyes, lack of energy, dizziness and sometimes fainting fits. Children may also have poor appetite, show signs of irritability, become breathless after exertion and may be very easily tired.

TREATMENT

Simple iron deficiency anaemia can be diagnosed by a blood test and is normally treated with a course of iron tonic, tablets or injections.

PREVENTION

Iron is needed to produce haemoglobin, so eating an iron-rich diet, including meat (especially liver and kidneys), oily fish and eggs will contribute to good health.

If your child is a fussy eater and you don't want to turn mealtimes into a major battle scene, consult your pharmacist. He will be able to recommend a pleasant tasting and safe tonic to supplement your child's diet. You should try and persuade him to take this. If you are satisfied that he is having the right diet, do consult your doctor about a blood test.

LYNDON PARKER

Lack of iron in the diet is the most common cause of anaemia. Eating any of the above foods will help.

YOUR QUESTIONS

Q My mother suffers from anaemia and I worry that my children might have inherited it. Is this possible?

A It depends on the type of anaemia. The common form is that caused by lack of iron, which is not inherited but some rare anaemias such as thalassemia are passed on. In cases like pernicious anaemia the disease is not transmitted but other family members are more likely to be affected.

Q I didn't know anaemia could be so serious. How does this happen?

A Growing bodies need iron and anaemia tends to diminish the appetite which makes the problem worse.

Q What is sickle cell anaemia?

A Sickle cell anaemia is an inherited abnormality of the blood common in people of African origin. If the oxygen level of the blood falls too low, the red cells become twisted into a sickle shape. It is a serious condition but can be controlled.

■ ANTIBIOTICS

Antibiotics are so commonly prescribed for adults that it is easy for us to forget that they are powerful drugs and should never be taken unless the doctor has prescribed them for a particular disease or illness.

HOW THEY WORK

Antibiotics can kill bacteria and are useful against throat infections, tonsillitis, abscesses and septic fingers. They are vital in the treatment of bacterial meningitis. They have no effect on viruses.

Side-effects Some children may be

Always finish a prescribed course of antibiotics, even if your child seems to have recovered.

A. SIEVEKING/NETWORK PHOTOGRAPHERS

YOUR QUESTIONS

Q Can antibiotics be taken during pregnancy? Will they harm my unborn child?

A No medication should be taken during pregnancy unless your doctor advises that it's necessary for your health or that of your baby. However, if you need to take some antibiotics, your doctor will prescribe ones which are considered safe for use in pregnancy.

WATCHPOINTS

- Never give your child antibiotics unless prescribed by a doctor.
- Go back to the doctor if you're worried about side-effects.
- Always finish the prescribed course.
- Lock medicines away.

allergic to penicillin and may come out in a rash if they are given it. You should always tell the doctor if you know this is the case with your child.

Many antibiotics can cause side-effects ranging from indigestion and diarrhoea to [rarely] deafness and loss of balance. It may be worth putting up with some discomfort for the sake of the cure, but if you are at all worried, go back to the doctor.

There are many different kinds of antibiotics and your doctor should be able to find one to suit your child.

Taking antibiotics These drugs work very quickly but, although your child may feel better within a few hours, you must make sure he finishes the whole course prescribed. This is extremely important, otherwise the bacteria causing your child's illness can build up a 'resistance' to the antibiotic or the infection might persist.

■ APPENDICITIS

The appendix is a narrow, tube-like piece of gut resembling a tail, which is located at the end of the large intestine. The tip of the tube is closed; the other end joins on to the large intestine. It can measure up to 10cm (4in) long and about 1cm (⅝in) in diameter.

For reasons that are not understood, the appendix may become inflamed and this condition is called 'appendicitis'.

In most cases, the start of appendicitis can be recognized by general 'tummy' pains that will not go away. Always have these checked.

CAUSES

It is thought that recent emphasis on healthy eating may make appendicitis less common; the modern Western diet, high in refined and processed food, may be causing blockages in the intestine because of its low fibre content. Pips, fruit stones and other foreign bodies that have been swallowed accidentally can also block the appendix.

THE 'GRUMBLING' APPENDIX

Some doctors believe it is possible to have recurrent attacks of appendicitis, each lasting a day or two. The theory is that the appendix gets inflamed, the intestines nearby close round it to wall off the infection. If the inflammation clears up, the intestines may still be left stuck around the appendix. This can restrain the normal movement of food around the system, resulting in colicky (griping) pains which may then be felt in the appendix region during normal digestion. This 'grumbling' appendix may settle by itself but always seek medical advice if you are worried.

SYMPTOMS

Acute appendicitis is a common emergency which virtually always requires surgery to cure.

The early symptoms are not easy to distinguish from any other form of tummy ache. Pain which may come and go in a colicky fashion is felt around the tummy button.

After six to 12 hours, the symptoms will change as inflammation builds up around the appendix. Your child will feel more pain but the site of maximum pain varies and often the child has to press her own stomach to establish exactly where it hurts most. The most common site is two-thirds of the way along a line between the tummy button and the right hip. Your child will feel increasingly ill and may vomit as the infection progresses.

The right leg muscle may feel stiff, so the child naturally bends the leg up to gain relief. Stretching it down again will produce pain.

Appendicitis — Recognizing the Symptoms

Early symptoms	Action	Later symptoms GET MEDICAL HELP AT ONCE
Colicky (griping) pain in stomach	Give mild painkiller eg. Paracetamol	More pain in appendix area (right lower abdomen)
Loss of appetite	Try a soothing drink: warm milk or weak tea	Pain may move up or down from tummy button
Constipation	Use a hot water bottle. Do not give a laxative – this will be harmful, causing painful contractions of the appendix and increasing the chance of perforation	Slight rise in temperature eg. 37.5°C (99.5°F)
		Child may lie with right leg flexed up; stretching it down produces pain
		Slight increase in pulse rate
In children, a respiratory infection may imitate appendicitis.	Tell the doctor about your child's tummy symptoms – just in case	Nausea
		Vomiting – usually once only
		Foul-smelling breath

DIAGNOSIS

It is particularly difficult to diagnose appendicitis in children as they may develop symptoms and signs which are not caused by an inflamed appendix but, most probably, by a chest infection or glands in the tummy. In this case, the child may have other symptoms as well, such as a sore throat or maybe a cough. Even if your child seems to have obvious signs of tonsillitis, it is very important to tell the doctor if he or she has complained of tummy ache.

WHEN TO SEE THE DOCTOR

If the pain has continued for a whole day or night, becoming increasingly severe, or if the child is feeling awful and unable to get up, it is clearly time to seek medical help and you should do so without delay.

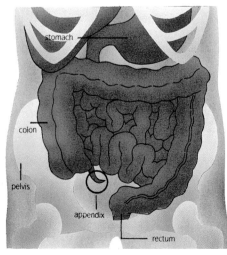

An inflamed appendix is easily removed through a small incision.

JOHN HUTCHINSON

TREATMENT

Do not try painkillers and soothing drinks at this stage. An operation may be urgently needed and the stomach must be empty at least four hours before an anaesthetic.

COMPLICATIONS

If the problem is neglected, the situation can become dangerous as the appendix could burst. This is unlikely to happen within the first 24 to 36 hours of the illness, but the risk increases considerably if it is left much longer than this. If the appendix does perforate, an urgent operation will be necessary.

The risks of neglecting appendicitis are so much greater than the risks of an unnecessary operation that the surgeon will *always* operate.

If the symptoms are inconclusive, however, the child may be put to bed and kept under observation. If things do not improve, the appendix will be taken out. The operation is quite simple and takes less than half an hour to perform.

CONVALESCENCE

Once the stitches have been taken out, the scar still has to heal so you will be advised to keep the child quiet for a while. Don't worry about the scar – in a few weeks it will be visible only as a reddish mark and later will fade to a hardly noticeable line.

After the operation, the bowels stop working for a short time and it may be a few days before they return to normal. The child may also develop severe wind, which is a good sign as it shows that things are getting back to normal.

■ APPETITE

There is an important difference between appetite and hunger. When you want to eat something because it looks good, smells nice and tastes delicious, your appetite is working. When you want to eat something because your stomach is rumbling and you feel in need of food, then your hunger drive is working hard.

It is quite an important difference because it is not hunger that makes people overeat, but appetite. In the same way, your child might actually

YOUR QUESTIONS

Q I prefer not to eat during the day, and just to have an evening meal when my husband comes home from work. Is this a suitable routine for my three-year-old daughter, too?

A No, not really. As a general rule, it is better for children to have several small meals throughout the course of the day, rather than one big meal, and to avoid too many 'snack' foods such as biscuits and sweets.

be hungry and need food but his appetite will stop him eating if, for example, he is ill.

Developing an appetite When a baby is born, one of the very first things he or she feels is the need for food. In most cases, this need is satisfied with milk and it is only later that babies will learn what foods they really like.

With this learning, the growing child's tastes are gradually developed. It is because human beings are so complex that we have such different appetites and likes for different foods.

How appetite works An organ below the brain, the hypothalamus, collects signals from the intestines, blood, mouth and stomach. When enough signals have been collected, the part of the hypothalamus concerned with eating tells the brain that the body has had enough and eating stops. This all sounds very simple but, unfortunately, it does not always work like this.

EATING PROBLEMS

Many children develop erratic appetites, suddenly refusing to eat a particular food or developing a taste for one food to the exclusion of anything else.

Eating patterns may also vary — some children are happy with a routine of two or three meals a day, while others prefer several small snacks. Some children need a lot of

Children often take a sudden dislike to food for no apparent reason.

IAN WEST/BUBBLES

Q My little boy is just getting over a nasty cold and doesn't want to eat anything. What can I do?

A Try to tempt him with foods he really likes — though avoid indulging him with sweets and ice-creams.

If this fails, try one of the food substitute drinks you can buy from the chemist, which will provide adequate nourishment.

food, others require much less.

Eating patterns can also be affected by illness or emotional stress.

TREATMENT

Unless your child is ill, little harm can come from short phases of fussy eating or appetite loss, though it's important he has enough to drink. Adequate fluids are essential to keep a child's body working.

Never force a child to eat — this will simply make an issue of every meal — but make sure all the food you offer him is as tempting and nourishing as possible.

■ ARTIFICIAL RESPIRATION

see also SMOTHERING, STRANGULATION, SUFFOCATION

If your child has stopped breathing, you must use artificial respiration to get air into her lungs as soon as possible.

The chances of saving your child's life will be greatly increased if you have been taught the proper technique by a qualified instructor.

Do not carry out the technique on anyone who is breathing normally.

WHEN BREATHING STOPS

Your child's breathing could be stopped for a number of reasons:

● The nose and mouth could be covered by a pillow, the airway between mouth and lungs could be blocked by food or a small object that has gone down the 'wrong way', the child's own tongue, vomit or broken teeth.

● The airway can also be closed by swelling caused by swallowing a scalding or corrosive liquid or by an insect sting.

● Any constriction of the neck, as in strangulation, has the same result.

● Sometimes the airways close up naturally, because of noxious gases or medical conditions such as bronchitis or asthma.

● Breathing may also stop if the child has inhaled smoke, gas or dust.

● Electrocution, pesticides and damage to the spinal cord can all stop your child's respiration, as can an overdose of drugs such as barbiturates or morphine which is why lockable bathroom cabinets are essential.

WHAT TO LOOK FOR

Whatever the cause, the outcome of asphyxia (suffocation) is the same. If obvious, remove the cause of the difficulty immediately as breathing may start. Breathing may become deeper and more rapid while the

FIRST THINGS FIRST

Do not rush in and start artificial respiration without thinking first. What has stopped the breathing?

● **If the room is filled with gas,** open the windows.

● **In the case of electrocution,** switch off the electricity supply before you touch the child.

● **If the child is choking,** turn her upside down and slap her on the back.

● **If the child is drowning,** rescue him from the water, and start artificial respiration immediately.

Always use the 'kiss of life' or mouth-to-mouth unless there are severe facial injuries, in which case use the Silvester method (see box – page 18).

SILVESTER METHOD

The Silvester method should only be used when facial injuries prevent you giving the 'kiss of life', if strong poison has been swallowed, or if copious vomiting means that mouth to mouth would push vomit into the lungs.

1 Place the child on her back with a cushion or blanket under her shoulders.

2 Bend the head well back to clear air passages.

3 Kneel facing the child's feet with your knees either side of her forehead.

4 Grasp the child's wrists and cross them over on her lower chest.

5 Rock your body forward and keeping your back straight, press down lightly and steadily, using your body weight for two seconds.

6 Lean back on your heels, bringing the child's arms up and out in a wide arc until her hands are on the ground with arms fully extended. Hold for three seconds then repeat until breathing begins.

CORAL MULA

ARTIFICIAL RESPIRATION

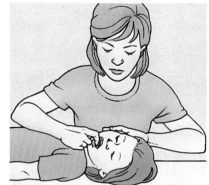

Remove any obstructions from the mouth and throat. Tilt the head back with one hand holding the chin to get maximum access to the airway.

Pinch nostrils, take a deep breath and after firmly sealing your lips over the child's mouth, blow steadily and gently into the lungs until the chest rises.

Take your mouth away and watch the chest sink. Give five more breaths quickly. Continue at a normal breathing pace until her breathing starts again.

If you are giving the 'kiss of life' to a small baby, place your mouth over his mouth and nose together when you gently breathe out. Repeat at three-second intervals.

pulse speeds up as heart and lungs fight to get oxygen into the blood.

As the blood's oxygen content falls, the skin turns blue, particularly in the face, neck, hands and feet.

The child eventually loses consciousness and may go into convulsions. Finally, respiration fails and the heart stops beating.

EMERGENCY

The brain will suffer irreversible damage if it is totally starved of oxygen for more than about four minutes. Everyone should know how to give artificial respiration — *when an accident happens, there will be no time to look it up in a book.*

CHECKLIST

• Think before you start — should you open windows, switch off electric current? (See FIRST THINGS FIRST.)

• Give the first six breaths as quickly as possible to get a surge of oxygen into the blood and prevent irreversible brain damage.

• Do not blow too hard — remember a child's lungs are smaller than your own. Watch her chest fall before breathing again.

• Keep a close watch on the heart. Check for a pulse at the sides of the neck just below the corner of the jawbone.

• If there is no pulse, start cardiac massage (see entries under 'C').

• Keep going — the child's life may depend on it.

• When the child starts breathing, place her in the recovery position on her stomach with her head to one side.

■ ASTHMA

see also ALLERGIES

About one child in ten develops asthma at some stage in childhood. It is one of the commonest chest problems in children and can cause endless misery unless it is treated properly. Fortunately, many children outgrow it and those who don't need not be protected as they were in the past. With proper treatment, they can lead as full a life as others.

Asthma involves a severe narrowing of the bronchial tubes which lead from the windpipe into the lungs. They carry the oxygen we breathe in into all parts of the lungs and the carbon dioxide we breathe out back into the windpipe. The narrowing of the tubes results from the contraction of the muscle lining them. The difficulty is most obvious when breathing out. For this reason, asthmatics tend to inhale in short gasps and breathe out with a long wheeze — a result of the effort required to breathe against the obstruction.

CAUSES

Asthma is brought on by a number of different factors, ranging from breathing polluted air to emotional upset, which makes it rather a complex problem to treat. The most common cause of asthma is the body's own release of histamine in response to breathing substances as varied as house dust containing house mites, animal fur, pollen and fungal spores among others. In some children, asthma is an allergic reaction to substances such as these.

Viral or bacterial infections of the throat can cause similar irritations which is why asthma tends to get worse with chest infections or colds. We also know that emotional upsets or anxiety may occasionally worsen an asthmatic condition, though how this happens is not clear. Cold air or vigorous exercise, especially running, can also trigger an attack. Certain drinks, foods and preservatives can also produce an asthmatic response, though rather than being a straight-forward allergic response, it is often the result of the body's sensitivity to certain substances. Again, the mechanism involved is still not fully understood.

SYMPTOMS

The typical asthma attack is characterized by a sudden shortness of breath and wheezing, which is sometimes accompanied by coughing. The bringing up of phlegm is not a prominent part of the attack and suggests that the child may also have bronchitis. Generally speaking, asthmatics are more prone to chest infections caused by a failure to clear the lungs fully. Some children develop a hunched look which is brought about by the constant effort of breathing.

In some cases, the onset of asthma follows a seasonal pattern as the pollen count rises. This pattern is often accompanied by irritations to the nose and sneezing, which we usually refer to as hay fever.

Of course, allergies to house pets and the house mite will occur all through the year as the allergen is constantly in the air. The house mite is particularly keen on living in warm places, like beds, and for this reason

An aerosol inhaler will help relieve an asthma attack.

JANINE WIEDEL

YOUR QUESTIONS

Q My father had asthma when he was a child and I have it, too. Can it run in families, and will I pass it on to my son?

A Asthma does tend to run in families, though the inherited link is not yet fully understood. So there is a possibility that your son will inherit the condition.

asthma attacks often seem to happen at night. In fact, coughing at night in children may well be a result of this allergy and is often an early sign of the onset of asthma.

TREATMENT

The treatment given for asthma largely depends on the type of asthma and the severity of the attacks, but it is broadly divided into two: emergency treatment for severe attacks, requiring a visit from the doctor or admission to hospital and everyday self-medication to prevent an attack occurring, which is known as prophylactic or preventive treatment and can be carried out at home. **Emergency treatment** is designed to bring relief as rapidly as possible by getting drugs quickly into the system to help the body's natural chemicals which dilate the bronchial tubes to do their job. These drugs can be given by injection or inhalation but they are most effective when given by a 'nebuliser'. This device is powered by electricity and produces a fine mist or spray of the drug dissolved in sterile water. The mist can be inhaled through a mouthpiece or a mask. Your child should obtain relief in a few minutes. In the case of a very severe attack, the doctor will often give a steroid drug to be taken by mouth for a few days. This reduces inflammation in the lungs and prevents the attack from developing any further.

Regular treatment is designed to prevent severe attacks and to allow the sufferers to lead as normal a life as possible. Asthmatic children may be tested for allergies so that steps can be taken to avoid the allergen that upsets them, although in the many cases where the child is allergic to house dust mites, this is difficult.

PREVENTIVE DRUGS

A number of prophylactic drugs are available which cut short the abnormal response that asthmatics suffer. These may be taken by mouth or by inhaler three or four times a day. These drugs all considerably reduce the risk of asthmatic attacks.

Steroid drugs can also be taken in very low dose by inhaler to prevent asthmatic attacks. Since they are inhaled directly into the lungs, there is practically no absorption of the drug into the system and negligible risk of any side-effects.

In addition to a prophylactic drug, most asthmatics use a bronchodilator from time to time. Usually this is given in the form of an aerosol inhaler. Children may be given it as a liquid medicine. These preparations will help to relieve an asthma attack; prophylactic drugs can do nothing once an attack has started.

PREVENTION

Most asthmatics will have their condition worsened or even triggered by everyday substances and once the cause is identified, the only course is to avoid it by, for instance, keeping the house as clear of dust as possible, avoiding petrol fumes and tobacco smoke, certain 'reactive' foods and also sudden exertion and emotional stress. However, it is difficult to be specific as what affects one asthmatic may not actually have any effect on another. But it is accepted that regular, controlled exercise rather than sudden exertion does have a beneficial effect and all asthmatics should be encouraged to take as much regular — but strictly controlled — exercise as they can manage.

REGULAR TREATMENT

Although there is no absolute cure, regular treatment with prophylactic drugs will do much to reduce the occurrence of attacks.

HOW TO KEEP DUST MITES DOWN

- use lightweight curtains and wash them every six weeks
- clean carpets thoroughly with a vacuum cleaner – daily where possible
- use pillows and duvets containing artificial fibres rather than feathers. Use synthetic sheets, pillowcases and duvet covers and wash them every week
- vacuum clean the mattress about twice a week and turn it at regular intervals
- dust with a damp duster
- put all clothes away in a wardrobe

YOUR QUESTIONS

Q My two young children are both asthmatic, but they are full of energy and vitality. Should they be allowed to play sports?

A Of course! However, some sports may be more likely to bring on an asthma attack than others, so make sure your children keep their inhalers handy at all times. Of all sports, swimming is the least likely to cause an asthma attack.

ASTHMA: ITS CAUSES AND PREVENTION

Although an asthmatic condition must always be treated and never ignored, there are some preventive measures that can be taken.

Causes	Preventive measures
Allergens breathed in: pollens, house dust, feathers, fungal spores, animal hair.	Keep house as dust-free as possible. Use foam pillows; avoid animals.
Allergens in food: can include milk, eggs, strawberries, fish, tomatoes.	Isolate allergen with doctor's help and then avoid it.
Drugs: can include penicillin, vaccines, anaesthetics.	Identify and avoid drugs that cause allergic reaction.
Infections: common cold, some viral infections, sinusitis, bronchitis.	Keep your child away from people with colds. Make sure he has a balanced diet, adequate sleep and takes moderate exercise.
Irritants breathed in: paint fumes, tobacco smoke, air pollutants, cold air.	Keep your child away from fumes. Keep him indoors when it is cold.
Psychological changes: stress, emotional disturbance.	Reduce or eliminate causes of stress; stop your child worrying.
Trigger mechanisms: physical exertion; sudden changes in temperature.	Make sure your child approaches exercise in a relaxed way and avoids sudden exertion and temperature changes.

■ ATHLETE'S FOOT

Athlete's foot is an annoying and unpleasant fungal infection. Fortunately, it usually responds well to treatment and can be prevented fairly easily. It is not very common in small children, but anyone in the family can get it and pass it on if precautions are not taken.

CAUSES

People who suffer from sweaty feet are particularly prone to athlete's foot and the infection can be aggravated by wearing airless, plastic shoes which prevent the feet from breathing. Care should always be taken in drying the feet thoroughly.

The fungus lives on dead skin shed from the moist, sweaty areas between the toes. However, it may also inflame and damage surrounding areas of live tissue which is when the discomfort starts.

SYMPTOMS

The first signs of athlete's foot are irritation and itching between the toes followed by the skin beginning to peel. The feet may smell too.

In bad cases, painful red cracks,

PREVENTION

• Wash your child's feet daily with soap. Clean any dirt from under the nails and between the toes.

• Dry between each toe thoroughly with your child's own towel. Do not let anyone else use this towel.

• Dust the feet with antifungal powder. To prevent re-infection, put powder in the child's shoes as well.

• Make sure your child has clean cotton or wool socks every day. Avoid nylon socks and plastic shoes. Put your child in open shoes if her feet feel sweaty.

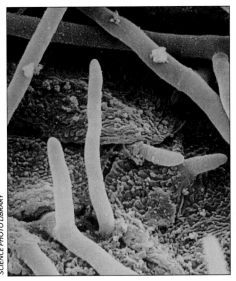

SCIENCE PHOTO LIBRARY

Athlete's foot is caused by a fungus on the surface scales of skin. This electron micrograph shows the branching filaments of the fungus, which feeds on the protein keratin *in skin and hair, and also causes ringworm.*

known as fissures, appear between the toes. In more severe cases the toe-nails can even be affected, becoming either soft or brittle as the fungus invades them.

TREATMENT

Modern antifungal creams and powders are very successful in the treatment of athlete's foot. These need to be applied daily until two or three weeks after the symptoms have disappeared.

Where the infection is severe and the nails have been affected, your doctor may prescribe a medicine to be taken orally which is effective within a few weeks. To prevent re-infection however, it is necessary to dust your child's feet, socks and shoes daily with antifungal powder.

■ AUTISM

Autism is a rare and distressing disability, but specialist teaching and a constructive approach can do much to help autistic children.

The word 'autism' is used to describe an extremely complex form of

learning difficulty. It is taken from the Greek word 'autos' and means being turned in upon the self.

Autism, also known as Kanner's syndrome, has been a recognized — that is to say medically classified — condition for 45 years. Today, it is believed that autism cannot be exactly separated into a category of its own. Many children possess autistic features who cannot be said to have Kanner's syndrome. Such children still need the specialized education essential to the truly autistic, though 20 years ago they would have slipped through the diagnostic net.

SYMPTOMS

What most parents usually notice first in their young autistic child is the inability to look others in the eye – an autistic child tends to look past the shoulder of whoever is speaking to them in a way which, if he or she were older, might well be thought impolite.

In fact, this puzzling aloofness is only the tip of the iceberg. As the toddler develops, the parents slowly realize that he or she is unable to fully participate in any of the normal social activities of the family and this can be very distressing.

TANTRUMS

An autistic child's fits of screaming and tantrums far outdo in length and volume those of even the most violent normal toddler. This is at least partly because autistic children, while seeing and hearing normally, appear to be unable to make sense of what they see and hear. Their everyday world becomes terrifying.

Nor is there any refuge in the world of the imagination. The autistic toddler does not develop 'pretend play' – a box remains a box and can never be transformed into a garage, a dolls' house or a fort.

EFFECT ON SPEECH

Abnormalities of language vary from total muteness (inability to speak) to a literal, pedantic use of words. An autistic child, asked, 'What do you do if you cut yourself?', might answer 'I bleed!' instead of 'I ask Mummy for a plaster'. Echolalia — repeating the question instead of answering it — is frequent.

STRANGE RESPONSES

Autistic children also have misplaced fears. They may be scared of harmless objects such as a garden rake but not register fear when there is real danger. This is probably connected to their inability to make sense of what they hear and see.

Then there is a fascination with bright lights, or with strange objects such as bits of broken plastic or elastic bands. Additionally, an autistic child may well show a disturbing indifference to heat and cold — being capable, for instance, of stewing in a hot bath without showing any reaction. Strangest of all, perhaps, are the odd body movements — grimaces, arm or hand-flapping and jumping or springing from one foot to the other.

Many autistic children possess what are known as 'islands of normality'. These islands of normality usually affect activities where the development of language and certain other skills are not necessary — such as music, maths or art. A child who is incapable of uttering a single spontaneous word may be a near genius at mathematics or have an extraordinary memory.

These islands of normality have even led parents of young autistic children to believe that they had an exceptionally gifted child, putting all other oddities of behaviour down to the quirks of genius, until the increasing number of 'quirks' eventually disillusioned them.

A SHELTERED LIFE

Other autistic children may develop a certain amount of useful speech and acquire many practical skills, but cannot tolerate the whirl of everyday modern life.

Whilst they will always need to live in a sheltered environment, they are, however, capable of making important contributions to the success of that environment and of living full lives themselves.

At the other end of the scale there are those who are so severely disturbed that their parents never had much doubt. In the most severe cases, these children can turn a normal home to wreckage — tearing clothing, curtains, bedding and even turning their rage on to themselves.

CAUSES

The cause of autism is not known. Over the years, many theories have been suggested but none have been proved conclusively.

TREATMENT

Until the cause of autism is found, it is unlikely that there will be a cure, although special teaching can do a lot to help the autistic. Most autistic children remain handicapped for life. Very rarely, a sudden easing of the symptoms occurs, usually when the child has been severely affected in the first instance although no-one knows why this should be so.

TEACHING AUTISTIC CHILDREN

There cannot be one single teaching method or technique to be applied to

A school for autistic children (left) has to cater for a wide range of abilities and usually offers a number of learning programmes.

Obsessive play (below) is a common autistic feature and may alternate with tantrums, hyperactivity or a total lack of interest.

all the children (like Braille for the blind or sign language for the mute). Different abilities and degrees of autism have to be catered for in individual learning programmes.

Language problems are given constant attention since they are linked with the problems of behaving properly and learning to think. Parents have an important role to play here too. It is essential that all those engaged in teaching the child, at all levels, should themselves speak simply and in short sentences.

The child's lack of natural interest, motivation and concentration demand the teacher's careful organization of all daily situations and fairly constant supervision.

AUTISTIC CHILDREN AT HOME

It is very important that parents should be closely involved in the work and techniques of the school. Autistic children are unable to transfer the training they have received in one environment to another, so parents need to be familiar with the methods used in the school if the training is to be constant.

BAD BREATH – see HALITOSIS

■ BANDAGES

Bandages are available in a variety of sizes and shapes and can be made from any cloth-like substance such as calico, linen, cotton, muslin, crêpe, flannel or even paper.

A good chemist's shop will stock those illustrated here.

Triangular bandages can be used as a whole cloth to hold a dressing in place or as a sling.

Roller bandages are rolls of open-weave cloth of different widths for varying parts of the body. Their advantage is that they cannot easily be applied too tightly, but they are more difficult to secure.

Types of bandage
Roller bandages (1) and crêpe bandages (2) are essential items in your first aid kit but ideally it should include a triangular (3) and tubular bandage (4) too. Also keep a stock of sterile dressings (5). The easiest ways to secure bandages are adhesive tape (6), fabric strapping (7) or safety pins (8).

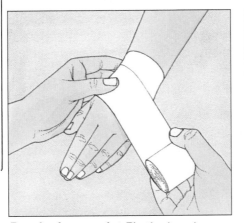

Bandaging a wrist *Fix the bandage round the wrist and take it diagonally across the back of the hand, round the palm and under the fingers.*

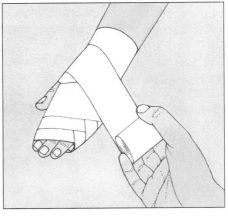

Carry the bandage across the top of the fingers to the little finger, round the palm again and across the back to the wrist. Continue until the hand is covered, and secure.

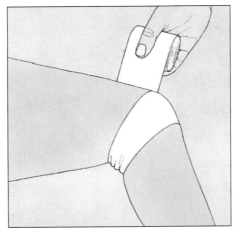

Bandaging a knee *Start from the inside of the knee and make one straight turn, carrying the bandage over the knee cap and right around the leg.*

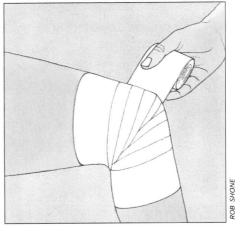

Take the bandage round the thigh, then round the calf. Continue turns, covering a little more each time. Finish off with a spiral turn just above the knee.

ROB SHONE

CHECKLIST

Bandages are a vital part of first aid, and can be used for many different purposes:
• to hold a dressing in position and give added protection
• to prevent movement of an injured part of the body
• to stop bleeding or reduce a swelling by applying pressure
• to give support
• to hold a splint in position

Crêpe bandages are the most popular type of bandage. Their elastic strength makes them easy to apply and ensures that they stay firmly in place. Care has to be taken not to cut off the blood supply by bandaging too tightly. Release the pressure immediately if you suspect this.

Tubular bandages are used to bandage fingers or limbs with the aid of a special applicator.

SECURING BANDAGES

Adhesive tape is the easiest way of securing bandages. However, as children often pull and tug at them, it is better to use small elastic bandage clips, a small safety pin (through the outer two layers) or a reef knot when tying the ends of a bandage.

TIGHT BANDAGING

Any bandage that is applied too tightly will cut off the blood supply to the injured area and may cause permanent damage. If the bandage isn't loosened or is left for too long, gangrene may develop.

To test for good circulation in a bandaged limb, press one of the nails. The skin beneath should go white immediately and, when released, the blood and the pink colour of the nail should return within two seconds.

Do not use bandages if the area requires regular observation, if a limb is broken or if the child is seriously injured and you have called an ambulance to take her to hospital.

◼ BAT EARS

Some children may have ears which protrude at an angle from the head rather than lying flat against the skull. This is a purely cosmetic condition which does not affect hearing ability. If your child is very self-conscious about his ears, try to reassure him. In some cases, a minor operation can

be performed. In small babies, the ears may appear to stick out but later lie flat as the baby 'grows into them'.

◼ BED-WETTING

At some point between the ages of two and four, most toddlers manage to stay dry through a whole night. No two children are the same however; some may take longer to achieve this milestone.

A sudden regression to bed-wetting is often an indication that your child is worrying about something.

Staying dry has more to do with bladder size and family traits than anything else. A toddler's bladder may not be large enough to hold the overnight build-up of urine. Boys are more prone to bed-wetting than girls, and the tendency seems to run in families.

If your child is still wetting by the age of five, ask your doctor to check there is nothing wrong physically. He may suggest ways of encouraging your child to stay dry — or prevent you trying things that could make the problem worse.

The vast majority of children simply grow out of wetting the bed. Half of all the children who are still doing it at five have stopped by the age of

YOUR QUESTIONS

Q I had to bandage my daughter's leg which since seems to have swollen up. How can I tell whether the bandage is too tight?

A Elasticated bandages are the best ones to use because they allow for the swelling which accompanies most injuries. If the bandage gets too tight, you will be able to see swelling above and below it. If the area below your child's bandage seems blue or white and if she complains about it feeling painful and numb, the bandage could be blocking off the blood supply, and should be loosened immediately.

Protruding ears do not affect your child's hearing. Do reassure him if children try to tease him about it.

seven. Only a few are still wetting the bed at puberty – and at every stage, help is available with training, via your family doctor.

CAUSES

Bed-wetting sometimes afflicts a child who has already successfully reached the dry night stage. In this case, stress is very probably the cause. Common reasons for stress in toddlers are the arrival of a new brother or sister, starting a new school, or even illness.

If your child suddenly starts to wet his bed again, find out what is worrying him and try to minimize the problem. Indulge him, let him behave a bit babyishly – some children revert to thumbsucking or demanding a bottle for example, when a new baby arrives. Don't let him know you are bothered about the bed-wetting until he is used to the new situation, or you may end up in a vicious circle.

Bear in mind that stress may also affect a child who has not yet quite managed the dry night stage and may be what is preventing him from getting there.

■ BEE STINGS

Bee stings can cause severe pain and, for the very young, the old and those prone to allergies, are potentially the most dangerous of insect stings in this country. Most other insect stings cause only minor irritation that can be cooled with a cold compress or calamine lotion. A bee sting requires a little more care.

SYMPTOMS

A bee always leaves its sting behind. So, if your child is stung, always first suspect a bee if you have not actually seen the insect and look for the black sting which may still be embedded in his skin. The puncture area around a bee sting is surrounded by a blanched area and then a reddish area, usually swollen.

Bee stings can be dangerous and extremely painful. Even a professional beekeeper has to take elaborate precautions when handling bees.

TREATMENT

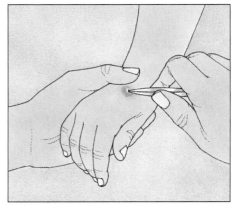

Gently pull the black sting out with a pair of tweezers if it is still embedded in the skin.

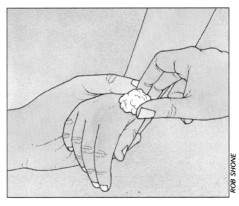

With a clean cotton-wool pad, apply some alkaline solution to the puncture area.

Either gently scrape the sting away with a clean finger nail or ease it out with a pair of tweezers, without squeezing the attached poison sac.

The venom of bee stings is acid. Treat the puncture area and surrounding swelling with a counteracting alkaline solution from your pharmacist. Then make your child rest and watch for any signs of shock.

If your child is stung more than once at the same time, his body will have a lot of poison to cope with, which may make him very ill. He may suffer from breathing difficulties or signs of shock such as faintness, a shallow rapid pulse and sweating. This severe reaction is known as *anaphylactic shock.* Take him to a doctor immediately.

PREVENTION

• If there is a bees' nest in your attic or near your house have it removed by an expert as soon as you spot it.

• Don't allow your child to approach a swarm of bees, or play close to flower beds where there are bees.

STING IN THE MOUTH

A sting in the mouth can also be serious as any swelling might impair breathing. Give the child a mouth-wash of one teaspoon of bicarbonate of soda in a tumbler of water, then make him suck an ice cube. To reduce the swelling of the tongue or throat, put a cold soothing compress on your child's neck. Take him to a hospital emergency unit immediately, and also the dead insect if you can find it.

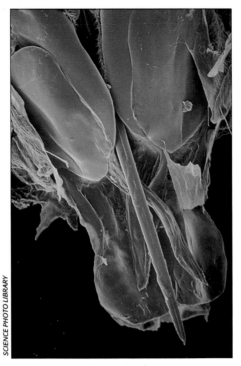

An electron micrograph of a bee sting and the two glands, one of which carries poison to hurt humans and paralyse other prey.

YOUR QUESTIONS

Q Will it help if I give para-cetamol for pain relief if my son is stung by a wasp?

A Paracetamol won't do any harm but local remedies such as a soothing ointment would probably relieve the pain better. The pain should soon subside. If the sting remains very itchy, give antihistamine tablets.

Q Is there a soothing ointment I can apply to insect stings?

A Try dabbing the affected area with a cream recommended by your pharmacist. Alternatively, apply a cold compress to the area as soon as possible.

Common bites and stings

Source	Prevention	First aid	Later treatment
Jelly fish	Do not bathe in water known to be frequented by jelly fish.	Get child to shore and pick off pieces of jelly fish with sandy hands. Cleanse the area stung, and apply antihistamine cream.	Seek medical help, especially for the sting of Portuguese Man of War.
Mosquitoes	Wrap up after dark. Avoid stagnant water. Burn a mosquito coil by the bed. Apply insect repellent.	Apply antihistamine cream, or surgical spirit; cologne or cold water will do if these are not available. Repeat as necessary.	Avoid scratching. Take antihistamine tablets if swelling is severe.
Ants	Do not sit on uncovered grass or disturb ants' nests. Wear an insect repellent.	Treat them with bicarbonate of soda paste or dilute ammonia.	None is usually necessary.
Ticks	Do not sit on grass used normally by sheep or cattle. Keep dogs and cats free of ticks.	If the tick is embedded in the skin use petroleum jelly, oil, alcohol or petrol to loosen its grip and remove it with tweezers.	Soothe tick bites with calamine lotion.
Fleas	Keep dogs and cats free of fleas.	Treat bites with calamine or antihistamine cream. Badly affected children should see a doctor.	Use a suitable powder on animals, clothes, bedding and cushions.

■ BIRTHMARKS

A birthmark is any noticeable 'abnormality' such as a swelling or mark on the skin of a baby at birth or appearing soon after. There are several types of birthmark which can be pink, red, mauve, pale brown, or a light skin colour.

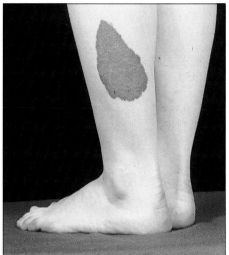

Birthmarks may look distressing but are almost always harmless.

CAUSES

Birthmarks are caused by one of three irregularities in the development of part of the skin: groups of abnormal blood vessels, concentrations of pigment or colour producing cells, or defective groups of cells that form the skin surface.

If your baby is born with such a

YOUR QUESTIONS

Q I am expecting a baby and have heard that birthmarks can be caused by a shock during pregnancy, Is this true?

A No – this is an old wives' tale. There is no evidence that birthmarks are caused by any external influence in pregnancy, be it emotional or physical. In fact, there is no known cause at all for any birthmarks.

mark, or develops one soon after birth, don't worry. Birthmarks are quite harmless, and often fade away in early childhood.

TEMPORARY MARKS

Reddish birthmarks are caused by abnormal blood vessels and are of two main types. Most of them are temporary and disappear quite quickly.

If your baby is born with a flat red patch on his eyelid, mid-forehead or nape of his neck near the hairline, he has the most common birthmark — the 'stork's beak' mark. It is called this because the marks occur just

YOUR QUESTIONS

Q Can my baby's strawberry birthmark give rise to side-effects or complications?

A The strawberry mark is one of the most common and may become sore and ulcerated, but this can be prevented with careful washing and powdering.

Q If I have a difficult labour and birth will it give my baby birthmarks?

A There may be some red marks on the skin if there was pressure during the birth, but these soon fade, usually within a week.

where a stork's beak would hold the baby when delivering it! Similar pale pink marks elsewhere on the body are called salmon patches.

In reality these stains are caused by wider than normal capillaries (the smallest of blood vessels) just beneath the top layer of skin. Although they will show up more when your baby cries, stork or salmon marks require no special treatment and these areas of skin are no more tender than anywhere else.

In most cases, the facial marks disappear after a few months. Marks on the neck, however, sometimes

remain throughout life, but they are usually covered by hair.

STRAWBERRY MARKS

The second most common kind of birthmark is raised, soft and reddish, resembling a strawberry. It is due to the blood contained in extra capillaries and occurs in ten per cent of babies. It may not be present at birth, especially if the baby is premature. Either there at birth or appearing a few days later, it starts off as small as a pin prick, then grows rapidly for six to nine months before gradually fading away. You can tell when it is beginning to disappear as the colour in the centre develops into pale patches which grow to fill the centre; at the same time it becomes flatter. Eventually the mark disappears altogether.

Should the surface of a strawberry mark be damaged and ooze blood, apply pressure to stop the bleeding as a surface break will leave a scar.

PERMANENT MARKS

The least common type of red birth mark does not fade away. It is dark red or purple and consequently is called the port wine stain. It is usually flat, although its surface may be knobbly, and it varies from a few millimetres across to several centimetres. It is most common on the upper trunk and face.

The mark is almost always harmless, but when it occurs on the face, some parents are concerned that the child may suffer from self-consciousness or teasing as a result. Consult your doctor who will give you the best advice for the condition.

BROWN BIRTHMARKS

Brown birthmarks, those caused by concentrations of pigment-producing cells, are also permanent.

Café-au-lait patches are flat, pale brown marks from 2–20cm across, usually on the trunk. Ten per cent of babies are born with these harmless marks.

Moles, whether black or brown, are collections of pigment cells and are uncommon in babyhood. They tend to appear later in childhood,

BIRTHMARKS

Type	Temporary or permanent	Treatment
Salmon patches (small pink marks)	Usually fade rapidly and disappear by age of one year.	Rarely need treatment
Stork marks (red marks on nose)	Usually fade rapidly and disappear by age of one year.	Rarely need treatment
Port wine stains (large red patches, often on face)	Remain indefinitely	Cosmetic camouflage. Can be cut out but may require skin graft. Directing X-rays on to blemish. Laser treatment. Occasionally tattooing. Freezing.
Capillary naevi (red stains under skin, caused by small blood vessels)	Permanent	Carbon dioxide snow may be used to destroy small ones. Radium therapy; large ones may be cut out. Cosmetic camouflage.
Strawberry marks	Usually temporary	90 per cent disappear without treatment. Occasionally steroid drugs are prescribed.
Café-au-lait patches	Remain indefinitely	Not necessary
Moles	Usually develop in childhood and adolescence, and unless removed are permanent. Rarely become malignant in later life.	Large ones should be removed. Moles that develop later in childhood do not usually require treatment. If they enlarge, they may be removed.
Epidermal naevi	Present at birth or soon after. Permanent.	Can be cut out, but sometimes return. Freezing effective in some cases.

TREATMENT

Special creams are now available to camouflage such marks. Applied like base make-up, they come in tones to suit your child's skin. Although putting on the make-up will take several minutes each day, it will ease any embarrassment.

Permanent, unsightly blemishes may be completely cut out and if they are not too big the wound will heal over. Unfortunately, surgical removal of large marks would usually necessitate a skin graft which may itself be unsightly.

YOUR QUESTIONS

Q Can birthmarks vanish by themselves without any treatment?

A The strawberry mark, and another common blemish known as the stork mark, usually do, but others tend to be permanent.

Q Is it true that moles can be dangerous?

A A very few moles can become what is known as malignant in later life. Signs that a mole is malignant are: sudden increase in size, bleeding, continuous itching, development of further moles nearby and darkening in colour of the mole.

If you suspect a mole of being malignant, see a doctor *immediately*. Removal of the mole usually prevents any problems developing.

especially in adolescence and are usually harmless although large ones may be removed. If they change size or shape, or bleed, consult your doctor. There is no need for anxiety should your baby be born with any moles, they too will generally be harmless. However, they do have a slight risk of becoming malignant later on, so it is wise to keep an eye on them and inform your doctor of any changes.

■ BITES

Families often live with a wide range of domestic animals which are all capable, under provocation, of biting children. Bites may be superficial needing only minor first aid and a cuddle, or they may be serious enough to require stitches.

Dogs make particularly good pets for children but it is important to teach your child to handle all animals gently and with confidence. Most animals will only bite if frightened or hurt.

TREATMENT

Where an animal bite has not broken the skin, gently wash the area and apply a soothing ointment. As long as there is no swelling or other symptom of infection, this will be sufficient along with loving attention.

Rabies is common in some countries, so if your child is bitten outside the UK you must take him immediately to a doctor to see if he needs protection against rabies. Most bites will heal over without any problems, although deep gashes could leave a scar.

PREVENTION

Teach your child to respect all animals and to treat them with caution and kindness. Don't let him use pets as toys; a mauled kitten, puppy, or even hamster can bite if handled roughly. Your child should never approach other people's pets until he has permission to do so and is sure that the animal is friendly. Some dogs are not used to children and might react to sudden movement. On the other hand, don't make your child afraid of dogs. A nervous screaming child can make a normally calm dog aggressive. Dog bites are the most serious danger to children. Make sure that you can control your own dog, under any circumstances; if necessary, take it to obedience classes. Never leave your child to play unsupervised with any animal even if you are told it is safe.

SNAKE BITES

Different countries have different species of snakes. Some are harmless, others are poisonous and require urgent action. The only poisonous snake in Europe is the adder, which is about 75cm long when fully grown, with a broad head. It may be grey, yellow or reddish brown with a black zigzag along its back.

Although the adder's bite is rarely fatal to an adult it will cause swelling and pain as well as possibly sweating and vomiting which can make a child seriously ill.

• If your child is bitten by a snake, wash the wound, but do not suck out the venom.

• Comfort your child, treating him for shock if necessary.

• Rush him to the nearest casualty department.

• Don't let him walk as this will move the venom around the body and make it worse.

IN AN EMERGENCY

• If the skin is broken, clean the wound, then take your child to the doctor, as an infection could occur and cause complications.

• Check that your child's tetanus immunization is up-to-date – he could need a booster.

• If the bite is deep or you cannot stop the bleeding, take your child to the hospital immediately in case he needs to have stitches.

YOUR QUESTIONS

Q My son was bitten by a dog. Should I take him to a doctor?

A In the UK and other countries without rabies, animal bites should be seen by a doctor if the skin is broken, as an infection could occur. The doctor may give a tetanus injection. With a severe cut stitches may be needed. However, if the skin is unbroken after a bite, cleaning the skin and applying soothing ointment are all that is necessary so long as no swelling or other symptoms of infection develop. In countries where rabies exists, medical help for animal bites should be sought immediately.

Q When I was on holiday last year, a mosquito bite on my arm swelled into a big lump. Does this mean that I am allergic to mosquitoes?

A It may mean that the bite you had became infected and healed by itself, or it may mean that a mild allergic reaction occurred. If you use an antihistamine cream it will help to counteract such a reaction. Where a swelling becomes larger than expected following a bite or sting, it is a good idea to see your doctor. Infections can be dangerous, and allergies can get worse as time passes, and may require special care.

OTHER BITES AND STINGS

There are several kinds of insect, especially during the summer months, which can give unpleasant bites or stings and of course you may encounter jellyfish and so on while on holiday. Most will not be serious – unless the victim has an allergic reaction – though they can be painful. See the chart under **BEE STINGS** for more information.

■ BLACK EYE

See also BRUISES

In the rough and tumble of everyday life, energetic young children can suffer all kinds of bumps and bruises, including black eyes. Although alarming, they are rarely serious.

S Y M P T O M S

The first sign of a black eye is a yellowing of the tissues around the eye, which will gradually turn black. There may also be rapid swelling, even to the point where the eye is almost closed. The swelling should go down in a couple of days.

C A U S E S

The most common cause of a black eye is a direct blow to the eye area. The skin here is thinner and more easily damaged than on the rest of the face, so a blow to, say, the eyebrow or cheekbone could cause the skin around the eye to discolour and swell.

SCIENCE PHOTO LIBRARY

Black eyes are one of the hazards of an active childhood. A blow to the eye area causes bleeding beneath the skin's surface which shows through as a discolouration of the tissues.

T R E A T M E N T

No treatment is usually necessary. If, however, you are not sure of the cause of a black eye or if the blow to the eye area was severe, take your child to your doctor or a hospital casualty department.

YOUR QUESTIONS

Q My son has a black eye. Might his eye be damaged?

A The eyes are set into bony sockets to protect them from injury, so a black eye seldom involves damage to the eye itself, only bruising to the surrounding tissues. Rarely, what looks like an ordinary black eye is caused by a fracture at the base of the skull, but then the bruising usually shows beneath *both* eyes. Seek hospital treatment immediately.

■ BLEEDING

See also ACCIDENTS

However badly your child is bleeding, your first priority is to make sure he or she is still breathing and the heartbeat is present. Then check for foreign bodies in the wound. Small pieces of gravel or dirt can be wiped off, but anything larger may be plugging the wound and stopping further bleeding. Do not attempt to remove it (see **FOREIGN BODIES – BANDAGING THE WOUND** below).

BLEEDING FROM THE EAR

Make the child comfortable with her head tilted towards the injured side. Do not put anything inside the ear to stop it bleeding as this could cause further damage. Cover the whole ear with a sterile dressing and secure with tape or a bandage. Watch for any signs of shock which may develop. Take him to the doctor as quickly as you can. If your child is not too distressed, do your best to find out what caused the bleeding to save time at the doctors.

FOREIGN BODIES – BANDAGING THE WOUND

After controlling the bleeding with pressure on either side of the wound, cover very gently with sterile gauze. Build up a layer of pads or cotton wool around the foreign body until you reach at least its own height. Do not pull the gauze tight over the object. Secure dressing firmly by bandaging either side of the object. Bandage once over the object only if you have built up the dressing round it.

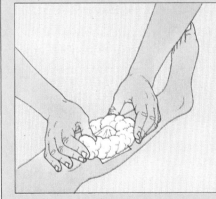

CORAL MULA

If part of the embedded object sticks up from the dressing, take care that nothing touches it.

Pass one turn of the bandage over the object only if the pads are built up to its height.

CONTROLLING BLEEDING

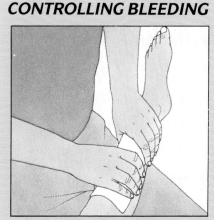
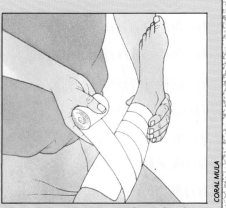

Direct pressure on a wound through a clean pad is the best and most effective way to control severe bleeding.

If the injured part can be raised and supported above the level of the heart, the bleeding will be more easily controlled.

1. Raise injured limb above level of heart. You may need to lie the child down.

2. Apply direct pressure to the wound with thumb or fingers, ideally through a clean dressing. Press the edges of the wound together if necessary.

3. If an object is sticking out of the wound, press around it, not on it. Maintain the pressure until you see a lessening in the flow of blood.

4. Cover wound with a sterile dressing large enough to overlap the wound.

5. If blood starts seeping through, place another dressing on top of the first one. Bandage in place. Do not try to use a tourniquet unless you have expert knowledge.

6. Treat for shock, if necessary (see ACCIDENTS, SHOCK) and seek medical help at the nearest hospital.

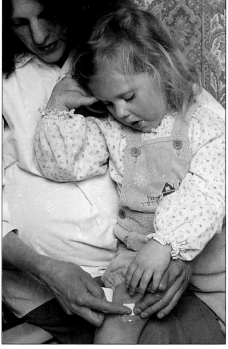

SCALP WOUNDS

The scalp bleeds very freely, so scalp wounds generally look much worse than they are. Control the bleeding by applying pressure through a pad and take the child to the doctor to check for concussion or possible fracture as soon as possible. Just because your child is still conscious does not mean that he is not concussed.

NOSEBLEEDS

Nosebleeds are quite common. If your child has a nosebleed, sit him on your knee with his head forwards over a bowl. Loosen any tight clothing around the neck and pinch the soft part of the nose for about ten minutes. Your child will need to stop crying before he can breathe through his mouth, so comfort him as much as you can. If the bleeding has not stopped after ten minutes, apply pressure again for another ten minutes. If the nose continues to bleed after 30 minutes, take your child to a doctor. Do not let him run around or blow his nose for about four hours after the bleeding has stopped.

BLEEDING FROM THE EYE

Do not attempt to remove anything which may be embedded in the eye.

Lie your child on his back, supporting his head. Keep him as still as possible. Place a sterile dressing or pad over the closed eye. Secure with tape or a bandage. Take him to the nearest hospital.

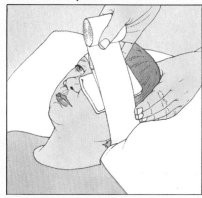

If his eye is bleeding, reassure your child and cover the eye before going to hospital.

IMPALEMENT

If your child falls on to railings or spikes and impales himself, do not attempt to lift him off. Support the weight of his body and limbs. Tell whoever phones the emergency services to give all the details so they can bring the equipment to cut the child free. This will normally involve the Fire Brigade. While waiting for the emergency services to arrive, keep the child as calm and as still as possible to prevent him from injuring himself any further.

AMPUTATIONS

If a child has lost the end of a finger or toe, for example, the doctors may be able to sew it back in place if hospital attention is received quickly enough. Control the bleeding as described on page 31, but take extra care not to damage the stump as you press. Pressure immediately above the wound rather than directly on it will help, though it may be less effective. Put the severed part in a clean plastic bag. If possible, wrap the bag in some material and put it in a container of ice. Make sure that the ice does not come into direct contact with the severed tissue. Get to hospital as quickly as possible.

EMERGENCY

INTERNAL BLEEDING

If you suspect internal bleeding, you must get your child to hospital as quickly as you can. It is not easy to diagnose, so play it safe and go to the hospital if you note any of the following symptoms:

• Shock after a violent injury but no sign of blood.

• Pattern bruising — the imprint of clothes can be seen in the bruise.

• Blood coming out of the mouth (especially bright, frothy blood), or the anus or passed in the urine.

• Severe swelling round an injury.

• Sudden severe pains in the chest or abdomen.

Internal bleeding can result from a number of causes including broken bones, crush injuries or simply a hard blow to the body, though it can also occur with a penetration injury. Tell the doctor if you know or suspect what the cause could be.

■ BLISTERS

Blisters can be extremely painful, but if left alone, most will heal by them-selves. Should one become infected, medical advice should be sought.

CAUSES

Blisters are most commonly caused by friction, for instance new shoes or walking long distances can chafe tender skin on the feet.

All types of burn, including sun-burn, may result in blistering of the skin. Sunburn blisters tend to be small and numerous; the skin will peel a few days later. Tiny blisters may form around a bite or sting.

Diseases such as chickenpox pro-duce small, extremely itchy blisters over large areas of the body.

SYMPTOMS

The common friction blister causes feelings of heat and pain, and by the time your child complains of these, the blister will have formed.

Blisters from stings and bites arise more slowly and cause itching and swelling of the surrounding skin. Chickenpox begins as small dark red pimples which within a few hours turn into blisters resembling droplets of water. Where there are a lot of blisters but no other symptoms, the cause is more likely to be eczema.

DANGERS

Ordinary blisters are rarely danger-ous, but in all types of blister there is a danger of infection. Once the blis-ter is broken, bacteria can enter and this will delay healing or spread infection. Try to stop your child scratching itchy blisters — this may take some patience.

TREATMENT

Never burst a blister unless it is really painful or very large. Small blisters usually heal on their own while large blisters usually burst themselves.

To treat a friction blister cool and clean the area. If the blister is small, then cover it with a plaster. If it has been caused by new shoes, pad the area with cotton wool.

Medical treatment is required for blisters caused by infection.

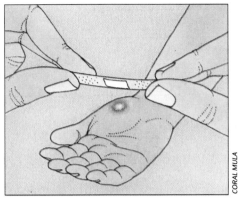

CORAL MULA

Once a blister has been broken or pierced, it very easily becomes infected. Rinse away any dirt under running water and apply a little mild antiseptic. Keep it covered with a plaster until it has healed.

PREVENTION

How to avoid blisters on feet:

• Make sure your child's shoes fit well. Too tight a shoe causes press-ure while too loose a shoe allows the foot to slide about.

• Make sure he has suitable shoes for walking or playing active games. Trainer style shoes are best as rigid shoes will rub against his feet.

• Choose soft socks without large seams. Cotton socks allow the foot to 'breathe' and sweat to evaporate.

• Try to avoid plastic shoes.

YOUR QUESTIONS

Q Should I pop the blister on my daughter's heel?

A Large blisters may be a little more comfortable if the fluid is drained with a sterile pin or needle but unless these blisters are really uncomfortable, they are best left, protected by a plaster.

Q My little boy has a blister at the side of his mouth, but there's no sign of a burn. What could it be?

A It is most likely a 'cold sore' caused by a virus. The doctor may prescribe an anti-viral cream.

■ BLOOD POISONING

The term 'blood poisoning', or septi-caemia, describes a condition caused by the spread of an infection in the blood. Since the discovery of antibio-tics, blood poisoning has become relatively rare.

C A U S E S

Any minor infection allows some bac-teria to escape into the bloodstream but the body's natural defences can

Even minor cuts should be cleaned to prevent the spread of infection.

usually cope.

Some major infections — of the kidneys, for example — can cause the bacteria to breed very fast as the child's resistance is already low.

S Y M P T O M S

If your child has a cut or boil which is healing slowly, seems reddened or weepy, ask your doctor's advice.

Severe blood poisoning will make the child feel feverish and unwell and can cause septic shock.

T R E A T M E N T

If symptoms persist your doctor may prescribe antibiotics.

Septic shock requires first aid and immediate medical treatment.

■ BOILS

See also STYES

Small boils will often clear up by themselves. However, treatment with antibiotics may be needed to prevent them getting larger and more painful.

There are three main types of boil — those caused by a hair follicle becoming infected; carbuncles, which are two or more boils occurring next to each other; and styes, a boil in one of the eyelash follicles.

LOCATION

Boils can occur anywhere on the body, but they appear most often on the face, eyelids, back of the neck, upper back and buttocks. They espe-cially favour places where clothing rubs, such as the neck area along the collar line.

C A U S E S

Boils are most commonly caused by certain bacteria, some of which live harmlessly on the skin all the time. These bacteria usually only cause trouble when excessive friction has buried them in a hair follicle.

Infection happens most easily when the child is tired or anaemic, or badly undernourished.

Some children who eat a very fatty diet may also be prone to boils, for they are probably increasing the greasiness of their skin, and the infection thrives in greasy, blocked-up pores.

Diabetics can have a series of boils when their blood sugar concentration remains high. This is because the bacteria breed fast when there is sugar present in the tissues.

When the skin is broken boils develop rather more easily.

S Y M P T O M S

A boil starts gradually with a tender area under the skin. It becomes hot and red and may be surrounded by swelling.

A centre of pus develops where the fight against the infection is fiercest. On places like the ear or nose, where

the skin is tight and the surrounding tissue cannot stretch, the condition is very painful indeed.

P R E V E N T I O N

• If your child is fit and healthy, he is much less likely to suffer from boils.

• Take extra care when washing areas where there is rubbing, such as the buttocks and neck.

• Powder neck and buttocks to re-duce friction and sweat formation.

• Always keep flannels and sponges clean.

• Avoid tight collars and underwear made of nylon.

T R E A T M E N T

Small boils usually clear up by them-selves but the larger ones might need antibiotics or even surgery. You can help them to form a head and ease the pain at the same time by bathing the area with hot water or by ap-plying a hot flannel or poultice. Your doctor might send a district nurse to help with the dressing. Painkillers such as paracetamol or ibuprofen can reduce pain and fever; and ibup-rofen also acts as an anti-inflammatory.

Magnesium sulphate paste (ask your pharmacist) has no effect in bringing a boil to a head, but will help to draw the pus out once the boil is open. The paste should be applied

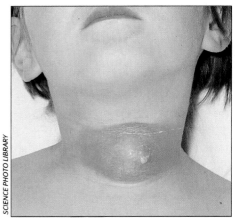

Large or recurrent boils can be a symptom of poor immunity. If your child is prone to boils, ask your doctor's advice.

thickly. Cover with a dry dressing. Keep the open boil covered until it has healed over.

SQUEEZING BOILS

Although small boils can be gently squeezed without much danger, it is wiser to leave them alone.

Large or painful boils must *never* be squeezed, nor should you squeeze any boils or carbuncles, large or small, between the eyes and the nose as you risk infection spreading and this could eventually reach the brain.

Once a boil has burst and the pus begins to drain, a dry dressing should be applied daily.

HEALING

As soon as the pus from a boil has been released and the central core of dead tissue is gone, the boil heals. This may take about a week. Occasionally the body's defences will get the best of a boil, and the inflammation will subside without bursting.

SCARRING

A small boil will heal without leaving a noticeable scar, but large boils and carbuncles do form scar tissue which may shrink over the months, but never disappear altogether. The best way to reduce the risk of scarring from a large boil or carbuncle is by early treatment. The sooner you take your child to the doctor, the sooner the boil will be brought under control and damage kept to a minimum.

■ BOW LEGS

During the first year of life, the shape of your baby's legs is influenced by the position they held in the womb — tucked up and crossed over the tummy. As the baby grows, his legs straighten out. This is a gradual procedure so there is little need to worry if your child seems very slightly bowlegged for the first couple of years. His or her walking ability will not be affected although if you have serious worries, mention it to your health visitor.

Rickets — softening of the bones —

is now very rare because most children get enough vitamin D and calcium from their diet — from fish, milk and eggs, for example. However, vitamin supplements are still recommended by the government for all children under the age of five, starting at six months for breast-fed babies and one year for bottle-fed ones.

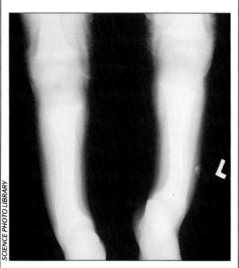

Rickets, the vitamin D deficiency disease, can cause severe bowlegs as this X-ray of a young child shows.

■ BOWEL
— see also CONSTIPATION and DIARRHOEA

The content and regularity of bowel movements varies greatly between babies and young children. A breast-fed baby's bowel movements may be

Bowel control usually comes at some stage between 20 and 24 months, though it's often later.

almost entirely liquid, while a bottle-fed baby's bowel movements are likely to be more solid and smellier. What is the same for both breast and bottle-fed babies, however, is that they have no control over their bowel movements. Control comes at 20-24 months or later.

It is important to remember that each child develops at his own rate and that there is no point in getting angry with your child for dirtying himself. Once he is physically capable of controlling his bowels, he will do so but if you upset him, it will take him longer to achieve control.

The regularity and consistency of your child's bowel movements are a good indicator of his general health. If there is a sudden change, it could be the first sign of an illness.

A diet containing plenty of fibre — green vegetables, baked beans and other pulses, wholegrain bread and so on — will help keep his bowels healthy and the motions regular.

■ BREATH HOLDING

Small children will sometimes scream so hard from temper, shock or pain that they fail to breathe properly and

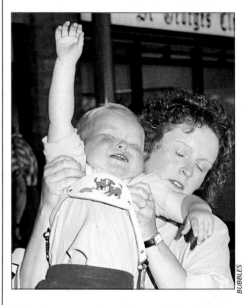

A tantrum can turn to a sudden fit of breath holding.

may turn greyish blue in the face. Alarming though this may be, if your child holds his breath, don't worry! It is physically impossible for anyone to harm themselves by holding their breath. Even if your child faints, reflex breathing will start immediately and he will be none the worse.

However, if you panic and make a fuss of trying to make him breathe during a temper tantrum, he may realize that this is a good way of getting your undivided attention and do it again another time.

BRONCHIOLITIS

This illness, which usually starts off as a cold, is similar to bronchitis, but potentially much more serious. Fortunately it is less common.

It is a contagious viral infection of the bronchioles – the tiny air tubes that carry air into all parts of the

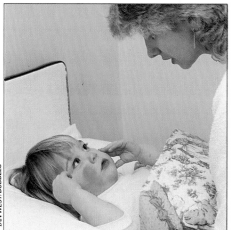

Warmth and rest are very important in the treatment of bronchiolitis. As it is contagious, restrict visitors.

lungs. The bronchioles become inflamed and this restricts a child's breathing. In extreme cases, the lungs fill with mucus which makes breathing even more difficult.

The illness strikes mostly in a child's first and second years, usually when the child is about six months old. It is most prevalent in winter and early spring.

SYMPTOMS

A child developing bronchiolitis will lose his appetite and have a slight temperature. His breathing will

gradually become more difficult and eventually he starts to take very short shallow breaths. He will also cough a lot and wheeze. If your child develops these symptoms, call your doctor immediately.

TREATMENT

Your doctor will prescribe a course of treatment for your child. It is important that you follow the doctor's instructions precisely, as this illness could become dangerous if not properly treated. If the child's breathing is extremely difficult, the doctor may recommend a short stay in hospital until the infection is cleared up, just in case he needs any special treatment or medication.

With proper care and treatment the illness should run its course within three days and your child will soon recover.

Try to make your child as comfortable as possible. Make sure he gets plenty of rest and that he doesn't come into contact with many people.

To assist his breathing, use a cool-mist humidifier or vaporizer which will loosen the mucus in his lungs. Sitting with him in a steamy bathroom can also be very effective. If your child is very young, shift his position frequently in his cot to help his lungs drain more quickly.

SIGNS TO WATCH FOR

Your child should drink a lot of liquid whilst he is recovering. If he refuses to drink for a whole day, or if he vomits after taking fluid, inform your doctor. Telephone your doctor also if you notice his lips or fingertips turning blue.

WATCHPOINTS

Bronchiolitis may strike after a cold.
Look out for:
• loss of appetite
• slight temperature
• **rapid and very shallow breathing**
• **coughing**
• **wheezing**

BRONCHITIS

There is a lot of confusion about the word 'bronchitis' because it is used to describe two totally different conditions. *Acute* bronchitis occurs in children; *Chronic* bronchitis occurs in adults. Acute bronchitis is an inflammation of the main bronchial tubes – the bronchi – caused by a bacterial or viral infection. It may develop suddenly, following a head cold or a sore throat.

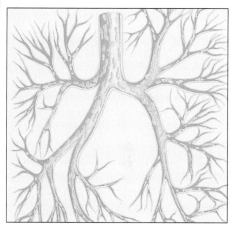

Difficulty in breathing is caused by mucus blocking the bronchi, the main tubes from the windpipe to the lungs (above), or the smaller bronchioles and alveoli. An alveolus (below) functions by picking up air from the blood.

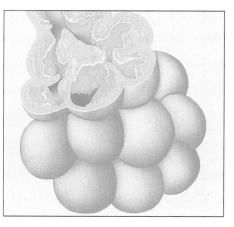

CAUSES

Bronchitis usually occurs more frequently in winter, in damp cold climates and in heavily polluted environments. Chilling, overcrowding, fatigue and living with parents who smoke can all help cause bronchitis in young children.

SCIENCE PHOTO LIBRARY

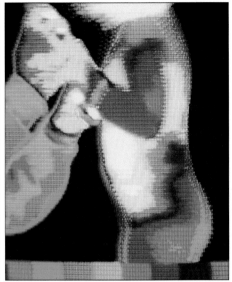

Burns are especially distressing in children. The white areas of this thermograph represent burned tissue.

YOUR QUESTIONS

Q Both I and my husband smoke quite heavily. Could this aggravate bronchitis?

A Yes. A smoky atmosphere irritates the lungs and may worsen a child's cough. If you can't give up, try not to smoke when you are in the same room with your children.

SYMPTOMS

The initial symptoms are often a head cold, running nose, fever and chills, aching muscles and possibly back pain. This is soon followed by the most obvious feature: a persistent cough. At first it is dry and racking, but later it becomes phlegmy. It is worse at night.

TREATMENT

The best treatment is bed rest in a warm room. Paracetamol will reduce the fever and cough medicine will relieve the cough. If your child is very young, your doctor will tell you what is best to give her. Antibiotics are usually needed to eliminate bacterial infection.

■ BRUISES

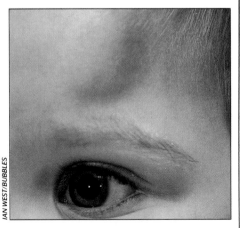

IAN WEST/BUBBLES

Bruises can look alarming but have to be expected when curious toddlers begin exploring their world.

Bruises are formed by small blood vessels breaking and bleeding beneath the skin. As the blood collects, dries and is then reabsorbed by the body, a bruise runs through its familiar pattern of changing from purple to greeny-yellow and finally disappearing altogether.

All children will bump and bruise themselves regularly when they are growing up. In most cases no treatment beyond 'a kiss to make it better' is necessary. If the skin is broken, it may need a little more attention.

If the bruise is under a finger or toe nail and is very painful, you should ask the doctor about it as he may feel it should be let out. If the blood underneath the nail is released, this will relieve pain, reduce the risk of infection and help prevent the nail turning black. However, it will not always be necessary. Bruises where the skin is very near the bone, as on the skull, ribs, arms and legs, may also need to be checked in case the bone underneath is fractured.

TREATMENT

An icepack or a cloth soaked in cold water will limit the pain and swelling if applied quickly. Severe bruising should be checked by a doctor as it is likely to be accompanied by swelling which may make a broken bone difficult for an inexperienced person to diagnose.

■ BURNS AND SCALDS

See also SAFETY

Burns Toddlers who do not understand the dangers of playing with fire are especially vulnerable to burns.

Burns are medically classified according to the depth of damage to the skin — first, second and third degree. A first degree burn harms only the top layer of skin: sunburn and the slighter burns that happen in the kitchen are examples of this. A second degree burn penetrates the outer layer and damages the underlying layer, while third degree burns destroy all skin layers.

Hospital treatment is needed for all serious burns, but prompt first aid can do a lot to reduce pain and damage.

Scalds A scald is a burn produced by steam or boiling fluid such as water or fat. The treatment is the same as for burns.

A scalded mouth or throat can be caused by your child drinking a very hot fluid or inhaling steam. If the thin layer of skin that lines the mouth and throat gets damaged it will swell very quickly and, in severe cases, can block your child's breathing. Make him wash his mouth out to cool the tissues, then give him frequent sips of water to drink.

ELECTRICAL BURNS

These may look quite small on the surface but serious damage underneath can result.

All electrical burns must be seen by a doctor.

CHEMICAL BURNS

Battery acid, drain cleaners and lime used in building are some of the commoner causes of chemical burns.

Wash away the chemical with running water. Chemical splashes in the eye must be flushed out immediately for about ten minutes. Take your child to a hospital as soon as you can for follow-up treatment.

TREATING BURNS

The first treatment for every burn is to cool it off. For scalds, remove any clothing that has become hot from boiling fluid, fat or steam. If the clothing has already cooled, however, do not remove it.

A chemical burn can be nasty, so quickly remove any soaked clothing without touching the chemical yourself. Immediately wash away the chemical by flooding with water for about ten minutes.

An electrical burn requires quick action. First of all, switch off the current. If this is impossible, break the contact by standing on something dry and pushing the victim away with a wooden chair.

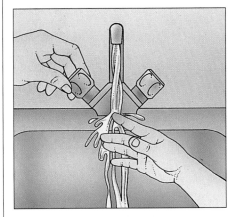

Always begin by cooling the burn. Major damage can be done by the heat from a burn penetrating deep into the body, and the application of cold water will help reduce this effect. A small part, like a fingertip or wrist, can be held under a running tap; a larger area should be plunged into a bucket or sink full of cold water.

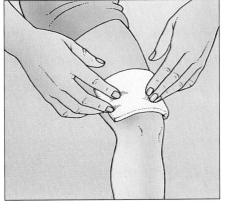

Areas like the face or chest that cannot be kept under water should be covered by a thick cloth, soaked in cold water. If the cloth gets warm and dry, renew cold water and re-apply. Continue cooling the burn for at least ten minutes. This quickly relieves pain and reduces the formation of blisters. Repeat until pain is relieved.

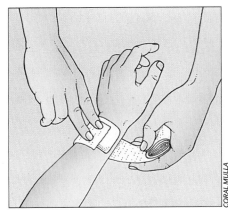

A large burn or a burn on the face should be covered with a non-fluffy dry dressing after cooling. Do not apply a lotion or ointment, and avoid touching the burn itself. Use the inside of a sterile surgical dressing or a clean handkerchief, handling it as little as possible. Cover with more folded padding and loosely bandage.

CORAL MULLA

CLOTHES ON FIRE

• Get the child on the floor, flames uppermost so they rise away from the body.

• Use water if possible to extinguish flames. If not, smother the flames with a rug or heavy coat. Press it firmly round her body so as to extinguish all burning.

• Remove smouldering clothes but do not try and tear away any material sticking to the skin.

• Never roll the child around. This will only expose different areas to the flames.

• Remove anything such as a bracelet which could constrict the burnt area if it swells.

• Do not prick any blisters or apply anything but cold water.

SAFETY CHECKLIST

MARSHALL CAVENDISH LIBRARY

Most burns are easily prevented. Look around your house and check for the following:

• Are there any open fires without guards?

• Have you left any matches or lighters lying around?

• Trailing electrical wires and sockets – are they within reach? Loop wires out of the way and fit sockets with safety plugs.

• Kettles and pans of boiling liquid – could your child pull them over herself?

• Are there any dangerous chemicals where a curious child could find them?

• Have you got a fire extinguisher or fire blanket?

■ CANCER

See also LEUKAEMIA

Fortunately, cancer is fairly rare in childhood, so it is unlikely that you will have to face the great ordeal of looking after a child that suffers from this condition.

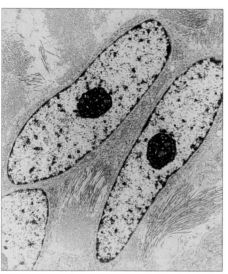

This electron micrograph shows two this is a correction line inserted as the 2nd and 3rd lines of this caption. tendon or other connective tissue.

Nonetheless, the fact is that there are two 'peaks' in the cancer figures during human life: a big one shows up in old age, and a much smaller peak in early childhood.

C A U S E S

We don't know why there is a 'mini-peak' in the cancer figures in early childhood. In fact, doctors have no idea of the cause of most cases of childhood cancer.

However, there is some evidence that radiation plays a part in causing at least some of the childhood cancers which occur today – particularly

in the case of leukaemia.

Recent evidence does suggest that there may be an increased risk of childhood cancers in the region of nuclear power stations. This would suggest they are due to radiation.

However, some authorities have claimed that the apparent increase in childhood cancer around nuclear installations could be due to viruses – brought in by people coming to work on the site.

But at the moment, very, very few cancers are known to be due to viruses – and they are all rare tumours which occur in Africa. In Britain, a child with cancer is regarded as being *non*-infectious.

INCIDENCE RATES

Bear in mind that the risk of childhood cancer in the UK is very low. Although there are far more than 100,000 *adult* cancer cases each year, the figures for children are much lower.

In the under-fives there are only about 600 cases of cancer a year. About 200 of these are cases of leukaemia.

CHILDHOOD CANCERS

The main other types of cancer are:

Hodgkin's disease is a disorder of the lymph glands. It has a lot in this is also a correction line inserted much 'milder' disorder, and the survival rate is very good. Treatment is with radiotherapy and anti-cancer drugs.
Brain tumours are fortur ately rare. They are treated with radiotherapy and/or surgery.
Wilm's tumour is a type of cancer of the kidney. It is also known as 'nephroblastoma'. The symptom which it produces is a rapidly growing abdominal swelling. As soon as the diagnosis is made, the cancer must be removed surgically.
Neuroblastoma is a cancer of the child's adrenal gland, which lies just above the kidney. Surgery, radiotherapy and chemotherapy now offer a good chance of a cure.
The same is true of **sarcoma:** a form of childhood cancer which affects bones and can be cured by surgery.

■ CARBOHYDRATES

See also CHOLESTEROL

About half of our daily energy supply comes from carbohydrates, which contain carbon, hydrogen and oxygen.

Carbohydrates are found in the foods we describe as 'starchy' or 'sugary' and are an essential part of our diet. However, it is best to avoid 'straight' sugar.

Most of the foods high in carbohydrates (bread, pasta, potatoes, cereals and biscuits) are very good for you and your family as they provide the major source of energy and many of them contain other valuable ingredients such as fibre (wholegrain bread, potatoes), protein (oats, barley and rice) or iron (bread). Such foods are a much better source of carbohydrates than cakes and biscuits as these have a high sugar content and added sugar is not an essential or desirable part of a balanced diet.

Carbohydrates can also be found in fresh food such as root vegetables, peas and bananas. These are very good for your child and will provide energy and take the edge off hunger without encouraging tooth decay.

■ CARDIAC MASSAGE

Cardiac massage, or cardiac compression, is the name given to the First Aid technique which is used to start the heart beating again by pressing on the chest.

SYMPTOMS OF HEART FAILURE

Six to 12 seconds after the heart has stopped, the child will lose consciousness. No pulse can be felt. Within 15 to 30 seconds, breathing will stop. The skin turns grey and the pupils dilate (enlarge).

First Aid is urgently required to re-start circulation and breathing. Within three or four minutes of circulation stopping, the heart will become damaged because of lack of oxygen. Although the heart may be re-started, the brain will suffer irreversible damage.

If cardiac massage is successful, heartbeat may be restored within a few minutes. It is worth continuing for at least 10 minutes even if there is no sign of a returning pulse.

TREATMENT

Give cardiac massage immediately, combined with artificial respiration, as breathing will also fail. If possible, one person should give artificial respiration – one breath after every five heart compressions – while another concentrates on the cardiac massage. You should not interrupt the heart massage to give a breath, if it can be avoided.
- Make sure the child is lying on her back on a hard surface.
- Check for a carotid pulse by extending the head backwards and feeling with all four fingers (one or two in very small children) in the groove between the Adam's apple and the strap muscles of the neck. Allow at least ten seconds to be sure no pulse is present.
- With the side of your hand, hit hard on the lower left side of the breast bone: this may start the heart beating.
- Give one breath (**see ARTIFICIAL RESPIRATION).**
- Move your hand to the lower third

HOW TO GIVE CARDIAC MASSAGE

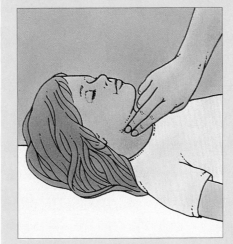

Lay the child on a hard surface and feel her carotid pulse.

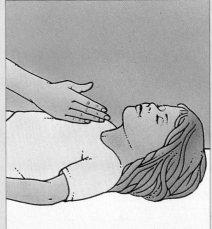

A sharp hit with the side of the hand on the breast bone may help.

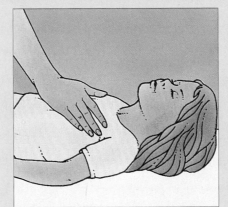

Otherwise, press firmly on the lower breast bone and repeat.

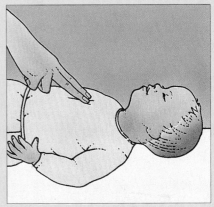

For a very small child or baby, use two fingers only.

CORAL MULA

of the breastbone. Place your palm at the point where the last ribs join it. Use two fingers only for a baby.
- Press down: the movement should be regular and rhythmical at a rate of about 100 beats per minute.
- Check carotid pulse every two minutes.
- Stop cardiac compression once you feel the pulse again.

DANGERS

On occasion, ribs are broken, but this is one of the hazards of performing a life-saving procedure. Generally, if the hands are placed in the right position and heart compression is done properly, no damage should be done to the child.

YOUR QUESTIONS

Q What should I do if my child has a cardiac arrest and his mouth is full of food?

A Turn your child's head sideways and use a finger to clear any obstruction. Then begin cardiac massage and artificial respiration.

Q Where can I learn to do cardiac massage?

A Ask your doctor about local First Aid courses. Expert training will give you confidence in an emergency.

■ CAR SICKNESS

see also TRAVEL SICKNESS

Car sickness is likely to be the most common form of travel sickness from which your child may suffer. However, many children will also feel sick when riding on anything from fairground rides to cable cars.

CAUSES

The feeling of sickness is caused when the balance organs in the ear are upset. Anxiety worsens the situation so a child who has previously felt sick in the car may well vomit during the next ride, simply through misery at the prospect of more nausea and discomfort.

No one knows why some children are quite immune to motion sickness while others feel sick watching car chases on television. Most will outgrow car sickness, but while it lasts it can be very distressing for both you and the child.

SYMPTOMS

An island of silence among chattering, singing or squabbling will probably be the first sign that all is not well. The child may look pale and complain of feeling sick. The skin on her forehead may feel cold and clammy. Sudden visible sweating, loss of colour and a watering mouth are signs that she is about to vomit.

PREVENTION

There are several brands of car sickness remedies available over the counter at the chemist's and you could try a number of these to see which is the most effective. If the standard children's tablets do not seem to help very much, other remedies include medicated plasters to stick behind the ear, wristbands with buttons which lie on acupressure points or tablets containing ginger, which is reputed to be very effective. If you are really worried or have to do a lot of driving with your children, ask your doctor's advice.

Small children can find motoring an unnatural experience and suffer car sickness before they adjust.

It is better not to give the child a large meal immediately before you set off but don't let her travel on a completely empty stomach. Stick to small snacks of light, non-greasy foods and keep some dry biscuits or salty snacks in the car. Iced water in a thermos flask is the best drink.

DO'S & DON'TS

DO
• try different anti-nausea remedies
• make regular halts on long journeys
• take iced water and dry biscuits or salty snacks on long journeys
• keep a supply of strong brown paper bags in the car in case of emergencies

DON'T
• let a carsick child ride in the front seat
• give your child a big meal before a long journey
• let children read or draw in the car – it brings on nausea
• travel in the morning if you can avoid it

TREATMENT

If you cannot stop, open a window in the car to let fresh air circulate. Try to stop when you can and let her walk around in the fresh air for a while.

Keep a stock of sick bags in the car, but don't make an issue of their presence as this will raise associations of being sick. Strong brown paper bags are better than plastic bags which look revolting when filled with vomit.

■ CATARRH

This common complaint may be no more than a temporary irritation which can be relieved by treatment at home. But if it lingers, see the doctor.

The membranes lining the nose and the windpipe help to warm and moisten the air flowing into the lungs, but they also help to trap dust and germs in the mucus. It is therefore quite normal for the nose to have some mucus present at all times, but an excess of mucus in the nose is usually called 'catarrh'. Since the mucous membranes extend to the windpipe, excessive mucus may be produced in the chest.

CAUSES

The commonest causes of catarrh are an allergy, infection or other irritation of the mucous membrane lining the nose. The membrane responds by producing more and more mucus.

Physical irritation of the lining of the nose can occur with dusts or cigarette smoke, so if your child is in a dusty or smoky atmosphere, he may be prone to catarrh.

SYMPTOMS

The most obvious symptom is a runny, irritated nose with some blockage. If catarrh persists for more than a few days, a cough may follow because the catarrh tends to run down the back of the nose into the windpipe. The cough is often worst at night and in the morning but clears during the day.

TREATMENT

The treatment depends to a large extent on the cause. If your child's catarrh is caused by dust or smoke in

Breathing in steam helps a blocked nose, but care needs to be taken with the boiling water.

the atmosphere, then try to remove the irritant from the air he breathes. For a cold, you can help to relieve catarrh by using a steam inhalation. This will liquify the thick mucus and allow you to blow the child's nose more effectively. A decongestant nose spray from the chemist may help for a few days.

Hay fever and other allergies do not respond well to these sprays but may be helped by antihistamine tablets which can be bought over the

---

STEAM TREATMENT FOR CATARRH

• Pour boiling water into a heatproof basin and add a few menthol crystals or a proprietary inhalant.

• Put a towel over the child's head so that the ends drape down over the basin and trap the steam. Let the child breathe the steam deeply for about five minutes.

• Repeat three or four times a day.

• If catarrh persists for more than four or five days, take your child to the doctor.

---

counter on prescription. The doctor may also prescribe a spray.

If the catarrh is caused by allergy to fur or feathers, your child should avoid animals and feather-filled pillows in the house.

■ CEREBRAL PALSY

Cerebral palsy is the description of a physical impairment that affects movement: the movement problems vary from barely noticeable to extremely severe. They are the result of damage to parts of the brain usually before, during or just after birth. In the past, the term 'spastic' was used to describe cerebral palsy, but this is no longer so.

CAUSES

It used to be thought that cerebral palsy resulted from lack of oxygen to the child's brain during delivery, but the damage is now believed to occur more often before birth. It is most probably caused by a viral infection such as rubella (German measles) which affects the developing foetus, although the mother may not necessarily feel very ill.

After birth, a head injury, meningitis or a stroke can cause brain damage which may lead to cerebral palsy, but unfortunately there is often no identifiable cause.

Specialist teaching methods ensure that the effects of cerebral palsy need not be entirely disabling.

SYMPTOMS

Abnormalities in the development of muscular movement and control are the most immediately obvious symptoms, but some children may also suffer convulsions, impaired sight, hearing or speech and learning disabilities.

The symptoms are not always immediately apparent and may change as the child grows.

TREATMENT

There is no cure for cerebral palsy,

WATCHPOINTS

There are combinations of several symptoms the doctor may wish to look for before diagnosing cerebral palsy.

• Poor head control after three months

• Problems with sucking or swallowing

• Persistent dribbling

• Persistent arching of the spine

• Restricted movement of arm or leg on one side of the body

• Unusual crawling

• Poor balance

• Persistent walking on toes

• Late motor development

but if it is spotted early, physiotherapy can prevent muscle deformities and teach the child to move more smoothly and with greater control.

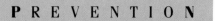

PREVENTION

It is not possible to prevent all the causes of brain damage, such as strokes, severe head injuries or congenital defects. However, it is possible to receive immunization against rubella and most women will have been immunized at age 11. If you do not know whether or not you have had the rubella vaccination, take all precautions to avoid exposure to German measles while you are pregnant and see your doctor about being vaccinated before you next get pregnant.

If your child seems to be slow in developing motor control, see your doctor about it.

■ CHEST INFECTIONS

Chest infections are common in childhood. This is not surprising when you think about the way in which chest infections arise.

CAUSES

They are caused by germs which are breathed in through the child's nose or mouth. From there, they pass

WHEN TO SEE THE DOCTOR
You should definitely contact the doctor if your child has any of the following symptoms:
- Cough that has gone on for more than two days
- Wheezing in the chest

EMERGENCY
- Difficulty in breathing
- Very rapid breathing
- Ribs 'pulled in' with every breath
- Noisy breathing may be an emergency too

If in doubt, ring the doctor.

down through the child's windpipe (trachea) and into her large air passages (her bronchi) and her lungs.

Children are of course exposed to a whole range of germs which they have never met before (particularly when they first go to playschool or to 'real' school), and they usually have no immunity to these.

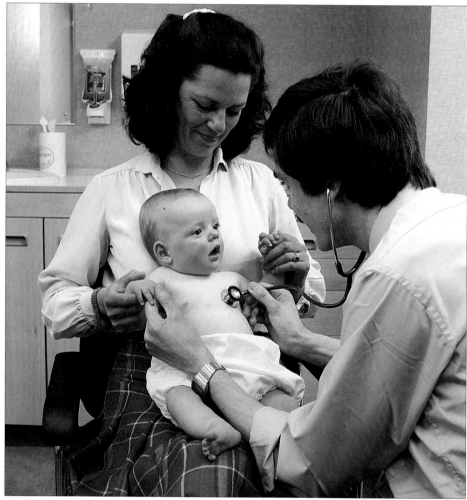

JOHN WATNEY

COMMON INFECTIONS

Common childhood chest infections include acute bronchitis, bronchiolitis, and pneumonia — though this last infection is less common than it used to be. Tracheitis is an infection of the windpipe, which leads down into the bronchi — the two major air passages of the chest.

Pleurisy is an inflammation of the 'lining' of the child's chest. It often follows other infections.

Chest infections due to tuberculosis (TB) are rare nowadays in Western countries but are more common-

ly seen in babies and children from the Asian and African communities.

RESISTANCE

Children vary greatly in their resistance to infection. For instance, if a toddler is extremely fit and healthy, it may well happen that a germ which enters his chest does not cause an

Chest infections are common in small children until they have built up their immunity.

infection, and is just killed by the body's defences.

On the other hand, a youngster who is already under the weather, and perhaps suffering from some other medical condition, is all too likely to fall victim to a germ which she breathes in.

In particular, it is very common indeed for a child to develop a chest infection immediately after she has had an infection higher up in the air passages. That's why a cold, or a bad bout of catarrh, or tonsilitis may be followed by a chest infection.

.S Y M P T O M S

The main symptoms of chest infections are cough, soreness in the chest and breathlessness.

■ CHICKEN POX

Being so easily caught, chickenpox is almost a natural hazard of childhood. It does not last long, it rarely has serious complications and effective home nursing is a simple matter.

It is a childhood illness because although babies are born with a natural ability to resist the infection (passed on by their mother), by the age of one or two this wears off.

HOW IT IS CAUGHT

The chickenpox virus is present in the child's spots, but it is chiefly transmitted by droplet infection. A child who already has chickenpox spreads clusters of the virus in the tiny droplets of water which are exhaled as a matter of course with every breath. When another child breathes in an infected droplet, the virus starts to multiply and another case of chickenpox begins.

S Y M P T O M S

Once the virus has entered the child's body, there is an 'incubation period' of about a fortnight while the virus spreads. After this, the first a child will know of his illness may be a 24-hour period of vague headache, feeling unwell, occasional slight fever and sometimes a blotchy red rash which quickly fades.

The first spots will appear within 24 hours. They usually start on the trunk and face, only mildly affecting the arms and legs.

The spot starts as a pink bump which within five or six hours becomes raised to form a tiny blister containing clear fluid which is full of viruses. These 'teardrop' spots gradually become milky in colour. Then they form a crust and finally a scab.

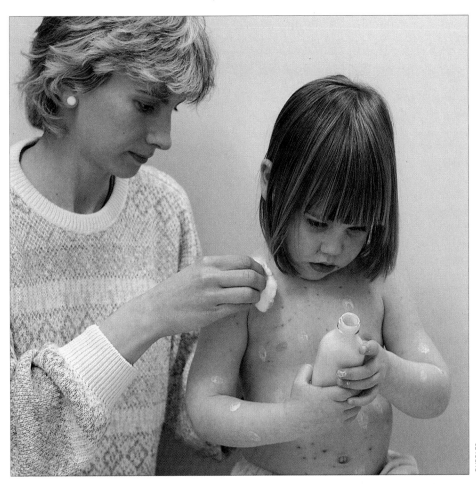

During this period, the child may be fretful and run a temperature of around 38°C (which is 100.4°F). Some children may only have 30 to 50 spots while others may have several hundred.

Immediately the crust forms, the spots begin to itch and this may last until the scabs drop off, leaving your child with normal skin, after one or two weeks.

THE COURSE

Chickenpox spots come out in crops, new ones will appear every day for three or four days.

When examining the skin, you will notice that the spots will be at different stages even in the same area. This is typical of chickenpox and quite normal.

COMPLICATIONS

The dangerous complications of chickenpox are extremely rare. Most children feel well enough to play around the house during the illness.

Children who are taking steroid

Chickenpox spots can be very itchy, but scratching may cause scars. Calamine or antihistamine lotion will give some relief.

HOME CARE OF A CHILD

• Allow the child freedom and do not insist on bedrest. Give paracetamol for sore throat or headache. Reassure the child. The spots may look dramatic, but the patient is rarely unwell.
• Consult your doctor if the spots are massive, infected or exceedingly painful (for instance in the ear).
• Cut down on food when temperature is raised, but offer plenty of fluids.
• Explain the need not to scratch.
• Apply plenty of calamine lotion or ask the doctor for an antihistamine drug to reduce irritation.

drugs or those suffering from leukaemia are the likeliest to be seriously affected and in whom the condition may be fatal. In a very small number of cases, a severe form of pneumonia is caused by the virus.

TAKING CARE

In other rare cases, there may be bleeding into the spots so that the patient becomes ill from loss of blood. Brain inflammation may also occur — particularly if the child has mistakenly been given aspirin. (Do NOT give this to under-12s — especially in chickenpox.) Children with chickenpox are traditionally isolated from old people as the virus can cause shingles.

The most common complications arise from infection of the skin at the spot, causing boils, or one or two other skin conditions.

YOUR QUESTIONS

Q Can babies get chickenpox and, if so, is it more serious than in children?

A Babies seem to have some immunity to chickenpox and when they do get it, it tends to be less severe than in older children.

Q My son seems to have chickenpox for the second time. Is this possible?

A It is highly unlikely. In general, chickenpox is a once-only infection. The first attack might have been scabies (severe itching and spots caused by a mite) or even a number of gnat bites occurring together.

TREATMENT

Children with a high temperature who feel unwell may prefer to stay in bed or lie downstairs. Otherwise, there is no medical reason to enforce strict bed rest. The majority of children require no treatment at all.

Any pain from sore throat or headache is best relieved with paracetamol. As there is no medical cure for the virus, the condition is left to take its natural course. Severe itching can be helped with application of calamine lotion or an antihistamine drug. Should any of the spots become infected, they will take longer to heal. Try to persuade your child not to scratch the scabs as this will increase the risk of scarring as well as infection.

OUTLOOK

The majority of children with mild chickenpox start losing their scabs after about ten days and will then be completely clear of spots within two weeks. Scabs which fall off on their own do not leave a scar.

Chickenpox infection produces life-long immunity but does not give immunity to shingles, which may occur later in life.

■ CHILBLAINS

A chilblain is an area of soft tissue where the skin has become damaged by cold and damp.

SYMPTOMS

Chilblains usually affect the toes or outer side of the foot. The ears, nose and fingers can also be affected.

The skin becomes red and swollen and may itch. If the child scratches hard enough to break the skin, the chilblains can become infected.

Babies sometimes get red, swollen hands if they are out in cold weather without gloves. This condition has nothing to do with chilblains.

CAUSES

It is not known exactly why some children are prone to chilblains and others never get them. They are related to cold weather and poor circulation.

TREATMENT

Your doctor can prescribe ointment to reduce the itching, but there is no cure as such.

PREVENTION

You can help your child avoid getting chilblains by taking a few sensible precautions:
• In cold weather dress your child warmly all over.
• If he is going out, put warm gloves, socks and a hat on him.
• Dry his hands and feet carefully after washing and change damp clothing immediately.
• If your child is prone to chilblains, gently massage likely chilblain areas daily.
• Give him plenty of hot, nourishing food.
• Don't let him sit in draughts or overheat his hands or feet in front of a roaring fire, on radiators or in hot water.
• Make sure his clothes do not have tight cuffs which could restrict circulation to hands and feet.

SALLY & RICHARD GREENHILL

Chilblains often appear after exposure to damp and cold. Make sure your child is warmly dressed all over.

■ CHOKING

Choking is one of the most common accidents among babies and children. If the child can cough, there is less to worry about as obviously some air must be getting through. It is frightening for the child, however, so stay calm yourself. Food or drink which has 'gone down the wrong way' may be coughed back up the nose. This may be painful but it is not dangerous.

S Y M P T O M S

If the child does not cough, but gasps, turns red and then greyish or blue while obviously panicking, her airway is blocked and you must act quickly.

T R E A T M E N T

Open her mouth and hook your finger around the object or piece of food to see if you can get it out of her throat. Don't worry if you make her retch — it could help dislodge the obstruction.

If you cannot clear her airway with your finger and the child is under a year old, lie her head down over your knees and on top of your forearm

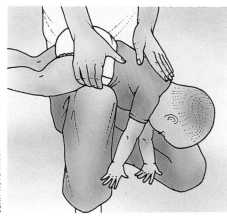

To clear a choking baby's throat, lay her across your thigh and give her four light but firm slaps on her back.

(see illustration). Give her four smart pats between the shoulder blades with the heel of your other hand. If she continues to choke, turn her over and put two or three fingertips on the

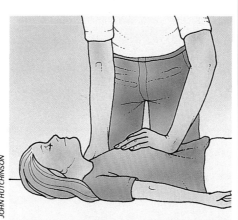

For an older child, apply pressure to the area beneath her ribs with the heel of your hand.

lower end of her breastbone. Press down quickly and smoothly four times. Repeat the sequence of pats on the back alternating with pressure on the front until the obstruction is dislodged. Be ready to give artificial respiration if breathing stops altogether.

Lie an older child on her back and put the heel of your hand just below her ribcage, above her tummy button (see illustration). Press smartly upward and inward between six and 10 times until the object is cleared. If she is still not breathing, give artificial respiration.

P R E V E N T I O N

Never leave your baby alone when she is eating or drinking — particularly if she is drinking from a bottle. Keep small objects such as beads, balloons and toy parts away from her. For older children, certain foods such as hard sweets or popcorn are easy to choke on. Peanuts should not be given to small children as they not only go down the wrong way easily but also contain an oil which can irritate and inflame the lungs even after the peanut has been removed.

■ CHOLESTEROL

Cholesterol is a fatty substance which normally forms part of the wall around each cell in the body. It is also a basic 'building block' of a major group of the body's chemical messengers called the steroid hormones which form a part of our defence against infection. Unfortunately, when it becomes lodged in the walls of the arteries, it contributes to the condition called arteriosclerosis, or hardening of the arteries, which causes heart attacks and strokes — the major scourges of the Western world. The cholesterol we need is normally made by the body itself, but this amount is increased by extra cholesterol in our diets.

A HEALTHY DIET

Cholesterol is a fatty substance found in animal fats and other foods. High levels are thought to contribute to the build-up of fatty deposits in the arteries.

However, while good eating habits certainly begin in childhood, toddlers and small children need a diet that's higher in fat than that needed by an adult. This is because their high energy requirements demand the concentrated calories present in fat, and also the vitamins A, C and D which are less likely to be present in lower-fat foods.

This is why most nutrition experts recommend full-fat, whole milk in preference to skimmed, for children under the age of five. Children over the age of two can have semi-skimmed milk as long as they have a varied and healthy diet.

If there is a history of heart disease in your family, the risk of your child developing heart disease in later life will be higher.

The other important factors are the total level of fat in your family's diet and whether that fat comes from an animal or vegetable source.

Some of the fat in the typical UK diet should be replaced by carbohydrates (starchy foods such as bread,

CHOLESTEROL IN FOODS

Foods high in cholesterol
Eggs
Saturated fats: dairy products (full-cream milk, cream, butter, cheese), processed fats (many types of cooking fats — such as lard — and margarines), meat (even lean meat), certain vegetable oils (coconut oil, palm oil)
Foods low in cholesterol
Monounsaturated fats: fish oils and some vegetable oils (such as peanut oil and olive oil)
Polyunsaturated fats: most vegetable oils (such as corn, safflower, sesame, soya, sunflower and oils derived from nuts), fish oils such as cod liver oil.

A diet high in cholesterol can lead to heart diseases in later life.

potatoes, rice and pasta) and this, according to official recommendations, is likely to lower cholesterol levels and to promote heart health.

Unsaturated fats from vegetable sources such as sunflower oil and corn oil are thought less likely to increase the cholesterol levels in the blood, compared with the saturated fats found in animal products such as meat and dairy products.

WHAT HAPPENS IN THE BODY

Only a quarter of the cholesterol that circulates in the blood comes directly from the digestive tract, where it has been absorbed from food. Some of the cholesterol in the blood returns to the liver, where it is broken down and secreted as bile by the gall bladder. The cholesterol which enters the walls of the arteries is carried in the blood.

It is thought that exercise improves the efficiency of the blood at 'mopping up' the 'loose' cholesterol and carrying it back to the liver, thus preventing it from settling in the artery walls.

Bringing up your child on a healthy, balanced diet can help to teach him good eating habits which last him a lifetime. Firstly, your consumption of sugar should be reduced to a minimum. Carbohydrate is best taken as bread, potatoes, rice and pulses. Meat is a convenient source of protein and other nutrients, but it is no longer thought to be an essential part of the diet. Reducing the amount of meat in the diet, or even switching to a vegetarian diet, can be a healthy alternative for adults and children alike.

Toddlers and children under five need sufficient fat and protein in their diet because of their calorie and vitamin requirements — however it is possible for these needs to be satisfied from a vegetarian diet or one free of animal fat.

Research is continuing into what constitutes a healthy diet, with some controversy about how the research should be interpreted.

■ CHORIONIC BIOPSY

Chorionic biopsy (or chorionic villus sampling), like amniocentesis, is a test carried out during pregnancy to check the foetus for any chromosome defect or other inherited disorder. It may be offered to you if there is a risk that your baby may have Down's syndrome or if you have a family history of an inherited disorder.

A sample of tissue from the placenta is taken with a hollow needle inserted through the cervix (the neck of the uterus) with the guidance of an ultrasound scan. The test is not painful and it can be done at nine weeks rather than 16 weeks, which is the earliest that an amniocentesis test can be carried out. The precise risk of miscarriage from chorionic biopsy is still being assessed.

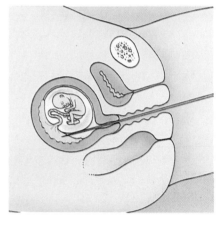

The chorionic biopsy test involves taking a small sample of placental tissue for analysis and it can detect a number of genetic disorders. To obtain the sample, a fine tube, guided by ultra sound, is inserted through the cervix into the uterus.

The chorionic biopsy technique has been associated with some limb deformities in babies born after the test, and while cause and effect has yet to be demonstrated, doctors are cautious about recommending it.

■ CHROMOSOMES

See also COLOUR BLINDNESS, CYSTIC FIBROSIS, DOWN'S SYNDROME, HAEMOPHILIA

You will often be told that your child 'takes after' you or your partner in character or looks.

Every child grows from a single egg produced by the mother and fertilized by the father. The fertilized egg 'knows' how to develop because it carries all the information concerning the number and position of limbs and so on right down to the length of eyelashes. This information is carried in a total of 46 chromosomes, arranged in 23 pairs. One chromosome of each pair comes from the mother and the other from the father. The chromosomes are made up of thousands of genes, each relating to a particular characteristic such as blood group and eye colour.

TWO OF A KIND

Each gene from one parent has its opposite number on the chromosome from the other parent. There are two kinds of gene, dominant and recessive, and it is this which helps determine what your child will inherit from each of you.

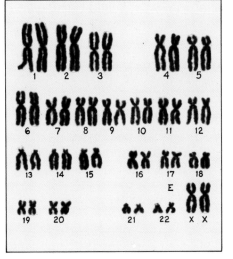

This illustration shows the chromosomes of a normal female child – 23 pairs of chromosomes.

Your child's sex is determined by the chromosomes relating to sex. There are two kinds, X and Y. A female has two X chromosomes and therefore can only pass on an X chromosome to her baby. A male has one X and one Y so if he passes on an X as well, the child will be a girl, while

Genes determine features such as hair colour which can result in different looking brothers and sisters.

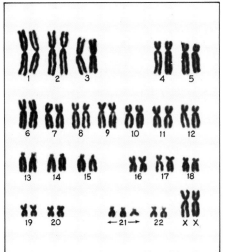

The extra number 21 chromosome above is a genetic abnormality and will result in a Down's syndrome child.

if he passes on a Y, it will be a boy.

The genes on the X and Y chromosomes can also affect other characteristics. For example, through these genes, women can give to their sons, but not their daughters, an inability for the blood to clot correctly. And their daughters are likely to have sons with the same problem. This inherited disorder is called haemophilia.

MIND THAT GENE

Most inherited diseases such as cystic fibrosis are caused by a defective gene, which is recessive, that is, the child will only inherit cystic fibrosis if *both* parents carry the defective gene – a chance of about one in 400. If only one parent passes on the defective gene, it will be 'overpowered' by its normal opposite number. The child will thus carry the disease but not suffer it.

However, a few are caused by a dominant gene, which means that any child who inherits that gene will suffer from the disease. An example of this is Huntington's chorea, a degenerative nerve disease in which body movement gradually becomes uncontrollable, memory is lost and the personality degenerates. Fortunately, it is very rare, but is particularly distressing because the symptoms do not appear until middle age. This means that some people do not

realize they have the defective gene until they have had children, while others suspect they may be carriers and refrain from having children, only to find out too late that they do not in fact have the disease.

The single gene disorders described above are easy to spot in families and clearly show how inheritance works. However, many less serious disorders are inherited through more than one gene and are far more complicated to trace. Asthma, for example, has a genetic element among its causes, but it is far more difficult to separate that element from other genetic traits and environmental influences such as diet, climate and upbringing. If you or your partner think you might pass on a genetic disorder to your children, speak to your doctor about genetic counselling.

YOUR QUESTIONS

Q What are the X and Y chromosomes?

A They are the chromosomes that determine the sex of your child. Females have two X and males one X and one Y chromosomes. If the sperm that fertilizes the egg carries an X, the baby will be a girl, if it carries the Y chromosome, it will be a boy.

■ CHOROIDITIS

Choroiditis is an inflammation of the choroid, a layer of blood vessels underlying the retina at the back of the eye, which usually leaves both scarred.

CAUSES

In many cases, the exact cause of this inflammation cannot be discovered. Occasionally, the disorder is the result of infection by a microbe acquired before birth. In children, it can be due to infection by a worm-like microbe that enters their system

after they've touched dirt fouled by dog faeces and then put their fingers into their mouth.

TREATMENT

If the inflammation causes any blurring of vision. consult your doctor.

Steroids will be prescribed to clear up the inflammation and blurred vision. Before giving the drugs your doctor may arrange for tests to be done to be sure of the cause.

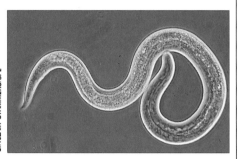

After touching dog litter, a worm-like microbe may enter your child's system and cause infection.

■ CHRONIC ILLNESS

A chronic illness is a long-term condition such as diabetes, epilepsy and cystic fibrosis. A child who is physically or mentally handicapped may not be ill as such, but still requires protracted care. While we all know that children are born with these probably lifelong problems, and pregnant women worry about the health of their unborn child, we always think of it as something which happens to other people's children.

A FAMILY PROBLEM

The impact of chronic illness is often unexpectedly far-reaching. The whole structure of your family life will be changed and you and your partner will be best prepared to meet these changes if you discuss your feelings towards the situation openly and honestly with each other. You cannot give your sick child or your family the best support if you and your partner are not supporting each other.

Other children may be bewildered and then jealous of the sick child who

takes up so much of your time and attention. It is not unusual for feelings of hatred to develop in younger children, while older children may worry about the future when you are no longer around.

The sick child himself will also have confused feelings about his place and value within the family and all these feelings should be discussed so that you can cope with them as a family to avoid further unhappiness.

A chronically sick child does not cause only anxiety and problems. Many parents say that despite the physical and emotional strain, the child gives them insight into the significant values of life, and the child has enhanced their lives in a way they could never have anticipated.

RE-ARRANGING ROUTINES

Both you and your child will need to know all about any medicines or courses of treatment which may be needed. You may need to re-think your shopping and meal planning to allow for a special diet, or be ready to spend sleepless nights with a child in pain or distress.

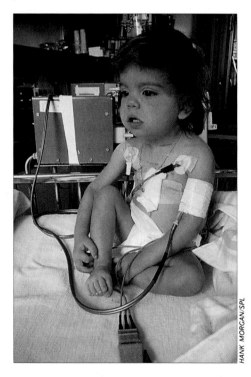

A child with kidney failure undergoing peritoneal dialysis, a treatment carried out in hospital to clean waste products from her blood.

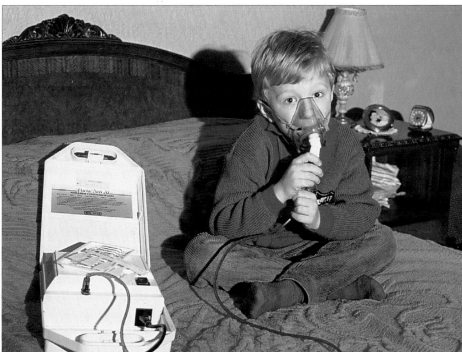

Luckily, more than half of young asthma sufferers grow out of their condition by the time they are teenagers.

Some children may have to go into hospital periodically, so that you have to fit hospital visiting into all the other demands on your time.

All these extra factors in addition to the everyday running of your home and family are exhausting, so do try to find out about day care facilities for handicapped children or short term hospital care. You will function far better if you can give yourself a break from time to time.

It is very easy to lavish too much care on a chronically ill child through feelings of guilt or worry. Your child will follow your lead in forming an attitude to his illness or handicap, so if you seem anxious, he will worry too. Likewise, if you do everything for him, he will become more dependent and demanding. Try to let him find the limitations imposed by his illness or handicap himself and take pleasure in the things he can do. If he can look after himself to any extent, this will reduce any guilt he might feel at making extra work for you and help his self confidence.

Ask friends and family to help out so that your family don't have to watch you exhausting yourself on their behalf. If you allow yourself time on your own, you will be able to replenish your resources and your family and friends will be able to show their love and support for you.

■ CIRCULATION

The circulation is a closed network of blood vessels – in other words, tubes which carry blood around the body. At its centre is the heart, a muscular pump with the job of keeping the blood in motion.

Blood starts its journey around the circulatory system by leaving the left side of the heart through the large

YOUR QUESTIONS

Q Will eating too many sweets make my child more likely to develop diabetes?

A No. If a child is going to get diabetes it will be caused by failure of insulin, a hormone produced in the pancreas. Eating sweets has nothing to do with the functioning of the insulin-producing cells in the pancreas.

PLACENTAL CIRCULATION

While you are pregnant, the baby does not share your circulation but picks up certain substances from it through the placenta and the umbilical cord. In this way, the baby gets all the oxygen and nourishment necessary for growth, as well as a certain amount of immunity to disease which will protect him throughout pregnancy and for a few weeks after he is born. But as soon as he is born, the baby relies on his lungs for oxygen, not the placenta.

artery known as the aorta.

At this stage, blood is rich in oxygen, food (in microscopic particles) and hormones – the chemical messengers. The arteries take this rich blood away from the heart and into smaller tubes known as arterioles. The arterioles take the rich,

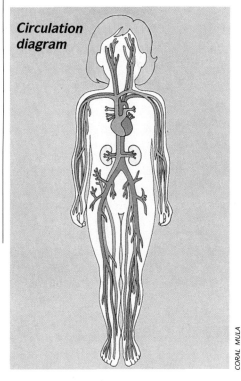

Circulation diagram

Blood pumped by the heart circulates round the body; the arteries (red) carry oxygen to nourish tissues, the veins (blue) take away waste products.

TONY STONE ASSOC.

Handling snow makes the hands feel numb because the capillaries contract and restrict blood circulation.

oxygenated blood to every organ and tissue in the body. The food and oxygen is actually transferred to the tissues through the capillaries, a vast network of minute vessels. In return, the capillaries take up the waste products which are taken away again by the blood.

The blood returns to the heart through first the venules (tiny veins) and then the veins themselves. Two major veins, the superior and inferior vena cava, take the blood into the right side of the heart. From there, it is pumped into the lungs through the pulmonary artery (the only artery to carry non-oxygenated blood). In the lungs, oxygen from the air we breathe is absorbed into the blood, and the carbon dioxide is released and breathed out.

THERE AND BACK

The blood then goes back to the heart again through the pulmonary vein (the only vein to carry deoxygenated blood) and into the left side of the heart to begin its journey again.

Blood from the intestine passes through the liver on its way to the heart. Some substances are then sifted out for immediate use, others are put into storage and toxic substances are broken down.

GIVE AND TAKE

When extra blood is needed for a special purpose in one part of the body it is taken from another part. For example, during exercise, the blood vessels in the leg muscles expand and those in the intestine are shut down so that it is directed to where it is needed. This is why it is best not to exercise soon after eating, as the blood is needed in the intestine for digestion.

■ CIRCUMCISION

see also GENITALS

Baby boys are born with a sheath of skin, known as the foreskin, which covers the tip of the penis. In circumcision, this foreskin is cut away so that the tip is permanently exposed.

Deciding whether or not to circumcize your baby is a personal decision, but is unlikely to be necessary on medical grounds.

RELIGIOUS REASONS

In certain cultures, baby boys are circumcized because of religious tradition. The reasons for this custom are not clear, although the ideas of ritual cleansing and initiation into manhood may explain it. Jewish babies are circumcized when they are eight days old, Muslim boys between the ages of three and fifteen.

The tip of the penis produces secretions known as smegma which can collect under the foreskin. Some parents are concerned that this may set up a bacterial infection, so they have their babies' foreskin removed to make the penis easier to keep clean. In fact, circumcizing a baby because it seems more hygienic can actually have an adverse effect because the foreskin protects the tip from infection by wet nappies.

Forcibly pushing the foreskin back to clean beneath it can also lead to infection because it can cause the tissue to tear. The foreskin will normally loosen in its own time when you can gently push it back and bathe away the smegma.

PHIMOSIS

This is a condition in which the foreskin is too tight to be pulled back over the tip of the penis. Although some parents may be worried by this, it is in fact perfectly normal in babies and young boys. At birth, the foreskin is joined to the tip of the penis, and gradually separates by itself over the first three or four years, making circumcision unnecessary. If the condition persists after this time, you could have a chat with your doctor, but treatment is unlikely

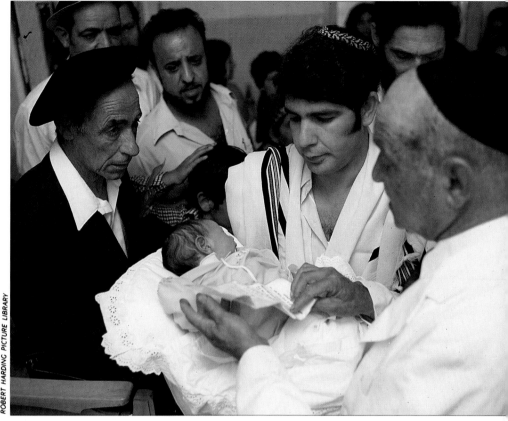

An Israeli baby boy is circumcized ritually. In some communities, such as the Jewish and Muslim, circumcision is an ancient religious tradition.

to be urgently needed.

Do not be tempted to push a tight foreskin back: you could make it tear and the resulting scarring would permanently seal the foreskin to the glans — then circumcision really would be necessary.

If circumcision is being done for medical reasons, a surgeon will perform the operation by carefully lifting the foreskin and cutting it away close to the base of the glans. On a young baby, the area of skin to be removed is so tiny that he will hardly notice; on an older child, a local or general anaesthetic will be used. If circumcision is being done for religious reasons, no anaesthetic is traditionally used.

After the operation, there will be a raw area on the penis that you will have to dress until the wound heals. Regular dressing will also reduce the risk of scarring. You can use gauze covered in soft paraffin jelly or an antiseptic cream. Obviously a baby

or young infant has a higher chance of irritation or infection from wet nappies, which can cause a small ulcer to form at the tip of the penis. You should therefore bath your baby and change his nappies more often than usual during the healing period.

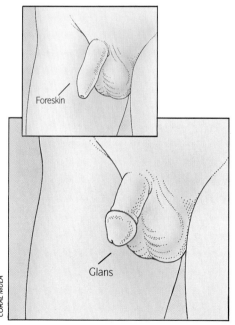

Foreskin

Glans

In circumcision, the foreskin (see above top) is cut back to reveal the tip of the penis (below).

■ CLEFT PALATE

Cleft palates vary in size and type, but always consist of a gap between the internal parts of the nose and mouth. A cleft lip occurs when the two halves of the lip fail to join together. This condition is also known as hare lip.

The palate, or roof of the mouth, is hard at the front and soft at the back. The hard front palate is part of the upper jaw bone, and the soft back palate is made of muscle and ends in the uvula (the piece of tissue which

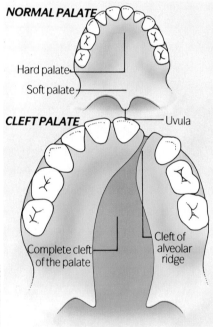

NORMAL PALATE

Hard palate

Soft palate

CLEFT PALATE

Uvula

Complete cleft of the palate

Cleft of alveolar ridge

JOHN HUTCHINSON

Unlike a normal palate (top), the two sides of a cleft palate do not come together during the development of the baby's mouth and face while it is still in the womb.

hangs at the back of the mouth).

In normal growth in the womb, the palate develops from two halves. In about the sixth week of pregnancy they grow together, spreading upwards to join above the tongue in the eighth week.

THE DEVELOPING PALATE

The join then slowly moves forward to the lip and backward to the uvula. By the tenth week of pregnancy, the two halves are usually fully fused together and the nose is separated from the mouth.

In a few cases, these normal stages of development do not take place, and gaps are left in parts of the mouth or lip.

CAUSES

No one knows exactly what causes cleft palate or cleft lip. One of the most likely possibilities is that the condition is inherited. Clefts run in families, with relatives frequently showing the same type of cleft. There are some interesting tendencies, though. Cleft lip appears to be more common in boys and cleft palate in girls. In a pair of identical twins, if one twin has a cleft, the chances are three to one that the other will have a normal palate and lip.

Another possible cause of clefts is a deficiency in tissue development at a certain stage in the growth of the foetus. Poor blood circulation in the face as it develops is another theory.

SYMPTOMS

Clefts are divided into types, depending on where they occur. The types are lip only, in the ridge behind the teeth (alveolar), or in the palate. All three types can occur together, but because the areas of the lip and uvula are the last to join, clefts here are more common.

Clefts vary in their seriousness. A cleft lip may look more alarming than a cleft palate but can actually be less of a problem to a baby because it does not interfere with feeding. A cleft soft palate is less serious than a cleft running into the hard palate as well, while a cleft uvula is least serious of all, and needs no treatment at all.

TREATMENT

In a baby born with a cleft palate, one half of the palate is likely to be smaller than the other. In this case, the baby will have a plate inserted into the roof of his mouth soon after birth. The plate will be fitted so that it encourages the smaller half to grow faster than the bigger half. As the palate changes, new plates will prob-

ably be inserted until the two halves have achieved the same size, usually after several months. An operation can then be performed to join the two sides of the palate together.

There are two advantages to this type of treatment: it gives better results than operating when the two halves of the palate are different sizes and it also helps to prevent milk escaping up into the nose when the baby is feeding.

If the palate is divided exactly in half, surgery can be carried out without the use of a plate, between the ages of 12 and 18 months.

Surgery for cleft lips is normally delayed until a baby is about three months old. It is usually highly successful, with little visible scarring.

■ CLUB FOOT

Club foot – or talipes – affects about one in 500 babies. It is a congenital disorder of the skeleton, which means it is not usually inherited but more often happens as a result of an abnormality in the baby's development while it is still in the womb.

SYMPTOMS

Your newborn baby will undergo some simple routine tests when it is born, one of which will be checking the feet to discover any abnormal twisting which would indicate a club foot. One or both feet may be affected and the signs will be a foot bent either downwards and inwards or upwards and outwards. Either way the foot will look twisted and the sole will face in or out rather than down.

The feet of a newborn baby sometimes look turned in like club feet, but in most cases won't be. If the foot can be pushed gently forward so that the little toe almost touches the shin, the baby does not have a club foot.

TREATMENT

A club foot is always correctable. If the defect is only slight, you will be shown by the doctor how to manipulate the foot gently every day until it has gone back to a normal position. If it is more severe the foot might be bound or put in a plaster cast in addition to manipulation in order to stop the foot growing back to its former position.

Very rarely, for a severe case, it may be necessary to have the foot operated on. This operation is usually very successful.

Best foot forward. In spite of being born with club feet, Michael Aldred became an ice skating champion.

SYNDICATED FEATURES LTD

YOUR QUESTIONS

Q You don't often see people with a club foot nowadays. Is this becaue we have a better diet, or because people have it operated on to correct it?

A Being born with a club foot has nothing to do with diet. But, yes, it can be corrected with an operation. The most likely reason, however (because as many babies are born with it now as before) is that these days a club foot is detected at birth so manipulation can be started immediately.

Q My mother tells me that I was born with a club foot, which was corrected when I was still a baby. I'm getting married soon and want to have children one day. Will they inherit the defect?

A A club foot is not hereditary, so there is no need to worry — it is highly unlikely you will pass it on to your children.

■ COELIAC DISEASE

Coeliac (pronounced 'see-lee-ack') disease is an allergy of the small intestine. The lining of the intestine cannot absorb gluten — a protein found in cereals such as wheat, rye, barley and oats. When it comes into contact with gluten, the lining loses its 'fluffiness' and becomes smooth because the microscopic finger-like fronds, called villi, disappear.

Coeliac disease will reveal itself early in childhood, when the baby is first introduced to cereals. Thus, it is very rarely diagnosed for the first time in adults.

SYMPTOMS

The baby will have a poor appetite and she will fail to put on weight when you expect her to — when she goes on solids; she may lose weight.

Other symptoms include diarrhoea with foul-smelling bulky stools and a bloated stomach caused by excess wind, which contrasts with the rest of her undernourished frame.

If you suspect your child has coeliac disease, see your doctor. She may arrange for tests on the blood and faeces to be carried out at a gastro-enterology clinic. If the tests prove positive, a biopsy of the intestinal lining will be carried out.

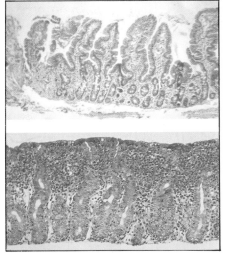

WESTMINSTER CHILDREN'S HOSPITAL

The lining of a healthy intestine has villi (top), which disappear (bottom) with coeliac disease.

NORMAL AND CLUB FEET

In a club foot (below) the foot turns inwards or outwards and unlike a normal foot (left), the sole cannot be placed down.

Bone structure of club foot

Bone structure of normal foot

CAUSES

It is not known quite why gluten has this effect on coeliac sufferers. It could be due to an allergy, to the lack of an enzyme which is supposed to break down gluten, to an abnormality in the intestinal membrane, or to a combination of all or some of these possible causes.

There is a slightly higher risk of a child being born with the disease if there is a family history of it.

TREATMENT

Coeliac disease is not very common; only one in 500 are affected. But it can be a permanent condition.

There is, as yet, no cure for the disease; the only effective treatment is a gluten-free diet. If gluten is avoided, the villi in the intestinal lining will grow again, but they will disappear once more if gluten is reintroduced in the diet.

Avoiding gluten is not always easy, as it is so much a part of the Western diet, but gluten-free products and alternatives are available.

Gluten is a protein found in some cereal products, such as bread. Coeliac disease sufferers need to exclude it from their diet.

WATCHPOINTS

If your child is diagnosed as having coeliac disease, you will have to make sure there is no gluten in her diet. This means she must avoid all foods made from wheat, barley, rye or oats.
● When in doubt, check the ingredients listed on the label.
● Use gluten-free rather than the ordinary varieties of:
  Baby foods (cereals, vegetables, fruits)
  Spaghetti and macaroni
  Semolina
  Biscuits
  Flour
  Bread (breadmix, canned white or brown)
  Baking powder
  Cakes
  Crispbread
  Topping and biscuit mixes
  Bedtime drinks
  Soup mixes
  Soya bran
● Some gluten-free products carry a special symbol: a circle containing a crossed-out ear of wheat.

ANDREW McCLENAGHAN/SPL

■ COLDS

See also ADENOIDS, BRONCHITIS, COLD SORES, CROUP, EAR PROBLEMS, PNEUMONIA, TONSILS

If you have young children in the family, one illness from which you are not going to be able to protect them is the common cold. Children's immune systems are immature and will not yet have learned to cope with the numerous viruses that cause colds. As a result, they can suffer quite a few such infections each year. The problem can be at its worst when they start school, and any colds they catch there will then be brought home and possibly infect other members of the family.

SPREADING IT

A baby with a cold can be quite distressing for parents. Babies have small nasal passages and a cold makes breathing through the nose difficult and can interfere with their ability to feed.

Contrary to popular wisdom, colds are *not* caused by sitting in a draught, or by getting cold and wet — although it is true that these can lower the body's resistance and make it easier for an infection to take hold. The common cold is in fact not one disease but many, produced by at least 20 different types of virus. To complicate matters further, within any one of these groups of viruses there are hundreds — possibly thousands — of variations.

Colds are transmitted in droplets and are spread when breathing out, sneezing and coughing. The virus attacks the mucous membrane of the nose, causing a clear discharge which gradually thickens. The mucus can spread to other parts of the respiratory system, causing secondary infections like sinusitis or bronchitis.

SYMPTOMS

The first signs that your child is developing a cold may be loss of appetite and generally seeming 'off colour'. In more severe cases, he may look feverish and even vomit. He

COMPLICATIONS OF COLDS

Complication	Possible symptoms	Cause	Treatment
Otitis media (infection of middle ear)	Earache	Infection by bacteria in mucus from nose or throat; violent nose blowing can push mucus along Eustachian tubes, or swollen tonsils and adenoids can cause blockage and build-up of mucus	Antibiotics and probably nose drops (to aid drainage) from doctor. 'Runny' ear may indicate a burst ear-drum and needs urgent treatment to prevent later deafness
Tonsillitis and infected adenoids	Sore throat; general aches and pains; headaches; vomiting; fever	Infection by germs entering through the mouth or nose; can lead to otitis media	Antibiotics from doctor; paracetamol for pain and fever; tonsils only removed after repeated tonsilitis, and adenoids if causing repeated otitis media.
Sinusitis (infection of sinuses, the small cavities in the skull)	Pain above or below eyes; fever; thick discharge from nose; persistent catarrh	Infection from mucus which has filled sinuses	Antibiotics and nose drops to reduce swelling of membranes; physiotherapy if catarrh is persistent
Cold sores	Painful ulcers in the mouth, spreading to form sores around the lips and nose	Infection by the Herpes Simplex virus which attacks when resistance to infection is lowered	Ointment prescribed by doctor. Sores should disappear in a week or so

may also complain of a sore throat, although children seem to suffer less from sore throats than adults. He will sneeze frequently and his nose will produce a large amount of watery catarrh which, after a day or two, will become thicker and block the nose. The glands in his neck may also become swollen.

As the cold progresses, mucus from the nose may trickle down to the throat and the resulting irritation may lead to a cough. This is more likely to happen when a child is lying down in bed, so you may find that your child's cough is worse at night. If this is the case, try raising the bed slightly at the headboard end.

All this may or may not be accompanied by a higher-than-normal temperature although you should note that in babies in particular, you should not use temperature as a guide to the degree of illness as babies can be quite ill without having a fever.

COMPLICATIONS

As well as the usual runny nose, sneezing and coughing, the flow of bacteria-laden mucus and the overall lowering of the body's resistance can lead to various secondary infections. One of the most common in children is otitis media, or infection of the middle ear. Mucus from the back of the nose can travel up a Eustachian tube (one of the tubes leading from the throat to the ear) to the middle ear and infect it. Pus then collects inside the middle ear, behind the ear drum, which causes earache and often a high temperature. If you suspect your child has an ear infection, consult your doctor.

Another common complication is infected tonsils and adenoids. These act as a filter against germs entering the body via the nose or mouth, and if a cold virus is present, they will become inflamed and swollen.

Acute inflammation of the tonsils is known as tonsillitis and should be investigated by a doctor.

TREATMENT

Despite vast amounts of medical research, so far no cure exists for the common cold. Antibiotics are ineffective against the cold virus itself, although they may be used for secondary bacterial infections, such as otitis media.

No protective vaccine for colds has as yet been developed either. This is hardly surprising when you consider that such a vaccine would have to prime the cells of the body to recognize literally thousands of different types of virus.

The only treatment for colds is to ease the symptoms of the illness, and

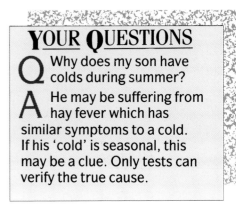

YOUR QUESTIONS

Q Why does my son have colds during summer?

A He may be suffering from hay fever which has similar symptoms to a cold. If his 'cold' is seasonal, this may be a clue. Only tests can verify the true cause.

to make the patient as comfortable as possible while the infection runs its course. Unless you suspect that your child's cold is in some way unusual and that there may be secondary infection, there is no point in calling on your doctor: he will not be able to do any more for your child than you can yourself.

CARING FOR THE PATIENT

Doctors sometimes prescribe nose drops for a baby with a cold. These can be very effective in clearing the nasal passages, especially important

should not need nose drops — unless, of course, he sucks his thumb.

You should, in any case, show your child how to blow his nose correctly, blowing only one nostril at a time and closing the other with a finger. Blowing both nostrils at once can force mucus up the Eustachian tubes, and risk setting up infection in the middle ear.

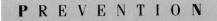

PREVENTION

There is very little you can do to prevent colds, except to make sure

Children mixing in groups are bound to spread and pick up colds. The virus is carried on droplets exhaled by the infected and inhaled by the others.

before a feed, but should not be used without a doctor's advice and are not recommended for more than about three days as they can damage the air passages.

Unlike a baby, an older child with a blocked nose can breathe effectively through his mouth instead, so he

that your child is generally healthy so that he can build up his resistance to infection (which increases with age).

There is no conclusive evidence that taking extra vitamin C, in the form of fresh fruit or supplements, helps either.

Protect a young baby by firmly keeping visitors with colds away from him — but if you or other members of your family have colds, you will probably already have infected him even before you know that you are ill.

YOUR QUESTIONS

Q Should I give my three-year-old anything for her cold?

A You should not automatically give medicines for a cold. If your child has a fever, you can give paracetamol, in tablet or syrup form and in the right dosage, to bring down the temperature and to help her sleep at night. Avoid medicines designed to suppress a cough — coughing is nature's way of loosening mucus in the throat. A cough linctus, however, can have a soothing effect.

Q Should I keep my child away from school when he has a cold?

A This depends on how ill you think he feels. Keeping him home would limit the spread of infection, but it may not be necessary from his point of view unless he seems too listless and tired to cope with school.

WATCHPOINTS

Colds are a very common childhood illness but may cause your child some distress if the symptoms persist over several days or keep recurring. See your doctor if:
• your child has a high temperature after the first day of the cold; or is suffering from earache, deafness, a very sore throat, a wheezy cough, or a thick, greenish discharge from his nose; or is listless and has no appetite
• your baby seems at all ill, with or without fever, and has gone off his food. Never give medicines to a young baby without a doctor's prescription.

■ COLD SORES

'Cold sore' is the term used to describe certain blisters that form in and around the mouth and near the nose. The name is rather misleading because they are not caused by a cold, but can appear at the end of one, when the body's ability to fight infection has been weakened.

Babies do not seem to get cold sores. Young children get them after the age of one, but by the age of about five, most seem to have built up immunity to them.

CAUSES

Cold sores are caused by the Herpes Simplex virus. The virus penetrates the skin and gets into the nerves beneath. It then lies dormant but flares up from time to time causing the 'cold sore' to appear.

SYMPTOMS

When your child has his first attack of cold sores in the mouth, he will suddenly produce a rash of flattish white ulcers; these may be on his tongue, on the roof of his mouth, on his gums or inside his cheeks. They will be very painful and, as a result, he may not feel like eating or perhaps even drinking.

Subsequent attacks around the lips and near the nose will begin with an itchy feeling in the affected area, up to two days before the sores themselves erupt. An inflamed cluster of tiny blisters will then develop; these will fill with a yellowish-white fluid, and will feel itchy, hot and can often be painful.

Sometimes these inflamed blisters burst within two to four days of appearing, but initially, all cold sores start to heal by drying up and forming crusts on top.

TREATMENT

Once the virus is in the skin, there is no way you can be rid of it; once the sores have developed, there is no treatment that will stop them running their course. Most sores will dis-

appear after about a week.

However, if the sore persists or is extensive, your doctor may prescribe an antiviral ointment to kill off the virus. The greasiness of these ointments will also help to stop the sores from cracking when they have dried up.

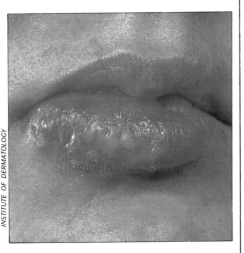

A cold sore is a cluster of tiny blisters caused by the Herpes Simplex virus. It can feel hot and itchy and will dry up as it begins to heal.

Discourage your child from picking the crusts off the sores: they could then be reinfected and this would prolong the whole healing process. Also discourage him from touching the sores, or he may spread the infection further.

YOUR QUESTIONS

Q My mother suffers from cold sores. Will she pass them on by kissing my daughter?

A Yes – cold sores are infectious and the virus can be passed on to very young children like this.

Q Do cold sores have a tendency to run in families?

A Yes, but no one really knows why. Possibly it is because some families are not very good at building up resistance to the virus.

■ COLIC

Colic, the term used to describe painful intestinal cramp, comes in many forms, such as intestinal colic, kidney colic, menstrual colic and so on. But most parents, when they talk of colic are referring to infantile colic which is suffered by many healthy babies. Its causes are not well understood. Both breast-fed and bottle-fed infants experience colic, so diet cannot be blamed for the condition. This problem is also known as '12 week colic' because the symptoms may end at 12 weeks.

SYMPTOMS

Persistent crying accompanied by legs doubled up and a hardened stomach are a sure sign of colic in a baby. This is very distressing to the

Rocking a baby with colic often eases the symptoms.

parents, yet there are no other signs of ill-health. The baby eats well and continues to put on weight.

TREATMENT

There really is no cure for infantile colic, but do not, therefore, just leave your baby to cry on his own. Try and soothe him in every way possible, carry him around, rock him, push him in his pram or take him for a drive in the car. Some of these measures work some of the time but, basically, if you do have a colicky baby, you have to resign yourselves to some months of crying, and just keep reminding yourselves that it will end.

PARENT CARE

A colicky baby will absorb your energies even more than usual in those very early months, and it is very important that parents take care of themselves too, by snatching rest and sleep whenever they can. Don't worry about the housework so long as you can get some time to relax.

Some doctors have a theory that if the parents are tense, their child is affected and this makes the cramp worse. But this is not a proven theory. After all, new babies suffer colic first, and the parents' tension comes second. But, still, it will help both of you to catch up on as much rest and sleep as you can.

YOUR QUESTIONS

Q My first child was a serene and happy baby. I am desperate with worry, however, because my new one-month-old cries and kicks all the time. Is there no medicine to help her?

A Your baby has the symptoms of colic and there is very little you can do, except hold and soothe her. You can give her small doses of gripe water, which brings relief, at least to the parents, for a while. Take heart — she will stop crying eventually and may well become as serene as your first child.

Q I'm worried that my baby who has colic, cannot digest properly and is not eating enough.

A Don't worry — a colicky baby will eat well and gain weight anyway.

■ COLITIS

Colitis is an inflammation of the colon — the part of the large intestine that loops around the abdomen. The function of the colon is to move solid material from the small intestine to the rectum, which leads to the anus. As the solids pass through, the colon absorbs salt and water from them. There are three main kinds of colitis — acute, and the more serious forms known as ulcerative (chronic), and ischaemic colitis. Acute colitis sometimes occurs in children, whereas ulcerative colitis rarely affects the young, and ischaemic colitis, when the blood supply is impeded, occurs only in older adults.

SYMPTOMS

The onset of acute colitis is usually quite sudden. The child will have diarrhoea, sometimes as often as once every half hour, and recurrent abdominal pain. The diarrhoea will be very watery, possibly accompanied by some mucus and, in more severe cases, blood as well. The child

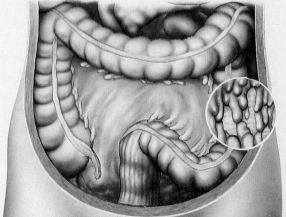

may be vomiting, and may have a fever. The diarrhoea can last between two days and several weeks, and the pains often continue for several days even after the diarrhoea has stopped.

Whenever diarrhoea occurs frequently, there is a danger that the child will become dehydrated as a result of fluid loss. The risk is greater if the child is also losing fluid through vomiting or excessive sweating. In

severe cases of acute colitis, there is also a danger that the colon wall could become perforated.

ULCERATIVE COLITIS

In ulcerative colitis, the diarrhoea, which usually occurs up to 15 times per day, tends to be semi-solid, mixed with mucus or pus and, often, dark-red blood. Abdominal pain may be experienced, but this is not always the case. In mild forms of ulcerative colitis, the symptoms may last for a few days, then disappear for months or even years before recurring.

CAUSES

Acute colitis usually occurs as a result of the child becoming infected with bacteria such as *Shigella*, *Salmonella* or *Campylobacter*. These bacteria are sometimes transferred from person to person by touch, but are most commonly spread in food that has been contaminated because of poor hygiene conditions.

In tropical countries, acute colitis is often caused by invisible organisms called amoebae which have got into

Colitis is inflammation of the colon (left). If caused by an ulcer (inset), it is known as ulcerative colitis but this is rare in children. Colitis can also be caused by bacteria, such as Salmonella (below)

FRANK KENNARD

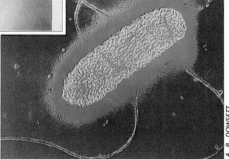

A. B. DOWSETT

the drinking water.

The cause of ulcerative colitis is not known, but one theory suggests that it is triggered off by a food allergy. An alternative theory blames a virus, and yet another idea links this disease with stress.

TREATMENT

For mild cases of acute colitis, the only treatment required is to give the child large quantities of liquid to drink in order to prevent dehydration. You can buy a mixture of salt and sugar from a chemist which you dissolve in water.

YOUR QUESTIONS

Q My daughter sometimes has diarrhoea. How can I tell if she has colitis?

A If the diarrhoea occurs every hour, or even more frequently, and your daughter has recurring abdominal pains, then it is likely that she has acute colitis and she should be seen by your doctor. Any more servere form of colitis is most unlikely in a young child.

Q How can I ensure that my little boy does not suffer from colitis?

A Taking care over hygiene in the kitchen will help to reduce the possibility of colitis and some other illnesses. Make sure that fresh food is stored at a low temperature (5°C or lower), and that cooked food is not stored near or directly under uncooked food which might infect it with bacteria. Also, ensure that all fish, meat, poultry and eggs are properly cooked, so that any harmful bacteria present are destroyed.

In more severe cases, the child may require hospital treatment. An intravenous drip will be used to maintain the level of liquid in the body, and laboratory tests will be carried out on specimens of the diarrhoea stool.

INTERNAL EXAMINATION

The doctor may also examine the lining of the child's colon by inserting a sigmoidoscope or a colonoscope. In the case of acute colonitis, a characteristic reddening of the colon wall will be seen. If this infection has led to a perforation of the colon, the condition will be corrected by perfoming an emergency operation.

If ulcerative colitis is diagnosed on examination, then a barium X-ray of the colon may be taken. In mild cases, ulcerative colitis is treated with a drug called sulphasalazine. Steroid drugs are given if the symptoms are severe, and the worst cases may require surgery.

■ COLOUR BLINDNESS

Colour blindness is the inability to distinguish between certain colours — usually red and green. This kind of condition affects about one in 20 males and one in 200 females. In a rare form of colour blindness, affecting males and females equally, all colours are seen in shades of grey.

SYMPTOMS

Many children are unaware that they are colour blind until they have a special test, usually at age seven. This is not so strange as they are usually able to distinguish some colours from one another. And although a red-green colour-blind child cannot distinguish these colours from each other, he will soon learn, for example, that the colour he sees when he looks at a ripe tomato is called 'red', and that the colour he sees when he looks at grass is called 'green'. So he becomes able to name the colours of common objects correctly, and it may be years before the child and his parents are surprised to find out that he has defective colour vision.

In young children, the symptoms of colour blindness are easily ignored because it is usually impossible to know whether a child is confusing one colour with another, or whether he has simply forgotten the correct name for a colour which he sees exactly the same as everyone else. If your child is old enough to communicate reasonably well and seems to have some difficulty in naming colours, it is advisable to take him to have his colour vision tested.

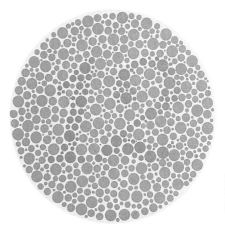

RAN DUNNS

Everyone can distinguish the number in the diagram, the first used in a series to test for colour blindness.

Colour vision is tested using a set of Ishihara cards. These have large numbers printed on them in dots of various tints against a background of differently tinted dots. A child will be able to see the numeral against the background if he can distinguish

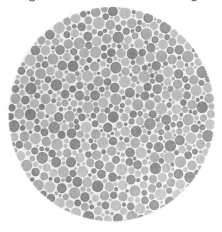

If your child cannot distinguish the squiggle from the background by tracing it with his finger, he may be 'blind' to certain colours.

between the different colours used. But, if his colour vision is defective, the dots in the numeral and background may appear the same, making it impossible for him to distinguish the numeral. By testing your child with cards printed in a range of colours, the extent of his colour blindness can be determined.

CAUSES

Colour is detected by cells called cones in the retina of the eye. Each cone contains a pigment that determines the colour it will respond to, so the absence of one of these pigments will mean that the child will confuse certain colours.

Colour blindness of this type is inherited, but may not appear in every generation. A woman with perfect colour vision can transmit red-green colour blindness to her children. But a girl born to a mother who is a carrier will suffer this defect only if her father is colour blind.

The rarer form of colour blindness, in which no colours can be distinguished, is caused by a diseased retina or optic nerve, which connects the retina to the brain. This defect is usually associated with a general deterioration of vision.

TREATMENT

Drug treatment will usually help to stop or slow down the weakening of vision associated with a diseased retina or optic nerve. No treatment is available for the inherited form of colour blindness. However, although it may, at times, be inconvenient, this condition never worsens, and the child's ability to see things in detail is not affected at all.

■ CONCUSSION

See also ACCIDENTS, FIRST AID and SHOCK

Concussion is a bruising of the brain, usually when the head receives a blow. It may also occur if the head is shaken violently. Young children are especially susceptible to concussion as their skulls are still relatively soft and more susceptible to blows.

The child may lose consciousness, usually for just a few seconds, but sometimes minutes. In very severe cases, he may remain unconscious for several weeks.

CAUSES

When the child's head is knocked or shaken, the brain may suddenly be forced against the skull with sufficient pressure to cause bruising. Shaking may result in bruising to several areas of the brain. A single blow tends to cause bruising below the site of the impact, where the skull is forced against the brain, and sometimes on the opposite side of the head too, possibly because of the jarring effect.

SYMPTOMS

In mild cases, the child may simply feel giddy for a little while and complain of a headache, which can persist for a day or two. If the injury was

caused by a blow, a painful bump will usually be found on the head.

If the child seems confused about what happened, or cannot remember, this indicates that he has prob-

If you suspect concussion, take your child to your doctor straight away.

ably been unconscious. In more serious cases, the child may remain unconscious for some minutes and, on coming round, may have problems with muscular control, you may notice slurred speech, for instance. The symptoms of concussion usually disappear as the damage to the brain gradually heals. However, a severe blow to the head could cause the child to remain unconscious 'in a coma' for several weeks.

YOUR QUESTIONS

Q I am worried that my son's colour blindness will make life difficult for him when he grows up, starts work and drives a car. What can be done to cure him?

A He cannot be cured of common colour blindness, but you should not worry. As far as driving is concerned, traffic lights can be distinguished by their positions, so colour blindness does not prevent a person from driving safely. However, a few jobs do require people with good colour vision. For example, a ship's navigator needs to be able to distinguish between the port (red) and starboard (green) lights on distant ships at night.

ACTIONPLAN

● If you find the child unconscious, check his breathing and heartbeat. If either is absent, start resuscitation immediately (see **ARTIFICIAL RESPIRATION**) and have someone send for an ambulance.

● If any blood or other liquid is discharged through the ear, call an ambulance immediately.

● Clean and dress any wounds. In the case of deep cuts, stop the bleeding first (see **FIRST AID**) and call a doctor or take the child to a hospital.

● Even if the child appears to recover quickly, take him to a doctor for a check-up. Watch out for signs of difficulties with muscular control.

■ CONJUNCTIVITIS

Conjunctivitis, commonly known as red eye, is an inflammation of the conjunctiva – the membrane covering the white of the eye and the inner surface of the eyelids. It frequently occurs in babies and young children, who get it from rubbing their eyes. This type of conjunctivitis is not serious and usually responds quickly to treatment. However, some more serious forms of conjunctivitis, including the type known as trachoma, can cause blindness, so it is important for the doctor to check any inflammation of the eye in order to have the infection correctly diagnosed.

C A U S E S

The most common cause of conjunctivitis is infection by bacteria. When a child rubs the eyes, she may transfer bacteria from the fingers on to the eye surface. Children with runny noses caused by a cold often develop conjunctivitis in this way. Bacteria from the nose are rubbed off on to the hands and transferred to the eyes.

PASSING IT ON

Bacteria may also be transferred to the eyes from infected face flannels or towels. Occasionally, a fly or other foreign body that gets in the eye leaves behind germs that cause conjunctivitis, even if the offender is removed almost immediately.

A particular bacteria called Chlamydia trachomatis gives rise to the very serious form of the disease called trachoma, which occurs in tropical countries. This kind of conjunctivitis is spread by touch, especially in overcrowded living conditions. In cooler climates, the Chlamydia organism gives rise to a less severe form of conjunctivitis.

ADULT CARRIERS

Between five and ten per cent of young adults carry *Chlamydia* in their genital tract, where it is responsible for the most common type of sexually transmitted infection, called non-specific urethritis (nsu). *Chlamydia* is present in the semen or vaginal fluid,

so there is a danger that parents may transfer the bacteria by touch to their child's eyes, either directly or via flannel or towel.

A woman carrying Chlamydia in her vaginal fluid risks passing it to her baby during the birth. Within a few weeks of delivery, the child may develop conjunctivitis as a result; this form of the infection is called

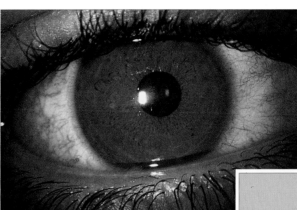

ophthalmia neonatorum.

Allergy is another cause of conjunctivitis. Children who suffer from hay fever often develop conjunctivitis when the pollen count is high. Grains of pollen from the air get into the eye and set up an allergic reaction. In some children, industrial dust, for example from wool or cotton, can have a similar effect, and chemical fumes can cause conjunctivitis too.

BLOCKED TEAR DUCT

Conjunctivitis usually affects both eyes, but babies occasionally become infected in one eye only. This usually happens when a tear duct leading from the eye to the nose becomes blocked. As the liquid from the eye cannot trickle down into the nose in the normal way, the eye becomes too moist, and tears run continually down the face. As a result, the baby frequently rubs the eye, which soon becomes infected.

S Y M P T O M S

The first symptom of conjunctivitis is usually a gritty feeling in the eye, with irritation just under the eyelids. The eye becomes red because blood vessels in the conjunctiva become

enlarged and inflamed, and pus forms, producing a discharge.

If the complaint is caused by a bacterial or viral infection, large quantities of pus may be produced. This clouds the child's eye, causing a sticky feeling and blurring vision. Overnight, the discharge may dry on the child's eyelashes and eyelids, temporarily sealing the lids together.

In conjunctivitis, the membrane covering the front of the eyes and the inside of the eyelids gets inflamed (left). Before applying the medication, gently wipe away any pus with a clean swab (below).

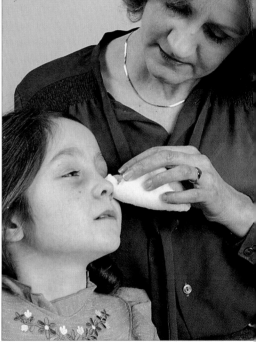

T R E A T M E N T

In most cases, a doctor can tell from a brief examination whether the conjunctivitis is an infective or an allergic type. In cases of infective conjunctivitis, the doctor may use a swab to take a sample of pus from the eyes for examination in the laboratory. This can determine whether the infection is bacterial or viral, and thus help in determining the most appropriate treatment.

For infective conjunctivitis, the

doctor usually prescribes antibiotics. Chloramphenicol and sulphacetamide are often used. Drops may be prescribed for use during the day, with an ointment for the night. This is particularly helpful in preventing the eyelids from sticking together. If there is a lot of discharge, it is advisable to bathe the child's eyes, or to wipe the surfaces of her eyelids with cotton wool dipped in warm, slightly salty water – about one level tablespoonful to half a litre (one pint) of cooled boiled water.

ANTIBIOTIC EYEDROPS

Chlamydial conjunctivitis is usually treated with the antibiotic tetracycline in the form of eye drops. In addition, the child is often given an antibiotic to be taken by mouth, such as xithromycin or erythromycin, as the infection may be slow to clear with local treatment alone. Chlamydial conjunctivitis occurring outside the tropics does not usually cause severe infection and generally clears without producing permanent eye damage. However, in the tropics, trachoma caused by a chlamydial infection should be treated quickly. Otherwise, the eye may require surgery and could perhaps suffer

permanent damage.

Allergic conjunctivitis is treated with drops containing anti-allergy drugs. Antihistamine eye drops are useful for short-term treatment but for long-term use, cromoglycate drops are usually prescribed to counteract the allergic response.

■ CONSTIPATION

Constipation is an interference with the process by which food passes through the intestines. It causes long, often highly irregular gaps between bowel movements – sometimes as long as one week.

VARYING INTERVALS

All children have their own particular patterns of bowel movements. These may occur several times each day or only once every two or three days. So if you have a child who defecates at quite long intervals, do not automatically assume that he is constipated. There may be nothing at all wrong with him.

SYMPTOMS

The abdomen of a constipated child will be enlarged, and he may complain of discomfort. This condition is often accompanied by flatulence

BUBBLES

Eating a cereal bar (above) provides more fibre than chocolate.
High fibre foods, such as whole grain bread, bran, dried fruit and beans (below) help to prevent constipation.

(wind), a furred tongue, bad breath and headaches. And the child may experience pain while eventually passing motions because his faeces will have hardened, as the moisture from them is absorbed into the body.

CAUSES

Solid food normally passes along the intestines by rhythmic waves of muscular action called peristalsis. Probably the most common cause of interference to this process is the food itself. Once the child's digestive system has fully developed, it is able to break up most kinds of solid food material eaten and extract the nutritious substances. However, the human digestive system cannot break down plant cellulose, which commonly occurs in fruit and vegetables and in the outer husks of corn grain, a form called bran. Plant cellulose in food is generally referred to as roughage, or fibre.

Although it is not digested, fibre plays an important role in the body because it stimulates peristalsis. So a diet lacking in fibre is a common cause of constipation. Some foods, such as meat, eggs and cheese, contain no fibre at all.

OTHER CAUSES

Another cause of constipation is simply a lack of food in the intestines. If a child has an illness that causes loss of appetite, his condition may become complicated with the onset of constipation. Also, lack of exercise, caused by a prolonged period in bed, can lead to constipation. The diseases of colitis and diverticulitis are sometimes a direct cause.

Some children experience pain on defecation because of damaged veins (piles) or cracks (fissures) in the anus. This condition makes the child reluctant to defecate, so the faeces accumulate in the body and become hard because water from them is absorbed into the blood stream. In turn, this makes them even more painful to pass from the body.

INVOLUNTARY INACTION

Sometimes, the cause of constipation is psychological, rather than physical. Like breathing and the heartbeat, peristalsis is controlled by a part of the brain that works without our direct control. However, a child soon learns to control *when* he defecates, and this ability to hold back a bowel movement sometimes causes a problem. Almost in an absent-minded way, the child may overlook signals from the intestine indicating that the bowel is full and a visit to the lavatory is now due.

YOUR QUESTIONS

Q Why does my son always suffer from constipation when we go on holiday?

A Many people blame holiday constipation on a change in the water, but it is more likely to be due to a change in your child's daily routine or a change in his diet. Even using an unfamiliar toilet causes constipation in some children. They become so used to defecating in places they know well that the brain tends to prevent the process happening elsewhere. Another possibility is that your son is relaxing for too much of the time when on holiday. If so, encourage him to take more exercise.

Q My daughter often suffers from constipation. Is this likely to cause blood poisoning?

A No. It is an old wives' tale that faeces retained in the body for a prolonged period will cause poisoning. Although the faeces are teeming with bacteria, these are harmless and they stay in the bowel, where they aid digestion. Constipation may make your daughter feel drained of energy and generally off-colour, but there is no risk of poisoning.

TREATMENT

If constipation occurs along with some other illness, then consult your doctor, as it could be dangerous to treat your child yourself. In other cases, the best treatment is a common-sense one. Make sure that he eats foods containing fibre regularly, and give him plenty to drink as this will help to soften the faeces. Encourage your child to exercise in order to tone up the abdominal muscles and also to relieve stress and promote relaxation.

Avoid giving your child laxatives, except as a last resort. Most laxatives work by stimulating the nerves of the intestine to encourage peristalsis, which sometimes causes pain and even diarrhoea.

OVERUSE

Once the child's intestine has been cleared out by the use of a laxative, it tends to hold the next lot of food for a fairly long time. Do not be tempted to give your child another dose of laxative. Simply give his digestive system time to return to normal, and make sure he has plenty of fibre in his diet and takes some regular exercise. Repeated doses of laxative may condition the intestinal nerves to the artificial stimulation so much that they fail to work without the laxative.

If you feel it is necessary to give your child a laxative, syrup of figs should be suitable. If you are unable to find a remedy for your child's condition, consult your doctor in case it is caused by some undiscovered underlying disease.

■ CONVULSIONS
see also EPILEPSY

Convulsions are violent, involuntary and irregular movements of the body. Also known as fits or seizures, convulsions are among the most distressing symptoms that the parent may have to deal with.

CAUSES

The most common cause of convulsions in young children is a high body temperature. The tendency to react to high temperatures by having convulsions is often present in other members of the family, but the child usually grows out of this condition and, after the age of five, febrile convulsions (those caused by fever) rarely occur.

Convulsions in newborn babies are rare but distressing. The baby will be tested for low blood sugar or calcium, but it may remain unexplained.

A baby is wired up for an electro-encephalograph to detect any disorders, such as epilepsy, that may lead to convulsions.

Another cause in children is a disorder of the central nervous system, such as epilepsy. And sometimes a child's temper tantrums are so severe that she has convulsions. In some children, certain drugs may cause convulsions, especially if the stipulated dosage is exceeded.

SYMPTOMS

Febrile convulsions may start with the child becoming unconscious and falling down. She usually twitches uncontrollably, and writhes and shakes. The teeth may be clenched violently at times and, if the tongue gets in the way, it may be bitten through. The eyes roll upwards, breathing becomes laboured and there is sometimes frothing at the mouth. She may also spontaneously empty her bladder or bowels.

AFTERMATH

Convulsions of this kind last for only a few minutes, after which the child may briefly regain consciousness. She then falls asleep, and may make peculiar facial expressions while snoring.

Epileptic convulsions may be similar, but they can take many forms. Sometimes only one part of the body is affected and the child may remain conscious throughout.

WATCHPOINTS

- If one of your children has had convulsions caused by fever, then be prepared for the same to happen to any brothers or sisters, as this problem tends to run in families.
- Any child suffering from a fever needs to be cooled, and this is particularly important with a child known to be susceptible to febrile convulsions. If you spot the temperature rise in time, bathing the child's skin with tepid water may be sufficient to prevent her from having convulsions.

TREATMENT

Stay with the child if she starts to have convulsions, as you will be able to prevent her injuring herself. Kneel beside her on the floor and lay her on her side so that, if she vomits, there will be no danger of her choking.

If possible, place a clean pad, such as a folded linen handkerchief, between the child's teeth. This will prevent her from biting through her tongue. But, if the teeth are clamped shut, do not try to force them apart.

A SAFE POSITION

Loosen the child's clothing, especially around the neck and waist. While the convulsions are occurring, try to prevent her from striking her head or limbs on nearby objects. If possible, pull her away from such hazards, but do not try to restrain her, and do not try to arouse her by slapping.

When the writhing stops, move the child into the recovery position and contact your doctor. While waiting for the doctor to come, stay with the child. If she has a fever, cool her by mopping with lukewarm water, or wrap a damp cloth around her head.

After he has stopped writhing, place your child in the recovery position which will prevent him from choking on his vomit or saliva.

YOUR QUESTIONS

Q My toddler sometimes throws terrible temper tantrums. Could these bring on convulsions?

A Convulsions can sometimes be brought on by severe temper tantrums. It is possible that if your child is very worked up and she holds her breath for very long, this may make her unconscious. But, in spite of the distressing symptoms, the condition is not serious, and she will soon regain consciousness. Be attentive and wait for the symptoms to pass. However, try not to let her use this as a means of getting you to do what she wants.

■ COT DEATH

Cot death is a term used to describe the sudden death of an apparently healthy child, usually while resting in his cot or pram, or even in his mother's arms. The child may die in his sleep, but death sometimes occurs while a child is feeding or playing. In each case, the child dies suddenly, without warning, and for no obvious reason. Although any death of a young child is sad, an unexpected and unexplained death is particularly disturbing for a family.

BABIES AT RISK

Cot death, also known as sudden infant death syndrome, or SIDS, is among the commonest causes of death among babies, claiming the life of about one baby in every 800. Babies aged between four weeks and one year, and especially those between two and four months, are most susceptible. There are more cases among boys, twins, bottle-fed babies, those whose weight at birth was low, and those who were pre-term or who had breathing difficulties at the time of birth. The incidence of cot death seems to increase during autumn and winter.

SYMPTOMS

One of the most puzzling aspects of cot death is that there is no warning that it is likely to occur. Many babies who have died in this way appear to have had no prior symptoms of illness. In some cases, however, the child has had a cold, a runny nose, a slightly high temperature, listlessness, drowsiness or even a slight breathing difficulty. Such symptoms would not normally mean that anything was seriously wrong, and yet death occurs suddenly, the child usually appearing to have died peacefully while asleep.

CAUSES

It is usually a legal requirement that, whenever a child dies suddenly and for no obvious reason, a pathologist must make an examination. As a result, in about one-third of cases of sudden infant death, the cause is identified. It may be a previously undiscovered internal abnormality, such as a heart defect, or perhaps an unnoticed infection.

The unexpected loss of a baby is even sadder if it is through cot death, as the cause is often not known.

However, in the majority of cases, a routine autopsy fails to discover any apparent cause of death. This sad phenomenon is one of the most perplexing problems facing doctors, and research continues in an effort to establish the causes of the mystery deaths.

INFECTIONS

When a baby is born, he has quite a high resistance to infection because his bloodstream contains various antibodies, transferred to him in the womb from the mother's circulation. But, over the first few weeks of life, these antibodies gradually disappear, and it takes several months for the baby to develop his own antibodies. For this reason, the level of antibodies in a baby's blood are at their lowest between the ages of two and four months, thus making the baby most susceptible to infection during this period. Some doctors think that certain mild viral infections, or toxins from bacterial infections, may have a much more severe effect on a baby at this time in his life than they normally do later.

ABNORMAL TEMPERATURE

As cot deaths are more common in winter than summer, it might be thought that a low body temperature would somehow make cot death more likely to occur. However, research into possible explanations associated with changes in the baby's body temperature suggests that the risk increases when this temperature is excessively high, rather than low. This apparent paradox is explained by the fact that, when the weather becomes cooler, parents often put extra clothing on their baby and keep him in a warm room. The advice to make sure babies are put down to sleep on their backs — which has been part of the UK's information campaign to reduce cot death — may be effective because it helps the baby regulate his own temperature, and prevents overheating.

OTHER REACTIONS

Cot death occurs more frequently in bottle-fed babies. This may be because some babies become allergic to cow's milk protein and this triggers an abnormality in the way the breathing passages work. Or, because breast milk boosts the immune system, breast-fed babies may be able to fight whatever causes cot death. Parents are also advised not to smoke or at least to confine smoking to rooms where the baby is not present. Smoking has been shown to be a factor in the rate of cot death. Other research has looked at the way substances in the cot mattress may degenerate and poison the baby — but this is far from proven. Nevertheless, parents are advised to buy a new mattress for each child.

BREATHING PROBLEMS

Recently, it's been thought that apnoea, or the cessation of breathing, is a cause of cot death. Many people have periods of apnoea lasting a few seconds. It usually ends with the person taking a deep breath,

But, in babies, a developmental defect of immaturity in the brain centre that controls breathing involuntarily may prevent the normal breathing pattern from being resumed.

However, the relationship between the number of apnoeic attacks that a child has and the chance of cot death occurring is still unclear. A child who often suffers from apnoea may cope well with the problem and not necessarily be at greater risk.

YOUR QUESTIONS

Q I lost my first child through cot death at the age of four weeks. I am now pregnant again. What is the risk of my next child suffering the same fate?

A Many parents who have lost a child through cot death have a great fear of losing their next child in the same way. Fortunately, although this sometimes happens, the chance of a cot death occurring in a family that has already suffered in this way are little greater than in any other family.

Q I have been told I should not let my baby sleep face down, in order to protect her from cot death. Is this correct?

A Yes. It's thought that the 'back to sleep' campaign run in recent years has caused a significant fall in the cot death statistics. Your baby can be placed on her side if she doesn't seem comfortable on her back. Other measures you should take are to stop smoking, or to avoid smoking near your baby, and to make sure your baby isn't over-heated. Your baby doesn't need any more clothing or bedding than you do, once she gets beyond the newborn period. Always seek your doctor's advice if you are worried about your baby's health.

PREVENTION

Cot death may occur even when a baby has had the best care, for there are many possible causes. However, various measures can be taken to reduce the chances (see left).

If possible, breast feed the baby, because your milk will provide additional antibodies to help your baby fight infection, and it will also reduce the risk of an allergy developing.

Keep a thermometer in your baby's room so that you can check that the air never becomes too hot or cold. The temperature should be between 18°C (65°F) and 20°C (68°F). Make sure that the baby's bedclothes are warm, but not too heavy. If, however, your baby's temperature rises and cannot be brought back to normal by cooling or giving the child paracetamol syrup, seek advice from your doctor.

■ COUGHS

A cough is the forcing of air from the chest in a sudden, usually noisy, action. Coughing is the body's way of helping to clear the air passages of obstructions or other irritants that may cause harm. It is a reflex action triggered by the presence of the foreign material. In the case of an obstruction, such as a piece of food lodged in the throat, coughing stops as soon as the item has been dislodged and coughed up. But usually, coughing is associated with infections, and is more persistent.

SYMPTOMS

Coughing is a symptom that something is wrong in the air passages, but more important than the cough itself is the material (if any) coughed up. A productive cough is one that brings up phlegm, and this may be white, yellowish or, if blood is present, pink. A dry cough is one that does not bring up any material from the air passages.

Other important features are the frequency at which the coughing occurs and whether there is any

SHEILA TERRY/SPL

Cough linctus will soothe a dry cough, while an expectorant cough medicine will loosen phlegm.

accompanying pain. The child may also suffer from hoarseness, a certain breathlessness and fever.

CAUSES

In the early stages of a cold, the lining of the breathing passages becomes inflamed, and this may cause a dry, irritating cough.

A persistent dry cough associated with a fever may be the first sign of a lung infection such as pneumonia. If there is hoarseness as well, there is a possibility of laryngitis — an infection of the larynx, or voice box.

Coughing that brings up a little clear, white phlegm is common in the later stages of a cold. But thick, yellow phlegm usually indicates an infection, such as bronchitis, which may also cause wheezing.

If the child has breathing difficulties as well as a cough, the cause may be more serious.

Persistent coughing is commonly one of the first signs of asthma in children, and may occur long before a child has any difficulty with breathing. The coughing is often worse at night, and the child may later develop chronic nasal catarrh and a characteristic wheezing, finding it more difficult to breathe out than in.

Croup usually gives children a cough that is initially dry, later becoming productive and then noisy, with laboured breathing.

Violent coughing that occurs in spasms, with vomiting and sometimes a crowing noise, may indicate whooping cough.

MORE SERIOUS COMPLAINTS

Coughing accompanied by pain may indicate that the child is suffering from a serious condition, such as pleurisy. This infection of the lung and its covering membrane produces a sharp pain in the chest whenever the child coughs or breathes deeply.

Coughing that produces blood may be caused by lung infections, such as tuberculosis, or may, in extreme cases, mark the onset of heart failure.

In cases where the shortness of breath is severe, the cause may, again, be imminent heart failure, and a doctor should be called at once.

TREATMENT

Most coughs, especially those accompanying colds, are not dangerous and get better on their own within a few days, without any treatment. Using medicines to suppress the cough can be harmful, especially if it is a productive cough, and may delay recovery.

A productive cough may be eased by using the type of medicine known as an expectorant. It will help to liquefy the sputum, thus making it easier to cough up. However, if your child is old enough to use a steam inhaler, this may prove to be more effective as a remedy.

DECONGESTANTS

For a cough associated with a cold, the child may get relief from decongestant drops or a spray to relieve nasal catarrh. Otherwise, this may trickle down the back of the throat and cause more coughing. A warm, soothing drink, such as honey and lemon, often helps. Some children may prefer a fruit-based medicine, although this may be no more effective than an ordinary drink.

A dry cough may be treated with a suppressant, such as pholocodeine linctus. Call a doctor if any type of coughing persists, and seek medical advice immediately if a child has a painful cough, is having difficulty breathing or is producing blood.

YOUR QUESTIONS

Q Why can't my son stop coughing when he has a cold?

A Coughing caused by an illness is a reflex action and is carried out automatically by a part of the brain not normally affected by any decision of the patient. Your son simply has no control over the matter – if he needs to cough, his brain will make him cough. But do take him to see a doctor if this condition persists for long.

Q I have four children. If one starts coughing, it's not long before all the others are coughing too. How can I prevent this from happening?

A Prevention is certainly better than cure, and one of the main things to guard against is spreading germs by coughing. So teach your children to hold a handkerchief in front of their mouths whenever they feel a cough or sneeze coming on.

■ CRADLE CAP

As the name implies, cradle cap affects the heads of young babies. It is a greasy scalp condition that often develops when a baby is four to six weeks old, and some babies seem to be more susceptible than others to this complaint. Your baby's appearance may upset you but, although it looks unpleasant, cradle cap is not harmful, and it will not infect other children in the family.

SYMPTOMS

Very unattractive, greasy, yellow-brown or grey patches or crusts form on the baby's head. These formations are usually just on the scalp, but they may spread on to the forehead, and are sometimes found in the eyebrows. Occasionally, the cradle cap is accompanied by weeping red eruptions in the skin creases behind the ears, around the neck, under the arms and in the groin.

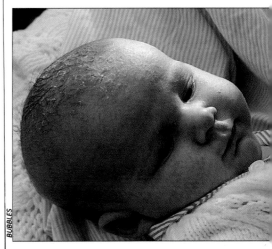

Cradle cap shows up as dry patches of skin on the scalp. Gentle washing with a special shampoo will help.

CAUSES

Sebacious glands all over the body produce an oil called sebum, which stops the skin and hair from drying out. The sebaceous glands in the young baby's scalp, and sometimes other areas, may produce too much sebum. If a mother is nervous about washing her baby's hair, she may not do it properly or often enough, and there is a possibility that the excess oil will build up, clog the pores and form the blemishes which are typical of cradle cap.

TREATMENT

Although cradle cap is harmless, it should be treated promptly because it becomes more awkward to deal with as the baby's hair grows. The treatment is simple and can be carried out quite easily at home.

Wash your baby's scalp every day,

YOUR QUESTIONS

Q My six-week-old baby has mild cradle cap. I don't like the idea of using a harsh shampoo on her as she is so young. Will it clear up if I rub in some baby oil and then wash it with baby shampoo?

A No. Ordinary baby oil and shampoo will not clear up cradle cap. Even if the condition is not very bad, you should still switch to a special antiseptic shampoo. If the cradle cap is hard to dislodge, rub in a little olive oil, nut oil or medicinal liquid paraffin – not baby oil. When the crusts have softened, carefully wash or comb them out.

Q I know that it is important to wash my baby's hair regularly to prevent cradle cap, but I am frightened of touching the 'soft spot' on top of his head. What exactly is the soft spot, and can it be easily damaged?

A There are two soft spots, or fontanelles – one on top of the baby's head and another, smaller one at the back of the skull. They are areas of soft cartilage, where the bones of the skull have not yet joined together. The fontanelles make the birth easier by allowing the skull to be compressed. But there is no need to worry about damaging them as they are covered by a very tough membrane which will easily withstand normal handling.

or every other day, using water and one per cent centrimide shampoo. This is an antiseptic shampoo with a mild detergent action. Your local chemist should stock a type suitable for babies. Simply shampoo the scalp in the normal way, taking extra care not to get any of the solution in your baby's eyes.

If the cradle cap does not come off easily, it should be loosened by rubbing a little olive oil, nut oil or medicinal liquid paraffin into your baby's scalp and leaving it on for several hours – overnight may be convenient. Then the softened crusts will be easy to wash out. Or you can remove them using a fine-toothed comb, but take care not to scratch your baby's scalp. The cradle cap should clear up after a few days of treatment. If your baby is affected on other parts of the body besides the scalp, consult your doctor, who will prescribe suitable treatment.

GONE FOR GOOD

Once it has gone, cradle cap is unlikely to return as long as the child's scalp is kept clean and washed regularly. Even babies with a tendency towards developing cradle cap will eventually grow out of it by the time they are two years old.

■ CROUP

Croup is the common name for various conditions that cause the larynx (voice box) or trachea (windpipe) to become partially blocked, resulting in breathing difficulties and a harsh cough. The term is also used to describe the characteristic sound heard when the child breathes in. Children are most likely to suffer from croup when aged between six months and three years.

Croup is more serious in a very young child because there is a danger that the child's much smaller windpipe may become completely blocked as a result.

SYMPTOMS

Attacks of croup usually start suddenly and occur mostly at night. The child has difficulty in breathing in, and makes a growling or wheezing noise. The cough sounds like the bark of a small dog. These unusual sounds often frighten the child, causing panic and making it even more difficult for him to breathe properly.

CAUSES

Various childhood infections, especially the common cold, can give rise to swelling of the larynx and trachea, thus causing a partial blockage. Another possible cause of swelling is an allergic reaction. Occasionally, croup is caused by the child inhaling a small object, such as part of a toy or a piece of food. The foreign body may itself cause sufficient blockage to give rise to croup, or it may irritate

When your child has an attack of croup, boil up a kettle in her room (above) to create a humid atmosphere which makes breathing easier. Otherwise, take her into the bathroom, turn on the hot water taps to produce steam and, holding her upright in your lap, get her to inhale (left).

the air passage and cause inflammation and constriction later.

TREATMENT

Comfort and calm your child and call a doctor immediately if you are worried about coping with the problem. Keep your child in a warm room and increase the humidity by boiling some water in an electric kettle and allowing the steam to fill the room. The moisture will help to relieve your child's discomfort.

Alternatively, take your child into a warm, steamy bathroom. Sit him up on your lap, as he will find it easier to breathe in this position.

If the symptoms do not disappear by themselves, call your doctor, who will try to ascertain the cause of the croup so that he can determine the best treatment to prescribe.

SEEK HELP AT ONCE IF

- **The child has severe difficulty in breathing**
- **You suspect that he has inhaled a small object**
- **The lips appear blue, indicating that the child is not getting sufficient oxygen**
- **The skin is unusually pale or even grey**
- **The child seems distressed or very unwell**
- **The child's temperature is abnormally high**
- **Any other symptoms cause you concern**
- **You are unable to calm the child or relieve his suffering**

◼ CRYING

Crying is sometimes a natural and often involuntary reaction caused by an emotional state, such as anxiety, or produced in response to pain. In such cases, the purpose of crying is to release tension. At other times, it is a way of expressing pain, grief or

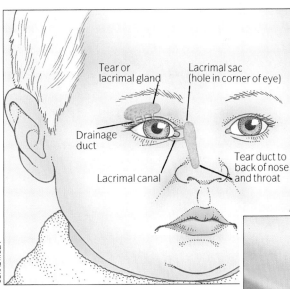

Crying is your baby's first way of communicating and getting your attention (below). Tears, produced by the lacrimal glands (left), keep the eyes moist; crying produces an excess which fills the eyes and overflows.

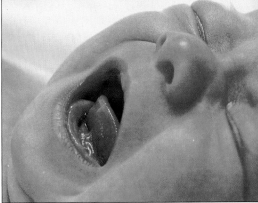

need, when words cannot be used. During the first weeks of life, the only way an infant can communicate is through crying.

Tears consist of a watery, salty fluid, which is produced continuously by the tear, or lacrimal, glands. These are situated above the outer corners of the eyes. The flow of tears keeps the eye clean and free from germs. It also lubricates the eyeballs, to let the eyelids move smoothly over them during blinking.

Each time the eyelids blink, the fluid drains away into small holes in the inner corners of the eyes. From here it passes down the tear ducts to the back of the nose and throat.

When your child cries, or if an eye is irritated by dust or grit, the flow of tears increases.

SYMPTOMS

Besides having tears running down his face, your child may appear flushed in the cheeks and his forehead may become wrinkled. The corners of the mouth often turn down and there is a marked change in the breathing pattern. The general rate of respiration gets much faster, and a deep initial breath may be followed by sobbing or wailing.

CAUSES

The most common causes of crying in young children are hunger, wind, general discomfort, pain (especially during teething), boredom and loneliness. A frightening noise can also set off crying, as may over-stimulation and tiredness. Rough handling, and dressing or undressing can bring on tears very easily although, strangely, wet or dirty nappies are unlikely to cause much distress. Another possible reason is the onset of illness.

TREATMENT

Try to establish the cause of the crying and deal with this first. Then various soothing techniques can be used. Some babies like being swaddled tightly in a blanket, being rocked or carried around the room. Others will relax to soft music or singing. A dummy may provide comfort, but never use one to replace the affection and physical reassurance that all babies need. Older children can get their tears under control quickly, but a young baby may continue sobbing long after it has been soothed. If your baby keeps crying a lot, let your doctor give him a check to make sure there is no serious underlying cause.

CUTS see ABRASIONS

■ CYANOSIS

Cyanosis is a condition in which some parts of the body are blue. A child born with this condition is sometimes referred to as a 'blue baby'.

SYMPTOMS

The nails of the fingers and toes, and the face, especially the lips, appear blue. The blood in these parts is blue in colour, instead of red. In some cases, the baby appears to be normal at birth, the blueness developing later on in his development.

A child with cyanosis may also have respiratory problems, or difficulties during swallowing or crying. This usually indicates that there is some kind of heart abnormality.

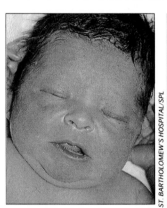

Cyanosis turns a baby blue (above). A hole in the heart lets some used blood (blue) mix with healthy blood (red), thus preventing full oxygenation of the used blood (right).

CAUSES

One of the functions of blood is to carry oxygen around the body. Oxygen-rich blood is red, whereas oxygen-deficient blood, such as that in our veins, is blue. Cyanosis occurs when blood that should be rich in oxygen has not absorbed enough of this gas to turn it from blue to red.

Normally, air, which is mostly oxygen, is breathed into the lungs and absorbed by the blood. The heart pumps the blood around the body, thus keeping it supplied with the oxygen it needs. Cyanosis, therefore, may be caused by a blockage in the air passages, or by the lungs or heart not functioning properly.

A common cause of cyanosis in babies is a 'hole in the heart' at birth. This is a general term for a group of congenital heart defects. Some of the oxygen-deficient blue blood from the veins is pumped around the body again instead of first going to the lungs to collect oxygen. If one-third or more of this flow consists of de-oxygenated blood, because of an abnormality of the heart or blood vessels, the baby's lips take on a purplish-blue colour.

The abnormality may consist of a hole between the heart's left and right atria (collecting chambers), or

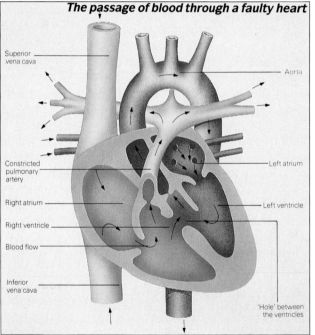

The passage of blood through a faulty heart

Superior vena cava

Aorta

Constricted pulmonary artery

Right atrium

Left atrium

Right ventricle

Left ventricle

Blood flow

Inferior vena cava

'Hole' between the ventricles

ST. BARTHOLOMEW'S HOSPITAL/SPL

left and right ventricles, which are chambers below the atria. Or there may be a mix-up between the large vessels that take blood to and from the heart. A child may have one or a combination of these abnormalities. The two most common heart problems that cause cyanosis are called ventricular septal defect and tetralogy of Fallot. Together these two problems account for one-third of all congenital heart abnormalities.

Only about one baby in every thousand born alive will have a con-

genital heart defect. The causes of these conditions are not fully understood, but there may be a hereditary link in some cases. And it is known that exposure to German measles during the first three months of pregnancy can affect the development of a baby's heart. Other possible causes during the pregnancy include virus infections and certain drugs.

TREATMENT

If the doctor suspects cyanosis, he will first have the child's chest X-rayed and an electrocardiogram (ECG) taken to diagnose the abnormality causing cyanosis. Other painless, non-surgical tests may be made to determine the amount and direction of blood flow.

One or more of these tests are usually carried out within the first few weeks after birth.

SURGERY

If an operation is contemplated, a cardiac catheter test may be carried out under anaesthetic. A surgeon passes a fine tube into the baby's heart from a vein or artery in the leg. The pressures in the various chambers of the heart are then measured and, with special X-rays, an accurate diagnosis can be made.

The various heart abnormalities that cause cyanosis require different forms of treatment and the operations are performed at various ages.

The most common heart abnormality requiring surgery is ventricular septal defect — a hole between the left and right ventricles. The operation, which has a success rate of over 95 per cent, consists of opening a ventricle and stitching up the hole, or putting a plastic patch over it if it is too large to be closed.

Once the operation has been carried out, it is necessary for the doctor to check the child from time to time to make sure that the heart and lungs are still functioning normally. However, it is generally agreed that, if the heart can stand the strain of the defect for the first year of life, it will probably continue to work well for some years.

■ CYSTIC FIBROSIS

Cystic fibrosis is a genetic disease, caused by an abnormal inherited gene. Glands in the lungs and pancreas secrete an extremely sticky mucus, which usually makes the baby ill soon after birth. Although treatment is available, no cure has yet been found.

Another name for the disease is mucoviscidosis. Although it is the most common of all hereditary diseases in the UK, affecting about one person in every 2,000 of the population, it is still quite rare compared with other kinds of illness.

SYMPTOMS

The first sign that anything is wrong may be an intestinal obstruction caused by the abnormally sticky mucus. Later, the pancreas becomes gummed up and fails to secrete the enzymes essential to normal digestion. This, in turn, may cause obstruction of the liver, which can lead to cirrhosis.

The most serious complication is in the lungs. The mucus produced blocks the bronchial tubes and this causes repeated infections, such as pneumonia. Finally, the lungs become filled with little cysts containing pus, and the delicate elastic tissue in the air sacs is replaced by a much more rigid substance called fibrin — hence the name, cystic fibrosis.

One unusual feature of this disease is the very high level of salt in the body sweat.

CAUSES

Cystic fibrosis is caused by the presence in the body of an abnormal gene — a complex chemical that determines hereditary features. A child may inherit cystic fibrosis from his parents if both of them are carriers of the gene. If only one parent is a carrier, the disease will not be passed on, although the child may become a carrier. A parent who is actually suffering from the disease could pass it on to the child but this is unlikely to happen unless the other parent, though not a sufferer, is, however, a carrier.

TREATMENT

Pancreatic extract will be given to overcome the lack of digestive enzymes, but the child must stay on a special low-fat diet. Many children are able to withstand the repeated lung infections with the aid of modern antibiotics, nursing care and physiotherapy to drain secretions from the chest. Some hospitals have units specializing in the care of patients with this disease.

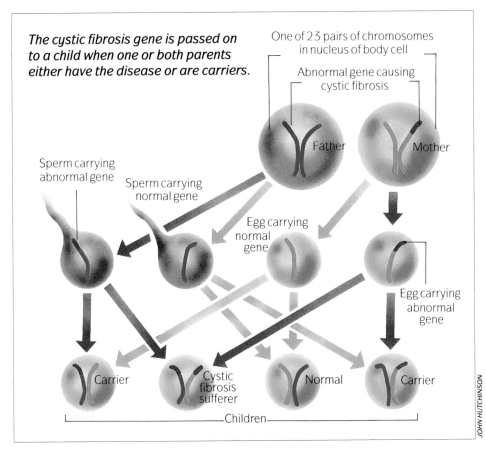

The cystic fibrosis gene is passed on to a child when one or both parents either have the disease or are carriers.

One of 23 pairs of chromosomes in nucleus of body cell

Abnormal gene causing cystic fibrosis

Father

Mother

Sperm carrying abnormal gene

Sperm carrying normal gene

Egg carrying normal gene

Egg carrying abnormal gene

Carrier

Cystic fibrosis sufferer

Normal

Carrier

Children

JOHN HUTCHINSON

■ DANDRUFF

Dandruff is an excessive scaling of dead skin, usually on the scalp, although it sometimes occurs on a child's eyebrows.

SYMPTOMS

Dandruff appears as small whitish scales of skin, which come loose when the hair is brushed or combed. The scaling is sometimes accompanied by itching, which may be intense at times. In severe cases, the skin and hair become excessively greasy, patches of scalp redden, and a fluid oozes from tiny openings that appear, forming hard, yellow crusts.

OTHER AREAS AFFECTED

The skin on the face, especially on the forehead, cheeks and eyebrows, becomes reddened, and scaling occurs in the skin of the ears and on the front of the chest, over the breast and collar bone. Occasionally, dandruff may be associated with other skin conditions, such as eczema and impetigo, or to otitis externa — an infection of the outer ear canal.

CAUSES

Contrary to popular belief, dandruff is not an infection. It is part of a condition that doctors call a seborrhoeic tendency — an overproduction of sebum, the oil secreted by glands in the skin. However, recently it has become clear that some cases of dandruff are linked with a micro-organism called pityrosporum. An anti-fungal shampoo called ketoconazole is available on prescription from your doctor. The shampoo kills the pityrosporum and can often make a significant improvement to the dandruff.

BUBBLES

Regular gentle shampooing with a medicated shampoo may eradicate dandruff or keep it under control. Otherwise, your doctor may prescribe a special one.

TREATMENT

There is no cure for dandruff, which may disappear for good at any age, or disappear for a while and then return for no apparent reason. However, the condition may be treated by regular washing with baby shampoo. Avoid excessive shampooing or massaging of your child's scalp as this may overstimulate the skin and make the condition worse.

SPECIAL SHAMPOO

Some medicated and anti-dandruff shampoos are suitable for young children and may be used occasionally. However, others are not and could make the dandruff worse.

Only severe cases of dandruff require medical treatment. Consult a doctor if your child has severe flaking, itching and cracking of the scalp, or if there is also hair loss.

CHECKLIST

• Find a shampoo that suits your child's hair by trying out various kinds, but make sure that they are stated to be suitable for young children.
• Wash your child's hair as often as it needs. This may be twice a week or every other day. Avoid washing the hair every day, unless absolutely necessary: this could make the dandruff worse in some cases.
• Trim your child's hair regularly, keeping it as short as possible. Dandruff often disappears after a radical haircut.
• Brush out the scales from your child's hair every day with a soft brush. Avoid hard brushes and sharp combs, which can tear the scalp and lead to crust formation.
• If these common-sense measures don't work, ask your doctor about ketoconazole.

■ DEAFNESS

see also GLUE EAR

Deafness is a partial or total loss of hearing. It may affect one or both ears, and the onset may be slow or sudden. Mild or partial hearing loss can slow down a child's general ability to learn and speak, and may make her more accident prone.

To understand deafness, it is necessary to know what sound is and how the ear works. Objects emit sounds by vibrating. The vibrations travel in waves through the air.

HOW THE EAR WORKS

Normally, the sound waves pass along the outer ear to the ear drum, or tympanic membrane, making it vibrate. In the middle ear are three tiny bones called the malleus (hammer), incus (anvil) and stapes (stirrup). These bones, known collectively as the auditory ossicles, transfer the vibrations from the ear drum to a spiral-shaped pitch-sensing organ called the cochlea. This converts the vibrations into electrical signals, which pass along nerve fibres to the brain, where they are interpreted as sounds. As the process is relatively complicated, there are many possible causes of deafness.

S Y M P T O M S

A child with normal hearing will easily hear words or numbers whispered softly from a distance of about 1.5m (5 ft). A slightly deaf child will miss most of the words whispered from this distance, and a very deaf child will be unable to hear speech 15cm (6 in) from the ear.

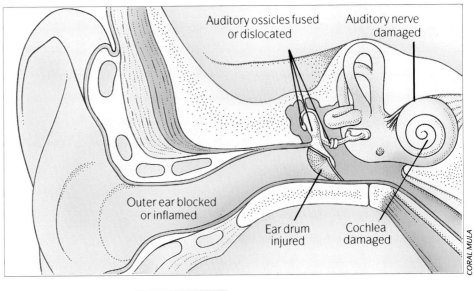

Auditory ossicles fused or dislocated

Auditory nerve damaged

Outer ear blocked or inflamed

Ear drum injured

Cochlea damaged

CORAL MULA

C A U S E S

The two main types of hearing problems are called conductive deafness and nerve deafness. In conductive deafness, sound waves are not transmitted properly to the inner ear.

YOUR QUESTIONS

Q My little girl's ears get very waxy. Why does this happen, and what is the best way to clean them?

A There are two possible explanations for this common condition. Your child may simply produce more ear wax than others, or she may have a fairly narrow ear canal, which could become blocked by a normal amount of wax. If the wax seems to be affecting your child's hearing, take her to the doctor, who will remove the wax by syringing. It may be necessary to have this done as often as once every six months. All an untrained person should do is to wipe off any wax that appears around the outside of the ear. Never use cotton buds or anything else in an attempt to clean inside the ear. You are likely to push the wax further in, and you risk damaging the lining of the ear canal.

Deafness can have many causes. Infection or damage through injury to any of the parts of the ear may result in loss of hearing.

This may be because of wax in the ear canal, or because the bones in the middle ear cannot move freely due to glue (hence glue ear).

In nerve deafness, the sound waves reach the inner ear, but a malfunction in this area, or a disease of the nerves leading to the brain, prevents the child from hearing.

T R E A T M E N T

Your child will receive regular hearing tests, starting in infancy. If your doctor or health visitor notices any problem, they will try to determine the cause. Similarly, if you suspect any deafness, make an appointment for your child to see the doctor. He will first inspect the ears for wax or other material that might be causing a blockage. Should this fail to reveal the cause of deafness, the doctor may then carry out some simple tests to determine the severity of deafness.

FURTHER TESTS

If your child is old enough to understand, there are play tests which health visitors or doctors might do to find out what your child can hear. Older children, over five years, can have a hearing test using an audiometer, just as an adult does.

YOUR QUESTIONS

Q My three-year-old son is very backward with his speech and his doctor said he might need grommets. What exactly are these and will he need to go into hospital to have them put in?

A If your child has what is known as glue ear, and it is a recurrent problem, he may need to be admitted to hospital to have the excess fluid drained from one or both ears and then have tiny plastic tubes inserted. These tiny tubes are called grommets and they prevent a further build up of mucus in the ear. It is a simple operation to insert them and they generally fall out after several months, when the ears may well be healthy again. If your son does have them, it is as well to stop him diving when swimming.

Deafness need not mean shutting out the world. A hearing aid, sometimes in conjunction with sign language, can help most deaf children communicate successfully.

In play tests, the tester will speak to the child in a low voice and ask him or her to identify objects or items in pictures or among toys.

If there is any cause for concern, the doctor will arrange for your child to see a specialist. If your child is old enough to co-operate, the specialist can accurately assess your child's hearing ability by means of an instrument called an audiometer. This is an electronic device that plays a range of notes at various volumes through an earphone. Besides testing the child's

WATCHPOINTS

• Teach your child never to put objects in his ear.
• Do not push cotton buds or other objects in your child's ears.
• Never slap your child on the side of the face, as there is a danger that it could rupture the ear drum.
• Do not expose your child to loud music or to any other very loud noise.
• Seek medical attention if your child has hearing difficulties or a discharge or pain in the ear.

hearing through the ear in the normal way, the audiometer can also test for conductive deafness by transmitting the sounds directly through the bone of the skull to the cochlea. If this produces better results, it indicates that the problem lies in the outer ear or middle ear, which provide the normal route to the cochlea.

Once the specialist has found the cause of your child's deafness, he will prescribe appropriate treatment or tell you the course of action to take if the condition cannot be treated. For example, in cases of glue ear, your child may need to have her ears drained and have grommets inserted.

YOUR QUESTIONS

Q My little girl seems to go deaf when she has a head cold. Why is this?

A In the same way that a viral infection makes the nose run, it causes catarrh to be produced in the middle ear. The catarrh blocks the Eustachian tube, making the patient feel 'blocked up', and impairing the hearing. When the cold goes, the Eustachian tube clears and the hearing returns to normal.

Q Since my little boy developed a hearing problem, he has been having trouble with his balance. Why is this?

A There is a very close connection between balance and hearing. The organs of balance are situated in the inner ear, near the cochlea. And the same nerve carries balance and sound signals to the brain, so some problems that affect one sensation may well affect the other sensation too. Be sure to tell your doctor about this difficulty with balance as it may give him a better understanding of your son's hearing problem.

DENTAL CARE

By the time your child is about two years old, her first set of teeth should be complete. These 20 primary teeth are commonly called the baby or milk teeth. Regular cleaning is vital for keeping the teeth and gums healthy and for fresh-smelling breath. Although a secondary set will start to replace the primary teeth from the age of about six, it is important to teach your child how to clean her first teeth properly as soon as possible. If she has not got into the habit of keeping them clean by the time her second set come through, she is likely to neglect these too and suffer pain and other problems later.

SYMPTOMS

Bad breath, soreness and inflammation of the gums, toothache and visible damage to the teeth are common symptoms of inadequate dental care. Even if they are brushed hard, your gums should not bleed if they are strong and healthy.

If allowed to get worse, gum disease, technically known as periodontal disease, can make the gums recede and may eventually affect deeper tissues, including the jaw bone. In some cases, the teeth become permanently loose.

Sometimes the child may complain of earache when a tooth is giving trouble. This is because the nerves in the side of the face are very close together and the pain caused by an inflammation of the ear may be easily confused with a toothache.

CAUSES

If the teeth are not cleaned regularly and thoroughly, unpleasant substances develop in the mouth and may cause tooth decay.

The most dangerous substance that damages teeth is plaque. This is an almost invisible layer of sticky, yellowish-white material, composed of saliva, microscopic particles of food and millions of bacteria. Plaque clings to the teeth and changes sugar in the mouth into acid, which attacks the enamel surface of the teeth. This is the start of tooth decay and, once it is established, it slowly moves deeper into the tooth, resulting in holes in the enamel which are known as cavities.

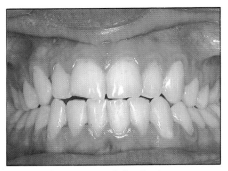

Although your teeth look clean, there may still be a build-up of plaque.

Gum disease is caused by plaque accumulating around, and just under, the edge of the gums. If only the gum tissue is affected, the condition is called gingivitis.

TREATMENT

Because plaque is such a sticky substance, the child's teeth must be brushed thoroughly at least twice a day to remove it. Being thorough is more important than cleaning the teeth frequently. On average, it takes about three minutes to remove all the plaque if you brush the teeth properly. Brushing your child's teeth quickly several times each day is not as effective as a really good clean after breakfast and before putting the child to bed. When your child is old enough to clean her own teeth, she will tend to copy what you have done, so always take time when cleaning her teeth.

BRUSHING THE TEETH

When brushing, work steadily around the outside of the teeth, and then clean the inside surfaces. Moving the brush around in small circles is the safest and most effective method, as it cleans the teeth without damaging the gums. Also, massage the gums by brushing them gently. Afterwards, make your child rinse out her mouth with water.

When cleaning your child's teeth, the quality of the brush is considerably more important than using lots of toothpaste. A blob of paste about the size of a pea will be sufficient. But teeth cannot be cleaned properly with a frayed toothbrush, so check

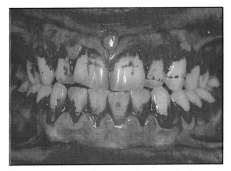

Chewing revealing tablets will show up areas of plaque as bright red.

its condition and replace it when necessary – perhaps every three months or so.

Most dentists recommend a flat-headed nylon toothbrush with a short, straight handle as being the best for reaching the awkward corners of the mouth. Use a fairly soft brush to avoid damaging your child's delicate gums. She can progress to a slightly harder brush when she becomes older.

It is important that you teach your child how best to clean her teeth. Help her to brush until she's at least five.

Another way of cleaning the teeth is with a tooth-cloth. This ancient technique has been gaining popularity since research showed that it can help prevent tooth decay. Any small piece of clean cloth may be used. Dampen the cloth, apply a little toothpaste to it, then hold the cloth over a finger and rub the paste on to the teeth and between them. The toothcloth may be used in addition to brushing, but should not be regarded as an alternative.

Although dental floss is not recommended for children, it is still a good idea for you to floss your teeth as children learn by copying adults, and they will need to know how to floss when they are older.

Dental floss is useful for cleaning the spaces between the teeth, where food particles can be trapped. Floss is a thin, silky yarn which is sometimes waxed to make it feel

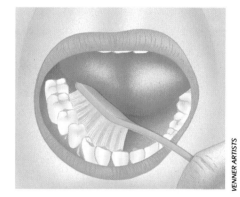

Using a flat-headed nylon toothbrush, brush the upper teeth downwards from the gums and the lower teeth upwards from the gums.

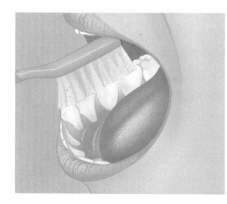

Don't overlook the inner surfaces of your teeth as these are just as important. Brush all round these upper and lower surfaces.

WATCHPOINTS

• Try to reduce the amount of unnecessary sugary food that your child eats as this is one of the main causes of tooth decay. Within minutes of eating anything containing sugar, bacteria on the teeth form acid. This helps to rot the teeth. Any type of sugar can contribute to decay.

• Do not prevent a youngster from eating honey and fruit as they are highly nutritious. However, as they contain sugar, make sure that her teeth are cleaned afterwards.

• Reduce the number of times per day that your child eats sugary food. If she eats small amounts of sugar at intervals throughout the day, her mouth will have traces of sugar in it most of the time. This is much worse than eating the same total amount all at once.

• If your child becomes hungry between meals, offer her a savoury snack, rather than cakes, biscuits, chocolate, sweets or ice cream.

smoother. The waxed and unwaxed types are equally effective. A length of floss is drawn back and forth between the teeth to remove the plaque. Your dentist will be glad to demonstrate the most effective way of using it.

FLUORIDE

Some dentists believe that the best way to prevent tooth decay, especially in children, is to brush the teeth with fluoride toothpaste, and to use fluoride in other forms as well. In some regions, fluoride occurs naturally in the water supply; in other areas, fluoride is deliberately added to drinking water because of its effectiveness in protecting the teeth. Your local water authority will tell you whether your supply contains fluoride. If it does not, ask your dentist their advice about whether to buy

fluoride drops or tablets for daily use. Another way to help protect your child's teeth is to get her to use

Occasional – small – lollipops are fine, but beware the sugar content.

a fluoride mouthwash.

If using fluoride drops, tablets or mouthwash, be sure to follow the directions as exceeding the dose does not offer extra protection and could, in extreme cases, cause mottling of the teeth.

DETECTING PLAQUE

To discover whether all the plaque has been removed from your child's teeth, obtain some revealing tablets from a dentist or chemist. Get your child to chew one of the tablets after her teeth have been cleaned. Any remaining plaque will be dyed bright red. If you find it impossible to remove the plaque from your child's teeth, get this done by the dentist.

Better still, arrange for the dentist to check your child's teeth and gums regularly, even when they appear to be healthy. Any problems will be spotted before they become serious, and will be easier to treat.

■ DENTIST

Many children are not taken to see a dentist until they have a severely decayed tooth and are in pain. And often, the only possible treatment at this stage is extraction. As a result, a child may come to associate a visit to the dentist with discomfort, and may become extremely nervous at the thought of a future visit, even for a routine inspection when his teeth and gums appear to be in good condition. The fear of going to the dentist may never be overcome, so try to make sure that this situation does not arise.

THE FIRST VISIT

The best way to get your child accustomed to going to the dentist is to take him as soon as he can walk. Ideally, you should take him with you when you attend for a routine checkup. You should take great care not to say anything frightening about dentistry before the visit, even as a joke, and you should try not to show any concern while the dentist is looking at your teeth or giving you any treatment.

Then your child will probably be quite happy to let the dentist inspect his teeth too. If, however, your child does show some signs of fear, it may be best for him to sit on your lap, rather than alone in the chair.

At such an early age, your child is unlikely to need any treatment. But the dentist may like to polish one or

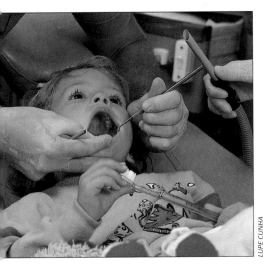

Visits to the dentist need not be scary. Start taking your children early – and they may always have healthy teeth.

two teeth to get your child used to having dental instruments in his mouth. As there will be no pain, your child is unlikely to make much fuss when he has to go for proper treatment in the future.

FILLING A TOOTH

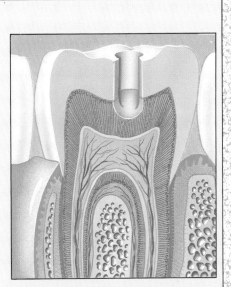

This diagram shows the spread of decay from the outer enamel down into the inner core of the tooth.

A hole is drilled to remove the decay but a filling cannot be inserted yet as it would fall straight out.

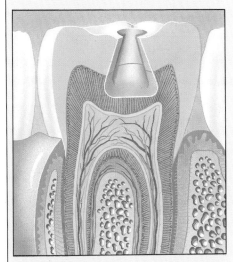

Your dentist has to shape the cavity to give it an 'undercut', so that it is wider at the bottom than at the top.

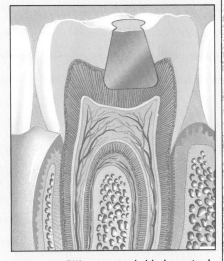

After the filling material is inserted, your dentist will check that it does not impair your bite.

TREATMENT

The most common form of dental disease is tooth decay, and this is usually treated by having the affected teeth filled. The dentist may take one or more X-rays of your child's jaw to establish the extent of the decay. If the teeth are severely decayed, they may have to be extracted. But it is sometimes possible to relieve the pain from a decayed tooth by removing just the sensitive pulp from its centre. Teeth may also be extracted if advanced gum disease has made them so loose that they have become difficult to bite on.

Sometimes, some healthy teeth are extracted if your child's jaw is too small to hold all the teeth in even rows. A slight unevenness in an older child's permanent teeth may be corrected with a brace.

FILLINGS

Having a filling will prevent decay spreading. First, the decayed part of the tooth is removed, mainly by drilling, then the tooth is filled with material that sets hard.

As the teeth are very sensitive to pain, a local anaesthetic is usually given by means of an injection in the mouth. The child remains conscious, but feels no pain when the dentist gets to work on the teeth. Some children have had fillings carrried out painlessly under hypnosis, but this technique does not work with all children, and relatively few dentists offer this alternative.

REMOVING DECAY

A high-speed drill, cooled by a water spray, is used for the removal of decayed enamel and some dentine, but a slower drill may be used to finish the cavity. The high-speed drill produces a characteristic whine, but there is no noticeable vibration; the slow-speed drill is quieter, but your child will feel his mouth vibrating when it is used. Very soft decayed material is often scraped away with an instrument called an excavator.

FILLING THE CAVITY

When all the decayed or weakened tooth material has been removed, the cavity is usually lined with an insulating material. This also protects the pulp from the chemical constituents of the filling while it is setting.

The material commonly used to fill teeth is called silver amalgam. It consists of a mixture of silver, tin and mercury, and has a pasty consistency when prepared. The silvery paste is packed into the cavity and then smoothed off to try to restore the original shape of the tooth, and to not interfere with the bite.

Teeth near the front of the mouth are usually filled with material that is tooth-coloured to give them a more attractive appearance, although this never sets as hard as amalgam.

Various hand instruments are used to carve the outside of the filling into shape and, at this stage, the dentist will check that any large fillings do not protrude and prevent the upper and lower teeth from coming together normally when the mouth is closed. While the filling is setting, it may be supported by means of a

plastic or metal strip, which the dentist fits around the tooth.

Once the filling has hardened, your child should be able to use the tooth normally. But should further decay occur in or near the same place, it will be more difficult to construct a satisfactory filling. If there is too little of the original tooth left to hold the filling, it may be necessary to have the remains extracted to avoid further decay and pain.

HAVING AN EXTRACTION

Before a tooth is extracted, your child will be given a local or general anaesthetic. Then the dentist will normally use a pair of extraction forceps to remove the tooth. These instruments have sharp 'beaks' which are forced down between the tooth and its supporting bone. However, if a tooth is badly damaged and tends to break when gripped with forceps, it may be removed using an instrument called an elevator. As your child's jawbone is softer than that of an adult, extracting your child's tooth is usually easy.

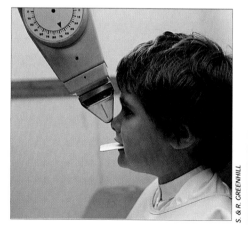

X-rays are painless and may even be fun, if your dentist takes time to explain what he can see in them.

After extraction, the wound will bleed a little until a blood clot forms in the socket of the tooth. Eventually, this will become converted into a soft, fibrous repair tissue and finally into bone. Tell your child not to investigate this blood clot with his tongue as he might disturb it.

If bleeding starts again, it can usually be stopped by taking a clean

linen handkerchief, rolling it up and placing it over the socket. Tell your child to bite gently on this pad for ten minutes. If this does not work, take your child back to the dentist, who will look into the problem.

PREVENTION

The best precaution against your child developing dental disease is to make sure that his teeth and gums are cleaned regularly and thoroughly. When necessary, the dentist will remove any plaque build-up by scaling your child's teeth, and will also give them a polish. But such treatment only removes substances that should not have been allowed to accumulate, and is no substitute for proper dental care in the home.

YOUR QUESTIONS

Q How often should I take my child to the dentist?

A At least every six months, although some dentists suggest every four months for young children, as their teeth decay more rapidly.

Q My six-year-old daughter has a decayed front tooth, which is rather unsightly. Is it worth having it filled as it is only a milk tooth?

A Any decaying tooth should be filled. If the decay is untreated, it will eventually cause pain and then have to be extracted. And losing milk teeth too early can lead to the permanent teeth being irregular when they do finally emerge.

Q When should I start taking my daughter to the dentist?

A As soon as she can walk. An early visit to the dentist when no treatment is required may well be an interesting experience rather than an ordeal.

DERMATITIS

The term dermatitis covers a variety of skin complaints, the most common forms being eczema, or atopic dermatitis, and contact dermatitis. These are widespread and often affect young children. But, although uncomfortable and unattractive, most types of dermatitis are temporary, harmless and not contagious.

SYMPTOMS

The main symptom of dermatitis is itchy skin, accompanied by a patchy rash, especially in the creases of the arms, legs and hands. The affected skin may be cracked and dry, or wet and weeping. In some cases, the child's scalp is itchy and inflamed, with peeling skin and dandruff.

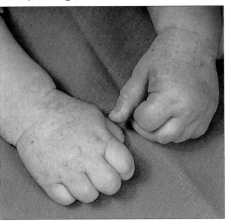

Eczema, a form of dermatitis, often affects the hands. It itches and looks bad but is not infectious.

CAUSES

Allergies are the most common cause of eczema, which is closely related to hay fever. There are many substances, notably pollen and animal fluff, that can cause allergies, and almost all of them can bring on eczema. This can also be brought on or aggravated by other factors, especially anxiety or stress as well as diet.

A common cause of eczema in young children is an allergy to milk, eggs or other protein-rich foods. Some allergens − substances that trigger off allergic reactions − can enter a baby's body through the mother's milk. So, eczema in a breast fed baby may be caused by something that the mother happened to eat. Such allergies often disappear as the baby grows older.

Contact dermatitis is also an allergic complaint but, unlike eczema, it is confined to those parts of the body that come into direct contact with the allergen. Metals, especially nickel and chromium, are common causes. The hands are often affected as they are so frequently exposed to contact allergens. For example, a baby's hands could be affected by contact dermatitis through regular contact with chromium-plated parts of her pram.

Some children are allergic to rubber, and their skin becomes inflamed where it is in contact with the rubber elastic in their underwear. Perfumes and other substances in soap and washing powder sometimes cause an allergic reaction that may appear as eczema on any part of the body.

Seborrhoea, or **seborrhoeaic dermatitis**, is brought on by over-production of oil by the skin's sebaceous glands, usually in the baby's scalp.

Solar dermatitis, or **photo-dermatitis**, is brought on by exposure to sunlight. In most cases, the sunlight is not directly responsible for the condition, but it aggravates an allergy that would not, by itself, be strong enough to produce symptoms. Certain drugs, such as the antibiotic tetracycline, may make the situation worse by increasing the skin's sensitivity to light.

TREATMENT

There are no cures for many forms of dermatitis, but your child can be given relief from discomfort, and the condition can be kept under control. A wide range of ointments, creams, pastes and lotions is available to treat the inflammation. But the most important treatment is to keep the affected area clean, using liquid paraffin instead of soap, and to discourage your child from scratching it. This will allow the skin to heal naturally and will reduce the risk of infection.

Dry, flaky inflammations can be soothed and protected with oily preparations, such as lanolin or petroleum jelly. Wet, weepy inflammations are better treated with starch-based applications or astringents. Among the more potent treatments available to fight inflammation are steroids, which are made into creams and ointments. The mildest type is hydrocortisone, which can be bought from a chemist. But the stronger steroid creams and ointments are available only on prescription, as their use must be carefully controlled and supervised.

ELIMINATING THE CAUSE

Although they are undeniably effective, these drugs have their drawbacks. If used for long periods on the same area of skin, they can damage its underlying layers. However, if they are abruptly abandoned, the dermatitis may suddenly recur. This is because while steroids may suppress the symptoms of dermatitis, they will not dispose of its cause. So, if the condition is caused by an allergy, the

YOUR QUESTIONS

Q My neighbour's eczema was cleared up by the use of a steroid cream that the doctor prescribed. She has some left over and says that I could try it on my daughter's eczema. Is there any reason why I should not do this?

A There are a number of reasons why you shouldn't. Firstly, it is a bad idea to use any medicines that have been prescribed for another person, especially steroids and other powerful drugs. These do not suit everyone and have to be used sparingly. Also, left-over drugs may have been stored in warm conditions and may no longer be effective. Instead, take your daughter to your doctor, who will decide which course of treatment will be most suitable.

inflammation is likely to return once you stop the treatment. However, if the allergen can be identified and avoided in future, then the dermatitis may be permanently cured.

To help determine the substance responsible for an allergy, dermatology departments in hospitals keep stocks of all the major allergens so that they can be tested on patients. But finding the cause of an allergy is not always easy, as the dermatitis may not show up until several days after the child is exposed to it.

YOUR QUESTIONS

Q My little boy's best friend has dermatitis and I am afraid that my son will catch it too. I would hate him to have scars when he grows up. What should I do?

A Stop worrying. Dermatitis does not cause scarring and, because it is not infectious, your son will not catch it from his friend.

Q My little girl likes wearing a metal ring that she got from a Christmas cracker, but it seems to cause a rash on her finger. Why should it do this?

A Your daughter is probably allergic to the metal in the ring. Many items of cheap jewellery contain chromium or nickel, and these metals commonly cause allergies. Try persuading her to wear a plastic ring instead and see if her skin gets better within a few weeks. If it does not, take her to the doctor.

If your child has sensitive skin, make sure that she uses only hypoallergenic soap. This contains none of the perfumes and other allergens that are present in many ordinary soaps and cannot, therefore, cause contact dermatitis. Your doctor may also be able to recommend a suitable barrier cream or spray to protect your child's skin against irritating substances, or a sun screen to filter out some of the sun's ultraviolet rays, and so provide effective protection from solar dermatitis.

■ DIABETES

What is commonly referred to as diabetes is a condition in which the blood contains an abnormally high level of sugar. The full name for this is *diabetes mellitus*. *(Diabetes insipidus* is an extremely rare disease resulting from a failure of the pituitary gland in the skull and is unrelated to *diabetes mellitus*.)* Diabetes can start at any age, although children do not usually suffer from it before they are five years old.

CAUSES

The form of the disease that affects young children most often is insulin-dependent diabetes. This occurs when the body fails to produce enough insulin, which is a hormone or 'chemical messenger', or when the body does not react in the normal way to the insulin produced. Usually, the problem is due to a failure of insulin-producing cells in the pancreas. It is not known why they should stop producing insulin, and research continues in this area. However, it seems that some event, possibly an infection, may trigger the onset of diabetes.

BLOOD SUGAR LEVEL

Some hormones, including cortisone and adrenalin, tend to increase the amount of sugar (glucose) in the blood. The purpose of insulin is to keep the sugar content of the blood down to normal levels by directing sugar into the cells, where it can be converted into energy.

Normally, if the level of sugar in the blood rises above certain limits, insulin is released into the bloodstream by the Islets of Langerhans, clusters of cells in the pancreas. As a result, more sugar passes into the cells, so the level in the blood is brought back to normal. But, if there is insufficient insulin, the cells of the body may become starved of sugar, while the sugar level in the blood becomes too high. Without their normal 'fuel', the cells start using up fat, instead, thus causing a loss in body weight.

MC LIBRARY

All foods and drinks containing sugar are banned from a diabetic child's diet except in hypoglycaemic attacks.

In non-insulin-dependent diabetes, the pancreas does produce insulin, often in normal amounts, but the tissues in the body do not respond to its presence, so the sugar level is not controlled. Although this type of diabetes does occur in young children, it is fairly uncommon.

SYMPTOMS

Children with diabetes pass abnormally large quantities of urine, develop an abnormal thirst and lose a great deal of weight. The used-up fat in the body produces waste materials called ketones, so the presence of these chemicals is an indication that the body lacks insulin. Left untreated, diabetes is a serious disease. A child would become steadily weaker, losing weight all the time, and eventually lapsing into a coma and dying.

Diabetes can also lead to complications, including problems with the eyes, kidneys, arteries and nerves. It is, therefore, important to ensure that the child follows the prescribed course of treatment.

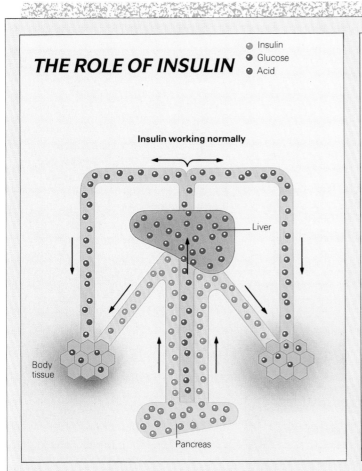

THE ROLE OF INSULIN

- Insulin
- Glucose
- Acid

Insulin working normally

Body tissue

Liver

Pancreas

When insulin is being manufactured by the pancreas it enables glucose — which the body needs in order to produce energy — to be stored in the liver. When the body cells need more energy, this is obtained from the glucose, which is released from storage. The insulin then allows the body cells to convert the glucose into the energy the body needs.

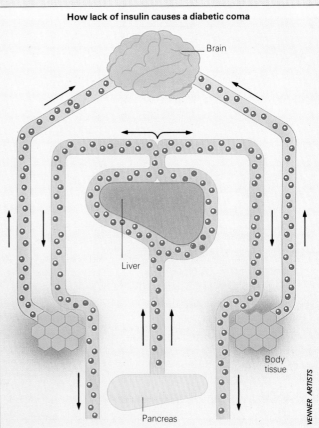

How lack of insulin causes a diabetic coma

Brain

Liver

Pancreas

Body tissue

VENNER ARTISTS

If there is insufficient insulin in the bloodstream, glucose cannot be stored and utilized. Sugar builds up in the blood and is excreted in the urine. The cells of the body produce energy by burning up fats, but as these cannot be burned properly without glucose, acids accumulate in the blood. These acids act as a poison on the brain, causing drowsiness and, eventually, coma.

TREATMENT

The treatment for insulin-dependent diabetes is to introduce insulin into the body. It would be destroyed by the gastric juices if taken by mouth, so it has to be given by injection. Most diabetics have two injections each day; when they wake up and before the last meal of the day.

Non-insulin-dependent diabetes often occurs when the child is overweight. In such cases, dieting may be sufficient to keep it under control. By losing weight and avoiding sugary foods, the child may be able to manage with the insulin his body produces. In some cases, however, tablets may be prescribed to en-hance the body's production of insulin, or to increase its effectiveness. Although this type of diabetes is described as being non-dependent on insulin, injections of the hormone may help in some severe cases. Some specialists feel that it is a good idea to teach children to inject themselves as soon as possible. Even children as young as seven may manage their own injections if given help and encouragement. Learning to do this will help the child to become independent.

THE HYPOGLYCAEMIA HAZARD

Once a child has had an insulin injection, his blood sugar level will start to fall. But, if it becomes too low, perhaps through taking too much insulin, other problems arise. Sugar is an essential food for the body tissues in general, and especially for the brain. If the sugar level becomes too low, the brain ceases to function properly and the child becomes unconscious.

Fortunately, the early symptoms of a low blood sugar level, known as hypoglycaemia, or 'hypo', are easy to recognize. These are shakiness, sweating, tingling around the mouth and, often, a muddled feeling.

The treatment for these symptoms is simple. If the child takes some sugary food or drink immediately, the symptoms of hypoglycaemia will usually pass within a few minutes.

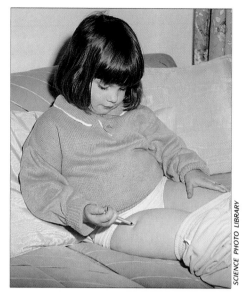

Given encouragement, even very young diabetic children can learn to give themselves insulin injections.

Occasionally, in a severe attack, the child may quickly become so confused that he does not know what he is doing. In these circumstances, it is important to give the child a sugary drink at once. Three or four tea-spoonfuls of sugar in a glass of water are usually sufficient. However, if the child goes into a coma, the doctor

should be called immediately. He will probably give an injection to bring the child out of the coma.

Because of the risk of hypogly-caemia attacks, parents or guardians must try to control their child's diet so that the sugar level in the blood is kept at about the normal level, with as little variation as possible. This means giving the child regular meals containing similar amounts of car-bohydrates — food that is broken down to form sugar in the blood. All diabetics, whether insulin-treated or not, should avoid sugar itself, and all foods that contain sugar except, of course, when trying to halt a hypo attack. Such foods include jam, sweets, cakes and commercial fruit squash drinks.

Diabetic children should be en-couraged to eat foods that are low in fats and high in fibre, such as

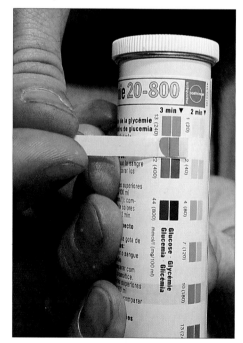

The level of glucose in the blood is measured by comparing the result of a blood test against a chart.

wholegrain cereals, vegetables and fruits. Such a diet encourages gra-dual absorption of sugars from the digestive system, and may also re-duce the risk of arterial disease even-tually developing.

Another factor to be taken into account is the amount of exercise that the child does. If he does a lot of

INSULIN

Most of the insulin now produced for diabetics is chemically identical to the body's own insulin and is called human insulin. Insulin for diabetics was once extracted from the pancreases of cattle and pigs, and was known as beef insulin or pork insulin. The body would sometimes produce antibodies to these forms of insulin, so that they would gradually become less effective. No antibodies are produced to destroy human insulin.

Human insulin is made artificially by genetic engineering. Special bacteria, bred in the laboratory, are given a gene that causes them to produce human insulin. This is then extracted and purified.

YOUR QUESTIONS

Q My son was recently found to be diabetic and has to have injections of insulin. Will he have to remain on it for the rest of his life?

A Your son will probably have to continue taking insulin. However, in a few cases, the insulin is needed only during a particularly difficult time, after which a special diet may be all that is required.

Q My little girl has diabetes and I am afraid that it might alter her personality. Is this likely?

A Like any illness, diabetes may put the patient under strain, but it does not cause personality changes.

extra exercise, he will need more food and, possibly, more insulin.

SUGAR TESTS

To check that the child's diet and insulin injections are resulting in an acceptable blood sugar level, the parents usually carry out tests daily or once per week. The traditional way of doing this is to measure the amount of sugar in the urine, as this is easy to do and gives a reasonable idea of the amount of sugar in the blood. However, this technique is now used only in the case of dia-betics who do not use insulin.

For children who are taking insulin, a more accurate test is used so that the dose of insulin may be correctly adjusted according to the level of sugar present. The child's finger is pricked to produce a drop of blood, which is then chemically tested.

In the case of insulin-dependent diabetics, the blood sugar level is usually checked at various times throughout the day, on one day per week. But, in some cases, tests must be carried out every day so that the insulin intake can be adjusted according to the child's needs.

DIARRHOEA

Diarrhoea is a symptom of a disorder, usually an infection in the intestines, although it may sometimes indicate a more serious problem. Diarrhoea can be dangerous in babies and young children if it lasts more than a day or two, so it is important to seek advice from a doctor in such cases.

SYMPTOMS

Diarrhoea is an uncomfortable symptom, and may be accompanied by pains in the abdomen. The stools are much more fluid and less well formed than usual. In severe cases of diarrhoea, the stools are very watery and may be passed very frequently. In some cases, the child may also have attacks of vomiting.

Oral rehydration powders may be prescribed for the treatment of diarrhoea in small children.

Persistent diarrhoea causes considerable loss of water and salts, and may lead to dehydration which, if untreated, can be fatal. Babies are particularly at risk as they can become dehydrated much more quickly than older children. And the vomiting may make it very difficult for them to absorb the fluid given by mouth to replace that lost in the diarrhoea.

CAUSES

Diarrhoea occurs when the lining of the intestine becomes irritated. This may be due to an infection, the presence of a poisonous substance or some other cause. As a result, the lining of the intestine becomes unable to absorb water and salts from the food. In consequence, food and water pass through the length of the intestine much faster than usual and the stool becomes watery. In addition, the inflamed condition of the intestine walls may cause them to release water, thus increasing the amount of fluid lost in the stools.

ACUTE DIARRHOEA

One of the most common causes of acute diarrhoea is food poisoning; in this case diarrhoea often starts within a few hours of eating contaminated food. The most frequent causes of food poisoning are bacteria that grow on fly-blown food, producing toxins (poisons) in the process. This kind of food poisoning is often caused by toxins from *Staphylococcus* bacteria.

In other types of food poisoning, the bacterium itself may cause the infection. For example, the *Salmonella* bacterium causes diarrhoea, with pain and vomiting. The *Campylobacter* bacterium also causes diarrhoea, often with fairly severe stomach pains. This bacterium can spread by touch between members of a household, or may be spread in contaminated food or water.

Organisms called viruses sometimes cause diseases whose symptoms include diarrhoea. Some gastroenteritis is caused by viruses, rotavirus for example, which leads to diarrhoea, vomiting and abdominal pains. This complaint is also known as gastric flu and summer diarrhoea.

Gastroenteritis is a common affliction in babies but, to avoid making a wrong diagnosis, it is important to distinguish between loose stools and diarrhoea. Breast-fed babies often have very loose motions, and they may pass several stools each day. Bottle-fed babies produce stools with a consistency more like those of adults, but the colour varies greatly.

In spite of the appearance of the stool, a breast-fed baby is less likely to have gastroenteritis, as the breast milk protects the intestines from infection, and in breast feeding there is no risk of infection from unsterilized bottles and teats.

Highly spiced foods, or large quantities of fruit or shellfish can also cause acute stomach upsets and loose bowels.

Infections completely unconnected with the bowels sometimes cause diarrhoea in children. This typically happens to toddlers with ear and throat infections.

Diarrhoea also accompanies various epidemic diseases, including typhoid, dysentery and cholera, which, however, have practically disappeared from Western countries. Typhoid and dysentery are spread by bacteria, often injested with food, whereas cholera is spread by drinking water that has been infected with faeces. The difference between food poisoning and dysentery is that the symptoms of dysentery can take up to 24 hours to develop and are longer lasting than in food poisoning.

Traveller's diarrhoea occurs when new strains of bacteria replace the normally beneficial ones residing in the large intestine. Such bacteria are commonly acquired from the water supply, and do not affect local people, who have built up an immunity to them through long exposure.

CHRONIC DIARRHOEA

If parasites get into a child's food and water, they may cause diarrhoea. One such parasite is the amoeba, a single-celled organism, which causes amoebic dysentery, a common disease in the tropics. The diarrhoea alternates with periods of constipation, and the condition may persist for some years.

Diarrhoea also occurs when some other disease of the intestinal wall prevents the proper absorption of foods (*see* Coeliac Disease). These malabsorption problems also leave patients badly undernourished.

TREATMENT

Although the course of action to be taken depends on what the cause of the trouble is, the basic treatment for diarrhoea is very simple. The priority is to keep up the level of fluid intake by getting your child to drink plenty of liquids. Eating is not essential and, if he isn't hungry, he shouldn't be forced to eat, especially if he has been vomiting earlier.

TREATMENT OF BABIES

Diarrhoea may be serious for a baby and you should contact your doctor. You may be advised to cease solid foods if your baby is old enough to have them. If you're breast feeding, continue, as this will boost your baby's defences against the problem. If you're bottle feeding, you may be advised to give half-strength feeds, though don't do this without your doctor's support. Your baby may be prescribed a preparation to combat the dehydration caused by the diarrhoea.

If, apart from having diarrhoea, the baby appears to be well and is taking fluids, then keep a careful watch for the next 24 hours. If your baby develops other symptoms, such as vomiting, or if the stools are tinged with blood, then call your doctor. Retain a soiled nappy for the doctor to examine when he calls.

Your doctor may advise stopping all milk and giving your baby only clear liquids. He may prescribe a balanced sugar/salt solution to make up for the salts lost in the diarrhoea and restore the normal absorption of water from the intestine. It is unlikely that your doctor will suggest a medicine to 'dry up' the diarrhoea in small babies. Mild attacks will soon be over, while seriously ill babies should be treated in hospital.

DRUG TREATMENT

Drugs may reduce the level of activity in the intestine and slow down the passage of its contents but this will not reduce the duration of the illness.

Antibiotics, usually sulphonamides or erythromycin, may be prescribed for some forms of food poisoning, especially if the cause is found to be bacteria such as *Salmonella* and *Campylobacter*.

YOUR QUESTIONS

Q My little girl seems to get diarrhoea whenever she eats cheese. Could she be allergic to it?

A She might well be allergic to cheese. Food allergies seem to be quite common and can cause a wide range of symptoms. Try excluding cheese from your daughter's diet for a few weeks, but let her have all the other kinds of food that she normally eats. If the diarrhoea does not return until she eats cheese again, she probably does have an allergy to this food.

Q I am breast feeding and a friend told me not to eat grapes as my baby would get diarrhoea. Is this true?

A Loose stools are normal in a breast fed baby anyway. It's unusual for a baby to get diarrhoea when he is being fully breast fed. Some mothers do feel that things they eat while breast feeding affect the baby, but there's not a lot of good evidence available to prove this one way or the other. If you notice what appears to be a reaction in your baby, stop eating that particular food until your baby is older.

■ DIPHTHERIA

Diphtheria is a disease that occurs mainly in children under the age of ten. It is an acute infection of the nose and throat and can prove fatal if not treated at an early stage. The disease is still very common in some

tropical countries, especially those in Africa, and it is only by widespread immunization that diphtheria has been largely eradicated from Western countries.

SYMPTOMS

There are several forms of diphtheria, and these can sometimes, though not always, be distinguished from one another by the different symptoms they produce.

Nasal diphtheria The mildest and most common form of the disease is nasal diphtheria. Some white 'membrane' may be visible in the nostrils, and the child has a runny nose, the discharge sometimes containing blood. However, there is little discomfort with this form of diphtheria.

Tonsillar diphtheria Diphtheria of the tonsils is a more serious form of the disease. A membrane forms on the tonsils and the child may have a high temperature. She may have some difficulty in swallowing because the palate becomes paralysed. Usually the illness lasts about a week, and there are generally no long-term effects.

Naso-pharyngeal diphtheria The throat and nose infection known as naso-pharyngeal diphtheria is a dangerous disease. The onset is rapid, with the child developing a fever, sore throat and nasal discharge. A heavy, whitish membrane builds up over the back of the throat and can then spread down the windpipe. After a few days, the membrane may change to a dark greenish-grey colour.

Glands in the neck become so enlarged that the child is described as having a 'bull-neck' appearance. In the acute stage, within the first week or two, the pulse may become weak or irregular, heart failure may occur and the child may die.

If she survives the first few weeks, the child may then suffer from various complications. Apart from paralysis of the palate, and the resulting difficulty in swallowing, paralysis of the whole throat may occur, with consequent difficulty in breathing. This may then be made worse by

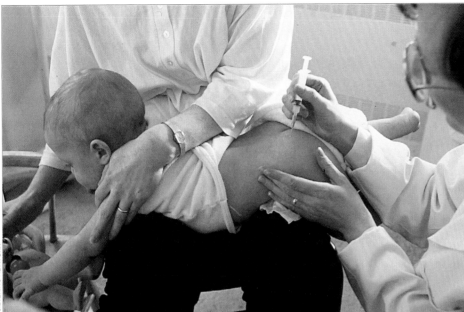

SIEVEKING NETWORK

Babies are usually immunized against diphtheria, whooping cough and tetanus all together, with three injections at monthly intervals..

paralysis of the chest muscles as well. Paralysis sometimes affects the limbs, especially the legs, and this condition may persist for several weeks. The disease can still be fatal at this stage.

Laryngeal diphtheria Diphtheria of the larynx is another dangerous form of the disease. The diphtheria membrane forms in the larynx, giving rise to cough, croup and fever in the early stages. The child can become unwell rapidly and may die.

Skin diphtheria The same bacteria that cause diphtheria in the nose and throat can also affect the skin, producing small sores on the trunk or limbs, especially the legs. This type of diphtheria spreads rapidly by direct contact and may take a long time to heal. Complications sometimes arise, but these are rare.

CAUSES

Diphtheria is caused by a bacterium called *Corynebacterium diphtheriae*. This tends to settle in the throat or nose, where it grows on the tissues, causing a membrane to form. The main threat from diphtheria usually comes not from the local growth of bacteria, but from a powerful toxin

produced by them. This is a poison that spreads into the bloodstream from the area where the bacteria are growing. It is this toxin that, in some cases, affects the function of the heart, or causes paralysis by affecting the nerves.

FORMS OF DIPHTHERIA

There are several varieties of the diphtheria bacterium, each having a different capability of producing toxin. The more serious forms, called *gravis* and *intermedius*, produce severe symptoms. The mildest form, called *mitis*, produces little toxin, and infection with it is unlikely to prove fatal. And, after being infected with this mild bacterium, the child will become immune to diphtheria for the rest of her life.

TREATMENT

Once diphtheria has been diagnosed, early treatment can save your child's life. Antibiotics, such as penicillin, are given to stop the growth of bacteria, but the most important treatment for a child with diphtheria is the injection of anti-toxin. This is a serum that is an antidote to the diphtheria toxin. If given early enough, it can prevent heart complications and paralysis. But, if diphtheria is not diagnosed at an early stage, and there has been time for the toxin to form in the child's body, the heart and nerves

may already be affected and the anti-toxin may take time to act.

A child who has developed paralysis or difficulty in breathing as a result of laryngeal diphtheria needs intensive nursing care. She may also need a tracheotomy — a surgical opening made in the windpipe to ease the breathing difficulty. In some cases, continuous artificial respiration is required as well.

VACCINATION

Although diphtheria may have tragic results, the disease is easily avoided by having your child vaccinated. This is usually carried out during the first year of life. The vaccine consists of a specially treated form of the diphtheria toxin, called a toxoid. A course of three injections is sufficient to build up immunity.

YOUR QUESTIONS

Q Is it really necessary for a child to be vaccinated against diphtheria? My little son seems so healthy that I'm tempted not to bother.

A The vaccination is extremely important. Deaths from diphtheria are now rare in Western countries, but this is due mainly to the fact that most children are immunized against the disease. However, outbreaks of diphtheria often occur, and any child who has not been vaccinated is in danger of catching the infection.

Q Can a person's immunity to diphtheria wear off?

A Yes. For this reason, booster doses are now recommended not only at 3½–4½ years old but also again at 13–14 years before leaving school. The recommendation to give this last dose is a recent introduction and is thought to give long-term protection against the disease.

The diphtheria toxoid is usually given at the same time and in the same injection as vaccines against whooping cough (pertussis) and tetanus, in the so-called DPT vaccine. Currently, this is given in three separate doses, at about two months, three months and four months of age; with a further DT booster at age four, just before school entry. Side effects are rare but your child may be sore at the site of the injection for a few days.

■ DISLOCATION

see also HIP

Joints are the junction points between the bones which allow us to move, and a joint is dislocated when a bone in the joint is displaced.

The joints in the arms and legs, hands and feet, and even in the spine, can all be dislocated, but some joints dislocate more readily than others. The joints of the fingers are relatively unstable and are liable to give in an accident, and the jaw bone can even be dislocated in a particularly wide yawn!

Playground accidents can cause joint dislocations. A child's shoulder blades, fingers and thumbs are especially vulnerable.

Active children who play sports are especially susceptible to dislocated joints in fingers and thumbs while catching balls, and to dislocated shoulders when falling or raising their arms too high. But luckily, although painful, these injuries can usually be put right quite easily.

S Y M P T O M S

A dislocated joint looks misshapen and cannot work properly. Movement is difficult and there is considerable pain, especially if the bone is pressing on a nerve.

Dislocated shoulder The joint between the bone of the upper arm (the humerus) and the shoulder-blade (the scapula) is a ball and socket joint, with the top outside corner of the shoulder-blade providing the socket. To allow for the wide range of movements the arm needs to make, the socket is very shallow, and the joint is therefore unstable.

The humerus can slip out of the socket forwards, backwards, up or down, but in most accidents it slips forward (called an anterior dislocation), making the shoulder appear square in shape.

Dislocated finger or thumb The finger or thumb will look shorter, and will be swollen and painful.

Dislocated elbow This can result from a fall on an outstretched arm, when the bones in the forearm are pushed backwards and laterally. It is extremely painful and the elbow looks out of joint, and can't work properly.

Dislocation in the neck This is a more serious form of injury, which usually occurs on the sports field. Due to pressure on the spinal cord, the child is unable to get up, and complains of numbness or paralysis in the legs and arms. In this event, call an ambulance immediately.

Dislocation of the hip This is an unusual injury, as the hip joint is very stable. The most frequent cause is a car accident. There will be extreme pain in the thigh and lack of movement in the leg, usually with additional injuries.

Occasionally, babies are born with dislocated hips (*see* Hip).

EMERGENCY ACTION

If you suspect that your child has dislocated a bone, do NOT try to put it back in place. Instead, try to immobilize it as best you can and see your doctor at once. Dislocations must be put right within 24 hours, as after this the tendons begin to shorten, and the dislocation is more difficult to correct.

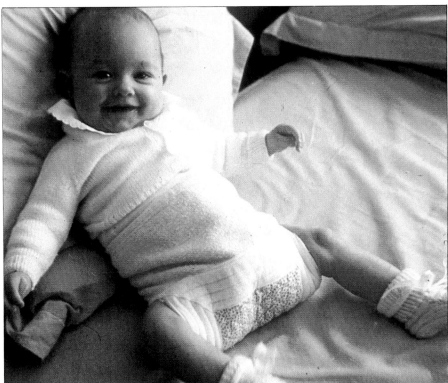

CNRI/VISION

Occasionally babies are born with dislocated hips. It is more common in girls than boys and is quite painless. Provided it is caught early enough – within the first three months – the condition is easily corrected, with excellent results, by the baby wearing splints for a while.

YOUR QUESTIONS

Q My little boy has to keep his arm in a sling since he dislocated it in a fall. Can you explain why?

A After a dislocation the injured limb or finger has to be kept immobile to make sure that no further damage is done to the tendons. Encourage your son to be patient and make sure he wears his sling until you are advised to remove it.

Q My little boy dislocated his thumb recently when he was playing ball in the garden. Is the joint likely to be permanently loose now?

A Fortunately, the thumb is a joint which can dislocate without causing too much damage to the surrounding soft tissue. If your son wears a splint for about three weeks, his thumb should heal perfectly.

TREATMENT

Neck dislocations have to be treated as emergencies, in a hospital. It is important not to change the position of the head and especially not to bend it forward but to support the head on each side of the face while waiting for the ambulance.

A dislocated hip will usually be one of several injuries in a serious accident and will be treated in hospital. **Dislocation of the elbow** is also best dealt with in hospital, as a general anaesthetic is usually required. If you suspect that your child has dislocated his elbow, take him straight to the nearest accident and emergency ward. It must be corrected, under anaesthetic, within 12 hours.

OTHER DISLOCATIONS

With other dislocations it is enough to take your child straight to the doctor, who will usually give a sedative and pain killer by injection before manipulating the slipped bone into position.

Shoulder dislocations may be so extremely painful that the doctor will arrange for the child to be taken to hospital for a general anaesthetic.

Once the dislocated bone has been put back into place the worst of the pain usually goes, but there may be some pain and stiffness for a few months. After treatment, dislocated joints in children are generally immobilized by means of bandages or slings for about three weeks. With a dislocated finger a finger splint may have to be worn.

With most dislocations your child will probably have physiotherapy after immobilization is over to help to restore full movement to the joint. But as long as the dislocation has been dealt with in time – within 24 hours – and as long as the child does any exercises advised, you can expect a complete recovery.

YOUR QUESTIONS

Q When a dislocation is obvious, should an adult try to manipulate the slipped bone back into place?

A No, definitely not. An untrained person should never try to put right a dislocation, as doing so can cause further injury.

■ DISTURBED CHILDREN

It is natural for children to exhibit disturbed behaviour when they are in particularly stressful situations, but it generally passes. Probably only between five and ten per cent of children are actually classified as disturbed. It is only when a child fails to adjust to a difficult situation, and when disturbed behaviour goes on for months rather than weeks, that a more serious problem should be suspected and professional help should be sought.

CAUSES OF DISTURBED BEHAVIOUR

Sometimes a dramatic event can cause long-term disturbed behaviour, and parents and teachers should be watchful if a child experiences a car accident, any physically violent encounter (such as being bitten by a dog), and of course being battered or molested.

Equally, long-term disturbance can be caused by a problem in the relationship between parent and child. For instance withdrawal of a parent's love and attention, or, at the other extreme, too much obsessive attention, both put a child at risk.

RON SUTHERLAND

Aggressive behaviour, turned inwards or outwards, is a common symptom.

SYMPTOMS

Anxiety can cause a variety of symptoms in a child — bed-wetting, nightmares, aggressive or explosive behaviour, excessive fear of people, animals or particular situations, nailbiting and periods of day-dreaming or lack of co-operation at home. Mostly these symptoms will disappear as the child adjusts to the source of anxiety.

CAUSE FOR CONCERN

It is always as well to be on your guard when a child shows any of the symptoms mentioned and notice how long they last. For instance, if bed-wetting which began when a child attended school for the first time then goes on for months, something may be wrong, and the same applies to the other symptoms.

In addition to the time factor, watch out for the severity of signs and their number.

If, for example, on top of bedwetting and nail-biting and consistently poor school performance your child is displaying aggression towards other children and has an inability to make friends, if her teachers tell you that she is daydreaming at school and if you notice a lack of co-operation at home, pro-fessional help could be needed to help sort out the problem.

TREATMENT

There will always be a reason for the child's disturbed behaviour and it may be possible to guess at what it is yourself. Perhaps the problem stems from your own treatment of, and attitude to, the child, for example you and your partner are not getting along and your child is responding to the constant tension at home, or perhaps you are worried about the state of your health and you are failing to give your child the attention she needs.

SELF-HELP

Once you recognize the root of the problem you should be able to start resolving it. If you think that your child may need more attention, try to set aside a recognized part of the day when you spend time together. Encourage older children to talk about any fears and anxieties.

PROFESSIONAL TREATMENT

If you feel you cannot cope alone and need outside help, ask your health visitor for advice or consult your family doctor. Most doctors will probably start by making a regular appointment to see the child and try to treat the problem themselves, with the emphasis on making as little fuss as possible.

However, if this does not work the doctor will probably refer the child to a psychiatrist or to the child guidance clinic at the local hospital. Here quite often the child will be seen with the parents, and possibly any brothers and sisters. The first stage will be an investigation of the problem, and the psychiatrist or counsellor will study school reports and listen objectively to what the relevant people have to say to form an overall picture and understand the background.

THE COUNSELLING PROCESS

The psychiatrist or child guidance officer will try to build up a trusting relationship with all concerned, and will attempt to identify the problem and to solve it by talking to both the child and the parents. If, for example, the parents are getting divorced, their child may feel terrified as the security of her home and family is threatened. She needs to be made to feel safe and loved, whatever else is going on between her parents.

An experienced counsellor will be able to help, although the process may take a matter of months or even longer. In most cases, this type of treatment is a complete success, and the disturbed behaviour will become a thing of the past.

YOUR QUESTIONS

Q My five-year-old still wets her bed. Do you think she is disturbed?

A Ten per cent of children still wet their beds once a week at the age of five. On its own, this is not enough to suggest that a child is disturbed. If your daughter seems generally happy and outgoing, don't worry; but mention it to your doctor just in case it's caused by a physical problem.

■ DIZZINESS

See also ANAEMIA, CONCUSSION, CONVULSIONS, FEVER, INFLUENZA, SUNSTROKE

Dizziness is fairly rare in children and if it does occur the cause will probably be obvious. If your child has unexplained prolonged or frequent dizzy spells, always take her to your doctor for a check-up.

CAUSES

In children temporary dizziness can be caused just by being out of breath after running about, or by spinning and whirling round, which children sometimes do deliberately to make themselves feel 'giddy'. Cartwheels, head-over-heels and hand-stands are also a perfectly normal cause of short-lived dizzy spells.

More prolonged dizziness can be the result of sun-stroke. And a frequent cause of dizziness is a viral infection such as influenza, which often makes adults and children alike feel light-headed, especially if they sit up or get out of bed suddenly.

Children who have epileptic attacks often have a dizzy spell at the onset of an attack. They and their

S. & R. GREENHILL

Fairground thrills will make even the most robust child feel temporarily dizzy – it's all part of the fun, and it wears off very quickly.

parents learn to recognize this as a useful warning that an attack is about to take place.

UNSUSPECTED CAUSES

Sometimes, however, the cause is not obvious and dizziness can be an indication of an unsuspected condition or illness, which needs to be diagnosed by your doctor. Children who are anaemic may complain of feeling dizzy, or dizziness may be a symptom of middle ear infection (otitis media), or simply of impacted ear wax, all needing treatment.

If the child has received a blow to the head an attack of dizziness could be the result of potentially serious concussion or skull fracture. In some cases the attack comes on several hours after the injury, so parents should be on the look-out.

SYMPTOMS

A child who has not had a dizzy spell before may not know how to describe it. She may describe it as a floating or spinning feeling, or may complain that she can't see properly. You may also notice that the child walks unsteadily.

TREATMENT

If the dizziness is the result of an illness or medical condition, then the treatment will depend on the cause and on the doctor's advice.

If a child has a sudden dizzy spell, encourage her to sit with her head between her knees to increase the flow of blood to the brain. Get her to take slow, deep breaths, and to rest until the spell has passed.

YOUR QUESTIONS

Q My son has dizzy spells and occasionally even faints. The doctor has told me to give him a sweet drink or a biscuit afterwards. Why is this?

A Dizzy spells are often caused by low blood sugar level, especially if the child has not eaten for some time. A sweet drink or a biscuit will quickly remedy this, although it is better to make sure that your son eats regularly and heathily rather than relying on sweet snacks which interfere with the body's natural regulation of the blood sugar level. So sweets are necessary after a dizzy spell but *not* as part of the normal diet the rest of the time.

YOUR QUESTIONS

Q My teenage daughter has had several dizzy spells this year. Is there anything to worry about?

A Quite often dizzy spells precede a viral infection, but in your daughter's case it is just possible that they are linked to the onset of her periods.

Take her to the doctor, who will check this out. If it is anaemia, a course of iron tablets will soon set it right. It is a good idea generally to make sure that growing girls have plenty of iron-rich foods. These include liver, eggs, sun-dried raisins, cereals, and leafy green vegetables.

■ DOCTOR

In recent years there has been a move away from the individual family doctor, working alone or with one partner, towards group practices. Your doctor is now much more likely to be one of a group of doctors working in partnership, sometimes with a trained nurse to help with routine matters. These people, together with health visitors and district nurses are collectively known as 'the primary health care team'.

FAMILY PRACTICE

You will probably find that your doctor (or the doctors in your local practice) prefers to treat everyone in a family to get an overall picture of the pattern of health in the family, and you will in any case probably prefer this. Usually in a practice with several doctors you will be allocated, or be able to choose, a particular doctor who is the one you normally see, except in an emergency.

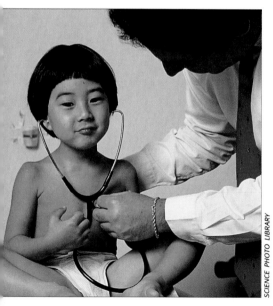

A young patient is given confidence during a routine check-up as the doctor lets him listen to his own heartbeat through the stethoscope.

The doctor's work is to resolve all the medical (and often emotional and psychological) problems that are brought to the surgery. Many of these problems can be dealt with immediately, but sometimes another

opinion or special tests may be needed, and you may have to take your child for an X-ray or blood test, to a specialist, for out-patient treatment, or for admission to a hospital as a result of seeing your doctor.

CONSULTING YOUR DOCTOR

Make sure that you know your practice's routine for making appointments and visiting the surgery or clinic. For example, your group practice may have a special 'Well Baby' clinic for routine health checks, immunizations and so on, while you may only need to visit the surgery for appointments when the child is ill.

If you are not sure whether a visit is necessary, remember that many doctors are happy to give advice over the phone, and may have times of day allocated for this. They may also prefer to telephone you back rather than receiving a call from you. Check this out with the receptionist, and arrange to be available at the appropriate time.

Remember, too, that the receptionist can often give advice on whether it is necessary to see the doctor, and if so, how urgently.

CALLING THE DOCTOR OUT

If you are worried about your child yet feel reluctant to call the doctor out it may be possible to arrange to take the child into the surgery and be seen without waiting. This has the advantage that all the doctor's facilities are at hand for any tests, and, especially if you have a car and live not too far away, it is often the best solution. Some practices even have a special waiting room for anyone who may be infectious, or who needs to be kept comfortable.

But do not hesitate to call the doctor out if you feel it necessary. He or she would rather be called before an emergency sets in, which may often be in the middle of the night.

THE CONSULTATION

Children over the age of five can often speak for themselves and answer the doctor's questions about what is wrong with them, but for younger children you will need to tell

VISITS TO SEE THE DOCTOR

- When you are making an appointment, let the receptionist know if you want the doctor to see you as well as your child, or if there is more than one child to see.

- If you are taking your child for pre-arranged treatment, such as injections, let him or her know, without dramatizing it, what will be involved and why it is necessary.

- Take toys or books to keep your child or children quietly occupied while waiting.

- Encourage your child to see the doctor as a friend, and this will help the doctor to provide the best health care.

the doctor about the symptoms.

The doctor will also want to know all the details of the illness from you, and it may be a good idea to make a note of all the details you think relevant beforehand, to make sure you don't forget anything. You should be able to say how long the symptoms have been observable, whether there have been fluctuations in temperature, or any swellings of

WHEN TO SEE THE DOCTOR

Arrange to see your doctor without delay if your child has any of the following:
- high temperature (over 39°C/102°F, or over 38°/100°F for over two days)
- difficulty in breathing, with wheezing
- severe pains in the abdomen
- fits, or unconsciousness
- diarrhoea or vomiting in a baby or young child, if the attack carries on for more than a few hours
- persistent headaches or dizziness or disturbed vision
- prolonged loss of appetite

glands, puffiness, changes of skin colour; whether there has been vomiting, diarrhoea, lack of appetite, headache, pain, loss of consciousness, blurred vision, convulsions. Other questions that may be relevant are what and when the child has eaten, whether you have tried any remedies, and to what effect; whether the child has been in contact with anyone ill, and any relevant family health matters.

In turn, you may want to ask the doctor some questions, and again, it may help to have these written down.

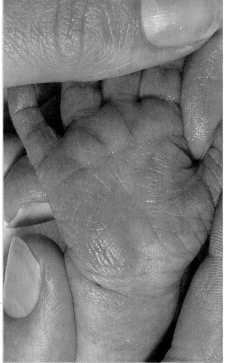

One of the characteristics of a Down's syndrome baby is abnormal skin creases in the palm of the hand. The little finger generally curves inwards.

Questions may include: How long can the illness be expected to last? Can the child mix with other children? Will you need to bring your child to see the doctor again? If medicine is prescribed, should the treatment be continued until the end of the prescription or only until the child is better? Should medicine be taken before or after meals, and is it crucial to take it at regular intervals?

FOLLOWING ADVICE

Make a note of any advice the doctor gives you as it is surprising how easy it is to forget, because of your anxiety about the child's health. If the doctor gives you advice only rather than a prescription, don't worry, but do make sure that you understand the advice and follow it carefully. Make sure too that you get from your doctor an idea of how long the symptoms can be expected to last, and don't be afraid to seek his or her advice again if the course of the illness doesn't go as predicted.

■ DOG BITES see BITES
■ DOWN'S SYNDROME

Down's syndrome, which used to be known as mongolism, is caused by a chance genetic error, which is to say that it does not usually run in the family. An irregularity of the chromosomes produces a collection of abnormalities while the baby is in the womb. These cause the child to suffer varying degrees of learning difficulty as well as affecting her appearance.

SYMPTOMS

There may be few symptoms to notice just after the birth, but a very striking and characteristic feature of the Down's syndrome baby is its floppiness.

By careful examination other features become obvious — the eyes are rather small, almond-shaped and slanting, and the bridge of the nose is small too, giving the nose an upward curve which can cause the baby to

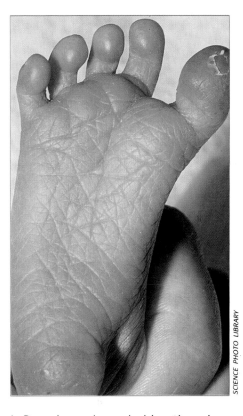

In Down's syndrome babies, the soles of the feet are deeply creased, like the palms, with a pronounced gap between the first and second toes.

YOUR QUESTIONS

Q My doctor doesn't seem to have a very good manner with children and my two little boys are quite frightened by him. Is it possible to change doctor?

A Yes, you can change doctor if you are unhappy with yours. First you must find another within your area who is willing to take you and your family on to his list. Then, out of courtesy, you should let your doctor know that you are leaving his practice. Your family's medical records will be forwarded to your new doctor in a few weeks.

Q When is it advisable to take a sick child to hospital rather than calling out the doctor?

A If the condition seems life-threatening, then call an ambulance or take the child straight to hospital yourself. If the condition is serious (for example if a baby or small child has been vomiting for several hours, or if any child has a temperature of 40°C (104°F) or more which you cannot reduce by sponging and paracetamol), call your doctor urgently, but take the child to hospital if the doctor can't be contacted.

snuffle. The mouth is also small, but the tongue is of normal size and so it tends to protrude.

Then as the baby grows, other abnormalities begin to show. The child's hands are short and broad, with a short little finger which curves towards the thumb. Also, the gap between the big toe and the other toes is unusually large and the feet tend to be rather square.

Many Down's syndrome children also have problems with their internal organs which might require surgery. About 40 per cent have heart defects, and hernias are common too, with intestinal problems often causing severe constipation.

BELOW AVERAGE IQ

As the child grows, learning difficulties soon become apparent. The Down's syndrome child's IQ ranges from 30 to 50 (while the normal average is 100). Given the right encouragement, the IQ can sometimes be raised by up to 20 points.

One positive characteristic of the Down's syndrome is that these children are usually easy-going, happy and friendly, responding well to love.

CAUSES

Down's syndrome is caused by an extra chromosome. Normally, people have a total of 46 chromosomes, in 23 matched pairs, which are numbered from the largest (number one) to the smallest (number 23). A child inherits 23 chromosomes from the mother and 23 from the father.

For reasons which are not really understood, a Down's syndrome child has 47 chromosomes, instead of 46. This abnormality in Down's syndrome always occurs in chromosome number 21, and usually, but not always, the extra chromosome comes from the mother's egg, not the father's sperm.

The condition is very closely related to the age of the mother, even though there is some evidence that the father's age is relevant too. A mother aged 20 has only a one in 2300 chance of having a Down's syndrome baby, whereas for a woman aged 35 the chance is one in 290, and at 45 the chance is one in 30. The chances of having a second Down's syndrome baby are doubled once a woman has had one.

HOW TO DETECT IT

Tests can be performed at the 14th to 16th week of pregnancy to determine whether the foetus will develop into a Down's syndrome child. With mothers over the age of 40 it is now routine to perform a test known as amniocentesis, and women over 35 may request the test if they wish. The test is simple, quick and painless, and involves using a needle to draw off a small amount of the amniotic fluid from inside the womb in order to study the cells shed by the baby.

As an alternative to amniocentesis, another test, called chorionic villus biopsy, is now sometimes performed. In this test — which can be performed in the third month of pregnancy — an obstetrician removes a small piece of tissue from the inside of the uterus through the vagina. This tissue contains cells with the same chromosomes as those of the baby and laboratory analysis will detect any abnormality.

These tests show conclusively

Older brothers and sisters often help stimulate a Down's syndrome child's mental potential.

whether Down's syndrome is present, and if it is the parents may wish to choose to have an abortion. On the other hand, if they choose to continue with the pregnancy they can contact an appropriate organization, or parents in a similar situation, for help, advice and support.

While there is no cure for children with Down's syndrome, any of the illnesses or internal problems they may have as a result of the condition can of course be treated.

TREATMENT

The success of treatment depends on the severity of the problem. Unfortunately there is a risk of severe infections of the lungs during childhood, and abnormalities of the heart may be so severe as to result in early death. But if the child passes her first five years without trouble, there is no reason why she should not live quite healthily into middle age.

On the whole, Down's syndrome children grow up to be happy and contented people. The important factor in their development is that they should receive as much stimulation as possible from the earliest possible age and through childhood. Parents should try to stimulate all the baby's

YOUR QUESTIONS

Q I am 38 and expecting a baby. Is the Down's syndrome test advisable?

A Yes. You will probably be offered an amniocentesis (an examination of the fluid in the womb to check whether the baby is normal) as a matter of routine. The test is usually done at 16 weeks, when it is not too late to have the pregnancy terminated if this abnormality is found and the parents decide that this is the best solution.

Q Why are older women more likely to give birth to Down's syndrome children?

A The answer to this is not really known, but it is thought to be related to the fact that the woman's eggs, which have been in her ovaries since birth, are ageing.

YOUR QUESTIONS

Q What are my chances of having a Down's syndrome child?

A It depends on your age. The overall average is one in 660 births in Britain, but at the age of 20, the chance is one in 2300. The chances are still fairly low until the mid-30s (when they become one in 290), and they reach one in 30 at the age of 45 plus.

Q Can a Down's syndrome child be toilet trained?

A Yes. There is usually no difficulty in toilet training these children, or in teaching them to feed and dress themselves.

■ DRESSINGS

see also BANDAGES

A dressing is a protective covering that is applied to a wound. It is used to absorb blood or pus, to control bleeding, to prevent infection or dirt from entering the wound, and to protect it from further damage.

Dressings must naturally be clean, sterile, non-irritant and porous, so that air can enter and sweat can get out. They must also be large enough to cover the wound completely. Dressings are held in place by bandages or adhesive tape.

TYPES OF DRESSING

Usually a dressing is made of layers of gauze, and is applied dry to a bleeding wound, helping the blood to clot. Dressings for burns, which heal to form a crust that would stick to a dry dressing, are impregnated with paraffin, and there are also more complex dressings, which involve layers of packing, and medicated dressings for ulcers, discharging abscesses and large wounds. These complex dressings are usually applied by a nurse or doctor.

Keep a supply of adhesive dressings (known as plasters or sticking plasters) in your medicine chest for use on the small wounds that children get so frequently. These dressings consist of a pad of absorbent gauze or cellulose on an adhesive backing which is perforated to allow sweat to evaporate.

For larger wounds, non-adhesive dressings can be bought in sterile packs for use with bandages or sticking plaster. In emergencies a clean, ironed handkerchief or piece of cotton sheeting can be used to stem the flow of blood while waiting for medical treatment. It is important to apply pressure on the wound through the dressing to help stem blood flow.

APPLYING DRESSINGS

Wash your hands thoroughly, and put on thin plastic gloves if available. Use cotton cloth to clean the wound by dabbing it from the centre outward, using a fresh area of cloth for each stroke. Do not use cotton wool as this leaves 'hair' that may stick to the wound and become infected.

A sterile dressing held in place with bandage will protect a wound from dirt and infection while it heals.

Ensure that the wound looks clean and healthy and that any major bleeding has stopped. Dry the wound with gentle dabbing movements, and decide whether to use adhesive dressing (better for a small wound) or non-adhesive dressing (better for a larger wound).

Adhesive dressings Make sure that the dressing is large enough (i.e. that the adhesive part is *not* on the

senses, moving the baby's limbs, playing a variety of sounds to stimulate hearing, placing the baby in contact with different textures, and keeping the baby visually interested. As soon as possible parents should read to the child, play with her and so on, to stimulate her mentally.

Without this treatment Down's syndrome children will not show a great deal of interest in anything and their condition will deteriorate. But if they are given sufficient care and attention as they are growing, there is even a chance of their developing sufficiently to earn their own living.

EDUCATION

Keeping up with children at a normal school is possible, but it is best for some children with Down's syndrome to be cared for in special schools. Very few of these children can learn to read and write well, but some experts now claim that with proper teaching their learning potential can be significantly improved.

Down's syndrome children vary enormously in their personalities — just like everyone else. Each individual should be treated in a way that matches his or her emotional and intellectual state.

DRESSINGS

Before dressing a wound, wash your hands and dry them on a clean towel. Try not to let your hands come in contact with the wound while dressing it.

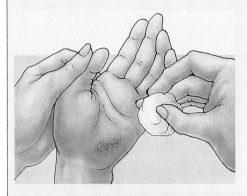

Clean and dry the wound gently, using sterile cotton soaked in fresh water. Use a little soap for a dirty wound.

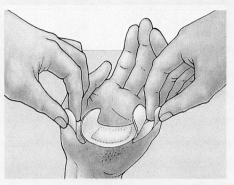

Peel away the protective strips on the back of an adhesive dressing and then lower it carefully onto the wound.

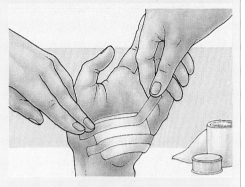

If the wound requires padding but does not warrant bandaging, use sticking plaster to secure the dressing.

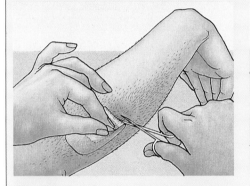

If hair is stuck to the sticky part of an adhesive dressing, cut away as you peel back the dressing.

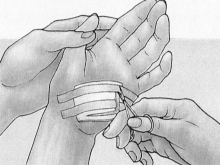

If the dressing is stuck, cut away as much as possible, then soak in warm, previously boiled water to loosen.

Layers of dressing should float off and the rest can be peeled back without pain or damage to the wound.

wound), and that the skin around the wound is completely dry. For a new wound it should not be necessary to apply any antibiotic cream, but if for any reason this has been used, wipe off any excess or it will prevent the dressing from sticking.

Hold the dressing over the wound and slowly peel off the strips while pressing the dressing on to the wound. Smooth down to make sure that the dressing adheres.

Non-adhesive dressings Use a dressing pad large enough to cover the wound completely, and gently lay the dressing over the wound. Secure a small pad with strips of sticking plaster, or hold a larger dressing in place with bandaging. To make your own dressing, apply to the wound pieces of gauze which have been taken from a sterile pack and cut to size, and on top of these put cotton wool padding, all held in place by means of a bandage.

REPLACING DRESSINGS

Dry dressings covering small wounds can be changed every three days, or whenever dirty, uncomfortable or wet. If the wound seems to be infected, change the dressing frequently, and ask your doctor for advice. (Signs of infection are increasing discomfort, swelling or discharge.)

Wet dressings, meant for infected or discharging wounds, and impregnated with an antiseptic or antibiotic substance or with soft paraffin, are usually used only on medical advice. They are replaced daily or more frequently if stained or wet.

YOUR QUESTIONS

Q Can my son go swimming with a dressing over his cut leg?

A No. Wet dressings delay the healing process. Consequently a dressing which has become wet must be changed as soon as possible.

Q How can I avoid changing dressings too frequently?

A Ideally a dressing should be left in place for three days to allow the wound to heal. Place an additional bandage on top of the dressing, and change this daily.

■ DROWNING

See also ARTIFICIAL RESPIRATION

Accidental drowning claims between 700 and 1000 lives each year in the UK alone. Many of the young children who have drowned would still be alive if they had been taught how to swim, the dangers to avoid, and what to do when in trouble in the water. However, even children who can swim should be supervised by someone who will be able to assist if they get into difficulties. For, contrary to popular belief, most people who drown are swimmers. And the majority die within ten metres of the shore. Often, parents are unfamiliar with the particular stretch of beach and do not realize that the current is too strong for a young child. If a toddler paddling in shallow water slips over, he may be quickly carried out into deep water by the tide.

Most of the deaths occur in inland waters, and this has led many people to assume that it is more dangerous to swim in fresh water than in salt water. It is true that fresh water is less buoyant than salt water, but the main reason for there being more cases of drowning in fresh water is the lack of rescue services in most of these areas. Canals, lakes and rivers are rarely adequately guarded, whereas many holiday beaches are protected by life-guards employed by the local authority. Even on beaches with no lifeguards, there are usually plenty of other people around who can assist a swimmer in danger or can go and fetch help.

Although swimming accidents account for most cases of drowning, it should be remembered that a young child may easily drown in a paddling pool, or even in the bath, if left unattended.

SIGNS OF DROWNING

Drowning can occur so quickly that the child may not be able to call for help or wave to attract attention. So anyone in charge of a child who is swimming should watch for any changes in behaviour. A swimmer in trouble will usually face towards the shore and use the breast stroke, which will cause the head to bob up and down. If the rate of bobbing becomes slower, this may indicate that the child is tiring. As the swimmer slows down, his body will be-

WATCHPOINTS

- **Never let young children out of your sight when you are near water.**
- **Make sure that your children learn to swim as early as possible** – preferably before they start going to school.
- **Don't let children float on a lilo in the sea.** They may easily be carried away from the shore by the wind or tide.
- **Don't let children swim after a beachball that is floating out to sea.** A child can quite easily be swept out too.
- **Never let a child go swimming straight after a heavy meal.** (A light meal should cause no harm.)
- **On beaches, look for any signs or flags warning of dangerous swimming conditions.**
- **Teach children never to stray out of their depth until they are strong swimmers.**
- **Make children wear life jackets when they go boating.**
- **Tell children not to panic if they get cramp while swimming.** They should float on their back or dog paddle until the cramp wears off.
- **Keep garden ponds fenced in while small children are about.** Even a few centimetres of water could cause drowning.
- **Never leave a baby alone in a bath, even for a few seconds.**
- **Ideally, try to ensure that all adults in the family learn resuscitation techniques** – *see* step-by-step **ARTIFICIAL RESPIRATION.**

JENNIE WOODCOCK

Children should be taught to swim at an early age. Even very young babies can learn to float and usually enjoy being in the water.

come nearly upright in the water. And, if he becomes exhausted, he will stop swimming and float vertically, with the head just above the water. He may be unable to raise his arms to attract attention as this would make him sink. Difficulties with breathing may prevent him from calling out. At this stage, he may also become disoriented and no longer be facing the shore.

CAUSES

In most cases of drowning, the victim panics and as a result loses control of his breathing. What then happens is that water enters the lungs and the victim suffers from a lack of oxygen. Technically, death results from asphyxiation.

TREATMENT

A child who has got into difficulties in the water can be saved by prompt, effective resuscitation. As soon as the victim has been brought to the shore, he should be turned on one side so that the mouth can be cleared of any obstruction. He should then be

YOUR QUESTIONS

Q My son was recently saved from drowning in the village pond. Might he have suffered any brain damage when he stopped breathing?

A This is most unlikely. If the breathing and circulation are re-established within five minutes or so, the victim usually makes a complete recovery.

Q Is it true that people come to the surface three times before drowning?

A No. Once the person has taken a breath under the water, he is likely to remain submerged for a long time. Eye-witnesses often report that the victim was swimming normally but then suddenly vanished.

rolled on to his back and the head tilted backwards to prevent the tongue from obstructing the passage of air. Then he should be given five rapid breaths of mouth-to-mouth artificial respiration.

This may be sufficient to ensure that the child continues breathing normally. To check, put your cheek in front of the child's mouth. The skin of the cheek is fairly sensitive and will normally detect even weak breathing. If the child is breathing, he can now be turned on to his side again and nursed in that position. However, if he is not breathing, artificial respiration should be continued for at least an hour. Children should be given one breath every three seconds – a faster rate than the one which is recommended for adults.

To check that the heart is beating, place your ear against the centre of the child's chest. In the event of a cardiac arrest, firm intermittent pressure on the chest must be given at the same time as artificial respiration. This makes the task of resuscitation very difficult for an unskilled

person so, if possible, it should be left to someone familiar with the technique. The layperson can learn this properly only by attending a course and practising on a dummy. Trying it on a healthy person may cause harm.

Even if the child seems to be recovering well, he should be taken to hospital. There a doctor will check the child's temperature, heartbeat and level of oxygen in the blood. The oxygen level is often low in such cases, so the doctor will probably give the child oxygen to breathe.

The doctor will also check the lungs to see how much water has been inhaled. A child who has inhaled water runs the risk of developing a form of pneumonia several hours after the accident in the water. Some years ago, this was nearly always fatal but, with a better understanding of the physiology of the lungs and with the development of improved hospital equipment, this rarely occurs today.

PREVENTION

The human body floats naturally in water until a large quantity of water is swallowed. Consequently children – and adults – should be taught how to float on their backs with their mouth, and nose, kept above water. If a child is in difficulties in the water he should roll on to his back with arms and legs outstretched until he is spotted and rescued.

■ DYSENTERY

Dysentery is a general term for intestinal infections causing severe diarrhoea and tummy pains. It is very rare in countries with good sanitation, but it is particularly threatening to small children and can even cause death through dehydration.

There are two types of dysentery, amoebic dysentery and bacillary dysentery. Both types are commonly found in tropical countries, but bacillary dysentery can occur anywhere in the world. Outbreaks have even occurred in Britain, where they tend to happen in schools and institutions.

SYMPTOMS

Symptoms of bacillary dysentery are abdominal pain with profuse diarrhoea, often containing mucus or blood. If properly treated, it does not last longer than five to seven days. Amoebic dysentery, on the other hand, is chronic and also causes flatulence. Bacillary dysentery takes 12 hours to three days to develop after ingesting the bacteria responsible, while amoebic dysentery develops more gradually and is more difficult to cure.

Dysentery is prevalent in countries with insanitary water supplies. Inset: magnified amoeba which causes amoebic dysentery.

PREVENTION

If you have to take your child to a country where dysentery is prevalent, make sure that the child drinks only bottled water and eats only tinned meat and vegetables, and fruit that has been peeled.

Outbreaks of the less virulent form of dysentery known in Europe are spread by lack of hygiene, and children must be encouraged always to wash their hands after going to the lavatory, as the bacteria are easily transferred from hand to mouth.

TREATMENT

Bouts of diarrhoea quickly rob small children of the water and mineral salts in their bodies. The treatment for this is to drink a solution of specially prepared salts and glucose (*see* Diarrhoea). It may be necessary to replace the lost fluids by intravenous injection, and medical help should always be sought. Antibiotics are used to treat bacillary dysentery. Amoebic dysentery is treated by drugs such as emetine or flagyl and chloraquine.

■ DYSLEXIA

Dyslexia is a condition that causes some children to have extreme difficulty with reading and writing. It is often called 'word blindness', but this term describes only one of the many features of dyslexia. About ten per cent of children are affected by dyslexia to some degree, and it is more common in boys than girls.

Because of their difficulties with reading and writing, dyslexics are sometimes thought to be lazy, ignorant or wilfully disobedient and are relegated to a slow learning group. However, dyslexic children may be highly intelligent and suffer greatly if asked to work at a slow pace.

WATCHPOINTS

• Always encourage a dyslexic child by praising his achievements. Do not compare him unfavourably with other children.

• Concentrate on what the child is good at, as this will help to build up his confidence.

• When teaching the child new words, give him only one or two at a time. A long list will only cause confusion. To help the child to read longer words, divide them into syllables with a pencil line.

• Teach the child to pronounce words correctly. But do not make him change his writing style for the sake of neatness.

• When helping the child with reading, do not rush him. Let him take his own time, and stop when he shows signs of tiredness.

If dyslexia is left untreated, the child will not be able to catch up in his schoolwork and will have difficulties in adult life. If dyslexia is recognized at an early age, however, there is much that can be done.

SYMPTOMS

Dyslexia can take many forms. In reading, the child may confuse letters of similar shapes, such as b and d, and u and n; or the confusion may be between letters with similar sounds, such as v, f and th.

He may have trouble in keeping his place on a line, and may go to the wrong place when moving from one line to the next. When reading aloud, he may lack expression, or put the

A CHAUMAT/PETIT FORMAT

A dyslexic child often finds it difficult to distinguish between letters that are similar in shape, but responds to individualized teaching.

stresses in the wrong places. In some cases, the child may mix some of the letters or reverse parts of words.

Writing also presents problems: individual letters may be hard to form and capital letters may be left out or put in the wrong places. Arithmetic can also suffer, although this may be due to a difficulty in writing the figures correctly.

YOUR QUESTIONS

Q My son is dyslexic and left-handed. Could there be any connection between the two?

A Yes, although these conditions do not always go together. This combination may occur because the left half of the brain controls the action of the right hand and also most of the speech-processing mechanisms. So a malfunction in the left half of the brain could result in the right hand losing its dominance, together with a form of dyslexia.

CAUSES

In some cases of dyslexia, a brain injury has resulted in an area of scar tissue, so some of the brain cells do not function correctly. In other cases, there is incomplete development in one part of the brain.

About half the cases of dyslexia appear to be inherited, but the condition does not necessarily affect all members of a family, and can be mild or severe.

TREATMENT

Occasionally dyslexia disappears by itself if the development of part of the brain was merely delayed. And, even if there is a permanent malfunction, the dyslexia may still disappear as the brain sometimes finds alternative ways of performing the required tasks. In other cases, skilled help with reading and writing is necessary.

Once dyslexia has been recognized, the child should be given a remedial course. Besides helping with the general difficulty in reading and writing, the course will also help the child to quickly recognize road signs and essential words, such as 'danger', 'no entry', and 'exit'.

While studying, the child can use aids such as tape-recorded notes, films, pictures and video tapes instead of note pad and pencil.

■ EAR

See also ADENOIDS, BAT EARS, DEAF-NESS, GLUE EAR

Our ears consist of three parts: the outer, middle and inner ear, which act as receiver, amplifier and transmitter in the process of hearing. The inner ear is also important for balance and movement.

A canal leads from the outer ear

A child with ear problems should always be examined by your doctor as soon as possible.

(the part we see) to the drum in the middle ear, and in this canal wax is secreted to lubricate the skin.

A narrow tube, called the Eustachian tube, which leads out of the middle ear and runs to the back of the throat, behind the tonsils, equalizes the pressure between the outer and inner ear. Nerve endings from the inner ear transmit electrical impulses to the brain, to be converted into 'sound'.

There are three types of ear infection, known as *otitis externa* (affecting the outer ear), *otitis media* (middle ear), and the rarer *otitis interna* (inner ear). Young children are particularly prone to ear infections.

Other common ear problems in children are impacted earwax, 'glue ear' and objects pushed into ears.

■ EARACHE

Earache can be caused by impacted wax or a bad cold, by tooth decay or even a boil. The outer ear infection, *otitis externa*, can also sometimes result in earache. But severe earache in children is usually caused by middle ear infection (*otitis media*).

SYMPTOMS

Often a child or baby with earache will be very distressed, and there may be a high temperature. Babies with earache may rub their ears, or be obviously in pain.

Children under five are particularly prone to middle ear infection, and the main symptom is bad earache. This is usually preceded by a sore throat or a cold, as the infection starts in the throat and travels up the Eustachian tube. Discharge from the ears and some loss of hearing can also sometimes occur.

Always seek medical attention for these symptoms, as untreated middle ear infection can spread, causing perforation of the ear drum and infection of the inner ear, which can lead to permanent deafness.

TREATMENT

If the earache is caused by an infection the doctor will prescribe a course of antibiotics.

A warm cloth held over the ear can help to soothe pain, and a cold one will help if the ear feels hot. The doctor may advise you to give para-

YOUR QUESTIONS

Q My little boy loves swimming, but the doctor has told him not to go as he is being treated for an ear infection. Why is this?

A While a child has an ear infection there is a slight risk that swimming will cause a perforated ear drum. He will have to give up swimming until the infection has cleared.

CARE OF CHILDREN'S EARS

The ears are very complex and sensitive, and you must treat a child's ears with special care.

• To clean a child's ears, wash them gently with soft cotton wool. Never insert any object (including cotton buds) into the ears.

• Any discharge, pain or loss of hearing should always be reported to your doctor straight away.

• If a child has pushed any object into the ear, see your doctor. Do not attempt to remove the object yourself.

• Remember that it is easy to inflict serious damage on children's ears.

cetamol to control the pain.

Earache caused by impacted earwax will be treated by syringing the ear. If the pain is caused by the child having pushed something into his ear, it should be better when the object has been removed.

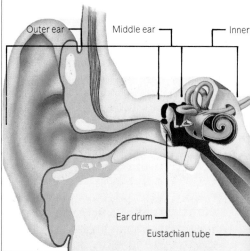

PARTS OF THE EAR

Outer ear — Middle ear — Inner

Ear drum —

Eustachian tube —

Colds and throat infections can travel up the Eustachian tube to the middle ear. If they are left untreated they can damage the ear drum and spread to the inner ear.

■ ECZEMA

Many babies and young children suffer from eczema and it tends to fade away as the child gets older. It usually runs in families, although often only one child in the family is affected. Eczema can be caused by an allergy but may be brought on by emotional upsets. Often, there is no obvious cause.

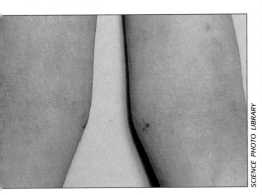

Although eczema rashes often appear first on the face, they usually also affect the folds in the skin and the bends in the elbows (see above) and knees.

S Y M P T O M S

Eczema is characterized by inflamed patches of skin, which soon become dry and cracked or covered with tiny red pimples or blisters. This is accompanied by severe itching, and scratching the rash makes it worse, causing wet, bleeding sores and encouraging it to spread.

Eczema usually starts on the child's face and scalp and spreads to the hands and limbs. It is at its worst in the skin-folds, or where clothing rubs against the skin.

WATCHPOINTS

It is essential that children with eczema do not come into direct contact with anyone with cold sores (*herpes simplex*). This is because eczematous skin is vulnerable to the herpes virus and liable to widespread infection if exposed to it.

YOUR QUESTIONS

Q My teenage daughter had eczema badly as a small child. We had forgotten all about it but now she is getting it again. What can I do?

A Eczema often makes an unwelcome return in adolescence. Emotional stress seems to be a possible cause, with worry about exams or a new job acting as a trigger. Uncomfortable and unsightly as eczema can be, it is not something to be brooded over. Encourage your daughter to see the problem as a nuisance that can be controlled, and not as a cause for alarm.

T R E A T M E N T

Babies who suffer from eczema are sometimes allergic to cow's milk. In families where the allergy is known to exist, breast feeding will give the child a good chance of avoiding the complaint. If this is not possible, or when the child is weaned, goat's milk or artificial milk based on soya are nutritious alternatives. Exposure to household pets can also, unfortunately, bring on attacks and should be avoided if it is suspected.

Eczema usually affects children with dry skin, so the most important part of the treatment is to keep the skin moist. It should not be washed too often, and soap should be avoided as it dries the skin and can also cause allergic eczema.

Ask your pharmacist for an alternative to soap, such as aqueous cream or emulsifying ointment, or add an oil containing liquid paraffin to the bath water. Use bland baby moisturizing creams and keep the skin well covered in cold weather to prevent it from drying.

Doctors sometimes prescribe creams or ointments based on coal-tar extracts or, for short-term use, steroids. These help to soothe the rash but there is no known cure. The main concern is to stop the child from scratching, which makes the rash worse and may lead to skin infection.

Little children can be protected from hurting themselves if they wear cotton mittens, and cotton underclothing and socks will help to stop the rash from getting worse. Wool in particular should be avoided as it can irritate sensitive skin.

■ ELECTRIC SHOCKS

Electric shocks can be fatal and it is vital to try to eliminate every risk of their happening. Check that you have taken all possible precautions to guard children from danger (*see* Safety in the Home, page 92).

Young children love to explore – to touch and to taste – and accidents can easily happen. Appliances should always be kept unplugged when not in use, and out of reach.

S Y M P T O M S

The effect of an electric shock varies from a mildly unpleasant tingling to severe muscle spasms, destruction of tissue, shock, and failure of heartbeat and of breathing. Even low

WATCHPOINTS

Even mild electric shocks can cause damage to the nervous system, so always get medical attention for any shock other than one causing only a brief, mild tingling and leaving no visible mark.

voltage electricity can kill in some circumstances.

TREATMENT

Although in some cases the severity of the shock can throw the victim aside, usually she is unable to let go of the appliance. In this case, **the first thing to do is to switch off the current.** If this is impossible, use a broom handle or a wooden chair to separate the child from the appliance. **You must act quickly.**

Treatment will depend on the severity of the case. If the child is not breathing, artificial respiration or mouth to mouth resuscitation are

SAFETY IN THE HOME

• Be sure that the wiring in your house is up to standard. If in doubt have it checked by a qualified electrician.

• Use shuttered or covered sockets so that young children cannot put their fingers, or poke objects, into them.

• If you have a standard fuse box, make sure that the fuse wire or cartridge is of the correct rating.

• Switch off, and unplug, any equipment not in use.

• Keep flexes as short as possible and away from children's reach. Do not run flexes under carpets.

• Make sure that plugs are correctly wired and earthed, and replace any damaged plugs straight away.

urgent and can take an hour or more. If possible, get someone to call an ambulance while you do this.

Do not move the victim unless you have to, as there is a danger of fractures if she fell or was thrown. If there are obvious burns or wounds, get someone to cover them with dressings while you continue to give resuscitation.

If the child is breathing, put her in the recovery position — lying on her side with lower arm behind her bottom, and lower leg stretched out straight, upper arm and leg bent at right-angles at elbow and knee, and with head back to prevent choking.

Keep the child warm and reassure her (if conscious) while you are waiting for the ambulance to arrive.

■ ENCEPHALITIS

The term encephalitis simply means inflammation of the brain, and this is usually caused by a virus. Sometimes the virus attacks the brain itself, but in most cases the encephalitis results more as a side-effect with the brain becoming inflamed in reaction to a viral attack on some other part of the body.

The attack can be mild, serious, or even fatal, especially in babies, where 5-10 per cent of those affected may die.

SYMPTOMS

Most cases start when a child is recovering from a rash. Mild encephalitis may merely cause a headache but in a serious attack the headache will be severe, with drowsiness which can worsen until the child falls into a coma.

There may also be convulsions, neck pain and stiffness, sometimes paralysis in one side of the body, with difficulty in passing water and opening the bowels.

If these symptoms follow an infectious disease, call the doctor.

CAUSES

The disease can be due to measles, now increasingly rare thanks to im-

munization, and to many other common viruses. For example, herpes simplex can cause the disease by attacking the brain. Polio, chicken pox, mumps and German measles can, without actually attacking the brain, cause it to become inflamed in reaction to the infection. This reaction is very rare and is becoming more so as more children are immunized against these diseases.

Very, very rarely, encephalitis can occur as a reaction to the whooping cough vaccine, but the chances of this happening are infinitely less than the risk of not vaccinating your child. Vaccination is the safest way to prevent encephalitis.

TREATMENT

Encephalitis has to be treated in hospital. To establish the cause, fluid is drawn from the base of the spine and tested. In most cases, however, there are no drugs to combat viral infection, and the treatment consists of nursing care to alleviate the symptoms while the body fights the infection. For example, inflammation can be reduced and convulsions controlled by drugs. If the disease is caused by the herpes simplex virus it may be treated with drugs which help to combat the virus.

Hospital treatment may last as little as two weeks, but it will usually be followed with physiotherapy over a much longer period.

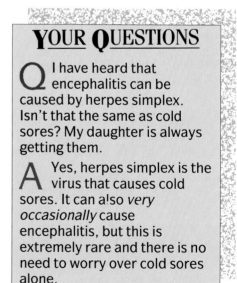

YOUR QUESTIONS

Q I have heard that encephalitis can be caused by herpes simplex. Isn't that the same as cold sores? My daughter is always getting them.

A Yes, herpes simplex is the virus that causes cold sores. It can also *very occasionally* cause encephalitis, but this is extremely rare and there is no need to worry over cold sores alone.

■ ENEMA

Enemas are occasionally prescribed by a doctor if a child is very severely constipated. A liquid is inserted into the rectum to encourage the bowels to open. Although the treatment is not painful, it may seem frightening and should be explained to the child.

Usually a laxative (taken by mouth) will be all that's needed for constipation, and a healthy diet with plenty of fibre, fruit and vegetables, will prevent it occurring.

■ EPILEPSY

Epilepsy, known as seizures, fits or convulsions, is not uncommon, especially in young children. About five in every 1000 children are sufferers. It is important for the epileptic child to regard the fits as an inconvenient nuisance, not as something shameful or dramatic.

SYMPTOMS

Grand mal A child having an epileptic fit will suddenly lose consciousness and fall rigidly to the ground. This is called the 'tonic' stage, and is followed by involuntary twitching and holding of breath lasting for a minute or two (the 'clonic' stage).

These attacks, known by the French name, 'grand mal' are often preceded by the child experiencing strange sensations, such as smelling an unreal smell, and this stage is known as the 'aura' stage.

After the attack, the child will probably feel drowsy and need to sleep. There can also be paralysis in one or more limbs for an hour or more. This grand mal form of epilepsy can also affect adults.

Petit mal A second form of epilepsy known as 'petit mal' develops in children and rarely persists into adult life. With petit mal the child does not fall down, but loses touch with the world for a couple of seconds.

Some children may have several such attacks a day, causing them to be confused and forgetful. If the condition is not recognized, the child may be labelled a slow learner or punished for appearing inattentive.

Focal seizure A third type of attack is known as 'focal seizure'. These attacks show themselves as a twitching of an arm or leg, or perhaps just of one side of the face.

Temporal lobe epilepsy This is a fourth type of epilepsy in which the patient may smack the lips, make licking movements with the tongue, jerk the head, and grimace.

CAUSES

Epileptic attacks are caused by periods of disordered electrical activity in the brain. Why these occur is not understood. The condition sometimes runs in families.

Sometimes what is known as acquired epilepsy may develop as a complication of a severe head injury. Many children have fits because their temperature is too high, but they usually grow out of this tendency.

Acute poisoning can also cause fits, and in days gone by children could have attacks as a result of licking lead-based paint on their toys.

TREATMENT

During an attack all you can do is to place the child in the recovery position. When the attack is over, reassure the child and help him to bed.

If the fit lasts more than ten mi-

GAILLARD/JERRICAN

Epileptic attacks can be brought on by disturbing visual effects, such as reflections from a computer screen.

Sites of epilepsy in the brain: in grand mal the motor and sensory areas are affected (top); petit mal is sited in the thalamus (bottom); focal seizures are often sited in the temporal lobe (top).

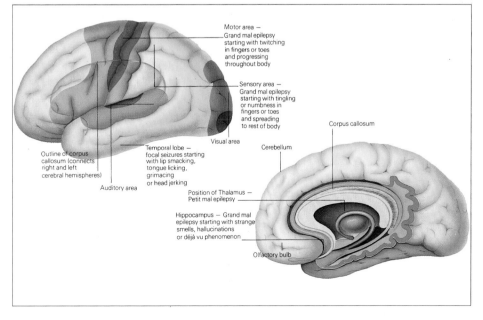

Motor area — Grand mal epilepsy starting with twitching in fingers or toes and progressing throughout body

Sensory area — Grand mal epilepsy starting with tingling or numbness in fingers or toes and spreading to rest of body

Visual area

Corpus callosum

Cerebellum

Outline of corpus callosum (connects right and left cerebral hemispheres)

Temporal lobe — focal seizures starting with lip smacking, tongue licking, grimacing or head jerking

Auditory area

Position of Thalamus — Petit mal epilepsy

Hippocampus — Grand mal epilepsy starting with strange smells, hallucinations or déjà vu phenomenon

Olfactory bulb

nutes, or if several fits follow one another, seek immediate medical attention, as persistent holding of the breath can cause brain damage.

Medical treatment Grand mal seizures can be treated by a number of different anti-convulsant drugs, whose effect is to bring the abnormal electrical activity in the brain under control. Under medication the incidence of fits will decrease, and the fits may stop entirely.

Unfortunately anti-convulsant drugs may have the undesirable side-effect of causing drowsiness. Your child's progress will be monitored, and you should tell your doctor of any worrying side-effects.

YOUR QUESTIONS

Q How can I protect my son from being hurt during an epileptic attack?

A Try not to over-protect your child, so that he can lead as full a life as possible. It is sensible to guard fires and stairwells, and leave the bathroom door open when he takes a bath.

As for activities, your child may be able to cycle, but only if the doctor is in agreement, and he can enjoy swimming under supervision.

Encourage your son to wear a special bracelet identifying his condition, so that people will know how to help him.

■ EYES

see also COLOUR BLINDNESS, EYESIGHT, LAZY EYE, OPTICIAN

Our eyes are often likened to a photographic camera because of the way in which they convert light into images in the process of seeing.

STRUCTURE OF THE EYE

The eye (which is spherical) has two lenses — the cornea, which is a fixed-focus lens and consists of five layers, at the front of the eye, and an adjustable lens, simply called the lens, within the eye.

Between the cornea and the lens is the outer one of two 'chambers' in the eye. At the back of this chamber, which is called the anterior chamber, is the iris, the coloured part of the eye. The anterior chamber itself is filled with a watery fluid called the aqueous humour, which is constantly

EYE INJURIES

An eye can be injured by a blow or by a foreign body such as a piece of grit. Other types of injury are caused by burns or dangerous chemicals.

• Always keep all chemicals, such as cleaning fluids and disinfectants, stored away safely, out of children's reach.

• Never let a child play with matches or fireworks, and keep all fires guarded.

• Remember that the cornea on the surface of the eye can easily be permanently damaged. Never attempt to remove an object that has become embedded in a child's eye, or that is on the iris (the coloured part of the eye). Seek immediate medical attention.

• For chemical or other burns, immediately apply plenty of cold water, making sure in the case of chemicals to flush the water away from the un-injured eye so as not to spread the problem. Call an ambulance or take the child to the nearest accident and emergency ward as soon as possible.

• If the child has been hit in the eye, make him rest with a pad soaked in cold water placed over the eye, to restrict any bruising.

• If the injured eye is bleeding, apply a clean pad and bandage and take the child to the nearest accident and emergency ward at once.

being drained away and replaced.

The iris is a circular, muscular diaphragm, in other words, a disc, with an opening (like the aperture of a camera) at its centre. This opening is the pupil, which is adjusted by two sets of muscles, causing it to narrow or dilate (enlarge) according to the amount of light falling on the iris. This controls the amount of light that enters the eye, with the pupils dilating to admit more light when the light is dim and narrowing to admit less light when the light is bright.

FINE FOCUS LENS

The fine-focusing of light rays is done by the lens, which is situated just behind the iris. The lens is soft and elastic, and held round the edges by a muscle which changes the shape of

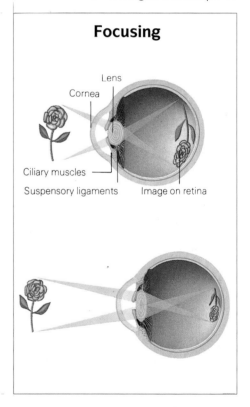

Focusing

Lens

Cornea

Ciliary muscles

Suspensory ligaments

Image on retina

The cornea at the front of the eye acts as a fixed-focus lens. Behind it is the lens proper, whose shape is adjusted by the ciliary muscles according to the distance of the object being focused on. The surface of the lens becomes more curved (top) to focus on close objects, and wider and flatter for distant objects (below). If the eyeball is too long the child will be short-sighted.

YOUR QUESTIONS

Q What exactly causes a black eye?

A The tissues of the cavities in which the eyes are set are very soft. Any injury (usually a knock or blow) to the face or scalp which causes bleeding beneath the skin tends to drain towards these cavities. Disrupted red blood cells which have escaped from the blood vessels look yellow at first and then turn black before clearing.

If your child suffers a blow to the face the eye itself is usually unhurt, being well protected by the socket, but a black eye may well result, and can look quite alarming, even though it is not a serious injury and soon heals itself.

Q Should I give my children vitamins for good eyesight?

A Although certain vitamins are connected with good eyesight, eyesight is only adversely affected by the kind of severe vitamin deficiency which occurs when a child is on the verge of starvation. Severe vitamin A deficiency causes night blindness, and can also cause a disease of the cornea which ultimately leads to blindness. Carrots, reputed to help you see in the dark, do indeed contain a rich supply of this vitamin, but no normal diet is deficient in it. However, by all means encourage your children to eat carrots as a healthy alternative to sweets.

Lack of vitamin B12 can interfere with the normal nutrition of the optic nerve, causing temporary blindness, but any normal diet in developed countries provides an ample amount of this vitamin, and supplements are quite unnecessary.

the lens to adapt it to focusing on a range of objects at different distances from the eye.

The lens too is relatively near the front of the eye, and behind it lies the second chamber, known as the interior chamber, which makes up a large part of the eyeball. The chamber is lined with a light-sensitive layer (equivalent to the film in a camera) called the retina.

The retina is actually made up of two different types of light-sensitive cells called rods and cones. The rod cells are sensitive to low-intensity light and are responsible for clarity of vision. The cones interpret colour and fine details of objects. They only function when the light level is high, explaining why we cannot distinguish colours and details in dim light.

The rods are most plentiful in the area of the retina at the back of the eye known as the macula, and this is where the lens focuses its sharpest image and where vision is best. Towards the edge of the retina is what is known as peripheral vision, which is all that indistinct area where we only half see.

OPTIC NERVE

At the back of each eye an optic nerve leads to an area of the brain called the visual cortex, where the information on the retina is processed and interpreted. We have a blind spot where the optic nerve leads away from the back of the eye, although we are not aware of this, as the eyes compensate for it by overlapping in their fields of vision.

The image transferred to the retina is in fact upside down, and in 'decoding' the information received from the retina via the optic nerve, the brain turns it back the right way round again.

TEARS

The lining of the eyelids and the front of the eye is known as the conjunctiva. This keeps the eye moistened by a film of tears, which protects the cornea from bacterial microorganisms, dust and other forms of pollution. The tears are secreted by the lacrimal gland, and are drained

into the nose through the tear duct which is situated at the inner corner of the eye.

HOW THE EYES WORK

In the process of seeing, light bouncing off objects enters the eye. As it passes through the cornea, or fixed lens, and then through the lens proper, the light is bent inwards and concentrated by the lens, so that tiny images are formed on the retina of the much larger objects we are looking at, in just the same way as images

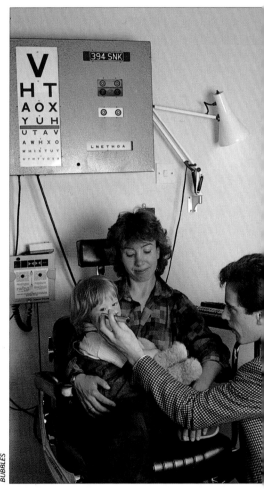

A young child can be reassured by a parent while having her eyes tested.

are formed on the film in a camera when the light has passed through the lens.

The degree to which the light is bent depends on the shape of the lens, and when the muscles around the lens are working properly, the shape of the lens is varied so that we can focus on near and far objects.

YOUR QUESTIONS

Q How often should my child's eyes be checked?

A There is no need to seek out routine checks. The usual developmental checks at the child health clinic and at school are likely to spot eye problems, but if you feel your child has a difficulty, then of course arrange a special test. If your child wears spectacles, your optician will arrange for regular checks.

Q My little boy is always breaking his spectacles. What can I do?

A It is worth investing in spectacles with plastic lenses, as these are almost unbreakable, even though they can easily be scratched. Persuade your son to tie elastic to the arms of his spectacles when he is playing sports, to prevent them from falling off. If he is dependent on his glasses, keep a spare pair in reserve.

■ EYE PROBLEMS

Conjunctivitis (*see also* separate entry) This is one of the most common minor problems in babies and young children. It is an inflammation of the conjunctiva, the thin membrane covering the whites of the eyes, and it makes the eyes red and sore. Sometimes pus sticks the eyelids together, especially when the child is asleep. Conjunctivitis is caused by bacteria, viruses, or irritation.

Even though it is rarely serious, conjunctivitis can be quite distressing. If the result of bacteria or a virus, the condition can cause a great deal of discharge and profuse swelling of the lids. Treatment with antibacterial eye drops or creams usually clears it up quickly.

Corneal problems Pain in the eyeball, redness, blurred vision or

A foreign body on the surface of the eye can usually be washed away with tears. If you get your child to rub the unaffected eye, this should get enough tears to flow in both eyes to solve the problem.

clouding of the cornea are all signs of various types of inflammation of the cornea and should be given immediate medical attention.

Diabetes-related eye problems Diabetes can cause the blood vessels in the eye to grow over the retina or to bleed inside the eye, and this can affect the retina. If the diabetes is kept under control the dangers are minimized, but any eye problems in a diabetic child should be reported to the family doctor.

Inflamed eyelids Eyelids can become inflamed as a result of an illness such as measles, when the child becomes run down. Lack of sleep, or dust or smoke irritating the eyes can also cause inflamed eyelids, as can some visual defects if not treated. Poor hygiene can sometimes cause the problem, and it can be a symptom of a sinus infection. Your doctor may prescribe antibiotic eye ointment or eye lotions.

Itchy eyes Itchy eyes can be caused by an allergy and the condition is

often related to eczema. It should be treated by your doctor, who will probably prescribe eye drops.

Squinting This is a fairly common problem in young children. In many babies, the eyes work independently at first, but in some cases this continues to happen, due to eye muscles of unequal strength, or to visual acuity being different in each eye.

If this condition has not righted itself by the time the baby is about 12 weeks old, or if the child has a permanent squint in one eye, consult your doctor who will probably refer your child to an eye specialist (ophthalmologist).

An older child with a squint should also be referred to a specialist or an optician. Wearing a patch, wearing glasses or doing eye exercises, de-

REMOVING A FOREIGN BODY

If a fly or speck of dust is visible on the eye, and if it is not embedded in the eye, it can usually be rinsed or gently wiped away.

• First try rubbing the unaffected eye, which should stimulate the flow of tears in both eyes, causing the foreign body to be washed away.

• Alternatively, pull up the upper eyelid and get your child to look up and down and to each side. Repeat with the lower lid pulled down, until you see the foreign body, which you can then remove with the corner of a clean handkerchief or rolled-up tissue.

• If this does not work, make the child sit with his head to one side and rinse the eye by pouring clean water into it from a jug.

• If these methods don't succeed, take the child to your family doctor.

• Always seek medical help if the surface of the eye appears to be damaged in any way.

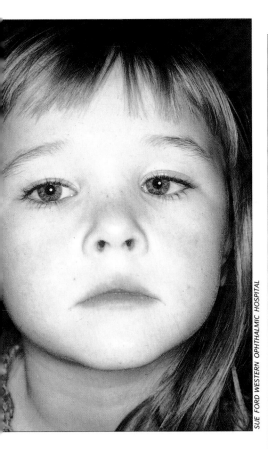

A squint does not usually right itself automatically, and a child who squints should be seen by her doctor, who will refer her to an eye specialist for treatment.

pending on the type of squint, will usually correct the problem, but in some cases surgery may be necessary in older children.

Sticky eye This is another common, minor problem in small babies, with the baby's eye getting gummed up with pus. It is really a mild form of conjunctivitis. It should be treated by washing the eye(s) several times a day with cotton wool soaked in water which has been boiled and allowed to cool. The eye should be wiped from the outer corner inward. If the condition persists or recurs, see your doctor or health visitor, who may prescribe ointment or eye drops.

Stye Children often develop styes, which are inflammations along the edges of the eyelids, at the root of the lashes, and which are usually caused by bacterial infections. Bathing the affected area in an eye lotion may clear them up, but if they do not clear within a day or two, take the

YOUR QUESTIONS

Q Should I encourage my children to use eye lotions to keep their eyes healthy?

A No. Do not use lotions, drops or ointments unless your doctor prescribes them. The tear fluid contains a natural antiseptic which keeps the cornea clean and healthy, and eye drops can interfere with this process.

Q How can a young child's eyesight be tested before he is old enough to recognize letters?

A A child's sight can be tested by using pictures. The health of the interior of the eyes can be checked by examining the eyes with an ophthalmoscope.

You yourself may be able to notice if there is anything wrong with your child's sight, for example if he squints or seems to have difficulty in following moving objects with his eyes, and if he wants to hold books very close, or sit close to the television set. Report any of these symptoms to your doctor.

You should also check with your doctor if your child complains of sore eyes or headaches or gives you any reason to think that he cannot see clearly, or if there is anything unusual about his eyes.

child to the family doctor, who will probably prescribe an ointment or an alternative eye lotion. Discourage your child from touching his eyes.

■ EYESIGHT

Imperfect eyesight is technically known as refractive error. It is usually due to physical defects in the eyeball, in the lens, or in the muscle which adjusts the lens.

The image on the retina will not be properly focussed if the cornea is imperfectly shaped, so that light rays are distorted by it, or if the lens is insufficiently elastic or the muscles controlling it do not change shape sufficiently (see diagram on p.102). If the eyeball is too long or too short, the image will not be accurately focused on the retina, and will be blurred.

Short sight If the eyeball is too long, or if the lens lacks elasticity, there will be good close-up vision, but poor distant vision. This is easily corrected by spectacles.

Long sight This is also frequently caused by the imperfect shape of the eyeball, with the eyeball being too short from front to back. This too can be corrected by spectacles. A child is usually born long-sighted, and diagnosis often follows complaints of eye strain or fatigue.

Astigmatism This is a very common defect, caused by the cornea on the front of the eye being imperfectly rounded, so that a distorted image is formed on the retina. Again spectacles can cure the problem by compensating for the defective cornea.

Most forms of imperfect sight can be corrected by wearing spectacles. If your child is particularly active, opt for plastic lenses and keep a spare pair of glasses in reserve.

F

FAINTING

Fainting, known medically as syncope, is a sudden loss of consciousness, usually preceded by a feeling of weakness and giddiness, and sometimes nausea as well. A child of any age can have an attack of fainting, but it is quite unusual except in adolescence.

SYMPTOMS

A child who is about to faint will feel weak and giddy. Her skin will look white and feel clammy, and her breathing will become quick and shallow. When she faints, she will fall to the ground and will usually regain consciousness within a couple of minutes. One cannot faint in a lying position – only when sitting or standing.

CAUSES

Fainting is caused by a reduction of the blood supply to the brain triggered by a reflex in the vagus nerve that slows down the rate of the heartbeat. It can also be caused by low blood pressure and by a low blood sugar level. In some children (and adults) the reflex in the vagus nerve is particularly sensitive, causing them to faint more readily.

Fainting can be caused by standing still for too long, which makes the blood accumulate in the legs rather than circulating in the body. It can also be brought on by standing up suddenly, if the blood vessels fail to adjust quickly enough as the body changes position.

SUDDEN SHOCK

As in adults, fainting in children can be caused by a stuffy room, which can affect the supply of blood to the

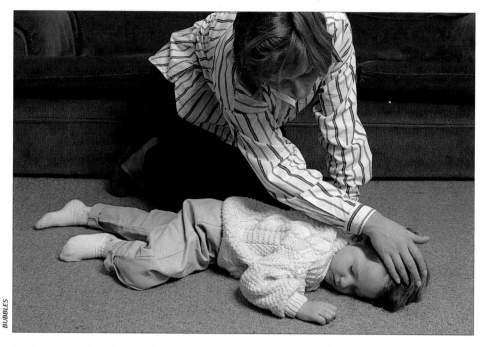

BUBBLES

brain. Emotional shock can cause fainting, triggering the reflex in the vagus nerve; as can excitement, for example at a pop concert or a party.

TREATMENT

In most cases fainting treats itself. Once the body is flat, blood reaches the brain and recovery is fairly rapid. Keep the child flat and in the recovery position while she recovers consciousness. Also discourage your child from getting up too quickly after a faint, to prevent another one.

If you see that a child is about to faint, encourage her to sit with her head between her knees or to lie down for five minutes.

A HEALTHY DIET

There can be a lack of nutrients, especially sugar, in the blood before breakfast, and it is wise to make sure that all children always eat something before rushing off to school, especially those prone to fainting.

Any parent concerned about fainting in a teenage girl should make sure that her daughter has plenty of iron in her diet by giving her liver, meat, cereals and green vegetables. Fresh fruit and vegetables supply the vitamins B and C without which red blood cells cannot function properly.

If you are worried by your child having frequent fainting attacks and

A child in a faint should be left on the ground, but place him in the recovery position while he comes to.

you know that she has a good diet and regular meals, see your doctor.

YOUR QUESTIONS

Q Why should a child who feels faint sit with her head between her knees rather than going outside?

A Although fresh air may help someone to recover from a faint it is dangerous to send anyone in this situation outside. She might still faint, and injure herself by falling.

Keep her indoors with her head below the level of her heart, so that the heart has less work to do, and open the window to let in fresh air.

■ FALLS

see also DISLOCATION, DRESSINGS, FIRST AID

As they begin to walk, young children fall constantly, and rarely come to much harm. Even children from about three to seven almost never hurt themselves seriously when they fall down because their joints and bones are very supple.

Older children are less prone to falling but when they do, their injuries are often more serious. This is partly because they are taller and heavier, and partly because their bones are not as supple as those of a small child. Furthermore, with older children, accidents often occur when they are involved in fast-moving athletic activities such as football, climbing or horse riding.

INJURIES AND SYMPTOMS

Even if there is no visible injury, any child complaining of pain some hours after a fall should see a doctor. Although a young child's bones rarely fracture, it is possible for them to be bent (this is known as 'green stick fracture'). Moreover, the main part of the thigh-bone is surprisingly brittle, even in a young child, and can easily be broken.

BUBBLES

Youngsters should not be discouraged from climbing as this develops useful skills. But try to teach them to be cautious as well as adventurous since falls can be dangerous.

TREATMENT OF INJURIES FROM FALLS

Serious head blow	See a doctor – the child may be kept under observation for 24 hours.
Unconscious and not breathing	Get someone to call an ambulance. Start mouth-to-mouth resuscitation at once (*see* **First Aid**), moving the child *only if absolutely necessary*.
Unconscious but breathing	*Do not move the child.* Cover with a blanket (or coats) and call an ambulance.
Suspected spinal or neck injury	*Do not move the child.* Keep her warm and call for an ambulance.
Suspected arm or wrist fracture	Support the arm in the most comfortable position and take the child straight to a doctor or hospital.
Suspected leg fracture	If the child is small (under 5), pick her up and drive her to hospital. With an older child, call an ambulance and keep the child warm while waiting. Allow the child to move her leg into a more comfortable position, but then keep her still. Do not give her anything to eat or drink in case an anaesthetic is necessary.
Bleeding	For serious bleeding get someone to call an ambulance immediately. Hold a clean pad over the wound, applying gentle pressure, while waiting. For less serious bleeding, hold a clean pad over the wound until bleeding stops. If bleeding is from an arm or a leg, keep the limb upright to reduce the outflow of blood from the wound.
Bumps and bruises	No treatment strictly necessary. A gauze pad soaked in cold water and applied immediately may minimize swelling and witch-hazel has a soothing effect.

Head injuries These are perhaps the most serious injuries resulting from a fall, and often need medical treatment. Any child who has had a bad blow to the head should be seen by a doctor, even if there is no visible sign of injury.

If you did not see the fall (and so do not know how hard it was) danger signs to look out for in your child are loss of memory about the accident (this could mean that the child was knocked out), persistent headache or nausea, giddiness, a squint, lack of balance or a staggering gait.

All these symptoms could indicate concussion. Blood or a straw-coloured discharge from the nose are signs of possible skull fracture. A child with any of these symptoms should be seen by a doctor at once.

Fractures In older children, injuries often take the form of a fractured wrist or fractured neck of femur (the part of the thigh-bone between the ball of the hip joint and the main shaft of the bone).

Both these injuries will cause severe pain and swelling, and they are not likely to be overlooked.

Cuts, grazes and bruises The most common result of children falling are cuts, grazes and bruises, which can usually be dealt with at home (*see* Bandages, Dressings, First Aid).

PREVENTION

Once a child is crawling, fix a stair gate to prevent her falling downstairs. Supervise young children on swings, slides, roundabouts and climbing frames as accidents can happen in an instant.

Remember that children slip easily when playing, so make sure they wear shoes that fit well and are securely fastened.

YOUR QUESTIONS

Q My mother always used to put witch-hazel on bumps. Does this really work?

A There is really no medical benefit in this, but since it is cool and soothing there is no reason why you should not use it as your mother did.

■ FATS

Fats (including oils) make up a large part of the human diet and are the most energy-rich of all foods. For example, if you were to make a comparison between butter and bread, 100 grammes of bread supplies 250 calories, while the same weight of butter (pure fat) provides 720 calories – which is nearly three times as much energy.

While too much fat in the diet will make children (and adults) put on weight, fats are nevertheless one of the three most important groups of foods, the others being proteins and carbohydrates.

TYPES OF FAT

Fats (including oils) are compounds formed by fatty acids and a substance called glycerol which binds the fatty acids together.

Technically, the 'saturation' of a fat is an indication of the ratio of hydrogen atoms to carbon atoms in each fat molecule. 'Polyunsaturated' fats have only one hydrogen atom for two or more atoms of carbon, and are easily broken down in the body.

As a rough guide, saturated fats are generally solid at room temperature, and of animal origin, while unsaturated fats are usually liquid, and come from fish or plants.

FATS AND HEALTH

Over recent years, saturated fats have been given a lot of bad publicity. This is because a high level of saturated fat in the diet may lead in many adults to a high level of cholesterol in the bloodstream. People with high cholesterol are more likely to develop fatty deposits in the arteries, and this condition is linked to artery and heart disease.

The body needs some cholesterol, and as well as getting some of it from cholesterol-containing foods such as

Providing a varied diet will help to ensure that a child receives the vitamins, carbohydrates, proteins and fats that he needs.

eggs, it also makes its own, partly from saturated fats in the diet. Saturated fat in the diet is much more significant in determining the amount of cholesterol in the blood than cholesterol in the diet itself.

Unsaturated fats These have the advantage that they are not transformed to cholesterol in the body; polyunsaturated fats may have the double advantage that they actually help the body to metabolize cholesterol, so that excess is not circulating in the bloodstream.

Diet Since good and bad eating habits are often established during childhood, it makes good sense to follow the advice of modern nutritionists, and make sure that children do not eat too much fat of any kind, but in particular that they have only a restricted amount of saturated fat such as butter and cheese.

Although carbohydrates could provide all the energy a child needs, the body does need some fat, and in any case food would be dull without it. So, to provide fats without incurring the risk of increasing blood cholesterol, use corn, olive, nut or sunflower oil as opposed to butter, lard or dripping (but avoid coconut oil which, although of vegetable origin, has a particularly high saturated fat level.

Encourage your children to eat more fish, and the less-fat meats such as poultry, and don't indulge them in cream cakes and ice cream.

Although fats in the diet tend to make adults put on weight, there is little need to worry about this with active and growing children. As long as they take plenty of exercise, the fat in their diet is quickly broken down to provide energy rather than excess weight. Encourage your children to be active and to enjoy a diet low in saturated fats and you will be helping them to grow into healthy adults.

YOUR QUESTIONS

Q Is it healthier for my children to have grilled meat rather than fried?

A It is certainly better to grill than fry any fatty meat, such as bacon or fatty pork or lamp chops. But it is better still to give your children lean meat. For example, there is less fat in chicken which has been fried in oil than there is in the equivalent weight of grilled bacon.

■ FEAR

see also DISTURBED CHILDREN

Fears and anxieties of all kinds are both common and normal in children. Babies and under-threes are usually fearful when separated from their parents, or at least when left with people they do not know. School-age children may develop fears of animals or of the dark, of going to the dentist or of having an injection, or even, sometimes, of having to go to school.

You can help your child to overcome these feelings by the way you behave and there is usually no need for medical help.

SYMPTOMS

A fearful child will usually make his anxiety quite obvious. For example, he will cry when separated from a parent, shrink away from a friend's pet animal, cling to a parent when taken to the doctor, and so on.

If a fear is more entrenched, as for example if parents are constantly quarrelling so that the child feels generally frightened, or if the child is being bullied at school, there may be less obviously related symptoms such as bed-wetting, not sleeping well or tantrums.

If your child is showing such symptoms and you cannot get to the bottom of the problem, or if he seems to be developing in general into a fearful, clinging and too readily upset child, you may need your doctor's help. If normal fears and anxieties become persistent and the child becomes upset or withdrawn, he may be developing phobias.

CAUSES

Fears and anxieties can be transferred to a child from a parent. If you are frightened of spiders and over-react whenever you see them, your child may believe that spiders are frightening. If you are anxious for the child to do well at school, the child may become anxious, too.

Sometimes fears can be caused by an incident in the child's life. Being

Some children are terrified of certain animals. Introducing them very gradually to the animal they dread can help them to overcome this fear.

bitten by a dog, for example, will naturally make most children fearful of dogs. Equally the child can be frightened of a genuinely frightening situation. If he is being bullied at school or has a strong dislike of a particular teacher, he will naturally fear going to school.

Fear may be aroused if the child has to deal with a new situation and feels he can't cope. But other typical childhood fears have no particular cause. Fears of the dark, being lost or being separated from one's parents and so on, are commonplace in young children and usually fade away as the child gets older.

TREATMENT

Never laugh at a child's fear or try to force him out of it, but gently explain why the fear is unnecessary. If possible, help him to deal with his fear by introducing him gradually to the cause, if it is something such as a particular type of animal, insects, heights or swings. Always be encouraging, and never push the child too far at a time.

Talk to the child and try to get to the cause of an unexplained fear. If it turns out that he is being bullied, or is worried about his school performance, reassure him, and go to the school and discuss it with the class teacher or the head, so that a solution can be found.

To help a child to overcome a fear of a new situation, talk it through with him and let him know you have confidence in him. Be prepared to listen, too. Try to be supportive but not over-protective, so that he can gradually learn to be independent. And encourage him to realize that fear of different things at different times is quite normal and that he will grow out of it.

It may also help to teach him simple relaxation techniques, such as deep, slow breathing or learning to relax all the muscles in his body so that he becomes floppy.

YOUR QUESTIONS

Q How can I help my three-year-old son overcome his fear of the dark?

A Put a night light in his room or leave his bedroom door slightly ajar, keeping the hall light on. Behave very calmly and reassuringly when you put him to bed, and never ridicule him.

Don't rush upstairs every time he calls out, but reassure him from downstairs.

Q My son gets frightened by the stories I read, but begs me to continue. Should I stop?

A Learning to fear evil is important, but try some less disturbing tales if the fear persists or leads to nightmares.

■ FEEDING PROBLEMS

Like adults, children have varying appetites, depending on mood, health and general inclination. Nevertheless, there are certain problems which are characteristic of many newborn babies, and others which affect children at different ages and which can be readily addressed by the parents.

BREAST FEEDING

With both breast and bottle feeding, problems often arise during the first six weeks. The usual reason for this is that both the mother and the baby are new to the process and need time to learn how to do it.

If your baby is having difficulty attaching to the breast, ask a midwife to help you. The size of your breasts is not important — even tiny breasts will make enough milk for your baby. Sometimes, engorgement — when the milk 'comes in' on about the third day after birth — can make it difficult for the baby to take the breast. Your midwife will show you how to express a little milk to make the breast rather softer and easier for the baby.

It's important to make sure the baby is 'latched on' to your breast correctly. Her mouth needs to be wide open, with her tongue forward, so she can take the breast into her mouth without making you sore. She can do this best if you hold her chest to chest with you, with her body across yours so she has no need to turn her head to feed.

Whenever your baby sucks, she stimulates the breast to 'let down' the milk that's stored there. The other response made by your body is to make more milk. So the more your baby feeds, the more milk you'll make. If you ever feel you aren't making enough, get an experienced person to check your baby's position at the breast, to make sure she can get a good feed, and 'tell' your breasts to make more. You may also need to feed more often for a while, to increase the production. Don't take your baby off the breast before she wants to come off. 'Demand feeding' is nature's way of making sure you make enough milk to match your baby's growth needs.

Soreness is almost always caused by poor positioning, which needs to be corrected before healing can take place. Occasionally, thrush is a cause of sore nipples. Your doctor will need to prescribe something for your nipples, and your baby's mouth, to eradicate the problem.

It's not a good idea to introduce bottles of formula while breast-feeding is getting established. Your baby may get used to sucking from a teat, and become confused when offered the breast again, which needs a rather different sucking technique. Bottles will reduce your baby's appetite for the breast, which will reduce the stimulation your breasts need in order to make enough milk.

BOTTLE FEEDING

If you are bottle feeding using powdered formula, observe scrupulously the sterilization routine and always follow the directions on the packet. After you have made up the feed and warmed it to the right temperature, make sure that the bottle is kept at an angle during feeding which prevents the baby from sucking in air.

POSSETTING

Possetting or regurgitating is when a small amount of food is returned on bringing up wind or between feeds. It should not cause concern and may indicate that a little too much feed is being offered.

VOMITING

This can occur when your baby has not been correctly winded, or if he has been sucking from a teat with too small a hole, or has gulped down a feed too quickly. These causes can easily be remedied, but if the vomiting persists or if vomiting even occurs between feeds, you should consult your doctor.

COLDS AND INFECTIONS

In small babies, feeding problems result if the baby has a cold and cannot breathe properly — he will not be able to suck and breathe through his mouth at the same time. In this instance, your doctor may recommend nose drops to clear the nose. While the baby is having difficulty sucking, feed him small amounts more frequently.

WEANING

Milk is enough on its own for a baby's growth until the age of four to six months. Your doctor or health visitor will help you decide when your baby needs to begin solid foods. Puréed fruit or vegetables are good first foods. You can also give a branded baby rice. Mix the foods with your baby's usual formula, with expressed breast milk, or with boiled, cooled water.

Manufactured baby foods are fine, although, as long as you stick to simple foods without added sugar or salt, a portion of your own meal, mashed, sieved or blended, will be fine. Making your own baby food will also be cheaper in the long run.

FIRST FOODS

Start by offering your baby small tastes of solid food to be sucked off the end of a spoon. Simple fruit or vegetable purées are good initial choices. Offer him one food at a time and give him the same thing for a few meals in a row. This way, you will find out whether your child has any allergies to any specific foods. You will find out, too, your baby's early likes and dislikes.

Good first foods to try are sweet ripe fruit, in particular apple, pear and banana, and cooked vegetables such as potatoes, carrots, parsnips or peas. Baby cereals are also popular as they are quite bland and taste similar to milk. Rice- or oat-based cereals are safer to start with than wheat-based ones as wheat can occasionally cause allergic reactions.

Most babies take to solids quite happily, but if yours shows no interest, it is best not to insist. A crying and hungry baby will almost certainly reject solid food, and forcing the issue will make matters worse. If this happens, it is best to wait a few days before trying again. Keep feeding times relaxed and happy, so that

LUPE CUNHA

Babies being weaned often refuse to eat from a spoon, and may show signs of distress. If this happens, simply feed the baby on milk for a few days and then try solids again.

your baby will associate food with fun and pleasure.

There is no need to worry if your baby shows no interest in baby food while other babies of the same age enjoy being spoon fed. As long as your baby is thriving, all is well, and

WATCHPOINTS

- Do not put salt or sugar in foods for babies.
- Never feed babies low-fat milk — they need the vitamins and calories.
- Never leave your baby alone when she is feeding, either with a bottle or with solids.
- Always allow 24 hours between portions of a new food to make sure there is no allergic reaction. And introduce new tastes little by little.

he will take to solids when he is ready and in his own good time.

EATING HABITS

Many parents create problems for themselves by over-conscientiously trying to make their children eat more than they want, or eat things they don't like, but which are 'healthy' and 'good for them'. This creates a vicious circle, with the child refusing to eat and the parents becoming more and more anxious.

Refusing food is rarely serious, and anxiety and making an issue of it usually make things worse. After the age of about 12 months most children change their eating habits and have a drop in appetite. They often acquire strong likes and dislikes at the same time; but this stage is usually short-lived. It is only if your child is not thriving or putting on weight that you need to worry.

■ FEET

see also ATHLETE'S FOOT, CHILBLAINS, CLUB FOOT, VERUCCA

Our feet have 26 bones, 35 joints and more than 100 ligaments. We use them to support the weight of the body and to lever us about when walking and running, but people without the use of their hands can educate their feet to achieve more dexterity, and can even learn to write or paint with them. It is vital to make sure that growing children's feet are allowed to develop properly, as foot problems dating back to childhood cannot easily be put right.

FOOTWEAR

In order for all the tiny bones, tendons, muscles and ligaments in the foot to develop freely, a child's feet must never be cramped. To make sure that this does not happen, check that your baby's all-in-one suits are not tight. Once your child begins to wear shoes, make sure that his feet are measured for length and width about once every two to three months as it is essential that young children wear shoes that fit them properly.

Shoes are expensive, but it is most important to buy them at a reputable shoe shop and to discard them as soon as they no longer fit. Preferably, babies and children should go barefoot as much as possible, indoors and in the garden, when the weather is reasonable.

FLAT FEET

Many parents worry unnecessarily about flat feet. The apparently flat feet that babies have are due to their having a large quantity of fatty tissue in the soles of their feet and a pad of fat filling up the arch in front of the heel. The arch develops as the foot is used and gains strength.

If you are worried about your toddler's feet, look inside your child's shoes. If they are markedly worn along the inside edge, it could be that the arches of the foot have not developed properly. Have this checked by your doctor or a foot specialist who may recommend remedial exercises to correct it.

BUBBLES

In a good shoe shop, an assistant will measure your child's feet with a gauge to measure both the length and width required. Badly fitting shoes can do life-long damage.

PIGEON TOES

The medical term for pigeon toes is 'in-toeing', and it describes the condition in which the fronts of the child's feet are turned inwards. It is common for children learning to walk to turn their feet in, and the problem usually corrects itself.

In-toeing can be to do with the feet but it can also be due to an inturning of the whole leg.

CARING FOR CHILDREN'S FEET

• Let children go barefoot whenever possible. (Naturally, you should make sure that it is warm and that there are no sharp objects about that could injure their feet).

• Make sure that a child's footwear is not tight. Even tight all-in-one baby suits can cramp and damage your baby's feet.

• Do not pass on footwear from one child to another, as shoes become shaped to fit their wearer and to form a personalized fit. No two children will have feet exactly the same shape.

• To encourage good foot hygiene and so prevent foot infections, make sure that your child's feet are thoroughly washed and dried at least once a day.

• Buy your children socks made of cotton or wool, which are better at absorbing perspiration than synthetic fibres. This helps to keep the feet free from infection.

• Dress your children in leather shoes whenever possible, to allow the feet to 'breathe' and minimize the build-up of stale sweat.

• As the child grows older, do not be tempted to yield to pressure for fashionable shoes that might deform the feet.

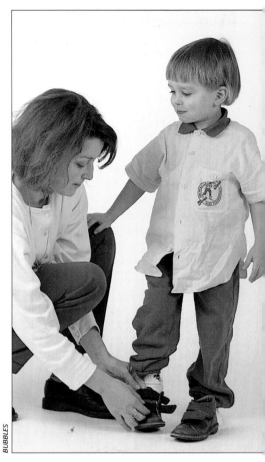

BUBBLES

Some shoes are fastened with straps, which can be adjusted to suit the width of the child's feet. The straps can be slackened a little as the feet grow, but change the shoes as soon as they start to pinch the toes.

TREATMENT

When the in-toeing occurs in the feet only, the problem usually resolves itself by the time the child is about three, without any treatment being necessary. If this does not happen, the condition can be corrected by plaster casts, or, occasionally, by means of surgery.

An inturning of the whole legs also usually puts itself right, by the time the child is six or seven. In earlier days, children were put in splints to treat the condition, but this method of treatment is no longer considered necessary. In the few cases where the child does not grow out of the condition, an operation is sometimes performed to realign the bones of the upper leg, with excellent long-term results.

■ FEVER

see also CONVULSIONS

Fever, or raised body temperature, usually indicates an infection of some sort, but the cause may not always be obvious. People often refer to fever simply as 'a temperature'.

Normal temperature The normal body temperature is 37°C (98.4°F) but this varies from person to person, from day to day, and even from one time of day to another. Some healthy children have temperatures as low as 35.6°C (96°F) or as high as 37.2°C (99°F).

Normally the body temperature rises during the day, reaching its peak at about 6pm. A temperature of 37.7°C (100°F) or more is considered to be a fever.

Temperature control The body temperature is kept fairly even by the region of the brain called the hypothalmus. When the body temperature goes up, for example after strenuous activity, the brain causes the heat to be lost by diverting blood to the skin as the skin surface cools through evaporation of sweat, and this brings the temperature down again.

SYMPTOMS

A mild fever may have hardly any symptoms, but the higher the temperature the more the child is likely to be 'feverish'. Symptoms will include sweating, restlessness, hot skin, flushed cheeks, and often the desire to sleep (which can be very beneficial). Extreme fever can cause hallucinations or febrile convulsions.

CAUSES

The reason why infections in children (and adults) are often accompanied by raised temperature is not fully understood. It is linked to the activity of the white blood cells, which play a key role in the body's defence system. They produce a substance called pyrogen, which acts on the hypothalmus and causes the body temperature to rise. The white blood cells multiply and become more active (and therefore produce more pyrogen) when there is an infection. Both viral and bacterial infections can cause a rise in body temperature.

Viruses cause such common illnesses as flu, measles, mumps and chicken pox, while bacterial infections cause sore throats, pneumonia, infections of the bowel and bladder, and abscesses, as well as more serious infections such as typhoid fever and tuberculosis, which are now rare in the developed world. All these illnesses are accompanied by a raised body temperature.

Finally, tropical diseases such as malaria which are caused by parasites are accompanied by very high fever. And, although this is extremely rare, fever can also be an indication of a tumour.

OTHER SYMPTOMS

Very high temperatures can accompany quite minor illnesses, so temperature alone is not an indication of the severity of an illness. Symptoms such as loss of appetite, vomiting and the child being miserable and lethargic are a much better guide to her general health.

TREATMENT

Viruses cannot be treated in themselves, although of course the child can be nursed and the symptoms of the illness relieved. But bacterial infections can be treated with antibiotics. This is not necessary for most infections, which can soon be overcome by the body's own defences.

A child with a high fever need not be kept in bed, but should stay resting comfortably indoors. She should not be forced to eat if she has no appetite, but it is important to encourage a feverish child to drink as much as possible to make sure that she doesn't become dehydrated.

In most cases high temperature can be brought down by sponging the child all over with tepid water. If the child is in bed, she should just be covered by a light sheet, which will need to be changed frequently as it will absorb a lot of sweat.

If you have a baby with a high temperature and sponging with tepid

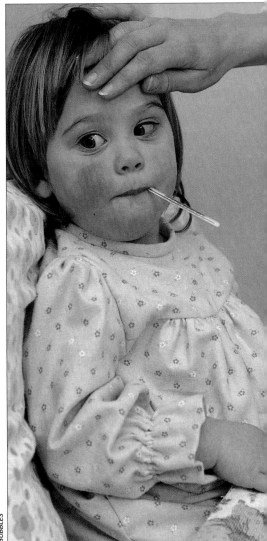
BUBBLES

If your child seems feverish, check her temperature to make sure it isn't abnormally high. She may need to rest and to sleep.

WATCHPOINTS

● Very high temperatures can cause hallucinations. They can also cause convulsions and can be fatal. Call your doctor if your child's temperature is 39.4°C (103°F) or above or if your baby's temperature is 37.7°C (100°F) or above.

● Never give aspirin to children under 12. Paracetamol is a safer option.

water does not bring it down, call your doctor. Do not let an older child's high temperature worry you unduly if the child seems otherwise well, but call the doctor if the child's temperature is 39.4°C (103°F) or above, or if it remains high despite home treatment.

Paracetamol lowers a high temperature by blocking the messages to the brain, and this can be given to a feverish child if sponging has not made a difference.

YOUR QUESTIONS

Q Should a child be kept warm when he has a high temperature?

A Keep the room fairly warm, but do not keep the child swaddled up in bedclothes. If he is very feverish, just a sheet will be enough to keep him comfortable.

Q Why do children become hot one minute and cold the next when they have a fever?

A Often in a fever the body temperature fluctuates wildly. When it rises the child becomes hot and sweats profusely, and should not be made hotter by blankets or by the room temperature being too high. But when the body temperature drops the child will become shivery and may even have uncontrollable shaking attacks, as the body tries to heat itself up again through muscular activity.

■ FINGERNAILS

See also RINGWORM, WHITLOW

Nails are formed from keratin, the substance that also forms the outer layer of the hair.

A child's nails should be kept short, as this makes it easy to keep them clean and to make sure that

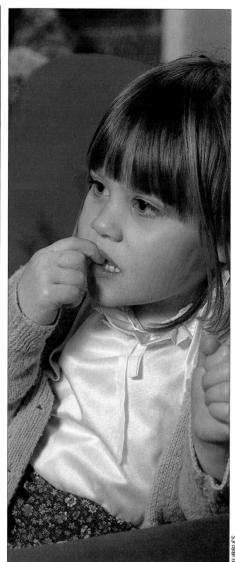

BUBBLES

A child who habitually bites her nails may be showing signs of anxiety. Try to find out if something is worrying her, and be reassuring. Most children stop nail-biting when they start to take pride in their appearance.

they will not be torn while the child is playing. It also minimizes the danger of other children getting scratched in over-active play.

The simplest way to cut the nails of a baby or small child is with a pair of small, blunt-ended scissors after a bath or while the child is asleep.

PROBLEMS

The nail bed is the name for all the part of the finger over which the nail grows. Any injury to the nail bed can be quite painful, but only a serious injury to the base of the nail bed can

actually cause the nail to be lost.

A nail being torn to below its usual level can cause some temporary pain, as can a splinter being pushed under the nail. But the main danger with any nail injury is infection.

TREATMENT

For minor injuries no treatment is necessary other than bathing the injured finger in warm water. The injury should be dressed if necessary, and kept clean. A little antiseptic ointment or cream, though not strictly necessary, can be soothing and comforting. If your child's finger is throbbing from a blow, you could rub an ice cube over it, or she can dip her finger in a bowl of cold water.

A small splinter under the nail is best left to come out of its own accord. Holding the finger in a bowl of very warm water may help it to come out more quickly. If the splinter does not come out after a day or so, and if the finger is sore, the child should see the doctor. Equally, if the finger swells or continues to feel sore after an injury, it is best to have it seen by your doctor in case it has become infected.

NAIL-BITING

Nail-biting on its own is not serious, but it can be an indication that the child is suffering from some stress.

Rather than fussing about the nail-biting, see if you can find out what it is that is making your child anxious. Help her to be relaxed by encouraging play and physical activity, and give her lots of cuddles and a happy, calm bedtime routine.

If the nail-biting persists over a long period and if the child shows other signs of anxiety (such as bed-wetting) it might be a good idea to have a word with your doctor, but without taking your child in the first instance.

A very bad blow to the base of the nail may need to be treated by your doctor. The worst of the pain will soon be over, but it will probably result in the loss of the nail.

■ FIRST AID

Specific first aid entries are given under separate headings. The key entries are as follows, and ideally should be looked at before any specific problem occurs:

- Artificial respiration
- Bleeding
- Burns and scalds
- Cardiac massage
- Choking
- Concussion
- Convulsions
- Drowning
- Electric shocks
- Head injuries
- Poisoning
- Shock
- Smothering
- Swallowed objects
- Unconsciousness

See also ABRASIONS, ACCIDENTS, BANDAGES, BEE STINGS, BITES, BLISTERS, BRUISES, DRESSINGS, FAINTING, GRAZES, HEAT STROKE, SPRAINS

BE PREPARED

The best way to be prepared for an emergency is to study these entries carefully *before* an emergency happens and takes you by surprise.

WHAT YOU SHOULD KNOW

Firstly remember that the risk of accidents other than cuts and scrapes can be kept to a minimum if you are aware of danger and observe safety codes (*see* Safety).

All parents need to know how to deal with cuts and grazes, but also what to do in the case of choking, burns and poisoning. For serious accidents, an ambulance should be called straight away, but it is as well to know what to do while waiting for the ambulance to come.

Doing the right thing could save a child's life. You should know how to do the following:
- Administer artificial respiration (see

pp. 9–10).
- Check the pulse and give cardiac massage if there is no pulse (see p. 31).
- Put the child in the recovery position (see this page).

CARDIAC MASSAGE

Cardiac massage can only be learned properly under instruction, but it is worth trying in an emergency if a child's heart has stopped beating, even if you have not been trained or the training took place a long time ago (see page 31).

WATCHPOINTS

- Do not move the victim of a serious accident unless you have to for safety reasons. There may be internal or spinal injuries.

- Loosen any tight clothing which might inhibit circulation or breathing.

RECOVERY POSITION

It is a good idea to practise putting a child in the recovery position, and children themselves can learn how to do this in case they ever have to look after an accident victim.

Put a child in this position if she is unconscious or semi-conscious after an accident, while her heart is still beating and she is breathing regularly. In this position the child can breathe easily and will not inhale any vomit in case she is sick.

The recovery position is for use in

ACTION FOR EMERGENCIES

1 Keep calm.
2 Eliminate danger (for example, separate child from electrical appliance in case of electric shock; turn off gas and open window in case of gas poisoning).
3 Check that the child's airway is clear with your finger.
4 If possible, get someone else to call an ambulance to prevent delay while you attend to the child.
5 Check breathing (watch for chest movement and place your face close to the child's nose to feel for breath. Give artificial respiration if the child is not breathing.
6 Check pulse at side of neck with fingers. Give heart massage if you are sure that there is no pulse.
7 Staunch any bleeding, starting with the worst wound, or attend to any severe burns (page 37). If blood is pumping from the wound, indicating that an artery has been cut, a tourniquet needs to be applied above the wound.
8 Place the child in the recovery position and keep her warm to prevent shock.
9 Call an ambulance if this has not already been done.

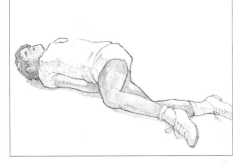

If your child is unconscious, put him into the recovery position. Pull his far hip over so that he rolls towards you.

Position his arms as shown. His head should be tilted backwards, with his chin forwards to facilitate breathing.

JOHN DAVIES

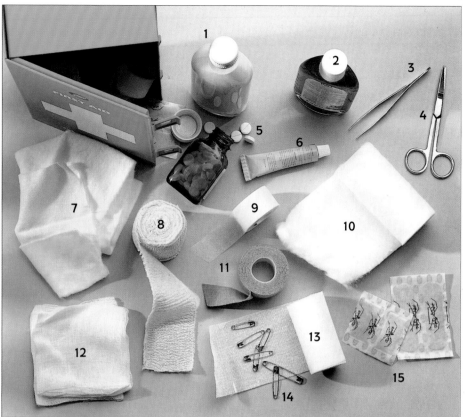

RAY DUNS

1 Calamine lotion for soothing bites, stings and burns 2 antiseptic liquid for cleaning wounds 3 tweezers for removing splinters   4 scissors for cutting dressings 5 paracetamol tablets (also include paracetamol liquid) 6 antiseptic cream 7 soft lint dressing 8 rolled crêpe bandage 9 thin adhesive tape 10 cotton wool roll 11 adhesive strapping 12 sterile gauze squares 13 rolled gauze 14 safety pins 15 sticking plasters

circumstances where there are not likely to be broken bones or internal injuries, for example: after a fit, after being saved from drowning, after asphyxiation, after a severe electric shock, after poisoning and after a deep faint.

FIRST AID KIT

Every household should have a first aid kit kept in a securely closed box in a safe place, high enough to be out of the reach of children.

Many chemists sell first aid kits complete with box, but if you make up your own it should include: sterile packs of gauze, lint and bandages, adhesive dressings, adhesive tape for securing your own dressings, cotton-wool, safety pins, scissors, tweezers, antiseptic ointment, small bottle of disinfectant, calamine lotion, ointment for burns and infant paraceta-mol (tablets or liquid).

EMERGENCY

To save yourself vital moments in an emergency, keep the telephone number of your doctor's surgery and the local accident and emergency unit by the telephone.

■ FITS

See CONVULSIONS

■ FLU

Properly known as influenza, flu is one of the most common and the most infectious of illnesses. It is caused by a virus and usually occurs in epidemics. Although it is mostly prevalent during the winter and early spring, it can be active at any time. Although not serious in itself, flu can make a child susceptible to other diseases if not watched carefully.

SYMPTOMS

Flu symptoms usually come on suddenly. Your child will complain of aching in the limbs and back, and will often have fits of shivering and a headache. His temperature will be high, and there may also be a cough, sore throat and runny nose, or sickness and diarrhoea.

It is quite possible for only one child in the family to have these symptoms. This is because although flu is infectious, people who have had a particular strain of flu develop immunity to that strain.

The symptoms of flu last for two to five days, and leave the child feeling tired and weak. The cough that goes with flu can persist for up to two weeks after the symptoms are over.

CAUSES

Influenza is caused by a virus, and this virus is unusual in that it is always changing its form. The body's defences are deceived by the slightly altered form so that normal immunity is interfered with.

The new outbreaks of flu that occur year after year are due to slightly changed forms of the virus which require the body to build up immunity all over again. These changes are known as drifts. It has also been found that every 30 or 40 years a completely different form of flu virus appears, and this causes world-wide epidemics. These bigger changes are known as shifts.

Occasionally, the flu virus reverts to a form that resembles a previous flu. When this happens, people who have had the original form will be immune. Young children, who are not old enough to have developed this immunity, will be susceptible.

HOW THE ILLNESS IS SPREAD

When a child or adult who already has flu coughs or sneezes, tiny droplets containing the virus are released into the air and these can be breathed in by people nearby. If they are not immune to the virus, these people will develop the illness in one to three days.

PREVENTION

As flu is caued by a virus there is no cure for it. However, even though the virus changes its form and catches people out, it may be possible to have your child vaccinated against it if he is particularly at risk, for example if he has a congenital heart condition, cystic fibrosis, severe asthma, emphysema or chronic bronchitis.

Vaccinations against the currently prevalent form of flu are available each autumn, and they may prevent or reduce the severity of an attack.

If your child is offered a flu injection, it will be given in a single dose and usually has no side-effects. There may be a slight rise in temperature and the child's arm may be slightly sore for a day.

TREATMENT

A child with feverish flu should be put to bed and kept warm. He should be given plenty of fluids to drink, especially sweet drinks such as lemon barley water or orange squash, which will provide some energy through the sugar they contain. If the child has a poor or no appetite at all, he should not be made to eat.

If the child is very feverish, he can

CNRI/SCIENCE PHOTO LIBRARY

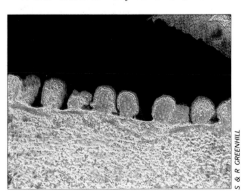

S & R GREENHILL

This electron micrograph shows what an influenza virus looks like. It has infected a cell and a row of virus particles bud from the cell's surface.

YOUR QUESTIONS

Q My little boy has asthma attacks. Does this make him more prone to catching the flu?

A A child with asthma is more likely to suffer from secondary infections if he does get flu, but is no more likely to catch the flu than any other child. If his asthma attacks tend to be severe, ask your doctor if he can have yearly flu vaccines as a precautionary measure.

Keep a watch on your son if he has an attack of flu, and call your doctor if he shows signs of developing a chest infection. Signs of this are a severe cough, with green or yellow sputum, chest pains and breathlessness.

Q Can flu affect the ears and lead to or occur with an ear infection?

A Yes, a flu which causes coughing and sneezing can set up a secondary infection in the ears especially in children. Signs of this will include ear-ache and discharge from the ear. See your doctor if you have any reason to think that your child's ears may have been infected, as the problem needs to be treated at once.

Your child will not get flu from being naked and 'catching cold' but from an infected person passing on the virus through the air.

be given infant paracetamol to bring down the temperature. If the child's temperature has not come down within a day and a half, or if he does not begin to feel better after two days, consult your doctor. Otherwise, keep him warm and resting and the illness should soon be over.

Remember that for some time afterwards your child will be weak and possibly tearful. Reassure him that this is quite normal, and that he will soon be out to play again.

■ FLUORIDE

Fluoride helps to fight tooth decay. It can be taken by children in tablet form or as drops while their tooth enamel is forming, until all their permanent teeth except the wisdom teeth have come through.

WHAT IS FLUORIDE?

Fluoride is a substance that contains the chemical element fluorine. It is present in all the body's bony tissues, including the teeth, and is vital to their development.

HOW DOES IT PROTECT TEETH?

The outer covering of the teeth is a tough layer of enamel which protects the rest of the tooth. The enamel can be attacked by acids in the mouth, and the process will then cause tooth decay.

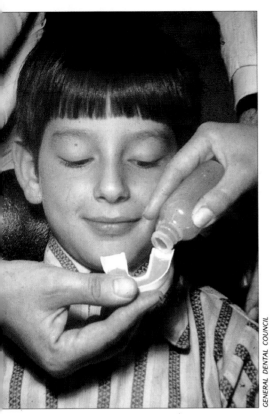

Most dentists offer fluoride treatment as a preventive measure against decay. Fluoride can either be painted directly on to the teeth or applied by means of a shield, as here.

The vulnerability of the enamel to attack depends on its hardness. Some children naturally have very hard tooth enamel, and this makes them less prone to have tooth decay, even when adults. It has been found that in areas where fluoride occurs naturally in the drinking water children and adults have tougher tooth enamel and consequently less decay.

Fluoride can be incorporated into the enamel of the teeth through the diet as the child's teeth are being formed and by direct application to the teeth themselves, and in both cases this reduces decay.

HOW IS FLUORIDE SUPPLIED?

Fluoride can be provided in a number of ways. In some areas it occurs naturally in the water, and in other areas it is added to the water. The child can take fluoride drops, and the mother can get the child's teeth off to a good start by taking a fluoride supplement herself before the baby is born. A dentist can apply fluoride gel directly to a child's teeth; or the child can use a fluoride toothpaste.

Water supply When fluoride is added to the water supply at a concentration of one part per million the incidence of dental decay in the area is reduced by 60 per cent.

Fluoride is however potentially toxic, and large doses of fluoride cause mottling of the teeth and brittle bones. Fluoride at the permitted level of concentration is not known to have any ill effects, but some people do not like the idea of having chemicals forced upon them through the water supply. In Britain fluoridization is only carried out by the local water authorities after consultation with the relevant health authority.

Flouride drops Your dentist or chemist can supply a suitable preparation to be added once a day to milk or other food, from birth until the child is weaned. After this a daily flouride tablet can be taken until all the permanent teeth are formed.

Gel Your dentist may advise you to strengthen your child's teeth by having flouride applied to the teeth. This is usually done once every year or every other year.

Toothpaste Daily use of a toothpaste which contains flouride helps to keep up the level of flouride in the enamel, although it is not as effective as flouride in the diet.

YOUR QUESTIONS

Q Do children really need fluoride supplements if they clean their teeth properly?

A It is true that one way to fight tooth decay is to clean the teeth properly. This removes particles of food which otherwise decay in the mouth and give rise to the development of the bacteria which can cause tooth decay.

Thorough cleaning also removes plaque, a film which builds up on the teeth and which appears to have the ability to turn sugars into acids which attack the tooth enamel. But it is impossible to banish plaque completely — it begins to build up as soon as it has been cleaned off. It therefore makes sense to give children's teeth an extra line of defence in the form of enamel-strengthening fluoride while their teeth are forming.

A child who regularly brushes his teeth with a fluoride toothpaste will be helping to protect them from decay. Fluoride toughens the enamel which covers the teeth.

■ FONTANELLES

Fontanelles are the soft spots on a baby's skull. If you run a finger gently over a baby's head you will feel several of these indentations and even a pulsing in places, but this is absolutely normal.

POSITION OF FONTANELLES

The largest fontanelle is positioned at the top of the baby's head. It is diamond-shaped and measures roughly 4cm (1½in) across and is known as the anterior (front) fontanelle. The anterior fontanelle pulsates noticeably to the baby's heartbeat, which can seem alarming to parents and give the impression that the brain is more exposed and consequently the baby more vulnerable than she really is.

There are five more fontanelles, one on its own and two in pairs. The other single fontanelle is known as the posterior (back) fontanelle. It is smaller than the front one and is situated about 5cm (2in) behind it, at the back of the head. The mastoid fontanelles are located at the back of the head behind the ears, and the sphenoidal fontanelles lie at each side of the skull, just above the baby's cheek bone.

FUNCTION OF FONTANELLES

In the skull of a newly born baby the bones are completely separate, but joined together by tough sheets of fibrous tissue, the fontanelles. This enables the baby's skull to change shape during the birth.

If the baby's head is large or the mother's pelvic opening very small, the bones of the skull actually overlap during the birth, and the baby is born with a very narrow head. The bones resume their normal position within 24–48 hours, completely without harm to the brain.

DEVELOPMENT OF THE HEAD

As the baby grows, new bone is laid down and the fontanelles gradually close, although very occasionally the anterior fontanelle does become larger and more noticeable during the first three months or so. At about three

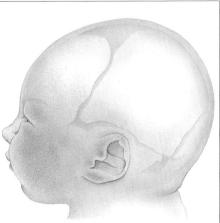

The fontanelles feel soft but are strong sheets of fibrous tissue.

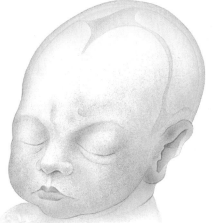

On top is the anterior fontanelle; at the sides, the sphenoidal.

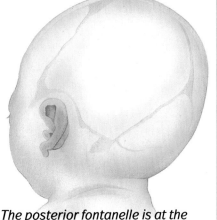

The posterior fontanelle is at the back; the mastoid behind each ear.

months the sphenoidal and posterior fontanelles close, by the time the baby is about a year old the mastoid fontanelles are closed, and the child can be up to two years old before the anterior fontanelle finally disappears completely.

New mothers sometimes worry that they could damage the baby's brain by touching the fontanelles, but this is not so. The tissue between the bones is very firm and it is perfectly safe to wash the baby's head, although not too roughly.

YOUR QUESTIONS

Q My baby had an attack of gastroenteritis recently, and I was sure that it made the dent on top of her head more noticeable. Was I imagining it?

A Probably not. Gastroenteritis can cause serious dehydration in babies, due to loss of fluids from vomiting and diarrhoea. The anterior fontanelle becomes more indented when this occurs, which can indicate that the child urgently needs fluids.

Gastroenteritis and prolonged diarrhoea should receive medical attention because of the danger of dehydration.

Q Is it true that the condition of the fontanelles can be an indicator of illness?

A Yes. The fontanelles become indented when the baby is dehydrated, but certain illnesses cause an accumulation of fluid in the skull, and this makes the anterior fontanelle feel tight and hard. Hydrocephalus and meningitis, which are serious, but rare, both have this effect.

■ FOOD ALLERGIES

see also ASTHMA, ECZEMA

Food allergies can be triggered off by any number of foods, and the substance causing the allergy (called the allergen) can be difficult to track down. Food allergies often run in families (although without affecting all members of the family) and are often linked to the incidence of eczema and asthma.

SYMPTOMS

There is a whole range of symptoms that can be caused by food allergies and they always arise a few hours after the food has been eaten.

Skin Some food allergies result in skin irritation. This ranges from a red, flushed rash to an eczematous condition, with a scaly rash on hands, face, neck and limbs; or hives, in which there are red, irritated swellings on the skin, with small white, very itchy points at their centre.

Digestion Upset stomach with diarrhoea, vomiting and nausea can be symptoms of food allergy. These symptoms usually become apparent within an hour of eating the food responsible, making it easier to identify the cause and eliminate the culprit from the diet.

Other symptoms Asthma is often caused by allergies, and food allergies are sometimes responsible. This is a fairly common, but distressing childhood complaint, in which the child wheezes, has difficulty in drawing breath and experiences tight pains across the chest.

Swollen tongues and lips are usually symptoms of food allergies, and again can generally be traced quite easily to the food responsible.

Migraine headaches are thought to be caused by allergic reactions to food in many cases, but these seem to affect adults more than children.

Many specialists now think that some behavioural problems, and in particular hyperactivity, are reactions to substances in the diet, although these may not be, strictly speaking, allergic reactions.

CAUSES

Any allergy is a sensitivity to a substance that does not normally cause any harm. The substance that causes the allergy is called an allergen, and among the most common allergens are eggs, cow's milk and fish, especially seafood.

Food allergens are absorbed into the bloodstream and can therefore cause reactions in almost any part of the body, and this is why it is often difficult to track down the precise cause if your child is suffering from a food allergy — and even, sometimes, that it is an allergy that is causing the symptoms at all. Swollen tongue and lips, and digestive disorders are usually more obviously linked to the particular foods that have caused these reactions.

ALLERGIC REACTIONS

An allergic reaction is the result of the body's defence mechanism coming into play when confronted with what should be harmless substances. The body tries to produce antibodies to these harmless substances and these antibodies cause certain cells to release histamine. It is the histamine, produced by the body itself, that provoke the symptoms of allergy.

Normally, the body is able to tell the difference between a dangerous foreign protein and a harmless one, such as a food protein. But, for reasons that are not yet understood, in an allergic person the body treats a harmless protein as if it were harmful.

The dyes used in some drinks can cause an allergic reaction in children and lead to behavioural problems such as hyperactivity.

Since, once a child is weaned, the diet normally contains so many different elements, it can be very difficult to isolate the foodstuff that triggers off an allergic reaction. An elimination diet is one way of diagnosing the cause.

At first a very plain diet is provided, often consisting of little more than water, one vegetable (usually potato) and one meat (usually lamb). If the child has no symptoms while following this diet, it is considered likely that food allergies are to blame for the condition.

After this, different foods are reintroduced, little by little, and any reactions noted.

Another approach to an elimination diet is simply to remove those substances (wheat and cow's milk, for example) most likely to be responsible, one by one, and keep a note of the results. Often nowadays the substances responsible are food dyes and additives, and if food allergy is suspected in children it may be worth feeding them fresh food without any additives for a while to see if the symptoms diminish.

PROVOCATION TESTS

To speed up the diagnosis, some doctors now use an alternative test in which a weak solution of various possible allergens including preserv-

YOUR QUESTIONS

Q I have suffered from food allergies badly over the years. Is there any way I can prevent my children from having similar problems?

A Specialists differ over this question. Some believe that the risk of a child developing allergies is reduced if the child is breast fed and not weaned onto solids before four months. And some specialists believe that if a child has a varied diet the risk of food allergies is reduced. But allergies do tend to run in families so your children might have inherited a tendency towards allergies.

ing agents is injected under the skin to see the reaction on the skin. This is known as a skin test.

TREATMENT

Unfortunately there is no effective treatment for food allergies other than avoiding the food that causes the problem. This means the parents

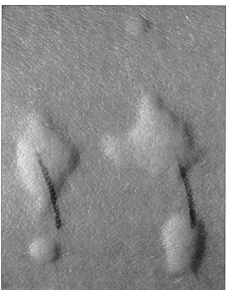

These raised areas follow skin tests for certain allergies and show a positive reaction.

SCIENCE PHOTO LIBRARY

must select food with care, reading packets and labels to check on the contents of pre-packed food.

Allergies to shellfish or a particular kind of fruit are relatively easy to cope with, but allergies to wheat or dairy food do demand a major revision of the normal diet. Your doctor will help with suggestions.

Sometimes suitable substitutes can be found fairly easily – for instance cow's milk can be replaced with goat's milk or soya milk, and potato flour or cornflour can replace flour from cereals to some extent.

DRUGS

Drugs can control some food allergy symptoms. Corticosteroid drugs have an anti-inflammatory effect and can be prescribed as a cream or as tablets for skin rashes and in liquid form to be taken by inhaler, for asthma. Asthma attacks can also be

controlled by drugs known as bronchodilators. Both drugs may be given by injection in particularly serious asthma cases.

However, these drugs are not cures – they simply relieve the symptoms. And usually they are not suitable for long-term use. So avoiding the allergen is really the only solution, difficult though this may be.

It is best not to make a fuss and to try to give the child the same diet as his brothers and sisters as much as possible. It is surprising how even quite young children can learn what they can and cannot have, and adapt to it. And children do frequently grow out of many food allergies.

■ FOOD POISONING

Incidences of food poisoning seem to be frequent, but they can usually be avoided by good hygiene.

SYMPTOMS

Food poisoning usually takes the form of tummy pain, vomiting and diarrhoea. This can be extremely debilitating and cause dehydration.

The pains are usually violent cramps that come on quite suddenly. They can continue for a few days, often becoming worse just before an attack of vomiting or diarrhoea. Vomiting tends to stop after a few hours, but diarrhoea can continue for a few days.

Especially in young children, diarrhoea and vomiting can lead to the loss of relatively large quantities of fluids and salts. This causes dehydration and affects the body's delicate chemical balance. In some extreme cases, when not treated promptly, this can lead to coma and even death, and this makes food poisoning potentially serious.

CAUSES

Food poisoning comes about as a result of the child eating contaminated food, and this contamination can be caused by bacteria, by toxins or by chemicals. Usually everyone who has eaten the same food is affected to some extent.

Bacterial food poisoning In this type of poisoning the cause is, as the name implies, bacteria (germs) which either were present in the food from the beginning or have been introduced, and which then multiply on the food before it is eaten. Once ingested with the food these germs continue to multiply inside the stomach or the bowel.

Perhaps the best known, by name, of such bacteria is *Salmonella*. This is often found in poultry and eggs, particularly duck eggs, and is killed by thorough cooking. The bacterium *Clostridia* contaminates food through dirt or flies, and *Shigella* and *Escherichia coli* can contaminate food through poor hygiene.

Toxins In toxic food poisoning the problem is caused by toxins released as germs multiply on the food, rather than by the germs themselves. Perhaps the best known form of toxic food poisoning is botulism which, although it is very rare, is very dangerous. It can be caught from badly tinned or bottled food.

Germs known as *Staphylococci* can be transferred to food from infected boils or cuts. Once they are on the food they grow rapidly and produce staphylococci toxin, which quickly affects anyone eating the food.

Bacillus cereus develops in cooked rice if it is kept warm for long periods before being reheated and eaten. The toxin produced survives cooking.

Chemical poisoning A few foods do contain chemicals which are

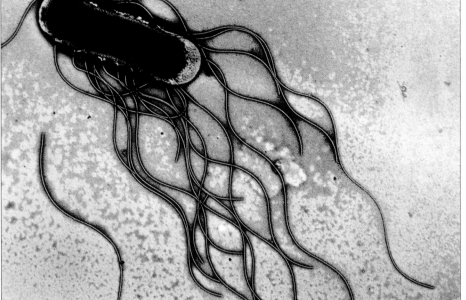

Salmonella bacteria are one of the well known causes of food poisoning. They can generate headaches, vomiting and diarrhoea.

poisonous to people, as in the case of poisonous mushrooms and toadstools. Sometimes this type of food poisoning can even result in death, and children should be warned against tasting or even touching mushrooms while on walks.

Some nuts contain small quantities of chemicals that can be poisonous if eaten in very large amounts, and the green parts of potatoes also contain poisonous chemicals.

Finally, foods that have been treated with pesticides could in theory cause food poisoning if the pesticides have not been used in accordance with official advice, if fruit skins are not washed or if the food is eaten in very large quantities.

ONSET OF SYMPTOMS

The interval between the contaminated food being eaten and the symptoms developing is an indicator of the type of poisoning. If the cause is a bacterial infection symptoms can take from 12 to 24 hours to develop.

Toxic food poisoning usually occurs almost as soon as the contaminated food has been eaten. If the toxins are from *Staphylococcus* there is vomiting and pain, but there is no

---

WARNING

Young children with food poisoning can become badly ill quite quickly. Any child under two who vomits for more than a couple of hours, or who has severe diarrhoea, should be seen by a doctor at once. Always give the salt and sugar mixture described below.

---

diarrhoea. However if the cause is botulism, symptoms arise after an interval of about 12 hours, and include vomiting, abdominal pain, paralysis and coma.

T R E A T M E N T

The most important treatment in most cases of food poisoning is to replace the fluid that is being lost as a result of vomiting or diarrhoea. If the child is over 12 she can be given plenty of water to which a little fresh fruit juice has been added.

Babies and young children should be given a mixture of two level teaspoonfuls of sugar and a generous pinch of salt in 200ml of water, or for severe fluid loss the doctor will prescribe powders containing a balanced mixture of salts and sugars which are mixed with plain water.

In a baby who is being breast fed

BOTULISM

Paralysis and death can occur if botulism goes untreated. A swiftly administered antitoxin and intensive nursing are necessary to counteract it.

The child's stomach is washed out, and she may be put on a ventilator. Once the acute stage is over, the outlook for a complete recovery is excellent.

---

as well as receiving solids, the breast feeding should continue. The child should be given additional clear fluids by bottle or spoon.

ANTIBIOTICS AND ANTIDOTES

Depending on the type of poisoning, antibiotics may be prescribed by your doctor to clear up the infection but they are not needed in all cases.

For fungus poisoning an antidote may be given, and the patient is taken to hospital for care and treatment. In serious cases intensive care may be necessary.

DEHYDRATION

Dehdyration is a serious threat to babies and young children. The early signs of dehydration are:
• dry mouth and lips
• sunken fontanelle (if the child is under 18 months)
• sunken eyes
• dark yellow urine, or no urine being passed at all
• drowsiness, lethargy and irritability in older children.

Call a doctor in the case of children under two who are vomiting for two hours or more or who have bad diarrhoea.

In an older child, if the symptoms of dehydration appear, take the child immediately to the nearest hospital accident and emergency department.

YOUR QUESTIONS

Q Is it really important to train a child to wash his hands after going to the lavatory and before eating?

A Yes. This reduces the number of bacteria on them, lessening the chance of transferring bacteria to the mouth and reducing the risk of many forms of food poisoning.

Q Why must frozen meat be defrosted thoroughly before being cooked?

A When meat is being cooked from a partially defrosted state, large parts of it will be warm rather than hot during the cooking, and this causes *Salmonella* and other bacteria to multiply rapidly.

Q Why should cooked and uncooked meats be kept separately in the fridge?

A All uncooked meats have bacteria on their surface, which are normally killed when the meat is cooked. If the uncooked meat comes into contact with cooked meats bacteria can be transferred to cooked meat, where they will quickly multiply.

It is also important not to use a knife that has been used for uncooked meat on any other food without cleaning it carefully first.

■ **FORESKIN**
see GENITALS, CIRCUMCISION

■ **FRACTURES**
see also DISLOCATION, FALLS

Fractures are broken bones, and they are usually caused by falls or car accidents. Fractures are fairly unusual in young children, as their bones are very supple. They are most likely to occur if the child is the victim of a car accident. It takes a great deal

of force to break a healthy child's bone in a fall, but some bones are more vulnerable than others.

SYMPTOMS

Perhaps the most obvious symptom of a fracture will be that the child is in great pain. He will probably be pale and sweating (signs of shock), due to loss of blood from the broken bone.

If a limb is fractured, it may be in an unnatural position, it may look bent or swollen and the child will be unable to move it. But some fractures, especially in the ribs or hand, may be almost unnoticeable and may take time to be recognized. Very young children have difficulty in explaining where the pain is, making it more difficult to spot what is wrong.

Bones are not necessarily displaced in a fracture, and sometimes an X-ray is necessary to identify the injury.

TYPES OF FRACTURE

Very young and supple bones are most susceptible to a type of fracture known as a greenstick fracture. This gets its name from the way in which a

willow sapling breaks when it is bent too far. A **greenstick** fracture is a crack that goes part-way across or part-way along a young bone.

Sometimes these cracks are so small that they do not show up in an X-ray. Their presence is diagnosed from the pain the child feels when using the bone. These are known as **stress** fractures, and heal with rest.

In a **simple** fracture the skin is undamaged, while in a **compound** or **open** fracture part of the bone is driven through the skin, and a **comminuted** fracture is one in which the bone is splintered. In a **complicated** fracture the broken bone causes other internal injuries. Finally, there are so-called **pathological** fractures, which are rare and occur only when there is an inherent weakness in the bone, usually due to disease.

CAUSES

The most likely cause of a fracture will be a bad fall, and the hand and wrist are most likely to be injured in breaking the fall (*see* Falls).

In older children fractures occur

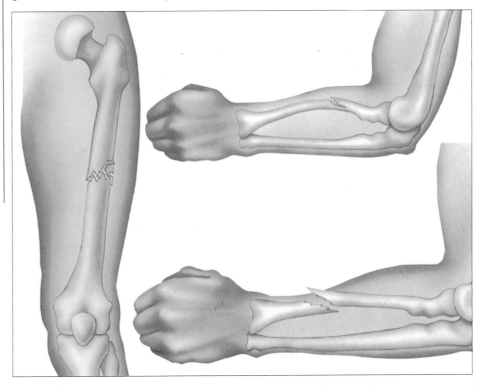

The diagram shows a comminuted fracture (left), in which the bone is shattered; a greenstick fracture (top), in which the bone is cracked; and a compound fracture, in which the bone pierces the skin (bottom).

HOW TO DEAL WITH FRACTURES

Do
- Keep the child warm and reassure him
- Handle the child with care, only moving him if absolutely necessary for safety
- Cover an open wound with sterile gauze and bandage
- Call an ambulance.

Don't
- Move the child unless you really have to
- Give him anything to eat or drink in case he needs an anaesthetic
- Transport the child to hospital yourself unless it is impossible to get an ambulance, or move him before immobilizing the injured limb.

more frequently, partly as the bones become less supple, and partly as the children become involved in sport. Ideally children should be supervised by a trained adult when they are playing sports, so that injuries will be recognized and properly attended to. But of course this will not always happen, and it is as well to teach older children about the dangers and symptoms of fractures (and other injuries) and what to do if they occur.

The most serious fractures of all are caused by road injuries. Even if one of the vehicles involved is not moving, the speed of the other intensifies the impact of the accident.

DANGERS

The chief danger from a fracture is shock, due to pain and loss of blood, especially if the broken bone cuts through surrounding blood vessels. If the skin is broken there is a risk of osteomyelitis (infection of the bone).

Fractures of the skull can cause damage to the brain, due to increased pressure from bleeding. If a fractured skull is suspected the child will automatically be taken to hospital and put under observation for 12 hours or more.

A rib fracture can cause a ruptured lung or liver. Again this will result in severe loss of blood. Likewise a fractured pelvis can cause damage to the bladder or urethra.

A fractured spine needs particularly careful, skilled handling to avoid damage to the spinal cord, because if this happens, permanent paralysis can be the result.

Special danger for children A fracture across the end of a bone, close to the joint, can stop the bone from growing properly. If this happens, the affected limb will not reach the same size as its opposite partner.

Nevertheless, most fractures in children are not particularly serious, as long as loss of blood is controlled and infection prevented. As well as being more supple, children's bones also heal much more quickly than adult bones if they do fracture.

TREATMENT

Shock will be treated first and a blood transfusion given if necessary; the pain of the fracture is relieved with drugs. Only then is the fracture itself attended to. Muscular spasm usually pulls apart the broken ends of the bone, and the child usually has to be given an anaesthetic so that the ends can be realigned. When this has been done, the break is encased in plaster to hold the bone in place while it heals. Fractured ribs do not need to be immobilized in this way while they heal.

In comminuted fractures, where the bone is splintered, it may be necessary to join the bone by screwing a metal plate along it to act as a splint. This often has to be done if the thigh bone is broken. A plaster cast is then applied to keep the bone still while it heals.

Continuous traction If it is impossible (when the pull of the muscles is too strong) to stabilize the broken bone by using plaster, then the child has to be put in continuous traction. This means that he has to be kept in a hospital bed with the broken bone

WARNING

It is important not to move anyone with a suspected spinal injury. This is most frequent in falls from a height.

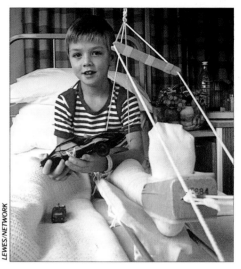

LEWES/NETWORK

Continuous traction is helping to mend this little boy's leg.

held in place by weights adjusted to counteract the pull of the muscles.

Recovery period The speed at which healing takes place depends on the blood supply at the site of the fracture. A fractured leg usually has to be kept in plaster for about 12 weeks, while a broken arm may take only six weeks to heal. Bones possess remarkable healing powers.

During the recovery period the child will be encouraged to do exercises to keep the muscles strong.

YOUR QUESTIONS

Q Do fractures leave abnormalities after they have healed?

A If the broken ends have been correctly aligned the break usually heals so well that later the fracture may not even show up on X-rays. If not, the bone will usually heal well and straighten itself.

■ FROSTBITE

Lengthy exposure to extreme cold can damage the tissues by affecting the blood circulation. But frostbite proper causes ice crystals to form in the skin as circulation ceases altogether in the affected parts, and this is even more serious.

SYMPTOMS

Frostbite is most likely to occur in the extremities: the nose, ears, fingers and toes. The skin starts to become red and hard, and gradually becomes pale grey. The frostbitten area has no feeling, and a rash of little blisters may develop.

CAUSES

Through exposure to extreme cold the circulation gradually fails to carry blood to the extremities, and the parts of the body that are frostbitten become lifeless, void of any sensation and literally frozen.

TREATMENT

Frostbite is an emergency, and correct treatment is essential. The most important thing is to get the child out of the cold and wrapped up in blankets or coats.

It is equally important not to rub the affected areas — by doing this you are not improving the circulation, for it has stopped altogether in the frostbitten parts. Rubbing will make the damage worse.

The aim is to thaw out the frostbitten areas, and the way to do it is by

WARNING

• Do not use hot water to thaw out frostbite. Anything hotter than blood heat can cause more serious damage.

• Do not use friction to try to restore the circulation. This will further harm the already damaged tissues.

YOUR QUESTIONS

Q Where I live winter days can be literally freezing. What can I do to prevent frostbite?

A Always wrap up babies and little children well when taking them out in the cold, and particularly make sure that fingers, feet, heads and noses are well protected. Never leave babies outside in their prams in cold weather.

applying warm water. The water should be kept at blood heat, and if the hands or feet are affected they can be immersed in water. The face or other parts of the body can be warmed by your own body heat, as can hands and feet if warm water is unavailable. (You can put hands or feet in your armpits, or the child's face against your face or body.) If possible, feed the child sips of a warm drink.

When the damaged skin is pink again it should be covered with sterile

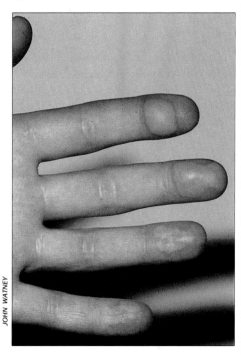

JOHN WATNEY

Frostbite typically affects the extremities of the body and the result is very much like a burn, as this child's fingers show.

dressings, just as if it were burnt. Now the child should be taken to hospital, still warmly wrapped and preferably lying down to keep the frostbitten areas level with the heart.

In hospital the child will be seen by a doctor to check that blood circulation has been restored, and if necessary drugs will be given to improve the circulation. The affected areas will be properly dressed and the child may be kept in for observation or further treatment.

■ GAS

see POISONING

■ GASTROENTERITIS

see also DIARRHOEA, FOOD POISONING

Gastroenteritis is an inflammation of the lining of the intestine and stomach which causes diarrhoea, vomiting, stomach pains and sometimes fever. It is a fairly common infection in both children and adults but should be treated as a serious illness when babies and young children become infected, since it can lead to complications. Children under the age of four are most at risk from fluid loss which in turn can lead to brain damage if not treated promptly.

CAUSES

In children the most common cause of gastroenteritis is a virus that is inhaled, rather like the common cold. Outbreaks, which usually occur in winter, can often spread rapidly in nursery schools and kindergartens and in other places where groups of children congregate.

Gastroenteritis can also be caused by bacteria on contaminated food which may be ingested or may be transferred to the mouth by dirty

LUPE CUNHA

Gastroenteritis can be caused by bacterial infection. To prevent the spread of bacteria, observe a strict hygiene in the kitchen.

fingers. Contaminated food is often the result of poor hygiene in the kitchen. Your baby, for example, may become infected because of faulty cleaning and sterilization of bottles and teats; it is less common, of course, in breast fed babies. Also, by not washing your hands thoroughly after going to the toilet or changing nappies, you or a member of your family can spread infection when handling food or feeding bottles.

SYMPTOMS

The main symptom is diarrhoea with greenish, watery stools but children may also be vomiting, have a fever and show signs of drowsiness and general illness. Older children and adults usually complain of loss of appetite and 'griping' pains in the stomach. Your child may have the symptoms within a few hours of eating contaminated food but if it is a viral infection symptoms may take a couple of days to develop.

Dehydration is a danger when a child – and more seriously – a baby is losing a lot of fluids through vomiting and diarrhoea. The sick child is usually very thirsty but can only suck, or sip, feebly and then is unable to retain even small amounts. If your child's condition does not improve within 24 hours, or if his skin and mouth look dry and warm, and his eyes are sunken, call a doctor im-

mediately. Bear in mind that babies are much more vulnerable to fluid loss than older children; if your baby has vomiting and diarrhoea for more than four hours you should always consult your doctor.

TREATMENT

In gastroenteritis, the first aim is to restore fluids to the body. Your doctor may suggest giving a glucose electrolyte solution such as Diorolyte to replace sodium lost in the diarrhoea. This special preparation will promote easy absorption of water, sugar and salt back into the body. If a baby is not able to retain liquids, he may need to be treated in hospital with an intravenous drip until the water balance is restored. Some children continue to have diarrhoea after the infection has passed and this can be due to damage to the inflamed intestine by sugar or protein, espe-

YOUR QUESTIONS

Q My son is recovering from a fairly severe bout of gastroenteritis, but after I gave him orange juice he began vomiting again. Why is this?

A Acid drinks such as orange or lemon can cause irritation. Yeast extract or clear soups are more suitable fluids to give your boy. When he is able to take some solid food, start with dry biscuits, cornflour jellies and blancmanges until his stomach has fully settled.

YOUR QUESTIONS

Q My young son gets diarrhoea and stomach pains every time we go to Spain on holiday in the summer. My neighbour says that it could be caused by recurrent bouts of gastroenteritis. Is this so?

A Your son probably suffers from enteritis – not gastroenteritis – in Spain. This is simply an inflammation of the intestine caused by mile food infections; your son's body as not built up a resistance to the different type of bacteria found in local food. Gastroenteritis affects the stomach lining as well as the intestine and tends to have more severe symptoms. To prevent enteritis, make sure your son drinks and washes in bottled or boiled water, and avoids salads and uncooked food and shellfish for the first few days.

cially milk protein. If this is the case, talk to your doctor. In instances where the attack has been caused by bacteria, antibiotics may be prescribed, but usually are not necessary.

Your child should rest in bed until he is completely recovered. Give him an easily digested diet of mainly liquids and bland foods.

PREVENTION

Gastroenteritis caused by poor hygiene can be prevented by taking a few simple precautions. Be specially careful about preparing food and washing hands after going to the toilet. Make sure all food from the freezer is thoroughly thawed and thoroughly cooked; heat kills bacteria. Be particularly vigilant about cleaning and sterilizing feeding units and bottles.

■ GENITALS

The genital organs in men and women are those that nature designed for the purpose of sex and reproduction. They are fully formed at birth but only function as reproductive organs from puberty onwards when hormonal development makes this possible.

THE MALE GENITALS

In boys and men, the genitals consist of the testes and the penis which lie outside the body; the prostate gland, seminal vesicles and various tubes linking the genital system are found inside the abdomen. The two testes, which lie one either side of the penis, are each enclosed in a pouch of loose skin called the scrotum. After puberty the testes are responsible for the production of sperm and of the male hormone testosterone (which is responsible for the sexual changes of puberty, such as the growth of body and facial hair and the breaking and deepening of the voice). The penis is a tube-shaped organ which has a collar of skin at the tip known as the foreskin. This foreskin is often removed for cultural or medical reasons by the operation called circumcision. The penis provides the exit for urine and, after puberty, for the ejaculation of sperm.

THE FEMALE GENITALS

The female reproductive organs – the ovaries, Fallopian tubes, womb and cervix (neck of the womb) lie inside the body. What we call the genitals consist of the vagina, a muscular canal situated below the neck of the womb, and the external genitals known as the vulva which protect the entrance to the vagina. The vulva consists of two folds of flesh called the inner and outer labia. The inner labia join together in front to form a small fleshy organ, the clitoris, which is covered by a flap of skin called the clitoral hood. The vagina is the vessel into which sperm is deposited in the reproductive process; the clitoris plays no actual part in reproduction.

MALE GENITALS AT BIRTH

At birth a boy's genitals are larger in proportion to the rest of his body than at any other time until puberty. They may even look red and inflamed. This is perfectly normal and is caused by the mother's hormones. The doctor or midwife checks for any abnormalities in any case and in a few days the swelling dies down.

Circumcision is medically necessary in only a small number of babies but when it is desirable for cultural or religious reasons, it is best done soon

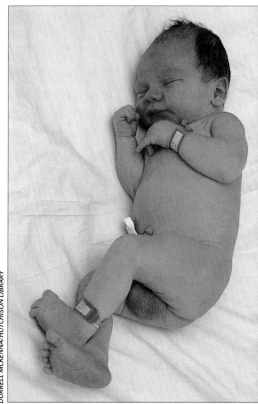

DURRELL MCKENNA/HUTCHISON LIBRARY

The mother's hormones in pregnancy can cause a newborn baby boy's genitals to look swollen and inflamed for a few days after birth.

after birth. If you want your baby circumcized in the hospital, consult your doctor about this.

UNDESCENDED TESTICLES

In some baby boys when the scrotum is touched – usually by cold hands – the testis retracts back into the abdomen. This condition usually rights itself within the first couple of years, with the testis becoming fixed in the scrotum and the passageway to the abdomen closing over.

Occasionally one or both testes do not descend before birth but in most cases this too rights itself within the first year. You can test that the testicles are descended and fixed by feeling for them as separate, walnut-shaped objects inside the loose scrotal skin. Your doctor will check for the presence of both testicles on your regular visits to the clinic and later in routine medical examinations. If one or both testicles have not descended or become fixed by the time your son is one year old, a simple

WATCHPOINTS

● Never pull back a baby boy's foreskin for cleaning or for any other reason; the foreskin will retract normally at about four years.

● Do not try to open the lips of your baby girl's vulva to clean inside; it is unnecessary.

● When changing nappies, always wipe from the front back towards the anus; this minimizes the risk of bacteria spreading from the bowels to the bladder.

operation may be necessary, since an undescended testicle may not be able to produce normal sperm.

FEMALE GENITALS AT BIRTH

Like a baby boy's genitals, a girl's labia may appear swollen and red at birth. A small amount of vaginal bleeding or a clear or whitish discharge is also quite normal in the first few days after birth. These are the result of the hormone oestrogen being passed from mother to baby.

There are few things that go wrong with the female genitals during childhood. If, however, there is any discharge, it is important to see a doctor as this could be a sign of infection, possibly as a result of a foreign object in the vagina. It is not uncommon for little girls to poke a bead or small object into the vagina when they are exploring their bodies.

HANDLING GENITALS

Babies usually become aware of their genital organs within their first year; when their nappies are left off it is only natural that they will explore

these areas of their body. Later they discover that touching or fondling the genitals give them a pleasurable sensation. Nearly all boys handle their penis and most girls also masturbate. This is perfectly normal and there is no need to discourage it. Above all, do not scold your child or stop him from masturbating; this could lead to problems with relationships in later life when sex and pleasure could be seen as something furtive and unhealthy.

Masturbation in public is embarrassing and the best you can do with a young child is to distract him. An older child can be told that it is simply bad manners to touch the genitals in public, like picking his nose — it is something not done in front of other people.

■ GERMAN MEASLES

German measles is an illness caused by the rubella virus. It is fairly common in both children and adults and is often undiagnosed because the symptoms are so mild. The rubella virus can, however, have a devastating effect if a woman catches it in the early months of pregnancy. Fortunately, vaccination is now available and is offered to toddlers between 12 and 18 months, with the measles and mumps vaccine.

COMPLICATIONS

An attack of German measles in the first four months of pregnancy can severely damage the growing foetus, causing a range of defects which includes deafness, eye and heart defects, developmental delays and bone deformities. Sometimes these are so severe that the baby is miscarried or dies soon after birth.

The reason for this devastation is that the virus attacks the foetus at a crucial stage in its development, and while it is growing the foetus has no defences, or antibodies, to protect itself against the onslaught. It is ironic that an illness that is hardly noticed by children and adults can have such dreadful consequences for an unborn child.

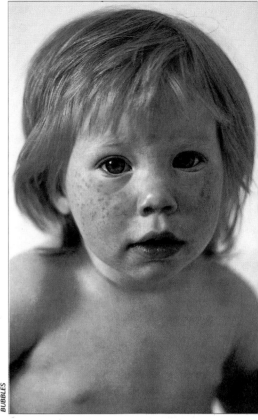

BUBBLES

The rash that accompanies German measles usually starts behind the ears and spreads to the face and body.

S Y M P T O M S

Children are most likely to get German measles in the spring or summer; it also appears to run in four- to

YOUR QUESTIONS

Q My two-year-old son has a tight foreskin and I'm worried that this is abnormal. Should I take him to see a doctor?

A This condition, known as phimosis, is very common in babies and young boys and is nothing to worry about. The reason for a tight foreskin is that at birth the penis and foreskin are fused together and only gradually separate during the first few years of the boy's life. Never be tempted to push a tight foreskin back by force; you could tear it and do damage that might make a circumcision necessary. If your son's foreskin has not retracted by the age of about four, mention it to the doctor on one of your routine visits.

WATCHPOINTS

• Inform the school or place of work if anyone in your family has German measles. Mention the risk to any pregnant women.

• Be especially sure to avoid your doctor's surgery or antenatal clinic if you or your child has German measles.

• There is no need for strict isolation but it is best to stay at home for four or five days if you have German measles.

• Mention you have German measles to all new contacts, especially female ones.

six-year cycles of minor epidemics. Like the common cold (and many other viruses) it is passed from person to person by airborne droplets. After an incubation period of about two to three weeks, your child may develop symptoms similar to those of measles, only less severe.

The two most noticeable are a rash of fine pink dots which first appears on the face and neck but spreads to the trunk and limbs, and swollen lymph glands behind the ear and the back of the neck. The child may also have a slight fever. The rash disappears within four or five days and may even go unnoticed.

Many cases of German measles pass undiagnosed since it seems hardly worth bothering the doctor over such a minor ailment.

TREATMENT

There is no treatment which will cure the disease but you can relieve some of the symptoms if your child is feeling unwell or suffering discomfort from, for instance, a sore throat. Rest at home and liquid paracetamol gargles will help. Most children however, are able to attend school as usual and play normally throughout the illness.

In theory, your child is infectious for seven days before the rash appears and for up to eight days after it has gone. In fact, once the rash appears, the child will be highly infectious for up to five days.

VACCINATION

A vaccination is available which gives protection against German measles. This is included in the MMR (measles, mumps, rubella) immunization which is offered to toddlers over the age of 12 months. Young women who may have missed out on the protection of the vaccination can ask for it from their family doctor, but they must do so before they think of getting pregnant. Once pregnant, it is unsafe to have the vaccine.

■ GLANDULAR FEVER

Glandular fever is a viral infection which mainly affects adolescents. Outbreaks often occur in schools and colleges where young people spend a lot of time in each other's company. Although babies under two have been known to get it, it is very rare; it is also uncommon in adults who are over the age of 30.

The virus is passed from person to person by close or intimate contact, including kissing (in fact, glandular fever is often known as the 'kissing

disease'). Some people are more susceptible to the virus than others but most cases are mild. Even so, it can take young people up to eight or more weeks to recover fully from the disease, during which time they may be moody and depressed.

SYMPTOMS

The first symptoms are listlessness and fatigue, which many parents dismiss as simply problems of adolescence in an older child. However, the youngster soon de-

A child with glandular fever will feel very tired and listless and the symptoms may even last for several months. There is no real treatment other than rest.

velops headaches and chills, followed by fever, a sore throat and swollen lymph glands in the neck and armpits. Sometimes a rash appears

LUPE CUNHA

CAMILLA JESSEL

Children are vaccinated against German measles at 12-18 months.

and, in severe cases, the liver may become inflamed and jaundiced. A blood test will confirm the disease.

TREATMENT

There is no special treatment for glandular fever except rest and symptomic relief for the sore throat and headaches. With mild cases the child may not need to take time off school but most patients need a couple of weeks at home since they feel generally unwell and any exertion can make them feel very fatigued. Glandular fever can be debilitating and it may take several months before the child feels really well again. Depression and listlessness can last for many months and it is important that you — and your family — are aware of this.

YOUR QUESTIONS

Q My son had glandular fever about ten months ago from which he seemed to recover completely but now some of the symptoms have returned. Is this normal?

A A small number of glandular fever patients do have a recurrence of the disease up to a year after first contracting it. Usually the symptoms are mild.

■ GLUE EAR

See also EARACHE

Glue ear occurs when the middle ear fills with a sticky mucus. The condition can affect one or both ears. It is common in young children and is usually the result of enlarged adenoids or of swelling of the lining of the Eustachian tubes from an infection or allergy. Although the fluid itself is harmless, it may cause discomfort and it muffles sound from the outside world so that the child does not hear distinctly.

YOUR QUESTIONS

Q My little girl has glue ear and the doctor says she needs an operation. Will she need to stay in hospital to recover after this and if so, for how long?

A The operation to drain fluid from the ear and to insert grommets is a simple one, usually carried out under general anaesthetic. There are rarely complications and your child will probably be sent home the next day.

Q My two-year-old son has glue ear which the doctor believes is due to enlarged adenoids. Does this mean that my child will have to have his adenoids taken out?

A Not necessarily. The doctor may prescribe antihistamines or other drugs to reduce the swelling, depending on whether an allergy or infection has caused the swelling. Only after other methods have failed will the adenoids be removed. The operation is a fairly simple one and often involves the tonsils also being removed.

SYMPTOMS

The child may complain of earache, and there may be a feeling of fullness in the ear and a sensation of clicking on swallowing or moving the jaw. Often, though, there is no pain with glue ear and the first signs are usually backwardness in speech. You may notice that your child is not repeating sounds correctly or that he turns one ear towards a sound in order to hear clearly. You can test your child by asking him to repeat certain sounds or words. If he cannot repeat them accurately, something is wrong and the problem needs to be diagnosed by a doctor. Hearing difficulties are common in young children but it is

A child who has earache, or who seems to have imperfect hearing, should be taken to the doctor for a check-up.

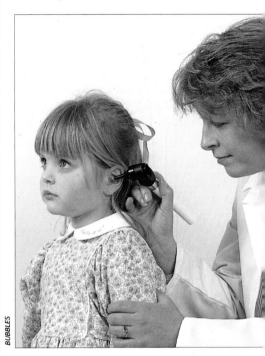

BUBBLES

very important that they are treated promptly or learning and speech development could suffer, particularly when the child begins school.

TREATMENT

Take your child to the doctor, who will look into the ear to see if fluid is there. He can also test the child's hearing. For a first attack, the doctor may prescribe antibiotics, decongestants and nose drops or antihistamines. These are not guaranteed to work and if the problem recurs or becomes chronic, a simple operation may be needed to drain away the fluid via a hole made in the eardrum.

A grommet — a tiny plastic tube — is inserted in the hole to keep the channel open. Later the grommets may be taken out by the doctor, or the grommets may fall out on their own, leaving the small hole in the drum to heal up. Hearing should then return to normal.

Once the grommets are in place, no specific precautions are necessary. Although swimming is allowed, diving is not recommended since water might enter the middle ear.

■ GRAND MAL
see EPILEPSY

■ GRAZES
see also BANDAGES, DRESSINGS, FIRST AID

Children regularly graze themselves in falls and minor accidents and although grazes can be painful they are hardly ever serious. A graze usually results from a sliding fall which damages the superficial layers of the skin, leaving a very tender raw area. This may bleed and ooze pus.

Because millions of tiny nerve endings are exposed in a graze, young children find the intense stinging pain quite distressing and so deserve sympathy plus a little fuss over treating the wound.

T R E A T M E N T

Most grazes are covered with dirt and grit and the first thing to do is to clean the wound. Soap and warm water are as good as anything but you can use a mild antiseptic instead. As it is impossible to get rid of all the germs, avoid rubbing the graze too harshly and making it even more raw.

Ideally, the graze should be left exposed to the air; within a few hours a tough scab forms over it, acting as a natural protective dressing. In practice it may be better, where young

YOUR QUESTIONS

Q I know many wounds leave scars, but what about grazes?

A You can only get a scar from a cut that goes through all the layers of the skin. A graze or abrasion only affects the outer layer of the skin, the epidermis, which is largely made up of dead cells. When the epidermis is damaged in a graze, cells move up from the dermis to replace the damaged ones, so no scarring occurs.

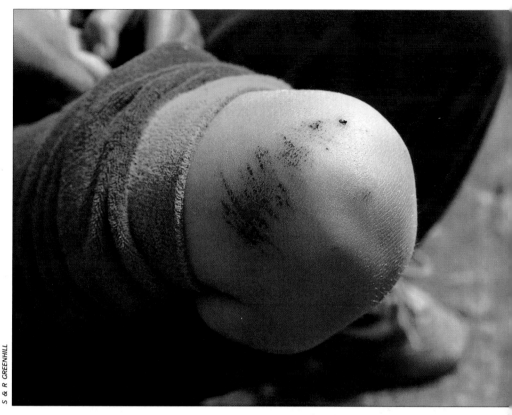

S & R GREENHILL

A graze is a wound on the surface layer of the skin, which usually heals without any problem.

children are concerned, to cover the graze with a dressing to prevent it from rubbing on clothing or becoming dirty. Also, children tend to pick at unprotected scabs and so delay the healing process.

For a large graze, cover with a dry gauze strip and hold it in place with surgical tape. Never apply any adhesive dressing directly on to a graze as it can be extremely painful to remove. Change the dressing daily and leave the graze uncovered at night to allow the scab to dry hard.

Although grazes rarely cause problems, some do become infected. If there is redness beyond the area of a graze which seems to be slow in healing, or if it is oozing moisture or pus after a couple of days, take the child to the family doctor.

■ GROWTH

Growth is an amazing process which is characterized by rapid development of the body in the first few years of life, after which the rate of growth slows down before a sudden spurt towards maturity in adolescence. Although every child follows this basic pattern of growth, there are wide variations in what is termed 'normal growth'; children, like adults, come in all shapes and sizes, very few of them abnormal.

The most important factor for growth is adequate nutrition. Very occasionally hormone deficiencies or genetic defects can cause growth problems, but these are rare and will almost certainly come to light early on in your child's life as your doctor monitors his height and weight. Nowadays, even these unusual growth problems can be successfully treated, so that a child grows in the normal way.

BABIES' GROWTH

When your baby is born, the first thing you are told after his sex is his weight. This varies hugely, from 2.78kg (6¼lb) to 3.82kg (8½lb) for boys, and from 2.54kg (5¾lb) to 3.64kg (8lb) for girls.

Whatever his birthweight, you can expect your baby to lose a little weight within the first five days of

Babies and toddlers are usually weighed and measured during visits to child health or 'well baby' clinics. This baby is being extremely helpful and co-operative!

birth. He will regain it within about ten days and then gain weight steadily. Your baby's weight will be monitored at your regular visits to the clinic, and you will be able to see this pattern for yourself.

There are a few exceptions to this pattern, such as premature babies or babies who have been ill in the early weeks of life. These frequently have a 'catch-up' spurt of growth.

Growth is rapid in the first six months (approximately 20g (0.7oz) a day) and then slows down towards the end of the first year (when it is

approximately 15g (0.5oz) a day). In general a baby of average weight will increase its length by a quarter during the first six months, and double its weight.

It is sensible not to be too anxious about your baby's weight. If, overall, he is growing steadily, and is happy and thriving, then he is perfectly normal; what matters is the overall regularity of his weight gain, not the amount gained at each weighing. Parents who keep a record of their baby's growth will see how quickly a baby tends to get over minor setbacks.

TODDLERS

Once he has passed his first birthday, your baby's weight gain begins to slow down. The average child gains

about 2.5kg (5½lb) in weight and 12cm (4¾in) in height during the second year. At this stage he needs to be weighed and measured about every three months to check his progress. Although he may still seem ill-proportioned and baby-like in appearance, this soon changes when he begins to walk and develops the sturdy little body of a toddler.

Between his third and fifth years your child's growth rate will slow down even more (to 2kg (4lb 6oz) and 7cm (2¾in), on average, per year); his body will lose much of its stockiness and he will become more elongated. He may even look quite thin but this is normal and nothing to worry about. At this stage of his growth he needs to be measured and weighed roughly every six months.

CHILDHOOD GROWTH

From the age of four or five, your child continues to grow at a fairly steady rate until the growth spurt of adolescence; on average this will be 10cm (4in) for boys and 8cm (3⅛in) for girls.

Children need to be measured and weighed about once a year throughout their childhood. Doctors have established a range of normal heights for different age groups and they will

YOUR QUESTIONS

Q My daughter was born last spring and has been a thriving baby with weight gains as expected. Now that it is getting colder and autumn is setting in, I've noticed that her growth rate has slowed down a little. Could this be the first signs of an illness or some kind of setback?

A As long as your baby is feeding normally and is happy and contented there is nothing to worry about. In fact, growth rate is at its slowest in autumn and at its fastest in spring; over the year these seasonal fluctuations even out.

Q My sister has just adopted a six-month-old baby but he seems to be very small for his age and is gaining weight at a very slow rate. Could he be subnormal?

A It is most unlikely. However, some babies who have been separated from their mothers soon after birth, for whatever reason, can be deprived of the love and attention that is so necessary for normal development. This can happen to babies who spend the first few months of life in institutions where they are physically well-cared for but cannot be given a great deal of individual attention. As a result, many such babies are slow in growing. Your sister's baby will certainly benefit from lots of love, cuddling and devotion to make up for his earlier deprivations.

use these 'percentile' charts — which are based on surveys of a very wide range of children — to determine whether your child is within the normal range for his age. The majority of children are, but with the few who are outside the limits, the doctor will look for an obvious cause, such as bad nutrition, or simply that the child has very tall or very short parents. In rare cases, the child may have a growth deficiency and this will be diagnosed and treated.

ADOLESCENT GROWTH SPURT

There is tremendous variation in the ages at which the adolescent growth spurt starts and this can cause anxiety in parents (and children) who see classmates and friends of a similar age developing into adulthood while their own child seems to lag behind. In fact, the growth spurt may be anywhere between the ages of 9½ and 13½ for girls and between 10½ and 16 for boys. Between the ages of about 11 and 15 a child's muscle growth rate almost trebles.

The adolescent growth spurt actually starts before the other changes associated with puberty in both sexes. This is particularly so in girls who may grow up to very near their full height without much change in the shape of their breasts and hips. The degree of sexual development

Q My son was a large baby weighing over 4kg (9lbs) at birth and I am now worried that he may be abnormally large, partly because few of the baby clothes I buy for him now, aged three months, actually fit him. Is it likely that there is something wrong with him — he seems quite well?

A It is highly unlikely. What you must remember is that baby clothes are made for the 'average' baby, so that a stretch suit suitable for 'birth to three months' will fit a 3–5.5kg (7–12lb) baby with length to match. If your baby has been gaining weight normally, he probably weighs about 6.25kg (14lbs) at three months, so the average size is obviously too small for him. When you shop, allow for this difference. There is absolutely nothing wrong with your baby, who is following *his* normal growth pattern, not some theoretical average.

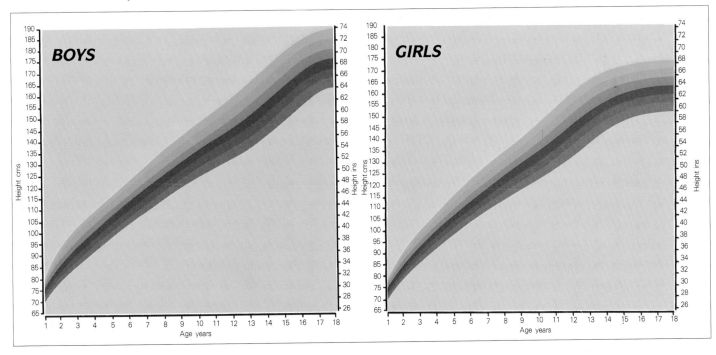

Percentile charts based on surveys of children aged from 1 – 18 are used by doctors to assess a child's growth.

BUBBLES

Children grow at different rates, but they all enjoy being measured to see how much they have grown.

varies greatly from individual to individual and the single factor that seems to have most influence is the age at which puberty occurred in the parents. If both parents had a late puberty, then the children can also be expected to be late.

BONE GROWTH

Growth in height takes place through an increase in the size of the bones of the arms, legs and back. Bones grow through new bone being added along their width and at both ends. By studying X-rays of their bones doctors can arrive at children's 'bone age'. This may differ from a child's real age by a couple of years, which is not unusual. Bone age is a useful way of detecting any growth abnormali-

ties early in a child's life when there is still time for treatment.

THE ROLE OF HORMONES

Growth is controlled by a number of hormones, of which the most important is growth hormone, produced by the hypophysis, a gland attached to the brain. A very few children do lack this hormone, which can be replaced if its lack is detected early in the child's life. Thyroid hormone is also essential for normal growth and if this is lacking, growth will fall away from the average but this too can be rectified with hormone therapy. At puberty the sex hormones are responsible for the bodily changes that take place in boys and girls.

GROWTH PROBLEMS

If a child's growth rate does not seem normal, particularly in the early years, you should take him to the

doctor who will first of all enquire about the diet. In special cases he or she will probably measure the child's bone age. If it lags more than two years behind the real age, the doctor may recommend that the child be taken to a 'growth clinic' for investigation. If growth hormone deficiency is detected, growth hormone injections will be given to restart normal growth, but they may not be able to make up for the height already lost. This is why it is important to get advice from the doctor early.

A very small number of girls are born with a faulty gene which results in a condition called Turner's syndrome. This affects only one in 3000 girls who remain small and who require sex hormone replacement in tablet form in order to acquire normal female characteristics.

Occasionally, poor growth starts in the womb. This can happen when the mother is in bad health, has a disease when pregnant or is undernourished. Smoking can also cause poor development. Although children suffering from this will be born small and remain shorter than would be ex-

YOUR QUESTIONS

Q My baby was born prematurely and although she is gaining weight quite steadily, she is still very small. Will she always be behind other children in terms of growth, and does this mean that she will be a late developer in other ways?

A On the whole, premature babies do remain slightly smaller than average throughout their growth period but this is not abnormal in any way. Your baby may seem small for a long time but may have a spurt of 'catch-up growth' after her slow start. Your baby's overall mental and physical development will in no way be affected by her premature birth.

pected from their parents' height, they grow up quite healthy and there is no need to worry about their overall development.

■ GUMS
see TEETH

■ HAEMOPHILIA

Haemophilia is a hereditary disease in which the blood fails to clot properly. As a result the flow of blood from even a minor wound or bruise cannot be stopped without medical attention. It affects boys almost exclusively and can be a mild or severe disorder. In its mild form the child bleeds for longer than normal after a slight injury but otherwise has no symptoms. In its most severe form,

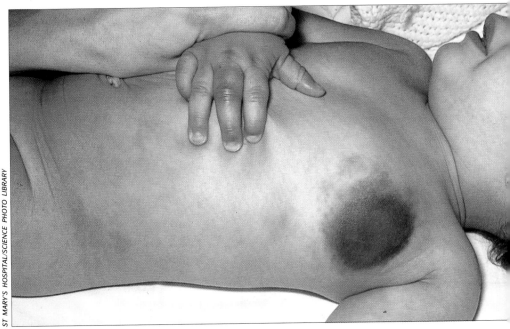

ST MARY'S HOSPITAL/SCIENCE PHOTO LIBRARY

This bruising shows the effects of haemophilia, which prevents the blood from clotting properly.

even a minor bruise can result in profuse bleeding which can only be stopped by immediate treatment in hospital. Like many inherited diseases, haemophilia cannot be cured but with care and the right treatment, many haemophiliacs can lead normal, active lives.

CAUSES

The disease is due to an abnormal gene. As a result of this abnormality, the body fails to make the blood-clotting agent, Factor 8. Haemophilia is always passed directly from mother to sons but daughters, who do not develop the disease, may become carriers, capable of passing it on to their sons. A haemophiliac father cannot pass the abnormal gene to his sons but he can transmit it to his daughters who become carriers, able to pass on the disease.

SYMPTOMS

Mild haemophilia is often discovered after a child has had a tooth extracted, when the dentist finds it difficult to stop the bleeding. Profuse or prolonged bleeding from a minor wound is also a symptom, as is heavy bruising, pain and swelling after even a light knock. In severe cases, stiff and painful joints and muscles can be caused by internal bleeding.

Haemophilia is diagnosed for certain when a measurement of the amount of Factor 8 in the child's blood is taken. In some cases, it may be only mildly lowered but in others there may be no Factor 8 at all and this is when haemophilia becomes a serious disease. Trivial injuries can cause massive bleeding which requires immediate medical attention.

PREVENTING HAEMOPHILIA

Most haemophiliac families are aware of the disease and boys of such families should be tested for the presence of the disease soon after birth; there is a 50 per cent chance that they will be normal.

Women who are carriers of haemophilia are strongly advised to consult their doctor or a genetic counsellor before choosing to have children. However, once they are pregnant a test can be carried out which can determine the sex of the baby and, if it is a boy, the level of Factor 8 in his blood.

TREATMENT

When a haemophiliac boy is injured, he needs medical attention immediately in the form of an injection

---

YOUR QUESTIONS

Q Our baby son has just been diagnosed haemophiliac. Not only has this come as a great shock to us, since my wife was not aware that she was a carrier, but we are desperately worried about how we can care for the boy and his special needs.

A Your doctor will be able to give basic advice on how best to protect your son against injury and put you in contact with any local organization dealing with haemophilia. They will be able to give you practical advice on how to look after your child and on the best type of school for him; and they can also put you in touch with parents of other haemophiliacs.

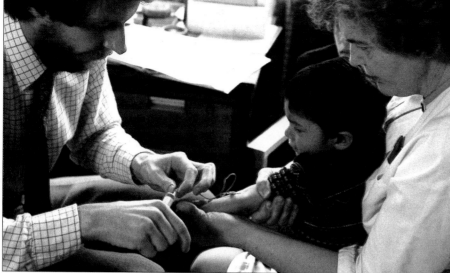

You can protect your child by taking some simple precautions. He should sleep on a low bed, avoid playing with hazardous toys and be careful when he helps in the kitchen where there are sharp utensils about.

A haemophiliac boy may have some difficulty in leading a completely normal life but there is no reason why he cannot be relatively active. Obviously he should avoid sports in which he might be injured but he can enjoy swimming, running and walking.

A haemophiliac child should wear a disc stating that he has the disease and indicating what should be done in the event of injury or emergency in case he has an accident when alone.

of Factor 8 (which is artificially produced or biosynthesized); the amount he is given depends on whether he has mild or severe haemophilia. Parents are often taught how to administer the Factor 8 injection at home for bruising and swelling.

In some cases though, the boy may need to be taken to hospital where blood transfusions will be given.

Haemophilia is usually suspected while the child is young and bruises too easily – and it is confirmed by a blood test.

PROTECTING THE CHILD

Parents of a haemophiliac boy need to be vigilant. Should the child suffer an injury, first-aid techniques must be quickly applied; firm pressure

Haemophilia need not prevent children from leading active lives if they are careful.

must be applied to the wound to reduce the flow of blood and the affected limb or part should be kept raised until medical help arrives.

YOUR QUESTIONS

Q My wife is a carrier of haemophilia and although we want to have a family, relatives and friends say that this would be unwise, since all our children would be affected by the disease. Is this so?

A Not necessarily. Each child born to you and your wife will have a 50 per cent chance of being normal.

One factor which should influence your decision about having children is the amount of Factor 8 any child is likely to have; this can be determined in a test during the 18th week of pregnancy, taking blood from the foetal circulation with a fine needle inserted through the abdominal wall, under X-ray. Haemophiliacs with a relatively high level of Factor 8 can lead virtually normal lives; those with almost no Factor 8 need to be extremely careful and may find their lives severely restricted. Talk to your doctor about the problem; he or she will almost certainly advise you to have genetic counselling before you make a decision about children.

■ HAIR LOSS
see also RINGWORM

Hair loss, medically known as alopecia, can sometimes affect children, but the hair often grows back to normal strength and thickness after a period of time.

SYMPTOMS

There are two kinds of alopecia, known as traction alopecia and alopecia areata. Traction alopecia is the less serious form, and the symptoms are usually a general thinning of the child's hair.

Usually with alopecia areata, a few small bald areas, two to three centimetres across, appear on the scalp, but occasionally all the hair is lost (known as alopecia totalis).

In some cases this may happen very suddenly, with tufts of hair being shed all in one go. Sometimes the hair grows again spontaneously between a month or two and a year later, but in some cases there is no regrowth at all.

Other parts of the body can be affected by alopecia areata, but this is unlikely to show, since children have such fine body hair.

If the hair loss is caused by ringworm, the bald patches will be red and itchy.

CAUSES

Traction alopecia is caused by the hair being pulled. This may be because it is scraped back into a tight pony-tail or plaits, or because the child herself sits and pulls at it, usually without realizing it.

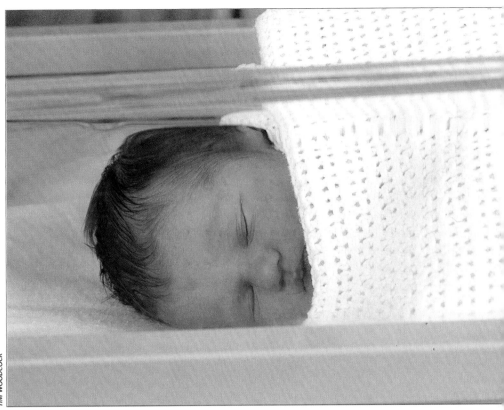

TIM WOODCOCK

HAIR LOSS IN BABIES

Babies who are born with hair often lose it soon after birth, and it may be some months before their new hair grows. Equally, babies may have bald areas where their heads rest against the pillow, as the slightest rubbing can affect the growth of their very fine hair.

YOUR QUESTIONS

Q Can frequent hair washing be the cause of hair loss in a child?

A No. Wash your child's hair as often as necessary. Hair which is oily attracts dirt more quickly and needs to be washed more often than dry hair — perhaps two or three times a week. It is better to use a mild shampoo for frequent washing.

The cause of **alopecia areata** is not known. Sometimes the condition arises if the child has suffered from a shock, and it also appears to be slightly more common in children who suffer from diabetes and pernicious anaemia.

POOR HEALTH

Protein and vitamin deficiencies and general ill health can also cause thinning hair. Illness such as flu can temporarily slow down hair growth and make the hair look lifeless and

This three-day old baby will probably lose her fine head of hair and be left bald for several months.

thin. In this case the hair gradually returns to normal as the child's health improves.

Disorders of the hormone glands can also cause a thinning of the hair, as can radiotherapy and some drugs used for cancer treatment.

TREATMENT

In the case of hair loss caused by the hair being stretched, or by illness or poor diet, the hair will grow normally again once the child stops pulling her hair or having it pulled back too tightly in plaits or pony-tail, or when the health or diet is improved.

If the hair remains thin for some time, and the cause is not apparent, it is a good idea to consult your doctor in case the condition is being caused by an illness that has not been diagnosed.

ALOPECIA AREATA

There is no very satisfactory treatment for alopecia areata. Sometimes it clears up of its own accord, as

A pony-tail may be fashionable, and it keeps long hair off the face for school and sports, but scraping a child's hair back too tightly can cause it to become weak and thin.

BUBBLES

much as a year after it first occurred, but in some cases the hair never regrows in the bald areas. The fewer the bald areas, the more likely it is that a spontaneous cure will occur.

It is important to give moral support to a child who has noticeable bald patches. Explain the situation to her class teacher in the hope that he or she will be able to discourage teasing, and help the child to take a pride in her appearance.

■ HALITOSIS

see also TEETH

Better known as bad breath, halitosis is quite rare in children. When it does occur it is usually a symptom of

CAMILLA JESSEL

poor dental hygiene, or of a minor health problem such as a stomach upset or throat infection.

CAUSES

The most common cause of halitosis is gum disease or tooth decay, when the bacteria in the mouth cause the breath to smell unpleasant. Food allergy is another possible cause.

DIGESTIVE TRACT

The workings of the digestive tract can also cause the breath to smell. Even when the system is working properly, onions, garlic and spices can cause the breath to smell as they are being digested, although not everyone objects to this.

Children with infections of the digestive tract such as gastric flu usually have bad breath. The breath can also smell quite foul for several hours after a child (or adult) has been sick for any reason. Tonsilitis, although not an infection of the digestive tract itself, can also cause the breath to smell unpleasant.

RESPIRATORY TRACT

Diseases of the respiratory tract can also cause bad breath. There is often temporary bad breath if the child has

heavy nasal catarrh or sinusitis (inflamed sinuses). More serious (and rare) illnesses affecting the bronchi or lungs, particularly if there is pus present, will also cause the breath to smell unpleasant.

In the very rare cases where a child has uncontrolled diabetes or kidney failure, one of the symptoms will be a distinctive smell (different in each case) on the breath.

SYMPTOMS

Bad breath is a symptom in itself. In most cases it will accompany other symptoms, but when it is caused by dental problems it may be the only indication that there is something wrong and it will not necessarily always be accompanied by toothache or painful gums.

PREVENTION

Decayed teeth and gum disease are the main cause of bad breath, and

Gum disease and decaying teeth cause bad breath and can be prevented by dental hygiene. The teeth should be brushed up and down, not from side to side, with the brush massaging the gums as well.

can be prevented. If the child cleans his teeth correctly and makes regular visits to the dentist, it is unlikely that

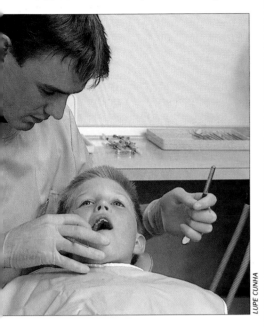

Regular visits to the dentist will help to keep teeth and gums healthy.

decay or gum disease will develop, and bad breath from this cause will be avoided.

TREATMENT

If there are no other symptoms, it will be wise to take your child to the dentist to see if poor teeth or gums are at fault. If dental hygiene has been neglected, it may be necessary to have decayed teeth treated or even extracted.

DENTAL TREATMENT

The dentist will probably scrape away hardened plaque which has formed in pockets between the teeth and gums and which sets up inflammation in the gums. Cutting and stitching of the gums may even be necessary if dental hygiene has been really neglected, so it is vital to make sure that your child looks after his teeth and gums to avoid the necessity for such drastic treatment.

Your dentist will show your child how to take proper care of his teeth and gums. Make sure that your child follows the advice on cleaning his teeth, and goes back afterwards

YOUR QUESTIONS

Q What has cleaning the teeth got to do with the occurrence of bad breath?

A If the teeth are not cleaned thoroughly a substance called plaque can build up on them and cause tooth decay. It also hardens into a tough material known as calculus which forms in pockets between the teeth and gums. This causes the gums to be inflamed and sometimes to produce foul-smelling pus.

At the same time debris from food that has not been cleaned away lingers on the teeth and is broken down by bacteria. The bacterial activity in the mouth in these conditions causes the unpleasant symptom of bad breath, and of course the child runs the risk of developing tooth decay as well.

for regular check-ups, ideally at three- to six-monthly intervals.

INFECTIONS AND DISEASES

Any other form of bad breath will usually be accompanied by other symptoms. Chest and sinus infections and any gastric complaints other than mild flu or colds should be seen by a doctor, who may prescribe antibiotics or other treatment.

Mouth washes, plenty of fluids to drink, and frequent cleaning of the teeth will help to make the breath fresh and will make the child feel better until the illness is over.

■ HARE LIP

see CLEFT PALATE

■ HAY FEVER

see also ALLERGIES

Hay fever is caused by an allergy to one or more of various substances in the air

The pollen shed by catkins can cause severe hay fever symptoms in susceptible people.

when inhaled. The most common allergen (substance causing an allergic reaction) is pollen.

SYMPTOMS

A child with hay fever sneezes a great deal, often particularly in the morning. Her eyes feel itchy and are watery, the head feels heavy as the nose and sinuses become blocked, and the throat may be sore too.

CAUSES

The nose, sinuses, eyes and upper throat react in hay fever because these are the parts that are most exposed to the air-borne allergen. The most common allergen is pollen from grass or trees, but the same symptoms can be caused by fungus spores, animal hair

WATCHPOINTS

Do not be tempted to treat a child who has hay fever with decongestant nose drops. These are intended only for short-term use, when the runny or blocked nose is caused by an infection. Prolonged use can cause further inflammation of the mucous lining of the child's nose and sinuses and make the problem worse.

DAVID SUTHERLAND/TSW

A holiday by the seaside is best for hay fever sufferers and is fun for everyone in the family.

and scurf, and house mites; and such attacks are still loosely referred to as hay fever.

SEASONAL HAY FEVER

Hay fever caused by pollen is seasonal and occurs only when the particular type of pollen responsible is in the air. The first pollens to appear each year are tree pollens. Plane trees and silver birches in particular are often responsible for cases of hay fever occurring in mid-March.

In mid-summer, grass pollens are released into the air, followed by nettle pollen, and from mid-summer until late autumn, fungus spores are abundant in the air. House mites and animal fur can cause trouble at any time of the year. A child can be allergic to more than one of these substances, so that hay fever can continue through the seasons.

REACTION TO POLLEN

Hay fever develops because of an error in the body's immune system. Normally it can tell the difference between a harmless substance like pollen and a dangerous virus or bacterium. But in an allergic person the immune system treats pollens and other allergens as if they were dangerous, and the white blood cells, whose function is to fight infection, start to form an antibody to neutralize the invader.

The antibody attaches itself to cells called mast cells, which contain, among other chemicals, histamine. In

YOUR QUESTIONS

Q My little daughter suffers badly from hay fever. Will she grow out of it?

A It is difficult to say. Children often do grow out of their allergies, but these sometimes return later in life.

Q My son has severe hay fever. Is there anything I can do to prevent an attack when he has to take an important school entry exam later this summer?

A Talk about this to your doctor, who may think that for an important event such as this your son should have a steroid injection to hold off an attack.

trying to neutralize the allergen, the antibody upsets the structure of the mast cells, and they release histamine. This release of histamine and other chemicals from the mast cells causes the blood vessels to dilate (increase in diameter) and this makes the mucous cells in the nose and sinuses become over-active.

Children whose bodies manufacture a great deal of antibody in response to allergens tend to develop asthma and eczema, rather than simple hay fever.

TREATMENT

By far the best treatment for hay fever is prevention — making sure that the child is not subjected to the allergen that brings on the symptoms. This means that if a family pet causes hay fever, the family pet will unfortunately have to find a new home. House mites can be kept under control by means of frequent vacuum cleaning and by using synthetic materials, as opposed to feathers and down, in the bedding.

Unfortunately there is no foolproof way of making sure that the child is not exposed to dust containing pollens or spores. Keeping away from trees and grass as much as possible helps — a day out at the seaside being preferable to a day in the country during the pollen season.

MEDICAL TREATMENT

Antihistamines are often prescribed to stop the allergic reaction of hay fever, but these can tend to cause drowsiness. Your doctor may prescribe a succession of types until a suitable one is found. Steroid injections can bring dramatic relief, but they are prescribed only if the condition is really incapacitating, since they usually have undesirable side-effects and are considered to be unsuitable for long-term use.

A low-dose steroid preparation may be prescribed to be puffed into the nose three times a day, or a solution of sodium cromoglycate may be prescribed to prevent the mast cells from releasing histamine. Both of these treatments have to be administered every day throughout the hay fever season to stop the symptoms developing, and have no effect once symptoms have occurred.

DESENSITIZATION

The doctor of a child who suffers badly from hay fever may decide to do a patch test in preparation for desensitization treatment. In this test, small patches of skin are exposed to the various possible allergens to see which allergen causes a reaction.

Following the result of this test, the child will receive a course of injections of minute quantities of the allergen in the hope that the immune system will learn to react normally to it. This treatment is always carried out by a specialist, as there is a danger that the child will have a severe reaction. The specialist will make a careful observation of the child for about two hours after each injection to make sure that no allergic reaction occurs.

■ HEAD BANGING

Some children go through a stage of head banging, and it usually passes as they grow older.

S Y M P T O M S

In head banging the child habitually makes a voluntary jerking movement of the head, usually banging against a chosen object. It is common in toddlers, who usually bang their heads against the side of their cots or on the wall by their beds.

C A U S E S

The likely causes of head banging seem to be frustration, anxiety, or desire for attention.

T R E A T M E N T

Small children get frustrated because their skills lag so much behind their perceptions and it is maddening for them to have so little control over the objects in their world. You can help

LUPE CUNHA

If her cot is well padded the baby will come to no harm should she go through a head banging phase.

YOUR QUESTIONS

Q Is head banging the same as a nervous tic?

A Head banging, nervous tics in the form of jerking the head or facial twitching, and mannerisms such as clearing the throat are all alike, in that there is no medical reason for them but they can indicate that the child is nervous or distressed in some way. These habits usually fade away as the child is helped to realize that there is no cause for anxiety and learns to enjoy independence.

Perhaps because it is a more conscious action than the other habits and mannerisms, head banging is usually only a short-lived phase although it is a worrying one.

by playing constructively with your child, encouraging her to manipulate objects and to feel a sense of achievement in what she can do. Make sure that she has toys to play with in her cot or bed, so that when she wakes up in the morning she has something to do.

There may be a reason for the child to suffer from anxiety or to demand attention. Perhaps she is finding it difficult to adjust to the arrival of a new brother or sister, to going to play-school or school, or to moving home. It may be that she is unsettled by disruption between you and your partner. It is important to give time to the child alone and to help her to feel relaxed and secure.

Usually there is no need for medical treatment, but you may find it helpful to talk to your health visitor or doctor. Do not pay too much attention to the head banging episodes, but try to make sure that the child cannot injure herself.

■ HEAD INJURIES

see also **BANDAGES, CONCUSSION, DRESSINGS, FALLS, FRACTURES**

The brain is the most important organ in our bodies, since it controls everything we do. This is why it is vital to protect a child's head from injury as much as possible and to seek medical help at once in the event of an accident in which the head is hurt.

TYPES OF INJURY

There are two ways in which the head can be injured, and these are known as deceleration and acceleration. In deceleration the head is moving and is suddenly brought to rest — as when a child falls and hits his head on the pavement or when he is flung against the windscreen in a car accident. In acceleration the head is still, and receives a violent blow — as when a child is hit by a moving swing or by a flying cricket ball.

In either type of accident, if the blow is violent, the soft tissue of the brain can be severely shaken inside

the skull. This may cause unconsciousness, and this is what is known as **concussion** (see separate entry).

CRITICAL FACTOR

The critical factor is whether damage has been done to the blood vessels. Bleeding in the brain rapidly causes pressure to build up, since the brain is encased within the inflexible shell of the skull and has no room to expand. Serious damage to the brain is caused if the bleeding does not stop or if the pressure is not quickly relieved.

SKULL INJURIES

It is also possible for the skull to be fractured as a result of a head injury (see **Fractures**).

MINOR INJURIES

Of course it is not always the case that a head injury results in serious damage to the brain or skull. In many cases there will just be cuts and bruises or a short episode of concussion with no lasting effects. Cuts and grazes on the scalp look worse than they are, because they bleed a lot, but they usually heal quickly. However, any injury to the head should be treated as potentially serious.

SYMPTOMS AND DIAGNOSIS

If the child is bruised and bleeding after a blow to the head, but has no other symptoms, it is unlikely that any serious damage has been done. But even so it is important to keep a close watch on the child over the next

Keep a watch over a child after any blow to the head, in case the injury has serious consequences.

24 hours to make sure there is no dizziness, loss of memory or blurred speech. Medical attention should be sought at once if any of these symptoms begins to develop.

Following a blow to the head, perhaps if the child falls heavily and the head hits something hard, the child may experience **concussion.** When concussion occurs, the child may be briefly unconscious, may feel dizzy and perhaps have a headache on recovering, and sometimes has no

WATCHPOINTS

• Always take your child to see a doctor after a head injury which made him unconscious for more than five seconds, even if there seem to be no after-effects.

• Be on the look-out for signs of brain injury after a child's head has been knocked —signs to watch for are headaches, dizziness, forgetfulness, confused speech, unsteady walk or further periods of unconsciousness. These may even occur several days after the accident.

• Always call an ambulance for a head injury when in doubt.

recollection of the events leading up to the accident or immediately after the accident. If the child has these symptoms he should be seen by the family doctor or taken to hospital straight away.

A **fracture of the skull** is not always as serious as it sounds. Strictly speaking all the bones of the face are part of the skull. Injuries here will usually be obvious. But if the base or lower part of the skull is fractured the only symptoms apart from dizziness, perhaps with a brief spell of unconsciousness, may be a straw-coloured liquid trickling from the nose or blood or discharge from the ear. As long as there is no bleeding in the brain a full recovery is most likely. But naturally it is essential to call an ambulance at once for suspected skull injuries.

BLEEDING IN THE BRAIN

If your child is knocked unconscious and does not regain consciousness an ambulance should always be called. A symptom of bleeding within the brain in these circumstances is one or both pupils being dilated (enlarged) and failing to constrict (get smaller) when a bright light is shone into the eye.

Another symptom of bleeding in the brain is the big toe pointing upwards if a blunt object is rubbed along the sole of the foot (normally this would make it turn down). Permanent brain damage can be the

Children's head injuries are often the result of playground accidents. Some children's playgrounds now have a special surface for safety.

Q One of my children's friends fell out of a tree recently and fractured his skull. His doctor said that he didn't need any treatment, Is this right?

A Yes. The fracture of the skull usually gets better by itself. To judge the seriousness of such an injury, the doctor will find out the length of time the child was unconscious and how quickly he recovered.

If the child is up and running around now, clearly the right decision was made.

Q Why do injuries on the top of a child's head bleed so much?

A There are two reasons why any injury to the head or face will bleed profusely. First, this part of the body has a very rich blood supply from vessels which tend not to constrict, and secondly, skin over the face and scalp forms an attachment for muscle. This is the reason why cuts on the face or scalp may gape open and why the wounds often need to be stitched.

result if the child is not given immediate hospital treatment.

Finally there may be an injury known as an **epidural haematoma** in which an artery within the skull is damaged, causing bleeding between the skull and the outer membrane of the brain and damage to the brain. The symptoms of this are a child relapsing into unconsciousness. This injury is usually caused by a blow to the temple, and needs immediate medical treatment.

TREATMENT

Usually the only treatment needed for **concussion** is rest, but the child will probably be kept in hospital for observation for at least 24 hours after the accident.

Fractures of the bones of the face are repaired as are many other complicated fractures, by being wired together for support until they have healed. Nursing care will be given in hospital while the child is recovering unless the injury was a minor one (perhaps to the nose). The cranium heals itself, and once it has been established that there is no damage to the brain, the child will be kept under observation in hospital for a while as the healing takes place.

Bleeding in the brain usually stops by itself. If there is **bleeding** between the skull and the brain a surgeon will try to stop the bleeding and relieve pressure in the brain to avert serious brain damage. Sometimes a small hole can be drilled in the skull to relieve pressure. The child may be put into intensive care to make sure the essential bodily functions continue while attempts are made to stop the bleeding, or while the body is trying to heal itself if nothing can be done surgically. There may be a long period of unconsciousness, but recovery is still possible.

Minor injuries should be cleaned and dressed (*see* **Bandages, Dressings**) and will soon heal. Stitches may be needed for large cuts.

■ HEAD LICE

see LICE

■ HEADACHES

see also OTITIS MEDIA

Headaches occur less frequently in children than in adults, but they are far from rare.

SYMPTOMS

An older child will be able to let you know that her head is aching, but a younger child may have difficulty in describing it, and it is even more difficult to identify the condition when it occurs in a baby.

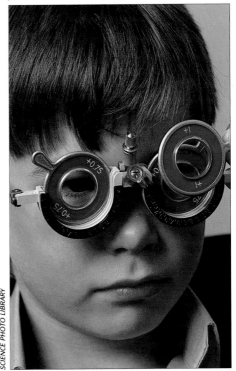

An eye test will confirm whether glasses are needed for eye strain.

The headache can be located in different parts of the head, giving an indication of the possible cause. If the child is able to tell you what sort of pain it is and where it is located this will help to establish what the cause of the headache is.

CAUSES

The most likely causes are eye strain, a virus infection, tiredness and lack of fresh air, infected sinuses, or (even in children) simple tension.

Less likely causes are meningitis (a potentially fatal inflammation of the membranes covering the brain), encephalitis (inflammation of the brain), brain tumour, or injury to the brain resulting from a blow to the head.

LIFE-THREATENING CAUSES

Headaches caused by meningitis or encephalitis are severe, and the child will also have a painfully stiff neck and high fever, often with inability to tolerate bright light. The child may also seem drowsy.

Headaches caused by pressure from a brain tumour are often accompanied by vomiting, becoming more severe as time goes by. There will usually be other symptoms, such as stumbling or confused speech.

A head injury could be the cause if the child has had a fall or any kind of blow to the head.

If you believe that your child's headache may have a serious cause, call your doctor without delay.

OTHER CAUSES

A headache caused by **eye strain** will be behind one or both eyes, or just above the eyes. Such a headache will probably occur after the child has been reading or doing close work.

If the cause is a **viral infection** there is likely also to be a raised temperature. This could be one of the first signs of mumps or chickenpox or part of the feverishness of influenza.

Circumstances should indicate when the cause is **tiredness**.

If the headache is caused by a **sinus infection**, the child's nose may well be blocked, and there may be a thick, yellowish discharge when she blows her nose, but this is not always the case. Sinus headaches are felt at the front of the face, and the area round the nose and under the eyes is tender to the touch. The headache feels worse if the child moves her head — especially if she bends over.

Tension headaches are not usually very severe, but they can recur in a child who easily gets 'keyed up'. It will often be clear to the parents that

Family walks in the fresh air keep everyone relaxed and free from headache-causing tension.

the child has become over-excited or over-anxious. Some tense children suffer from migraine headaches, which are usually preceded by nausea and are often located in one side of the head only.

Finally, **ear infections**, quite common in young children, can cause severe pain within the ear, and this may feel like a headache.

TREATMENT

The treatment for a headache will depend on whether it is part of another illness. You should call your doctor if the headache is accompanied by symptoms of any of the serious illnesses described above, or if the child's temperature is over 38°C (101°F). It is advisable for the child to see a doctor if the headache lasts for more than 12 hours; she should also be taken to the doctor if she has frequent headaches so that the cause can be investigated.

The headaches caused by **eye strain** will cease once the condition has been diagnosed and the correct spectacles have been prescribed. Make sure that your child wears her glasses as advised by the optician.

Paracetamol can be given to reduce fever accompanying an **infection**, and this should also control the child's headache.

If you think your child is **tired**, give her a light meal and let her play in the fresh air for a while before going to bed early. This is much better than getting her into the habit of taking paracetamol and retiring to bed, although there may be times, if the child is overtired and it is late, when this is the best treatment.

Sinus headaches will clear when the infection is cured, and this should be treated by a doctor. Getting the child to inhale menthol and eucalyptus, friar's balsam, or even steam alone can be helpful in many cases.

If you think your child's headaches are due to **tension**, try to get to the bottom of the problem by talking and listening. Seemingly minor features of a child's life can provoke major worries in a sensitive child. Children sometimes benefit from being taught

relaxation techniques. A relaxed bed-time routine, and plenty of outdoor exercise also help.

Pain caused by **ear infections** can be soothed by a warm cloth being held against the ear. If the pain is a burning sensation, a cloth wrung out in cold water may be more soothing. Your doctor will advise on any other treatment necessary, and will probably prescribe ear drops for the infection itself.

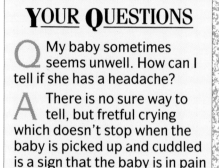

YOUR QUESTIONS

Q My baby sometimes seems unwell. How can I tell if she has a headache?

A There is no sure way to tell, but fretful crying which doesn't stop when the baby is picked up and cuddled is a sign that the baby is in pain of some kind.

Unless there is an obvious and safe explanation, any baby who continually cries should be seen by a doctor.

■ HEALTH VISITOR

Tending to be women, health visitors are state registered nurses who have special training in family health and the health of babies and young children, and their work gives them experience of all aspects of young children's health.

The health visitor visits you at home and can give advice on your own health as well as helping with all the problems concerned with the new baby (advising on breast feeding and bottle feeding and how to bathe the baby, for instance) and with toddlers (diet, behaviour problems, growth and so on). She can also give advice on any allowances and services to which you may be entitled.

The health visitor is usually very approachable and can give you the time to discuss problems that you feel you should not trouble your doctor with.

■ HEART PROBLEMS

See also CIRCULATION

The heart is responsible for pumping blood round the body. Blood pumped by the heart travels through the arteries to deliver oxygen and nutrients to all parts of the body. It returns via the veins to the heart, which pumps it on to the lungs where its supply of oxygen is renewed.

To operate this system the heart has four chambers, two on each side. Each chamber is a muscular bag with walls which contract rhythmically to pump the blood. This pumping mechanism is triggered by electrical impulses generated from the nerves within the heart.

The circulation in the lungs is called the pulmonary circulation and the circulation to the rest of the body is called the systemic circulation. As the blood delivers oxygen to the tissues it becomes blue in colour, and it becomes red again when the oxygen supply is renewed in the lungs.

HEART DEFECTS

Some babies are born with heart defects, and these are known as congenital heart defects. They can be so minor that they may remain undetected but in some cases they are apparent almost immediately and can be serious and life-threatening.

A child with congenital heart problems may need to avoid strenuous physical activity, but she can still enjoy watching, and can join in the gentler games.

A child with major congenital heart defects may die soon after birth or the foetus may die while it is still in the womb. If they survive, children with serious heart defects will need major surgery, and in some cases may never lead fully active lives. But children with minor defects often do not even need treatment.

A child with congenital heart defects has a heart which is imperfectly structured, usually with narrowing of the valves or a hole in the heart, or both conditions.

Narrowing of the valves decreases the volume of blood being pumped into either the lungs or the systemic circulation at each heartbeat. A hole in the heart is responsible for what is known as a 'blue baby' and both problems cause heart murmurs.

SYMPTOMS

Heart murmurs are detected when the doctor listens to the child's heartbeat through a stethoscope. An extra sound, something like a musical note, can be heard apart from the beating of the heart.

In many cases a child with a heart murmur seems perfectly well and has no symptoms, and often the murmur is found to be 'innocent' and not due to anything structurally wrong with the heart.

If this is so the murmur will only be audible when the child is in one particular position. But a murmur that sounds the same in all positions (when the child is standing, sitting, lying down, and so on) indicates that something more serious may be wrong, and the child will be sent for further investigations. These will probably include an X-ray and an electrocardiogram test to check whether the electrical impulses that cause the heart to beat are normal.

BLUE BABY

A hole in the heart can cause a baby to look blue. This happens because blood in the systemic circulation, which becomes blue as it releases oxygen (*see* introduction), is not returned to the pulmonary circulation, and is recirculated round the body

YOUR QUESTIONS

Q My child has been found to have a heart murmur, but the doctor has done nothing about it except to tell me to bring him back in six months time. Should I find another doctor?

A There should be no need to worry. A doctor can tell from the sound of a heart murmur whether further tests are needed. Obviously in the case of your son all the signs are that the murmur is 'innocent' and harmless. If there is any cause for doubt next time your doctor sees your son he will send him for further tests.

Q How many children have heart murmurs? I know of two among friends' children.

A About 50 per cent of babies and young children have so-called murmuring hearts. Mostly there is nothing wrong and the symptoms disappear as the child grows older.

without having had its oxygen supply renewed (*see* **Cyanosis**).

A serious hole in the heart may be obvious at birth, as the baby will probably look blue, and unlike other newborn babies, will remain blue. Even if this is not the case, the problem will be detected through routine examination with a stethoscope which will then be followed by further tests. A child who has a hole in the heart may seem very short of breath, and may have a poor colour if he is not actually blue. This and other heart defects may also cause swelling of the limbs.

CAUSES

Congenital heart defects can develop at an early stage of pregnancy (up to eight weeks), and if so they are

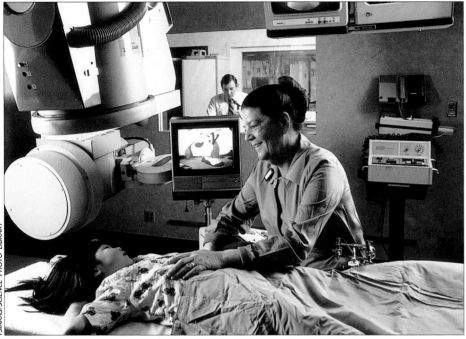

Nowadays everything possible is done to make a child feel at ease in hospitals. This little girl, about to undergo a detailed X-ray of the heart and major arteries, is watching cartoons on television.

usually very serious. Defects developing later in a pregnancy are not usually so life-threatening.

Although heart defects can run in families, this is by no means always the case, and frequently it cannot be ascertained why the abnormality has developed in a particular case. However, abnormalities are known to be linked with the mother having taken drugs (as in the thalidomide case), or having had German measles (rubella) early in pregnancy.

TREATMENT

It has been found that in many cases holes in the heart close up as the baby grows, and therefore surgical treatment may not be given when the problem is first detected. Instead, the condition will be regularly monitored. If possible most surgeons now prefer to defer any operation until the child is older.

If it is found necessary, corrective surgery will be performed. After the operation, the child will be kept in hospital for some time, at first under intensive care and then in a general ward where he will be given physiotherapy to help his recovery.

If surgery is not necessary or possible, the child may suffer some physical incapacity as a result of the heart condition. Your doctor will advise you on how much rest the child needs and how much activity (and of what sort) he can have.

Often the heart condition will make little difference to the child and he will find his own level and still be able to enjoy all sorts of physical activities. While it is important to make sure that your child follows your doctor's advice he should not be made to feel like an invalid.

■ HEARTBURN

see INDIGESTION

■ HEAT RASH

Heat rash is a common complaint in babies and children, and although it is not serious it can be troublesome.

SYMPTOMS

The child develops a rash of red spots which feel hot and cause itching. The spots are most likely to appear on the face, round the neck and in the elbows, at the back of the knees, and in the creases of the groin. These are all places where sweat glands are concentrated, and (except for the face) also where the increased amount of sweat can be trapped.

CAUSES

In babies heat rash normally occurs because the baby is hot, usually through being dressed in over-warm, constrictive clothing, and also if the room temperature is too high. However, it can occasionally develop without the baby getting too hot.

It is particularly prevalent in babies because their sweat glands are still developing and do not function as efficiently as in an adult or an older child. Young children are also prone to heat rash, and it may develop when the weather suddenly becomes hot (often on holiday in a hot climate) or if they get too hot in bed at night.

TREATMENT

Check that your baby is not over-dressed, and particularly that the clothes are not too tight, preventing the sweat from evaporating. Make sure that the room is not too hot (even though a small baby's room should always feel warm). Using cotton sheets and dressing your baby in

YOUR QUESTIONS

Q When my son goes out in the hot sun he often breaks out in a rash. Is this heat allergy?

A No. Although heat often makes an allergic reaction worse it does not actually cause allergies. The rash could be heat rash, which is a minor irritation, or it could be an allergic rash which is made worse by the heat. If it is causing problems it would be as well to seek your doctor's advice about it.

pure cotton, especially next to her skin, may help, as cotton is more absorbent than synthetic fibres, and

Heat rash particularly affects little babies and often appears on the face. This baby's warm clothing and the blanket she is wrapped in, are probably making her sweat, thereby aggravating the rash.

doesn't cause irritation as wool can sometimes do.

If the baby is outside in warm weather try to put her where there is a cooling breeze and in the shade. Heat rash is caused by body heat and sweat, and not by sun, but in any case it is not sensible to expose a baby or a young toddler to the direct rays of the sun.

Make sure that young children are not over-warm in bed on summer nights. Keep a window open to allow air movement, and, as with babies, try dressing them in loose cotton clothes. In hot weather, cotton sheets are best for children too.

COOLING THE RASH

The rash can be cooled by bathing the child in cool water, and she will find calamine lotion soothing. It is usually unnecessary to consult your doctor over a heat rash, and it is something that the child will grow out of as she gets older.

■ HEAT STROKE

Playing in the sun is usually beneficial, but overactive exercise and too much heat (especially when combined) can affect the body processes and lead to heat exhaustion. The problem is made worse in humid conditions where the body's sweat cannot easily evaporate. Heat stroke (also known as sun stroke) can be the result in extreme cases.

SYMPTOMS

A child who has heat exhaustion because he has been exposed to too much heat will feel weak, sick and dizzy. He may also suffer from cramps in the legs, he will certainly look pale, and he may have a raised temperature.

In the more serious form of heat stroke, the body temperature is always raised up to 40°C (104°F), and there may be fainting or even complete collapse. The most important symptom is that sweating ceases completely. When this happens the pulse will be rapid and the skin feel dry. Heat stroke can be very serious, and can cause coma, brain damage, and even death if left untreated.

CAUSES

Heat exhaustion is brought on by prolonged exposure to heat, especially if the weather is hotter than usual and the child has not been gradually acclimatized to the heat. The situation is made worse if the child is very active in his play, for this temporarily increases the body temperature and causes further sweating and loss of fluids and salts.

In these circumstances there is a loss of body fluids as the body sweats to cool itself down, and the loss of salts in the sweat causes an imbalance between salts and sugars in the bloodstream.

In extreme heat, the body's heat-regulating mechanism cannot cope at all and this is when sweating stops, high fever develops and the child may collapse with heat stroke.

TREATMENT

Minor cases of heat exhaustion respond well to treatment at home, but if the child is actually verging on

YOUR QUESTIONS

Q What can I do to ensure that my child doesn't suffer from heat stroke or heat exhaustion?

A Do not allow your child to play very active games in hot weather. Encourage him to spend time in the shade and to play quietly as well as running about in the sun.

When you go on holiday, break him in gently to give his body time to adjust. Make sure he spends plenty of time indoors or in the shade at the beginning of the holiday, gradually spending more time in the sun, and make him wear a hat to protect his head. Make sure he has plenty of cold drinks to satisfy his thirst when the weather is hot.

Letting a small child lie sleeping in the hot sun is exposing her to the risk of heat stroke.

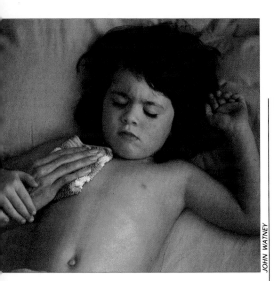

A child who has heat stroke is no longer able to sweat to cool the body down, and needs to be sponged all over with tepid water to reduce his temperature.

unconsciousness or has become unconscious, and if his temperature is at 40°C (104°F) or above, he should be given medical treatment at once, either by your doctor, or in hospital. If the child collapses artificial respiration must be applied.

HOME TREATMENT

Put your child to bed in a cool room, with windows and door open to encourage a draught, and with the minimum of clothing and covering. Give him salt to restore the salt-sugar balance and water to replace lost fluids. The best way to do this is to mix one teaspoonful of salt (5ml) to 1¾ pints (1 litre) of water and get the child to sip it.

To reduce body temperature, sponge the child with tepid water, leaving the water to evaporate on the skin. Take the child's temperature every half an hour or so, and as long as it is returning to normal all should be well within an hour or two.

MEDICAL TREATMENT

If the child does not respond to home treatment within a couple of hours, or if his condition is more serious (as described above) your doctor or the doctor at the hospital will decide on suitable treatment. Drugs may be given to help cool the body down and

fluids and salts may be given by intravenous drip feeding rather than by mouth as in less serious cases.

■ HEIGHT

see GROWTH

■ HEPATITIS

Hepatitis is an inflammation of the liver caused by a virus. Children are particularly vulnerable to a form of hepatitis brought about by a contagious virus known as type A virus. It is not normally life threatening, but it is debilitating and lasts a long time, and it can make your child feel very 'low'.

SYMPTOMS

The first symptom of hepatitis is usually lack of appetite, although this is not enough to establish the existence of the disease. Flu-like symptoms will develop, with digestive disorders and feverishness, and possibly aching in the limbs and back.

These symptoms may be very mild, and an exact diagnosis may be difficult until the symptoms of jaundice appear, with the child's skin and whites of the eyes taking on a yellowish tint, and the faeces ('stools')

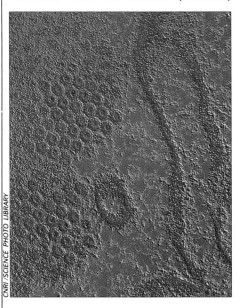

A false-colour transmission electron micrograph of the virus known as hepatitis A.

becoming light brown, while the urine becomes darker.

The incubation period (the length of time between the child's contracting the disease and showing the symptoms) is a long one — about 40 days. The child is infectious long before the jaundice develops and for about two weeks afterwards.

It is possible for the symptoms at every stage to be so mild that they pass unnoticed, although the illness can be detected by blood tests, even after the infection has passed.

CAUSES

Hepatitis A is caused by a virus which is very easily passed from person to person. It is found in saliva and blood, but also in faeces, and is chiefly passed on through contamination of food or water — usually as a result of poor hygiene and especially by people who are infected from not washing their hands after using the lavatory.

Because hepatitis A spreads so easily it can give rise to dramatic outbreaks, for example in children from the same school, or within a family. Although it is not common in developed countries, hepatitis A is often prevalent in less developed countries. This type of hepatitis may be introduced by an individual who has been on holiday in a hot country and has stayed in a place where sanitation is bad, and by the time the symptoms have developed it may have passed to other members of the family and to friends or colleagues.

HEPATITIS B

A second type of hepatitis, known as hepatitis B, is rare in children. This type takes even longer to develop and is transmitted in infected blood. It is this type that affects drug users who share needles, or people who have been tattooed in unsterile conditions. Hospital workers whose work involves handling blood are vulnerable to hepatitis B, and it can be transmitted sexually. Clearly then, it is unlikely to be passed about among children, but it can be passed by a mother to her unborn child.

JAUNDICE SYMPTOMS

In hepatitis the liver is inflamed, and this blocks the drainage of bile, causing yellow bile pigments produced by

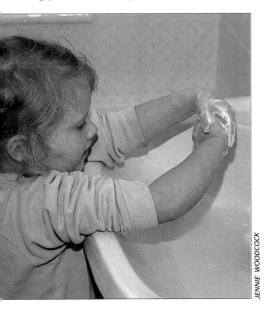

To help to prevent hepatitis from spreading, the infected child must wash her hands thoroughly before eating and after using the lavatory.

the liver to enter the circulation and then to pass into the urine instead of being eliminated through the intestine as happens normally. This is what causes the urine to become darker and the faeces lighter.

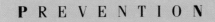

PREVENTION

Once you know that your child has hepatitis it is essential to do all you can to stop the infection from spreading. The patient is normally treated at home, and the strictest possible hygiene must be observed. The lavatory bowl should be cleaned with disinfectant after the child has used it, and the child herself must pay attention to washing thoroughly after using the lavatory.

The child must use only her own towel and flannel and these must be kept separate from those of the rest of the household and laundered separately. Her dishes and cutlery must also be washed separately and dried on a separate tea towel.

As an additional precaution your doctor will probably also give injections of immune serum globulin (ISG) to people who have been in close contact with the child.

ISOLATION

The child herself must be kept out of contact with the rest of the household for at least two weeks after the signs of jaundice have shown themselves. These measures may all seem drastic but they will help to make sure that the infection is not passed on (*see* box).

TREATMENT

As is nearly always the case with viral infections, the only treatment is rest while the body cures itself. However, an ISG injection can reduce the severity of the illness. The child should drink plenty of fluids, and as her appetite returns she should be indulged with tempting food. Do not put too much on her plate at once, and make it look attractive. But avoid giving her fatty foods, which she will find indigestible, however much she normally loves chips and ice cream.

There are usually no complications from hepatitis, but the child may well feel below par for weeks or even months after she has recovered.

■ HERNIA

A hernia (or rupture) is a protrusion through a weakness in a barrier of muscle and fibrous tissue separating one part of the body from another. It can be external (showing as a bump on the body surface) or internal and therefore not visible.

Although hernias are usually thought of as affecting adults — and particularly men — they can also occur in children, and may in particular affect babies within a few weeks of birth, when their muscles are still very weak.

SYMPTOMS

The hernias most likely to affect babies and children are those known as hiatus hernia, inguinal hernia and umbilical hernia.

Hiatus hernia, also known as diaphragmatic hernia, is a protrusion of part of the stomach or intestine through the diaphragm — the muscular wall which separates the thorax (chest) from the abdomen (belly). This protrusion bulges upwards into the chest and is therefore not visible.

Although hiatus hernia is far from common it can affect small babies, causing them to vomit up their feeds. This may happen immediately after a

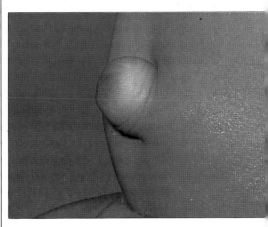

An umbilical hernia is a big bump which projects from the tummy in the area of the baby's navel.

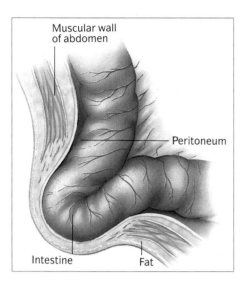

Hernias are caused by the lining of the abdomen pushing its way through weak muscles to form a sac in which part of an internal organ (here a loop of intestine) can fall.

feed or during a feed, and also at any time between feeds. The vomit may be bloodstained. In less severe cases the symptoms will be neither drastic nor frequent, but in more serious cases the baby will be vomiting and distressed much of the time and will not thrive through failing to absorb a large part of her feeds.

Inguinal hernia affects mainly little boys, and is the kind frequently referred to as a rupture. It shows itself as a soft lump in the groin, which often disappears when the child lies down, and is worse when he coughs or strains. There will be discomfort or pain, depending on the severity of the hernia.

Umbilical hernias frequently affect babies. The protrusion of the hernia is round the navel (tummy button), where it is very noticeable. Generally it can be pushed back into the tummy (though it will usually pop out again quite quickly) and it is usually completely painless.

C A U S E S

Hernias arise because of a weakness in the muscular wall through which the hernia protrudes. The thin membrane, known as the peritoneum, which lines the abdomen forms a little sac that pops through the weak

point, and part of an abdominal organ then fills the sac.

In the case of a hiatus hernia, part of the stomach pushes through to the wrong side of the diaphragm. In an inguinal hernia, a loop of intestine fills the sac that has worked its way through a weakness in the abdominal muscles, often following an attack of violent coughing, which strains the muscles. An umbilical hernia is caused by a commonly occurring weakness in the navel area of the abdomen of young babies.

DANGERS

Hernias in children or babies are not usually serious, but there is a danger that a hernia may become strangulated. This is a life-threatening development in which the blood supply to the contents of the hernia (whether part of the intestine or part of the stomach) is cut off by pressure on the blood vessels at the neck of the sac.

When this happens the contents of the hernia begin to swell and can become gangrenous. If the hernia is an external one you will notice it changing from being soft and merely uncomfortable to being very tense and tender. It will no longer go away when the child lies down, and the child may develop symptoms of intestinal obstruction — vomiting, abdominal pain, distension and constipation. In a strangulated hiatus hernia there will be a worsening of the vomiting and discomfort already being experienced. A strangulated hernia must be treated immediately.

T R E A T M E N T

All hernias or suspected hernias should be seen by your doctor.

HIATUS HERNIA

A hiatus hernia (which cannot be seen externally) will be diagnosed through an X-ray, following a barium meal or through an examination using a flexible endoscope, a tube which is inserted into the alimentary canal to allow a direct view of the oesophagus and stomach. Surgery is usually necessary to enable the baby

(or child) to digest food properly. Sometimes, however, in the case of mild hiatus hernias the doctor may simply give advice on how, when and what to feed the child, and the hernia may right itself by the time the child reaches 12–18 months old as the oesophagus grows longer and the child takes on an upright position through sitting and walking for most of the day.

INGUINAL HERNIAS

Even if an inguinal hernia is not causing pain and is what is known as reducible (which means that it disappears when the child lies down, or can be massaged away) it will probably need surgical treatment to make sure that it does not become strangulated and cause bowel constriction. A surgical operation will be performed to replace the protruding intestine and also to repair the weakened muscular wall if the surgeon finds this necessary. Occasionally the doctor may decide that the hernia should be left for a while to see whether it rights itself.

UMBILICAL HERNIAS

An umbilical hernia usually rights itself by the time the baby is a year old. Your doctor may advise you simply to massage the swelling gently and to keep a check on it. As long as it does not become hard or cause the baby pain, the chances are that no treatment will be needed.

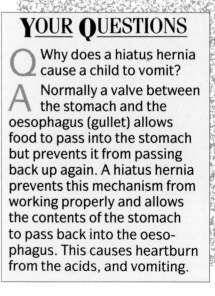

YOUR QUESTIONS

Q Why does a hiatus hernia cause a child to vomit?

A Normally a valve between the stomach and the oesophagus (gullet) allows food to pass into the stomach but prevents it from passing back up again. A hiatus hernia prevents this mechanism from working properly and allows the contents of the stomach to pass back into the oesophagus. This causes heartburn from the acids, and vomiting.

■ HERPES

See also CHICKENPOX

The most common form of herpes in children produces cold sores. These are painful blisters on the mouth and around the lips, which can be recurrent and troublesome.

Cold sores are caused by a strain of the virus Herpes simplex known as Type 1. There is also a strain known as Herpes simplex Type 2 and another form of herpes known as Herpes zoster, the last two being responsible for chickenpox — as well as shingles and sexually transmitted genital herpes, which rarely affect children.

SYMPTOMS

The first attack of Herpes simplex is usually the most severe. Small, painful blisters erupt on the child's tongue, inside the cheeks and on the lips. The whole of the affected area can be so painful that it makes eating and drinking difficult, and the child

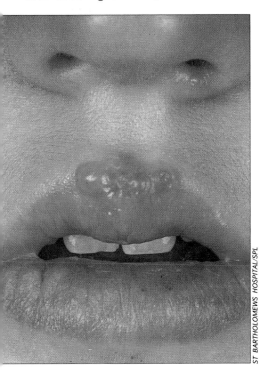

This little girl has a typical cold sore — blisters caused by the Herpes simplex virus. Cold sores usually affect the area round the mouth and can recur in some children.

ST BARTHOLOMEWS HOSPITAL/SPL

may also have a fever. Five to seven days after appearing, the blisters burst, and then heal, with a crust like the crust on a graze developing as this happens. Occasionally, symptoms affect the area round the eye rather than the mouth.

FURTHER ATTACKS

Although this first attack gives the body some immunity, the herpes virus then lies dormant in the body and can attack again. Subsequent attacks are usually less violent and cover only a small area at the edge of the lips or nose, but they are nevertheless a nuisance. They often seem to appear when the child has a cold, or at other times when his resistance is low, but they may be brought on by exposure to sun or strong wind.

CAUSES

Herpes simplex is an infectious virus which is transmitted through physical contact. About one in five children has contracted the virus from a relative or playmate by the age of six.

Direct contact through kissing is the most likely way to pass the virus on, so anybody who has a cold sore should avoid kissing until the sore has completely healed. As with all infections, scrupulous hygiene should be observed if your child has cold sores, as it is thought possible for the virus to be transmitted on towels and cutlery used by an infected person.

TREATMENT

As herpes is a virus, antibiotics do not help, but this family of viruses is one of the few that can now be treated by drugs — necessary only when the symptoms are severe. Creams are also available and can be very effective in mild cases.

In a more serious attack your doctor may prescribe a cream containing the drug acyclovir, which works well if used at an early stage. This drug may also be prescribed in liquid or tablet form, if the doctor thinks it necessary.

Sometimes herpes sores can develop into secondary infections which are caused by bacteria. If this happens the doctor may prescribe antibiotics such as penicillin. In minor attacks no treatment is necessary and the sores soon clear up.

Occasionally the first attack will be so virulent that hospital treatment is needed. This is the case when the inside of the mouth swells so much that swallowing becomes difficult. If this happens, drip feeding can be necessary while drug treatment is having an effect.

WATCHPOINTS

Herpes can cause severe complications in babies with eczema. The cold sores do not confine themselves to the baby's face but erupt wherever the eczema rash is present, and cause infections to set in.

If your baby suffers from eczema take extra care to keep her away from anyone with cold sores, and take her to the doctor straight away for early treatment if she does happen to contract the disease.

YOUR QUESTIONS

Q Why is it that Herpes simplex, which causes cold sores, lies dormant in the body, while once a child has had chickenpox, caused by Herpes zoster, she never has it again?

A A child will not suffer from chickenpox more than once because she develops immunity that modifies the body's reaction to the Herpes zoster virus. The virus does lie dormant in the body, however, just like Herpes simplex. When an adult is run down or emotionally upset (or sometimes for no apparent reason) this can flare up again in the form of shingles.

■ HICCUPS

Like adults, children of all ages get hiccups, and some babies seem to get them after every feed. Usually they do not last for long and no action is needed for them.

SYMPTOMS

The hiccups are a symptom in themselves. They usually cause no problem and it is rare for them to continue for more than a few minutes.

CAUSES

Sometimes hiccuping is brought about by eating or drinking something too hot or too cold, by eating too much or too quickly or by running about too soon after a meal. Suddenly gulping cold air can also upset the smooth breathing process and bring on an attack of hiccups. But often there is no apparent cause.

BREATHING AND HICCUPS

Normally as you breathe, air flows smoothly in and out of your lungs in time with the regular contractions of the muscular diaphragm, which moves up and down beneath the lungs, and the expansion and contraction of the ribs, which move in and out around the lungs.

When something goes wrong with this smooth pattern, hiccuping can be the result. So in a child who has hiccups the diaphragm, and usually the intercostal muscles that control the movement of the ribs, begin to move in twitching spasms.

This makes the child unconsciously gulp for air, and as this happens the epiglottis (a little flap at the top of the windpipe which prevents food from entering it) and the glottis (the opening between the vocal cords) both snap shut. This causes the flow of air being forced up through the windpipe to be cut off and produces the hiccuping sound.

NERVE MECHANISMS

This lack of muscular co-ordination is caused by an imperfect working of two sets of nerve mechanisms. There

YOUR QUESTIONS

Q Is it true that feeling nervous can cause a child to have hiccups?

A Yes, some people get hiccups when they are nervous because anxiety can set off abnormal impulses in the part of the brain that controls breathing.

Deep breathing exercises can help the child to relax. Chewing gum may also help to prevent hiccups in situations that make a child nervous.

is disturbance either in the nerve impulses sent out by the brain to control the rhythmical activities of breathing or in the impulses set off by one of the two phrenic nerves which serve to regulate the contractions of the diaphragm.

TREATMENT

Medical treatment is rarely needed for hiccups. You only need to take your child to the doctor if there are other symptoms of illness (even if they do not seem to be related) or if a

The old-fashioned remedy of drinking water out of the wrong side of the glass is often effective for an attack of hiccups – but can be messy!

bout of hiccups refuses to stop. For babies with hiccups there is little you can do, and usually they do not seem to worry the baby. If the hiccups go on for more than an hour, try giving a teaspoon of gripe water.

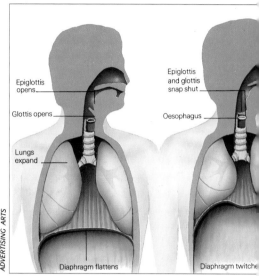

Epiglottis opens
Glottis opens
Lungs expand
Diaphragm flattens

Epiglottis and glottis snap shut
Oesophagus
Diaphragm twitches

In normal breathing, the glottis and epiglottis open so that air can pass into the lungs. If the diaphragm twitches as you breathe, air is forced up past the glottis and epiglottis, which then snap shut, causing the hiccuping sound.

For an older child one of the popular cures may help, even if they work only by causing a distraction. He should try holding his breath to the count of 20 or sipping water out of the wrong side of a glass.

Another remedy is to breathe in and out into a brown paper bag (holding it over the nose and mouth) for a minute or so. This is thought to be effective through causing the child to breathe in carbon dioxide from the air which has been breathed out, which depresses the activity of the nerves responsible for the hiccups.

■ HIP

See also HIP, CONGENITAL DISLOCATION, OSTEOMYELITIS, PERTHES DISEASE, SYNOVITIS

The hip joints are the biggest joints in the body and are of the type known as ball and socket. The hip bone provides a shallow, cup-shaped socket in which the ball-shaped top of the femur (the thigh bone) sits.

The hips allow for a wide range of movements in crawling, walking, running, kicking, raising the legs, bending and so on. These movements are all made possible by the numerous muscles of the pelvic girdle and the legs. Unlike its counterpart, the shoulder, the hip is very stable and hip problems are rare in children, except for the condition known as congenital dislocation of the hip.

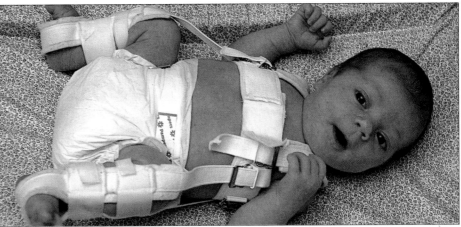

DURRELL-McKENNA/HUTCHISON

■ HIP, CONGENITAL DISLOCATION

Congenital dislocation of the hip is perhaps the most common problem found in newborn babies. To check for this, examinations are carried out at birth and at 6-8 weeks of age.

SYMPTOMS

The symptoms of congenital dislocation of the hip may not be immediately obvious when the baby is born but they are quickly discovered by a thorough examination.

The baby is placed on his back with his legs wide apart and held firmly by the feet. The doctor then bends the child's knees and moves the hips. If the joint is properly developed the movement will be smooth and soundless. If there is a clicking sound, this is caused by the top of the femur engaging in the hip socket, and another click will be heard when it disengages again.

YOUR QUESTIONS

Q Is there any danger that a child born with a dislocated hip will have problems later in life?

A Absolutely none. Once the growing hip has responded to treatment it will be absolutely normal, and will remain so.

Congenital dislocation of the hip is slightly more common in breech births, but is easily corrected. The baby is kept in a splint or brace (above) for six to 12 weeks, until the joint has developed properly.

As part of the check-up the doctor may also feel the baby's groin to check whether the femur is securely in its socket. If the head of the femur is easily moved by the doctor's finger the joint is what is known as unstable or irritable.

CAUSES

Congenital dislocation of the hip and unstable hip joints are a result of the joint not developing properly before the baby is born. For some reason, five times as many girl babies as boys have congenital dislocation of the hip. If it is not treated, the joints will be permanently affected.

TREATMENT

The treatment for this disorder is very effective and there are usually no long-term effects. Usually the baby is put in a plaster splint which keeps the legs in a frog-like position, and the joint is checked by X-ray after a few months. When the situation has been rectified the plaster is removed.

If the hip joint is unstable the mother may be advised to keep the baby in wide terry towelling nappies for a few months to keep the legs apart. This encourages the muscles to develop the necessary strength to make the joint stable.

■ HIVES

Also known as nettle rash or urticaria, this skin complaint is a common allergy symptom. Usually, attacks do not last for long and there is no need for treatment.

SYMPTOMS

Hives is a skin rash which looks very similar to insect bites or nettle stings on the skin. The spots of the rash are raised blisters, linked together to cover an area of skin which can vary a great deal in size. Sometimes the spots hardly differ in colour from the rest of the skin, but sometimes they form large red weals. The skin around the blisters often becomes red, and the whole area is burning and itchy, just like nettle stings.

Sometimes the rash appears in places where the child's skin has been in contact with the substance causing the allergy but in other cases it can appear on almost any part of the body. It also has the odd habit of disappearing in one place only to reappear elsewhere.

CAUSES

Hives is often triggered by an allergy. The allergen (the substance responsible) can be something that comes into contact directly with the skin or it can be something in food or breathed in from the air.

Thus there is a wide range of culprits, including wool, plants, eggs, strawberries, shellfish, fluff, perfumes, house mites, pollens and dyes.

In some children no independent substance is responsible and heat, cold or pressure – or even emotional stress – can bring on the same rash. Sometimes a child will get hives from sitting in a hot bath. In each case the skin over-reacts.

The rash is caused by a release of histamine in an allergic reaction which is fully described under other headings (*see* **Allergies, Food Allergies, Hay Fever**).

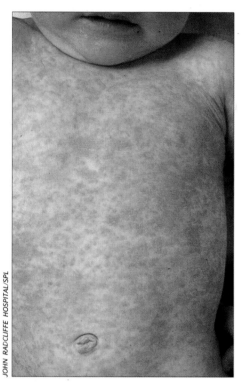

Hives or nettle rash can affect just tiny patches of skin or may cover large parts of the body with itchy blisters and inflammation (above). An attack usually dies down without treatment within an hour or so.

TREATMENT

As with all allergies, the best treatment is prevention, by identifying the allergen and trying to make sure that the child is not exposed to it. If the allergen is something that touches the skin the causal link will probably be apparent, and if it is a food that the child rarely eats the connection between eating it and having the rash will be noticed. But quite often, pin-pointing the allergen is not an easy task.

Fortunately the attacks are usually short-lived and not troublesome, and in these cases treatment is not necessary, although calamine lotion can be applied to soothe the rash. Your doctor will treat a child who has frequent and long-lasting attacks by prescribing anti-histamine ointment or tablets.

SEVERE FORM

Occasionally hives can take a more severe form known as angio-neurotic oedema or giant hives. This produces large swelling on the lips, eyelids, back or throat, and may cause difficulties in breathing. It is treated with adrenaline or corticosteroids, both of which are given only under strict medical supervision.

YOUR QUESTIONS

Q I suffer from hives and am worried that I might pass it on to my children. Can it run in families?

A Allergic complaints do tend to run in families, although this is not always so. But since the ailment is rarely severe, there really is no need to worry about passing it on.

■ HODGKIN'S DISEASE

Hodgkin's disease, medically known as lymphadenoma, is a form of cancer. It is rare in young children, but can affect teenagers and young adults. Although it is a serious illness, there is a chance of a complete cure if the disease is caught early.

The disease affects the glands in the lymphatic system — the network of vessels which carry a substance known as lymph throughout the body. At certain points in these vessels are the lymph nodes or lymph glands, which filter off bacteria and help to defend the body against illness. The little glands behind the ears and at the front of the neck that swell when the child has an infection are examples of lymph glands. In Hodgkin's disease, cells in one of the lymph glands multiply and spread.

SYMPTOMS

The lymph glands affected by Hodgkin's disease become enlarged as a result of the lymphocytes (a type of white blood cell) multiplying abnormally. Usually it is the glands in the neck, groin or armpit that are affected first, and the disease gradually spreads throughout the lymphatic system from one group of nodes to the next until the whole system is affected — unless, of course, it is diagnosed and treated.

The swelling may first be noticed when the child has a sore throat or some other minor illness. This is a common occurrence with infections, but in this case, as the child recovers from the illness the glands do not reduce in size as normal.

Sometimes there are additional symptoms in the form of fever, with sweating (especially at night), weight loss and general tiredness, but this is not always so.

CAUSES

It is still not known what causes Hodgkin's disease, although some medical scientists believe that a virus that has yet to be identified is responsible. It usually develops in older teenagers and young adults.

YOUR QUESTIONS

Q I have heard that Hodgkin's disease causes infections. Is this correct?

A Yes. Hodgkin's disease affects the immune system and anyone suffering from it is likely to be more prone to infections. Sometimes it is when a child goes to the doctor because of a string of minor infections that the disease is discovered.

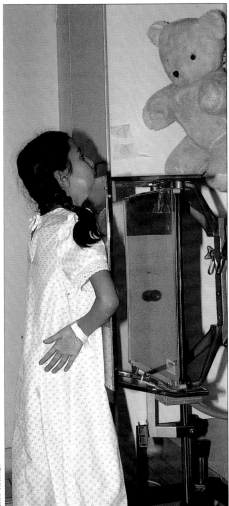

Hodgkin's disease starts in one of the lymph glands but can spread through the whole lymphatic system. Diagnosis may involve X-rays (above) as well as taking samples from the glands for laboratory tests.

DIAGNOSIS

If a child or young person has abnormally enlarged glands which are swollen for more than about two weeks, he should see the family doctor. If there is no obvious cause for the enlarged glands the child will probably be given blood tests to find out whether there is a cause such as glandular fever. But if the child has Hodgkin's disease the typical results of glandular fever will be absent.

This may lead your doctor to suspect that Hodgkin's disease could be responsible, and the child will then probably be sent for a biopsy, in which a sample from one of the enlarged glands is removed under anaesthetic and sent to a pathologist for examination under a microscope. The results will give a definite diagnosis if Hodgkin's disease is present.

TREATMENT

If Hodgkin's disease is found to be the cause of the swollen glands, further tests will be done to see how far the illness has spread. This involves physical examination of all the glands, X-rays and (probably) a scan on a computerized X-ray machine which can produce detailed pictures of the soft tissues within the body. It may also be necessary to take samples from glands within the abdomen (under anaesthetic) to see if these have been affected.

X-ray treatment to kill off the abnormal cells will usually then be given to the affected parts of the body. If the disease is found to be very advanced several courses of drug treatment will probably also be given to kill off the cells that are dividing abnormally, with up to four different drugs being given at once.

SIDE EFFECTS

Unfortunately the treatment, whether by X-ray or by drugs, can involve unpleasant side-effects, with vomiting, nausea and hair loss. Usually the child is old enough to understand that this will save her life and the side-effects will pass. It will help if the parents are supportive and show optimism and confidence, but it will be a difficult time.

It is encouraging to know that while 30 years ago most people who had Hodgkin's disease died within two years of diagnosis, it is now one of the most successfully treated cancers, and a complete cure is almost guaranteed.

■ HYDROCELE

This is a problem in little boys which takes the form of a swelling in the scrotum but usually needs no treatment. Many baby boys have swollen testicles at birth, due to their mother's hormones, but this swelling usually goes down within a few days. If the swelling is due to a hydrocele it is caused by fluid from the abdomen.

SYMPTOMS

Most hydroceles occur in boys when they are babies, and are visible soon after the birth. The scrotum of a baby with a hydrocele is swollen, often only on one side. The swelling is soft to the touch and the condition is quite painless.

A hydrocele may sometimes develop in an older boy, and if this happens it could be an indication that there is something wrong with the testicle concerned.

CAUSES

As a baby boy develops in the womb his testicles are formed in his abdomen (tummy). Shortly before the birth, or occasionally not long afterwards, the testicles descend through the abdomen and into the external sac called the scrotum.

If the channel down which the testicles descended on either side remains open in the abdomen, as it

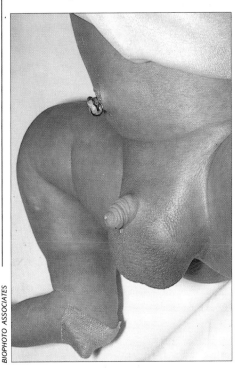

Swellings of the scrotum caused by a hydrocele look alarming, but are painless and almost always harmless.

sometimes does, fluid may drain from the abdomen and into the scrotum, leading to the swelling known as the hydrocele. It is fairly unusual for this to happen on both sides.

TREATMENT

It is a good idea to point out the hydrocele to your doctor or health visitor if it has not already been noticed. Usually no treatment will be necessary, and in normal cases the hydrocele will drain away and disappear before the baby is a year old. A minor operation to drain off the fluid may be recommended if the hydrocele has not disappeared soon after this time.

A hydrocele that appears in an older boy is potentially more serious. It could be a sign of some abnormality, and should be seen by a doctor to investigate the cause.

YOUR QUESTIONS

Q My baby boy had a hydrocele and now that he is ten months old it has disappeared. Does that mean that the channel inside him has disappeared too?

A Yes, the channel down which the baby's testicle descended does normally close up completely, and the disappearance of the hydrocele indicates that this has now happened in the case of your son.

■ HYDROCEPHALUS

Hydrocephalus literally means water on the brain. It is a rare and alarming condition but one which can now be treated successfully.

SYMPTOMS

This condition affects young children, causing their heads to swell. As it increases in size the head also takes on a characteristic shape with the forehead widening and deepening to make the face look small and doll-like, with rounded eyes.

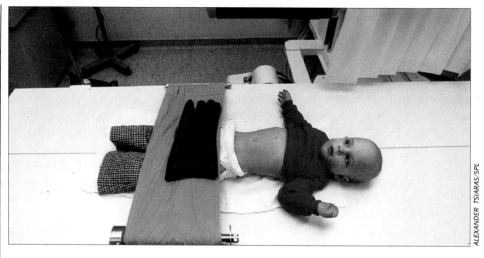

ALEXANDER TSIARAS/SPL

This 15-month old being treated for hydrocephalus has the typical enlarged head and doll-like features.

CAUSES

The immediate cause of hydrocephalus is an interruption in the flow of the fluid known as the cerebrospinal fluid, a liquid which flows round the brain and spinal cord to protect the tissues from injury. This brings about

YOUR QUESTIONS

Q If the head expands because pressure builds up and pushes the skull bones apart, what happens when an older child – or an adult for that matter – whose skull bones have fused together, gets hydrocephalus?

A Medically, the term hydrocephalus means an enlargement of the head due to excess fluid. So, strictly speaking, older children and adults do not get hydrocephalus. When they suffer from water on the brain the pressure from excess fluid causes the hollow ventricles of the brain to expand, resulting in progressive damage to the compressed brain tissue. This damage can be irreversible if treatment is not given soon enough.

increased pressure, which in children below the age when the small bones of the skull have not yet fused together, forces the bones apart and makes the head increase in size.

One of the chief causes of hydrocephalus is spina bifida, which has the effect of causing an obstruction in the circulation of the blood, leading to a build-up of fluid. Occasionally the condition is caused by pressure from tumours or cysts.

TREATMENT

Hydrocephalus must be treated as early as possible to make sure that no irreversible damage is done. If it is found to be present at birth, treatment may even be given before the child is 24 hours old.

Treatment involves a surgical operation, but is usually very successful. There are several different ways of relieving pressure and allowing the fluid to circulate properly, usually by inserting a small drainage tube left permanently in the brain.

■ HYPERACTIVITY

The term hyperactivity is widely used but has not been strictly defined. It is used to describe a child's behaviour rather than a definite medical condition, and many parents are tempted to describe their child as hyperactive at one time or another.

SYMPTOMS

Hyperactivity usually starts in children when they are still babies, but the symptoms become more obvious as they begin to walk, when they tear about in a completely disorganized way, unable to concentrate on anything, even for the short time of a normal toddler's attention span.

As these children grow older they show a complete lack of attention, while other children are becoming able to occupy themselves happily in their own activities. Inability to concentrate makes it difficult for hyperactive children to get on with other children. They cannot see the point of any game and cannot concentrate on it for any length of time, so that other children do not enjoy playing with them. The hyperactive child responds by being aggressive and so makes matters worse.

LEARNING DIFFICULTIES

A hyperactive child often seems of below average intelligence, and has difficulties with learning. He also finds it hard to distinguish between left and right and cannot understand the relationship between shapes or different sizes.

In addition to this the child is usually clumsy and can also be destructive. He has sudden, violent changes of mood, rapidly turning from rage to joy to misery, and he will frequently not sleep well. While normal children may show some of these characteristics from time to time, with hyperactive children they are always in evidence.

CAUSES

Hyperactivity can be caused by brain damage or epilepsy, or may be associated with psychiatric problems such as autism (a mental condition which prevents the child from communicating or having contact with even his own parents) or schizophrenia. But hyperactive behaviour can also be found on its own, without any apparent cause or associated condition, and some doctors refer to this as hyperkinetic syndrome (literally meaning moving about too much).

Some doctors believe that hyperactivity must be caused by a brain disorder or something in the genetic make-up, but there are therapists who believe that it is caused by problems in the child's relationship with the parents and with the rest of the family.

Other doctors now firmly believe that hyperactivity is a reaction to certain foodstuffs, and particularly to what are termed additives – artificial flavouring, colouring or preservatives – whereas some go as far as to blame the child's general diet for the condition. However, these theories are far from proven.

Your hyperactive child may be exhausting to look after. Be firm yet patient. Remember that she is not being deliberately difficult.

TREATMENT

It is important for parents and other children in the family to remember that the hyperactive child is not being deliberately difficult. He needs tolerance and patience, combined with firm handling on the part of the parents. The more secure the child feels the better he is able to cope.

Parents should talk about the problem to the child's teacher and head teacher. It may even be decided that he needs remedial teaching because of his learning difficulties.

It is important for the child to have plenty of opportunity to run about and let off steam in the fresh air. He will also benefit from all the attention you are able to give him. With your quiet encouragement he should be able to develop better concentration and to get satisfaction from finishing something, whether reading, drawing, putting toys away or making something in the kitchen.

MEDICAL TREATMENT

Your doctor may decide that the child needs drug treatment. Hyperactivity responds poorly to tranquillizers, but oddly enough, amphetamines, which speed up adults, can have a calming effect on hyperactive children. It may be necessary to try various drugs under medical supervision until the best treatment is found for the individual. It is very dangerous to give your child drugs without medical supervision.

The doctor may also refer the child for psychological therapy, which may help improve the child's attention span. Some therapists believe that the condition involves the whole family and will want to involve everyone in their treatment.

Some doctors recommend a strictly controlled diet, eliminating all additives, and some people have found this helpful.

Parents themselves will find dealing with a hyperactive child exhausting, but it is not helpful to get angry and impatient. It will help, if possible, for parents to be able to take time off regularly to free them from pressure.

OUTLOOK

It is reassuring for parents to know that in most cases the child eventually grows out of hyperactivity, although he may continue to have social problems through having found it so difficult to relate to other children for so long. Equally, learning may still be a problem after these difficult years, and remedial teaching or special support from teachers may always be necessary.

YOUR QUESTIONS

Q Is there physical danger in a child's being hyperactive?

A The condition is not a threat to physical health, except in a very general way. The only danger is that the hyperactive child might injure himself or other children. These children often do things rashly, and without thought for the consequences. Parents do need to be aware that the child is quite capable of rushing into the road without looking, or of tumbling out of a window or striking another child in a fit of rage.

Q I have never heard of a girl being hyperactive. Does the condition not affect girls?

A Oddly enough, statistically there are indeed four times as many hyperactive boys as girls, although there is no known reason for this.

■ HYPOGLYCAEMIA

See also DIABETES

Hypoglycaemia is the medical term for a low level of blood sugar. (This sugar is called glucose and it is a different substance from your everyday bag of sugar, which is sucrose.) It is often associated with diabetes, but almost anyone can have an occasional attack.

SYMPTOMS

Sugar in the blood gives us our energy. In an attack of hypoglycaemia, glucose levels fall dramatically and a child may show a number of symptoms. His hands may shake, and he may seem absent-minded, stubborn or ill-tempered; he may have an attack of sweating or a fit of hunger; and in a bad attack he may even become unconscious or have an epileptic fit.

Some children may have attacks whenever they are particularly tired or haven't eaten for a while.

Regular meals and healthy snacks, such as a fresh salad sandwich, will help ward off a child's attacks of hypoglycaemia.

CAUSES

Blood sugar is used to provide energy for all bodily activities, including mental activity. No matter how much energy-giving food we eat and how much sugar we convert into energy, the level of sugar in the blood is normally kept more or less constant.

This is because the brain needs a constant amount of sugar, and as the sugar in the blood is used up, the body converts reserves of a starch called glycogen into more sugar in the bloodstream to supply this need. When something goes wrong with the body's normal ability to call up reserves of glycogen and convert them into blood sugar, the lack of sugar causes a range of symptoms as the brain reacts to the short supply.

INSULIN

Insulin is the most important of several hormones that control the amount of sugar in the blood, and a low blood sugar level is usually associated with a high insulin level.

The cause of diabetes is usually a *low* insulin level, so it may seem puzzling that hypoglycaemia can occur in diabetes, but this is because it is difficult to control the insulin level precisely when treating diabetes, and it can therefore sometimes rise too high. When the level of insulin is too high the body stores more energy reserves in the form of glycogen instead of releasing them as sugar in the blood, and as supplies of blood sugar are used up as energy they are not replaced.

OTHER CAUSES

Hypoglycaemia can also occur when the body uses up energy faster than it replaces the lost sugar supply and therefore suffers from a temporary imbalance. But more seriously, in some rare liver disorders the body fails to store glycogen and has no reserves with which to supply more blood sugar. And apart from over-production of insulin, imbalances between the other hormones which are involved in regulating the sugar level in the blood can also be responsible for the condition.

TREATMENT

Sweet foods should normally be kept to a minimum in a child's diet, as in an adult's, but attacks of hypoglycaemia respond quickly if the child is given something sweet to eat. A child who is prone to attacks should carry glucose tablets about with her. She can learn to tell when an attack is coming on and can fend it off by sucking a tablet.

If a child does have frequent attacks of hypoglycaemia she should see her doctor, who will check that there is nothing seriously wrong, and will probably give advice on a suitable diet. A diet high in carbohydrates and low in sugars is particularly advisable.

SUITABLE DIET

The most important rule to avoid hypoglycaemia is to have regularly spaced meals in time to stop the blood sugar falling to a low level. Foods rich in carbohydrates, such as pasta, cereals, potatoes and bread provide 'slow release' energy, while sugary snacks produce 'quick release' energy. If your child is going to miss a meal, give him a snack to nibble away at, or something sweet. Among the high-energy, concentrated foods, chocolate is a good standby.

■ HYPOSPADIAS
See also GENITALS

In boys, the opening through which urine is passed is normally right at the tip of the penis. Hypospadias describes a condition where this is not so.

SYMPTOMS

Hypospadias is a condition which is present from birth. If a boy has hypospadias he will urinate from the underneath of the penis, or, in extreme cases, from somewhere in the area around the penis — wherever the wrongly positioned urethral opening happens to be.

There is no danger of hypospadias being overlooked in the routine examinations that babies go through, and there is no need to worry that your baby can be suffering from it without your realizing it.

CAUSES

As with many congenital problems it is not really known why this problem occurs. Hypospadias does seem to run in families to some extent.

Urination can be painless and normal in every way once an operation has been successfully performed to correct hypospadias.

TREATMENT

Unless the case is mild, and the urethral opening is very near to the tip of the penis, surgery will be necessary to make sure that the boy can urinate properly, and also that he will be able to function normally sexually when he is older.

A corrective operation is usually performed when the child is three to five years old, but sometimes the baby's existing opening has to be enlarged as soon as the condition is discovered so that the child can urinate without difficulty until he is old enough for the operation. This is quite painless and can be done without anaesthetic.

If the position of the urethra to be reconstructed is very long, the operation is performed in two or three stages.

■ HYPOTHERMIA

In cold weather the very young are almost as much at risk from hypothermia, or sub-normal body temperatures, as the very old. It is important to be aware of the dangers of letting children get too cold, as hypothermia can even cause death.

Hypothermia can happen, especially in babies, when the child is in an underheated room in very cold weather, but it is more of a risk for older children when they are out of doors. Particularly if the child gets wet, and if she is tired, the body temperature can drop quite quickly, and the early symptoms are not always obvious.

Experts consider that hypothermia is present if the body temperature is below 35°C (95°F). Taking the temperature by mouth is unreliable, as the mouth can become even colder than the body as a whole, so the most reliable way is take the temperature of the rectum (bottom). However, a mouth temperature is good enough as a general guide that the child needs to be warmed up.

SYMPTOMS

As hypothermia develops, the child will have violent attacks of shivering, which is the body's way of trying to warm itself up. Small babies cannot shiver, nor of course can they be physically very active which is why their bodies are more prone to suffer a drop in temperature.

Shivering stops as the child gets colder, and then if hypothermia is not averted, he will begin to be mentally confused. This is followed by him feeling sleepy and eventually, if his temperature drops to 32°C (89.6°F), falling into a coma.

If the temperature continues to fall, cell activity and breathing rate slow down, the oxygen supply to the cells is reduced and finally the heart beat is replaced by a rippling known as fibrillation, which does not pump blood. Unless something is done at once, blood circulation stops and the child will die. However, in infants and very young children the body temperature can be as low as 21°C (69.8°F) before fibrillation starts.

CAUSES

The main cause of hypothermia is exposure to cold. Older children, if they are warmly dressed, are quite safe outside in the cold, since they generate heat through being active. But babies and very young children are much at risk.

With older children, the danger arises when they become too tired to be active, or when they are forced not to be — perhaps during a long cold wait for a bus — after burning up a lot of energy. Also (as mentioned above) if the child is wet for any reason, body heat is quickly lost.

PREVENTION

Protect your baby from hypothermia by keeping his room warm in winter. Keep him warmly wrapped if you have to take him outside in abnormally cold weather and do not leave him outside in his pram. But do remember that it is very easy to make a baby too hot — check by feeling the back of his neck, which should be pleasantly warm.

Make sure that older children eat well to fuel them for playing outside in the cold. Dress them warmly in waterproof clothing if they are going to be out for long — perhaps for a country walk or on an outing to watch a football match.

A blanket kept permanently in the car is always a good idea (especially useful if your child gets his clothes really wet), and 'space blankets' (lightweight metallic sheets which can be bought in camping shops) can be folded into tiny packages for use in all emergencies. Remember that the body loses a lot of heat through the head, and always dress children in hats when it is cold.

Snow is fun to play in, but it is also cold and wet. So make sure your child is wearing waterproof clothing and that his head is covered.

JOHN WATNEY

TREATMENT

The main aim is to warm up your child gradually. Do not use hot water bottles or electric blankets, which will bring blood to the surface and cause further cooling of the internal vital organs. Instead, use your own body warmth, getting into a sleeping bag with your child or wrapping him up with you in a blanket.

If your child is wet, wrap him in something dry while he is still outside and do not remove the wet clothes until he is in a warm room.

If your child has passed the shivering stage and seems drowsy, call your doctor, and continue warming your child while you wait for the doctor to arrive. And if your child is unconscious, or if his temperature fails to rise after an hour or so of warming, take him straight away to the nearest hospital accident and emergency department.

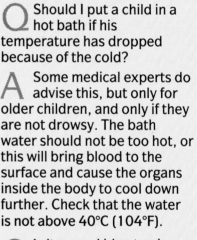

YOUR QUESTIONS

Q Should I put a child in a hot bath if his temperature has dropped because of the cold?

A Some medical experts do advise this, but only for older children, and only if they are not drowsy. The bath water should not be too hot, or this will bring blood to the surface and cause the organs inside the body to cool down further. Check that the water is not above 40°C (104°F).

Q Is it a good idea to give food and hot drinks to a child who is suffering from hypothermia?

A If the child is not too ill a hot drink can be soothing, but it should be warm, rather than hot, and the body warming method should not be abandoned.

On no account should you give your child any alcohol, as this causes the blood vessels to dilate and leads to further heat loss.

■ HYSTERIA

Hysteria means different things to different people and there is no precise medical definition of the term. Symptoms of illness are said to be hysterical if they are related to anxiety and not to a medical cause.

The term is also used medically to describe an immature personality of any age who cannot cope and who behaves in an extreme way instead — typically children who use temper tantrums in an attempt to get their own way.

Mass hysteria is a term used to describe the over-emotional and uncontrolled behaviour sometimes exhibited by fans at pop concerts.

SYMPTOMS

In the first type of hysteria the symptoms are those of a physical illness, and these symptoms are usually related to the anxiety at the root of the problem. There may be paralysis, blindness or inability to taste or sometimes the symptoms will be those of mild disorders, with coughing fits, blackouts, vomiting or diarrhoea.

Apart from temper tantrums, the symptoms of the second type of hysteria, known as dissociative hysteria, are amnesia (loss of memory), sleep-walking, refusal to eat and hysterical fits. These can be unnerving for parents as they resemble epileptic seizures.

CAUSES

The causes of hysterical symptoms or behaviour can range from anxiety to inability to cope. Children with extrovert (outward-going) natures are most likely to succumb to hysterical behaviour as a way of avoiding things, or of getting their own way.

The mass hysteria of pop concert audiences might be caused by the heightened emotions of young people en masse, whose emotions may be unstable because of their age.

TREATMENT

Treatment depends on the type and severity of the hysterical symptoms and the frequency with which they occur. By far the most likely cause with children will be the occasional

hysterical outburst over some trivial situation in which the child wants to get his own way. The best thing is to ignore these outbursts altogether.

You may be unaware that an illness is of a hysterical origin, and this will be diagnosed by your doctor when no other cause can be found. Your doctor may then refer you to a child psychiatrist or therapist for further help, especially if the symptoms are severe or frequent. But the hysterical symptoms or behaviour may pass with time, and it may be possible for you to get to the bottom of the problem without help once you realize that your child's behaviour could be an appeal to you to help shield him from what he considers an intolerable situation.

The most common form of hysteria in young children is in temper tantrums. Ignoring outbursts is the best way to deal with them.

YOUR QUESTIONS

Q My little girl has what I can only describe as hysterial fits when she can't get her own way. How should I react?

A It is best to ignore the outburst calmly, and not to give in. The more you give in, the more your daughter is likely to turn on the tantrums to get her own way. If she finds that her attacks don't further her ends she will gradually give them up.

■ IMMUNIZATION

The human body develops immunity to many viral and bacterial infections simply through exposure to them. This acquired immunity explains why children will generally get only one attack of an illness such as measles or chicken-pox during their life. Humans as a species are also automatically immune to some diseases that affect animals.

In addition to these two types of natural immunity, there is a third type that can be conferred by means of vaccination or immunization. Because of this there are some diseases which formerly caused serious illness and even death which have now been brought under control or even eradicated worldwide.

INFECTION

The body deals with infection by manufacturing antibodies, special proteins which are specific to each particular infection. It stores information on the exact nature of these antibodies in the lymphocytes, and if the same infection attacks a second time, identical antibodies are then manufactured to fight it.

Immunization by vaccination is a way of provoking the body into producing antibodies to an infection without being submitted to the full-blown infection itself. If the immunized person later comes into contact with the agent of that infection the lymphocytes will get to work to produce antibodies and the infection will not be able to take hold.

The number of illnesses for which immunization by vaccination is now possible is still quite small, but several illnesses which used to be a major threat to children's health are included. Immunization has resulted in great improvements to health and life expectancy generally.

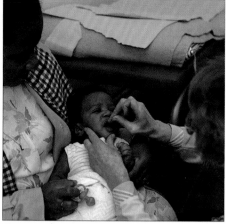

Thanks to widespread immunization programmes, polio has been virtually abolished in the Western world. The vaccine is given orally.

ACTIVE IMMUNIZATION

The usual form of immunization is active immunization. This involves injecting small amounts of the virus or bacteria, either in inactivated (dead) or in live but much weakened form. The body is encouraged to produce antibodies, without actually making the child ill and the usual result is that immunity develops. This kind of immunization is given to babies and young children, to protect against diphtheria, polio, whooping cough, measles, mumps, rubella and Hib.

PASSIVE IMMUNIZATION

This form of immunization is used to treat people who have already caught the disease in question, or who are at risk of having caught it. It involves injecting immunoglobulin, which is rich in antibodies to that particular disease. Immunoglobulin is extracted from blood plasma provided by donors who have had the disease.

This form of immunization gives immediate protection, and is the type used, for example, if a child has had the sort of injury that might lead to tetanus or if a child has been in contact with someone who has hepatitis B. The effect of these injections wears off over time.

Immunization by vaccination not only protects the individual child — it also protects society from epidemics.

Since an immunization campaign was put in hand in Britain in 1942 smallpox has almost ceased to be known, whereas in the 1930s there were about 3000 deaths a year from it in children under 15 in Britain alone.

Other diseases have now been banished. For example, poliomyelitis was also responsible for many deaths and many more cases of paralysis, and thanks to vaccination programmes put into effect, in the United Kingdom, since 1957 it has now been virtually abolished.

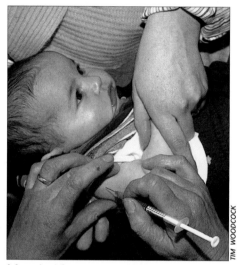

Most babies are vaccinated against diphtheria, tetanus and whooping cough, giving them immunity to these diseases.

A wide vaccination programme is now available to all children in developed countries, and most parents automatically take advantage of it. Some parents, however, do worry about the risks.

CONTROVERSIAL VACCINE

Only the whooping cough (pertussis) vaccination has proved controversial, since it was reported in 1974 that a very few children had to be admitted to hospital after the injection suffering from severe neurological illness. It could not be proved that the vaccination was responsible, but even so, as a result of this report many parents decided not to have their children immunized against whooping cough, and in the late 1970s and early 1980s there were new epidemics of the disease.

In extremely rare cases it is true that the vaccination has led to a child suffering from an illness related to the disease against which she has been vaccinated. But the risks of this happening are minute. For example, it is now estimated that the risk of side effects, including temporary ones, is something like one in 100,000 in the case of whooping cough vaccination, infinitely smaller than the risk of the child's having neurological complications as a result of actually catching a bad attack of the disease.

So the risk is really negligible and is completely outweighed by the advantages. But parents who are worried can seek reassurance from their family doctor.

YOUR QUESTIONS

Q Why are three tetanus injections needed, spaced out in the way they are?

A This is so as not to give too large a dose at once. After the first injection very little change in antibody level occurs. However, after the second dose there is a very large rise, and after the third dose an even bigger one. After this, booster injections have to be given occasionally to keep the level adjusted correctly.

Q What diseases will my child be vaccinated against?

A Diphtheria, tetanus and whooping cough (pertussis), polio, measles, mumps, rubella, and haemophilus influenzae b (known as Hib), plus tuberculosis are part of the UK immunization programme for babies, toddlers and children. Your child health clinic can give you information, plus a schedule of when you should bring your child for vaccination.

■ IMPETIGO

Impetigo is a highly contagious (catching) skin infection which mainly affects children. Although some people associate it with eczema it can equally affect skin where there are insect bites, scabies or cold sores, and it affects perfectly healthy skin as well. In new-born babies it can be serious, but otherwise it is not a threat and can easily be cured.

SYMPTOMS

Impetigo first appears on the face, scalp, hands or knees. It begins as little red spots which soon become blisters and quickly break, exuding a pale yellow, sticky liquid. The blisters then dry to form large, irregularly shaped, brownish-yellow crusts.

If only a small area of skin is affected, there are usually no other symptoms, but if large areas are involved, or if the surrounding skin is also infected with other bacteria, your child will feel unwell, and will have a high temperature and swollen lymph nodes (for example the glands in the neck).

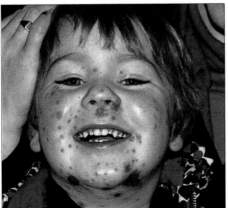

JOHN WATNEY

Even though this child looks quite happy, impetigo can cause children to be feverish and unwell.

CAUSES

Impetigo is caused by the staphylococcus bacterium, which is found in the nose. It can be transmitted by breathing or sneezing, particularly on to damaged skin, and it soon causes inflammation and weeping blisters.

PREVENTION

Unless precautions are taken, impetigo can quickly spread to other members of the household or school, either through infected flannels and towels, or by direct contact. As always when a child is ill, it is very important to keep flannels and towels used by the affected child away from other members of your family. If possible these should be boiled after use, as should your child's bed linen and clothes.

Children with impetigo should be told not to scratch the crusts, which can cause the infection to spread as well as running the risk of scarring. They should also be kept away from school until the infection has cleared.

TREATMENT

The earlier treatment begins, the better. If the area affected is small the doctor will prescribe an antibiotic cream to be applied to the blisters three or four times a day until the crusts have healed. For larger areas additional antibiotics will be prescribed, to be taken by mouth or occasionally by injection. Thick crusts may have to be soaked off with liquid paraffin or salt water.

If left untreated, impetigo can cause abscesses elsewhere in the body, and very occasionally may even be responsible for nephritis (an inflammation of the kidneys). But as long as your child sees the doctor and starts the treatment straight away there is usually no problem. Very young babies may need to be treated in hospital.

WATCHPOINTS

As new-born babies have no immunity they can suffer badly if they catch impetigo, and it can occasionally even be life-threatening. It is extremely important that no-one with the disease should come into contact with young babies or their mothers.

YOUR QUESTIONS

Q In my mother's day, impetigo was a frightening word – people dreaded their children getting it. But now it doesn't seem to be very serious. Why is this?

A This is simply because modern treatment of the disease, with antibiotics, is so effective at curing it in the early stages.

■ INDIGESTION

See also COLIC

Indigestion is a common complaint in children and can cause considerable pain in the bowel. It is often referred to as colic in babies and simply as tummy-ache in older children.

SYMPTOMS

A tummy-ache can be a constant pain or it can come and go in waves. If the pain keeps recurring, this is a sign of colic when the stomach or intestine goes into spasm. A baby will invariably start to cry during a spasm and will be difficult to comfort as he draws his legs up to his stomach. Colic can last for hours and it may not appear to have any relation to feeds. Most babies will probably be sick, which is undoubtedly the best way of dealing with the problem.

A constant pain is more common in older children and adults. It is usually situated in the pit of the stomach or in the chest (heartburn). Nausea, a bloated feeling, or flatulence (wind) frequently accompany indigestion. Further symptoms include acid being regurgitated into the mouth and experiencing pain just before opening the bowels.

CAUSES

Indigestion is most commonly caused by over-eating, eating too quickly, or eating unsuitable food. When this happens, the stomach produces an excess of acid in a bid to digest the food. This in turn leads to heartburn or tummy-ache.

It is possible for psychological reasons to be behind bouts of indigestion. Anxiety and tension often affect that part of the nervous system which controls the acid production in the stomach. Acid is poured into the gut and painful cramps are the result.

Colic in small babies can be brought on by emotional tension but it is usually a reaction to food. Even breast milk can induce colic as minute traces of certain foods, especially dairy products for example, may disagree with the baby's digestive system. Older children can get colic after eating acidic food, such as unripe fruit.

Indigestion occasionally has a more severe cause. Both measles and mumps can cause it, as can something that the child has swallowed, like a button or a wad of cotton wool.

TREATMENT

Alas, there is very little you can do to ease the pain in a baby or small child. Reassure him by holding him close to you or alternatively keep him active to take his mind off the pain. Some breast feeding mothers discover that if they eat little but often, their babies appear to be happier.

An antacid such as bicarbonate of soda is the usual way of treating indigestion in children over the age of five. As the name suggests, an antacid neutralizes the acid in the stomach and brings prompt relief. But make sure you follow the manufacturer's instructions to the letter and never attempt to give more in the belief that the antacid will work better or faster.

Most children want to lie down when they have indigestion but this is not a good thing to do and it is better to keep active if possible. If your child becomes so listless that he has to rest, encourage him to sit up and let him have a few sips of water.

If you suspect that the indigestion might have been brought on by an emotional problem, try to find out the cause and, if necessary, ask the child's teacher, or the doctor or health visitor for advice.

If you know your child has swallowed something small such as a button, there is little cause for worry as it will pass harmlessly through the digestive system. However, if you are uncertain of what was swallowed let your doctor take over treatment. If you know he has swallowed a poisonous chemical, take him to the local hospital immediately.

When children get excited, and eat rich foods they may not be used to, indigestion often follows.

PRODEEPTA DAS

PREVENTION

Indigestion can usually be avoided if you encourage your child to chew food slowly and thoroughly, as this will make it easier to digest. It is also a good idea to avoid giving your child meals when he is cold or wet, as the digestive mechanism of the body slows down when it is cold. Making sure that your child has plenty of exercise and including plenty of fibre in his diet will also help keep indigestion at bay.

WATCHPOINTS

Isolated bouts of indigestion are not dangerous but if your child has any of the following additional symptoms, consult your doctor:
• persistent diarrhoea or vomiting
• passing blood-stained faeces (*see* Intussusception)
• a fever or any signs of a rash or swelling
• a tummy-ache that refuses to go away after several hours
• a pain that is so acute that he has to lie down or draws his legs up to his chest.

YOUR QUESTIONS

Q Our entire family suffers from indigestion. Does it run in families?

A It really depends on the exact nature of the symptoms. Indigestion is so common that you could say that every family has sufferers because most people get indigestion at some time or another. Try altering your family's diet slightly for a while and see if it makes any difference. Stay clear of rich and spicy food and avoid giving meals just before going to bed.

■ INFLUENZA
see FLU

■ INGROWING TOENAIL
see TOENAIL

■ INSOMNIA

Insomnia — not being able to sleep — is most usually associated with older people but children can suffer from it too. Insomnia really means habitual sleeplessness over a substantial period.

SYMPTOMS

The symptoms of sleeplessness are obvious enough. But diagnosing genuine insomnia (being unable to go to sleep on a regular basis) in children is not always so easy. It is only when the problem recurs night after night, week after week, that you should take the matter in hand. The older your child is, the more you should take note of the problem. A two-year-old is bound to be wakeful for short periods during most nights but a five-year-old should be able to sleep more consistently through the night (except when ill).

There are essentially two forms of insomnia. As with adults, some children find it hard to go to sleep, but others wake up in the middle of the night and only then find it hard to nod off again.

Of the two, the latter is more significant as it usually betrays signs of deep anxiety — something that should be tackled quickly before it becomes a problem.

A child who wakes up in the night often needs a reassuring cuddle before she can go back to sleep.

CAUSES

Reasons for insomnia are legion but only a few of them need medical treatment, especially as far as children are concerned.

Babies tend to evolve their own sleep patterns which may not, unfortunately, coincide with yours. It is perfectly natural and normal for a baby to wake up in the middle of the night and this should not be misconstrued as insomnia.

However, a two-year-old who is familiar with a routine should go to sleep readily and should sleep for at least eight hours out of 24. She may wake up in the middle of the night, possibly several times, but again this is not considered unusual. The cause may just be a bad dream that has disturbed her and all she needs is some comforting. Most children go back to sleep again without too much trouble.

A sick child may sleep soundly if she is on medication, but a mild illness like a common cold will be more likely to keep her awake as breathing and relaxing can become extremely difficult. Anybody with a fever, whether child or adult, is prone to waking up in the middle of the night bathed in sweat. This can be extremely distressing and scaring to a child and she may even be reluctant to try and go to sleep again.

Another common reason for children being unable to sleep at night is a change in routine or a change in surroundings. A new cot or strange wallpaper can make a child feel scared or insecure and going to sleep is the last thing she will want to do until she is convinced that she is safe.

A heavy meal before bed-time can make children wakeful. And so can a badly ventilated bedroom that lacks fresh air. If your child is listless and complains of no sleep one morning, these could be the cause.

Anxiety is the most common cause of insomnia in adults and it can also keep children awake at night. Children are remarkably quick at picking up family tensions that create doubts about their security and will sleep badly when this happens.

A glass of warm milk at bedtime is a well-known way of ensuring a good night's sleep.

TREATMENT

As far as babies are concerned, there are, broadly speaking, two ways of coping with disrupted sleep patterns. On the one hand, you can let your baby dictate her own routine — sleeping when she wants to, for as long as she wants to — or you can impose a regime. For many parents, imposing a regime is the most practical option.

Whichever option you adopt, it is imperative that you are consistent — a change in routine will almost certainly lead to restless nights. If you go away on holiday or stay with relatives for a weekend, make sure that you take a supply of teddies, dolls or other familiar toys as well — they will help to provide the necessary comfort in an otherwise strange house.

Older children also need reassurance at night, which can be a frightening time, especially if they have vivid imaginations and can see monsters looming out of the curtains or wallpaper. Try not to ridicule your child's perceptions. Although they may seem silly to you, they may be extremely frightening to her — to the extent that they will keep her awake night after night.

Comfort your child by reading her stories and, if needs be, show her that there is nothing sinister under the bed or in the cupboard.

If your child goes to school and persists in waking up in the middle of the night, it may be something at school, rather than at home, that is making her panic. Try to find the cause and act on it immediately, if necessary with help from teachers.

The one thing to bear in mind is that drugs (sleeping pills or depressants) should be used only as the very last resort. Consult your family doctor if the problem becomes unduly worrying and never give your child drugs unless they have been prescribed for her.

ACTIONPLAN

There are several things you can do to help your child sleep better.

• Try to ensure that she gets plenty of exercise and fresh air during the day – this will encourage sleep later on.

• If your baby has difficulty in getting off to sleep, don't try to keep her up late in the belief that this will make her more tired and therefore more likely to get to sleep. She will undoubtedly get tired but this will probably make her bad-tempered and upset, so instead of going to sleep, she may end up crying.

• Check that your child's nightwear isn't restrictive in any way. It should be soft and loose all over. Some nylon garments can irritate children's sensitive skin.

• Some fresh air at night encourages sound sleep and an open window or a door left ajar is always a good idea even in chilly weather.

• Avoid giving your child a late-night snack last thing before bed as this will stimulate rather than pacify. A hot, milky drink at bedtime, however, is a good idea.

YOUR QUESTIONS

Q We seem to be a family of insomniacs. Can insomnia in fact run in families?

A There is some evidence that shows that this is possible but it is more likely that you share the same habits and it is these that are keeping you all awake. Try changing some of your routines – for example, eat earlier in the evening, avoid stimulating drinks like coffee and tea, take more exercise, and sleep in well ventilated rooms.

■ INTUSSUSCEPTION

This is an illness which, although it is not common, particularly affects babies under the age of about 12 months. It is a condition in which one part of the intestine is drawn into the next and doubles up inside it. The action of the intestinal muscles draws the intestine further and further inside itself, causing a blockage of the bowel, and sometimes requiring surgery. If the condition is not diagnosed and treated quickly, it can cause the child's death.

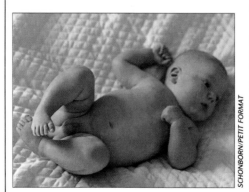

Intussusception, a distortion of the bowel, mainly affects babies who are under 12 months old.

SYMPTOMS

As the intestine is drawn inside itself it goes into spasm, and this causes the child severe tummy pain which will make him cry and draw up his legs in pain. But there may be fairly long periods between the spasms during which he seems quite normal, and will often sleep with exhaustion from the previous fit of pain.

At first the baby will have normal bowel movements, but after a few hours the condition will cause his faeces ('stools') to be jelly-like with mucus and red with blood. The child will probably be pale, especially during the attacks, and may also have a fever. The condition can also cause attacks of vomiting.

CAUSES

It is not known what causes intussusception. Although it is very rare, it often seems to occur out of the blue, suddenly attacking an otherwise completely healthy baby. But it may follow on from a cold or other viral infection which has caused the glands in the abdomen to become enlarged.

DIAGNOSIS

If your baby suddenly has colicky attacks which make him scream with pain, and has the bowel movements described above, you should take him to the doctor's surgery or call the doctor out straight away, saving a sample of the faeces for the doctor to examine.

If your doctor suspects that intussusception is the cause, he or she will arrange for hospital tests to be done. These will involve pumping air into the bowels through the rectum (known as an air study), so that any problems will show up clearly on an X-ray. This is quite painless, and sometimes even rights the problem, with the pumping of air pushing any inverted parts of the intestine out again, making further treatment unnecessary.

TREATMENT

If an intussusception shows up on the X-ray and is not put right during the air study, an operation will be performed to correct it. Depending on the severity of the case this operation can be quite straightforward or it may mean removing a part of the child's bowel. The outlook for a full recovery is good.

■ IRON-DEFICIENCY

see ANAEMIA

■ ITCHING

Annoying though they are, itches are essential to the well-being of the body as they can be a warning of an illness or disease that may require treatment. Itches can appear any-where – from the toes to the scalp – and they are not always just on the skin. They can affect the eyes, ears, palate of the mouth and even the area around the anus, which are all covered by mucous membranes.

SYMPTOMS

Itching sensations vary greatly, de-pending on their cause. They can be mild, localized tingling feelings that are easily relieved by a quick scratch,

or they can be so severe, or all over the body, that the sufferer is driven into a complete frenzy.

One of the dangers with itches, particularly with children, is that they are often made worse by scratching and if the skin is broken, infection can soon follow. For this reason alone they should be tackled as quickly as possible when they crop up.

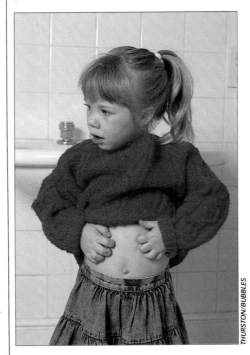

Wool worn next to the skin can easily cause irritation, but a vest or blouse will help to prevent this.

CAUSES

Itching is caused by the stimulation of the tiny nerve endings which lie just under the skin or the mucous mem-brane. This stimulation can be local as, for example, when a shirt collar rubs against the neck, or it can be brought on by the release of hista-mine, a chemical substance which inflames the nerve endings. For inst-ance, histamine is released when a person is stung by an insect or nettle or due to the presence under the skin of some virus or fungi.

Many children have sensitive skins that are allergic to lotions, shampoos and even anti-septics, drugs and certain foods. Such allergies can lead to a condition called urticaria – a short-lived but intensely irritating

skin rash which is red and lumpy.

Urticaria, which is sometimes cal-led hives (*see* separate entry), often appears around the mouth or genit-als and the swelling can be quite severe. Sometimes, urticaria is associated with aching joints and difficulty swallowing or breathing.

Skin diseases and conditions are some of the most common causes of itching. Dermatitis, eczema, and psoriasis all produce severe itching in the affected area, as do chilblains, lice, ringworm, scabies, infestation with threadworm, and athlete's foot. Sunburn is another common culprit.

MORE SERIOUS CAUSES

If your child has other symptoms that accompany itching – is listless or has a fever, for example – it is always as well to play safe and consult a doc-tor. Similarly, if a rash breaks out, consult your doctor in case it needs treatment. Itching can be an early sign of diabetes, kidney failure, chick-enpox or jaundice.

In addition, some itching can be totally psychological in cause, result-ing from tension or anxiety. If you think this may be the case, try to find out what the problem is and if needs be ask for professional help.

TREATMENT

How you treat an itch depends very much on the cause. Severe rashes or uncontrollable itching should always be tackled by a doctor but minor cases can be safely tackled at home.

You can ease the irritation from insect bites or stings by applying calamine or antihistamine lotion. Witch hazel also helps to relieve itching as it cools the skin and re-duces local swelling. Urticaria can be treated in much the same way but if it is very severe and if your child is having trouble breathing or swallow-ing, go and see your doctor. Urticaria usually clears up after approximately 48 hours.

Fungal infections, such as athlete's foot between toes, are easily treated with an anti-fungal ointment or pow-der. Thrush, another itchy rash caused by a fungus, is quite common in children and is also easily treated with a prescribed ointment, as are scabies and worm infestations.

Most itchy spots benefit from being left uncovered but if the skin is broken, cover it with a sticking plaster so that dirty finger nails don't cause infection. Scabs and old wounds can cause itching — try to prevent your child from touching them and if absolutely necessary cover them up.

If you are in any doubt about what is causing your child to scratch, do not hesitate in seeing your doctor.

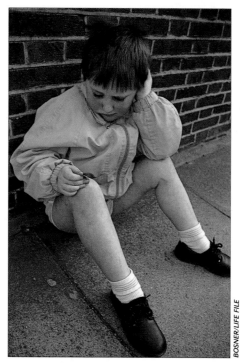

Some children are affected by adhesive dressings and it is better not to use them for small wounds.

■ JAUNDICE

see also HEPATITIS

A child or adult who looks yellow is described as being jaundiced, but jaundice is not actually a disease in itself. Rather it is a symptom of a disorder, usually in the liver. Prompt diagnosis and treatment of the disorder is important.

TYPES OF JAUNDICE

Although jaundice is often associated with a liver disorder, this is not always the case. If excessive numbers of blood cells are being broken down there may be jaundice but no actual problem with the liver. This is called **pre-hepatic** jaundice and it is comparatively rare. But there are certain congenital, hereditary disorders which affect the function of

the red blood cells and there are other circumstances in which too many red blood cells are broken down (called excessive haemolysis).

Any condition that upsets the function of the liver cells may cause jaundice by interfering with the conjugation process. This is known as **hepatocellular** (liver cell) jaundice. The most common disease to affect the liver is hepatitis (in fact there are two types of the disease — type A is most frequent in children *see* separate entry).

Hepatitis inflames the liver cells and jaundice follows quickly. Type A hepatitis is very contagious and can quickly spread through a family or even a school. The virus is found in saliva, blood and faeces and is most often passed on through contaminated food.

Certain drugs, such as some antidiabetic and certain antimalarian drugs, can adversely affect the liver but such cases are rare.

Obstructive jaundice is not very common in children. It is brought about when the bile duct from the liver to the gall bladder becomes blocked. The usual cause for this obstruction in adults is gall stones, but in children it may be something more serious such as a tumour that is causing the obstruction.

JAUNDICE IN NEWBORNS

Jaundice in new-born babies is very common. The usual cause is that the baby's liver is underdeveloped and not quite mature enough to cope with the normal breakdown of red blood cells. Rarer cases are due to infections contracted from the mother. Severe cases of jaundice in babies have to be dealt with quickly as high levels of unconjugated bilirubin in the blood may lead to it being deposited in various parts of the brain, causing permanent damage.

SYMPTOMS

Yellowness is usually the first symptom of jaundice, showing first in the whites of the eyes and then in the skin and this is a symptom which cannot be missed. The disease or problem that is causing the jaundice may lead to pain.

If you suspect that your child may be jaundiced, take note of her stools and urine – pale stools and dark urine often indicate that jaundice is developing.

CAUSES

Red blood cells are constantly being broken down by the spleen and replaced so that they can carry out their vital functions in the body efficiently.

A substance called bilirubin is released during this process and is carried to the liver where it is subjected to a process called conjugation. This makes the bilirubin soluble in water so that it can be excreted by the liver as bile product.

If there is a problem in the production, conjugation or disposal or bilirubin, then it builds up inside the body. It is the raised level of bilirubin in the blood that gives the yellow colour of jaundice.

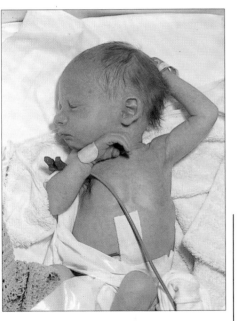

STEVENSON/SCIENCE PHOTO LIBRARY

New-born babies are particularly vulnerable to jaundice because of their immature livers.

TREATMENT

Pre-hepatic jaundice can be tackled in many ways, depending on what is causing the problem. It may be necessary for the child to take drugs or some hormones.

Hepatocellular forms of jaundice due to hepatitis often clear up by themselves without any specific treatment. Rest is often the best cure but it can take a very long time.

The most common way of treating jaundiced new-born babies is to place them under a powerful light as this helps to break down the bilirubin that is causing the problem. In very extreme cases, a badly jaundiced baby may have to have a complete change of blood but this is not normally necessary and after a few days the liver will be able to conjugate the bilirubin without any help.

YOUR QUESTIONS

Q My daughter looks quite yellow when she is very tired. Could this be jaundice?

A It is possible that your child has a slightly higher level of bilirubin in her blood stream than is normal. There is a congenital disorder called Gilbert's syndrome where people suffer from a long-term, low-grade jaundice. The condition is extremely common and can be made worse by infection. Although it does not usually cause any trouble, it is always worth consulting your doctor to seek advice.

■ KIDNEYS

The kidneys are two of the most vital organs in the body. Their main purpose is to filter out impurities from the blood but they also regulate the balance of salts and water that is kept in circulation. The two kidneys are located on either side of the spine, just under the rib cage.

Kidneys in both children and adults are so efficient that it is perfectly possible to live a normal life with just one. However, kidney disease and renal failure (renal means 'of the kidneys' in Latin and is a medical term often used by doctors) usually affect both organs. Consequently, it is important to act as quickly as possible if you detect that something could be wrong.

KIDNEY FUNCTIONS

Like all organs, the kidney has an extremely complex structure. Under the microscope it reveals a maze of tiny tubes which are all mixed together. Some of these tubes (capillaries) are part of the blood circulation system and the rest, tubules, carry urine and are connected to the bladder through the ureter. The capillaries and tubules come into close contact in bunches, called nephrons. It is in the nephrons that impurities and water are filtered out of the blood stream into the tubules to be discharged to the bladder. It is also in the nephrons where the body's chemical balance is maintained. For example, on a hot, dry day, the kidneys will conserve water in the blood stream, but if it is cold and there is a lot of water already in the blood, the kidneys will get rid of the excess water.

Many of a kidney's functions are governed by hormones which are secreted into the body by glands situated in different regions of the body. For instance, the pituitary gland in the brain releases a hormone (antidiuretic hormone) that dictates how much water should be retained by the kidneys.

KIDNEY PROBLEMS

Remarkable and efficient though they usually are, kidneys do occasionally fail. And unfortunately, renal collapse is not unheard of among children.

Shock, severe dehydration, kidney disease, and infection can all reduce the filtering powers of the kidneys and this inevitably leads to chemical imbalance in the body.

SYMPTOMS

If the kidneys fail quickly – as the result of acute renal failure, an infection, or because of shock – your child will pass little or no urine and will look puffy, possibly with swollen ankles. She may also feel sleepy depite breathing fast. In more severe cases, she may have convulsions. Other signs that something is wrong include blood or pus in the urine and pain in passing urine.

Dehydration in particularly hot, dry weather can lead to a failure to produce urine, but provided your child drinks plenty of liquid this should not develop any further.

If a progressive disease is to blame, the symptoms of chronic kidney failure are not so obvious. Your child may have headaches, look pale and go off her food. She may also feel sick or even vomit. After some time, you may notice that she stops growing and complains of aching joints, and a dry itchy skin.

If you have the slightest reason for considering chronic kidney failure, take your child to the doctor. He will carry out routine tests on your child's urine to see if it contains any proteins that should have been dealt with by the kidneys.

CAUSES

A number of diseases can affect the kidneys, the most frequent in children being infectrion of the kidneys (nephritis) and degeneration of the renal tissues (nephrosis). Or the streptococcus bacterium that causes sore throats can enter the blood stream and infect the kidneys. However, this type of infection is comparatively rare these days, thanks to antibiotics. Other bacteria can travel up the ureters, the tubes that link the bladder to the kidneys.

TREATMENT

Most kidney infections can be treated quickly and efficiently by antibiotics. Your doctor may try several different antibiotics to find the most efficient one to beat the disease.

Apart from treating the underlying cause for the kidney failure, your doctor will attempt to correct any chemical imbalance in your child's body and may suggest a special diet. In addition, he may prescribe drugs if there is high blood pressure.

It is only if the kidneys have been severely or irreparably damaged that dialysis may be recommended. This process involves being 'plugged' into a kidney machine that filters out impurities in the blood. Each session on the machine can take up to five hours and it may be necessary to have several sessions every week. This can be extremely distressing for an adult, let alone a child, and the alternative may be to have a kidney transplant.

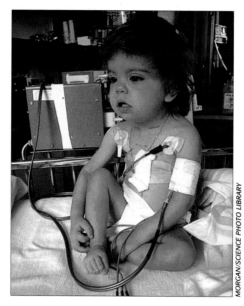

This little diabetic girl has to undergo regular renal dialysis.

MORGAN/SCIENCE PHOTO LIBRARY

WATCHPOINTS

Contact your doctor if your child has:

• discoloured urine, particularly if it is red and leaves a red deposit

• pain experienced while passing urine

• pain in the lower back or in the abdomen

• a puffy appearance, possibly with swollen ankles.

YOUR QUESTIONS

Q If one of my child's kidneys were to fail, would the other one be able to cope on its own?

A Yes. Each kidney has so many nephrons (filtering units) that it is perfectly possible to live a normal, energetic life with just one. In fact, a healthy person doesn't really need all of the second one either.

For this reason, it is quite reasonable to remove a kidney from a healthy person and donate it to someone else. The donor can live with one kidney for the rest of his or her life, provided it stays healthy.

Q My child seems to drink a lot of water and juice. Is this a good thing or does it mean that something is wrong with her kidneys?

A Babies and children need plenty of liquid, especially during hot weather or if they are highly energetic. This is because water is lost in sweat and unless it is replaced, the chemical balance in the body will be upset.

If your child appears to be healthy in every other respect, there is nothing to worry about. The important thing to note is how much urine she passes over a period of many hours. If this is very little, it could be that something is wrong and you should take her to the doctor.

■ KISS OF LIFE

see ARTIFICIAL RESPIRATION

■ KNOCK KNEES

Many children have knock knees – it is quite common and is only occasionally caused by dietary deficiencies. The condition usually puts itself right without medical attention as they grow up.

SYMPTOMS

Knock knees is a condition that hardly needs description. The lower legs, instead of appearing straight and parallel, seem to splay outwards from the knees, and the knees often actually meet. Many children are born with their knees bowing out, and then develop knock knees as they learn to walk. But the knock-kneed child usually has no problems in walking or running and there is no pain or discomfort.

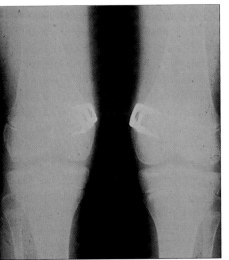

Occasionally metal staples – inserted in the bones of the leg – are used to correct knock knees.

CAUSES

Having knock knees seems to come about as a result of a stage of development in early childhood when the inside of the knee tends to grow faster than the outside. Often the condition develops when the child is about two years old, and becomes worse during the following year or so, before the legs gradually become normal. By the time the child is six or seven the legs are usually straight.

The disease known as rickets can cause knock knees and other types of bone deformities. Rickets is caused by a deficiency of vitamin D in the diet and is now very rare in developed countries. If knock knees are caused by rickets there will be other problems such as enlarged ankles and wrists.

In sunny countries the necessary vitamin D (needed for the absorption of calcium) is produced through the action of sunlight on the skin. Because of this people from Asia or the Caribbean who immigrate to northern countries may be prone to vitamin D deficiency unless they make up for the lack of sun by eating more fish (especially cod liver oil), milk and eggs to supply vitamin D, rather than following the diet they have traditionally been used to.

DIAGNOSIS

If you are worried about your child's knock knees, mention it to your health visitor or family doctor. If there seems to be any cause for concern the doctor may assess the condition at intervals by checking the distance between the ankles. He or she may also check the other joints in the body for evidence of rickets or for any early signs of arthritis, and may even test the child's blood or urine.

TREATMENT

There will rarely be anything to worry about and treatment will seldom be required. Usually the doctor will simply monitor the condition every few months to make sure that all is still well.

Very occasionally the doctor may prescribe wedges to be put inside the child's shoes to change the angle of the heels and encourage the legs to develop as they should. In the past children were sometimes made to wear splints to correct the condition but on the whole these are thought to have very little or no effect, and consequently are now rarely used.

It is only if the child still has knock knees by the time that she is about ten years old that surgery is considered. In the operation most commonly performed, metal staples are inserted in the inner side of the knees as shown in the photograph on this page. Once in position these are quite painless. They inhibit bone growth so that the outer part of the knee can catch up with the inner part. Once the knees are normal, another small

Many young children have knock knees and the condition usually rights itself without treatment by the time they are about seven years old.

operation is performed to remove the staples.

RICKETS

If rickets is found to be the cause of the knock knees, the child will be treated with calcium and vitamin D supplements. If the child is young enough this will lead to a complete recovery.

YOUR QUESTIONS

Q If a fully grown child has knock knees, can anything be done to correct them?

A Yes. An operation can be performed to realign the legs by taking a wedge-shaped piece out of the bone on the outside of the leg, just above the knee. After the operation the bones heal completely and the legs remain straight. This is very rarely necessary, however.

Q Is there anything I can do to help my two-year-old's knees to straighten out? He is very knock-kneed at the moment.

A It is worth stretching the knees gently every night by pushing lightly on the insides of the knees. This stretches the ligaments and helps straighten the knees.

■ LACTOSE INTOLERANCE

Lactose is the sugar found in cow's milk, and it is made up of two simple sugars known as galactose and glucose. Normally lactose is broken down in the digestive tract to reduce it to these two sugars, but some children, either temporarily or permanently, lack the ability to break down lactose. This is what is known as lactose intolerance.

SYMPTOMS

A child who has lactose intolerance suffers from a swollen, painful abdomen (tummy), with wind and diarrhoea whenever he drinks milk or consumes lactose in any form. The faeces (stools) are watery and often look frothy.

YOUR QUESTIONS

Q What is the difference between lactose intolerance and cow's milk intolerance, or are they the same thing?

A Cow's milk intolerance is a much more generalized complaint than lactose intolerance, and medical opinion differs concerning even its existence.

Many conditions have been blamed on cow's milk, from asthma and eczema to nettle rash, colic, migraine and catarrh, but the mechanisms involved have not been explained, even though in some cases cures do seem to be effected by withdrawing cow's milk from the diet.

It is more generally agreed that digestive disorders such as diarrhoea, colitis and vomiting can be caused by cow's milk, regardless of whether or not the child (or adult) concerned can produce the lactase that breaks down lactose. If eliminating cow's milk is found to cure a troublesome condition there is no reason not to do it, but care must be taken to make sure that the child has an adequate diet if it does not contain milk and milk products.

A child with lactose intolerance must avoid any foods containing milk, including yogurt.

CAUSES

Normally the body produces an enzyme known as lactase, which is used to break down lactose into its simple sugars. In children who have lactose intolerance this enzyme is not produced and the lactose passes through the digestive tract without being broken down. The undigested lactose draws water from the small intestine and makes the faeces watery. When the lactose reaches the large intestine fermentation takes place through the action of bacteria normally present there, causing the swelling and pain and introducing the froth.

Lactose intolerance can be the result of an inbuilt ability of the body to produce lactase, but it may also be a temporary condition brought about by gastroenteritis, which damages the digestive tract and stops it from functioning normally.

Sometimes children grow out of their lactose intolerance, but it does also occasionally develop in older children who have not previously suffered from it.

TREATMENT

The best way to prevent lactose intolerance is to breast feed, as human milk contains no lactose. When this is not possible, and your baby shows signs of lactose intolerance when first given cow's milk or formula, your doctor should be able to recommend a lactose-free milk powder.

For older children it may be enough to reduce the amount of milk in the diet, but sometimes milk (and butter and cream) will have to be eliminated altogether. Trial and error will be necessary to find out whether complete elimination is necessary, but it should be a simple matter to gauge your child's reaction to milk, once you are aware of the problem and the exact nature of the symptoms. Soya milk is a good substitute for cow's milk, if this does have to be eliminated from the diet.

■ LARYNGITIS

Laryngitis is an inflammation of the larynx or voice box, which may be caused by an infection or by over-using the voice. It usually gets better quickly if the child rests the larynx completely for a few days.

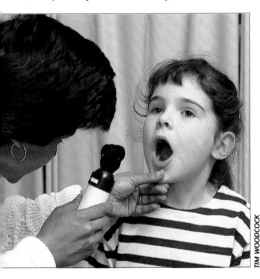

Laryngitis affects the very back of the throat and the doctor may have difficulty detecting it.

SYMPTOMS

Laryngitis can be acute (sudden) or chronic (continuous). In both cases the symptoms are hoarseness, with difficulty in speaking or even com-

plete loss of voice. Usually there is soreness at the very back of the throat and the neck feels tender to the touch.

CAUSES

Laryngitis can be caused by a viral or bacterial infection such as a cold or flu. Most frequently the infection will be one which spreads downwards from the nose, but in unusual cases there can be infection in the lungs or trachea (windpipe). Chronic laryngitis is commonly caused by continuous irritation from dust or smoke. A child whose parents smoke heavily can be affected by laryngitis in this way.

YOUR QUESTIONS

Q My little girl lost her voice after the school Christmas carol concert. Can singing cause laryngitis?

A Yes, although laryngitis is often caused by an infection it can also be a result of over-using the larynx. A hot, dry atmosphere, such as that in an over-heated school hall, can make this happen all the more quickly.

TREATMENT

Usually laryngitis is not a serious complaint and it is quickly cured by giving the voice a complete rest. Try to persuade a child with laryngitis to talk as little as possible, and to talk in a whisper. (You can whisper back to make it fun.)

Plenty of warm drinks, such as sweetened lemon juice and hot water or squash diluted with hot water, will soothe the child's throat, and it is also helpful to maintain a moist atmosphere by bringing a bowl of hot water into the room and replenishing it when the water cools.

The child can also get relief by inhaling steam, holding her head, covered with a towel, over a bowl of steaming water. Traditional remedies such as some eucalyptus oil or friar's

balsam in the water often prove helpful in soothing the throat.

MEDICAL HELP

If the condition lasts for more than a week, medical help may be needed, and your doctor may decide that antibiotics are necessary. If your child has frequent, troublesome or long-lasting attacks of laryngitis, take her to the doctor to see if a reason can be found.

WARNING

In young children, laryngitis may cause the windpipe to become so swollen that it is difficult for the child to breathe. Croup (*see* separate entry), a barking cough, can be a sign that this is happening.

If your child has croup, or if there is any indication that her breathing is difficult, immediate treatment must be given. The child should be taken at once to your family doctor or to the accident and emergency ward at your nearest hospital.

■ LAXATIVES
see also CONSTIPATION

There are several types of laxatives, but it should not normally be necessary to give laxatives of any kind to children except on your doctor's advice — nor, indeed, should adults need to take them.

TYPES OF LAXATIVE

Some laxatives, such as castor oil and senna, act on the nerves in the bowel and increase the power and frequency of the contractions that move the contents of the bowel through the bowel. Liquid paraffin has the effect of softening the faeces (stools) and consequently making it easier to pass them. So-called osmotic laxatives are drugs which draw water into the bowel, making the faeces softer and bulkier. Bulk laxatives — preparations based on vegetable fibre — are also designed to have this effect.

NEED FOR LAXATIVES

Laxatives are not necessary if children follow a healthy diet with plenty of cereals and other vegetable matter and fresh fruit. Taking laxatives can be harmful as it damages the nerve endings in the colon (large bowel) and eventually causes the colon to lose its ability to make proper contractions at all.

Exercise and adequate fluids are also necessary for good bowel movement, and a child who is ill in bed may become temporarily constipated through loss of fluids from sweating and lack of exercise. A child should always be given plenty of fluids when ill, and this may help a little.

Usually any problem with constipation will not last more than a few days if your child eats lots of fruit, but if you are worried, consult your doctor. He may prescribe a mild laxative for short-term use, especially if the constipation is causing the child pain.

A healthy diet with plenty of fruit, cereals and vegetables should prevent the need for laxatives.

DURRELL MCKENNA/HUTCHISON

■ LAZY EYE

see EYE PROBLEMS

■ LEAD POISONING

Lead is a metal which can be inhaled (breathed) or ingested (swallowed) in minute particles in the air and on food. Without help the body cannot eliminate it and it accumulates in the body to cause a variety of symptoms. Whereas small traces of other metals, such as zinc and copper, are necessary to health, lead is poisonous in any quantity, however small.

Although lead poisoning, leading to the symptoms described below, is nowadays extremely rare in children, and follows only ingestion of abnormal quantities of lead, the inhaling from the air of lead deriving from car and other industrial pollution can be harmful. In extreme cases it may lead to decreased intelligence and other impairments in the mental development of children, although a direct link has never been proved.

SYMPTOMS

Lead poisoning can produce a wide variety of symptoms. In children, who are especially vulnerable, it is most likely to cause fits, weight loss, poor coordination, hyperactivity and disturbed behaviour, all of which may be very difficult to pin down as being caused by lead in the body. In serious cases there is also mental retardation and blindness or deafness.

Other common symptoms of lead poisoning are abdominal pains and constipation, loss of appetite, and a metallic taste in the mouth. Lead in the body can also cause general ill-health, tiredness and disturbed sleep — again all rather generalized symptoms.

In its extreme forms, lead poisoning can affect the nerves, causing a condition known as peripheral neuropathy. This usually affects the nerves controlling the muscles in the hands and wrists. Anaemia is another problem that can be caused by long-term absorption of lead.

CAUSES

In the nineteenth century, many adults were subject to lead poisoning through their work before the dangers of lead were understood and legislation was passed to protect people who were brought into contact with it through their work. Paint was made up largely of lead, and the main danger to children was through their licking their toys, painted with innocent-looking, lead-based paints.

In present times the main source of lead is through car exhausts, since lead is added to petrol to improve performance (although, of course, lead-free petrol is now available, and diesel oil is increasingly being used). There is also a danger of children (and adults) ingesting lead if they live in housing with old paint containing lead, or old-fashioned plumbing in which the water pipes are made of lead. Also vegetables grown near roads may contain unacceptable levels of lead.

Traditional lead soldiers, handed down from father to son, are only suitable for older children who would not put them in their mouths.

PREVENTION

Since the major source of lead in the air is from car exhausts, curbing the use of lead in petrol is the main hope for prevention of any ill effect from small amounts of lead. At present this is still an individual choice, but clearly lead-free petrol should be chosen if possible. (Some older cars cannot be converted to run on lead-free petrol.) Unfortunately, people living near busy roads cannot control the environment in which their children are growing up, but it is sensible not to let children play near traffic, difficult though this is to put into practice with active children.

At least individuals can control their own plumbing systems. Whenever possible, old lead pipes should be replaced with modern copper ones, and if this cannot be done, the tap should be allowed to run for a couple of minutes when drawing off drinking water.

YOUR QUESTIONS

Q If lead is a metal, how does it get into drinking water?

A Lead is a metal which dissolves in water. In old plumbing systems the pipes are made of lead, small quantities of which dissolve in the water passing through them. This is why it is advisable to renew at least the pipes that supply drinking water. However, the problem is less serious in hard water areas, where pipes get 'furred' with lime.

TREATMENT

Lead absorbed into the body gradually replaces the calcium in the bones. From this store, lead gradually escapes into the bloodstream, and this will continue to happen for a long time after the source of poisoning has been controlled. This means that the level of lead in the blood is not an accurate guide to the total amount accumulated in the body. However, lead in the bloodstream can be eliminated by the kidneys, and the rate of excretion can be increased by giving the child drugs which encourage the lead in the bones to dissolve in the blood. This helps the kidneys to clear the store of lead in the bones, drawing it out gradually into the blood. Large doses of calcium also assist this process.

Unfortunately, however, in the case of children treatment can be too late. The developing brain is more sensitive to lead than the brain of an adult, and the few children who are affected by lead poisoning are permanently mentally retarded and suffer from fits. There is every reason for

parents to keep up the pressure for a lead-free atmosphere and limit their children's exposure to lead.

UPDATE

However worrying the dangers of lead in the air, it must be made clear that children are not likely to get lead poisoning in the medical sense from lead in the air. A recent report by the European Economic Commission stated that the link between lead in the blood and the IQ of children could not be definitively proven since IQ depends on so many other variants, including social factors. The conclusion of the report, however, was that lead has to be eliminated from the human environment, as much as possible.

While it is not enough to cause true lead poisoning, the air-borne lead from petrol fumes is still harmful.

■ LEG

From the waist to the end of the toes there are more than 60 different, interlinking bones. The femur (thigh bone) is the longest bone in the body; and the second longest is the tibia (shin bone), the main bone at the front of the pair of bones in the lower leg.

The femur and the tibia meet at the knee in a hinged joint which is protected at the front by the patella (kneecap). At the bottom of the tibia and fibia (the bones of the lower leg) are the complex bones of the ankles (tarsals), the foot (metatarsals) and the toes (phalanges).

MUSCLES

Corresponding to the bones, the muscles of the leg include some of the largest in the body. In the lower leg are three sets of muscles, the peroneal muscles on the outside of the leg, the flexors or calf muscles, and the extensors — the muscles in the ankle and foot.

The upper leg also has three sets of muscles: the quadriceps and hamstrings at the front and back of the thigh respectively, and the adductor muscles of the inner thigh. The muscles of the buttock connect with the upper leg and the pelvis.

BLOOD SUPPLY

All the tissues of the legs, and particularly their large muscle systems, need to be supplied with blood to provide oxygen and nutrients.

Blood circulation is perhaps at its weakest in the legs, and blood can easily collect in the veins, since it has to work against gravity. However,

inside the veins there are special valves that prevent the blood from flowing backwards.

Proper exercise is important as it protects children from heart problems later in life.

INJURIES

The legs are strong and flexible, and

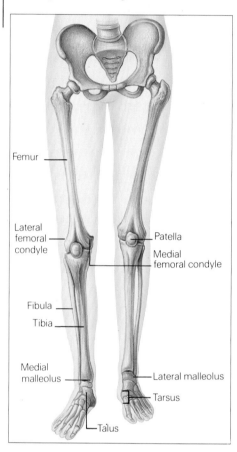

The bones of the leg are large and powerful, in contrast to the complex network of small bones in the feet.

in growing children they do a lot of work, quite apart from taking the weight of the body when standing.

But because of their flexibility they are surprisingly rarely injured. Cuts, bruises and grazes are the most common types of injury. As children grow up and begin to use their legs fully, one of the most vulnerable spots is the shin, which is easily bruised as the shin bone is protected only by a thin layer of skin, The malleolus — the part of the shin bone at the outer ankle — is another vulnerable spot, and the kneecap is prone to dislocation and fracture.

While children are still growing, their legs take a lot of the strain, and benefit from play and exercise.

■ LEG PAINS

see also FRACTURES, LEG, LIMP, OSTEOMYELITIS, STILL'S DISEASE

Children can complain of leg pains, but usually there is nothing really wrong. Adults may refer to these as 'growing pains', but they can be quite a problem for the child — and worrying for the parents.

SYMPTOMS

So-called 'growing pains' are most likely to affect children from four to eight years old. They are felt in both legs as a dull, aching pain, sometimes down the whole length of the thigh or, more usually, all down the lower leg. Often these pains are

Massaging an aching leg – a common problem with active children – will help to alleviate the pain.

worse at night, when they can disturb the child's sleep. The normal aches and pains may become worse after the child has been taking part in sporting activities.

OTHER LEG PAINS

Although most generalized leg pains will be simply 'growing pains', there are a few, quite rare, conditions

which also cause pains in the legs. Certain distinct types of leg pains, sometimes linked with other symptoms, can be an indication of more serious illnesses. (See box for details of these symptoms.)

CAUSES

It is not really known what causes generalized leg pains. Some doctors believe that they are connected with growth spurts and that they may be the effect of the muscles not growing at quite the same rate as the bones. Others argue that there can be no medical reason to explain why growing causes pain.

In some cases, of course, aching in the legs is a natural consequence of taking an unusual amount of exercise and giving the muscles more work than usual, but in this case the connection will be obvious.

TREATMENT

As long as there is no medical reason for pains in the legs, the only treatments are the old-fashioned remedies of warmth, relaxation and sympathy. A warm bath or a hot water bottle may help to take the pain away, and soothing massage can

CLARKE/SCIENCE PHOTO LIBRARY

Warm baths are soothing for most aches and pains and in the case of growing pains, may even stop them from developing.

TYPES OF LEG PAIN

- **Generalized aches** – probably 'growing pains'
- **Severe pain in one area,** deterring the child from using the leg
  - could be a fracture if the child has recently had an accident
  - could be a symptom of osteomyelitis
- **painful knee, with swelling**
  - could be a dislocation if it follows an accident
  - could be Still's disease or arthritis

See your doctor if your child has leg pains other than generalized pains, and if generalized pains last continuously for longer than a day.

THURSTON/BUBBLES

help to relax tense muscles. While there is no need to make a fuss, you may find that a cuddle and a show of concern do wonders for your child.

Finally, if there seems to be any chance that he is tense and anxious about something that is happening to him at the time, uncovering the cause and getting your child to talk about any worries may solve the problem. Reassurance may be all that is needed.

YOUR QUESTIONS

Q Can I give paracetamol to my little boy when he wakes up in the night with growing pains?

A If this happens frequently it would be a good idea to take your son to the doctor to make sure that there is no medical reason for the pains. If there is not, it could be that a warm bath before bed and a hot water bottle will bring relief. Paracetamol may be given once in a while if the pain really is keeping the child awake, but do not give it on a regular basis, and do seek your doctor's advice.

■ LEUKAEMIA

Leukaemia is a form of cancer that affects white blood cells. Although it is rare, it is very serious. Unfortunately, when children are affected with leukaemia, it often gets worse very quickly if left untreated.

Unlike other forms of cancer, which develop in and spread from one particular area of the body, leukaemia immediately affects the whole body, since it is a disease which involves the blood.

TYPES OF LEUKAEMIA

Leukaemia may start in the bone marrow, where both red and white blood cells are made, or in the lymph system, where a type of white blood cell known as lymphocites circulates.

Leukaemia which starts in the bone marrow is called either *myeloblastic* or *myelocytic* leukaemia, depending on its exact nature, and leukaemia of the lymph system is known as *lymphoblastic* or *lymphocytic* leukaemia. In both cases the leukaemic cells invade each other's territory so that the bone marrow and lymphatic system are always both affected.

LYMPHATIC SYSTEM

Leukaemia of the bone marrow is no more common in children than in adults, but leukaemia of the lymphatic system is far more common in children and affects 50 in a million children between the ages of two and four years. It represents 90 per cent of the cases of child leukaemia. These two forms are acute (developing rapidly) but there is also a chronic (developing over a period of time) form of myelocytic leukaemia.

SYMPTOMS

Anaemia is one of the main, and earliest symptoms of leukaemia, since the illness causes immature white blood cells to develop at the expense of red cells. These blood cells also prevent the formation of sufficient numbers of platelets, which enable the blood to clot, and this leads to excessive bleeding from wounds and unusual bruising, as well as bleeding from gums and also from the nose.

Leukaemia also causes generalized ill health related to anaemia, with tiredness, pallor and general sickliness. The child often also has aching limbs, headaches, and swollen glands. And, because the white blood cells which normally fight infection are being replaced by immature cells that do not have this power, the child with leukaemia falls prey to all sorts of infections. This often results in conditions such as dental abscesses, ulcers and sores in the mouth and throat, sinusitis, and even pneumonia.

Sometimes the liver, spleen and lymph nodes in the thorax become so enlarged that a doctor can feel them on examination. There is often also

considerable pain as the disease progresses. If the illness is chronic, symptoms can be very mild, but eventually they rapidly become marked.

CAUSES

It is thought that a virus is involved in at least some types of the disease. It is also well established that leukaemia is likely to develop in people exposed to atomic radiation, and it has been suggested that there is a special danger to children living in areas near atomic power stations. This could even be because male workers in the stations may have their sperm affected in such a way that their future children get leukaemia.

Chronic myelocytic leukaemia is associated with a chromosome abnormality, but it is not known whether this is merely a result of the disease or whether the abnormality

This girl is receiving an infusion of white blood cells to attack the leukaemic cells in her blood.

PALILLY/SCIENCE PHOTO LIBRARY

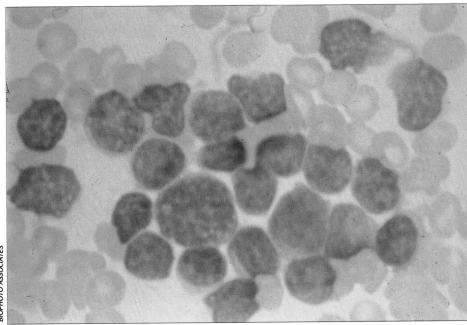

In leukaemia the number of white cells, here stained purple, are greatly increased and are unable to fight infection.

was present before the disease developed. However, leukaemia does not seem to be inherited, as its incidence is not sufficiently high in children whose relations have had the disease; the chance of having a second case in the family is approximately one in 720.

ABNORMAL CELLS

Normal white blood cells have a life-span of a few days, after which they are replaced by new cells. When a child has leukaemia, excesive numbers of immature white cells are produced, unable to fight infections as normal white cells do, and clogging up the bone marrow and invading the lymph system, liver and spleen. Normal production of both white and red blood cells in the bone marrow cannot be maintained.

DIAGNOSIS

Leukaemia is diagnosed by studying a blood sample under a microscope. Leukaemia cells are readily recognized. Sometimes a diagnosis can be made from a sample of bone marrow, taken under local anaesthetic by inserting a needle into the cavity of one of the bones (usually the breast-

bone). This often reveals the presence of the disease before it shows up in the blood.

TREATMENT

Leukaemia is usually treated by specialists in centres where all the necessary facilities are available, including so-called 'bubble' units which prevent the spread of infection. This can cause extra worries and problems, since in addition to the strain of seeing your child undergo such a worrying illness, it can be difficult to organize the travel back and forth to the hospital and to make arrangements for any other children to be looked after. Medical treatment and nursing skill is of an extremely high order in specialist hospitals, and staff there are also aware of practical problems and do all they can to help.

Treatment may be by chemotherapy (drugs), by radiation, or ultimately by a bone marrow transplant.

DRUG TREATMENT

Two courses of drug treatment are given. The first aims at killing all the white cells in order to get rid of the leukaemic cells. After this, normal bone marrow should be able to grow again to produce normal white cells. This intensive treatment is followed by a less intensive course of treatment designed to keep the remission

under control, and the child may be able to spend most of the time at home while undergoing this. .

RADIATION TREATMENT

Radiation is sometimes used to suppress the reproduction of cells. An accurately judged amount of radiation will affect only the abnormal, leukaemic cells, which are more susceptible to the effects of radiation than are healthy cells.

All children with acute lymphoblastic leukaemia are now given routine X-ray treatment of the brain and spinal cord, to reduce the potential risk of leukaemic cells invading the nervous system.

BONE MARROW TRANSPLANT

Bone marrow transplant is a relatively new development in the treatment of some forms of leukaemia. The disease is first controlled by chemotherapy, and this is followed by a high dose of X-ray therapy to kill all the cells in the bone marrow. This is aimed at eradicating every single leukaemia cell in the body before the child is given a transfusion of suitable bone marrow from a donor — usually a relative.

If this is successful the bone marrow cells multiply and a healthy new system for the manufacture of new blood cells is established. Unfortunately the patient is extremely susceptible to infection after the X-ray treatment, and the treatment itself involves a high risk of infection, hence the necessity of having the

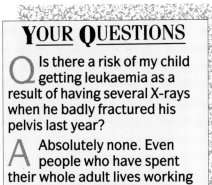

YOUR QUESTIONS

Q Is there a risk of my child getting leukaemia as a result of having several X-rays when he badly fractured his pelvis last year?

A Absolutely none. Even people who have spent their whole adult lives working with X-rays have only a very slightly increased risk. There is no need to worry about the occasional X-rays.

child in a protective 'bubble' unit.

OUTLOOK

The outlook for children diagnosed as having leukaemia, even though it is still serious, is at least not without hope — and treatment is constantly improving. In acute lymphoblastic leukaemia, roughly 25 per cent of children are completely cured. Even though a complete cure is by no means certain, at least in many cases life can be prolonged and suffering alleviated.

■ LICE

There are three types of lice — head lice, body lice and pubic lice. Children are most likely to be affected by head lice.

It has now been established that head lice, once thought to be associated with poor hygiene, thrive in clean hair. Many children suffer from an infestation at some stage, as it is so easily passed from child to child in group situations, and there is no shame involved.

The eggs of the head lice are laid in the hair, close to the scalp, and secured to it by a cement-like substance. After about eight days they

begin to hatch and the new lice feed off the scalp by sucking blood. If left untreated the young lice moult three times after a period of about nine days, and after this they are fully formed adults with the ability to reproduce. Female lice lay up to ten eggs a night.

SYMPTOMS

An itching scalp is the main symptom of head lice. If you inspect the child's scalp you should be able to see either the eggs, which are about 1 mm long, or the 'nits', which are actually the discarded egg casings, still cemented to the hair.

CAUSES

An infestation of head lice is the result of head-to-head contact with someone who is already host to the lice.

PREVENTION

Since lice are not put off by cleanliness, washing the hair frequently makes no difference. Keeping the child's hair short, or pinned back, so that hair-to-hair contact with other children is less likely, may help a

WARNING

Do not rely on medicated shampoos to kill head lice. These are not effective against the lice.

As lice move easily from head to head, it is sensible for every member of the family to be treated once any child in the family has lice. Parents and grandparents can carry head lice too!

little, but there is not a great deal that can be done to protect a child from infestation.

TREATMENT

The safest way to deal with head lice is to use a specific lotion which is sprinkled onto the scalp and rubbed into the hair. The lotion has an alcoholic base and is inflammable, so it must be used carefully, and in a well ventilated room.

Ask you doctor's advice before buying a treatment for head lice, because the lice and eggs can become resistant to particular forms of treatment. Your doctor will know

Close contact between children can spread head lice, if one child is infested. Nits (see inset) are louse eggs which are laid near to the scalp.

TIM WOODCOCK

HOW TO SPOT HEAD LICE

Head lice like clean, shiny hair and the best way of controlling them is to look regularly at your child's hair. The louse is a small greyish insect (which darkens after its feed) living close to the scalp. It gets its blood supply from the scalp. The eggs are laid just above the root of the hair. They are plump, shiny, scalp-coloured and about the size of a pin head.

Treatment

If your child's head is infested:

• Ask your family doctor for a prescription or buy the necessary preparation directly from your chemist.

• Do not wash your hair before treatment as the hair's natural oil helps it work.

• In the evening sprinkle the lotion on the hair and rub gently into the scalp, taking care to avoid the eyes. Repeat until the scalp is thoroughly moistened.

• Allow hair to dry naturally.

• Once the scalp has been properly treated, the lice and nits will be dead, thus preventing further infestation.

• After 12 hours, shampoo the hair in the normal way.

YOUR QUESTIONS

Q I am woried that my daughter's head lice can have spread to other parts of the body before I treated her hair. Can this happen?

A No. Head lice always stick to the head, and the treatment will have successfully eradicated it. There is no danger of the lice appearing anywhere else on your daughter's body.

PREVENTING HEAD LICE

Do

• Look regularly in your child's scalp every week, under a good light, especially around the ears, crown and neck line. An itchy scalp is a suspicious sign and be on the lookout if you hear of an outbreak in your child's class.

• Get a prescription from your family doctor if you find that anyone in your family is infested. You may also ask for advice from your School Nurse, Health Visitor or District Nurse, but remember the clinics and School Nurses cannot supply the lotion.

• Carry out the treatment that is recommended.

• Treat the entire family if one member is infested.

• Inform the class teacher so that other parents can be told to check their child's head and take action if necessary.

Don't

• Feel ashamed if your child catches lice. Lice actually prefer clean hair and no amount of washing with ordinary shampoo will get rid of them once they are there.

• Use the recommended lotion to *prevent* infestation – only use it if a member of your family has head lice.

• Encourage your children to share each other's comb and brushes as this can spread the problem.

• Just treat one member of your family if he catches head lice – it's wiser to treat the whole family at one go.

• Forget that regular combing, brushing and checking the hair will help to prevent infestation.

• Go swimming while treatment is in progress, as the lotion is affected by chlorine.

which treatment is being used successfully in your area at the particular time of the infestation.

■ LIMP

see also BLISTERS, FRACTURES, LEG, OSTEOMYELITIS, PERTHE'S DISEASE, RHEUMATIC FEVER, SEPTIC ARTHRITIS, SPRAINS, STILL'S DISEASE

There are many possible causes for a child's limp – a congenital difference in the growth of the two legs, a minor injury to the foot, perhaps, a hip or knee problem or even, occasionally, a more generalized disease.

SYMPTOMS

A child who limps does not place the full weight of his body on both legs when walking and develops an uneven, loping walk. If the foot or leg is injured, it may hurt only when the child walks on it or, depending on the severity of the injury, may give pain all the time.

CAUSES

A limp may be a congenital problem in which the child's legs develop at different rates. Even a minor differential in the length of the legs can cause a child to limp. If your child suddenly develops a limp and you cannot find a simple explanation such as tight shoes, an ingrowing toenail or a blister, splinter or cut on the foot, you should take her to the doctor for an examination.

It could be a **sprain, strain** or **fracture** in the leg or ankle that is causing the limp. Ask your child to tell you of any falls or bumps she has had, and check the leg for any areas of tenderness or swelling while she is sitting down. Then get her to move the leg gently to see whether any movement causes pain. Pain to the touch could indicate a fracture (which may have gone undetected for some time), while pain on movement suggests a sprain (damaged ligaments) or strain (pulled muscle). All may be accompanied by swelling or soreness and a fracture may also be accompanied by bruising.

A less common cause of limping in a child is the condition known as Perthe's disease, in which the top of the thigh bone collapses over a period of time. In this case there will be pain in the hip on moving, and also in the knee. Despite this being

which are bacterial infections respectively of joints and bones, are both quite rare, but need to be recognized and treated early.

Another possible but rare cause of swollen and extremely painful joints and consequent limping is **rheumatic fever**, which may also cause a blotchy rash and a headache with a high temperature. Rheumatic fever can follow an infection of the throat, up to a month after the infection, and it requires urgent medical treatment.

Rheumatoid arthritis or **Still's disease** is another possible, though infrequent, cause of similar symp-

If there is a **splinter** in the foot, this should be removed with sterilized tweezers, and there should be no further problem.

If you suspect a **sprain** or **strain**, apply a cloth wrung out in cold water to the swollen area to help reduce the swelling, then bandage the ankle or knee (the most likely areas to be affected) with a crêpe bandage to give support. If this has not brought considerable improvement after 24 hours, and definitely if the leg is not fully better within two days, you should take your child to the doctor, in case there is a fracture or some other condition.

To tell whether there is a fracture in the leg, the child will probably be sent to hospital for an X-ray and, if a fracture is found, the leg will probably be put in plaster. A minor fracture however, may be left to heal on its own.

If one leg is slightly shorter than the other, special shoes or boots may remedy the difference. In more extreme cases, callipers or braces can be worn, either occasionally or permanently, and can be quite comfortable to wear.

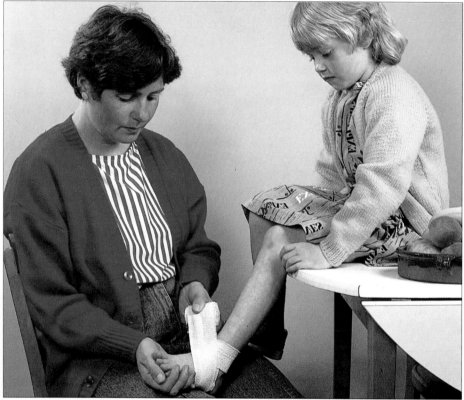

A child with a sprained ankle will limp, but only for a day or two. If it persists, see your doctor.

HOSPITAL TREATMENT

If the cause is found to be **Perthe's disease**, the child will probably be treated in hospital and the damaged bone may be put into a splint to encourage it to regrow properly. Sometimes the child's condition will simply be monitored while the bone regrows properly without the need for any medical help.

If it is found that **septic arthritis** or **osteomyelitis** are responsible, these will be treated by antibiotics, often given by intravenous injection. If osteomyelitis has developed fully, a surgical operation may be needed to remove damaged bone, but it is usually successfully treated by antibiotics some time before it has reached this stage.

Rheumatic fever affecting the joints can be very mild, causing only temporary pains and resolving itself without treatment. If treatment is needed it will be in the form of anti-inflammatory drugs, followed by

OTHER POSSIBLE SYMPTOMS

If there is swelling and extreme tenderness in the knee joint, and if the child has a fever or fluctuating temperature, it is possible that the limp is a symptom of **septic arthritis**, while swelling in the leg, accompanied by tenderness, especially if the child has a fever, could be a sign of **osteomyelitis**. These illnesses,

serious and causing pain and restricted movement, it often cures itself, but only over quite a lengthy period of time.

toms. This causes inflammation of the tissue around the joints, but not due to an infection (unlike rheumatic fever).

TREATMENT

Minor injuries such as **cuts, grazes** and **blisters** will need a dressing to keep them clean while they heal. Usually they will heal up quickly.

a long-term treatment with penicillin to prevent a recurrence.

Equally, **rheumatoid arthritis** or **Still's disease** is treated with anti-flammatory drugs to control the inflammation and ease the pain. Hospital treatment may be necessary for some time, with physiotherapy, and possibly the wearing of splints.

All these illnesses are covered more fully under separate entries.

YOUR QUESTIONS

Q My little girl cut the underside of her big toe badly. The wound had to be stitched and took some time to heal. But now that it is better she is still limping. Can there be any reason for this?

A While your daughter's toe was healing she will have taken the weight off it by limping. This can become a habit, and as long as the cut really has healed properly it should soon pass. However, do encourage your daughter to try to walk without limping.

■ LISPING

see SPEECH IMPEDIMENTS

■ LOCKJAW

see TETANUS

■ LONG SIGHT

see EYESIGHT

■ LUNGS

The lungs occupy most of the thorax or chest cavity, where they are protected by the rib cage. The air we breathe passes into the lungs, and from them oxygen is absorbed into the blood stream, while waste carbon dioxide is breathed out.

The right lung is larger than the left, since the heart takes up some of the space in the left side of the chest.

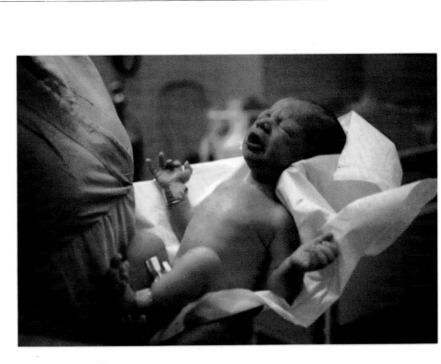

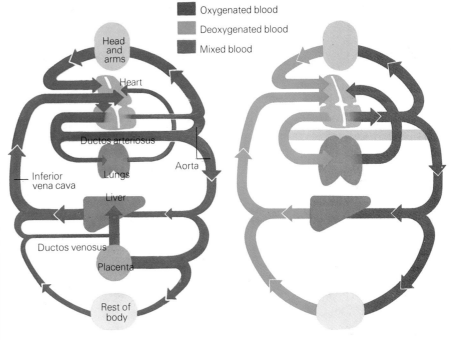

- Oxygenated blood
- Deoxygenated blood
- Mixed blood

Head and arms · Heart · Ductos arteriosus · Aorta · Inferior vena cava · Lungs · Liver · Ductos venosus · Placenta · Rest of body

Breathing is started by the baby's first cry. Before it is born, the foetus gets oxygen from the mother's blood via the placenta. Blood passing to the liver or the inferior vena cava via the ductus venosus is fully oxygenated, but blood in the rest of the body is mixed. A large proportion of the blood reaching the atrium of the heart is shunted to the left atrium through an opening which closes after birth. Much of the blood that reaches the right ventricle goes via the ductus arteriosus. Before birth, very little blood passes through the lungs, which contain no air and are not yet functioning (left). After the child is born, its oxygen supply from the blood in the placenta is cut off, but its first cry expands the lungs so that they start to work (right). There is no more need for the ductus arteriosus, which closes naturally after a few days. If it does not, it can be corrected.

BEGINNING BREATHING

Naturally, a baby does not use its lungs while it is still in the womb and surrounded by fluid. All the oxygen the foetus needs is obtained from the blood in the mother's placenta, so the alveoli (air sacs) are flat, like tiny, deflated balloons.

At the moment of birth a startling change takes place as the placenta separates from the uterus and ceases to supply oxygen to the baby, and the baby spontaneously takes her first breath.

Breathing starts with little gasps, followed by a prolonged cry, showing that the alveoli and lungs are expanding. It takes several months before all the alveoli have expanded and the baby's lungs are fully in use.

The lungs themselves are made up of a dense network of little tubes, some containing blood (blood vessels) and some containing air (bronchi).

INTERNAL STRUCTURE

The right lung is divided into three separate parts (lobes) and the left lung into two, and each lung has one air passage or bronchus, connected to the windpipe which divides and subdivides somewhat, like the branches of a tree.

The subdivisions of the bronchi are

If there is a history of asthma or other respiratory problems in the family, your doctor will listen for any tell-tale signs in your child's lungs.

known as the bronchioles and at the end of the tiny final branch of each of these are little air sacs known as alveoli. The lungs are surrounded by membranes in two layers, known as the pleura, and the bronchi are lined by a self-cleaning mucous membrane which causes invading particles of dust, smoke and bacteria to be coughed out.

BREATHING

When we breathe in our chest muscles and diaphragm (the band of muscle separating the upper from the lower chest) cause the ribs to rise and expand and air is drawn in. The air passes via the bronchi into the alveoli, where oxygen is taken up by the red cells of the blood to be transported to all the tissues of the body. Carbon dioxide, a by-product made when the body produces energy, is carried back in the blood to the lungs and breathed out.

SOME LUNG DISORDERS

Asthma
Constriction of the bronchial tubes, often as an allergic reaction to something breathed in.

Bronchitis
Inflammation of the lining of the bronchial tubes, with or without an infection.

Pleurisy
Inflammation of the pleura (the membranes surrounding the lung), usually caused by an infection.

Pneumonia
Inflammation of the bronchi and lung tissue caused by an infection.

Pneumothorax
A result of injury to the chest or of a lung disease in which air escapes from the lungs into the pleural cavity.

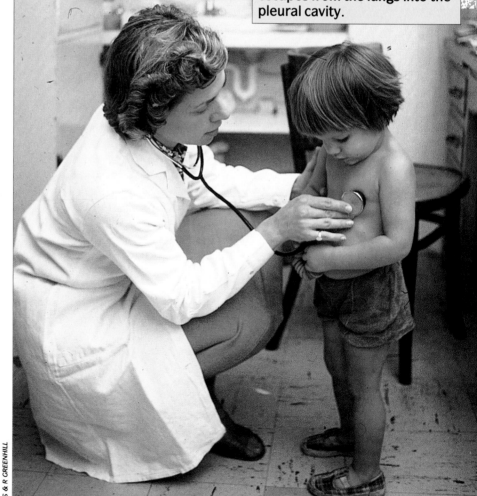

S & R GREENHILL

MALARIA

Even in adults, malaria is one of the most serious major infectious diseases in the world, causing severe bouts of illness and sometimes even death. When travelling to those parts of the world where the infection is rife, every possible precaution must be taken to prevent your child (and yourself) from catching it.

Malaria is a tropical disease, but it may be found a good distance north and south of the tropics. It is particularly prevalent in Africa and is becoming more common in India and other parts of Asia. The only parts of the world from which it has been eradicated are Europe, Australia, the USSR (where it formerly affected the Asian areas), and North America.

SYMPTOMS

Although there are several forms of malaria, the most significant (and sometimes the only) symptom is always fever. When the disease first develops, fevers may be fairly continuous; as it progresses, a cycle develops in which fevers usually occur in phases. A typical pattern is for a fever to break out on every second or third day (usually in the evening), depending on the type of malaria. There is only one form of malaria which generally shows an irregular fever pattern.

The fever often has three distinct stages: a cold, shivering stage, a hot, delirious stage, and finally a sweating stage when the temperature returns to normal. Other possible symptoms are similar to those of flu, with headaches, sickness and diarrhoea. The most dangerous form of malaria causes a fever known as malignant tertian fever ('MT fever'). Attacks are frequent but completely irregular, and their characteristic is that they can be mistaken for almost any kind of acute illness imaginable. As well as severe dysentery, MT fever can cause cerebral malaria which may be fatal in children.

One of the main complications of malaria in general is anaemia, resulting from a recurrent breakdown of the red blood cells. Liver and spleen problems also commonly occur.

CAUSES

Malaria is caused by a parasite — a form of animal life which lives and breeds in a human host. The parasite involved in malaria is the most minute form of animal life imaginable, a one-cell organism known as *plasmodium*, of which there are four types which cause malaria. The parasites are transmitted by mosquitos.

Mosquitos do not automatically

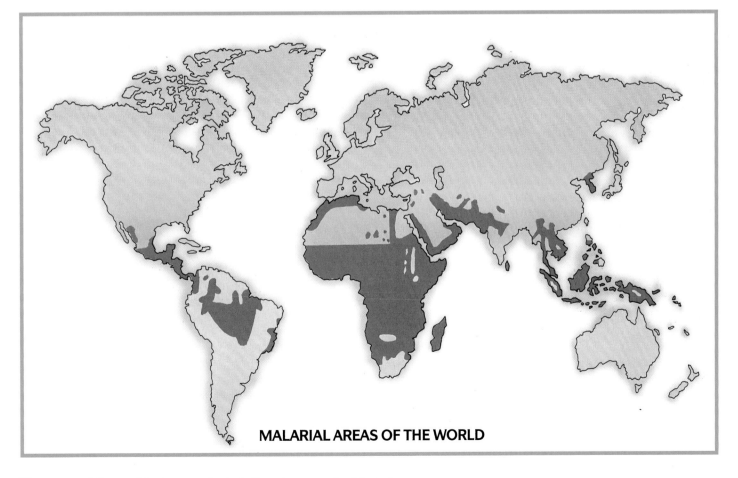

MALARIAL AREAS OF THE WORLD

The areas of the world where malaria is found are marked in red.

harbour the *plasmodium* parasite, but they become infected with it if they bite an infected person. After an incubation period of about ten days, the parasite invades the saliva of the mosquito and when the mosquito attacks again the malaria parasites are passed on to the next person.

Of the four different forms of *plasmodium* – causing malaria, the most dangerous is *P. falciparum*, since this is responsible for the form of malaria which causes MT fever and is most likely to have serious or fatal complications. The three other forms cause less malignant types of malaria, although all are serious.

CYCLE OF INFECTION

After a female carrier-mosquito has bitten a human being, the parasites are transported to the liver and other organs via the bloodstream. After a period of time, during which they multiply, parasites are released back into the blood. They then begin to multiply in the red blood cells, and when these cells are destroyed as a result, huge numbers of the parasite invade a further lot of red cells. It is when the red cells break down and the parasites are released that an attack of fever occurs.

In the three forms of malaria least likely to cause dangerous complications, the parasite continues to inhabit the liver, where it lies dormant. This is why some types of malaria can recur after very long intervals as the parasites become active again.

PREVENTION

If you are taking a child to an area where there is malaria infection, you must make sure that you and the child take anti-malarial drugs before you go. It is essential to take medical advice at least two weeks before you leave, to find out which drug is suitable for prevention in the particular country you are visiting.

Drugs will have to be taken for at least a week before you leave, all the time you are away, and for at least a month after you return, and they must be taken absolutely regularly,

as prescribed. As an additional precaution you and the child should sleep under mosquito nets and burn a mosquito coil in your rooms.

Remember when planning your journey that if you are passing through a country where malaria exists, there is a slight chance that you could be bitten by a mosquito even on a refuelling stop at the airport. Take this possibility into account when travelling anywhere with your child.

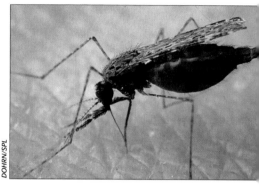

YOUR QUESTIONS

Q Is malaria very dangerous if you catch it when you are pregnant?

A 'Yes. In an affected area pregnant women lose their resistance to malaria and are often given anti-malaria drugs to prevent it. The disease must at all costs be avoided during pregnancy as it can cause miscarriage or abnormalities in the foetus.

TREATMENT

All forms of malaria would eventually clear themselves without treatment, but only after up to a dozen repeated attacks of fever, sometimes spread over many years. In all cases there can be serious liver disorders and dysentery, which need to be treated as they arise. The other common side effects, namely anaemia and general debilitation, can become very serious and require specialist treatment. If cerebral malaria develops as a result of MT fever, treatment may have to be given in specialist hospitals, as it otherwise often leads to death.

There are many drugs, however, that are effective in the treatment of the malaria itself. Of these quinine was the first to be used, but it is used rarely now as it is thought to be linked to a serious, but very rare complication known as blackwater fever, which involves the kidneys. Some of the safest drugs do not affect the parasites hibernating in the

liver, so that a stronger drug has to be given to eliminate these. And in some parts of the world the parasite is becoming resistant to treatment with quinine – though many other drugs are now available.

This all stresses the importance of taking full precautions if you and your child are travelling to or through any part of the world in which it is possible to be infected.

A female mosquito passes on malaria while feeding on human blood.

TRAVEL PRECAUTIONS

Precautions against malaria should be taken when travelling to:
• Mexico (though not Mexico city) and many parts of South America.
• North Africa and most parts of central, southern and eastern Africa (though not Tunisia or Morocco).
• Parts of coastal Turkey.
• Most Middle-Eastern countries.
• Sri Lanka, parts of India, Nepal, Pakistan and Bangladesh.
• Most Far-Eastern countries, such as Borneo, Thailand, Malaya, the Philippines, and Burma (though not Bangkok, Singapore or Hong Kong).

Travellers to Jordan, Egypt, China and the Seychelles do not normally need to take precautions against malaria.

Your doctor will be able to give you further information.

■ MALNUTRITION

see also COELIAC DISEASE, CYSTIC FIBROSIS, LACTOSE INTOLERANCE

Malnutrition is not confined to the Third World, where children suffer as a result of too little food being available. It also affects the developed countries where, though large quantities of food are available for most people, making the wrong choices from what is available can lead to an unbalanced diet that is low in protein or in essential vitamins and minerals, or too rich in fats and carbohydrates.

Any form of illness or poor health caused by an inadequate diet can be said to be a form of malnutrition, whether it be starvation, a poorly balanced diet or over-eating that is responsible for it.

In the Third World most people are starved even of the necessary calories to give them energy, while in the developed world families on low incomes tend to fill up on carbohydrates at the expense of other types of food, and even people with adequate resources may indulge themselves and their children in the wrong kind of food.

However, not all forms of malnutrition are due to a poor diet. It can also be caused by certain types of illness, which prevent nourishment being absorbed from food.

SYMPTOMS

Extreme malnutrition can cause kwashiorkor, the disease that affects thousands of newly weaned infants in the tropics. In its early stages this disease causes a pot-bellied appearance in the starving child and it often results in death from lack of resistance to minor ailments.

In the industrialized world these extremes are seldom, if ever, seen and the effect of malnutrition is general ill-health and poor resistance to infection. The under-nourished child is small, thin and pale, and does not thrive. She often has cold, inelastic skin, sparse, dry hair and a poor complexion; she is usually anaemic and falls prey to attacks of boils, abscesses and ulcers. There are also

several specific conditions that are now recognized to be the result of a lack of specific elements in the diet (*see* Box overleaf).

At the other end of the scale, a child who is malnourished while having plenty to eat will be overweight and will puff and pant when exerting herself mildly, as in running a short distance or going upstairs. If you allow your child to over-eat and put on too much weight you are storing up trouble for her in later life.

DANGERS

Underfed children have a lowered resistance to bacterial and parasitic infections and have no reserves to fall back on. In extreme cases, vitamin deficiencies can cause permanent damage (lack of vitamin D leading to rickets and lack of vitamin A leading to blindness), although it must be stressed that these are rare in the developed world.

Obese children run the risk of suffering from heart problems and artery problems later in life, and are susceptible to joint and bone damage, hernias and varicose veins. Other illnesses such as diabetes, gallstones and degenerative diseases of the kidneys are statistically related to being overweight.

YOUR QUESTIONS

Q My nephew and niece seem to eat a lot of crisps and biscuits, and sometimes refuse proper meals. Can this cause malnutrition?

A As long as it is the exception rather than the rule for them to refuse their meals, the children should not come to any harm.

Whenever possible, children should be steered away from crisps, biscuits and similar over-processed foods in favour of fruit, raw vegetables and wholemeal snacks. Sometimes a flexible approach to mealtimes can stop them eating snacks before meals.

In the West, malnutriton is more likely to result from eating too much of the wrong food rather than from not having enough to eat.

CAUSES

At present, the causes of widespread malnutrition in the Third World are war, drought and the economics which prevent imported food from being available or available food from being distributed. Eating habits can also be to blame — for instance beri-beri is common in the Far East and could be alleviated if whole rice were eaten instead of refined rice.

In the developed world a similar lack of knowledge can lead to bad eating habits and these are made worse by a low income which makes it all too tempting to fill children up on chips and burgers or similar 'convenience' foods, given the high cost of fish, lean meat and cheese. Equally, it must be repeated that affluence alone does not lead to a healthy diet, especially as small children can become fussy eaters, choosing biscuits and chocolate in preference to meat, fresh fruit and vegetables.

Medical conditions such as a cleft

palate can restrict food intake and cause mild malnutrition. Certain illnesses, such as cystic fibrosis, coeliac disease, and lactose or carbohydrate intolerance can also cause malnutrition due to malabsorption of molecules of broken-down food from the intestine, or to the body's inability to break down certain foods during digestion.

CONDITIONS DUE TO DIETARY DEFICIENCIES

- skin diseases
- conjunctivitis
- night blindness
due to lack of Vitamin A
corrected by milk, cod-liver oil, fresh vegetables (especially carrots, tomatoes and apricots)
- diarrhoea
- dermatitis
due to lack of Vitamin B (nicotinamide)
corrected by liver, kidneys, yeast
- anaemia
- bleeding from gums
- wounds slow to heal
due to lack of Vitamin C
corrected by fresh fruit and vegetables

TREATMENT

If the cause is diet, following the right diet should produce dramatic improvements in the child's health after two or three weeks, and even obesity should respond fairly quickly to a change in eating habits. Children may be given vitamin supplements and parents may need advice on how to provide a healthier diet.

Malnutrition due to medical causes will respond to successful treatment of the illness, but dietary supplements may be given to speed recovery. Avoidance of certain foods may be the only way of treating such problems as lactose intolerance or carbohydrate intolerance, and expert medical advice will be needed in devising suitable diets.

■ MASTURBATION
see GENITALS

■ MEASLES

see also BRONCHITIS, CONJUNCTIVITIS, CROUP, ENCEPHALITIS, FEVER, OTITIS, PNEUMONIA

Until recently measles (medically known as rubeola) was a very common childhood illness, but it occurs less frequently now that many children are immunized against it. Although it is highly contagious, it is very rarely a serious disease in developed countries.

The most likely age for contracting the disease is from one to six years, and a baby is protected by inherited resistance, which wears off after six months. Having the disease once gives immunity for life.

SYMPTOMS

Although measles is commonly recognized by its rash, the first signs of the disease are a high temperature (about 38°C/100·4°F), with a runny nose and eyes. These symptoms are often mistaken for a cold, and this is known as the catarrhal stage because the virus is confined to the mucous membranes of the eyes, nose and mouth.

A cough soon develops, together with a sore throat. Sometimes a red flush appears at this stage and disappears again after a few hours. The child is usually upset and off-colour, with a loss of appetite, and there may be sickness and diarrhoea, but symptoms can be very mild. Usually the inside of the child's cheeks are lined with tiny white spots, known as Koplik's spots, which are unique to measles. These may be difficult to notice as they are so small, and you may not think to look for them, since you are likely to think that your child merely has a bad cold or flu.

After anything from a couple of days to a week, the child's temperature drops temporarily, and then the measles rash appears. This is a rash of raised, dusky-red spots, grouped together in patches to give a blotchy

appearance. It appears first behind the ears, then spreads to the neck and forehead, eventually covering the face and trunk, and, in severe cases, the limbs. Any itching accompanying the rash is usually slight. Over the next three days or so the rash disappears, leaving a brownish stain on the skin which usually disappears with a peeling of the skin.

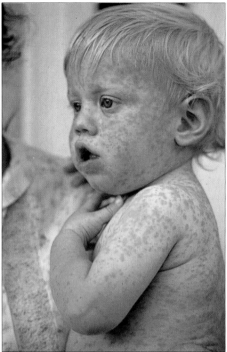

GEORGIA/SPL

The measles rash starts behind the ears, then spreads to the face and body. It varies in severity and usually fades in four or five days.

COMPLICATIONS

Complications are rare. In a few cases, however, the appearance of a rash is accompanied by a new bout of fever, and the eyes can be very irritated by the light. This indicates that complications have arisen.

Middle ear infection (otitis media) is the most commonly found complication of measles, and is especially likely to attack a child who is already prone to ear infections. Some children develop **croup** — a harsh, barking cough. **Chest infections** such as bronchitis and even pneumonia are also possible complications. Any ear problems, coughing up of phlegm or wheezing should always be reported to your doctor so that they can be treated properly.

The eye irritation and sensitivity to light often found with measles can become serious and may develop into a severe form of **conjunctivitis**, with a thick, sticky discharge from the eyes. This too needs to be treated urgently.

Finally a tiny minority of children develop **encephalitis** as a result of measles, with headache, high fever, drowsiness and a pain in the neck. This is potentially fatal and must be given urgent medical attention.

YOUR QUESTIONS

Q I have heard that measles is becoming less and less severe. Is there really any need to bother with immunization?

A Measles is certainly becoming less common, and the complications are found less frequently, but this is only because of immunization preventing the disease and ensuring that if it is contracted it is mild in its effects. It is well worth having your child immunized to ensure that if he does catch measles he will not suffer badly and that there will be no risk of complications developing.

WARNING

Persistent earache, a chesty cough, widespread bleeding of the spots or unexpected drowsiness are all signs of possible serious complications and should be reported to your doctor without delay.

CAUSES

Measles is caused by a highly contagious virus which is passed from child to child in air-borne droplets. A child who has not been immunized or has not gained immunity by having the disease is almost certain to contract it if he comes into contact with a child who is carrying measles. Since there is an incubation period of from seven to fourteen days, children can pass the infection on without their parents knowing they have it, before any of the symptoms have appeared.

YOUR QUESTIONS

Q Is it impossible to catch measles if you have been immunized against it?

A No. The vaccine does not give 100 per cent protection. If a child does become infected, however, the attack will be extremely mild, with no danger of developing complications.

TREATMENT

Mild forms of measles can be treated at home, without the need for a doctor to see the child. The doctor must be called, however, if the child shows symptoms of any of the complications described above. The more severe cases of measles may also require medical attention. The doctor will, if he or she believes there is a threat of complications, prescribe antibiotics to prevent them; if other illnesses have already developed they will be treated as necessary.

Meanwhile, in normal cases your child will almost certainly need extra rest, although not necessarily in bed, and should drink plenty of fluids. If he has a high temperature it can be brought down by sponging with tepid water, and it is safe to give paracetamol in the dose appropriate to the child's age to help bring down the temperature and subdue the feverish symptoms. Gargling with a mouthwash bought from the chemist will help soothe a sore throat. If the child's eyes are irritated he will need to have the curtains closed.

The child will probably have little appetite for a while, but glucose drinks will help to provide energy until he is able to eat again, when you should give him a light diet.

The measles rash is usually not particularly itchy, but if it is, it can be soothed with calamine lotion. It goes without saying that since measles is highly contagious the child should be kept away from school – and, where possible, other children – until all the symptoms have disappeared.

IMMUNIZATION

Immunization against measles is usually given at 12 months. Side effects are normally mild, and the injection continues to provide a high level of immunity. A second dose is given later.

Immunization against measles is often combined with an injection to give immunity to mumps and German measles (rubella) – this injection is known as the MMR vaccine.

■ MENINGITIS

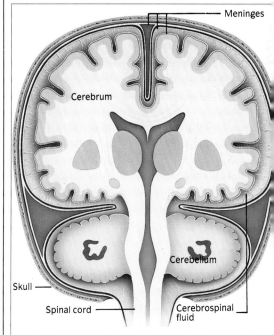

The meninges become temporarily inflamed in an attack of meningitis.

Meningitis is a rare disease which causes inflammation of the membranes enclosing the brain and spinal chord (the meninges). Although it can be mild in its effects, it can also be fatal if left untreated. Very young children are particularly susceptible to the disease.

SYMPTOMS

The onset of meningitis often occurs in a matter of hours, frequently following an infection. The most important symptoms are an unusually severe headache, associated with pain in the eyes on looking at a light, and stiffness in the neck. Additionally, the child feels unwell, and is feverish, and may have nausea and vomiting. There may be a mild skin rash which looks like slight bruising over most of the body. She may also be extremely drowsy, and will possibly have a fit.

In a baby, the main indications are fever, vomiting, poor feeding, general irritability, convulsions and bulging of the top fontanelle.

DIAGNOSIS

A doctor must be called straight away if there is any suspicion that a child may have meningitis, as prompt treatment is essential. The doctor will check for stiffness in the neck and will bend and straighten the child's legs to see if this causes similar pain. The doctor may also examine the inside of the child's eyes to see if the nerve to the eye has been affected. If meningitis is suspected in a baby, the doctor will need a full description of the symptoms from the mother.

If meningitis is suspected, the child will be sent to hospital for investigation. There will be blood tests, skull and chest X-rays and, most importantly, a lumbar puncture to remove some fluid from the spine as a sample for analysis.

CAUSES

Meningitis can be caused by many common viruses and some bacteria — most frequently the *Meningococcus* bacterium, which often lives quite harmlessy in the throat. Viral meningitis is most frequently caused by the virus that causes mumps, and follows on from mumps.

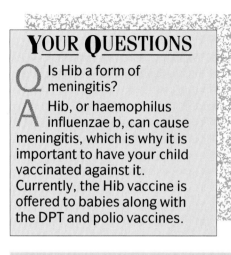

YOUR QUESTIONS

Q Is Hib a form of meningitis?

A Hib, or haemophilus influenzae b, can cause meningitis, which is why it is important to have your child vaccinated against it. Currently, the Hib vaccine is offered to babies along with the DPT and polio vaccines.

TREATMENT

Bacterial meningitis can be cured by antibiotics, usually given intravenously over a period of up to two weeks. The main danger is that it may have progressed too far before it is identified. If left untreated for too long it can cause permanent damage to the brain and may even be fatal. This is why it is essential to get early medical treatment and to call your doctor at once if you have the slightest suspicion that your child is suffering from meningitis.

Viral meningitis is usually fairly mild and, as with all viral infections, there is no treatment for the infection itself. Pain-killing drugs or other treatment may be given, however, to alleviate the symptoms and prevent complications. In most cases the child will have to stay in hospital during treatment of the disease.

OUTLOOK

When treatment begins early enough recovery from meningitis is usually good. A small proportion of children who suffer from the disease and are not treated early enough, die of it, however, and of those who survive some have serious and lasting disabilities as a result. This may include deafness, mental deficiency, cerebral palsy and epilepsy.

WHEN TO CALL THE DOCTOR

Call your doctor immediately if your child has any of the following symptoms in connection with a headache:
• vomiting
• a pain in the neck
• pain on looking at a bright light
• drowsiness and a desire to lie down
• a fit
• a high fever
• a rash, like a lot of small reddish bruises

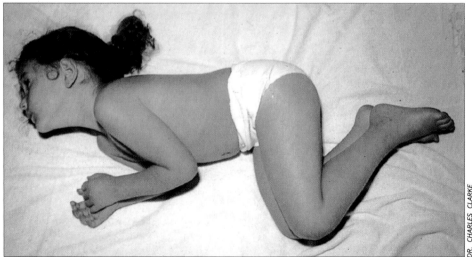

A child with meningitis may lie down in this characteristic posture.

DR. CHARLES CLARKE

■ MENSTRUATION

Menstruation – the monthly bleeding from the uterus (womb) in girls and women of childbearing years who are not pregnant – does not usually begin until girls are about 12 or 13. It can occasionally, however, begin when the girl is as young as nine or as old as 15 or 16.

SIGNS OF PUBERTY

Starting her periods is part of the lengthy process of a girl's growing up. Usually about two years before this, she will suddenly have a great spurt in growth and her breasts will begin to develop. The age at which these two events happen is by no means the same in all girls, and not all girls follow exactly the same pattern. Sooner or later, however, girls have a spurt in growth, develop breasts, start having periods, and then stop growing – usually before they are 16.

The first signs of pubic hair normally show at around the time the breasts begin to appear, and underarm hair usually begins to grow about two years later, when the underarm sweat glands develop. While all these changes are taking place, girls are often temperamental and emotional.

GARRETT/BUBBLES

There is no need for your daughter to give up any of her favourite activities when she starts her periods.

HOW IT STARTS

When a baby girl is born, her ovaries already contain all the eggs (ova) that will be released month by month when she matures, and that, if fertilized, will become new human beings. The uterus is very small.

During puberty the uterus enlarges, because the production of the female sex hormones by the ovaries increases rapidly at this time. Then, under the regulation of certain hormones, a monthly pattern of secretion is established, which causes eggs to be released and the lining of the womb to be thickened about once every 28 days. If the egg is not fertilized, about two weeks later the womb sheds its lining, and the process begins again. It is this shedding of the lining of the womb that causes the monthly bleeding.

It often takes up to a year for the regular pattern to develop, and it is quite normal for a girl to have periods irregularly and infrequently at first. During this time she may be moody and difficult as the hormone levels fluctuate. The first few menstrual cycles do not usually involve the production of ripe eggs, but within a year or so it would be possible for her to become pregnant, even though she has a long way to go before she is physically completely mature.

PROBLEMS WITH PERIODS

There is nothing abnormal about periods being irregular in frequency during the first year or so. If bleeding is very persistent or heavy, you should consult your doctor. Equally if your daughter's periods start at a very early age (nine years or below) or if they have not started by the time she is 16 or 17, or if they are particularly painful right from the beginning, you should take her to see the doctor, to check that there is no medical reason for this. Problems with periods can be caused by a number of factors. Delayed onset of periods can be a sign of anaemia, but can be caused by hormonal upsets, possibly of an emotional origin.

REMEDIES

The girl should be prepared for the start of her periods, and should be told about the choice between tampons and pads. She should know in advance what periods are like and why they occur.

Some of the problems mentioned above will respond to hormonal treatment, and very occasionally psychotherapy may be advised.

Period pains normally respond to painkillers such as aspirin or paracetamol, but if they are severe, your daughter should see the family doctor. Unfortunately, painful periods (known medically as dysmenorrhoea) are quite common in young girls, and often the girl will just have to learn how to put up with it (at least until she is older, when the problem may disappear), but sometimes hormone treatment is possible.

■ MIGRAINE

A surprising number of children suffer from migraine attacks, and being prone to these attacks seems to run in families.

SYMPTOMS

Migraine symptoms are the same in children as in adults – the main one being an incapacitating headache. The headache is often, but by no means always, on one side of the head and it may be preceded by the child 'seeing' bright, blinding lights or zig-zag patterns. There is usually an intense feeling of nausea, and often the child actually is sick, which sometimes relieves the headache.

When children have a migraine they often complain of tummy ache as well. A child will be unusually quiet before and during an attack, and will be pale and possibly sweating. Not all children will display the full symptoms of migraine and sometimes in children the headache itself is absent.

CAUSES

The causes of migraine are not fully understood. As in adults, certain foods, notably cheese and chocolate, may provoke attacks in some children, and tension is often to blame. But why these trigger attacks is not known; and exactly what happens physiologically is only partly understood. It is thought that the arteries inside and outside the skull contract and expand abnormally to cause migraine and that histamine and serontonin — substances produced by the body — are involved.

This eight-year-old's drawing depicts one of her migraine attacks.

TREATMENT

In most cases the best treatment for a child with migraine is to put the child to bed in a darkened room, and this is often what the child wants anyway, as he will usually be sensitive to light during an attack and will probably also want to sleep. If he can sleep for a quarter of an hour or so at an early stage the attack will often be

A child with a migraine attack needs to rest. A cloth soaked in cold water can help to soothe the headache.

less severe and will hopefully be over more quickly.

You can give your child a junior dose of sodium bicarbonate to help to settle the stomach, but it is a good idea to put a bucket by the bed as well in case the child is sick. He will certainly not feel well enough to find his way to the bathroom, and may not be able to tell until the last minute that he is going to be sick, rather than simply feeling nauseous.

MEDICAL TREATMENT

If your child has frequent attacks of migraine, you should take him to see your family doctor. Different patients respond to different drugs, but the main types used are antihistamine and ergot-based drugs. Your doctor may have to experiment with several prescriptions before a suitable one is found. A child who frequently suffers migraine attacks will learn to recognize the symptoms before an attack reaches its worst stage and it is important for him to take the drugs at this early stage, so that they can be absorbed before vomiting starts.

IDENTIFYING TRIGGERS

If you can detect a link between migraine attacks and certain foods it would be sensible to cut these out of the child's diet. It may also be possible to recognize a behaviour pattern in the attacks. For instance they may come on whenever the child has had to rush to get ready for school after going to bed late, or whenever he has an exciting day out, a long journey, unusual food, or late meals. Often it only takes small changes to avoid migraine-provoking situations.

Finally, if your child seems to have migraine attacks when he is tense or anxious, relaxation techniques can often help. Yoga is one possibility and swimming also seems to help.

■ MILIA

Milia is a rash which is usually brought on by extreme heat, and which may particularly affect babies and young children being taken abroad into hot climates. Newborn

babies are also prone to attacks, even when it is not particularly hot.

SYMPTOMS

Milia (or miliaria, as it is properly called) gets its name from the word for millet seeds, because the rash is like a sprinkling of tiny white seeds — usually just across the child's face, and particularly over the nose. The rash tends not to cause any trouble, but occasionally it is itchy and so it is sometimes known as prickly heat. Some parents might find this condition a little unsightly.

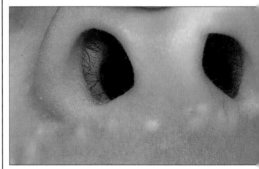

The rash of milia looks like a sprinkling of little white seeds. The spots are nothing to do with pimples or white heads and they should never be squeezed or picked.

CAUSES

Milia is brought on by blocked sebaceous (sweat) glands, and it occurs frequently in newborn babies because their sweat glands have not developed fully. Young children are more readily affected in less strong heat, as their sweat glands are still immature. In adults the rash usually occurs only when it is exceptionally hot — particularly affecting people visiting the tropics.

PREVENTION

There is no way of preventing milia in babies (although not all babies suffer from the rash). Children who are being taken to hotter countries need to wear loose, cool cotton clothes to encourage sweat to evaporate, and this will help to prevent milia from developing. It is always important for children to have plenty of fluids, and more salt than usual, when the weather is hot, to make sure that the sweat glands can function properly.

TREATMENT

No treatment is necessary for milia, and it is usually trouble-free. In small babies it gradually disappears as the child gets older and the sweat glands begin to function properly. When the condition is caused by heat it soon vanishes when the child comes back from holiday or as the weather cools.

It is important not to squeeze the spots (which do look a little like pimples or white heads), as this can damage children's fine skin. Normally it is quite unnecessary to apply any creams or ointments to the rash, but if it causes itching, calamine lotion can be soothing. Only if the rash persists, or if it causes a great deal of irritation, should you take your child to the doctor.

YOUR QUESTIONS

Q Is there anything I can do about my baby's milia rash? It is so unsightly.

A If it isn't upsetting your baby, you really shouldn't let it upset you. It is very common in newborns and will clear up of its own accord within a matter of weeks.

■ MOLES

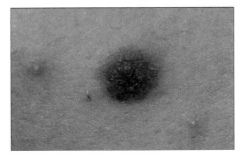

A mole may be dark or light brown in colour and can occur almost anywhere on the body.

Some moles may be present at birth, but on the whole they develop as children get older. Usually they cause

absolutely no problem, and some people even consider a mole to be 'a sign of beauty'.

SYMPTOMS

Most people are familiar with the appearance of a mole – a circular mark on the skin which varies from pale to deep brown in colour. Moles are usually slightly raised above the rest of the skin and occasionally have hairs growing out of them.

CAUSES

Moles are little areas of skin which are more highly pigmented than the rest of the skin. Pigment (skin colour) is produced by cells known as melanocytes, and the pigment they produce is called melanin. There seems to be no reason why melanin should occasionally be concentrated in a few small areas of the body.

There are in fact three types of mole. These are known as intradermal moles, which lie in the second layer of the skin, the dermis; junctional moles, which lie between the dermis and the epidermis (the top layer of the skin); and compound moles, which lie in both layers.

TREATMENT

Moles do not usually need any kind of treatment, especially on children. When the child grows up, if she feels that a mole is disfiguring it will be possible to have it removed safely and painlessly, leaving an almost invisible scar; but most people consider moles to be attractive rather than unsightly.

Occasionally your doctor may decide that it would be wise for your child to have moles removed as a precaution if they are of a type liable to become malignant. And in the very rare case when a child has a mole which shows signs of being malignant, this too will be removed by minor surgery.

Any mole that is removed will be analysed in a laboratory afterwards. This will show whether any further treatment is necessary, but usually

once the site of the mole has healed there is nothing to worry about.

WATCHPOINTS

● Put extra sun-screen, in cream or lotion form, on your child's moles when he is out in the sun, as it is thought that being exposed to sun can slightly increase the risk of moles becoming malignant later in life.

● Never let a child apply any chemical to the mole in the hope of removing it. This could cause severe irritation as well as increasing the possibility of the mole becoming malignant.

● If the child is worried by hairs growing out of a mole, remove these by cutting them carefully with nail scissors – never try to pluck them.

DANGERS

Most moles are absolutely harmless, but there is a very slight risk of a mole becoming cancerous (known as a malignant melanoma). This is most likely to happen with junctional moles situated on the palms of the hands, the soles of the feet and the genitals, where there is constant rubbing. Malignant melanomas very rarely affect children, but if your child has moles which increase in size or deepen in colour, or if they bleed, become itchy or feel sore, she should be taken to the family doctor, just to make sure there is nothing wrong.

■ MOUTH

See also TEETH, TEETHING, THRUSH

The cavity of the mouth is lined with mucous membrane. The roof and the lower part of the mouth are rigid, but otherwise it is surrounded by muscles. We use the mouth to speak and sing, to chew, yawn, whistle and make facial expressions, and it is linked to breathing and digestion, with the back of the mouth connecting with the entrance to the digestive tract and the respiratory tract.

Even though the mouth is full of bacteria and prone to minor injury it is surprisingly resilient at all ages and recovers fast from injury and common ailments. In a healthy child or adult the membrane lining of the mouth has a remarkable capacity for regeneration, so that any form of mouth infection is usually a sign of poor general health.

PARTS OF THE MOUTH

The lips are made of soft muscle fibres interspersed with elastic tissue. They have a generous supply of nerve endings, which is what gives them their essential sensitivity – after all, the major part of a baby's experience is gained via the mouth and lips.

The lips are covered by a modified form of skin, which, unlike true skin, has no hairs, sweat glands or oil-secreting glands. (This is why the lips easily become dry and chapped.)

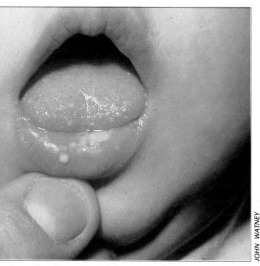

A common mouth problem in babies and young children is that of thrush. In some cases this can cover the inside of the mouth as well as the tongue.

JOHN WATNEY

LINING OF THE MOUTH

The mucous membrane lining of the mouth has glands which produce mucous – a slightly sticky, clear fluid. The action of these glands, helped by that of the saliva-producing salivary glands, keeps the mouth moist.

The roof of the mouth is known as the palate and, covered with tiny organs known as taste buds, is partly responsible for our sense of taste. The front of the palate is the hard palate, against which the tongue presses in the first stage of mixing and softening food, and in making certain consonants (known as hard consonants) in speech.

The back of the palate, known, appropriately, as the soft palate, is mobile, and closes off the nasopharynx (the entrance to the respiratory system) when food is being swallowed. This is to prevent the food from being forced up into the nose, which is linked to the back of the mouth.

The piece of tissue you see hanging down from the soft palate is known as the uvula, and some anatomists think that it helps to form a seal at the top of the air passage to help prevent choking while eating. The tongue strikes against the soft palate in making the sounds that are known as soft consonants.

THE TONGUE

The tongue consists mainly of muscles, which children learn to control in the most intricate way as they master the skills of eating and speaking. It is attached to the base of the skull, to the lower jaw, and to a bone called the hyoid bone above the larynx, and is much bigger than the part we see.

Our tongues are very sensitive to touch and heat, and contribute to our sense of taste through the many taste buds which cover them. Together with the teeth (once they are through) the tongue plays a vital part in the first stage of the digestive process.

THE BABY'S MOUTH

We all depend on our mouths for survival, but particularly when we are babies. A baby is born with the instinct to suck, and for a baby the sensitive mouth and tongue provide most of the information necessary about the outside world.

This is why, until the age of about two, babies and toddlers tend to examine things by putting them in their mouths. Although worrying and irritating to parents, it is inevitable.

All parents can do is keep objects that would be dangerous to swallow away from children while they are at this stage.

USING THE MOUTH

Food is chewed before being swallowed. Chewing, technically known as mastication, involves the tongue, as well as the teeth. The tongue places the food first to the teeth, which mince it, and then to the back of the mouth to be swallowed. This, of course, is why babies have to be given puréed food when they are first being weaned, and why they have to graduate to adult food via mashed food and food that has been cut up into small pieces.

In the mouth, the food is mixed with saliva produced by the three pairs of salivary glands. The saliva reaches the mouth through small channels or ducts and is produced in response to the sight and smell of food, as well as to food being put in the mouth.

Saliva is slightly alkaline and contains the catalyst called ptyalin. This begins the breakdown of starchy foods, and is the first stage in chemical digestion.

Once the food has been chewed and softened, it is ready to be swallowed. It is pushed up against the hard palate, and the soft palate dilates to allow it to pass.

A flap of tissue known as the epiglottis, positioned behind the tongue, closes off the passage to the lungs to prevent choking as the food is swallowed and transferred to the oesophagus (gullet). Contractions of the oesophagus then move the food on to the stomach for the digestive process to continue.

MOUTH PROBLEMS

Most problems arising in the mouth indicate poor general health or poor dental hygiene. However, since the mouth is closely linked to the ears, nose and throat, any infection such as a cold can also produce symptoms in the mouth.

Dribbling, ulcers and thrush are perhaps the most common mouth problems in babies and small children. Swollen lips (cheilosis) and swollen and sore mouths (stomatitis) and cold sores can also be troublesome. Gums can be sore in babies when they are teething (see **Teething**), and if the child has gingivitis.

SYMPTOMS

Dribbling is a symptom in itself.

Ulcers are little white or yellowish patches in the mouth, surrounded by an area which is red and sore. They can also cause bad breath, and are often linked to cold sores.

Thrush in the mouth is indicated by white patches on the tongue and also on the roof of the mouth and inside the cheeks. This is particularly common in babies.

Cheilosis and **stomatitis** are characterized by swelling and inflammation of the lips and mouth respectively. In the latter, the tongue is coated with a white substance.

Cold sores, or herpes, are inflamed blisters on the lips.

In a teething baby the **gums** are sore, swollen and inflamed, and the baby's cheeks are often flushed. The teething baby tends to dribble.

The symptoms of **gingivitis** are bleeding and soreness in the gums, especially when the teeth are brushed; the child may also have bad breath.

CAUSES

Dribbling is usually caused by teething, but it can also be associated with mouth ulcers and colds. Certain types of mouth ulcers can be caused by viral stomatitis, and the condition is usually associated with poor general health.

Thrush is a fungal infection caused by the fungus *Candida albicans*, which is always present in the mouth and intestine, but which is normally kept under control by other bacteria. It is a common problem in babies.

Cheilosis is caused by bacteria, as is **stomatitis,** which may be triggered by anaemia, vitamin deficiency or gastro-intestinal diseases.

Cold sores are caused by the virus *Herpes simplex*, which is usually caught in early life, and which then remains dormant in the body, flaring up from time to time. It is especially virulent in babies and young children with eczema.

Gingivitis is caused by a bacterial infection of the gums, and this seems to be related to poor dental hygiene and the build-up of plaque around the teeth.

TREATMENT

The treatment of **dribbling** will depend on the cause. In itself it is not, of course, a problem. Babies who are dribbling because of teething may find it soothing to have a hard rusk or a cool spoon to suck.

Children showing symptoms of mouth infections should be seen by a doctor. For **mouth ulcers** the doctor may prescribe soothing lozenges or ointment. The child should not eat chocolate or acid foods such as oranges or tomatoes which will make the ulcers more painful.

Thrush will probably be treated by anti-fungal drops or gel, and children with sore and swollen lips (**cheilosis**) may be prescribed an analgesic ointment to soothe the pain. The doctor may also give antibiotics.

In the case of the sore mouth of **stomatitis**, the doctor will probably want to make tests to uncover the underlying cause, as this can be a sign of a more serious complaint. In mild cases, stimulating the flow of saliva by sucking sweets or chewing gum could be all that is needed, but the doctor may prescribe a mouth rinse, or swabbing the child's mouth.

A child with **cold sores** need only be seen by a doctor if these are large and painful or if they occur frequently. Ointment may be prescribed to soothe and treat the sores. Preparations available from the chemist are all that is required in many cases. Make sure that the child has a healthy diet, with plenty of fresh fruit and vegetables, and is not allowed to get over-tired.

Children with **sore gums** (except teething babies) should be taken to a dentist at once. Gingivitis can cause loss of teeth. The dentist will probably scrape the teeth and give advice on good dental care.

YOUR QUESTIONS

Q When children cut their lips, why do even small wounds bleed so much?

A The lips are richly supplied with tiny blood vessels, and this explains why minor damage can result in so much bleeding. Rubbing an ice cube on the cut may help the blood to clot and take away the pain.

■ MUMPS

Mumps can make a child's face dramatically enlarged, but some children have only slight swelling.

Mumps, medically known as epidemic parotitis, affects many children from four to 14 years old, although it is slightly less infectious than some of the other common childhood illnesses such as measles or chickenpox. It can now be prevented by immunization. Mumps causes general symptoms, and characteristically, swelling of the salivary glands (six in total) situated around the mouth. A child who has had mumps gains lifelong immunity to the disease as a result.

SYMPTOMS

As with some other viral infections, the symptoms of mumps take a while to develop. Roughly two to three weeks after being exposed to the virus a child with mumps may have flu-like symptoms, with a slight fever, sore throat and shivering. She may also feel pain around her ears and find swallowing difficult.

Soon the large salivary gland between the upper and lower jaws (known as the parotid gland, from which mumps gets its medical name) becomes tender and swollen. Sometimes only one side of the face is affected, but usually both sides of the child's face become noticeably swollen round the jaw, and the child finds it very painful to open her mouth wide or to swallow.

At this stage the temperature often rises further, often as high as 39.4°C/103°F. All six salivary glands can be affected, making the whole jaw area swollen and painful at once, but sometimes only one gland is affected at first, with the infection gradually passing from one gland to another.

At the height of the attack the child with mumps can feel quite 'poorly'. Apart from being tired, hot and cold and shivery, and probably a little tearful, she will usually have no appetite, and will not be inclined to eat because of the pain on swallowing.

Two to three days later the swelling begins to subside and the temperature begins to fall. The child will soon feel more perky and her appetite will return. In some cases a child can have mumps while hardly showing any symptoms at all, and without noticeable swelling of the face.

Even in these mild cases, having the disease will give lifelong immunity to further attacks.

YOUR QUESTIONS

Q Could my daughter have passed on mumps to other children before we realized she had caught it? I understand the illness has a long incubation period.

A Although it can take up to a month for the symptoms of mumps to develop, the child is only infectious for about six days before the swelling appears. She remains infectious while her face is swollen.

DANGERS

Although mumps is not a serious disease, it is slightly more likely to cause complications than other common childhood illnesses, and parents need to be on the look out for signs that complications may be arising.

The most frequent complication of mumps is **pancreatitis**, or inflammation of the pancreas. This causes tummy-ache and sickness, which usually last for a day or two.

Orchitis (inflammation of the testes in boys) and **oophoritis** (inflammation of the ovaries in girls) are also possible developments. Orchitis causes pain and swelling in one or both of the testicles, and this occasionally occurs even when the child's face is not swollen. It is not unusual, and in all but very rare cases everything returns to normal within a week. Oophoritis in girls is less common. It causes severe pain in the lower abdomen and bouts of vomiting and usually lasts for two or three days. It has no long-term effects.

Two other possible complications can be very serious — **encephalitis** and **meningitis** (*see* individual entries). The former is characterized by severe headache, high fever and vomiting and the latter by neck stiffness with headache and, often, vomiting. Both complications must be treated urgently by your doctor as

they can even be fatal, especially in very young children, if left untreated.

Although it is very unusual for any of these complications to develop, it is as well for parents to be on the look-out for them, and it is important to let your doctor know at once if any worrying symptoms arise.

CAUSES

Mumps is caused by a virus which is passed from child to child through coughs, sneezes and the breath of someone who has the disease. The germs are breathed in and begin to act on the respiratory system. The symptoms of the disease do not begin to show until from two to four weeks after it was contracted.

YOUR QUESTIONS

Q How common is meningitis as a complication of mumps?

A Meningitis develops in only about one in a hundred cases of mumps, and even then it is usually mild, clearing up of its own accord within three or four days. However, your doctor's advice should always be sought if symptoms such as headaches, vomiting or stiff neck appear after a child has mumps.

TREATMENT

Your family doctor should be called to confirm that the child is suffering from mumps, and if this is the case treatment will depend on the severity of the mumps. The child should be kept at home for about ten days after the symptoms appear, but need not necessarily stay in bed.

Fever can be reduced by tepid sponging, or by paracetamol, which will also help to calm any aches and pains. The throat will be very sore for a few days, and the child will probably be unable to eat solid food. She will need plenty of cool drinks, and you may be able to tempt her to eat soups and purées. A wrapped hot water bottle placed against the sore face may be soothing.

VACCINATION

All babies are offered a routine immunization against mumps in the MMR vaccine, which also protects against measles and German measles. The current programme schedules this vaccination at about 12 months. Your health visitor or baby clinic will be able to answer any questions you may have about the vaccine and its safety. The vaccine will protect your child against the possible complications of mumps.

■ MUSCLE PROBLEMS

Healthy children make such active use of their muscles it is little wonder they sometimes injure them.

There are two different kinds of muscle in the human body: those that are under our conscious control and which are used in making voluntary movements; and those we do not control consciously and which work automatically, as in breathing and bowel movements. Voluntary muscles, known as striated muscles, number over 400 in the human body and account for 40 per cent of the body weight. Most, if not all, of the problems dealt with here refer to this type of muscle.

Muscles are connected to the skeleton by means of tendons, and nerves running down the spinal cord from the brain feed into the muscles. Electrical impulses passing down the nerves stimulate the muscles into action. Every movement we make is made possible by muscles, and it is surprising how rarely anything goes wrong with them. There are various types of muscle disorder — all fairly uncommon — and these are listed in the box, with their symptoms. But most diseases affecting the muscles are actually caused by disorders of the nervous system.

SYMPTOMS

The muscle problems your child is most likely to encounter are those of damage through **injury**, loosely referred to as pulls, tears and strains. Commonplace **cramps** are also a familiar minor muscular problem, but here there is no injury involved.

In all cases of **injury** the child experiences pain in the injured muscle and finds movement difficult in the affected part of the body. The pain may not come on properly until a day or two after the injury. It may be accompanied by some bleeding, which slowly surfaces as a bruise under the skin. **Cramp** is a sudden, painful tightening of the muscles which makes movement temporarily impossible. It most often affects the calf muscles.

CAUSES

When muscles are injured the muscle fibres are torn, and this is followed by bleeding and swelling in the muscle. **Injuries** usually arise when the child is being overactive — reaching too high and too suddenly to catch a ball, doing the 'splits' and so on. But, especially if the child is tired and cold, a muscle can be injured by less dramatic movements.

Sometimes there is such a time gap between the muscle being damaged and the pain being felt that the child will not remember how the injury occurred.

Cramps are not caused by injury but by the muscle going into spasm. This may be brought on by the body becoming low in salt or by a deficient blood supply to the muscle following very strenuous physical exercise. However, cramps may also be due to dehydration which may be caused by illness or heat stroke.

Eating a banana a day may help to prevent cramp by increasing the amount of potassium in the diet.

TREATMENT

Muscle **injuries** respond best to treatment with ice packs or immersion in cold water to reduce inflammation. (A pack of frozen peas makes a good ice pack and is often recommended by physiotherapists.) However, if there is bruising, applications of warmth help to clear the bleeding and ease the pain. Paracetamol can be given to reduce both pain and inflammation.

Crêpe bandages, if the pain is in a leg or ankle, arm or wrist, where a

Sternocleidomastoid
turns head

Trapezius
*maintains shoulder
position*

Deltoid
moves shoulder

Biceps
*bends and
rotates arm*

Rectus
abdominis
*strengthens
abdominal
wall*

Brachioradialis
bends elbow

Sartorious major
bends leg

Quadriceps magnus
straightens leg

Tibialis anterior
aids walking

Pectoralis major
*moves shoulder,
assists breathing*

Serratus anterior
supports shoulder

JOHN DAVIES

*The main muscles involved in body
movement are shown in the diagram.*

bandage can be applied, can give some relief straight away, and rest is the main treatment. A child's muscles repair themselves quickly, and after a day or two of rest your child should be encouraged to get the injured muscle working again.

Cramps can be overcome by stretching the affected muscle, even though this may seem impossible and may cause the child pain. If the child has been ill with diarrhoea and thus may be dehydrated and deficient in salt, give him salt to lick and

make him drink a pint of water. Doctors who are interested in alternative medicine may suggest giving a banana a day to a child who frequently suffers from cramps, as bananas supply potassium (one of the salts needed by the body and which is thought to get out of balance with the sodium derived from table salt).

If the child's cramps come on when he is taking exercise, as is most often the case, check that he is not doing this too soon after eating, as blood being diverted to the stomach to aid digestion causes less blood to be available to the limbs. Make the child rest before exercising after a meal.

If your child frequently suffers from severe cramps, take him to your doctor for a check-up. It may be possible to find out what the cause is. Equally, the doctor may prescribe quinine as a remedy in bad cases.

YOUR QUESTIONS

Q What is the difference between a strain and a sprain?

A The terms are used quite loosely, and in practice it hardly matters, as sprains and strains are minor injuries which respond to the same treatment of ice packs or cooling by some other method, support, and rest. Most doctors use the word sprain to refer to injury to a ligament and strain to refer to muscle damage.

WATCHPOINTS

• If in doubt about the cause of your child's pain, take him to the doctor. He may have a fracture or some other form of injury that needs medical treatment.

• Consult your doctor if an apparent muscle injury gets worse with treatment, and if it causes severe pain.

MUSCLE DISORDERS

Painful muscles

Polymyalgia rheumatica — inflammation of the muscles. Symptoms: pain in shoulder and buttocks.

Myositis — inflammation of the muscles, often accompanied by inflamed skin, possibly caused by a virus. Symptoms: pain and weakness.

Inherited muscle disease

Muscular dystrophy — abnormalities in the working of the muscle cells (*see* separate entry). Symptoms: progressive weakness of muscles, varying according to the type of disease.

Hypokalaemic paralysis — caused by a low level of potassium in the blood. Symptoms: periodic attacks of paralysis and weakness in the limbs.

Hyperkalaemic paralysis — caused by a high level of potassium in the blood. Symptoms: periodic attacks of paralysis with muscular rigidity.

Enzyme defects — an enzyme defect affecting the handling of glycogen, a source of energy, by the muscle cells. Symptoms: floppiness, a delay in beginning to walk (in young children), fatigue on taking exercise, and heart problems.

Apply a barrier cream such as zinc oxide cream to prevent the urine from irritating her skin. Change your baby's nappies and wash her bottom at least every three hours and immediately after she has opened her bowels. Leave her with no nappies on as often as possible.

INVOLVING THE DOCTOR

See your doctor if the rash is not better within two or three days or if you think your baby has thrush. Your doctor will be able to identify the cause of the rash and will make sure you've been using the correct home treatment. If the rash has become infected, he may prescribe an antibiotic ointment; if it is caused by thrush he will prescribe an anti-fungal cream. If he suspects the rash is caused by eczema, he may also prescribe a cortisone ointment to be used sparingly.

■ NAVEL

See also HERNIA

The navel or umbilicus is the scar on the tummy formed from the remnants of the umbilical cord. Immediately after birth the cord is cut. It contains no nerves so cutting it is painless. It is then tied to ensure that the blood vessels do not bleed as the cord shrinks. After a few days the stump shrivels and turns black, and after about ten days all that is usually left is a dry black string that soon falls off leaving a rough scab. It is very

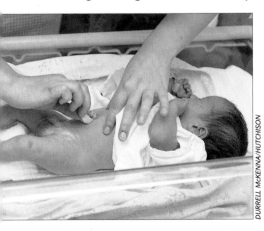

The skin round a newborn baby's umbilical cord can be cleaned gently at each nappy change.

important that you never pull or twist the stump to encourage it to fall off.

CARE OF THE STUMP

When the navel is healing over, it's important that the area around it should be kept clean. Opinions now differ as to whether this is best done by regularly swabbing it with antiseptic wipes, or whether plain water is sufficient. Too thorough cleansing could, it's thought, wipe away the natural defences the baby produces by himself. It is advisable to ask your midwife what she feels is best. In any case, you need to wipe gently round the navel area at each nappy change to prevent urine or faeces from remaining on or near the stump.

POSSIBLE PROBLEMS

If the stump weeps, crusts over, is pus-y or appears red or swollen, it has become infected. If this happens, consult your midwife or doctor. They will probably prescribe an antibiotic cream or powder to apply to the cord.

If the infection is spreading along the cord and into your baby's body your baby will need to be admitted to hospital and given antibiotics.

YOUR QUESTIONS

Q My baby's navel is rather large and protruding. Will he need plastic surgery to make it go down?

A No, it will almost certainly retract on its own as your baby grows. Some babies' navels stick out so much that their parents suspect an umbilical hernia, and babies with very little fat on their tummies occasionally have navels that stick out, but the condition usually rights itself with time.

If, however, your child is seriously worried about the shape of his navel, plastic surgery would be an option when he's older, although this is very rare indeed.

YOUR QUESTIONS

Q Can I bath my baby before the cord stump falls off?

A Yes, as long as you dry the stump and the area round it very carefully and gently. If you see any signs of redness or discharge, talk to the midwife or doctor. They will tell you if any treatment's needed.

■ NEPHRITIS
See KIDNEYS

■ NEPHROTIC SYNDROME
See KIDNEYS

■ NERVOUSNESS

See also DISTURBED CHILDREN

We tend to describe people as 'nervous' if they show outward signs of anxiety, fear or apprehension. However, it is worth remembering that everybody feels nervous in certain circumstances.

CAUSES

Nervousness is part of a person's temperament. It may appear to run in families or seemingly calm parents may produce a nervous child. Signs of nervousness may also appear in a previously calm baby or child following an upsetting circumstance.

SYMPTOMS

Some babies seem very jumpy and nervous. Although all babies are startled by loud noises, turn away from bright lights and throw up their arms and cry if they feel they are going to be dropped, jumpy babies seem to take these feelings to extremes and tremble and cry at any stimulus.

Babies also often appear nervous around eight months, the age at which they seem to become aware o.

special people in their lives and become upset when they leave them. Older children may also appear nervous in unfamiliar circumstances such as a new playground or coming across a large group of noisy children in the park.

THURSTON/BUBBLES

The first day at school will make even the most confident child nervous.

NERVOUS BREAKDOWN

A nervous breakdown happens when a person becomes so confused, depressed, aggressive, or illogical that he no longer appears to be in control of his life. Although it is called a nervous 'breakdown', the nervous system does not physically break down, rather the mind has ceased to function as an organized whole. The sufferer needs urgent medical help.

Nervous breakdowns are rare in children and the normally developing child seems able to resist considerable stress and pressure without breaking down – at least until later life.

TREATMENT

Accept your child's personality for what it is and recognize that many

apparent signs of nervousness are just part of a phase that your child will outgrow. Do not try to shock your child out of his nervous behaviour, you will only make him more insecure and clinging. Remember that signs of nervousness in children do not mean that they are likely to have difficulties in the future, simply that these children are more sensitive than others.

■ NETTLE RASH

See HIVES

■ NETTLE STINGS

Nettles commonly grow on uncultivated land. The plant is covered with sensitive hairs which sting when brushed by naked skin.

WEST/BUBBLES

If your child is stung by nettles, look for dock leaves growing close by – they are still the best antidote.

SYMPTOMS

There will be some swelling and reddening of the skin with raised white patches.

PREVENTION

Check your own garden and teach an older child to recognize and avoid nettles. If your child is playing in wild ground, long trousers and long sleeves offer some protection.

TREATMENT

The stings will go down of their own accord but can be soothed by ap-

plying calamine lotion or by rubbing with a dock leaf. Dock leaves are often found growing near nettles

■ NIGHTMARES

Nightmares are quite common in young children and they are not usually a cause for concern unless they occur regularly or are accompanied by sleepwalking (when the child can injure himself on stairs or objects). Few children have nightmares before the age of three or four and generally they have outgrown them by ten or 12.

CAUSES

Nightmares can occur for a number of reasons. A fever or discomfort because of illness can cause a child to wake hot and frightened in the night. More usually though, the cause is likely to be a disturbing incident or a frightening story or television programme.

When nightmares occur frequently, it is often because of some underlying anxiety such as the arrival of a new baby in the house or starting at nursery school.

SYMPTOMS

The child may wake screaming or sobbing and with a frightened look on his face. His eyes may be open but he will seem to be in a state halfway between consciousness and sleep and he probably will not recognize you or understand what you say.

Night terrors are even more distressing for the parent. In this case the child will shout angrily and abusively at you, often in a strange, babbling language. This can sometimes last for up to half-an-hour and can be a harrowing and upsetting ordeal for the parent who experiences it for the first time.

TREATMENT

It is important to realize that your child is not in touch with reality when in the grip of a nightmare or night terror, so there is no point speaking to him rationally; he cannot even understand what you are saying.

The best that you can do is to comfort him by holding him closely and speaking to him softly and soothingly. Soon the child will look less fearful and gradually you will be able to soothe him back to sleep. Never scold the child for being 'silly' and never ask him why he woke frightened or what the dream was about; this could make him more anxious and even hysterical.

It is most important that you stay with your child until he has drifted back to sleep. It is probable that your child will remember nothing about his dream in the morning.

WATCHPOINTS

• Leave a night light in your child's bedroom so that a nightmare is not made worse by fear of the dark.

• Fix a baby/child alarm to your bedroom so you can go to the child instantly in case of a night terror.

• Never lock your child's door; this in itself can cause anxiety and nightmares.

Witches and goblins make for good stories – but even bigger and better nightmares.

YOUR QUESTIONS

Q My normally happy and contented five-year-old has had recurrent nightmares since the birth two months ago of my baby daughter. I realize that the arrival of the new baby may be the cause, but what can I do to help my little boy?

A It is quite normal for an older child to feel disturbed by a new baby in the family and you should make up for this by being particularly loving and caring with your little boy until he becomes accustomed to his enlarged family. He naturally feels insecure, but if you take time to cuddle and reassure him, particularly at bedtime, he will feel more safe and secure and the nightmares will very likely disappear.

YOUR QUESTIONS

Q My aunt helped me with the children a few weeks ago but she frightened my daughter with stories of bogeymen who are able to come and get her when she misbehaves. A couple of nights later my daughter had a nightmare and I'm worried that she might have more nightmares. Is this likely?

A The fear of the bogeymen was probably a fleeting episode that your daughter has now forgotten, especially if nightmares have not recurred. It is important, though, that you talk to your aunt, and tell her that she mustn't frighten your child with such stories. Children have real fears to cope with without worrying about problems which do not exist. Ask your aunt to help by reading a bedtime story of your choosing.

Your child's nightmares will probably pass. Meanwhile, a night light or comforting friend will help.

■ NOSE

The nose, sinuses, mouth, throat and ears form an interlinked system of air passages along which infections can easily spread. For this reason you should see your doctor if any symptom in the ear, nose or throat lasts longer than one week.

The nose's primary function is for breathing. The lining has a rich blood supply which warms the air as it is breathed in. It also contains mucus producing glands which humidify the air and trap airborne particles such as dust and bacteria. The nasal passages contain hair which helps to filter the air. Finally nerve endings in the roof of the nasal cavity provide our sense of smell.

The nasal passages, the ends of which can be seen at the bottom of the nose (nostrils), continue backwards into the nasopharynx, which lies above and behind the mouth. The adenoids, a raised ring of tissue, lie to the rear of the nasopharynx. The nose is self cleansing and you should never put anything up it, especially not a baby's.

MOUTH BREATHING

Nature intended the nose for breathing and the mouth for eating and drinking. However, it is possible to breathe through the mouth and many people do so.

A cold often causes mouth breathing as do enlarged adenoids and tonsils, especially in children of four or five years old, the age at which both adenoids and tonsils reach their greatest size. If a child has enlarged adenoids, they may block her nose, and this will force her to breathe through her mouth.

Snoring and night-time coughs are also associated with mouth breathing. Coughing often happens when mucus builds up in the throat or is a result of post-nasal drip, when mucus drips from the back of the nose into the throat.

Structural abnormalities of the nose can also cause mouth breathing as can allergic conditions such as hay fever. If your child persists in breathing through her mouth when she does not have a cold or any other nasal obstruction, see your doctor to find the cause.

TIM WOODCOCK

Nose picking may look like a disgusting habit, but to a one-year-old it's a voyage of discovery!

STUFFY OR RUNNY NOSE

Stuffy or runny noses often accompany colds. A cold (see separate entry) is a viral infection which enters the body through the nasal passages and throat and causes inflammation of the mucous membranes lining these passages. There is no specific cure for a cold and it should normally be left to run its course with care as described under **Colds**. However, if any discharge changes from clear to yellow, this may be a sign of secondary infection and you should see your doctor, as you should if your child has catarrh or a runny nose for more than six days as this could be a sign of chronic sinusitis or chronic infection of the nose or throat.

A blocked or runny nose in a baby needs to be taken more seriously as this can cause feeding problems and there is a greater chance of complications. Your doctor will give you nose drops to use before each feed.

YOUR QUESTIONS

Q My three-year-old daughter picks her nose, shows everyone the contents and then eats them. Will this do her any harm and how can I stop this unpleasant habit?

A Young children are very interested in all parts of their bodies and love to explore them. Eating her finds will not do her any damage, but the habit is unhygienic as her nails may scratch the lining of the nasal passage and cause an infection. If her hands are not too clean she could transfer germs to her mouth when she puts her finger in.

Try to distract your daughter from this habit but do not make too much of your disgust.

SNIFFING

This usually accompanies a cold but it can be a habit or sometimes indicates an underlying problem such as enlarged adenoids. See your doctor if you are worried.

FOREIGN BODIES

Children are naturally curious and will often stuff small objects into their own or others' orifices such as noses and ears. Neither you nor your child may notice it at first but after two or three days your child may have a nosebleed or foul-smelling discharge from the affected nostril.

If you can remove the object easily with tweezers, do so, or if your child is old enough to blow his nose properly, ask him to blow down the affected nostril as you hold a finger against the good one. Do not ask a young child to do this as he may sniff the object back into his air passages.

If you cannot dislodge the object or if it moves further up the nostril, see your doctor or go to the nearest accident and emergency department. If your child shows any signs of breathing problems, call an ambulance or go immediately to the accident and emergency department. Do not to allow a child under three to play with objects small enough to swallow or put up his nose.

GIVING NOSEDROPS

Nose infections are generally treated with external drops. Most children will resist having drops put in, but these tips may help.

• Warm the drops before applying by standing the container in warm, not hot, water for a few minutes so your child doesn't get a shock when they enter his nose.

• Lie a baby or very young child on a flat surface and enlist the help of an adult or older child to keep him still and hold his head steady. Ask an older child to tilt his head back to give him drops.

• Make sure the head is tilted and gently drop the liquid into each nostril.

• Do not let the dropper touch your child's nose as you will transfer the germs back to the bottle. If the dropper does touch his nose, wash it thoroughly before putting it back in the bottle.

■ OBESITY

See WEIGHT PROBLEMS

■ OILS

See FATS

■ OPTICIAN

See also EYES, EYE PROBLEMS, EYESIGHT

There are two types of optician – a dispensing optician and an ophthalmic optician.

A dispensing optician makes up glasses to a prescription, while an ophthalmic optician is qualified to test the eyes and make up glasses.

If you are worried about your child's eyesight, the best thing to do in the first instance is to take him to your doctor. The doctor may give the child a few simple sight tests and check the eyes with an instrument known as an opthalmoscope. If he or she thinks that there may be something wrong with the child's vision you will be given a letter of referral to an ophthalmic optician.

WHAT THE OPTICIAN DOES

The optician will be looking for what is known as refractive error. In layman's terms, this is long sight (when the child can see distant objects clearly, but nearer ones are blurred), short sight (in which near objects are clear and distant ones are blurred) or astigmatism, in which the eye is unable to focus equally well on horizontal and vertical objects.

If the optician finds that the child's eyesight is imperfect he or she will prescribe corrective spectacles. If any other eye problems come to light during the sight test or during the doctor's examination, the child will be referred to an eye specialist or an oculist or ophthalmologist.

THE EYE TEST

The optician uses a chart set at a fixed distance from the child. The chart has seven rows of letters, which become smaller in size towards the bottom, and which can be read by a person with normal vision at set distances from the chart.

The child will wear a special frame in which a whole range of lenses can be fitted for each eye, and will be asked to read off letters from the chart. For smaller children, who cannot read, shapes are used. The optician will then adjust a suitable combination of lenses until he or she is satisfied that the right prescription has been found.

The optician will also shine a light into the child's eye to check on the condition of the optic nerve and will make an examination of the retina at the back of the eye. The lining of the eye is the only part of the body in which the blood vessels can be examined without surgery, and equally the optic nerve is the only part of the nervous system that can be seen. Their condition not only tells the optician about the state of the child's eyes but can also give a clue to the child's general health – for example diabetes can be detected from the condition of the blood vessels. Very occasionally, therefore, your child may be referred back to the doctor after an eye test for what may seem to be an unrelated condition.

CONFIRMING THE FINDINGS

To confirm the evidence of the letter-reading test the optician also checks the reaction of the eye to looking at objects through a number of selected lenses, using an instrument known as a retinoscope.

To prevent the muscular adjustment of pupil and lens which in young children can mask a defect in the

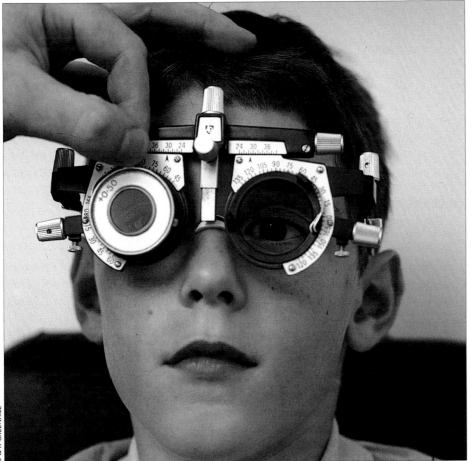

When having his eyesight checked, the child wears a spectacle frame into which a variety of lenses can be inserted to find the right combination.

S & R GREENHILL

An optician may check the child's sight for colour blindness, using patterns made up of coloured dots.

shape of the eyeball that is the cause of refractive error, young children are given drops to dilate (enlarge) the pupils. They sit in a dimly lit room while the drops take effect, and it takes some time afterwards for the pupils to contract and dilate normally again. This means that if the child goes outside into bright light he is unable to adjust his eyes, and while this is in no way painful, it can be rather alarming if the child is not prepared for it.

NEED FOR TESTS

Your child's eyesight will be tested during routine medical examinations, but if you have any reason to be worried about it you should take him to the doctor yourself. In a pre-school and pre-reading child it is more difficult to spot sight problems, but there are still some indicators (*see* Box, above right).

Once it has been established that your child needs to wear spectacles, he will need to have his sight checked regularly to make sure that the prescription is still correct. Most opticians send regular reminders about

the need for new appointments and it is important to fit these in. If you do not hear from your optician, try to keep a check on dates yourself and make sure that your child has his eyes checked once a year.

WHEN TO SUSPECT YOUR CHILD HAS POOR EYESIGHT

- if your child fails to recognize you from a distance
- if your child bumps into things or misjudges distances
- if your child crouches close to the television set
- if you get reports of ill-attention at school, which could be due to your child's being unable to see the board
- if your child is bad at ball games but normally enjoys sports
- if your child complains of tired eyes

YOUR QUESTIONS

Q My little girl often complains about headaches. Could this be a sign of poor eyesight? Both my husband and I are short-sighted.

A It could be that eye strain linked with short sight is a possible cause of your daughter's headaches, though unlikely. More commonly, headaches in children are caused by stress, tiredness or simply a bad cold. Take your child to your doctor if the headaches persist and ask him or her if an eye test would be advisable, just to make sure.

■ OSTEOMYELITIS

See also FRACTURES

Osteomyelitis is an infection of the bone that can come on either quite

gradually (chronic) or very suddenly (acute). The disease is extremely rare, but children under the age of 12 years are more likely to be affected than older children.

The name of the disease is still frightening, as until the days of antibiotics it always had serious consequences. Nowadays, however, there is usually a complete recovery.

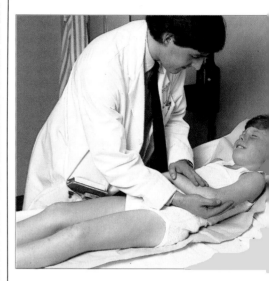

Osteomyelitis causes severe pain in the limb affected. The doctor checks pain and tenderness in the child's arm.

SYMPTOMS

Although in theory any bone can be affected by osteomyelitis, it usually affects a limb, and the symptoms in the acute form are severe pain and tenderness. The child will be unable to use an affected arm, or if it is a leg that is affected, she will begin to limp. A little later, the limb swells, and sometimes an abscess forms on the child's skin at the site of the infected bone.

Additional symptoms are vomiting (though this is not always present) and high temperature. If left untreated, the affected skin area will become red and swollen within one or two days. The symptoms of the chronic form generally develop gradually.

Osteomyelitis can follow an injury such as a compound fracture (*see* **FRACTURES**) but it can also develop as the result of generalized infection. If osteomyelitis is caused by an injury it naturally affects the bone involved in the injury, but when caused by an infection elsewhere in the body it often affects the bones of the leg or arm at the knee joint or elbow.

CAUSES

Osteomyelitis is caused by a bacterial infection. It can be the result of a compound fracture being exposed to infections in the air, or the infection may travel to the bone through the blood from another part of the body.

Often in this case the bacterium responsible is one of the streptococci or staphylococci, and it often travels through the bloodstream from an infected throat.

Osteomyelitis causes abscesses to form in the bone marrow at the site affected. The pus discharging from these abscesses can come out through the skin or can be trapped in the bone where, since it cannot escape, it builds up to cause the violent pain and swelling associated with this infection.

DANGERS

If the disease is not treated and cured in time the discharge that causes the pain affects more and more of the bone, and it can cut off the blood supply to these parts of the bone, so that they become 'dead', causing chronic osteomyelitis.

If this happens, the 'dead' bone cannot cure itself, does not respond to antibiotics and behaves like a foreign body within the body, harbouring the infection. The child will then need surgery to remove parts of the bone and will have to spend some time in hospital for the operation and during recovery.

DIAGNOSIS

If your child complains of a severe pain in a limb, check to see if the limb is swollen and painful to the touch. If so, this could be due to an undiagnosed fracture or tissue injury, especially if the child has recently been in an accident, but osteomyelitis is a very unusual possibility. This is slightly more likely if the child has had a very bad throat infection.

Check the child's temperature and

if she has a fever, make an urgent doctor's appointment, just to be sure. If there is no fever, treat the limb with cold compresses and rest, but again consult your doctor if there is no immediate improvement as some form of medical supervision will be needed, whatever the cause.

If, as a result of examining the limb, the doctor has any reason to suspect that osteomyelitis may be present he or she will make an immediate appointment for your child to be examined in hospital. Here blood samples will be taken, and X-rays may be made. X-rays do not show up the disease in its early stages, but if it has been present for some time and has spread through the bone, this will be revealed.

YOUR QUESTIONS

Q Can osteomyelitis ever cause cancer of the bone?

A No. Osteomyelitis does not lead to cancer, but some forms of cancer may have symptoms which are similar to those of osteomyelitis.

TREATMENT

If the child is found to have osteomyelitis she will be taken into hospital for intensive treatment with antibiotics. The drugs will probably be given intravenously.

If there is no improvement within about two days, this treatment may be followed by an operation to drain the pus from the abscesses and remove any small part of infected bone to prevent the infection from spreading. Sometimes this form of treatment will be given without waiting to see what effect the antibiotics have, and antibiotics will be given afterwards.

The treatment will involve a fairly lengthy stay in hospital, but there is almost certain to be a complete recovery. Many hospitals encourage parents to stay with the child in hospital, and if you can arrange to do

this, or to take turns with your partner or perhaps another member of the family such as a grandparent or aunt, this will be very reassuring for the child.

It will take about six months for the bone to heal completely following an operation, and physiotherapy will be given to help the child recover full use of the limb. You will need to encourage your child to do the daily exercises recommended by the physiotherapist and to give moral support as she makes her recovery.

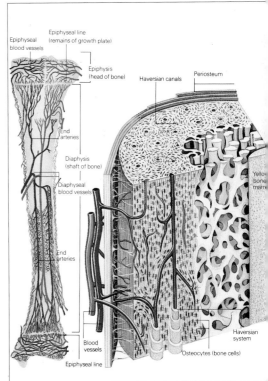

Bacteria can get trapped in the end arteries supplying blood to the bones, and cause osteomyelitis.

YOUR QUESTIONS

Q Can an abscess or a boil develop into osteomyelitis?

A Nowadays this never happens, as antibiotics can cure an abscess or boil and prevent it from infecting the bloodstream long before it poses the threat of osteomyelitis.

■ OSTEOPATHY

Osteopathy was developed in the 19th century as a system of medicine stemming from the belief that the body has powers to keep itself well and to heal itself, as long as it is structurally sound. The techniques involved are similar to those used in massage and manipulation which have been practised the world over since ancient times, but osteopathy was developed as a scientific system by one man, Andrew Taylor Still.

Still was an American who was trained as a doctor, but who became sceptical of the way medicine was practised. He chose the name osteopathy (meaning bone disease) for his system of healing, because he believed that a wrongly structured body was prey to disease and that by manipulating the bones and massaging the muscles that keep the bones in the correct relationship to each other he could prevent people from being ill and cure them when they were ill.

With their boundless energy, children run the risk of suffering from muscle and ligament injuries which can cause slight misalignment of the bones.

MODERN MEDICINE

Still's principle was that 'structure governs function', and modern research has shown that there is a lot to be said for it. Many body functions are inter-dependent and a malfunction in one part has repercussions in another. Most of all, the peripheral nervous system, through which conscious activity is controlled, and the autonomic nervous system, which regulates the working of the heart and lungs and digestive system, both consist of nerves situated in the spine and diseases of the spine may affect their functioning. Nerves are affected by pressure and this can be caused by a wrongly aligned spine. Whereas doctors were once sceptical about the benefits of osteopathy, they now generally accept that there are conditions that can be successfully treated by an osteopath.

COMPLEMENTARY ROLE

Most osteopaths in practice today do not claim that their methods are preferable to modern medicine or surgery, but rather they see their role as complementary to that of the doctor or surgeon. However, for the treatment of muscle and bone disorders, especially when caused by accidents or constant bad posture, osteopathy is often the only effective treatment possible. And many people find that it can also treat chronic disorders such as migraine, asthma and 'tennis elbow' where more conventional treatment has failed.

YOUR QUESTIONS

Q The osteopath said that my son has a curvature of the spine. Is this as serious as it sounds?

A A few children do develop a fairly severe curvature of the spine known as scoliosis, but in most cases curvature of the spine is caused by an accident or by bad posture and this can be successfully treated by osteopathy. Even scoliosis (which is inherited) can sometimes be helped by regular treatment from an osteopath while the spine is still growing.

OSTEOPATHY AND CHILDREN

Osteopathy is a suitable technique for the treatment of children, but if your child is being treated for a medical condition by your doctor it is sensible and courteous to discuss the possibility of osteopathy with the doctor first. If your doctor has had no success in trying to rid your child of chronic asthma or pains in the shoulder he or she may be quite happy for you to see an osteopath.

There are some conditions which should not be treated by an osteopath. These include fractures, arthritis and various types of bone disease. A qualified osteopath will be able to detect these conditions and refer your child to the appropriate specialist, and if your doctor is already treating such conditions in the child he or she will be able to advise you on the suitability of complementary medicine.

A child who has muscle or ligament injuries, perhaps resulting from a fall, an accident in games or over-enthusiastic dancing, can often be quickly cured by a session or two with an osteopath, who will also give advice on any exercises that may help complete the recovery. This can also prevent long-term ill effects developing as a result of minor injuries. Osteopaths also claim that they can detect and treat problems in the bone structure in young children and prevent these from developing into much more serious disorders.

CRANIAL OSTEOPATHY

Some osteopaths practise a form of manipulation known as cranial osteopathy, which involves manipulation

Ballet and other forms of dance can cause the type of injury that responds well to osteopathic treatment.

applied to the head and upper neck. This is a gentle form of treatment and it is claimed to be particularly suitable for babies with birth injuries, and for helping to improve the condition of autistic children.

Proper, registered osteopaths are highly trained practitioners with qualifications in the medical disciplines of anatomy, physiology, pathology, biochemistry and neurology as well as their own specialized subjects of osteopathic diagnosis and treatment. Unfortunately, however, in some countries (including Great Britain) there are no restrictions on someone calling himself or herself an osteopath. It is therefore important for you to make sure that the practitioner you consult is fully qualified.

TREATMENT

Osteopaths have developed great sensitivity in their hands, and treatment begins with a diagnosis in which the osteopath assesses the problem by touch. Sometimes X-rays will be taken in addition to this. The treatment consists of a mixture of fairly gentle kneading and massaging of the tissues together with some rather violent-sounding manipulation of the joints. This causes clicking sounds like the sound made when people crack their knuckles.

Treatment will probably be in sessions of from 20 to 30 minutes, and the number of treatments needed will depend on the condition. After a session the child may feel a little sore, but this is nothing to worry about. The treatment itself is usually painless. Although there are cases of a child limping in in considerable discomfort and later being able to skip away, usually a course of treatment will be necessary.

■ OTITIS

See also EAR, EARACHE, GLUE EAR, MENINGITIS

Otitis is an inflammation of the ear, which has an outer, middle and inner part. There are three kinds of otitis, depending on which part of the ear is affected, and these are known as otitis externa (outer ear), **otitis media** (middle ear — this is often known as middle ear infection) and **otitis interna** (inner ear).

Otitis externa is not usually very serious; but **middle ear infection**, although it usually responds to treatment, can become serious if it is not treated in time, as it can spread to the inner ear, to the mastoid bone behind the ear, or even to the skull-cavity, as well as occasionally causing a perforated ear drum. This is quite a common complaint in young children. **Otitis interna** is more serious, but also much rarer.

SYMPTOMS

Otitis externa is an inflammation of the ear canal which causes discharge from the ear, and earache. The flap itself may also become red and feel sore, and it may be dry and itchy. This complaint is particularly common in children who swim a lot. In babies the ear may be red and hot, and the baby will be fretful and restless, and will probably rub at the affected ear or ears.

Otitis media causes severe earache, and, sometimes, temporary deafness. It occurs quite frequently in young children, particularly after they have had a cold or throat infection or if they have enlarged adenoids. It may also follow on from measles or other infections that cause cold-like symptoms. In babies and very young children there may also be feverishness, vomiting and diarrhoea. Sometimes there is a sudden discharge from the ear, which may make it feel better. Although the attack of middle ear infection is usually preceded by a cold, sometimes a child is subject to chronic infection (attacks that follow on from each other and never clear up properly).

Otitis interna is a much rarer condition that occurs only in conjunction with other diseases. It may spread inward from the middle ear if the child has middle ear infection, or outward from the meninges (the lining of the skull) if the child has meningitis (*see* **MENINGITIS**). In either case the symptoms already present with the primary illness will worsen and there will be severe ear pain, but there should be no danger of the symptoms going unrecognized, as the child will already be treated for the primary infection.

CAMILLA JESSEL

Children with ear infections must wear a hat when playing outdoors to prevent the infection from lingering on.

CAUSES

Otitis externa may be caused by a bacterial or fungal infection, and it can be brought about by an abscess or boil in the ear, a foreign body in the ear or damage caused by probing the ear to clean out wax. Children who spend a lot of time at the local swimming pool may be prone to infection as the skin is more susceptible when wet, and there can be infection in the water.

Otitis media (middle ear infection) can be caused by an infection travelling inward from an infected outer ear, but is often a secondary infection resulting from a cold or sore throat. The bacteria or viruses responsible pass down the Eustachian tube, which links the back of the nose and the middle ear cavity.

Young children are particularly prone to middle ear infection because their Eustachian tubes are short and narrow, and infection can easily pass down them.

Especially when it is bacteria that are responsible for middle ear infection, the infection can become chronic if it is not treated successfully. This means that it lingers and recurs, and this can lead to glue ear (*see* separate entry).

Otitis interna is a much rarer infection, which is usually caused by meningitis or by unsuccessfully treated otitis media.

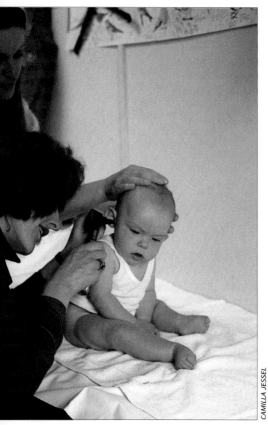

A child with ear problems should be seen by the family doctor without delay for an examination of the ears.

TREATMENT

The treatment of **otitis externa** will depend on the cause. The child should always be taken to your family doctor, but in the meantime you can gently wipe away any discharge with a clean flannel dipped in warm water. Look inside the child's ear in case there is an obvious foreign body which you could easily remove, but do not try to remove anything that you cannot get hold of easily and do not put anything in the child's ear as this could damage the ear as well as pushing the object further down the ear canal.

While waiting to see the doctor you can give the child paracetamol to soothe the pain, and fix a pad of cotton wool over the ear, using adhesive dressing, to absorb any discharge. Alternatively a wad of warmed cloth or a hot water bottle wrapped in a towel can be placed against the ear to ease pain.

Your doctor will then remove any foreign body, lance and drain an abscess or boil, and clean the ear. If the condition is caused by an infection, he or she may prescribe antibiotic or other ear-drops or antibiotics to be taken by mouth.

The child will not be allowed to go swimming until the inflammation has cleared and will be advised to keep her ears dry when bathing. It will also be as well not to wash her hair until the condition has cleared. This may take up to a week or ten days, although if the trouble is caused by a fungal infection it may be more persistent and a further course of treatment may be necessary.

OTITIS MEDIA

Home treatment is the same as for otitis externa. Any pain can be eased by paracetamol or by a warm cloth or wrapped hot water bottle being placed against the ear, and the child should be taken to the doctor.

The doctor will probably prescribe an antibiotic to clear up the infection if it is caused by bacteria, or to prevent bacterial infection from developing if the cause of the otitis media is a virus. Additional drugs may also be given as nose-drops or nose spray, to help to unblock the Eustachian tube. It may also be necessary to make a small surgical incision, under anaesthetic, to relieve the pressure on the eardrum and prevent the eardrum from becoming perforated. This will involve a short stay in hospital.

Sometimes the pressure relieves itself as pus perforates the eardrum. If this happens the pus will usually drain away to the outside of the ear, or down into the throat through the Eustachian tube, the eardrum will soon heal, and the child's hearing will return to normal. The doctor will keep a close check on the child's progress to make sure that complications are not developing.

OTITIS INTERNA

If the child has otitis interna as a complication of another disease the strong antibiotic treatment being given for the main disease will also treat the otitis. There is, however, a slight risk that permanent damage may be done to the ear.

YOUR QUESTIONS

Q My son loves swimming but he often complains of earache. Are the two likely to be related and is it alright to give him ear drops, when he has pain?

A No. Never treat a child's ears with anything that has not been prescribed, and always seek medical attention for ear problems. If treated early these can nearly always be sorted out, but if they are neglected they can become more serious.

And, yes, children who swim a lot do sometimes suffer more from ear infections, from infections in the water and from having damp skin (the skin is more susceptible to infection when wet). Try to persuade your son to wear a cap to keep his ears dry when swimming, and make sure that he has a clean towel and that he dries his ears properly.

P

■ PARACETAMOL

Paracetamol is an effective pain reliever which can also help to reduce the temperature when there is fever. It is considered to be the safest drug to give to children (and adults) with a high temperature or aches and pains.

Doctors now use paracetamol rather than aspirin for children since it is less likely to have harmful side effects and its use is not associated with any illness. Aspirin is known to play a part in the occurrence of Reye's syndrome, a disease affecting the liver and brain, and is banned for children under 12 years unless prescribed by a specialist.

Nevertheless it must not be forgotten that, like aspirin, paracetamol is a powerful drug and its use should be

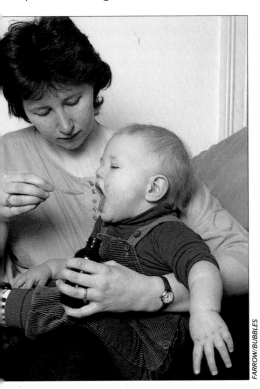

Paracetamol is now considered to be the safest painkiller to give to a child. It is best given to small children in liquid form.

the exception rather than the rule. Taken in excess paracetamol can affect the function of the kidneys and the liver, so recommended doses should always be observed.

WATCHPOINTS

- Keep *all* drugs safely locked away out of children's reach at all times.
- An overdose of paracetamol can be fatal.
- If your child does swallow more than two paracetamol tablets together, get medical help at once.
- Ask your doctor or a qualified pharmacist for advice if you are in doubt about the type of paracetamol to give or about the correct dose.

YOUR QUESTIONS

Q My doctor told me to give my daughter junior aspirin when she sprained a wrist recently. I thought aspirin was harmful?

A Aspirin should never be given to children who are under twelve years old, but after this it can be given in the appropriate dose when there is inflammation present. Though paracetamol is now normally used instead of aspirin as a pain-killer, there are some conditions for which aspirin is more effective. These are where the pain is caused by inflammation. Aspirin reduces inflammation as well as pain and therefore works on the cause of the pain.

ALTERNATIVES

Before resorting to giving your child a drug, always consider the alternatives. High temperatures can often be reduced quite effectively by undressing the child and putting him to

All drugs are potentially dangerous. Paracetamol should only be given in the recommended dose and children should never have access to drugs.

bed covered only by a cotton sheet. The doors and windows should be open to allow air to circulate (although the room should not be allowed to get too cold).

If the child's temperature is very high (over 40°C/104°F) it can often be lowered by sponging the child in tepid water while he is lying in bed (with towels to mop up any drips). As the water absorbs the child's heat, keep rinsing the sponge or cloth in more tepid water and gently sponge the whole body. Afterwards, cover the child with a cotton sheet.

Pain can often be soothed by applying cold or heat. A headache should be treated by placing a cold compress (a cloth rinsed in cold water) on the child's forehead. As this becomes warmer it should be refreshed again in cold water, and the child should be left to rest.

The pain of earache or tummy ache can be soothed by the warmth of a well-wrapped hot water bottle. It is better to use warm water and refill frequently than to use too-hot water. Always wrap the bottle, anyway, to make sure there is no risk of the child being burnt. It is not safe to give a hot water bottle to very young children, and for them warmth can be supplied by warming up a pad on a radiator or in front of a fire.

TYPES OF PARACETAMOL

There are several types of preparation containing paracetamol that are especially produced for the treatment of children. It is available in tablet form – both soluble (to be dissolved in water) and non-soluble (to be swallowed) – and as a suspension, syrup or elixir (to be taken by spoon). If in doubt as to whether a preparation contains paracetamol, consult your pharmacist.

■ PENIS

See CIRCUMCISION, GENITALS

■ PENIS, CAUGHT IN ZIP

Little boys who are not quite used to grown-up trousers with zip fronts do risk getting their penises caught when they are zipping or unzipping their trousers in a hurry.

CAUSES

This form of accident happens most often when the child is in a rush after going to the lavatory and is rapidly trying to get zipped up and back to what he was doing. Equally, if he is not paying attention when he gets dressed or if he is hurrying because he is late when going out, he may catch himself in his zip.

It makes sense not to dress your little boy in zipped trousers until he is old enough to handle a zip competently. Make sure he knows that he must take care when fastening a zip, and never hurry him when he is in the lavatory or dressing for school. It is much better to help him with dressing if there is a need for speed.

TREATMENT

Having his penis trapped in a zip's teeth is painful as well as alarming for the child. Stop him from panicking by being calm and reassuring. It can help to put an ice cube wrapped in a clean handkerchief on the penis to numb it while you check to see what has happened. If you think you can safely deal with the problem yourself, get the little boy to sit or lie comfortably while you do so.

When the zip's teeth have safely been extracted gently apply a soothing antiseptic ointment to the injury, and continue to do this several times a day until the penis is no longer sore. If the child complains of pain it is safe to give him paracetamol in the correct dosage for his age. He will probably feel more comfortable dressed in pull-on trousers or shorts for a few days afterwards.

MEDICAL HELP

If you think that you cannot free the penis yourself, get the child to your doctor's surgery or the nearest accident and emergency ward, holding

Zipped trousers make a little boy feel really grown up. Teach your son to pull up his underpants properly before pulling up his trousers.

CAMILLA JESSEL

some wrapped ice over the injury to numb it. If you do not have your own transport, it may be necessary to call an ambulance.

In the surgery or hospital, the child will be given a local anaesthetic and then the zip will be removed. Afterwards he will be quite sore for a few days, especially after passing water, and you will be advised if any further treatment is necessary.

> # YOUR QUESTIONS
>
> **Q** What after-care is necessary when a little boy has caught his penis in his trouser zip?
>
> **A** This injury is bound to take several days to heal, and it will be best to dress your child in comfortable, loose clothes during this time. Try to let him go without trousers or underpants if possible to aid healing, and apply antiseptic ointment several times a day to soothe and to prevent infection. (The child may prefer to do this for himself.)
>
> Try not to get in a panic if this ever happens as it will make the child feel even more upset. Just be sympathetic without making a fuss.

■ PEPTIC ULCER

See also PERITONITIS

Surprising as it may sound, children do sometimes fall prey to peptic ulcers. This is very rare, but is slightly more likely if there is a family history of ulcers or indigestion. Peptic ulcers can occur either in the stomach (when they are known as gastric ulcers) or in the duodenum (the first part of the intestine – when they are called duodenal ulcers).

SYMPTOMS

Pain in the middle of the chest is the main symptom of a stomach ulcer, and the child may find this worse at night or when she is hungry. (If the cause is a duodenal ulcer, she may complain of pains more towards the back.) The pain appears at regular intervals, two to four times during the day and at night, and lasts for less than half an hour. Occasionally, she may also be sick, and the vomit may be stained with blood. Some ulcers also cause blood to be present in the faeces, making them very dark — almost black — in colour.

A child with a peptic ulcer must follow a special diet, eating little and often. Milk will line the stomach and prevent digestive acids from attacking it.

CAUSES

Ulcers in the digestive system occur when the mucous lining of the digestive tract is attacked by the acids produced by the body itself to aid the process of digestion. But although most cases of ulcers are found in people whose systems over-produce acids, this is not always so, and exactly why these people develop ulcers is not fully understood. Nor is it clear why some people's systems over-produce acid, although it is known that this can be caused by continuous stress — and even young children can suffer from stress.

YOUR QUESTIONS

Q Why is a peptic ulcer painful, and why does the pain come and go?

A The pain is caused by the action of the digestive acid eating away at the raw, ulcerated lining of the stomach or duodenum. The pain is usually felt when acid is produced while there is no food passing through the system to absorb it.

DIAGNOSIS

You should always consult your doctor if your child frequently complains of pains in the chest at regular intervals and at night, or has any other symptoms to indicate that there may be an ulcer. If the symptoms are not too severe, the doctor may decide that the child should be put on a suitable diet and should take a mild antacid, but in some cases the child may be sent to hospital for diagnosis.

If this happens your child will be given a barium meal, followed by X-rays to see whether there is an ulcer. This is not painful, but it is rather unpleasant and if your child is old enough to understand, you should explain to her in advance what will be involved in the test.

Sometimes an examination using a flexible tube called an endoscope will also be necessary. The tube is passed into the stomach via the mouth and gives the doctor a view of the inside of the stomach. Very young children may be given an anaesthetic for this operation, and older children will probably be sedated.

TREATMENT

Hospital treatment is not necessary unless there are complications, and it will simply be necessary for the child to follow a suitable diet. Drugs that control the production of stomach acids will also be prescribed. As part of the treatment you will probably be advised to make sure that the child eats frequent small meals so that there is always food passing through the stomach for the digestive juices to work on. Milk is also often recommended. Any drugs must be taken strictly as prescribed.

WATCHPOINTS

- A child with a peptic ulcer or symptoms of an ulcer should never be given aspirin as this can irritate the lining of the stomach (and no child under the age of twelve should ever be given the drug).

- If a child with an ulcer suddenly complains of intense pain, following which she may collapse, call an ambulance. This may be peritonitis, and requires urgent treatment (see separate entry).

■ PERFORATED EARDRUM

See also EAR, GLUE EAR, OTITIS

The eardrum can be perforated (or ruptured) in a number of ways, and it usually heals itself within a few weeks. There is usually no danger unless the eardrum is perforated frequently.

SYMPTOMS

When the eardrum is perforated there may be some very slight bleeding from the ear. There is usually also mild pain, accompanied by buzzing noises in the ear, and sometimes slight loss of hearing. If the perforation is caused by a burst abscess or boil (*see* Causes) it can cause pain to be relieved as the build-up of pus is released. The symptoms often last for only a matter of hours. It is therefore quite possible for this form of injury to go undetected unless the child is already being treated for an ear infection, or unless it causes complications.

An eardrum can be perforated by a sudden burst of loud sound, such as a blast from an amplifier. If repeated, permanent damage can result.

CAUSES

Perforated eardrum can be caused by an infection of the middle ear (*see* **Otitis**), particularly that of an abscess or boil which bursts suddenly to discharge its build-up of pus.

Other causes can be the child's putting a foreign object such as a bead or a pencil into the ear. Unfortunately, eardrums have also been perforated by parents attempting to clean a child's ear with cotton buds. This is something that should never be done. Neither should a parent ever hit a child on the face, even in play, as a blow to the ear can cause a perforation of the eardrum.

Finally, a very loud sound can cause a perforated eardrum. This is a very unusual occurrence, resulting from the child being near the site of an explosion or perhaps from a sudden blast from a malfunctioning amplifier at a pop concert.

YOUR QUESTIONS

Q How long does it normally take for a perforated eardrum to get better?

A If all goes well, the eardrum completely heals itself in about a fortnight, but it can sometimes take up to three months.

TREATMENT

Surprisingly enough, a straightforward case cures itself, but it does need care and if you suspect from the symptoms and the circumstances that your child has perforated an eardrum you should always take him to the family doctor for a check-up.

The doctor will examine the ear with an otoscope, and if he or she finds that the eardrum is perforated, antibiotics will probably be prescribed to make sure that infection does not enter the ear through the perforation. The whole course of treatment must be taken at the prescribed intervals to make sure that it is effective. The doctor will also want to see the child regularly until the eardrum is fully healed.

If, in the early stages, the child has a pain in the ear as a result of the injury you can put a clean, warm pad over the ear to soothe it. The

CAMILLA JESSEL

A perforated eardrum is often the result of otitis media, which affects many little children and usually causes severe pain.

appropriate dose of paracetamol may be given, particularly at bedtime if the pain stops the child from sleeping properly.

COMPLICATIONS

It is very unusual for complications to arise following a perforation of the eardrum. In some cases, however, the injury makes it possible for an infection to enter into the middle ear, but this is unlikely to happen as long as the child takes the antibiotics prescribed by the doctor.

If the child suffers from persistent ear infections which result in frequent perforations, causing scarring, or if for some reason an ear infection does not heal up, a small operation may be performed to graft a new piece of skin onto the damaged area. This usually provides a complete cure to the problem and resolves any hearing problems that the child may have been experiencing.

■ PERITONITIS

See also ABDOMEN, APPENDICITIS, PEPTIC ULCER

Peritonitis is an inflammation of the peritoneum, the mucous membrane that forms the lining to the abdomen. This usually comes about as a result of a burst appendix or of a severe peptic ulcer perforating the wall of the stomach or duodenum. It is a fairly rare complication and is most unusual in children.

S Y M P T O M S

The main symptom of peritonitis is acute, violent pain in the abdomen. The pain will be felt at the site of the inflammation and its position will therefore vary depending on the exact cause. The wall of the tummy becomes rigid and the child stays very still. The condition will usually cause severe vomiting, and the child is likely to have a slight fever.

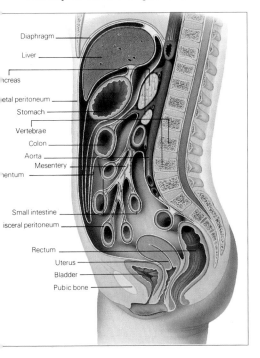

The organs in the abdomen lie close together, but are kept separate by a membrane called the peritoneum.

Diaphragm
Liver
Pancreas
Parietal peritoneum
Stomach
Vertebrae
Colon
Aorta
Mesentery
Omentum
Small intestine
Visceral peritoneum
Rectum
Uterus
Bladder
Pubic bone

C A U S E S

It is caused by infection of or damage to the peritoneum from one of several possible causes. Fortunately the peritoneum heals very quickly as long as it is treated in time.

APPENDICITIS

If a child has appendicitis which flares up very quickly, the appendix can burst before the condition has been diagnosed and treated. This causes pus from the appendix to be released within the abdomen, and the part of the peritoneum affected becomes inflamed. In this case the pain will normally be felt in the lower right side of the abdomen. Especially in young children, who have little resistance, the whole peritoneum can then quickly become inflamed, and immediate treament is vital.

PEPTIC ULCER

If an ulcer in the stomach or duodenum becomes unusually severe, the site of the ulcer becomes eroded. This development is known as a ruptured or perforated ulcer, and leads to severe inflammation of the peritoneum. The condition is unusual in children. The pain will be felt higher in the abdomen.

YOUR QUESTIONS

Q How would I know if my child had peritonitis?

A She would be in constant, severe pain, which was made worse by any movement. This would make her want to lie very still, often with her knees drawn up to her tummy, in a 'foetal' position.
She would probably vomit frequently, which would cause more pain, and her temperature would be raised. She might also look very pale and feel clammy.

INJURY

The peritoneum can also be damaged through injury. If anything pierces the abdomen in such a way that the peritoneum is cut through, infection can quickly enter and spread. The injury involved would be from a violent incident such as a bad car accident, or stabbing, kicking or punching.

DIAGNOSIS

If a child has severe abdominal pain which lasts for ten to twenty minutes or more, and if there is shock, vomiting or fever, you should call an ambulance straight away as peritonitis is an emergency and needs medical attention straight away.

In hospital a doctor will examine the child, pressing the abdomen to assess the exact location of the pain, and to see how severe it is. He or she will feel for lack of movement in the abdominal wall, a feeling of rigidity when the abdomen is pressed, and an absence of bowel sounds. The child may also be sent for X-rays to determine what is wrong.

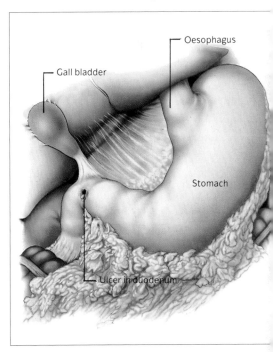

Oesophagus
Gall bladder
Stomach
Ulcer in duodenum

When an ulcer in the duodenum ruptures, this is known as a perforated ulcer or peritonitis.

T R E A T M E N T

Treatment will involve surgery to remove the appendix or repair the site of the ulcer. If there is an injury, the appropriate treatment will be given. The peritoneum itself, which heals very quickly, will be repaired and the abdominal cavity will be washed out with warm salt water. Naturally, the child will need to have a full anaesthetic for this.

In addition to surgery, antibiotics will be given to treat the infection, and if the child is dehydrated through vomiting, she will be given fluids intravenously.

The child will need to spend some time in hospital recovering from the illness, and if possible a parent or other member of the family should stay with her, especially during the early stages, when she will be very weak. There is every prospect of a complete recovery, however.

WATCHPOINTS

Do not give anything to eat or drink to a child showing symptoms of peritonitis, as an anaesthetic will almost certainly be necessary.

◼ PERTHES DISEASE

See also HIP

This is a rare disease that affects children between the ages of five and ten. It causes hip and leg pain and makes the child limp, but usually a complete cure is possible.

YOUR QUESTIONS

Q Can a child who has had Perthes' disease play sports and have a normal life when he has recovered?

A Yes. This is something to keep in mind if your child does suffer from the disease. There is usually a complete recovery. Once he has built up his strength he will be able to enjoy games and sporting activities like any other child.

SYMPTOMS

The symptoms of Perthes' disease are pain in the hip joint, or sometimes in the knee, and muscle spasm when movement is attempted, causing a characteristic limp. The hip joint at one or both sides can be affected.

CAUSES

Perthes' disease is caused by an abnormality in the blood supply to the top part of the femur (thighbone), which is the growth point of the bone. It is not known why this happens, and it frequently resolves itself over a few years. For some reason, boys are more likely to be affected than girls. In a small proportion of cases both hip joints are affected by the condition.

DIAGNOSIS

In the early stages of the disease the abnormality does not show up in X-rays, and a bone scan may be necessary. When the disease has developed and the bone is knitting back together again, areas of increased bone density will show up on an X-ray indicating that healing is taking place.

YOUR QUESTIONS

Q My little boy has irritable hip. Is this the same as Perthes' disease?

A No. The symptoms are almost indistinguishable, but irritable hip causes pain and limping for only a few days at a time and is caused by an inflammation of the hip joint. Irritable hip is most likely to affect children who are under six years old, and Perthes' disease usually affects slightly older children.

TREATMENT

Usually Perthes' disease does not need to be treated surgically, although some surgeons recommend grafting some normal bone from another part of the body onto the femur to speed up the natural healing process. (The bone used for the graft will grow again.)

Normally rest is the treatment that is advised. This means that the child must put no weight on the leg until the condition has cleared up – a process which may take two to three years or more.

Special arrangements will have to be made for your child's education while he is incapacitated like this, as he will not be able to attend school, and you will have to be very resourceful to make sure that his spirits do not sag during this time. You, too, will find the situation very stressful and frustrating at times. Your family doctor will be able to give advice and support, and you may be able to find a support group through which you can meet and exchange ideas with other parents whose children are suffering from the disease.

The main consolation during this time is that the outlook for the child's making a full recovery is very high. And the younger the child is at the onset of the disease the better the outlook, as there will still be many growing years ahead after the disease has passed.

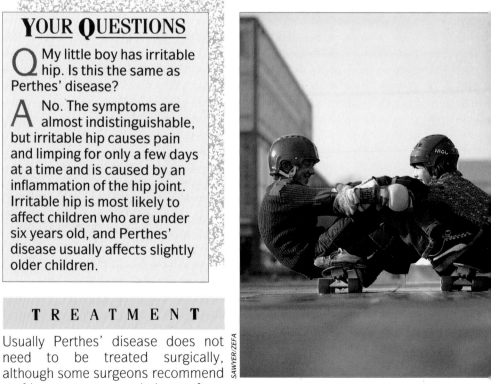

A child with Perthes' disease will have to have complete rest in order to recover, but eventually he will be skate-boarding once more.

PETIT MAL
See EPILEPSY

PHENYLKETONURIA

Phenylketonuria (PKU) is a very rare disorder, affecting only one in 10,000 babies. An affected baby lacks the enzyme which deals with a type of amino-acid, phenylalanine (a component of proteins). An excess of phenylalanine then accumulates, affecting the nervous system, although doctors do not yet know why. If the disorder is not treated, it can result in mental retardation, often associated with convulsions.

SYMPTOMS

In most countries in the western world, babies are tested for PKU at about six days old, in other words before any symptoms become apparent. Commonly known as the Guthrie test (which also reveals cretinism), the test consists of pricking the baby's heel with a needle and testing a drop of blood.

Routine blood tests taken within a few days of birth will show whether or not the child has phenylketonuria.

CAUSES

PKU is an inherited disorder. Parents who are carriers (but who may themselves be unaffected) can pass on either a normal or an affected gene. Babies are only affected if they inherit affected genes from both parents. If both parents carry the abnormal gene, there is a one in four chance that their child will develop the disorder.

TREATMENT

If discovered within a few days of birth, PKU is treated with a special diet which will need to be continued at least until the age of ten or 12. This diet excludes, or reduces the foods that contain much phenylalanine, and is supplemented with protein substitutes and vitamins. If the child sticks to this strict diet he will develop absolutely normally.

YOUR QUESTIONS

Q When my baby was six days old she was diagnosed as suffering from phenylketonuria and I was told that I would not be able to continue breast feeding. I feel very disappointed and wonder if this was really necessary?

A Unfortunately, it is necessary to stop breast feeding a baby who has PKU. This is because your baby cannot digest the phenylalanine that is present in your breast milk, and must be given a special milk which is very low in phenylalanine in order to thrive. As the disorder was picked up at this early stage, your baby should develop happily on her special diet and you will soon find other ways to feel close to her.

PHIMOSIS

See also FORESKIN

When a boy's foreskin is too tight to be drawn back over the glans.

SYMPTOMS

Phimosis cannot be detected before a boy reaches the age of about five as until then the foreskin is normally small and tight. If after this age the foreskin still cannot be retracted (drawn back) easily, it is worth mentioning this to your doctor. A child will sometimes feel pain when passing urine, but often he will not notice any symptoms until adolescence, when having an erection is painful.

Many little boys under the age of five have phimosis or tight foreskin, but it usually causes no problems.

WATCHPOINTS

Never try to force the foreskin back over the glans (tip of the penis) as this can tear the tissues and the resulting scarring as they heal will cause the foreskin to stick even more tightly to the glans, making circumcision inevitable.

TREATMENT

If the tightness persists after the age of about five and your child feels pain on urinating, your doctor will probably recommend circumcision (*see* separate entry).

◼ PIGEON TOES

See FEET

◼ PIMPLES

Isolated pimples and spots are usually associated with adolescence, but they can occur in young children and even in tiny babies. Acne is a separate medical condition characterized by the outgrowth of multiple, large pimples on the face, chest and shoulders, and affects adolescents, especially boys.

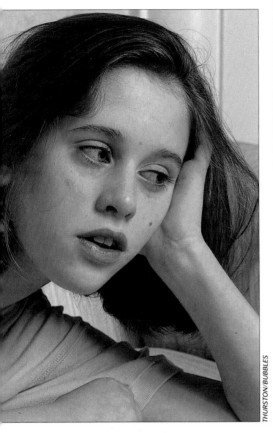

Almost all children can suffer from the odd pimple, and it is really nothing to feel gloomy about. There is little you can do about them, and they will clear up very quickly.

SYMPTOMS

A slightly raised, sometimes shiny, area of skin at the opening of a hair follicle, with a black, white or red centre. Pimples are most common on the more oily areas of the face (the forehead, nose and chin) and on the back, particularly round the shoulders.

YOUR QUESTIONS

Q My two-week-old baby's skin is so spotty that it looks like that of an adolescent. In fact it looks so awful that I'm afraid to take her out as people may think that I don't keep her clean. My health visitor says it's nothing to be concerned about and to leave the spots alone apart from washing her face with clean water. Surely she needs some ointment to clear up these spots?

A Your health visitor is absolutely right. Spots are very common in newborn babies and they will clear up on their own as her skin matures. Carry on keeping her skin clean and just don't worry about what other people may think.

CAUSES

Pimples are the result of overactive sebaceous glands, which produce too much sebum (an oily secretion). This is why they often occur in adolescence, when hormonal changes encourage over-production of sebum. Sebum is normally discharged from the hair follicles but if there is too much of it the excess sebum and dead cells form a blackhead or whitehead which blocks the follicle. Sebum continues to build up and the follicle may become inflamed and a red spot appears.

ACNE IN CHILDREN

A few young children do develop acne, even below the age of five. Most grow out of it, but it may return in a more severe form during adolescence. See your doctor, who may prescribe antibiotics or other drugs to decrease sebum production.

PIMPLES IN BABIES

New babies are subject to many different types of pimples. Some, known as neo-natal urticaria, can worry parents as they can look like true pimples. However, they are nothing to worry about and form because the baby's skin is not yet working efficiently. They need no treatment and will vanish after the first couple of weeks.

Milia are small white spots over the bridge of the nose and are caused by a temporary blockage of the sebaceous glands. Again, these are nothing to worry about and nearly always disappear after a few days (*see* separate entry).

TREATMENT

Never pick or squeeze pimples. This may spread infection and also cause scarring. Keep the skin clean with soap and water, and encourage your child to spend time out of doors as sunshine and particularly sea air seem to help clear up pimples. If the pimples persist or if you think they may be a symptom of disease, consult your doctor.

PREVENTION

Unfortunately pimples cannot be prevented and some children, especially those with oily skins, are particularly prone to them. Good hygiene, fresh air and sunshine can make them less likely to occur.

◼ PINK EYE

See CONJUNCTIVITIS

◼ PLASTERS

See also BANDAGES, DRESSINGS

Plasters (also known as sticking plasters or band aids) consist of a pad of

A sticking plaster will not stop a cut knee from hurting but it may help psychologically, especially if it is applied with a kiss and a cuddle.

absorbent gauze or cellulose on an adhesive backing which is perforated to allow air to get in and sweat to evaporate. They are used to cover smallish open wounds such as cuts and grazes while they heal, absorbing blood or pus, controlling bleeding, preventing infection, and keeping the wound clean. They should be changed at least once a day, or whenever they get wet. Plasters are not usually sufficient for large wounds, and non-adhesive dressings or bandages are used for these.

Plasters also have a psychological effect – small children love them and will request one for the smallest hurt.

WHEN TO USE A PLASTER

Although wounds heal fastest when left exposed to the air, it is best to apply a plaster if the wound is deep, is likely to become dirty or is in a place where it may be knocked causing the scab to reopen. You may also find that applying a plaster, even if it is to be kept on for just a short while, will make your child forget the hurt faster as she will feel you have taken it seriously.

Keep a supply of plasters, perhaps of the ones with cartoon characters or TV favourites, for fast recovery of wounded dignity. Assorted sizes are best, including some that are specially shaped for awkward areas like knuckles and knees. Although waterproof plasters are available they should be avoided where possible, as stopping the air getting to a wound will slow recovery. If the wound is a minor one, remove the plaster as soon as you can as it will recover faster if the air can get to it.

YOUR QUESTIONS

Q My young son always asks for a plaster when he has hurt himself – however slightly. I usually oblige as this seems to make him feel better but how often should I change the plaster?

A If the plaster is needed purely for psychological reasons and not for a bleeding cut or graze, it does not matter how dirty it gets. If it is covering an open wound, however, it should be changed at least once a day when you will be able to check the progress of the wound.

WATCHPOINTS

Try not to let your child become squeamish about minor injuries. Let her see what you are doing and if she can, let her clean the area and apply the plaster herself. If you dislike the sight of blood try not to let your child become aware of this as she will play up minor injuries instead of letting them become a normal part of everyday life.

APPLYING A PLASTER

The plaster should be large enough for the absorbent pad to cover both the wound and some of the surrounding whole skin. Plasters will not stick on skin that is damp or covered in antiseptic cream, so dry the area around the wound before applying the plaster. Hold the plaster over the wound, press the pad lightly on it and slowly peel off the protective coverings on the adhesive strips. Smooth the adhesive strips down on the skin to make sure the plaster stays on.

REMOVING A PLASTER

If the wound has healed, remove the plaster quickly in one smooth movement. If an older child is willing, let her remove the plaster herself. If hair is stuck to the plaster or the pad has become attached to the wound, you will need to proceed more slowly. Cut away any hairs as you peel the plaster back and if the pad is stuck to the wound, soak it in warm water until it will come away.

PLASTER OF PARIS

Plaster of paris is still used to immobilize a broken bone, although modern lightweight alternatives (resin and plastic) are sometimes used instead. The plaster or plaster substitute holds the bone still while healing takes place, enabling the two broken ends to knit together perfectly as long as they have first been correctly 'reduced' (aligned).

Plasters should never be allowed to get wet. If a child's plaster cast cracks, you should let the hospital know straight away, and you should also let your doctor know if the plaster causes pins and needles or numbness. Try to prevent your child from fiddling with the edges of the plaster, but by all means allow friends to sign it in the time-honoured way.

■ PLEURISY

This is an inflammation of the pleura (a double layer of thin membrane surrounding the lungs). There are three types: dry pleurisy, pleurisy with effusion (when fluid leaks into the chest cavity because of inflammation), and empyema (a type of abscess that occupies a natural cavity in the body).

SYMPTOMS

It is possible to suffer from pleurisy without any direct symptoms although most types will cause pain in the chest. A child suffering from **dry pleurisy** will feel pain when he coughs or takes a deep breath. However, if your child is suffering from **pleurisy with effusion**, when fluid accumulates in the space between the lung and the chest wall, he may not feel the pain any more, because the fluid protects the inflamed membrane from friction. He may however suffer from breathlessness as the fluid accumulates. **Empyema** also may not cause pain.

CAUSES

Pleurisy is nearly always caused by infection by bacteria or viruses. When a virus is the cause, the pleural membranes become inflamed and sore in just the same way as the membrane lining the nose does when you have a cold.

Bacterial pleurisy often occurs when there is an underlying infection in the lung, and especially if your child is suffering from pneumonia. This causes infection to spread through the lung tissue until it eventually leads to inflammation of the outer surface of the lung.

YOUR QUESTIONS

Q My doctor tells me that my son is suffering from viral pleurisy, but he has not prescribed any drugs, telling me simply to keep him warm and comfortable. I'm worried because I'm sure I've heard that people can die of pleurisy so surely he needs some medication?

A There are several different types of pleurisy and viral pleurisy does indeed get better on its own.

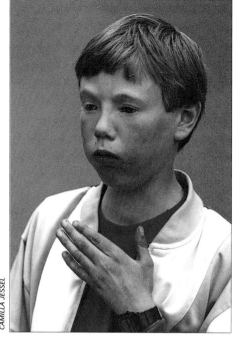

CAMILLA JESSEL

One sign of pleurisy is pain in the chest whenever the child coughs or breathes in deeply.

TREATMENT

All forms of pleurisy should be taken seriously, especially if there is no apparent cause, as this may be the first indication of a serious underlying disease. If your child has a temperature and seems unusually short of breath, whether or not breathing hurts, see your doctor. He will listen to the child's chest through a stethoscope and will percuss (tap) the chest to listen for the sounds that accompany irritated pleurae and pleural effusion. He may also send the child for a chest x-ray and tests which involve drawing off a sample of the fluid using a needle and syringe.

If the pleurisy is caused by bacteria, the underlying infection rather than the pleurisy is treated and the pleurisy will disappear with the infection. Viral pleurisy will disappear on its own with no treatment. Empyema is always treated surgically. The pus is first drawn off with a hollow needle and syringe and later, when the lung is firmly stuck to the chest wall around the abscess, a hole is made in the chest wall to enable the pus to drain away completely. All types of pleurisy respond to warmth, restric-

tion of chest movements on the affected side to relieve the pain, and the removal of any fluid.

EPIDEMIC PLEURISY

This is also known as Bornholm disease as it was first noticed on the island of Bornholm. It is a virus infection with fever and pain in the muscles of the ribs and abdomen. Attacks last a few days and sometimes return a few days later. Fortunately, this disease rarely causes complications.

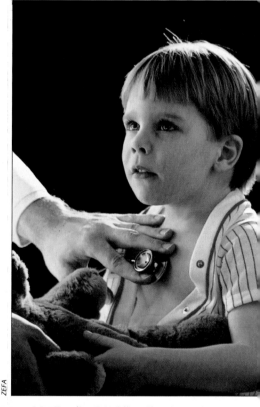

ZEFA

If your child seems short of breath or finds coughing or taking a deep breath painful, he should have his chest examined by the family doctor.

PNEUMONIA

Pneumonia is an infection of the lungs. It can affect children of all ages but is most common in the first year. There are three types: broncho-pneumonia, hypostatic pneumonia and lobar pneumonia. Broncho-pneumonia occasionally occurs as a complication in measles. If your child is suffering from measles and does not appear to be getting better two or three days after the rash has developed, or if he is very short of breath and has a persistent cough, consult your doctor. Similarly bronchopneumonia can occur after an attack of influenza, whooping cough, diphtheria, bronchitis or even a severe cold when the child's resistance is lowered, but again this is very rare. It can also occur after a child has come close to drowning if he has swallowed dirty or polluted water.

The other two forms of pneumonia

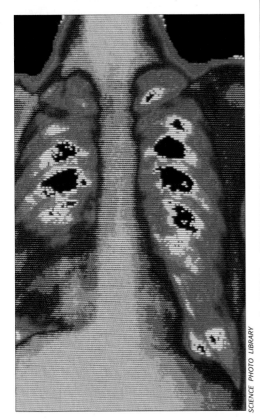

False-colour chest x-ray showing damage caused by lobar pneumonia (bottom left of picture). The condition is treated using antibiotics. The lung on the right of the picture is normal and healthy.

arise quite suddenly, sometimes preceeded by vomiting or convulsions.

SYMPTOMS

Your child will probably have a runny nose, a high temperature and fast breathing. He will feel very ill and will be listless and show no interest in anything. He may also be flushed or, in severe cases, his skin may appear grey and sweaty and he may make little grunting noises as he breathes. In some cases he will also have a cough which is, generally dry (i.e. not producing phlegm), and if the pneumonia is affecting the outer surface of the lung, the pleural membranes may be affected and breathing will be painful.

YOUR QUESTIONS

Q My little boy got very cold and wet the other day after being caught in the rain. He seems to have developed a heavy cold and I'm worried that he may develop pneumonia. Is this likely?

A Pneumonia can develop after a severe cold but this is very unusual. It is more likely to happen if your son's general health is poor, perhaps after a series of illnesses. Getting soaked does not lead to pneumonia and your child should recover from his cold in a few days.

CAUSES

All forms of pneumonia are caused by a bacterial or viral infection affecting the alveoli (air-pockets in the lungs where oxygen seeps into the blood and carbon dioxide escapes from it). The infected alveoli become blocked with fluid that in time forms a solid clot. The position of the blockage varies with the type of pneumonia. With bronchopneumonia, the blockage affects the small alveoli and is scattered all over the lungs. In lobar pneumonia the whole of one segment of the lung, called a lobe, is involved,

while hypostatic pneumonia affects the lowest parts of both lungs. The more severe bacterial pneumonia is, fortunately, now much less common than it was and seems to be giving place to the less dangerous viral pneumonia.

REPEATED PNEUMONIA

Although pneumonia does not normally recur, if your child has inhaled a small object, perhaps a toy or nut, he may suffer repeated attacks of pneumonia. This is because the swallowed object causes an infection which leads to pneumonia and although the pneumonia responds to the antibiotics each time, the underlying cause has not been removed. If your doctor suspects this is the problem, he will give your child x-rays. If the diagnosis is proved to be correct the doctor will give a general anaesthetic and pass a tube down the airways to find and remove the object.

TREATMENT

Always consult your doctor immediately you suspect pneumonia. Pneumonia used frequently to be fatal but today it is easily cured by modern antibiotics. While you are waiting, prop your child up in bed with pillows to help his breathing, keep him warm and keep the air moist by boiling a kettle in the room. (Never leave your child alone in a room with a boiling kettle.)

Mild cases may be treated at home with antibiotics given by mouth but in more severe cases the child will need to be admitted to hospital. Your child will need a larger amount of antibiotics than can be swallowed and these are given by injection, either intravenously (into a vein) or into the thigh muscle. Injections into the muscle are painful and leave a dull ache so some doctors prefer to give them intravenously to avoid this.

Your child will also be given physiotherapy to help clear the infected parts of the lung. A child with pneumonia is usually better within two or three days and the illness does not recur.

PNEUMONIA AND CYSTIC FIBROSIS

Children with cystic fibrosis (a rare congenital disease that affects various glands in the body – see separate entry) frequently suffer from repeated attacks of pneumonia. This is because cystic fibrosis affects the glands in the lining of the bronchial tubes and instead of producing the normal thin mucus, the glands produce a thick, sticky phlegm (mucus). This phelgm blocks the air passages, and this leads to lung infections. Small parts of the lung then collapse and become infected and the child will suffer repeated attacks of pneumonia. At present there is no cure for cystic fibrosis and the pneumonia will be treated with antibiotics as it occurs.

■ POISONING

See also FOOD POISONING, TOADSTOOL POISONING

Many household substances contain poisons and with small children about it is important for parents to be aware of the dangers in the home and keep potentially harmful substances out of reach. Several common plants in the house or garden also have poisonous effects and children should be trained not to put any part of any plant in their mouths. With very young children it is advisable not to grow poisonous plants or to grow them only where children cannot get at them.

As soon as a baby begins to crawl, she takes a delight in exploring her surroundings and it is natural for her to put things in her mouth. Young children from crawling age until the age of about five or six are particularly at risk of poisoning unless all danger is kept out of their reach preferably in a locked cupboard.

Older children may deliberately put themselves at risk, sometimes simply because they are afraid to say 'no' to their friends. Glue sniffing, drug taking and alcohol abuse are all worrying possibilities for them.

SYMPTOMS

The symptoms of poisoning will differ according to the poison your child has taken. Corrosive poisons such as household cleaners have a burning action and a child who has swallowed them will scream with pain. Sleeping tablets and many other drugs will cause drowsiness. Solvents inhaled from lighter fuel, dry cleaning fluid and glues causes mental confusion. Many poisonous plants cause vomiting and nausea, stomach pain and diarrhoea. Many types of poisoning can lead to unconsciousness or convulsions. Finally, paracetamol poisoning shows no symptoms at all at first.

IDENTIFYING THE POISON

It is important to know what your child has taken. Keep any bottle or container so that you can show the doctor what the poison was. A sample of any vomit or diarrhoea should also be kept to help identify the poisonous substance involved.

TREATMENT

Seek medical aid for any kind of poisoning, but first do what you can to protect the child from further harm. If the child is unconscious, place her in the recovery position (see box). Check that she is breathing normally and give artificial respiration if necessary. Wipe the child's face with a dry cloth and then rinse with plenty of water to remove any of the poisonous substance that may be round the mouth. Now telephone for an ambulance.

If you know what the child has taken, tell the hospital staff so that you can be given advice on how to treat the child while waiting for the ambulance. The more information you can supply the better. If the child is unconscious or semi-conscious, keep a check for breathing and heartbeat and be ready to administer artificial respiration or heart massage (see pages 9–10 and page 31).

CORROSIVE SUBSTANCES

If the child is in pain from having swallowed a corrosive substance, DO NOT MAKE HER VOMIT. A corrosive substance does further harm to the oesophagus (gullet) if it is regurgitated. Instead, give the child plenty of milk if it is available, or water. (See box for list of corrosive poisons.)

MEDICINES

Medicines do not have a corrosive effect, and if you know for sure that the child has taken a large amount of a medicine, and if she is conscious, it is safe to make her sick. Do this by

Keep all medicines in a locked cupboard. Attractive packaging around tablets could fool your child into thinking they are sweets.

putting a finger down the child's throat rather than by giving mustard or salt which can aggravate the situation. It is not vital to make the child sick, however, and it is best to follow the advice given by the hospital.

MEDICAL TREATMENT

Once in hospital, the child may be given a drug to induce vomiting or may have a stomach pump or gastric washout. In certain cases an antidote to the poison may be administered, and if the child is unconscious she may be put on a ventilator.

Usually plenty of fluids will be given to help flush the poison through the kidneys, and in some cases the child may be put on a kidney machine. She may be kept under observaton for a few days, but will usually be allowed home after 24 hours, with no further ill effects. You will need to continue to give plenty of fluids and a bland diet for a few days until the child's digestive system is fully recovered.

SOME COMMON POISONOUS PLANTS

- Castor oil plant
- Lily of the valley
- Monkshood
- Oleander
- Yew

can all be fatal

- Cherry laurel
- Cuckoo pint
- Deadly nightshade
- Dieffenbachia
- Laburnum
- Lupin
- Privet
- Snowberry
- Woody nightshade

are all dangerous

Children should not touch or eat any wild mushrooms or toadstools as it is difficult to distinguish harmless from harmful types.

CORROSIVE POISONS

- Bleach
- Caustic soda
- Weedkiller
- White spirit
- Turpentine and turpentine substitutes
- Paint stripper
- Ammonia
- Washing soda
- Cleaning fluids
- Detergent
- Dishwasher powder
- Polish
- Petrol

If a child has taken any of these substances give plenty of milk or water to drink and call an ambulance. Wipe any traces of the substance off the child's skin with a dry cloth and rinse with plenty of water.

RECOVERY POSITION

If the child is unconscious or semi-conscious, put her in the recovery position. Lie her on her back. Cross left arm over chest and left ankle over right. Turn her towards you to lie on her right side, with right leg and arm extended. Make sure that her mouth is clear of any obstructions and turn her face upwards.

WATCHPOINTS

Some drugs have delayed effects. This is particularly true of paracetamol, which can be fatal and which can show no effect for up to three days. Always seek medical advice if your child has swallowed drugs and medicines of any sort even if you think they are harmless.

GAS POISONING

Gas poisoning has become quite rare since the widespread introduction of natural gas. The action required is simple — and vital.

- Turn off the gas. Open doors and windows. Better still, take the child outside if possible.
- Give mouth to mouth resuscitation if the child is not breathing. (Lie the child on his back, close nostrils with one hand and hold jaw with other hand, gently but firmly breathe into the child's mouth.)
- Give heart massage if the heart is not beating.
- Meanwhile, get someone to call an ambulance.

SALMONELLA

Salmonella bacteria can make young children very ill. It causes stomach pain, vomiting and fever with accompanying diarrhoea, causing dehydration.

Salmonella bacteria are found in meat and are not killed by freezing. They quickly multiply at room temperature which is why frozen meat should always be thawed in the fridge, then cooked right through.

■ POLIOMYELITIS

Since vaccines were developed in the late 1950s, poliomyelitis or polio (also known as infantile paralysis) has been almost eradicated from the developed world. Immunization can now be given orally, and it is important for parents to have their children immunized to keep this disabling disease at bay. The disease is unfortunately still common in many poor areas of the world through lack of a vaccination programme.

SYMPTOMS

It is possible for a child who develops polio to show only mild symptoms, with what appears to be a form of gastric flu. But in a small number of cases, further symptoms develop a few weeks later, with general aches and pains. Again, for some of the children affected, this is all there is to the disease, but in a few cases yet more symptoms arise.

In these cases there may be the development of meningitis (inflammation of the lining of the brain and spinal cord), with neck pain and acute sensitivity to light, together with increasing weakness in one arm and leg.

Poliomyelitis affects the nerve cells of the muscles so that there can be severe muscular weakness in the limbs. In the worst cases the muscles involved in breathing and swallowing can be paralysed so that the child cannot breathe without the aid of a ventilator. There can also be a drop in blood pressure and the heart's functioning can be affected.

Vaccination programmes did not begin until the late 1950s. Babies born before that time, such as pop star Ian Drury, contracted polio.

In countries where there is no vaccination programme, there can be epidemic outbreaks of polio (which is highly infectious). Many of the people affected show very few symptoms, and recover with no ill effects, but those who suffer more extreme symptoms never regain the use of some of the muscles affected, and this causes muscle wasting and, occasionally, disablement and paralysis to some degree.

WATCHPOINTS

Parents who have not been vaccinated against polio are not immune and can contract the disease (it is not confined to children). If you suspect, for any reason, that you may not be protected, speak to your doctor about being given the vaccine at the same time as your child.

CAUSES

Polio is a viral infection which affects the nerve cells that regulate the use of the muscles. When the infection is mild this has minimal effect, but in extreme cases some of the nerve cells are permanently damaged, leading to severe and irreversible paralysis of the muscles.

PREVENTION

Good sanitation did a great deal to suppress the disease before the development of the safe and effective vaccine now available. This is why there can be widespread outbreaks in countries where the vaccine is not used and sanitation is poor.

There are three strains of polio, and the vaccine now used gives lifelong protection against all three. Injection is no longer necessary, and the vaccine is usually given on a sugar lump to babies or young children, in three doses. This is a particularly safe form of vaccination and it would be foolhardy not to make sure that your child is protected.

CHARLES HENNEGHIEN/BRUCE COLEMAN

These African children have learned how to cope with the disabling effects of polio and happily play.

YOUR QUESTIONS

Q Is it really necessary to have children vaccinated against polio, now that it has become so rare?

A Although polio has been virtually eradicated from the West, it is still rife in many other countries, for example North Africa, Mexico and parts of the West Indies. Furthermore there are still occasional outbreaks of the disease in western countries and children who have not been vaccinated can be affected. Therefore it is important to make sure that your child is protected. The vaccine has no side effects and is easily given.

TREATMENT

Since polio is caused by a virus, the only treatment possible is nursing care. The majority of children affected recover as easily as from a dose of flu, but where symptoms become severe, bed rest – usually in hospital – will be necessary for a long period, with physiotherapy to prevent muscles from wasting. In the rare cases where respiration is affected the child may need to be put on to a ventilator to help him to breathe.

■ POLYNEURITIS

Polyneuritis is a fairly rare condition in which several nerves are inflamed. It can occasionally affect children who are recovering from an infectious disease such as measles or flu and even less frequently can occur on its own.

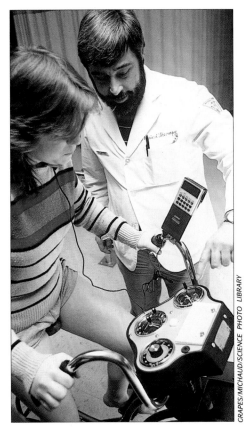

Polyneuritis causes loss of muscular control which can be helped with a course of physiotherapy.

SYMPTOMS

At the early stages the symptoms of polyneuritis are weakness in the legs, often with sensations of tingling, pins and needles or numbness. The child may be unable to use her legs, and this gradually develops over a day or two until, in the worst cases, the whole body is affected, including the face. Often in these cases the child is unable to control the muscles of the face and may become partially or completely paralysed in the rest of the body. If this happens, breathing can sometimes be affected.

CAUSES

The inflammation of the nerves in polyneuritis can be caused by a reaction to a viral or bacterial infection, but often it is not really clear what the cause is. The disease certainly seems to occur as a consequence of some of the commonplace infections experienced by children, especially herpes, measles and flu, in many cases.

If your child begins to show symptoms of weakness and tingling or numbness after an infection, it is advisable to report this to your doctor without delay. Although it is very unlikely that she is suffering from the condition, early treatment is important in these unusual cases.

YOUR QUESTIONS

Q How would I know if my child had polyneuritis?

A Although the first symptoms – weakness in the legs and tingling in the hands and feet – may pass unnoticed, these soon develop to the point where the child's legs are unable to take her own weight. The face muscles are also usually affected, so that the child is unable to open and close her eyes properly, or to smile and use her lips normally in speech. At the same time there is not usually any pain.

TREATMENT

A child with suspected polyneuritis will usually be taken into hospital and kept under observation to make sure that the muscles involved in breathing do not become affected. If this happens, the child will be put on a ventilator for a while.

Anti-inflammatory drugs may be given, together with antibiotics if there is a bacterial infection present. The child will be given nursing care to make sure that complications do not develop while she is recovering from the condition.

Although polyneuritis reaches its worst stage within a few day, the child may take about three weeks to recover after that. She will be given physiotherapy while still in hospital and this treatment, and the need to do set exercises, will continue once she is well enough to return home.

It will be several months before the child is fully well again. During this time she will have to remain at home, and arrangements will have to be made for her education so that she does not slip too far behind the other children in her class at school. However, there is every hope of a complete recovery being made in due course.

■ PRICKLY HEAT
See MILIA

■ PROJECTILE VOMITING
See PYLORIC STENOSIS

■ PROTEIN

Protein is made up of amino acids and is used in body-building and to replace the body's cells and produce the hormones and enzymes used in growth, digestion and many other bodily functions. Thus it is almost as important in the diet of growing children as are energy-giving foods.

If the body has inadequate fuel from carbohydrates and fats it can also use protein as fuel. Once protein has been broken down by the digestive system, the body is not able to store it in any form in any quantity. It is therefore important for children to have an adequate supply of protein every day.

GRAPES/MICHAUD/SCIENCE PHOTO LIBRARY

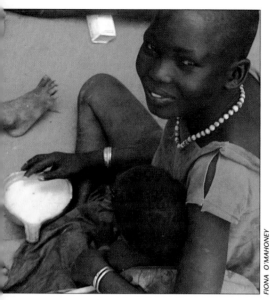

Third world people often have to make do with a diet inadequate in protein resulting in malnutrition. The children are particularly vulnerable and at risk.

SOURCES OF PROTEIN

g of protein (approx) per 100g

Fish 16–20

Lean red meat 13–15

Pork 12

Chicken 29

Eggs 12

Cheese (Cheddar types) 25

Cheese (cottage) 15

Milk (cow's) 3–5

Bread 8–9

Rice 6

Oatmeal 12

Lentils 24

Peas and broad beans (fresh) 5–7

Beans (dried) 20

Soyabeans 33.7

Brazil nuts 17.4

Peanuts (roasted) 28

SOURCES

In most diets the main source of protein is meat, fish and dairy products, especially cheese, and eggs. But many vegetables, especially cereals (for example rice and wheat), pulses (lentils, peas, beans of all kinds, and various seeds), and nuts also contain a large amount of protein.

While the protein from animal sources contains all the amino acids necessary to provide the essential building blocks for the body's own protein, no protein from a single vegetable source is complete on its own. Parents bringing up children on a strictly vegetarian diet need to be aware that vegetable sources must be combined so that lentils and rice, peas, beans and nuts can complement each other and yield up the full range of all the necessary amino-acids. A vegetarian diet may require more thought and care in preparation, but it can supply all the needs of growing children as long as it is well planned.

REQUIREMENTS

Children need large quantities of protein daily to sustain their growth, particularly when they are going through growth spurts. A child of seven to ten needs 54 grammes of protein a day, while an eleven to fourteen year old needs 63 grammes a day. This compares with an adult man's requirements of 62 grammes a day – the growing child needs more than an adult man!

PROTEIN AND DIGESTION

In the process of digestion, proteins are broken down into their constituent amino acids to be used in the body. This begins in the stomach, where hydrochloric acid and the enzyme known as pepsin begin to work on the food, and is continued in the small intestine, where enzymes known as trypsin from the pancreas and erepsin from the lining of the intestine complete the process.

There are approximately 22 types of amino acid in proteins, and these are carried in the blood to the tissues to be reassembled in different combinations to rebuild the cells of the body. Although the body can make some of its own amino acids, there are eight amino acids for adults and older children and nine for babies and very young children which have

to come from food. A diet with plenty of animal protein or protein from combined vegetable sources will provide all the necessary amino acids. See 'Sources of Protein' box on left for amounts of protein found in typical foods.

Protein is essential to a child's development. All the foods shown above are rich in protein.

YOUR QUESTIONS

Q What happens to any surplus protein if it cannot be stored in the body?

A Any excess amino acids are eliminated via the kidneys and the large intestine. Protein can be converted into energy, and if other foods are already providing enough energy this might spare burning of the fats from the diet. As a result surplus fat may be stored in the body.

■ PSORIASIS

This skin disease is in most cases very mild. It is quite common, especially in white people living in temperate climates, although it is fairly unusual to find it in younger children.

SYMPTOMS

The rash of psoriasis is characterized by scaling patches of silvery grey skin, with pink or red patches underneath, which are similar to the rash of eczema and which are often red and cracked. In its mildest form there may be just one or two very small patches of the rash, but in its much rarer severe form psoriasis can cover large areas of the body. The elbows and knees are the most likely areas to be affected. It is almost unknown for the rash to affect the face, but it often affects the scalp quite badly, causing considerable flaking.

Younger children do occasionally suffer from psoriasis, but it often appears for the first time in teenage children, when it can be a source of great anxiety to the child. Teenage children who develop the condition may need a great deal of reassurance.

In most cases the rash comes and goes. It often clears up of its own accord and disappears for months or even years at a time. Psoriasis does not hurt, but it can be itchy.

GUTTATE PSORIASIS

The type of psoriasis most likely to be developed by children is called guttate psoriasis, and appears as a rash of small spots all over the trunk and arms. This may last for a few weeks and then clear up completely, and for an unknown reason it often follows an attack of tonsillitis or sore throat.

CAUSES

Research is still being done as to what causes psoriasis, and as yet there is no clear answer. In susceptible people it may be triggered by an infection such as flu or by psychological causes such as emotional stress, perhaps at exam time. It is thought that in teenagers hormonal changes may be responsible, but what the mechanism is, is not clear.

CELL REPLACEMENT

Normal skin replaces itself by growing outwards from the deeper layers, and dead skin cells are gradually shed invisibly from the surface of the skin as they are replaced by new cells. In areas affected by psoriasis, the production of new cells is speeded up so that new skin is produced about ten times as fast as normal and the excess tissue comes away in visible flakes, while the cells reaching the surface have not had time to become as tough as they should be, causing the raw, pinky red appearance of the rash.

YOUR QUESTIONS

Q I thought that psoriasis was very serious, but my daughter has a small, scaly rash on her elbows, which the doctor says is psoriasis. Can this be right?

A Yes, in the majority of cases psoriasis is a minor inconvenience. In a very few cases, however, it can spread all over the body and the patient may need to be treated in hospital. In a very small number of cases it may also lead to arthritis.

TREATMENT

As yet there is no cure for psoriasis, but there are several forms of treatment that keep the condition successfully under control. Most forms of treatment involve applying creams, ointments or pastes to the skin. Tar preparations have long been found to be useful in many cases, and they work by making the skin more sensitive to light. Ultra-violet light, whether from sunshine itself or from artificial sources, has dramatic effects and the worst cases often clear up during a holiday by the sea. Treatment by artificial ultra-violet light is sometimes very effective.

Other creams contain corticosteroids, which must be used with care, especially on children. Zinc ointments and simple moisturizing creams have been found to bring relief to the condition, and some people find that vitamin E cream will clear it up, while recent research has suggested that taking cod liver oil can prevent attacks. In severe cases, new drugs are also prescribed which work by slowing down the rate at which new cells are formed.

LIVING WITH PSORIASIS

Often when the condition is not too severe the child can simply learn to live with psoriasis, knowing that it will flare up and die down again from time to time. The condition is surprisingly little understood, and it may help the child if parents speak to his teacher and the parents of his friends to explain that his rash is nothing to do with lack of hygiene and is not in any way contagious.

Ultra-violet light is good for psoriasis, and a sunshine holiday usually cures the rash for some time.

■ PYLORIC STENOSIS

Pyloric stenosis may be better known to parents as projectile vomiting. It is a fairly common but very frightening condition which needs urgent treatment to save the baby's life.

SYMPTOMS

The chief symptom of pyloric stenosis is that the baby starts to vomit up his feed violently – literally projecting it across the room. Within a few days of the vomiting developing the baby may start being violently sick after every feed. In addition to this, since almost nothing is being absorbed from the feed the baby fails to thrive and may also become very dehydrated.

This usually begins to occur when the baby is two to three weeks old, and the condition affects boys much more frequently than girls. It also seems to be more likely to affect first-born children.

CAUSES

The pylorus is a small, muscular ring which controls the passage of food from the stomach to the duodenum at the beginning of the intestines. In babies with pyloric stenosis, the muscular wall of the pylorus is over-developed and this causes the passageway to the intestines to be closed off. In an attempt to force the contents of the stomach into the duodenum the stomach contracts violently and the feed is forcibly ejected, much to the baby's distress.

It is known that the condition is congenital, but it is not known why some babies suffer from it. Nor is it known why it is more likely to be found in baby boys than in baby girls.

DIAGNOSIS

Occasional violent vomiting is not necessarily a sign of pyloric stenosis, but a doctor suspects the existence of the condition in a baby who frequently vomits after a feed in this characteristic way. He or she may decide to observe the child during a feed, as the spasmic contraction of

the stomach trying to force its contents past the pylorus can often be felt as the baby feeds. Usually the diagnosis will be confirmed by an X-ray after a barium meal.

COLLECTIONS/ANTHEA SIEVEKING

At a few weeks of age a previously contented baby may start vomiting violently and cease to thrive.

TREATMENT

The usual treatment is by an immediate surgical operation. A small cut is made in the baby's tummy and the muscles causing the constriction are cut lengthwise. This reduces their grip, and within two days the child is usually able to feed normally again.

If the baby has become malnourished and dehydrated before the condition was identified he may be put on a drip feed for a time to rehydrate him and strengthen him before the operation. Normally the baby will be out of hospital about five days after the operation.

Occasionally, when the symptoms are less severe, the doctor may try to treat the condition with drugs which act on the vagus nerve. These have

the effect of calming muscular contractions and can sometimes be effective. However, in most cases the operation will be necessary, and it is almost always completely successful. Once treated, projectile vomiting never recurs.

YOUR QUESTIONS

Q How vital is it to call the doctor if a baby is sick after feeds?

A Many young babies are a little bit sick after most feeds, but projectile vomiting is very different from this, with the feed really shooting out. If this happens more than two or three times in a row, or if it happens infrequently but your baby is irritable or listless and failing to put on weight, you should call your doctor straight away as small babies can very quickly become dehydrated.

■ QUARANTINE

Quarantine, or keeping a child in isolation during an illness to prevent infection from spreading, is not often heard of nowadays. This is partly because some of the major infectious illnesses of the past have now been controlled by immunization and partly because it has been realized that in many cases there is little point in isolating a child, since infections are passed on within 48 hours of the symptoms first developing. Nevertheless there are still some illnesses which require a child to be kept in isolation, at hospital or at home.

If your child has one of the forms of hepatitis or meningitis which are highly infectious, she will still have to

COLLECTIONS/ANTHEA SIEVEKING

A child who has to be kept in isolation will need lots of love and attention.

be kept in complete isolation, even if she is able to be at home. Your doctor, or the hospital staff, will advise you on what measures are necessary and these will include keeping her bedding, clothing and crockery separate from those used by everybody else in the household.

things in reserve and remember too that things will have to be sterilized after use. Ask your doctor or the hospital for advice on this, and inform the library before borrowing books for a child in isolation. The child will appreciate a personal stereo and tapes with messages from her friends. A television and VCR will also help to while away the time.

YOUR QUESTIONS

Q If a child has to be kept in quarantine, don't all his friends, who were playing with him before his illness was identified, have to be kept in quarantine too?

A This is not thought necessary nowadays, but everyone who has been in contact with the child will be put under observation, and also given suitable vaccines where these are appropriate.

FIGHTING BOREDOM

A child being kept in isolation may not necessarily feel all that ill, and you will need to use all your ingenuity to find ways to keep her occupied and stop her from feeling miserable. Books to read and to colour, games, puzzles and toys and her favourite teddy to keep her company can all be taken to hospital. Remember to keep

WATCHPOINTS

A child with chickenpox should be kept away from elderly people, who may develop shingles if they are in contact with the disease. A child with German measles should be kept away from any of your friends who are pregnant.

■ QUINSY
See TONSILLITIS

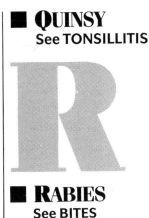

■ RABIES
See BITES

■ RASHES

Babies and small children often develop rashes, which frequently disappear as quickly as they came, without the child's having felt ill at all. A rash can be a symptom of an infectious disease such as chickenpox, or can be due to an allergy or a fungal or other infestation.

You should take your child to the family doctor for a rash that does not disappear within a day or two or if the child has a fever or other symptoms of illness. If it seems likely that the child has an infectious disease, call the doctor out even if the child is not too ill to go to the surgery, so as not to expose other people to the possibility of infection.

If a rash flares up when the child is taking medication you should let your doctor know at once. Consult your doctor or health visitor if the child seems prone to getting rashes.

SYMPTOMS

For more details of all the illnesses and conditions listed below, see the separate entries in the A–Z.

INFECTIOUS ILLNESSES

The most common infectious diseases of childhood cause their own distinctive rashes.

Chickenpox causes small, pimply spots which appear in fresh outbreaks at intervals of a few days, starting on the chest and back and spreading to the face and the rest of the body. The spots develop into blisters which then dry to form crusts, causing intense itching. Before the rash begins to appear the child usually feels off-colour.

German measles causes a flush of tiny pink spots, all over the body, sometimes starting behind the ears and spreading to the forehead first, and is sometimes very mild. The rash is short-lived, lasting two to three days. The child may have a fever, but may just feel slightly off-colour.

Measles causes dark red spots which start behind the ears and spread to the face and body. This usually follows the child having the symptoms of a bad cold and sore throat, and the appearance of small white spots inside the cheeks.

Nappy rash causes red skin in the nappy area or in the folds of the skin at the top of the legs. The skin may be broken and spots may develop.

Scarlet fever causes a flush of tiny red spots which spread from the face and chest to the rest of the body, and which always leave an area round the mouth unaffected. The child will have a sore throat and enlarged tonsils, and may also have a fever and vomiting and feel very poorly.

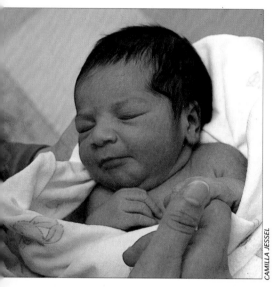

Rashes are common, especially in babies, but it is advisable to consult your doctor if your child has a rash.

YOUR QUESTIONS

Q Is there any general treatment for children's rashes?

A Rashes that itch or feel hot can often be calmed by an application of calamine lotion or by bathing them in a solution of sodium bicarbonate. It is also helpful to dress your child in cotton.

CONTAGIOUS RASHES

Cold sores (herpes) are itchy or painful blisters which develop round the mouth and nose and dry to form

a crust — similar to the rash of chickenpox. Some children seem prone to attacks of cold sores.

Impetigo causes red spots on face, scalp, hands and knees. The spots blister and exude a sticky, yellowish fluid which dries to form a thick crust.

Scabies (caused by a mite) is an itchy, red rash occurring in small areas usually between the fingers, or on the palms of the hands and soles of the feet, and itching more at night.

OTHER RASHES

Cradle cap is a yellowish brown or grey crust which forms on the scalps of young babies.

Eczema is a sore, red rash usually affecting folds in the skin or areas of the face. These become infected if the child scratches them, and the skin is dry and scaly.

Heat rash occurs especially on the face and neck, elbow creases, backs of knees and in the groin, usually when the child gets too hot. It causes irritation and feels hot.

Hives or nettle rash looks very much like nettle stings, with pale, raised spots surrounded by red and linked to cover an area of skin anywhere on the body.

Allergies, including allergies to food, can cause various types of skin rashes and flushes. Sometimes the link between the allergen and the rash it causes may be obvious, but often it can be difficult to track down.

Milia or prickly heat is a rash of tiny, white, pimple-like spots which particularly affects young babies.

TREATMENT

The treatment of a child's rash will of course depend on its cause. See separate entries for more details.

■ REYE'S SYNDROME

This is an extremely rare but very dangerous disease that sometimes affects children recovering from chickenpox or flu, or even a minor infection, and which is thought to be connected with the child having taken aspirin. Because of this, aspirin is now very rarely prescribed for

children and should never be given to children under the age of 12 except on a doctor's advice.

SYMPTOMS

The main symptoms of the condition are sudden and repeated attacks of severe vomiting in a child who is recovering from chickenpox or flu. The child usually has a fever, and may also become delirious. Reye's syndrome causes inflammation of the brain, leading to convulsions, lethargy, drowsiness and even unconsciousness. In some children there are fits of screaming.

YOUR QUESTIONS

Q I don't like making a fuss and wasting the doctor's time. How can I be sure the symptoms are serious enough to call the doctor out?

A Reye's syndrome is very rare, but if your child has sudden severe vomiting and fever and then develops delirium, has convulsions or becomes unconscious you will not be wasting the doctor's time by calling her out whatever the cause. So call the doctor or an ambulance at once. Immediate treatment could save the child's life.

CAUSES

The condition affects children under the age of about 12 to 14 and seems to be caused by viral attacks. It affects the liver as well as the brain and causes a change in the way the body deals with fats, but exactly what causes it is not yet known. Although it is linked to the taking of aspirin during the course of an infection, this is not entirely proved. However, in the United States of America, where the use of aspirin has been controlled, the number of cases has fallen, and doctors everywhere now treat aspirin as highly suspect.

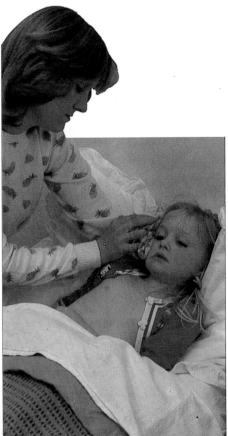

BRIAN NASH

The high fever that accompanies Reye's disease may be reduced by sponging the child with tepid water.

TREATMENT

Reye's syndrome requires urgent medical treatment. If your child shows any of the symptoms described above while recovering from a minor illness you should consult your doctor straight away. You should also call the doctor if a child becomes drowsy or delirious after an attack of vomiting, even if you are unaware of an infection being present.

While you are waiting for the doctor to arrive, you can try to reduce a fever by tepid sponging, and reassure and soothe a child who is distressed. But on no account give aspirin (or any preparation containing aspirin) or any other drug.

DIAGNOSIS

The doctor will send your child straight to hospital if he or she suspects that she has Reye's syndrome. In hospital it may be neces-sary to take a tiny tissue sample from the liver. This is a very simple procedure and is performed under local anaesthetic, using a needle. The sample will give a fully reliable confirmation of the diagnosis by showing up any abnormal distribution of fat which is characteristic of the disease.

CARE

The child will be kept in hospital on a glucose drip and will probably be put into intensive care. Doctors will attempt to control the inflammation of the brain and full nursing care will be given.

The stay in hospital may be quite a long one, and parents should arrange to spend as much time with the child as possible during this time. Recovery is slow, but parental presence and reassurance will be a great help.

■ RHESUS DISEASE

Rhesus disease is now extremely uncommon, thanks to reliable techniques for preventing it. The disease is a potential danger for the second and subsequent babies of women whose blood type is Rhesus negative when the father is Rhesus positive.

SYMPTOMS

In Rhesus disease the Rhesus positive foetus is affected by antibodies crossing the placenta from its Rhesus negative mother. In severe cases the foetus dies in the womb from anaemia and heart failure and if the baby is born it may be with a weak heart or severe jaundice.

CAUSES

The cause of Rhesus disease is an incompatibility of blood groups between a mother and her child, which causes the red cells in the bloodstream of the foetus to be destroyed.

In 85 per cent of people there is a factor known as factor D in the blood, and these people are known as 'Rhesus positive'. In the remaining 15 per cent, the factor D is lacking, and these people are known as 'Rhesus negative'. The blood group to which factor D belongs is known as the 'Rhesus group' – Rh for short.

As many more men are Rh positive than Rh negative, a woman from the Rh negative blood group is likely to be paired with a man from the Rh positive group. The man's Rh positive blood group is likely to be inherited by their children.

When an Rh negative mother is carrying an Rh positive foetus, occasionally blood cells manage to escape from the foetal circulation and enter the mother's bloodstream. This is particularly likely to happen if there is a threatened or actual miscarriage, and if not, it frequently occurs during the birth.

The mother's body usually reacts to this as though it had been invaded by a foreign substance and begins to produce antibodies to fight the invading red blood cells from the foetus. This has no effect on the child just born, but with future pregnancies, as the mother's blood crosses the placenta to the foetus the mother's antibodies come into play and the baby's blood cells can be severely damaged.

YOUR QUESTIONS

Q Can having an abortion risk causing the mother to develop factor D antibodies? I am Rh negative and had an abortion a couple of years ago, and now that I am pregnant I am worried about the risks.

A There is a strong chance that in an abortion – just as in a miscarriage – the foetus's blood could pass into that of the mother, and, if the foetus is Rh positive, antibodies could be formed. You should tell your doctor about the abortion so that measures can be taken now.

JAUNDICE

The jaundice of a Rhesus disease baby comes about through an excess of bile pigments building up in the baby's blood as a result of the large number of red blood cells being broken down. This can cause permanent damage to the brain if it is not successfully treated.

PREVENTION

The risk of Rhesus disease is just one of the reasons that blood samples are tested during pregnancy. If a woman is found to be Rh negative she can be prevented from forming antibodies to Rh positive blood by what is known as an 'anti-D' injection at the time of her first baby's birth. This means that any future children will not be at risk.

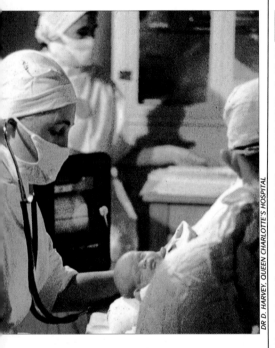

If a baby is born with jaundice as a result of Rhesus disease, the baby can be treated by 'exchange transfusions' when the baby's blood is swapped for Rhesus negative blood.

TREATMENT

If a baby is born with jaundice due to Rhesus disease she will usually be given an exchange blood transfusion, in which all her own blood is gradually replaced by blood containing no harmful antibodies, as a result of which the mother's antibodies cannot harm the child any longer.

In less severe cases jaundiced babies may be treated by phototherapy, or exposure to strong light, to break down the excess bile pigments. Thanks to prevention, this is now a very rare event.

■ RHEUMATIC FEVER

This disease of childhood and adolescence has become quite rare in the developed world, partly due to effective prevention. The disease affects the connective tissues, and those of the lining and valves of the heart as well as those of the joints are involved. The joints return to normal as the child recovers, but the heart can be permanently damaged.

SYMPTOMS

Some children affected with rheumatic fever have a very mild attack, which just makes their joints ache for a few days, but in most cases there is fever and tiredness and the child is pale and feels ill. He suffers from loss of appetite and loses weight.

The disease comes on as the child is recovering from an illness such as tonsillitis, sore throat or otitis media (middle ear infection), and its chief characteristic is that the joints become inflamed (rheumatism), causing pain and swelling. This especially affects the larger joints — those of the hips and knees. However, the rheumatic symptoms pass from joint to joint, making the joints painful and swollen as they are affected.

A bad case of rheumatic fever also produces the symptom of 'St Vitus dance' or Sydenham's chorea. This is a purposeless twitching of the body, sometimes accompanied by facial grimacing — a symptom which is only present when the child is awake.

Finally, rheumatic fever also affects the skin, producing a rash known as 'erythema marginatum', which consists of blotches of red surrounding a paler area. Nodules can be felt under the skin and at the wrists, knees, elbows and ankles.

CAUSES

Rheumatic fever is caused by a *Streptococcus* bacterium. This is the bacterium involved in many sore throats, tonsillitis and middle ear infections, explaining why these are linked with the fever. But what the link is, is not known. It is not clear why some children react to the bacterium in this way, but it is thought to have something to do with the immune system, as are other forms of rheumatism. For some reason the immune system seems to over-react to the presence of the bacteria, producing inflammation of the connective tissue.

It is thought that the disease is now so rare in developed countries partly because of improved standards of nutrition and hygiene, and partly because streptococcal infections are now treated with antibiotics in the early stages. It has also been suggested that the bacterium might have developed a new form which is more easily resisted.

TREATMENT

The main treatment of rheumatic fever is bed rest, and this is one condition for which children are still given aspirin. This is prescribed in relatively high doses for its anti-inflammatory effect. Specific antibiotics will be given to fight the infection. At least in the early stages the child will be treated in hospital, and in severe cases, where the heart has been affected, steroid drugs will be given to control the inflammation of the heart.

DANGERS

The main danger is that the disease will recur, and to prevent this from happening the child will have to take penicillin until she reaches the age of about 18, to protect her by making sure that she never suffers from a streptococcal infection.

■ RICKETS

Rickets is a bone disease that affects growing children, often causing permanent damage, and it was extremely prevalent among children during the industrial revolution. It is now almost a disease of the past, but certain groups are still at risk.

SYMPTOMS

The bones of a child with rickets cannot develop properly and become deformed at their growing points, causing wrists, knees and ankles to appear enlarged as the cartilage becomes misshapen. Bumps (once known as 'rickets rosary') may develop at the front ends of the ribs. The bones lack strength, and in a young child this may cause the knees to bow out.

If the disease is not arrested, it continues to affect the child's bones as she grows and the long bones of the legs become bent inwards to produce the knock-kneed appearance of an older child affected by rickets. The bones of the skull can become soft and the backbone and pelvis can also be affected.

CAUSES

Bone is formed from calcium and the diet has to provide the necessary calcium, but the body also needs a supply of vitamin D in order for it to put the calcium to use. Without vitamin D any calcium provided by the diet cannot be used, and the bones cannot grow properly. Rickets can therefore be caused by lack of either calcium or vitamin D, but it is usually the vitamin that is lacking.

Vitamin D is found in certain foods, and especially in dairy products and oily fish, but it can also be synthesized (made up) in the body through the action of sunlight on the skin. (Sunlight causes a reaction in a special form of cholesterol known as 7-dehydrocholesterol present in the skin.) During the industrial revolution children affected with rickets suffered from poor nutrition and were also deprived of sunlight. Their diets provided little calcium and less vitamin D, and they had no chance to make up the deficiency as they were always indoors.

RENAL RICKETS

In some rare cases rickets is caused by a malfunctioning of the kidneys. This causes calcium to be lost in the urine together with phosphates, so that there is not enough calcium left in the system for healthy bone formation. This type of rickets has to be treated by supplements of a special kind of vitamin D.

WATCHPOINTS

Too much vitamin D can cause too much calcium to be in circulation in the body and can lead to calcium deposits forming in the kidneys. But this will not happen as a result of a normal, varied diet nor if the child has taken prescribed supplements. However this is the reason that you should not give extra vitamin D unless your doctor has advised it.

PREVENTION

Rickets has largely been eradicated through improved nutrition and through the fact that young children now spend plenty of time outside. Since the disease causes so much harm, continued prevention, by making sure that babies and children have enough vitamin D, is essential.

Young babies get most of the vitamin D they need from breast milk or from modern milk substitutes. In the darker winter months, however, they may benefit from supplementary vitamin D drops. Children under the age of five and women who are breast feeding should take vitamin D supplements. Your doctor will advise you on whether these are necessary. Do remember to tell her if for any reason the child's diet may not provide adequate supplies of the vitamin (for example if the family is vegetarian). Supplements are sometimes necessary for people with dark skins living in less sunny countries as their skins let through less light, so that less vitamin D is formed.

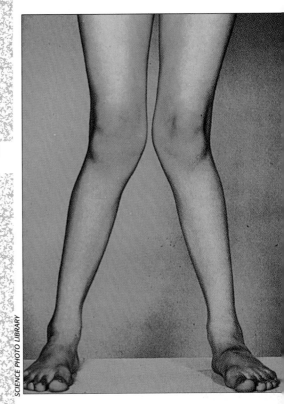

SCIENCE PHOTO LIBRARY

Without sufficient calcium, growing bones become weak and soft. In some cases, the bones become permanently deformed.

TREATMENT

Unless the disease is treated in time it can cause permanent damage to the skeleton. However, if a member of the health care team spots the condition early enough, a lot can be done to treat it. Treatment is by large doses of vitamin D supplement in the form of drops or tablets. It will also be ensured that the child has enough dietary calcium and supplements of this mineral may also be given.

Since rickets usually first shows itself when the child is under two years old, this treatment is usually enough to strengthen the growing bones and allow them to develop normally. However if the disease has progressed too far the child may need an operation on the legs before she can grow normally. In very advanced cases there is always the risk of permanent deformity to some degree.

YOUR QUESTIONS

Q Is it possible to have too much vitamin D? I am worried about giving my child supplements, but rickets sounds awful and I don't want her to get it.

A First, unless you and your child are vegans or the child does not eat dairy products for any reason, there is nothing to worry about. A normal, balanced diet will provide all the calcium and vitamin D necessary to prevent rickets.

But do tell your doctor if you think the child's diet may be inadequate and leave it to her to decide whether a supplement is necessary. Supplements should not be given to children except when the doctor advises it, and if they are prescribed they should be given only in the quantities prescribed.

■ RINGWORM

See also ATHLETE'S FOOT

Ringworm is a fungal infection that can affect the skin on the scalp, trunk and feet, fingers or groin and, less frequently, the armpits. It is intensely itchy and the infection develops in the shape of a ring, which gives the condition its name. (It is, however, nothing to do with worms.) Children can catch it from each other or from dogs or cats in the family. Country children can also catch it from cattle. Different varieties of the fungus can affect different parts of the body in slightly different ways.

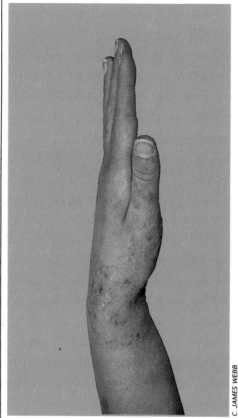

C. JAMES WEBB

Red itchy blisters or scaling skin are typical signs of ringworm, a common fungal infection.

SYMPTOMS

Ringworm of the **scalp** often causes a bald patch or patches. It usually spreads outwards in a ring, which is red, itchy and scaly. As the centre of the ring heals the ring itself grows bigger. The hairs within the ring are often broken off, and they begin to regrow from the centre of the ring as the skin starts to heal again.

On the **trunk**, ringworm is similar in appearance. An itchy patch is formed, which heals from the centre but grows larger in diameter as it heals. The skin is red and scaly, and within a few weeks small new patches may form.

The equivalent of ringworm on the **feet** is athlete's foot, which causes itchy, red patches between the toes. After a bath, or if the feet are sweaty, the skin can look soft and white, and dry crusts may form. The infection usually attacks the area between the toes, but can spread under the toes, and may also lodge under the child's

toe nails, causing them to be hard and ridged, and sometimes discoloured. Athlete's foot is more frequent in older children.

Ringworm on the **hands** or in the **groin** or **armpit** also causes red, scaly patches which itch and spread.

CAUSES

Ringworm is very common, particularly in children and is caused by one of several closely related fungi. In most cases it thrives on moisture and warmth, and all forms are highly contagious.

YOUR QUESTIONS

Q My little girl had ringworm which seemed to have gone within a few days of my putting on the cream the doctor prescribed, but now it has come back again. Why should this be?

A To make quite sure that the fungus causing the infection has been killed it is important to keep on applying the cream regularly for about two weeks after all signs of the infection have vanished. You should therefore begin to use the cream again and keep up the application. If the ringworm resists treatment take your daughter back to the doctor, who may decide to prescribe an antifungal drug.

TREATMENT

Athlete's foot can often be treated successfully by making sure that the child washes his feet at least once a day and dries them thoroughly after washing. Any of the preparations available from your local pharmacist will help rid the child of the condition, especially if the child wears clean cotton socks every day, to prevent moisture being trapped, and gives the feet an airing whenever possible. It is only necessary for him to see the doctor if the condition refuses to heal up, or if the toe nails are affected (when they begin to look gnarled and yellow).

All other forms of ringworm should be treated by your doctor and as the infection is highly contagious the child should be kept out of contact with other children as much as possible. He will have to take time off school for ringworm of the scalp or hands, and within the home he should not share combs, brushes or towels with the rest of the family.

In most cases the child will be treated with an anti-fungal cream, and it will also be important for you to make sure that the affected area is washed and carefully dried two or three times a day. When the armpits, trunk or groin area are affected loose clothing, made of cotton, should be worn to keep the skin cool and dry.

In severe cases an antibiotic drug, griseoflavin, may be prescribed. This is nearly always given when the child has ringworm on the scalp and will cure even the most persistent cases.

WATCHPOINTS

If you suspect that a family pet also has ringworm (signs will be scratching and bald areas) take him to the vet for treatment. Your pet will be grateful, and this will prevent the infection from being passed round the family.

YOUR QUESTIONS

Q My little boy has just had a bad case of ringworm on his scalp. Does this mean he will keep on getting the complaint?

A No. Oddly enough, although athlete's foot does tend to recur in susceptible children, ringworm affecting the scalp seldom recurs once it has been successfully treated.

■ ROSEOLA INFANTUM

Even though its name is not familiar, roseola infantum is a viral infection that quite frequently attacks babies and children under the age of three. It usually lasts for about a week and rarely causes problems.

SYMPTOMS

The first symptom of the disease is a fever. The baby's temperature goes up to as much as 40°C (104°F) and remains high for about three days. In rare cases the temperature may be high enough to cause convulsions (*see* separate entry), but more often the child will probably not seem particularly ill.

Three to four days after the fever began, the temperature falls and at this point the child breaks out in a rash. This is a flush of pinky-red spots which starts on the trunk and spreads to the rest of the body. It may be particularly noticeable behind the ears, but the face is not affected.

The rash of roseola infantum is not particularly itchy. It can be mistaken for scarlet fever, but unlike scarlet fever it is not accompanied by inflamed tonsils or sore throat, and the child does not feel nearly so unwell as when he has scarlet fever. Furthermore, as the rash appears the child's temperature quickly drops back to normal again and any slight irritability or lethargy vanishes.

After a couple of days the rash disappears and the illness is over.

CAUSES

Doctors think that the disease is caused by a virus, although this has not yet been isolated. It seems likely that the virus is caught from the breath of someone already suffering from the disease, and that the incubation period is about ten days.

Adults may suffer from roseola, but when they do the symptoms are hardly noticeable, and children have no sign of the rash until the illness is almost over. Thus the infection can easily be passed on without anyone realizing it.

WATCHPOINTS

A high temperature can be dangerous in babies and young children.

• If a baby under the age of six months has a fever the family doctor should always be called and you should ask your doctor's advice if any child has a temperature of 38°C (100.4°F) or more which lasts for a couple of days. The younger the child or the higher the temperature, the more readily you should call the doctor.

• If a baby or child has convulsions as well as a high temperature you should call the doctor at once.

COLLECTIONS/ANTHEA SIEVEKING

Roseola infantum is a viral infection causing fever and a rash. It is easily treated with paracetamol.

TREATMENT

When the fever first develops you can try to control it by sponging the child with tepid water or giving paracetamol in the appropriate form and dose for the child's age. If a fever is caused by roseola infantum it will usually rise again quite quickly.

The fever symptoms are likely to be enough for you to call the doctor out before the rash develops, and he or she may check for other possible causes of the fever and give advice on treating the fever itself. However, the rash will soon confirm what the illness is, and usually no special treatment is needed other than continuing to take measures to keep the fever down and making sure that the child has plenty of fluids to make up for the fluids lost in sweating.

The child will usually be feeling better by the time the rash appears, and will be completely recovered by the time the rash has gone.

YOUR QUESTIONS

Q How can I keep my child's temperature down if tepid sponging doesn't work?

A Call your doctor, who may prescribe drugs such as paracetamol.

Q Are there any dangers attached to roseola infantum?

A The only slight danger is that the child may suffer from febrile convulsions (convulsions associated with fever) in the early stages of the disease. This happens in susceptible children if the temperature gets too high.

Febrile convulsions are not unusual in children under the age of five or six, and because there is some risk of brain damage if there are repeated or sustained convulsions, you should call your doctor if this happens even if the child makes an immediate recovery. The doctor may decide to prescribe anti-convulsant drugs to be taken until the temperature is back to normal, and this will make sure that there is no recurrence.

■ SAFETY

While you do not want to molly-coddle your child, and you do want to encourage her to be independent, at the same time you want to do everything you can to prevent her from having accidents that could put her life or limb at risk. To make sure that accidents are prevented you need to be able to put yourself in the child's place and imagine what she might get up to from babyhood on.

EXPLORERS

From the time your child is born, go round your home making sure opportunities for accidents are all removed, and as she grows up, train the child so that accidents inside and outside the home are less likely. Remember that children are natural explorers, and love putting things into their mouths and grabbing at what they can't reach. They are single-minded when they want to do something and are quite unaware of danger. Until she is old enough to be alert to danger you must therefore try to keep it out of your child's way as much as possible.

TYPES OF ACCIDENT

With children under the age of five most accidents take place in the home, and as children get older they begin to be at risk from accidents in the street and playground as well. Possibilities to be aware of are:
- Falls
- Accidents with sharp implements
- Objects in nose or throat
- Burns and scalds
- Poisoning
- Electric shocks
- Road accidents
- Playground accidents
- Accidents on holiday.

CHECKLIST – OUT OF DOORS

Road safety:
- make sure brakes on prams and pushchairs are working properly
- train children not to run after balls into the street
- teach kerb drill as soon as possible
- don't let 'learner' tricyclists and bicyclists play on the pavement
- keep locks on gates to prevent a child from running out on to the street.

Safety at play:
- encourage a child to develop climbing skills to make her safe
- supervise young children in the playground
- make sure a child is aware of the dangers of moving swings
- make sure fairground rides are suitable for the child's age

- keep garden pools netted or fenced in
- make sure children have suitable footwear for active play and are wearing nothing to trip them up
- don't leave young children alone when playing on balconies or near garden walls.
- never let children play with fireworks
- have patio doors made of unbreakable glass, or leave doors wide open when children are running around
- never allow children to eat while they are running about
- store weedkiller, insecticides and other chemicals safely
- never put chemicals in other bottles or containers, and especially not in bottles that once contained soft drinks

CHECKLIST – IN THE HOME

To avoid falls:

• install stair gates when there are crawling babies and toddlers in the home

• make sure young children are not left alone in upstairs rooms unless windows cannot be opened

To avoid cuts, choking and suffocation:

• keep scissors, knitting needles, razors, screwdrivers, drills and similar tools, and kitchen knives safely out of reach

• don't let very young children play with beads or buttons and make sure that these are attached firmly if used on clothing or toys

• don't give small items of food such as peanuts or pieces of carrots to children until you know they can chew them

• remember plastic bags can cause suffocation

To avoid burns and scalds:

• keep saucepan handles turned inward on the stove

• consider installing a guard on the front of your hob

• keep kettles out of children's reach

• don't leave hot drinks where children can grab them.

• make sure fires have fireguards and never leave young children alone in a room with a fire (coal, gas or electric)

• keep matches, lighters and firelighters locked away

• don't let young children run their own baths unless you are there to test the water

To avoid poisoning:

• fit safety catches or locks to cupboard doors

• keep cleaning fluids,

detergents, bleaches, polishes, dishwasher powder, fabric conditioner safely out of reach, preferably in cupboards fitted with safety catches

• observe food safety codes for hygiene, storing and cooking

• keep pet food and litter trays and crawling children apart

• keep all medicines out of reach and use child resistant containers

• never encourage a child to take tablets by referring to them as 'sweets' – she may think they really are!

To avoid electric shocks:

• fit safety covers to sockets

• don't allow flexes and cables to trail along the floor

• make sure the flex of an electric kettle does not hang temptingly down when unplugged

• consider having hand-height sockets if rewiring

• never use electrical equipment with worn cables.

• be aware of danger when you visit other people

• keep poisonous plants and young children apart. Educate children so they learn which plants are harmful

Safety on holiday:

• make sure your child learns to swim at an early age

• teach her what to do when in difficulty in the water (see DROWNING)

• don't let children swim unsupervised until you are sure they are safe

• don't let a child float on airbeds at the seaside or swim out after beach balls

• protect children from hot sun

STEVE BIELSCHOWSKY

Danger lurks everywhere in the kitchen. Never put tempting objects next to dangerous ones, such as this boiling kettle.

■ SCABIES

Scabies is an irritating rash which is easily cured, but which can quickly be passed from person to person, so usually the whole family will be treated with a special lotion painted all over their bodies if anybody in the household is infected. The scalp is never affected.

SYMPTOMS

In children, scabies is most likely to appear on the hands and wrists. Other parts of the body that may be infected are the armpits, buttocks and the area round the genitals. The first signs are thin little red lines, but there may be no itching, and these can pass unnoticed. However, an itchy rash soon begins to develop, and if the cause is not treated this can bring about an allergic reaction within a few weeks. This leads to a generalized, blotchy rash which is intensely itchy, especially at night or whenever the child is warm.

The itching will make it impossible for the child not to scratch, and the skin may be broken. This can lead to bacterial infection and further complications but prompt treatment will prevent this.

STEVE BIELSCHOWSKY

Scabies, a skin disorder, is caused by mites burrowing under the skin and is very itchy.

CAUSES

Scabies is caused by tiny mites (*Sarcoptes scabiei*) which live on the skin, feeding on the dead cells which are constantly being shed as the skin renews itself. The mites are about 0.4mm (1/60 in) long, and just visible to the naked eye. The female mite burrows into the surface layer of the skin and lays her eggs along the tunnel she has made. This causes the first stage of the symptoms — fine red lines on the skin.

The female then dies, but the eggs hatch to form larvae which burrow their way out to the surface of the skin again, causing more irritation. Within a few days they are new mites and the process is ready to begin once again. The whole cycle from the eggs being laid to the next generation of mites beginning to breed takes about two weeks.

PREVENTION

It is not difficult to prevent your child from catching scabies, but if she does contract an infestation you must do all you can to prevent it from spreading to other people. Keep the child away from school until she has been treated and treat all other members of the family whether they show symptoms or not.

The mite usually travels from one person to another by skin to skin contact but it can also be transferred on clothing, bedding, towels and flannels. Therefore anything that has been in contact with the child should be washed and aired as a precaution.

DIAGNOSIS

If you suspect that your child has scabies, take her at once to the family doctor so that if there are mites they can be treated straight away before they multiply. This will prevent the rash from spreading and becoming more serious.

The doctor will probably be able to identify the condition on sight by looking at the skin, but he or she may also remove a mite with a needle to confirm the diagnosis.

If your child is at school you should advise the head teacher.

TREATMENT

Once the condition has been diagnosed, the treatment is simple. The doctor will prescribe cream or lotion containing an ingredient that kills the mites. The child (and everyone else in the family) has to be thoroughly washed from the neck down, and the lotion is then applied over the body and left for 24 hours.

The lotion has to be reapplied a couple of days later to kill any insects that have hatched out in the interval. The mites never infest the scalp or face, so the child's head does not need to be treated.

The rash itself may linger for a while after treatment. Your doctor may prescribe a suitable soothing ointment in some cases, but in many cases calamine lotion will be all that is needed. If there has been a secondary infection caused by bacteria, where skin has been damaged by scratching, this will be given suitable treatment.

■ SCABS

See ABRASIONS, DRESSINGS, SCARS

■ SCALDS

See BURNS

■ SCARLET FEVER

Otherwise known as scarlatina, scarlet fever is a fairly common disease of childhood which brings the child out in a characteristic reddish-pink rash. The disease is caused by the *Streptococcus* bacteria that also cause sore throats, and is easily treated. Nowadays it is often also very mild.

SYMPTOMS

In its worst form scarlet fever starts with the child suddenly having a high temperature, accompanied by vomiting. His throat becomes sore and the tonsils will be red and swollen and covered with a whitish crust. By the second day, the child's face will be flushed, except for an area of pale skin round the mouth, and by the third, the rash (which may be itchy) will have spread all over the body, and will have become more spotty in appearance, with tiny, deeper red, raised spots. The rash will be especially noticeable on the chest.

STRAWBERRY TONGUE

To start with the tongue may be white and 'furry', and as the disease progresses it begins to be covered with red blotches, giving the child the 'strawberry tongue' characteristic of scarlet fever. As this occurs the child's temperature begins to return to normal and the rash starts to fade.

During this time (about five to six days) the child may feel very 'poorly' and listless and have very little appetite. But as the rash fades, he will begin to feel better. His skin and tongue will peel for up to six weeks before returning to normal, but he will be well enough to return to school within about a week or ten days of first becoming ill.

These symptoms need not always be so marked. The disease is some-

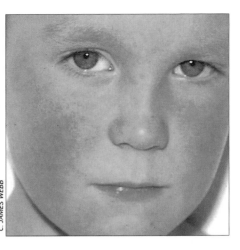

Scarlet fever was once one of the most dreaded diseases of childhood causing many deaths. Today it is easily treated with antibiotics.

C. JAMES WEBB

times so mild that the child will just be slightly flushed, perhaps with a slightly raised temperature and a bit of a sore throat.

CAUSES

The bacteria responsible for scarlet fever are *Streptococci*, which also cause tonsillitis and many types of sore throat. They are commonly present in people's throats, often without causing any symptoms at all.

The bacteria (a variety known as *Streptococcus pyogenes*) responsible for scarlet fever infect the throat and tonsils, where they multiply. As they do so, toxins are produced, and as these build up and begin to infect the whole body through the bloodstream, so the symptoms of scarlet fever develop.

Because the disease is often so mild, and because the *Streptococcus* bacteria is so common and can be present in people without making them ill at all, it is usually impossible to tell how the child caught the disease. The germs can be passed on through coughs and sneezes but also from contact with people who are carrying the infection (for example from hands they have coughed into), whether or not they have any symptoms. It can enter the body through wounds as well as through breathing. After contact, incubation takes up to six days.

TREATMENT

You should call your doctor if you suspect that your child has scarlet fever, as in most cases medical treatment will be necessary. Treatment is usually with penicillin, which kills the *Streptococcus* bacteria. Even minor cases are often treated for a couple of days so that the germs do not have a chance to multiply and so that the child does not pass on the infection to others.

If the child is feeling ill he may need to be kept in bed, and if his temperature is high he should be sponged with tepid water several times a day to help to reduce the fever. At night particularly, he can be given the correct dose of paracetamol for his age to keep the fever down and help him to sleep more restfully.

Children with a fever should always be given plenty of fluids to make up for the loss of body fluids through sweating and to prevent them from becoming dehydrated. There is no need to worry about any lack of appetite as long as the child drinks plenty of diluted fruit juices and squashes, as appetite will return. To tempt him to eat offer simple food in small portions, so as not to overwhelm the child when his appetite is poor.

COMPLICATIONS

Usually scarlet fever has soon run its course and the child makes a quick recovery with no problems. Very occasionally complications develop, but this is very rare, and is unlikely to occur if the scarlet fever itself is promptly treated.

Secondary infections that can occur if the *Streptococci* are allowed to multiply and spread include otitis media (middle ear infection), a type of nephritis (kidney disease) and rheumatic fever. Rheumatic fever and nephritis are serious illnesses so it is important to avoid any risk of their developing by making sure that your child takes the treatment prescribed by the doctor for scarlet fever until the whole course of tablets is finished, even if he feels better before this.

■ SCARS

See also BIRTHMARKS

The healing of all but the most superficial skin wounds involves the formation of scar tissue. Bad injuries can leave very noticeable scars which may make a child feel self-conscious, and moral support may be needed to help a child come to terms with this.

SYMPTOMS

Scars vary according to the type of injury. A small, clean cut will leave an almost invisible scar, while a larger cut needs to be carefully stitched (medically known as suturing) to encourage a neat scar to develop. A scar that crosses a joint will usually be very obvious, and can cause the joint to be bent during the period of healing, sometimes permanently. Grazing causes only superficial injury, whereas serious burns involving all the layers of the skin can cause a great deal of scarring.

A scar is formed during a long period of healing which takes up to ten months. During the first month the scar is fine and soft, and not very strong. During the next two months it becomes red, hard, thicker and stronger, and tends to contract to give a slightly puckered appearance to the skin. From then until the healing period is finally over, there is a gradual softening and whitening of the skin as the scar tissue relaxes.

The skin scars differently in different areas of the body, with the hairless skin of the lips, the palms of the hands and the soles of the feet giving rise to less conspicuous scars, and scars on the front of the chest, the shoulders and the upper part of the back being most marked. Different parts of the face scar in different ways, with the tip of the nose showing the most noticeable scars. Scars are much less obvious when they follow the lines of the skin.

UNUSUAL SCARS

Sometimes a scar becomes red and thickened instead of soft and pale, and forms either a **keloid** or a **hypertrophic** scar. Hypertrophic scars are particularly common in children and young people, and usually cause itching and discomfort, with the red scar tissue being noticeably raised. Keloids, which are less common, are even more raised scars which spread on to the surrounding skin and are tender to the touch as well as being itchy. Unfortunately, they get worse after a year and may continue to do so for up to ten years, while hypertrophic scars reach their worse level in about six months. Children with highly pigmented skins have more problems with scars than white children, and children of African origin suffer worst of all.

INTERNAL SCARRING

Healing after disease or injury (including surgical operations) causes scarring to the internal organs just as it does to the skin. The heart and brain are particularly affected by scarring. Scar tissue on the heart is less elastic than normal heart muscle tissue and can lead to the heart pumping less efficiently; and if (which is rare) a child suffers a stroke, the brain heals by forming scar tissue

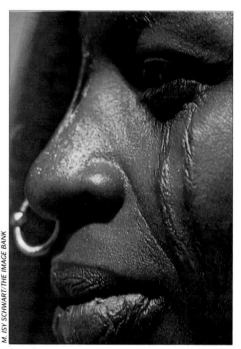

M. ISY SCHWART/THE IMAGE BANK

Self-inflicted tribal scars are prominent because the cuts are deliberately kept open during the healing process.

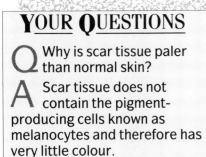

YOUR QUESTIONS

Q Why is scar tissue paler than normal skin?

A Scar tissue does not contain the pigment-producing cells known as melanocytes and therefore has very little colour.

Q Can pimples leave scars?

A Yes, unfortunately teenage acne affects the skin deep down and scar tissue is formed when the spots heal. Try to discourage a child from picking at pimples as this can make the scarring even worse. Picking at scabs when wounds are healing also has the same effect, but it is very difficult to stop children from doing it as scabs can itch so badly.

Q Is scarring just as bad at any age?

A No. Children under the age of one suffer very little scarring but older children can have rather heavy scar formation.

Q Do all skin injuries form scars? My little boy has had a bad fall and is covered with grazes. I am worried that he will be badly scarred.

A No. Luckily grazes do not leave scars as they affect only the top layer of skin and not the hair follicles or the sebaceous glands, from which a lining of skin grows to form perfect new skin.

which establishes a weakness that can cause epilepsy. Thankfully these problems are very rare in children.

CAUSES

As wounds heal they are first filled with blood clots. The outer layer of skin then grows in under the clot and dries to form a scab. Blood vessels and fibrous tissue then gradually cover the wound to form a scar. As this process takes place there is a contraction (shrinking) of the wound so that the final scar is much smaller than the original wound. Keloids and hypertrophic scars are caused by over-active scar formation.

TREATMENT

Usually no treatment is needed for scars, and although they never completely disappear they do fade slightly over the years. Children's hypertrophic scars eventually turn into normal, pale scars, although this can take two to three years.

In severe cases of scarring plastic surgery may be performed to improve the appearance of the scar, but this is never undertaken until at least a year and a half after the original injury, as scars continue to improve over a long period. During the period when the scar tissue is being formed the doctor may prescribe a steroid cream to be applied to badly itching scars, following serious wounds, and for hypertrophic scars and keloids.

Keloids present a problem, as they take so long to disappear, and they tend to recur after plastic surgery. An operation to remove them is not usually advised for this reason, and sadly, children suffering from them will have to learn to live with them.

Plastic surgery can be helpful for contracted joints caused by scarring. The scar is lengthened so that the joint can be straightened again, and healing leaves a neat scar with no other problem.

■ SCOLIOSIS

This is a condition in which the spine has a sideways bend so that the trunk looks crooked. It is also known as 'curvature of the spine'. It can be present from birth but it is more likely to develop during adolescence. It

In extreme cases, scoliosis can cause permanent curvature of the spine.

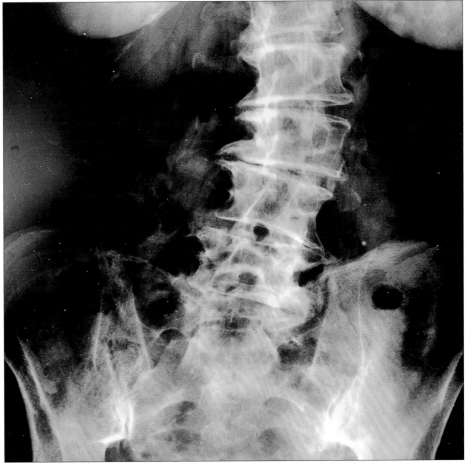

SCIENCE PHOTO LIBRARY

may come about as the result of a disease, but in many cases it is not connected with any other condition.

SYMPTOMS

In some cases scoliosis will be obvious even when the child is dressed because her trunk will be twisted so that her shoulders slope and she is much more 'wasted' on one side than on the other. In less extreme cases it may not be noticeable until the child is undressed; then if she bends over you may notice that her spine is curved to one side.

Scoliosis should come to light during routine medical examinations but if you are ever worried about your child's spine you should mention this to your doctor.

CAUSES

There are several possible causes of scoliosis. It can be the effect of a disease such as poliomyelitis, which can permanently weaken the muscles down one side of the back, and cerebral palsy can also have this effect. Untreated rickets can stop the vertebrae (the bones of the spine) from developing normally, again causing the spine to be curved.

Abnormalities in the pelvis can lead to the spine tipping over to compensate, and lung disease can cause the muscles on one side of the chest to be permanently tightened, pulling the spine out of true. But often there is no reason for the curved spine other than bad posture. Scoliosis may be present at birth and can be due simply to the way in which the baby was lying in the womb, but it may also show that the spine has not formed properly.

TREATMENT

If a child is found to have a curvature of the spine she will be sent to a specialist, and treatment will depend on the severity of the condition. In many cases the situation will simply be monitored to make sure that the curvature is not worsening, and physiotherapy may be given to correct the curve or to stop it from developing. In these cases, as long as the child does the necessary exercises the curve will cause no problem and may even be corrected through better use of the muscles. Even when the condition is due to a previous illness, much can be done through physiotherapy to make sure that the

YOUR QUESTIONS

Q After a school medical exam I was told that my child had a curvature of the spine. Yet I had never noticed it until it was pointed out and it is certainly very slight. Is treatment really necessary?

A Treatment is always necessary for scoliosis or curvature of the spine as the condition can become much worse if neglected, especially as the child goes through growth spurts.

In minor cases such as this sounds to be, the specialist usually arranges for the child to have physiotherapy. This will improve the condition and prevent any problems from developing. The specialist may then wish to monitor the condition as the child grows to make sure that all is still well.

Q What happens if scoliosis is not treated?

A This depends on the severity of the case. Minor cases may simply cause some muscular pain from time to time, but more severe cases can lead to chest problems as the muscles develop differently on each side of the rib cage, and the child can become vulnerable to chest infections. In the most serious cases the child may become deformed and develop a hunched back. But as long as the condition is spotted and treated in time much can be done to prevent this.

child or teenager uses the muscles to the full and to stop the curve from becoming worse.

In more difficult cases the child may have to wear a spinal brace to correct the spine as it grows. This will be worn until the specialist is sure that the curvature has been corrected and will prevent scoliosis from causing major problems. Wearing a brace will inevitably be quite a trial for the child, but parents and other children in the family can help her to take a positive attitude.

Where these methods do not succeed the specialist may decide that surgery is necessary to straighten the spine. This will involve lengthy preparation to strengthen the muscles and during the post-operative period a supportive jacket will have to be worn, but it may be the only way to prevent the child from becoming badly deformed as she grows.

If it is found that the spine has become curved in response to another illness, it will respond to physiotherapy given after the underlying cause has been successfully treated.

■ SEASICKNESS

See TRAVEL SICKNESS

■ SEPTIC ARTHRITIS

Thanks to antibiotics, septic arthritis is a rare disease these days. When it occurs it can usually be successfully treated.

SYMPTOMS

Septic arthritis is an inflammation of a joint. It causes the child to have a high fever (with a temperature up to 40°C (104°F)) and the infected joint will be swollen and painful and tender to the touch. Inflammation may cause the swollen area to be red. Usually only one joint is affected.

CAUSES

The disease is caused by bacterial infection settling on a joint. The infec-

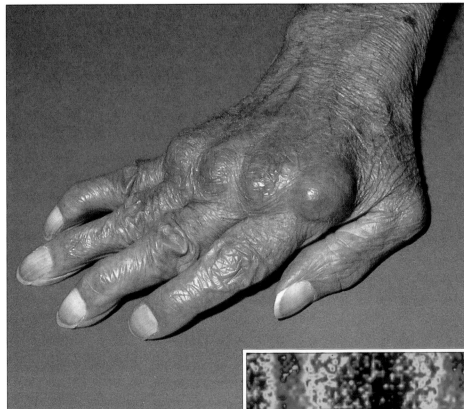

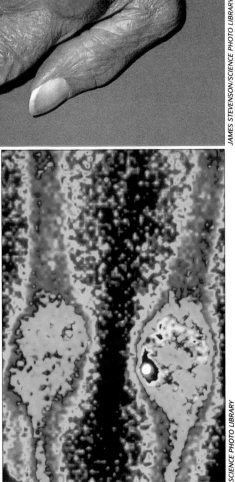

When left untreated a hand affected by arthritis (left) becomes severely deformed. The knee joint on the right in the picture below is affected by arthritis shown as 'hot spots' while the one on the left is normal.

JAMES STEVENSON/SCIENCE PHOTO LIBRARY

SCIENCE PHOTO LIBRARY

tion can be passed to the joint through the bloodstream if there is an infection elsewhere in the body, or may be the result of infection entering from a nearby wound. It may also spread from an infection near the joint. Since serious infections are usually controlled with antibiotics they now very rarely spread in this way.

If a joint becomes infected the germs multiply, causing pus to build up and making the whole area very inflamed and tender. The pain and swelling prevent the joint affected from being used normally, and if the hip joint is affected the child may not be able to stand.

TREATMENT

Prompt treatment is vital to make sure that no permanent damage is done to the joint. Your doctor should be called at once if your child has a very high temperature and associated swelling and tenderness of a joint.

If your doctor suspects that septic arthritis is present the child will probably be admitted to hospital at once.

High doses of antibiotics will be given intravenously to fight the infection, and if the swelling does not quickly begin to subside the child may have some of the pus drained off through a syringe under anaesthetic. Measures will also be taken if necessary to control the fever.

After about two weeks of intensive treatment a less intensive course of antibiotic treatment will be given, with the drugs being taken orally. The child will also be given phsyiotherapy to make sure that the joint does not

stiffen. When the child comes out of hospital he will continue with physiotherapy and exercises for some time to ensure that he regains full use of the joint.

YOUR QUESTIONS

Q Arthritis sounds like an old person's disease. Can children really suffer from it?

A The variety known as septic arthritis (also sometimes called infectious arthritis) can affect people of any age. Although it can be caused by a variety of infections, the chief cause is tuberculosis (TB), to which children are particularly vulnerable. In the many countries where this disease is now rare septic arthritis is equally rare, but it is still often found in some parts of the world.

Q I thought a lot of childhood illnesses caused swollen joints. Is this what septic arthritis is?

A You are right – measles, chickenpox and German measles can all cause the child's joints to be temporarily swollen. In these cases more than one joint is affected and the swelling and any pain or tenderness disappear as the symptoms of the illness die down. This is quite different from septic arthritis, when just one joint is extremely swollen and painful and symptoms become worse as time goes on. In this case infection has settled on a joint and there will be a high fever to indicate that something major is wrong.

■ SEX
See GENITALS

■ SEXUALLY TRANS-MITTED DISEASES
See also AIDS

We think of sexually transmitted diseases (venereal diseases) as being passed from person to person during sexual intercourse, and do not therefore associate them with young children. However disease can be passed from mother to child and for this reason, women are screened during pregnancy.

TYPES OF DISEASE

Syphilis is one of the more serious sexually transmitted diseases and unless an infected woman is treated she will pass the disease on to her unborn baby during pregnancy so that the child is born with congenital syphilis. Routine blood testing for syphilis is now carried out for all pregnant women and the treatment of any woman found to be carrying the disease has made congenital syphilis very rare.

If a pregnant woman is suffering from **gonorrhoea** the baby can be infected during the birth, causing conjunctivitis and possible long-term damage to the eyes. Again, the condition is nearly always detected and successfully treated. The disease can also cause infection to be passed on from mother to child through close contact so any mother who suspects that there is anything wrong should seek medical advice.

Chlamydia (non-specific urethritis) is a common sexually transmitted disease and can almost pass unnoticed in adults, with a very slight discharge and some discomfort on urinating. Yet it, too, can affect the baby's eyes if it is active during the time of the birth, so that detection and successful treatment during pregnancy are extremely important.

Finally, **genital herpes** is an infection similar to cold sores, which affects the genital area. It cannot be cured but it goes through dormant

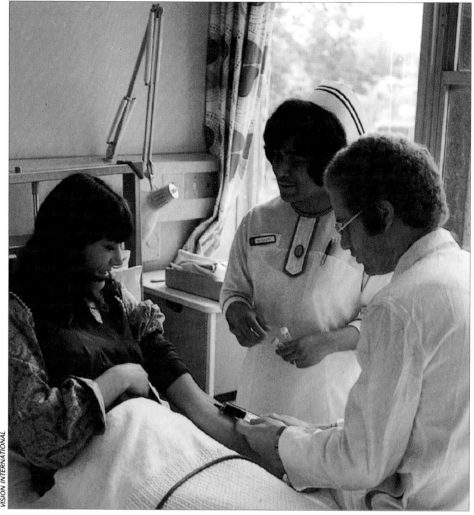

VISION INTERNATIONAL

and active phases and can be passed to a child during birth when in an active phase. Since this can be fatal, the child will be delivered by Caesarian section if the mother shows signs of infection.

PREVENTION

If you have any reason to suspect that you may have caught a sexually transmitted disease (symptoms such as discharge, discomfort on urinating or boils or ulcers) you must make an appointment at the special clinic at your local hospital so that treatment can be given. You do not need to be embarrassed about this — the medical staff know that you do not need to have been promiscuous, and in any case they are not there to judge you. Only correct diagnosis and appropriate treatment can protect the unborn baby from being affected if you do have a sexually transmitted disease.

The routine blood-testing of pregnant women for syphilis has helped to ensure that far fewer babies are born with this terrible disease.

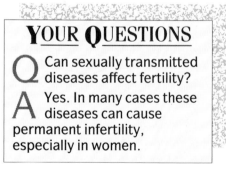

YOUR QUESTIONS

Q Can sexually transmitted diseases affect fertility?

A Yes. In many cases these diseases can cause permanent infertility, especially in women.

■ SHOCK

See also ACCIDENTS, FIRST AID

Shock has nothing to do with being startled. It is a potentially fatal condition that occurs when a person's blood pressure becomes too low for the blood to flow normally through the tissues of the body and back to the heart. It can happen when a person loses a lot of blood or when the heart stops working properly. Although most of the body's vital organs can function for a limited time without enough blood, the brain and the heart cannot and death is caused if prompt action is not taken.

CAMILLA JESSEL

Delayed shock can happen at any time after an accident.

S Y M P T O M S

A person suffering from shock may have one or several of the following symptoms: pale bluish or greyish skin (especially under the fingernails and inside the lips); shallow, fast breathing; cold, clammy skin; a rapid, weak pulse; dizziness; blurred vision; sweating; thirst; restlessness. She may also fall unconscious. Delayed shock can occur some time after an accident or injury so if your child is badly hurt get immediate medical attention even though she shows none of the symptoms of shock.

C A U S E S

These include: heavy bleeding (both internal and external), electric shock, which affects the heart, severe burns, which cause great fluid loss from the damaged skin, dehydration after severe vomiting or diarrhoea, an abnormal reaction to medicines, bites or stings (like an allergic reaction known as anaphylactic shock).

T R E A T M E N T

Always get medical treatment for shock. Meanwhile move her as little as possible as this can make an injury worse, especially if you suspect she may have a broken bone or an internal haemorrhage after an injury or accident. If you are sure there are no broken bones, lay her on a blanket

YOUR QUESTIONS

Q My son recently had a nasty fall from the swings in the park but although he was very quiet he seemed quite normal afterwards. However, after about 20 minutes he went very pale, his pulse started to race and he became clammy and sweaty. I took him to the doctor who said that he was suffering from shock and had broken a rib and was bleeding internally. I'm horrified that I didn't realize his condition was so serious, so how can I avoid making the same mistake again?

A Don't blame yourself. You did the right thing by taking your son to the doctor as soon as he showed symptoms of shock. It is always worth bearing in mind the possibility of internal bleeding following a serious injury, especially if your child is unusually quiet or complains of a pain in his chest. If this happens or if your child shows any of the symptoms of shock following what may seem to be even a trivial accident, always get medical attention as soon as possible.

or coat and raise her legs so that they are higher than her chest, supporting them on cushions or pillows. Loosen any tight clothing, particularly around the neck, chest and waist. Turn her head to one side. Cover her with a blanket to keep her warm but do not let her get too hot. Never use a hot water bottle or electric blanket as these bring blood to the surface of the skin, allowing even less to get to the vital organs. If your child is unconscious, check that her airway is free and give resuscitation if necessary (see pp. 18 and 39). Put her in the recovery position (p. 115). Call for an ambulance or, if no bones are broken, take her to your doctor or the nearest hospital accident and emergency department immediately. If she has lost a lot of blood, a blood transfusion will be necessary.

WATCHPOINTS

If you suspect your child is suffering from shock:

• don't move her more than is absolutely necessary

• stop any bleeding using light pressure over an artery or around the edges of a wound

• be calm and reassuring at all times

• don't let her get too hot, but keep her warm enough to prevent shivering

• get medical help immediately.

■ SHORT SIGHT

See EYESIGHT

■ SICKLE CELL ANAEMIA

This inherited blood disorder is most common in people of African origin, of whom one in 1000 is affected. It is also found to affect people of Asian and Mediterranean descent to a lesser extent.

SYMPTOMS

This particular form of anaemia is not present at birth, but develops during the first six months as the sickled cells gradually block up the small blood vessels. Symptoms include: pain, especially in the back, legs, arms and tummy; fever; swollen hands and feet; anaemia; extreme tiredness; mild jaundice; inefficient kidneys which are unable to concentrate urine effectively; an increased susceptibility to minor illnesses such as coughs and colds; a tendency to pneumonia-like diseases.

CAUSES

Sickle cell anaemia is caused by a defect in a person's haemoglobin (the red pigment contained in the 'red' cells of the blood). Haemoglobin takes oxygen from the lungs and carries it in the blood to the different parts of the body. In a person with sickle cell anaemia the haemoglobin carries the oxygen to the tissues in the normal way but once it has given up its oxygen the haemoglobin tends to solidify inside the red blood cells and eventually these cells become deformed and sickle-shaped. They also have a shorter life than normal so a child with sickle cell anaemia will have fewer red blood cells than a normal child. The condition is inherited: if both parents are carriers of the gene their child has a one in four chance of inheriting it.

TREATMENT

There is no cure for the disease, although research is going on. A healthy diet and good hygiene help to minimize the risk of illnesses and any illness that does develop should be treated promptly. Encourage your child to drink plenty of liquids to reduce the strain on her kidneys. It is especially important that a child with sickle cell anaemia should be immunized against all infectious diseases. A severe attack (known as a crisis), when the child suffers acute joint and abdominal pain, needs immediate medical attention and your doctor will give pain killing drugs. Blood transfusions can become necessary if the anaemia becomes much worse or if an anaesthetic is needed for any reason. However they only help temporarily and when the child starts to make her own blood again the sickle cells will return.

EVERYDAY LIFE

Most children with sickle cell anaemia can live an ordinary life. However it is important that anyone who is caring for your child knows of her condition and to call for a doctor if a crisis occurs. While your child can join in normal activities she should avoid anything too strenuous.

Babies of African origin are most likely to develop sickle cell anaemia, an inherited blood disorder.

YOUR QUESTIONS

Q My little girl has been diagnosed as suffering from sickle cell anaemia. Will iron injections or pills cure it?

A No. Unlike ordinary anaemia, sickle cell anaemia is an inherited condition and iron will not cure it. However, a balanced diet which includes lots of iron-rich food will help her fight off infections and generally make her feel better. Your doctor may also prescribe special vitamin supplements.

Q I know that there is no cure for sickle cell anaemia but I wonder if it is possible to prevent it?

A Yes. People who are carrying the disease can now be identified through blood tests, even if they are healthy, and can be given genetic counselling to help in prevention.

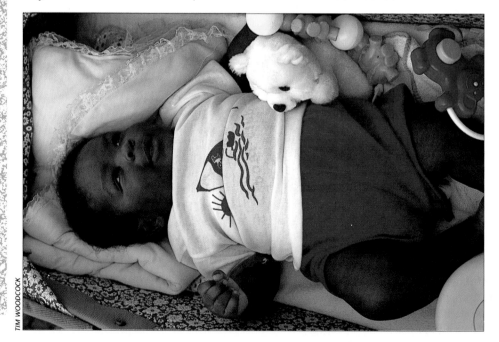

TIM WOODCOCK

■ SINUSITIS

This is an infection of the sinuses (the air-filled spaces inside the bones around the eyes and nose which make the skull bones light and give the voice its resonance). The sinuses are narrow passages lined with the same mucus membrane as the nose. They are connected to the upper part of the throat and drain into the nose so an infection of the nose or throat can easily spread to them. Their lining then becomes inflamed and clogged with mucus. Sinusitis tends not to affect babies as their sinuses are not fully developed but is fairly common in children over three.

S Y M P T O M S

The main symptom is usually an ache or pain over the infected sinus, either in one or both cheeks or in the forehead. The affected area will feel tender when touched and the pain usually feels worse when the child bends forward or lies down. She may also have a fever, a greenish or yellowish discharge from her nose and watering eyes.

C A U S E S

Sinusitis usually follows a cold, cough or sore throat. If the central cartilage of the child's nose is at all mis-shapen, this may predispose her to sinusitis as her sinuses will not be able to drain freely.

T R E A T M E N T

Mild sinusitis will clear up on its own in two or three days. Severe attacks are rare in children but if your child should suffer one, consult your doctor who may prescribe antibiotics or decongestants. Steam inhalation can loosen the mucus and helps the sinuses to drain, but must be done very carefully in order not to burn your child with the scalding water. Many children also dislike the sensation of inhaling steam. If the sinusitis recurs frequently, your doctor may advise a minor operation to wash out her sinuses.

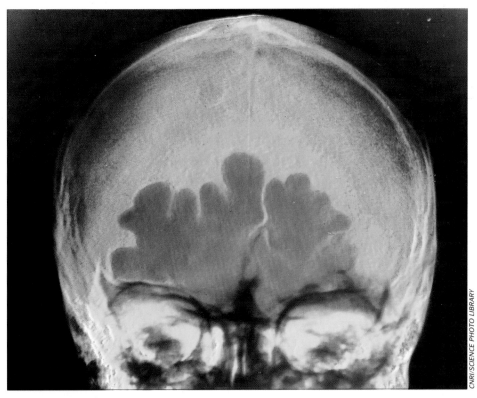

CNRI/SCIENCE PHOTO LIBRARY

YOUR QUESTIONS

Q My daughter suffers from frequent attacks of sinusitis. Would the nasal decongestants you can buy at the chemist's help clear it up?

A Nasal decongestants are sometimes prescribed by doctors to help in a severe attack of sinusitis because they work quickly. However, they offer only temporary relief and if they are used too often they can actually make the condition worse. See your doctor and ask what he recommends for your daughter.

■ SKIN

See also ALLERGIES, ATHLETE'S FOOT, BOILS, BURNS, CHILBLAINS, DANDRUFF, DERMATITIS, ECZEMA, HIVES, IMPETIGO, MOLES, NETTLE STINGS, PIMPLES, RASHES, RINGWORM, SCABIES, SPLINTERS, SUNBURN, VERRUCAS, WARTS

Sinusitis is inflammation of the sinus cavities in the skull, causing pain in the forehead and behind the eyes and nose.

The skin is the body's largest organ. It is made up of two layers: the epidermis (surface layer); and the dermis (lower layer). On most of the body the average thickness of the skin is 2mm ($\frac{1}{12}$ in), but on the palms of the hands and the soles of the feet the epidermis in particular is much thicker than elsewhere. There is a layer of fat under the skin which helps to insulate the body.

THE EPIDERMIS

The epidermis forms a tough protective layer on the outside of the body. It contains no blood vessels and the top layer that you can see and touch is made up of dead cells which are continually rubbed off and replaced by new cells. This happens because the cells in the lowest part of the epidermis are continually dividing and working their way to the surface. As they work their way upwards they fill up with a hard substance, keratin (a type of protein), and then die. Nails and hair are also derived from the epidermis.

SKIN STRUCTURE

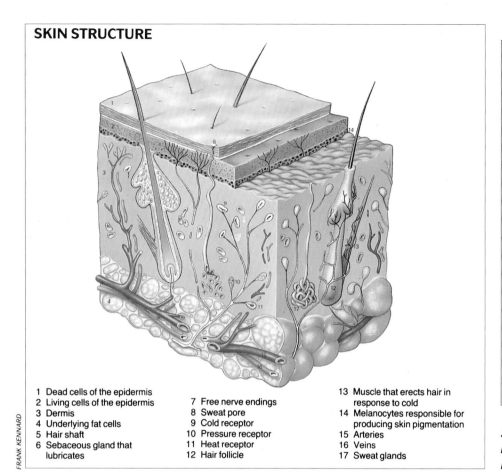

FRANK KENNARD

1 Dead cells of the epidermis	7 Free nerve endings	13 Muscle that erects hair in
2 Living cells of the epidermis	8 Sweat pore	response to cold
3 Dermis	9 Cold receptor	14 Melanocytes responsible for
4 Underlying fat cells	10 Pressure receptor	producing skin pigmentation
5 Hair shaft	11 Heat receptor	15 Arteries
6 Sebaceous gland that	12 Hair follicle	16 Veins
lubricates		17 Sweat glands

Skin is a tough, flexible and self-renewing covering made up of two interconnected layers.

THE DERMIS

The dermis contains a fibrous elastic tissue which gives the skin its strength and elasticity. It also contains blood and lymph vessels, nerve endings, muscles, hair follicles, sweat glands and sebaceous glands.

SKIN COLOUR

One in every ten cells in the lower part of the epidermis is a melanocyte or pigment-producing cell. These melanocytes produce melanin, the pigment that gives skin its colour. Everyone has approximately the same number of melanocytes, but in darker skinned people the melanocytes produce more melanin.

SKIN FUNCTION

The skin protects the underlying tissues from heat, cold, sun, wind, chemicals and injury. As it is almost waterproof, it also keeps body fluids in and other liquids out and being supple it allows the body to move freely. The skin also plays an important part in keeping the body's temperature regular. If you get too hot, perhaps with a fever, sweat then evaporates and helps to cool the skin. The layer of subcutaneous fat just under the skin helps to keep heat in and the sensitive nerve endings in the dermis recognize touch, pressure, pain, cold and heat and transmit these messages to the brain. Urea and other waste substances are excreted in sweat through the skin, and one vitamin, vitamin D, is synthesized when the skin is exposed to light.

SYMPTOMS OF ILLNESS

The condition of the skin often mirrors a person's health as both physical and mental upsets are reflected in it. If your child's skin is flushed, pale, excessively dry or sweaty, or if rashes or spots break out, it is always worth looking for an underlying cause and consulting your doctor if you are at all worried.

■ SLEEP PROBLEMS

See also INSOMNIA, NIGHTMARES

Many sleep problems in babies and young children actually belong more to the parents than to the child. Babies naturally fall asleep when they need to and sleep for as long as they need. It is the way in which they take their sleep that can cause their parents problems. Human beings are diurnal (they sleep at night and are awake during the day) but babies and young children have to learn this pattern and they vary enormously in the length of time this takes.

NEW BABIES

At first, unless he is in pain, ill or extremely uncomfortable, your baby will sleep in short bursts and wake for frequent feeds. While he is getting enough sleep, you are probably not and interrupted sleep over a period of weeks or months can leave you feeling very tired and edgy. Unfortu-

WATCHPOINTS

Remember:

• your baby will get as much sleep as he needs and fretting about it will only make you miserable, it will not make him sleep more

• a young baby's stomach is too small to allow him to sleep through the night without food so don't try to drop night feeds before your baby is ready

• leaving your baby to cry to 'teach' him to sleep is worse than useless – he wakes because he needs something. Hunger is the main trigger or perhaps he is too hot or cold, or has colic or a dirty nappy

• it is normal for a young baby to spend a considerable amount of time neither properly awake nor properly asleep

• you may inadvertently be keeping your baby awake by stimulating him when he shows signs of tiredness

A favourite teddy is a good companion for a child who suffers anxieties about going to bed. If necessary, also leave a nightlight in her room. It will help you find your way too.

nately, there is very little you can do about this in the early days.

You can however start as early as possible to make your baby aware of the difference between night and day by putting him to bed in a cot or pram as soon as he shows signs of being sleepy so that he comes to associate these places with sleeping and by getting him up and bringing him into the living area when he is awake during the day. Make the difference between day and night clear by changing and feeding him quietly with no stimulation at night and encouraging him to go back to sleep immediately after a feed or a nappy change.

OLDER BABIES

After about six weeks, although the time this takes varies enormously, your child's sleep pattern will become more regular. He will still sleep for as long as he needs and is

certainly not able to keep himself awake on purpose but he should be more aware of the difference between night and day.

EXTERNAL DISTURBANCE

You may be waking your baby if he still sleeps in your room, as no matter how quiet you try to be you will still make some noise when you come to bed and your movements in your sleep may disturb him during the night. If he has his own room you may wake him by going in to check on him while he is sleeping. Your baby is also now more aware of loud noises; perhaps traffic outside is disturbing him. Being too hot, too cold or hungry will also wake him, as will nappy rash. He may also kick his covers off as he sleeps and a sleeping bag could be useful at this stage.

EARLY WAKING

If your baby wakes early and stays awake, it is because he has had enough sleep. You will have to decide whether you want quiet evenings or quiet mornings and adjust his schedule accordingly.

ESTABLISHING A ROUTINE

You can help to minimize sleep problems as the baby develops by estab-

lishing a clear bedtime routine so that your child gets used to the idea of there being a set time to go to sleep. This will probably consist of a bath, followed by a feed, a story or nursery rhymes then a kiss good night to everyone in the family before going off to his cot with his toys or comforter. If he cries go back and reassure him, but do not lift him out of the cot and he will soon associate being put in his cot with going to sleep.

COMFORTERS

A soft toy, a piece of blanket or even an old nappy can help your child doze off so it is worth popping the same object into his cot with him every night. A dummy may also help, but never dip it in anything sweet. And do not let your baby doze off with a bottle as this can rot his teeth even before they come through.

ALEX BARTEL/SCIENCE PHOTO LIBRARY

Similarly, if the child wakes and cries in the night after giving up night feeds but is not ill or teething, leave him in his cot. Reassure him, change his nappy in his cot if necessary, but don't take him out.

NINE MONTHS PLUS

Your baby will now be able to keep himself awake. Sleep problems from this age onwards may come from being overtired and too tense to go to sleep at bedtime. Concentrate on a relaxing bedtime routine with no rough or boisterous games.

A change in routine of any kind can easily disrupt your child's sleeping patterns for some time afterwards. This is especially likely if he has to spend some time in hospital or goes to stay with relatives without you. Even going on holiday or moving to a new and unfamiliar room can disrupt his routine and you will need to spend time reassuring him and re-establishing the routine.

NIGHT WAKING

All adults go through periods of light and heavier sleep and also occasionally wake without even realizing it and babies and children do the same. Some frequently wake completely. If you just leave the child to cry when

YOUR QUESTIONS

Q My two month old baby seems to need very little sleep – about eight to ten hours a day. He seems perfectly happy but I've heard that babies usually sleep for about 16 hours a day. Will lack of sleep damage his development?

A All babies sleep for as long as they need, and you have a baby who needs very little sleep. This will not affect his development. Accept that your baby will probably carry on needing little sleep and don't worry about it unless he seems ill, when you should consult your doctor.

FEAR OF THE DARK

Many children, and adults, are afraid of the dark and this naturally prevents them falling asleep peacefully. Accept this as something the child will grow out of and leave a nightlight in his room or the hall light on. If he is afraid of monsters or other scary creatures in his room, you may find it best to 'chase' them away. But most children are quite able to be rational, and can be shown confidently that there really is nothing there.

this happens he will become more and more distressed and difficult to settle, so go to him immediately and reassure him but again without lifting. He should soon learn to go back to sleep on his own. A comforter or soft toy may also help to reassure him with its familiar presence.

SLEEP WALKING

Many children do walk in their sleep and it can be very alarming for parents to find their child wandering about in a daze with open, expressionless eyes. Sleepwalkers often do not recognize or even see other people. If your child sleep walks simply lead or carry him back to bed; do not try to wake him. Try not to mention these night wanderings to him during the day as he will not like to learn that he is doing things he

BEDWETTING

Some children have their sleep disturbed because they wet the bed at night, although others sleep calmly through it. Most children can go through the night by the time they are two or three, but about one in ten children cannot, and some children have still not learned by the age of five or six.
If your child is not continent during the night he can be put in nappies to keep his pyjamas and bed clothes dry and stop him waking. Taking him to the bathroom before you go to bed, may keep him dry for the rest of the night.
Never scold your child for wetting the bed at night. If a child reverts to bed wetting after having been dry this could be a sign of anxiety or illness, but otherwise it is quite normal for some children to take longer than others to learn to be dry all night.

can't remember and it will make him more anxious and less likely to go to sleep calmly. Most children soon grow out of this phase. Always fit a safety gate at the top of the stairs in case your child begins to sleep walk.

Young children sometimes resist daytime naps but a special comforter like a teddy bear can help.

SALLY & RICHARD GREENHILL

■ SMOTHERING

See also ARTIFICIAL RESPIRATION, CONVULSIONS, FIRST AID

Smothering is not a medical term, but it is commonly used when a baby or child is suffocated or nearly suffocated. This happens when the nose is blocked, preventing the child from breathing. This causes asphyxiation (lack of oxygen in the blood).

SYMPTOMS

When a child is asphyxiated he has difficulty in breathing. His breathing may become characteristically noisy and unless something is done may stop completely. This will cause the child to turn blue, then grey, and to become unconscious. It can also cause convulsions.

CAUSES

Asphyxiation, the result of smothering, is usually caused either by bedding, pillows or clothing covering the child's face and obstructing the airways when the child is asleep or by the child's face being covered by a plastic bag. It is tempting to a child to put things on his head and a plastic bag looks like an ideal dressing-up accessory. The bag clings to the child's face and makes him unable to breathe properly. The child panics, finds the bag is clinging to his nose and mouth and is unable to remove it, and eventually passes out through lack of oxygen.

PREVENTION

Smothering can be fatal or it can cause irreversible brain damage if treatment is not given within a few minutes. To prevent accidents, make sure that children are told how dangerous it is to play with plastic bags. Keep in a safe place any plastic bags that are being saved for re-use and put them away immediately as shopping is unpacked.

Children should have firm pillows and babies should not have them at all. Choose night-clothes that will not ride up when the child is asleep and

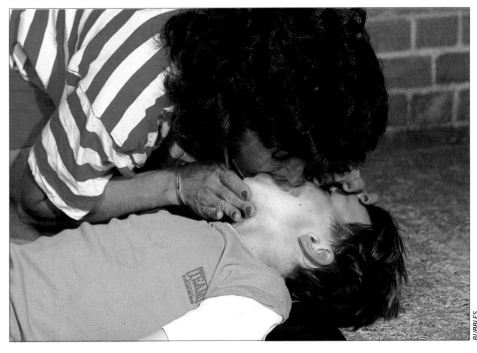

BUBBLES

make sure that bed covers are well tucked in at the bottom to prevent them from being pulled up over the child's face.

TREATMENT

Immediate, cool-headed action is vital if you find a child being asphyxiated. If possible get someone else to call an ambulance while you attend to the child, but if there is no one else there, deal with the child first, losing no time.

First remove the obstruction by ripping off the polythene bag or pulling away bed clothing and make sure that there is good ventilation.

Check that there is no other reason for the child's airways being blocked (vomit or some object in the mouth, for example). Run your finger round the inside of the mouth to make sure that it is clear.

Put your cheek to the child's nose to feel for breathing and check whether the chest is rising and falling. Feel the pulse to check that the heart is beating.

FIRST AID

If the child is still breathing and his heart is beating (even if he is unconscious) all you need to do is keep him lying down, in the recovery position (see p. 107), call an ambulance and

If you have a family, it's always useful to take a First Aid course but even if you have no training and the need arises, it is worth trying artificial respiration.

watch over him while you wait for the ambulance to arrive.

If he appears not to be breathing you must administer artificial respiration at once, and if his heart is *definitely* not beating cardiac massage should be given. (Ideally these techniques should be learned in first aid classes, but in an emergency they should be tried regardless.)

To give artificial respiration, lie the child on his back with his head tilted back. Close his nostrils with one

YOUR QUESTIONS

Q If I have to give artificial respiration, how can I tell when to stop?

A Stop when the child has started to breathe deeply and rhythmically. It is safe to give artificial respiration to a child whose breathing is faint and irregular, and you should be prepared to resume the treatment if the breathing begins to fail again.

hand, support his head with the other and breathe into his open mouth about once every two seconds (gently) for a baby and once every five seconds for older children. With a very small child it is easier to cover both the mouth and the nose with your mouth.

If there is no heart beat, give cardiac massage by pressing rhythmically on the breast bone – do not press too hard with babies – pausing after 15 presses to give two breaths (see p. 31). If possible, get someone to help so that you can concentrate on one function each.

If an ambulance has not been called, call one yourself once you are sure that breathing and heart beat have been restored.

WATCHPOINTS

It is dangerous to give cardiac massage if the child's heart is beating, however faintly. Check the pulse carefully before you start.

■ SNAKEBITE

In Britain and parts of Europe the only venomous snake is the adder, or viper, as it is also known. The other continents all have their share of deadly snakes, especially in tropical regions, but very few snakes bite unless provoked and it is very unlikely that you are running the risk of your child getting bitten when on holiday, in any part of the world. However, you should be on the alert for adders when walking in the countryside, even in Britain, as they are sluggish creatures that do not get out of the way, and there is a small risk of stepping on one by accident.

SYMPTOMS

A child who is bitten by a snake will first of all be extremely frightened and may be pale, sweating and shaking. The area around the bite will begin to swell and will be painful, and the site of the bite itself will show the puncture, or usually a pair of puncture marks, in the skin. As the poison begins to spread, so will the pain of the bite, and this may be followed by a feeling of numbness.

CAUSES

Poisonous snakes have fangs in their mouths, through which they can release venom (poison), which is injected into the victim when the snake bites. Most snake venom works by affecting the central nervous system and causes paralysis, or by interfering with the clotting of the blood. The puncture marks left on the skin by a snake bite are the fang marks through which the venom has been released. In most cases, shock is as great a danger as the poison itself.

The male adder (Vipera berus) can be recognized by its dark patterning on a silver to dark grey skin (below). The female's skin, however, is redder in colour and has a less sharply contrasting patterning. It is one of a few snakes that has different colouration for each of the sexes.

YOUR QUESTIONS

Q How dangerous is an adder bite? We want to go camping in the Pyrenees, but I don't want to risk it with a small child if there is a danger of snakebite.

A Firstly, the danger of being bitten is very slight, especially if you are on the look out for snakes; and secondly it is very rare for anyone to die as a result of being bitten by an adder (the most common poisonous snake in Europe). However, the risks are real, and you should take local advice on whether snakes are a danger in the area and whether it would be wise to have your own supply of serum (as many local people do.) Remember that the main danger is from shock, and reassurance rather than panic is essential. Do not let the very slight risks, however real, spoil your holiday.

S. S. TURNER/FRANK LANE PICTURE AGENCY

PREVENTION

When you are away on holiday ask local people for advice before walking in the countryside. In most parts of Europe local pharmacists are well informed about the likely dangers of snakebites. If you are told that snakes are to be found in that area, make sure that you and your child are wearing trousers tucked in thick socks or long boots when walking. Carry a stick, and make sure that the grass is clear before sitting down. Remember that in the tropics there are many poisonous snakes and take the risk of meeting one seriously.

TREATMENT

If your child is bitten by a snake you must get her to the nearest place where medical treatment is available as soon as possible. In Europe, local pharmacies stock serum against adders and it is usually best to take the child straight to the nearest pharmacy. In the tropics, where snakebites can be more serious, take the child straight to the nearest hospital, where the appropriate serum will be given. Most hospitals stock all-purpose serum in areas where there is danger from a variety of snakes. But it will also be useful if you can describe the snake to help to identify it.

FIRST AID

Before getting medical treatment, if possible you should wash or wipe clean the wound and cover it with a clean dressing. Reassure your child and keep her warm to help prevent shock. If she complains of pain it is safe to give her the appropriate dose of paracetamol for her age.

You should not apply a tourniquet, which can do more harm than good, nor should you try to suck out the poison. Try to immobilize the limb with an improvised splint, if possible, to slow down the rate at which the poison can spread. Whether or not you are able to improvise a splint, keep the child lying down, and transport her in this position.

■ SNEEZING

Sneezing is very rarely anything to worry about. It is a way of reacting to irritating substances which have been inhaled or of getting rid of a discharge which has built up as a result of infection. However, in children under the age of one, all symptoms should be watched carefully.

SYMPTOMS

There is no need to describe sneezing – a symptom in itself which is familiar

There are many causes of sneezing but none of them is serious.

to everyone. Usually any form of continuous or frequent sneezing is accompanied by a runny nose, and often by other symptoms too. These give an indication of what is wrong.

CAUSES

The most likely causes of sneezing are flu, colds, hay fever or a foreign object in the nose. When the cause is flu the child may have a slightly raised temperature. The discharge from the nose may start off being thin, but will usually soon thicken, causing congestion which makes the child feel 'bunged up' and unable to breathe properly. A cold also usually produces a thick discharge, but the child's temperature is less likely to be raised. In both cases the sneezing and runny nose may last for five to ten days.

A thin nasal discharge together with sneezing can also sometimes be a prelude to measles. If a runny nose or 'bunged up' feeling and sneezing last for longer than ten days, and if the child otherwise feels well, or if she suffers from frequent attacks of sneezing, and her temperature is normal, this could be hay fever. All these conditions are described more fully in separate entries.

IRRITANTS

Many airborne substances can cause irritation and make a child sneeze without causing all the symptoms of hay fever. Perfumes, dust and tobacco smoke can all cause sneezing, and in particular you should not subject your child to tobacco smoke, which can cause short-term and long-term respiratory problems as well as the odd sneeze.

Finally if the child's sneezing is accompanied by a discharge from just one nostril, it could be that there is a foreign body in her nose. A very young child will not be able to tell you whether she has pushed something up her nose, and an older child may not remember having done so (the sneezing may not begin immediately). If your child shows these symptoms it is advisable to ask your doctor's advice, whether you can see something in the nostril or not.

TREATMENT

For colds, flu, hay fever and measles, *see* separate entries. Isolated attacks of sneezing cause no problem and need no treatment, but if your child is constantly sneezing (whether or not she has the full symptoms of hay fever) you may be able to identify the substance causing the irritation and

keep the child away from it. If the child has a foreign body up her nostril the doctor will either remove it or send her to hospital to have it removed.

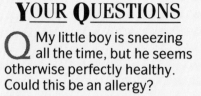

YOUR QUESTIONS

Q My little boy is sneezing all the time, but he seems otherwise perfectly healthy. Could this be an allergy?

A It does sound as though this might be a form of hay fever. But sometimes attacks can be very mild, and as long as there are no other symptoms, such as sore, runny eyes or nasal congestion, there is really no need to worry about this.

Adenoid problems can cause a child to snore, the blocked nose forcing her to breathe through the mouth.

■ SNORING

Snoring affects as many as one in eight people and while it does the snorer no harm it can be intensely irritating for those within earshot.

CAUSES

Snoring is an involuntary act — you cannot make yourself do it, nor can you make yourself stop. It happens when a sleeper begins to breathe through her mouth and the muscles of the soft palate (the soft part of the roof of the mouth behind the back teeth) and the uvula (the part of the soft palate that projects downwards into the mouth) relax. The passage through which the air passes are then narrowed and as the sleeping person breathes in, the air drawn into the lungs causes the soft palate and the uvula to vibrate. The type and volume of snoring depends on the shape of the mouth, how elastic the tissues are and how vigorously she inhales.

TONY STONE WORLDWIDE

YOUR QUESTIONS

Q My two children share a room and the older one often complains of being kept awake by her brother's snoring. The doctor has checked him and can find no physical cause for the snoring, so what can I do?

A If there is no physical cause and you find that encouraging your son to sleep on his side or front does not stop the snoring, check to see if the atmosphere in the bedroom is either very dry or very humid. If correcting the atmosphere doesn't work, there is nothing you can do. No one knows the cause of most snoring and there is no cure. Your son may grow out of his snoring but in the meantime your daughter will sleep better if you can move her into her own room.

Snoring is most likely to happen when a person sleeps with her mouth open, so it often accompanies a cold or blocked nose. Enlarged tonsils or adenoids can also lead to a stuffy nose, making snoring more likely as can falling asleep sitting up or lying on her back. Sleeping in a very dry centrally heated room or a damp room can also make a child more prone to snoring.

Some pregnant women snore even though they have never snored before. This is thought to be caused by fluid retention in the tissues which affects the breathing passages.

TREATMENT

If the cause is a cold the snoring will clear up with the cold. If you suspect your child has enlarged tonsils or adenoids, see your doctor, who may advise removal if the problem is persistent. Moving your sleeping child off her back may also help, but she may change her position again as she sleeps and start snoring again.

■ SORE THROAT

See also THROAT

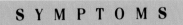

A sore throat is a common complaint that can occur on its own or as one of several symptoms. Even though it is so common, a sore throat has to be taken seriously in children as there is always the danger of the infection spreading to the middle ear.

SYMPTOMS

Young children are often not able to recognize a sore throat and may complain of their mouth hurting or may simply have difficulty in swallowing and perhaps be a little off their food and generally unwell.

If you look inside the child's mouth you may see that the area round the back of the tongue is inflamed and if you feel the child's neck from ear to chin you may be able to detect hard little swollen glands, or you may find that the whole area feels swollen and tender.

In babies the signs will be difficulty in feeding and general unhappiness and irritability.

Depending on the type of sore throat, the child may also have a high temperature.

CAUSES

Sore throats are usually caused by an infection. They may be one of the symptoms of colds and flu or the child may also have tonsillitis or laryngitis. The swelling of the glands in mumps can also make the throat feel sore and a sore throat can be a symptom of scarlet fever.

TREATMENT

More often than not the infection responsible for the sore throat is a viral rather than a bacterial one and antibiotics will make no difference. In the main the infection will clear itself within two or three days.

Make sure that a child with a sore throat has plenty of rest and keeps warm. Plenty of warm drinks such as lemon and honey or hot blackcurrant juice will help to soothe the throat as

YOUR QUESTIONS

Q How can I get my little boy to eat when he has a sore throat? He still seems hungry but it hurts to swallow.

A Try giving your son soups and purées. Cold puréed fruit, yoghurt, and ice cream are particularly easy to swallow and also soothing.

Q My daughter has had several attacks of tonsillitis in the past and used to be given antibiotics. Now I have a new doctor and he is most reluctant to prescribe antibiotics. Why is this?

A Most sore throats are caused by viruses which are not affected by antibiotics at all. Sometimes tonsillitis is caused by bacteria and will respond to antibiotics – but not always. There is a considerable controversy among doctors over exactly when antibiotics should be used for sore throats. There is also some evidence that antibiotics do not help much even for tonsillitis and it has been found that the condition may clear up just as quickly without them. So some doctors are reluctant to prescribe antibiotics for any sore throat, preferring to allow the natural defences of the body to clear up the infection.

Q If my child has his tonsils taken out will this stop him getting sore throats?

A Many parents believe that a tonsillectomy will stop sore throats, but it will not. What it will do is to reduce the number of attacks of tonsillitis, although often these reduce as the child gets older even without a tonsillectomy. But a child who has his tonsils out will still be at risk from 'ordinary' sore throats.

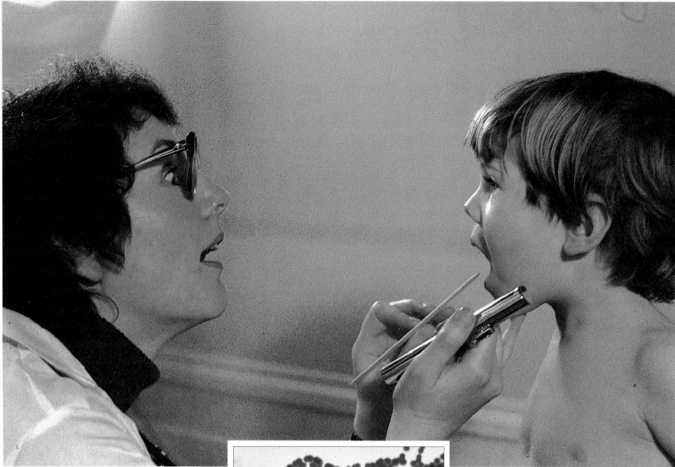

ANTHEA SIEVEKING/VISION INTERNATIONAL

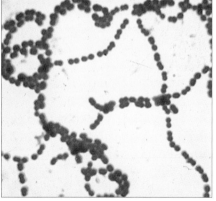

BIOPHOTO ASSOCIATES

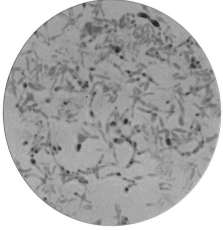

A doctor examining a sore throat. She may also take a swab to be sent to a laboratory for identification of the germ involved. On the right is streptococcus bacteria. Below is the organism that causes diphtheria (Cornyebacterium diphtheriae).

well as providing vitamin C and keeping the child's fluid level up.

If the child is not sleeping properly because of the sorenesss, or if his temperature is raised, he may be given the correct dose of paracetamol for his age to ease the pain or reduce the temperature.

CALLING THE DOCTOR

For a straightforward case there is no need to call the doctor, but if the child is feverish, if there is a rash, if the sore throat lasts for more than three days or so, or if the child has earache or any other symptoms that worry you, call your family doctor.

The doctor will use a light to examine the child's throat and check that the tonsils and adenoids are not affected. The child's ears may also be examined to make sure that the infection has not spread to the ears. Antibiotics may be prescribed if the signs are that the child has a bacterial infection and the doctor may prescribe lozenges to soothe the throat, and give advice on how the child should be cared for. You may be asked to bring the child back for a check-up if the throat is not better by a set time.

If the sore throat is a symptom of another illness the doctor will prescribe the necessary treatment for that illness.

■ SPASTIC DISORDERS

See CEREBRAL PALSY

■ SPEECH IMPEDIMENTS

See also CEREBRAL PALSY, CLEFT PALATE

Speech involves the use of dozens of muscles in the lungs, throat and mouth, controlled and co-ordinated by the brain. It is little wonder that, especially between the ages of two and five when they are learning to speak, many children have minor speech impediments – even when there is nothing physically wrong.

Speech disorders can be divided into several different types. These are problems of the voice itself (disorders of the larynx or voice box), abnormalities of the mouth, and damage to the areas of the brain involved in speech. Disorders of the nervous system (such as cerebral palsy) and deafness can also be the cause of problems with speech. However, the two chief speech problems that affect many children are lisping and stammering rather than major disorders, and in the main children grow out of them in time.

A baby can communicate with sounds long before he really learns to talk. From a very early age he tries to imitate the sounds and facial expressions his mother makes.

SYMPTOMS

Lisping and stammering are so familiar that they hardly need to be described. A child who lisps has difficulty in pronouncing the sound of the letter 's', so that it is spoken more as a 'th' sound. Oddly, this is often accompanied by difficulty with the 'th' sound, which often comes out as 'f'.

A child who stammers gets stuck on the first parts of words, so that they get pronounced several times, interfering with the fluency of the child's speech. This can vary in severity from the occasional stutter when the child is excited to continual stammering which makes it very difficult to understand the child's speech. Generally, children who stammer can

speak perfectly fluently when they are singing or reciting poetry.

Children with more serious speech disorders may have difficulty in forming words or in putting words together to make sentences. The problem can be one of articulation (forming sounds) or of comprehension (understanding).

TREATMENT

All children benefit from being patiently helped and encouraged to speak. From being quite young, babies enjoy trying to imitate the sounds that adults or older brothers and sisters make to them and watching their mouths to see how the sounds are made; and as they get older, children learning to speak are usually keen to be shown how those awkwards 's's and 'th's are made.

LISPING AND STAMMERING

Lisping can be helped in this way, but there is no need to make it into

YOUR QUESTIONS

Q My three-year-old son still makes no effort to speak, even though I am sure there is nothing wrong with his hearing. Is this anything to worry about?

A Many children do not begin to speak until quite late, and this is particularly so with boys. However you should discuss this problem with your doctor, who may decide that speech therapy would help your little boy to make a start to prevent him from developing any long-term difficulties.

SPEECH THERAPY

Depending on the child's speech problems, the speech therapist may concentrate on helping the child to use language or on helping her to make sounds. In both cases children will be encouraged to learn through play for much of the time; and parents will usually be involved, too, so that they can help the child between sessions.

To help her to understand how language works, the child will perhaps play with things in a doll's house, learning about nouns through naming the objects in the house, and then getting to understand verbs through doing things with the objects. A child with delayed development may learn partly through pointing at objects as the therapist names them, and children who have difficulties in making sounds will imitate the therapist to form a sound and will be shown how the same sound is used in different parts of words.

Part of the therapy may involve giving the child exercises to help her to form sounds and to strengthen the muscles used in speech, with the emphasis on learning through fun.

Children who stutter may be helped to speak fluently and rhythmically partly through the use of metronomes.

Speech therapy is a relatively new area of practice, and new developments are still being made all the time.

whether speech therapy is needed.

Equally, a mild stammer is nothing to be concerned about. But if your child stammers so badly that she has difficulty in making herself understood it could be that treatment could help her. Your doctor may refer her to a therapist who will assess how serious the problem is and whether treatment is necessary.

STAMMERING AND EMOTIONAL PROBLEMS

Stammering or stuttering, especially when severe, or when combined with other problems such as facial tics, can be a sign of emotional disturbance. Try to assess whether for any reason your child is feeling insecure, tense or anxious, and see if there is anything you can do to help solve the problem. Do not be afraid to ask your doctor for advice.

Meanwhile, try not to fuss about the stammer. Help your child with words if she really wants you to, but otherwise patiently wait for her to get them out, and never hurry her or tease her about her stammer.

SEVERE DIFFICULTIES

More severe difficulties can be an important sign of serious conditions such as deafness, brain damage or

Speech therapy is a specialized and relatively new area of medical practice. Through close contact with the therapist, deaf children can be helped to speak.

LEARNING TO SPEAK

Although the rate at which children learn to speak varies from child to child, there are various landmarks that all children go through.

Until the child is about three or four months old the only sound she makes is that of crying. After this babies begin to babble and gurgle in a speech-like way. The sounds they make at this stage seem to be much alike, whatever the language of their parents, and even deaf babies make them.

The next stage is cooing and chuckling, until, usually around the age of six months, the baby starts to imitate the sounds that people make at her. By the time she is a year old she is usually able to say one or two simple words, naming people and pets and asking for things.

She gradually becomes able to use more and more recognizable words, and can understand many words that she cannot say. From the age of two or so the child begins to learn how to put words together, and from then until she is about five she learns to use longer and more complex sentences as she gradually masters language.

something important. Most children will grow out of it by the time they are about six years old. In the majority of cases there is no need for special treatment, but if your child continues to lisp badly after she is five or six, or has other speech problems as well, ask your doctor's advice about

congenital problems such as cerebral palsy, but may also possibly be due to delayed development. Children affected can be helped considerably by speech therapy.

When there is nothing physically wrong, for example if the child speaks fluently at home but otherwise refuses to speak, the doctor may refer the child to a child psychiatrist to help resolve the emotional problems that seem likely to be at the root of the speech difficulties. The child's parents and brothers and sisters may also be asked to join in the therapy.

■ SPINA BIFIDA

Spina bifida is one of the more common congenital disorders. Even though the condition can cause severe disablement, in some cases spina bifida babies are only very slightly affected, and successful treatment can, in these cases, be given for the disorder so that the child grows up quite normally.

SYMPTOMS

The condition — a malformation of the spine — is present from birth and newborn babies are always examined for spina bifida. Symptoms vary from a cyst towards the base of the child's spine (or sometimes elsewhere on the spine) to severe spinal damage causing varying degrees of paralysis from the waist down, with (often) incurable incontinence and (sometimes) mental retardation.

Children with these more serious forms of the condition often also suffer from hydrocephalus (water on the brain) which causes the child to have an enlarged head. They are also prone to contracting meningitis.

CAUSES

The spines of children suffering from spina bifida have failed to form properly and one or more of the vertebrae (bones in the spine) lacks its arch at the back. In a normal spine the vertebral arches link together to form an unbroken column which protects

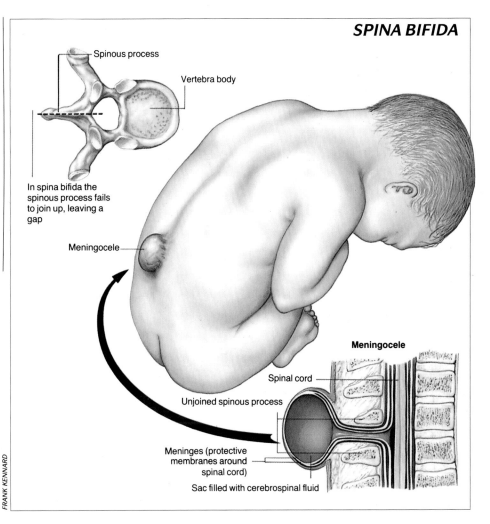

SPINA BIFIDA

Spinous process

Vertebra body

In spina bifida the spinous process fails to join up, leaving a gap

Meningocele

Meningocele

Spinal cord

Unjoined spinous process

Meninges (protective membranes around spinal cord)

Sac filled with cerebrospinal fluid

FRANK KENNARD

In spina bifida the spinal column fails to form properly.

the spinal cord, but in the case of spina bifida there is a break in this column, leaving the spinal cord unprotected. The swelling to be seen on the child's back marks the site of the break in the spinal column. This is covered either with skin or with a thin membrane, and in the worst cases the nerves themselves are exposed within the thinly covered swelling.

Why this happens is not really understood. It does seem to occur more commonly in some families than in others, and research has also suggested that it is more likely to occur in the babies of mothers who have an inadequate supply of folic acid before and during pregnancy.

TREATMENT

Treatment depends on the severity of the condition, but little can be done

to improve the condition of the spinal cord itself. Surgical treatment is usually limited to repairing the damage to the back and treating hydrocephalus where it occurs. But much can be done to help the child to cope with the disabilities resulting from the damaged spine.

YOUR QUESTIONS

Q Is there anything I can do to reduce the chances of having a baby born with spina bifida?

A Women planning a baby, or in the early stages of pregnancy, should ensure their diet contains folic acid, one of the B vitamins. In the UK, women are advised to take a daily supplement as it appears to help prevent neural tube defects.

DETECTING SPINA BIFIDA

Although there is some evidence that spina bifida is linked to a lack of vitamins in the mother's diet, there is no definite way to prevent it. Therefore, in many areas, pregnant women are offered a test to determine whether the foetus has spina bifida.

The first stage of the test is a blood test which indicates whether the condition is likely to exist. This is performed within the 16th to 18th weeks of pregnancy.

If the results are positive, the mother then has an ultra-sound test to check whether she is carrying twins (which can make the blood test results positive). After this an amniocentesis test is performed, in which a sample of fluid is drawn out of the uterus, using a needle.

If the results of this test show that the foetus has spina bifida, the parents are offered the option of having an abortion.

Since spina bifida tends to run in families it is particularly important for a woman to have the test if anyone in the family has had a spina bifida baby.

COMPLICATIONS

One of the chief complications of spina bifida is that infection can enter the spinal cord if the skin or membrane covering the affected part of the spine is damaged. As this can happen very easily, often causing meningitis, most specialists believe in operating within the first day of the child's life to repair the tissue. This usually means the baby having to be taken straight to a special hospital.

OUTLOOK

A successful operation protects the baby from further harm, and her future development will depend on what damage has been done to the spinal cord. Some babies will grow up to be entirely normal or to have only minor difficulties, typically with the feet and hip joints, which can be largely corrected by physiotherapy. However, in the worst cases the child will be paralysed from the waist down and may also be mentally retarded.

In the minority of cases the baby is so badly affected that there is unfortunately no hope of survival, and she will soon die. If necessary, nursing care and pain relief are given to the child in hospital, but sometimes it is possible for the parents to look after her at home.

Although damage done to the nerves can never be repaired, many children who survive can be helped by orthopaedic and other specialists as they grow older. This can in many cases help the child to walk independently, and enable her to gain bladder control.

A child who has hydrocephalus as a result of spina bifida can have a drainage tube inserted to allow the fluid to drain away (see **Hydrocephalus**), and if she develops meningitis this can be treated by antibiotics. The great majority of children who survive being born with spina bifida are able to go to normal schools as they grow up, although in most cases their condition has to be regularly checked by specialists and they may need continual physiotherapy, or other forms of treatment from time to time, including corrective operations.

■ SPLINTERS

Active children frequently come home with splinters in their fingers or elsewhere. Usually these are a very minor matter that can easily be dealt with at home and only very occasionally is medical help needed.

SYMPTOMS

Everyone knows what a splinter looks like. A small, rough fragment, usually of wood — from a fence, a wooden roundabout, an old spade handle, the seat of a swing, or something else that the child has been playing with or on — has pierced the skin and is embedded there.

A bad splinter can cause some bleeding, and the surrounding skin may be slightly inflamed and swollen. Occasionally a fragment of broken glass or metal may pierce the skin in the same way, depending on what the child has been doing, and thorns and prickles are the same as splinters for all practical purposes.

CAUSES

Children usually get splinters from contact with rough objects through climbing, falling, trailing their hands as they run, and so on, and splinters are just a normal part of childhood.

PREVENTION

It would be difficult and unnecessary to try to prevent splinters completely. Nevertheless, there are some precautions it is sensible to take. For example, if you have an old swing in your garden, make sure that the seat is smooth, and if necessary smooth it with sandpaper, to prevent a painful

YOUR QUESTIONS

Q My son got a little splinter in his hand about four weeks ago, and I could not remove it. It has still not worked its way out and you can see it under the skin. What should I do?

A If there is no inflammation or soreness there is really no need to do anything. The splinter will work its way out in due course.

However if there is any inflammation, soreness, swelling or pus, take your child to the doctor as there is a danger of the area becoming infected. The doctor will remove the splinter and prescribe antibiotics if they seem necessary.

WARNING

If your child gets a splinter in the garden, and especially if it is from something muddy, take him to the doctor, who might advise an anti-tetanus booster to guard against tetanus (lock-jaw). Keep a record of all boosters your child has had.

splinter in the soft skin at the back of the knee. Generally be aware of any rough surfaces that a child is likely to come into contact with, and give them the sandpaper treatment.

Although splinters are not on the whole serious, there is one exception to this, and that is splinters from glass. These can be much more dangerous, causing greater injury and needing medical attention. It is important to train your child to be aware of the dangers of broken glass, making sure that she knows never to run about when carrying glass bottles and jars in case she slips and falls.

Finally it makes sense to dress your child in tough clothing for tough play. This makes splinters and grazes less likely to occur and minimizes damage to clothes as well.

TREATMENT

Most splinters can easily be removed with a pair of tweezers. The tweezers should be sterilized first, by passing them through a flame (let them cool before using them) or standing them in disinfectant for a few minutes. To distract the child and to numb the skin slightly it is a good idea to rub an ice cube over the splinter before trying to remove it. Then grasp the end of the splinter firmly with the tweezers and pull it out.

Afterwards you can wash the area with mild soap and water and, if the skin is inflamed, apply a little antiseptic ointment. There should be no need to apply a dressing.

EMBEDDED SPLINTERS

Sometimes a splinter is firmly embedded and its end is no longer protruding from the skin, making it impossible to get hold of it with tweezers. In this case it is usually possible to remove it with a fine needle, by piercing the skin.

Again, the needle should be sterilized before use. Ice to numb the area and a certain amount of sympathy are also required, as the operation can be slightly fiddly as you try to raise one end of the splinter through the skin. You may find it possible to extract the splinter while the child holds her finger under cold running water. Once the end has been raised, it can be grasped with tweezers and the splinter can be extracted.

If you cannot easily remove a small splinter there is no need to worry. If you leave it alone it will almost certainly work its own way out within a day or two. During this time, apply a little antiseptic cream to guard against infection, and if the splinter is in a finger, get the child to keep his finger in very warm water for five minutes from time to time to help to draw the splinter out.

GLASS AND METAL

It is unwise to attempt to remove splinters of glass or metal yourself. For minor splinters take your child to the doctor's surgery, and if the damage is serious (for example if the splinter is large or seems to be deeply embedded, or if there are multiple splinters), take the child to the accident and emergency department of the local hospital.

Most splinters can easily be removed using sterilized tweezers.

BUBBLES

■ SPOTS

See PIMPLES

■ SPRAINS AND STRAINS

See also FALLS

There is some confusion about the difference between sprains and strains. Both can occur together, but strains are more common on their own. The symptoms are much the same and both injuries can result from the same kind of accident. In fact a sprain involves damage to the ligaments (the tough, fibrous and inelastic tissue between the two bones of a joint), while damage to the elastic muscle is known as a strain. Treatment is the same for both, but ligaments can be slow to heal, while muscles respond quickly.

SYMPTOMS

The symptoms of sprains and strains are swelling, pain, causing stiffness and preventing normal movement, and tenderness at the site of the injury. Especially in the case of sprains there is often also bruising, and the pain can be severe.

Sprains frequently occur in the ankles (known as 'twisted' ankle) and wrists, fingers and knees. Muscular strains can occur anywhere in the body, but in children they are mostly in the same areas as sprains.

CAUSES

Strains often occur as the result of falls and tumbles when children are playing and the muscles get over-stretched as the child falls or lands. Sprains result from a joint being forced to bend beyond its normal capacity, damaging the ligaments, which have very little 'stretch'. They become more likely as the child begins to take part in organized sport and they affect the knees and ankles as a result of football, dance, high jump and long jump or the wrists and elbows from playing tennis and netball. Like strains, they can also be the consequence of a bad fall.

TREATMENT

Children's sprains and strains usually respond quickly to home treatment. The swelling can be reduced by holding a cold compress (a pad of cloth soaked in cold water and wrung out) or a pack of frozen peas over the swollen area. This also soothes the pain for up to half an hour at a time.

When the initial swelling has gone down, support the injured muscle or joint with a crêpe bandage. This should be slightly stretched while you are applying it, but not applied so tightly that it affects the circulation.

YOUR QUESTIONS

Q My little boy is always twisting his ankle. Is there anything I can do to prevent this?

A Next time this happens it would be a good idea to take your son to the doctor for an examination. Frequent injury suggests that the ligaments may have been damaged at some time and physiotherapy may be needed to help them to heal properly and regain their strength. There is a slight risk of long-term weakness in the joint if full healing does not take place after a sprain.

Q When my little girl strained a muscle in dance she recovered very quickly, but my husband strained a muscle playing football recently and is making a terrible fuss. Why should this be?

A Children's muscles heal more quickly than an adult's muscles. As people grow older they can suffer much greater damage from a strained muscle and are more likely to need medical care.

SALLY & RICHARD GREENHILL

Active children can suffer from strains and sprains.

The child should be discouraged from using the affected muscle or joint for a day or two. After this the swelling should have completely subsided and there should be little or no pain. If any bruising remains it can be made to disappear more quickly by using a warm hot water bottle. It is now important for the child to exercise the injured area frequently but gently to restore full use. To encourage healing the child should still rest it when not doing the exercises.

MEDICAL CARE

In the vast majority of cases, the injury will soon heal, and the child will not need medical attention, but if the pain is severe, or if the swelling and pain continue for more than a day or two, you should take the child to the family doctor. He or she will examine the injury and decide whether further treatment is necessary. Painkillers may be prescribed to subdue the pain, and if an arm is affected the child may have to have it put in a sling. The doctor may also refer the child for physiotherapy.

In some cases a very bad sprain can be as troublesome as a fracture, and in others what appears to be a sprain can actually be a small fracture. The doctor may decide that the joint needs to be supported by a plaster for healing to take place properly, and may first send the child for X-rays to establish whether there is a small fracture. More intensive physiotherapy may be necessary when this type of injury is healing, to make sure that the joint returns to normal strength and to prevent it from being susceptible to more injury in future.

■ SQUINT

See EYE PROBLEMS

■ STAMMERING

See SPEECH IMPEDIMENTS

■ STILL'S DISEASE

Still's disease is a type of rheumatoid arthritis that affects children only. Most patients make a complete recovery, but this is usually only after having several attacks over a number of years. The disease is extremely rare, and usually attacks for the first time when the child is from two to five years old.

SYMPTOMS

This disease is also sometimes known as juvenile chronic arthritis, because of the fact that attacks recur over a long period of time. The first attack can be very severe, but subsequent attacks gradually become less and less violent.

The first sign of Still's disease is often a fever, especially in very young children. The child's temperature can be as high as 39.5°C/103°F, although it may fluctuate, dropping almost to normal in the morning and rising in the evening. A red, pimply rash often appears on the child's body while the fever lasts.

Symptoms differ widely from child to child, but all children with the disease develop arthritic symptoms of some kind. There is usually pain, discomfort or swelling of the joints and this may affect one or several joints. Knees, elbows, ankles, fingers and neck are most frequently affected, and sometimes these symptoms of inflammation occur before there are any signs of fever, especially in older children.

The inflammation can also affect other parts of the body, and other symptoms may be swelling of the lymph glands of the neck and armpits. In severe cases the eyes can be inflamed and sore, and the child

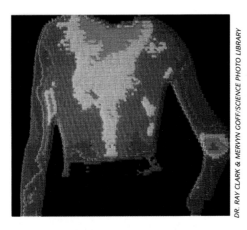

DR. RAY CLARK & MERVYN GOFF/SCIENCE PHOTO LIBRARY

Areas of inflammation caused by Still's disease are shown in red on this thermogram of a boy's back.

may also complain of pains in the chest, and may have a bad cough, if the heart or lungs are affected. As the symptoms persist the child becomes weak and tired, and loses his appetite. He may also become anaemic.

Although these attacks are extremely debilitating, in the majority of cases there will eventually be a complete recovery.

CAUSES

The cause of Still's disease is still not fully understood. It is thought to be what is known as an auto-immune disease, in which the body produces antibodies which are meant to attack harmful invading organisms, and which instead are turned on the body's own tissues.

YOUR QUESTIONS

Q Can anything be done to prevent Still's disease?

A Unfortunately, no, but this is an extremely rare disease. It is important for children who suffer from the disease to do their exercises and wear any splints or braces prescribed during the recovery periods. This prevents them from having any long-term disabilities, but it does not stop the disease from running its course.

DIAGNOSIS

If your doctor suspects that your child has Still's disease he will probably send her to hospital for tests. The child may be kept under observation, and blood tests will be taken. It may also be necessary to take a sample, under local anaesthetic, of the tissue that surrounds the inflamed joint for laboratory analysis.

TREATMENT

During attacks, the child may have to be treated in hospital. Treatment will partly depend on the severity of the symptoms, and on which parts of the body are affected. A blood transfusion may be necessary if the child becomes badly anaemic and measures will be taken to control any fever. The child will usually be given pain-killing and anti-inflammatory drugs, and it may be necessary to protect the affected joints by putting them in splints. Physiotherapy will be given so that the child does not lose the mobility of her joints.

HOME CARE

Attacks usually last for several weeks, but the child may be allowed home before she is completely better. Your doctor may prescribe aspirin to relieve the pain and inflammation at this stage, even though it is not generally recommended for children. The child will probably need to rest in bed for most of the time, and you will have to make sure that she does the exercises recommended by the physiotherapists.

Your child may have a very poor appetite until she is completely recovered, but you must try to encourage her to eat, and make sure that she has a nutritious diet with plenty of vitamins from fresh fruit and vegetables, and adequate protein — especially easy to eat in the form of fish and white meat. Your doctor will probably prescribe an iron supplement if the child becomes anaemic.

You will need to be able to spend a great deal of time with your child during the recovery periods and much moral support will be required.

If you are worried about a long absence from school, it should be possible to arrange for her to have home tuition as soon as she is well enough. This will make sure that she does not fall behind at school through being ill.

OUTLOOK

Although your child may suffer from several attacks of Still's disease, it is unusual for the attacks to continue beyond puberty. With early diagnosis and modern treatment at least 75 per cent of children with Still's disease enter adult life with little or no disability.

■ STINGS

See also BEE STINGS, NETTLE STINGS, WASP STINGS

Most insect stings and bites are completely harmless, merely causing temporary irritation. Bee and wasp stings (*see* separate entries) can be painful, and can have severe effects in a few susceptible children; the stings of jellyfish can sometimes be troublesome, as can multiple stings, and bites from mosquitoes, ants and

Some children can be quite badly affected by insect stings. If this affects your child, make sure that you pack the appropriate treatment for holidays and outings.

Some jellyfish can sting quite badly, but the severity of the sting is not always matched to the size of the creature. This large jellyfish has little sting.

even gnats. In a few, rare cases children can have severe allergic reaction to stings, but normally they are a very minor problem.

SYMPTOMS

When a child has been stung, his skin becomes red and swollen in the area round the sting. The skin may feel hot, and will be itchy or throbbing.

UNUSUAL EFFECTS

In a very few cases children have abnormal reactions to stings, with exaggerated swelling and soreness, and very occasionally being stung by a wasp or bee can produce symptoms of shock, with pallor, dilated pupils, shallow, fast breathing, cold, clammy skin and possibly unconsciousness. This is known as 'anaphylactic shock' and is treated as a medical emergency.

TREATMENT

Normally, the only treatment needed is to cool the area by bathing it in cold water or rubbing it with an ice cube. When the skin is dry, calamine lotion can be applied to soothe it, and this treatment can be repeated

YOUR QUESTIONS

Q Is there anything I can do to help my little girl, who seems to suffer very badly if she gets a sting of any kind, with swelling and irritation that last for days?

A It sounds as though it would be a good idea to take one of the special preparations containing antihistamines away with you when you go on holiday or out for the day so that if your daughter does get stung she can be treated straight away. If you find the choice in the chemist's confusing, ask the pharmacist for advice or see your doctor. These will calm down the reaction to all stings and insect bites (including jelly fish stings).

frequently until the irritation has subsided. Even the more irritating jelly fish stings can be treated in this way, but first any traces of jelly fish should be wiped off the child's skin, and if possible the area should be washed with soap and water.

When stings cause severe irritation, this can be numbed by using one of the many preparations that are available in cream or aerosol spray form. These are particularly useful at night, when the warmth of the bed can make the irritation worse and the child's sleep can be disturbed. Do not use them for more than a day or so, and if the problem persists see your family doctor.

MEDICAL TREATMENT

If a child has an adverse reaction to a sting or is stung in several places, take him to your doctor. The doctor may prescribe antihistamine cream or tablets or may give an antihistamine injection where there is a violent reaction. If a child shows signs of shock (*see* SHOCK), call an ambulance or get her to hospital yourself as soon as possible as emergency treatment will be necessary.

Some of the blood vessels in the skin burst, causing a rash of tiny, bleeding points. Within two or three minutes she loses consciousness, and within another three or four minutes she will die if she is not resuscitated.

CAUSES

Anything tight round the neck causes compression of the jugular veins on either side of the neck. These are the veins through which blood from the head is returned to the heart to be supplied with fresh oxygen. When they are compressed the blood circulation is interfered with, and the brain is deprived of oxygen as blood is trapped in the head and its supply of oxygen is used up.

PREVENTION

Babies and young children are most at risk from accidental strangulation

Parents have to learn to be aware of danger, as young children play without a thought for their own safety. A child could easily meet the same fate as this doll.

■ STOMACH ACHE
See TUMMY ACHE

■ STRAINS
See SPRAINS

■ STRANGULATION

We use the term 'strangulation' to mean compression of the neck, which reduces the supply of blood to the head, although medically strangulation is the cutting off of the blood supply to any part of the body, caused by local compression. However, in this entry 'strangulation' will be used in its everyday sense.

Strangulation causes irreversible brain damage and death unless the constriction is quickly removed and the child resuscitated, so rapid action is required. The risks should be avoided as much as possible.

SYMPTOMS

A child who is being strangled begins to struggle for breath and her face turns a livid purple or blue as the level of oxygen in the blood falls.

YOUR QUESTIONS

Q Is it true that a baby can be strangled on his own umbilical cord during the birth?

A Although in theory this could happen, good obstetrics ensures that if the baby is in any difficulty during the birth the problem will be identified and dealt with.

as they do not understand the dangers of forcing their heads into restricted spaces or playing with loops of cord, and they are likely to panic and be unable to extract themselves if they do find themselves getting entangled.

Sources of danger for you to be aware of are long cords attached to clothing or toys, fold-down washing lines with their loops of cord, and restraining apparatus from which babies and small children may be able to wriggle only to be strangled as they then fall out of bed or try to crawl away. You should also check for widely spaced slats or rails in cots. The ties on your child's cot bumpers should be kept short and should be regularly checked.

Parents can considerably reduce the risks of accidents by being aware of potential dangers when choosing and using restraining apparatus, toys and clothing.

As children grow up they should be taught about the dangers of having anything tight round the neck. They should not wear trailing scarves when on bicycles or tricycles because of the danger of the scarf being caught in the wheels, and they must be aware of danger when playing with ropes in 'cowboys and indians' or when swinging by ropes from trees or playing on swings.

TREATMENT

If you have to treat a child who is suffering from strangulation, try if possible to get someone else to get medical help while you give first aid. First, remove whatever it is that is constricting the throat as quickly and calmly as you can (cutting it through if necessary). Next, if the child is not breathing or if breathing is faint, give mouth-to-mouth resuscitation after clearing the child's mouth with your finger to make sure that there is nothing blocking the airways. See step-by-step diagrams on p.18 for method if you have not been trained. If you are sure that there is no pulse, give cardiac massage as described in the step-by-step diagrams on p.39, stopping to give two breaths after

approximately every 15 presses on the heart.

When the child begins to breathe spontaneously again, place her in the recovery position as shown in the diagram on p.115. Keep her warm and reassure her until medical help arrives, or call help if this has not already been done.

■ STRESS

See also FEARS

Odd though it may sound, children can be prey to stress just as adults can, and the results of this are emotional and behavioural problems, compulsive habits and ill health.

'Stress' is used to refer to a build-up of strains and pressures which disturb the child's normal balance — physical or emotional.

SYMPTOMS

There are many possible symptoms of stress. Perhaps the easiest to spot

YOUR QUESTIONS

Q What professional help is available for a child suffering from stress?

A If the child goes to school the head teacher may be able to refer him to a child psychologist attached to the school, and if not your doctor may be able to refer the child to a child psychologist or child psychiatrist. These are counsellors who have special experience in children's problems and there is absolutely no need to feel embarrassed or worried about seeking this kind of help.

If you think that you yourself are suffering from stress and that this is affecting your child, speak to your doctor about this. It may be that counselling could help you too, individually or as a family.

are behavioural problems and neurotic or compulsive behaviour or mannerisms. Of course some children are naturally boisterous, while others are more withdrawn, but if a child suddenly starts to be unruly or, on the other hand, to become nervous and withdrawn or unduly anxious this may be a reaction to stress. Equally, stress may cause the child to develop nervous tics, to want to stick obsessively to meaningless routines or to revert to more childish behaviour. In more severe cases he may pull his hair or fidget and lose all ability to concentrate.

Other symptoms that may arise in reaction to stress are loss of appetite (which can of course be caused by various purely physical conditions as well), reverting to bed-wetting after having been dry, soiling, frequent nightmares and sleeping problems. The child may develop a stammer, or in a child who already has speech difficulties these problems may become more marked.

POOR HEALTH

As in adults, stress in children can cause muscular tension and can affect the rate of the heart-beat and cause blood pressure to rise. The child may complain constantly of feeling sick or having tummy ache or may often feel faint. Stress can cause tummy upsets — tummy aches, diarrhoea and constipation — and headaches. A child suffering from the effects of stress can succumb more readily to infections, and certain illnesses or conditions, such as asthma, eczema and allergies, can be triggered or aggravated.

CAUSES

There are almost as many possible causes as there are effects of stress. Change is a key factor, and even changes they are looking forward to can be stressful for little children, just as they can for adults. Changing schools, having music or swimming lessons for the first time, going to a birthday party, on an outing or to stay with granny can all be just a bit too much to cope with. Reactions can

GEOFFREY COVE/IMAGE BANK

Many situations can cause stress in children, but parents quarrelling is often to blame.

be very short-lived, disappearing quickly as the child adjusts to the situation, but sometimes pressures can build up and symptoms may become more worrying.

SCHOOL AND HOME

Without realizing it, you yourself may be making your child feel under pressure by expecting him to do well at school or having high expectations of him in other ways. And pressures at school can include a new teacher, a playground bully and changes in teaching methods.

Major causes of stress for a child include the birth of a new baby, parents quarrelling or separating, and, of course, a death in the family – even that of a pet. Children in these circumstances need sympathetic support to help them to cope, and they may make their needs felt even more indirectly than adults do.

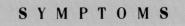

T R E A T M E N T

If your child has symptoms that could be signs of an illness, the first thing to do is to make an appointment for a check-up with your family doctor. If there is nothing medically wrong, and

the symptoms are suspected to be due to stress, tension or anxiety, try to find out what is worrying the child. He may have to be coaxed into admitting that he is afraid of his new teacher, is unable to face using the school lavatories or feels nervous in the school dining room, or into telling you about whatever other apparently small thing has blown up into an overwhelming problem in his mind.

Once you have uncovered the problem you will have to decide whether the child simply needs reassurance, or whether you need to get further advice. It may help to discuss any problems at school with the head teacher or to make an appointment on your own with your doctor to discuss whether professional help is needed for the child.

Try to think of ways of taking pressure off your child and also of helping him to cope with and even learn to enjoy a challenge. Remember that knowing that he is loved and that you have confidence in him is very important, and never ridicule him or try to laugh him out of his worries. However busy you are, try to make sure that you regularly have time for the child on his own. Relaxation helps children as well as adults to cope with pressure, and enjoyable exercise in the fresh air, cuddles and a story at bedtime can do wonders.

■ STUTTERING
See SPEECH IMPEDIMENTS

■ STYE
See EYE PROBLEMS

■ SUFFOCATION
See SMOTHERING

■ SUNBURN
See also HEATSTROKE

Most babies and young children have skins that are very sensitive to the sun, particularly if they are fair-haired and fair-skinned. However, it is always possible to prevent sunburn by controlling the amount of exposure to the sun a child has, and parents should always do this, as sunburn can ruin the holidays.

S Y M P T O M S

Sunburnt skin is red and sore, and feels hot and burning. In severe cases

WATCHPOINTS
Remember

• The sun can burn without seeming hot, especially if there is a cooling breeze, and when light is reflected by sea and snow.

• Burning can take place on days of thin cloud, and the burning rays of the sun can also pass through very light clothing such as fine cotton lawn.

• To prevent burnt shoulders you should always apply protective cream when the child is swimming and re-apply it to all exposed parts afterwards.

• Always use a sun block cream on the child's nose and re-apply frequently.

of sunburn the skin may blister, and there may also be intense itching. After several days the skin calms down, and then peels before returning to normal.

Resistance comes through the development of a tan, and this is best acquired through gradual exposure to the sun. The ultra-violet rays of the sun stimulate cells known as melanocytes to produce more of the skin pigment melanin, which darkens the skin and protects it from sunburn. The more gradual the exposure, the better the protection.

PREVENTION

To prevent your child from getting sunburn, keep him out of the sun as much as possible until he has built up a tan. If you're holidaying somewhere hot, avoid going out at the hottest times of the day. Even then, use a high factor sun screen at all times, and re-apply after he has been swimming or playing in the water. Put your child in a tee shirt and hat

IMAGE BANK

YOUR QUESTIONS

Q Why are fair-skinned children more susceptible to sunburn?

A This is because their skins produce much less melanin, the pigment that helps to protect the skin from burning.

Q Can sunburn do any harm?

A Although sunburn causes discomfort and spoils the holidays, it heals quite quickly and without problems. However it is now known that frequent and prolonged exposure to the sun may cause skin cancer, and too much heat can cause heat stroke, particularly in very young children. It is therefore a good idea not to allow children to be over-exposed to the sun even on hazy days.

whenever he is in direct sunlight. Build up your child's exposure to the sun very gradually.

Young babies and fair-skinned children are best kept away from direct sunlight or allowed to play in it only with head and shoulders covered, with, of course, a high factor sun screen on all exposed areas of skin. If you use a push-chair, buy a sun shade for it, and use it whenever you are out-of-doors. Heat stroke (see separate entry) is another, separate hazard you need to be aware of.

Children with darker skins are lucky and their parents do not need to be so cautious. But even these children can get burnt if they spend hours in the strong sun when they are not used to it.

TREATMENT

If the child does get sunburn, the best treatment is to dab on calamine lotion with cotton wool, and keep him indoors with the burnt parts exposed to the air. When he goes out, dress him in something loose and made of cotton, such as a soft old shirt or tee shirt, and at night make sure that the sheets on his bed are not rumpled, as the creases will make the sunburn more painful.

If the sunburnt skin causes pain this can be relieved with paracetamol in the dose recommended for the child's age, and it is safe to use

Children should not spend too much time in the sun at the beginning of the holiday and should wear sun-hats at all times.

antihistamine creams or creams containing local anaesthetic as long as you use them according to the instructions. These can be obtained from a chemist without a doctor's prescription, and if in doubt about whether a cream is suitable for your child you can ask the pharmacist's advice. If the sunburn is severe, and if the skin is blistered, you should take the child to a doctor.

HEAT STROKE

Too much exposure to heat can cause severe dehydration, which can lead to heat stroke with dizziness and high temperature. If these symptoms develop, the child may need to see a doctor (*see* separate entry).

■ SUNSTROKE

See HEAT STROKE, SUNBURN

When children have been exposed to too much sun they may suffer from heat stroke as well as getting sunburn. Mild cases of heat stroke caused by being in the sun are often referred to as 'sunstroke'. See the entry on HEAT STROKE for symptoms and treatment.

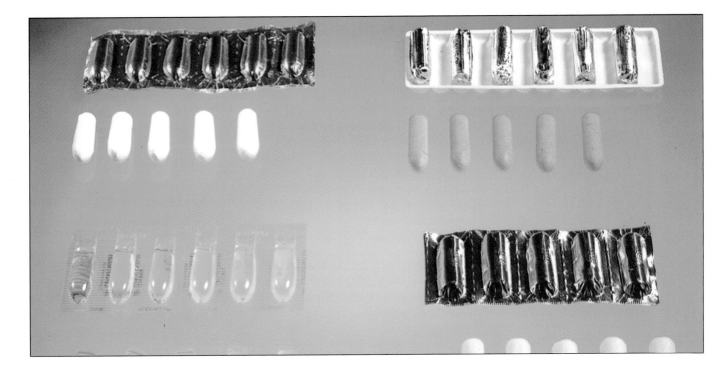

■ SUPPOSITORIES

Many of the drugs that can be taken by mouth can also be absorbed from the rectum (back passage) and can be given in suppository form. This method is sometimes preferable, although its use depends partly on the medical practices in the country concerned. For example, in Britain and the USA suppositories are used mainly just as a way of giving an enema or other treatment to the rectum itself.

ADVANTAGES

The use of suppositories may be preferred when a drug is likely to cause stomach irritation or indigestion. Some drugs are broken down by the gastric juices in the stomach and become useless. The suppository method prevents this as the drug is absorbed through the walls of the intestine. Taking drugs by suppository is also ideal when the child is vomiting so much that drugs taken orally are likely to be vomited back. It can also be useful if the child cannot swallow (for example when having fits). Giving drugs in suppository form has the advantage that the drug is absorbed more slowly, so that tablets do not have to be taken at frequent intervals, and of course it is the most obvious way of treating the rectum or anus.

USE

Suppositories are pellet shaped so that they can easily be inserted and are made of oily or greasy material which makes them as comfortable as possible. They are solid at room temperature, but dissolve once they are in the body so that the drug is slowly absorbed into the bloodstream. If it is necessary for your child to be treated with suppositories for any reason, your doctor will advise you on their use.

YOUR QUESTIONS

Q My little boy is constipated and has stools which are hard and painful to pass. Is there any harm in giving him an enema?

A You should take your son to the doctor, who will decide whether treatment is needed. It is much more likely that your doctor will prescribe a mild laxative and a fibre-rich diet than an enema.

A selection of suppositories prescribed for different purposes: they are all shaped so that they can be inserted with the minimum discomfort.

■ SWALLOWED OBJECTS

Babies and young children are always putting things in their mouths and as a result things sometimes get swallowed. If this happens to your child it is important for you not to panic. Many objects that were not intended to be swallowed will do no harm, but if the child swallows anything sharp, or small batteries like those used in calculators and musical birthday cards, or if he is choking and unable to breathe, swift action is needed.

SYMPTOMS

Especially when they are at the stage where they will put anything in their mouths (the worst time is usually between the ages of three to 18 months) children may swallow beads, pins, hairgrips, buttons, dried beans, washers, toy blocks, plastic bottle tops, metal can rings and all sorts of other objects.

You may actually see the child swallowing the object, but the first sign may be coughing or choking as the object gets stuck at the entrance to the airway. Sometimes there will be no sign that anything is amiss until the object gets further down into the child's digestive tract and causes a blockage with pains and bloating in the tummy.

TREATMENT

If the object was small and not sharp, and if there is no adverse reaction, there is no need to do anything but wait for the object to pass out at the other end. This does not apply to batteries – see Box. Keep a check on the child's faeces (stools) to check that this has happened (it is likely to take 24–48 hours). If the object does

YOUR QUESTIONS

Q Can a child come to any harm through swallowing a cherry stone? I have heard that it causes appendicitis.

A This is just an old wives' tale. Although it may feel a bit uncomfortable as it passes down the gullet, a cherry stone will do no harm and will be passed out of the body in due course.

Ring tops are particularly dangerous objects to swallow because they do not show up on X-rays. Keep them well away from children!

not appear in the stools or if the child has pain or swelling seek medical help, either by making an urgent appointment with your family doctor or by taking the child straight to the accident and emergency department of the nearest hospital if the symptoms are severe. An operation may be needed to remove the object.

COUGHING AND CHOKING

If the child is coughing, encourage him to continue as this should dislodge the object, but if he is choking, he will be unable to breathe and urgent action is called for.

Some parents find that their children swallow things so frequently that they soon learn how to scoop them calmly out of the child's throat with a finger. Quickly look into the child's throat and see if there is something you could easily remove. If so, do this deftly, making quite sure that you do not push whatever it is further down the child's throat.

If you cannot easily remove the object, you must hold the child upside down and hope that the force of gravity will do the job. For a baby hold him firmly along one arm, with his head downwards and supporting his jaw with your hand while you tap him firmly on the back between the shoulder blades with the other hand until the obstruction is clear. For a small child, sit down and hold him across your knees with his chest and head hanging down the side of your legs, and again tap him several times between the shoulder blades. (The strength of the tap should depend on the size of the child.) If you have nowhere to sit you can hold a baby or small child upside down by his feet and if possible get someone else to tap his back.

For an older, larger child who is too big to be placed across your knee the 'abdominal thrust' method may be used: stand behind the victim and place both your arms just above his waist. Feel for the bottom of the ribs, where they join the breastbone, and then, with his head, arms and chest hanging forward, grab the fist of one of your hands with the other hand so that your arms are braced and press

TOM BELSHAW

inward and upward quickly into the child's abdomen. Repeat several times if necessary.

DANGEROUS OBJECTS

A child who has swallowed batteries, or a pair of scissors, eyebrow tweezers or any other sharp object, needs immediate medical attention. Call an ambulance, or if you can get him to hospital quickly by taking him yourself, do so, if possible getting someone to telephone to say that you are on your way.

In hospital the child will be examined manually and by X-ray. Once

ANTHEA SIEVEKING/VISION INTERNATIONAL

CAMILLA JESSEL

When babies are teething they find it soothing to rub their gums on anything cool and hard (right). It is safer to give them a rusk or teething ring than a carrot (above), which can cause choking.

it has been confirmed that an object has been swallowed, and where it is, the object will then probably be removed surgically, although in some cases it may be thought preferable to leave it if it seems to be passing safely through the child's body.

■ TEETH

See DENTAL CARE, DENTIST

■ TEETHING

Babies usually begin teething at around six months, and the process is not complete until the first back teeth or premolars appear when they are up to two or three years old. The baby teeth or milk teeth, properly known as 'primary' teeth, begin to be replaced by permanent teeth from the time the child is about six years old, although the first permanent teeth to appear are usually the molars or back teeth, for which there are no equivalent primary teeth.

After the appearance of the molars the child's baby teeth gradually loosen and fall out and the permanent teeth take their place. It is not until the child is much older (usually

17 or 18) that the wisdom teeth grow and all 32 teeth are present.

The expression 'teething' is usually used to refer to the process of the primary teeth appearing. During the period of a year or so while this is happening your child may frequently be irritable and miserable as her gums will be sore and painful as new teeth push their way through.

SYMPTOMS

When a baby is teething, her gums will be red and swollen at the site of the tooth that is about to emerge. This may make her fretful and disrupt her sleep as the swollen gum throbs

YOUR QUESTIONS

Q My one-year-old is teething and her face seems very sore on one side. She cries a lot and keeps on rubbing her face. She seems to be having a lot more trouble this time than she had with earlier teeth. Do you think I should take her to the doctor?

A Yes, you should always take your child to the doctor if things don't seem right to you.

There may be nothing wrong, but it could be that your child has earache rather than teething troubles, and the sooner this is diagnosed and treated, the better.

Q Is it more painful to cut some teeth than others?

A Yes. The premolars (the larger teeth at the sides of the mouth), which are cut when the child is between one and three years old, can cause considerably more pain and soreness than the teeth at the front, which come through first. Plenty of cold drinks and food such as yoghurts and jellies will help the child to get through bouts of teething at this stage.

painfully. Teething usually makes a baby dribble more than usual and she may put her fists into her mouth and bite on them for comfort. Symptoms will not be continuous, but can be observed each time a new tooth is about to appear.

Other symptoms are sometimes wrongly connected with teething. Teething does not cause unrelated symptoms, such as vomiting, lack of appetite or diarrhoea, although it can sometimes cause the child to have difficulty with feeding.

TREATMENT

If your child is irritable or clinging look inside her mouth for any sign of sore and swollen gums, and feel the gum with your fingers. You will be able to feel the tooth under the gum if it is about to break through.

Give your child the cuddling she seems to be demanding as teething can be painful and she may feel very miserable. It is not a good idea to give pain relief medicines as the process will go on for such a long time as tooth after tooth breaks through.

Instead give the child a time-tested teething ring to bite on, or a rusk to chew. The child may also find it soothing if you cool your fingers in cold water and rub them over the sore gum.

You can still breast feed your child perfectly comfortably as her teeth appear, and she may actually need more nursing, partly just for the comfort and partly because when her gums are sore she may not feed as well as usual.

WHEN TO SEE THE DOCTOR

If the teething is going normally it is not necessary to see your doctor. However you should never put other symptoms down to teething and if your child has any other symptoms of illness while she is teething you should not hesitate to make a doctor's appointment — some parents have even been known to put a case of bronchitis down to 'just teething troubles'.

If the gum is unusually swollen, if

the baby is clearly in pain and not feeding properly, or if you are worried because a tooth seems to be taking a long time to come through, then you should see your doctor about it. He or she may prescribe a mild analgesic to help the child over the difficulty, and in rare cases you may be advised to see a dentist if the gums are badly swollen.

■ TEMPER TANTRUMS

Many children go through a phase of having temper tantrums, and although this is not a medical problem, it is a source of worry and alarm for parents when it happens.

RON SUTHERLAND

Temper tantrums are often a sign of an intelligent child, and most children grow out of them at around the age of five.

SYMPTOMS

Temper tantrums may begin to strike when the child is as as young as 18 months and are at their worst in two- to three-year-olds. Children can go on having them up to the age of four or five, when they usually begin to grow out of them. Temper tantrums seem to turn your sweet little toddler into a demanding monster with whom you cannot reason or communicate at all.

In a tantrum the child wants something or doesn't want something and screams and screams, demanding or refusing it. Often the child screams until he loses his breath, or he may hold his breath until he is blue in the face. Once the tantrum is over he is his sweet, sunny self again.

CAUSES

These displays develop as the child begins to assert himself as an independent human being. He has a strong will but his skills — both purely physical and in terms of understanding and self-expression — lag far behind. There are often provoking circumstances such as hunger, tiredness, momentary jealousy of a brother or sister or even over-excitement, but the tantrums may also come completely out of the blue. Very occasionally, if there are other symptoms, or if the tantrums go on well after the child is five years old, tantrums can be a sign of some deeper problem, but they are mostly just a normal part of the child's development.

TREATMENT

Most experts in child behaviour advise that it is best to ignore tantrums as far as possible, while making sure that the child does not hurt himself — as he may act quite violently. The child is incapable of understanding reason while having a tantrum; if he is demanding something and you give in this will encourage him to have more tantrums in future; if he holds his breath and goes blue, he will begin to breathe again quite automatically, and the tantrum will soon blow itself out.

You will find your own way of dealing with the situation, and you may find it is not always the same. Sometimes the best thing to do is to let the child get on with it, making sure from a distance that he does not hurt himself as he rolls on the floor or kicks about. Sometimes, however, you may sense that the child needs comfort and reassurance, and it will be best to hold him firmly on your knee while he storms. You may even decide occasionally that it is all right to give in, when you know that the child is tired and overwrought. Sometimes, also, it is possible to distract the child from his tantrum, with a joke (never at his expense) or by drawing his attention to something else.

Whatever happens, when your child has tantrums you must be calm yourself, and never show anxiety or anger. Some parents try slapping the child to 'bring him back to his senses', but this is something that should never be done.

MEDICAL HELP

You do not need to consult your doctor about temper tantrums unless these worry you unduly. But if they go on for too long or if they are accompanied by other symptoms which worry you, you may find it helpful to discuss this with your doctor. Make an appointment to go without your child if possible so that he does not realize you are worried. You will probably be reassured that everything is normal, but occasionally it may seem that the child is hyperactive or has some other problem, and further investigation may be needed to work out how the child can be helped.

■ TEMPERATURE

See also FEVER

Although normal body temperature is about 37°C/98.4°F when taken by mouth, the temperature does vary a little throughout the day and in different parts of the body. For instance, when a child's temperature is taken by placing a thermometer under his arm it will be 0.6°C/1°F lower than this and the temperature in the rectum is usually slightly higher. The temperature is normally slightly lower first thing in the morning and higher at the end of the day. It is also higher after exercise and hot drinks until the body has cooled itself down again. A child's temperature is a guide to her state of health, but it is not the only one.

YOUR QUESTIONS

Q Is there anything I can do to prevent my little girl from having temper tantrums? She tends to have them at the most inconvenient times — when we are in the supermarket or when my sister comes to stay for example. She is happy and good-natured the rest of the time.

A It is hard to accept that a good-natured little girl has this other side to her, but remind yourself that it is a normal part of development in many children, and she will eventually outgrow the tantrums. There is little you can do to prevent them, but you may learn how to defuse such situations.

Would it be possible for you to leave your daugher at home sometimes when you do the shopping or to have an arrangement with another mother to take turns with shopping and baby-minding? If it is other people's reactions that worry you, do not let them — just handle the situation as calmly and firmly as you would if you were at home. Make sure your daughter gets her fair share of your attention when you have visitors, and try not to let the visit disrupt her routine too much.

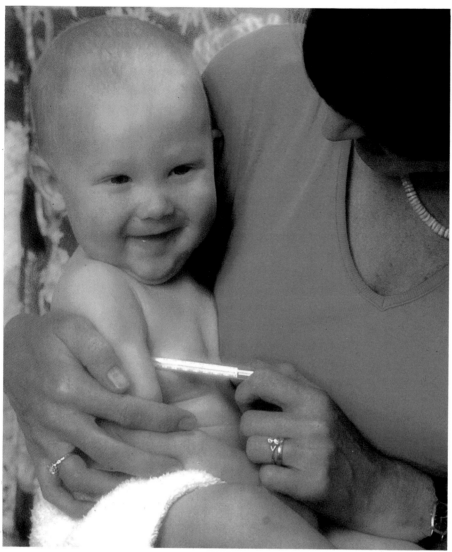

RON SUTHERLAND

TAKING A CHILD'S TEMPERATURE

Thermometers for use in the home are readily available at any chemist's shop. There are two types, the traditional glass mercury thermometer, which is placed in the mouth or armpit, and the more modern strip thermometer, which contains liquid crystals and is placed on the child's forehead.

Children who are over the age of six can usually have their temperatures taken by mouth, but with children under this age it is best to put the thermometer in the child's armpit or to use a strip thermometer. It is also possible to buy thermometers to take the temperature of the rectum (back passage) and these are sometime advised for babies under 12 months old.

For children under six it is best to take the temperature in the armpit unless you use a forehead strip.

HIGH TEMPERATURES

A temperature of over 37.7°C/100°F is considered to be a fever. Whether or not you call the doctor depends on a number of circumstances, such as the age of the child, exactly how high the temperature is, whether there are any other symptoms, and how long the temperature remains raised. If a baby under the age of six months has a temperature which is raised to this level, you should ask your doctor's advice, but with an older baby or child there is no need to inform the doctor every time the temperature is slightly raised. However, you will not have taken the child's temperature in the first place unless something

seemed wrong, and you must be guided by your instincts as to whether medical advice is needed. See the entry on FEVER for how to deal with a high temperature.

LOW TEMPERATURE

An abnormally low temperature can be just as dangerous as a high one. If a child is cold and his temperature drops to below 35°C/95°F he is suffering from hypothermia (*see* separate entry) and must be treated urgently. Remember that not all thermometers register temperatures as low as this and if you are worried about your child seeming cold you should contact your doctor.

The younger the child the greater the danger of heat loss if it is cold. Sometimes too, children who are ill have lowered rather than raised temperatures. Again, you have to be guided partly by other symptoms and partly by your instincts in deciding whether you need to call a doctor.

■ TETANUS

It is routine to immunize children against tetanus with the triple vaccine DPT (Diptheria, Pertussis, Tetanus). Otherwise tetanus, an infection of wounds, could be fatal.

S Y M P T O M S

Tetanus is commonly known as 'lockjaw' because the first major symptom is that the muscles of the jaw become rigid. This is usually preceded by vague symptoms of feeling 'ill' with headache and perhaps a slight fever.

The muscle rigidity which affects the jaw so noticeably also attacks the muscles of the back and the abdomen. Muscles go into uncontrollable spasm and if the illness progresses the back can be arched right over and the neck bent back. The child can also have severe difficulty in swallowing or breathing.

Lockjaw or tetanus can be fatal as the muscular spasms can cause severe exhaustion and asphyxia; pneumonia can be caused by the contents of the stomach entering the lungs, and heartbeat and blood pressure can be drastically affected.

P R E V E N T I O N

Parents should protect their children from this potentially fatal disease by having them immunized. The first series of injections are given to babies at 2, 3 and 4 months. Booster injections are given three years later and again before leaving school.

C A U S E S

A bacterium known as *Clostridium tetani* which is found in the soil and in animal dung is responsible for tetanus. The bacterium is resistant to heat and dry conditions and is also found in the dust and dirt of towns and cities and in gravel and rusty metal. Children playing in gardens, streets, playgrounds and waste sites are all likely to be in contact with *C. tetani*. The bacterium enters the body through cuts and gashes — the deeper and dirtier these are the more

SALLY & RICHARD GREENHILL

the child is in danger unless she has been immunized. Toxins produced by the bacterium are transported in the bloodstream and also travel down the nerves to the spinal column and brain where they act on the motor nerve cells and prevent the muscles from operating in a controlled way.

T R E A T M E N T

The incubation period for tetanus varies from the normal six to ten days to as much as several months. The first stage of treatment for a child who has not been immunized against tetanus is to give her an antitoxin injection. This is done as a matter of course if a child who has not been immunized has a deep cut, especially if dirt has entered the wound. If the child has already been immunized, a booster injection of antitetanus vaccine will be given, unless the most recent one was given within the previous six months.

If the disease is not successfully

Waste sites make great adventure playgrounds, but dust, dirt and rust harbour the bacteria that cause tetanus. Protect your child by making sure that her injections are kept up to date.

YOUR QUESTIONS

Q How great is the risk of anyone catching tetanus without realizing it?

A Although in many cases it is obvious, because a wound is deep and dirty, that there is a risk of tetanus, many people get it from minor wounds and it can sometimes take several months for the disease to develop. This is one reason why it is important to be immunized and to make sure you keep the booster injections up to date.

treated at this stage the child will be given large doses of antibiotics. Since tetanus is a reaction to the toxins produced by the bacterium *C. tetani*, rather than to the bacterium itself, antitoxins are also given, but these do not act as a cure, although they can stop the harmful toxins from spreading any further.

Treatment usually involves keeping the child under sedation, as any stimulus can trigger off convulsions. Nursing care appropriate to her condition will be given, and the child may have to be in intensive care and on a respirator for several weeks.

Even though, with the right treatment, most children do recover from tetanus, it is an extremely serious illness, and one which can easily be prevented. It makes good sense to make sure that your child is protected by immunization from the time she is a baby.

■ THALASSAEMIA

Thalassaemia is an inherited form of anaemia which occurs mainly among people from Mediterranean regions.

SYMPTOMS

The symptoms are those of anaemia, with extreme tiredness and pallor. The child loses his appetite and becomes breathless. The liver and spleen become enlarged, giving the child a bloated abdomen. Children who have thalassaemia often begin to show symptoms before they are six months old.

CAUSES

There are two main forms of thalassaemia, depending on whether the condition is inherited from both parents (thalassaemia major) or from only one (thalassaemia minor). Both forms affect the haemoglobin, the red pigment in the red blood cells which contains iron and carries oxygen round the body. There are many variations in the way haemoglobin is changed but the symptoms are always the same. For some unknown reason the condition seems to be confined to people from the Mediterranean and some people of Middle-Eastern and Asian origin.

When thalassaemia is inherited from one parent only, the result may be what is known as 'thalassaemia trait', which is symptom-free, but people who are affected can pass the condition on to their children. If both parents have the trait there is a one in four chance that their child will have thalassaemia major, the more serious form.

PREVENTION

Anyone (male or female) who may be a carrier of the trait can have blood

Thalassaemia is treated by giving the child repeated blood transfusions throughout his life. In between, he can usually lead a normal life.

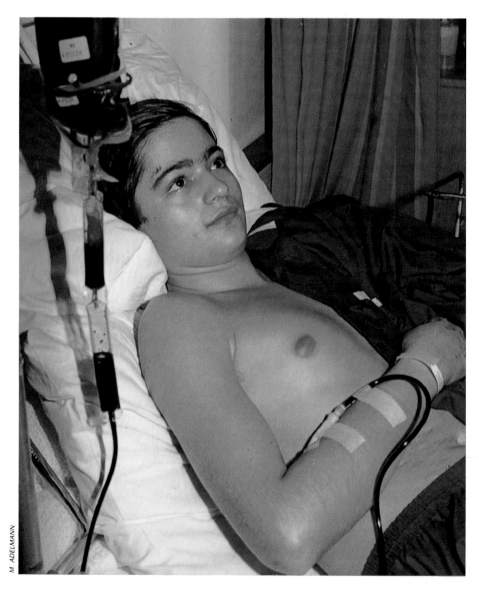

M. ADELMANN

SALLY & RICHARD GREENHILL

tests which will reliably establish what are the risks of producing a child who suffers from thalassaemia. It is now also possible to do reliable tests on the foetus and parents may wish to have the pregnancy terminated if the results show that the foetus is affected.

TREATMENT

The different types of thalassaemia are treated in much the same way. The child has to have regular blood transfusions to keep up the level of haemoglobin and so maintain the supply of oxygen to the tissues. In some cases this can lead to a dangerous build-up of iron, and some children need to be treated with a drug that enables the iron to be excreted in the urine. In some cases the child may have to have his spleen removed and some of the children affected need antibiotics to stop them from getting infections.

It is possible for children with thalassaemia to lead normal lives, but the need for frequent treatment makes demands on both parents and child. It may help to join a support group, in which families affected by the condition can give each other moral support.

■ THIRST

See also KIDNEYS

Delicate chemical processes ensure that the amount of water in the body is kept constantly in balance. The sensation of thirst is what usually enables us to satisfy the body's demands for water.

It is almost impossible normally to drink too much water as the excess is simply excreted in the urine, which becomes more or less concentrated according to the amount of surplus fluid in the body. Although the amount children drink is partly a question of habit, excessive thirst can nevertheless be a symptom that something is wrong.

CAUSES

Unusual thirst can indicate that there is an abnormality in the kidneys, and that they are not controlling properly the amount of fluid lost in the urine. It can also be a sign of sugar in the blood (as in diabetes) which causes excess water loss, and it may even show that there is damage to an area of the brain known as the hypothalmus. Normally when the hypothalmus senses that there is not enough fluid in the blood it stimulates thirst

When the body needs more water the mouth feels dry and this makes us want to drink. But the sight of running water will make anyone feel thirsty — dry mouth or not!

by making the mouth feel dry. For this reason dry mouth caused by a sore throat or by sleeping with the mouth open can also cause thirst, even though the body's fluid level may not be low.

It is also possible for a child to be so ill that he does not respond to thirst, even though his body badly needs more fluids. Because of this children who are ill can become dehydrated, especially if they are losing quantities of fluids through vomiting, diarrhoea or sweating. When a child is ill it is always important to make sure that he drinks plenty of clear fluids, or a balanced solution of salt and sugar (*see* DIARRHOEA).

TREATMENT

If your child seems to have abnormal thirst it is wise to consult your doctor, especially if there are any other symptoms that give cause for concern. The doctor may decide that tests need to be done, to make sure that nothing is wrong.

■ THROAT

The throat has a variety of functions. Firstly it acts as a passage-way for air to the lungs and food to the stomach and secondly it houses the larynx or voice box.

PARTS OF THE THROAT

The main part of the throat is known as the pharynx, and this is divided into the nasopharynx behind the nose, the oropharynx behind the mouth and the laryngopharynx behind the larynx. In the oropharynx the tonsils protect the food passage from bacteria and in the nasopharynx the air passage is protected by the adenoids. The nasopharynx is connected by a tube called the Eus-

---

CHOKING

What to do when a child has an object stuck in his throat.

If a child has swallowed something that has stuck in his throat he will begin to cough frantically in an attempt to cough up whatever it is. If the coughing does not work he will begin to turn blue in the face as he struggles to breathe.

• Hold the child across your knee so that his trunk and head are dangling down and give him several sharp smacks between the shoulder blades, coinciding with his coughs.

• When the object is dislodged get the child to spit it out or open his mouth and hook your finger round the object to remove it, being careful not to push it back down the throat.

• If the child is a baby, support him along your arm with his head below his chest and smack his back more gently with the hand of the other arm.

• If the object is a fishbone, get the child to eat chunks of bread if he is not coughing too much. This should dislodge the bone.

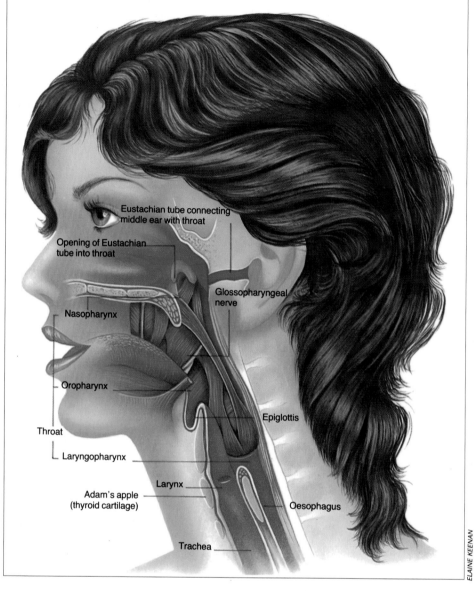

PARTS OF THE THROAT
The main part of the throat is the pharynx, consisting of the nasopharynx, oropharynx and laryngopharynx, and leading to the oesophagus and trachea.

Eustachian tube connecting middle ear with throat

Opening of Eustachian tube into throat

Glossopharyngeal nerve

Nasopharynx

Oropharynx

Epiglottis

Throat

Laryngopharynx

Larynx

Adam's apple (thyroid cartilage)

Oesophagus

Trachea

ELAINE KEENAN

---

tachian tube to the cavity of the middle ear.

The other important part of what we call the throat is the larynx at the top of the windpipe. The vocal cords, which vibrate to make sound when air is drawn through them, are situated in the larynx, and at the opening to the larynx is the epiglottis which closes off the windpipe as we eat and drink to stop food and drink from 'going the wrong way'.

THROAT DISORDERS

The disorder most likely to affect the throat is a sore throat. This is an inflammation of either the pharynx or the tonsils and is described by doctors as pharyngitis or tonsillitis according to the area affected. Pharyngitis and tonsillitis are both usually caused by infections which may be due to bacteria or to viruses. Pharyngitis can also sometimes be caused by irritation from smoke or dust or just by singing and shouting. Children of about the age of three to ten are particularly prone to attacks of tonsillitis.

Laryngitis is an infection or irritation of the larynx (see diagram). Occasionally the larynx may develop a tumour, either cancerous or non-cancerous. Although these are rare they are sometimes found in children, and when they occur, hoarseness without a sore throat can be the only sign at first. Hoarseness is also the symptom of laryngitis.

PROBLEMS AFFECTING CHILDREN

Although sore throats are usually over very quickly and do not usually cause children to feel particularly ill, both tonsillitis and pharyngitis can be a problem in children. Tonsillitis can cause a fever and make the child ill enough to need to stay in bed for several days, and it can also recur repeatedly and spread to the middle ear. Children who are affected in this way generally have to have their tonsils removed.

Laryngitis can be a problem if it occurs in a child, as the child's airways are very much smaller than those of an adult. When the inflammation of laryngitis causes the lining of the airway to be swollen the child can be prey to dangerous bouts of coughing and spasms of the vocal cords which make breathing difficult (known as croup, *see* separate entry). When it causes croup, laryngitis may have to be treated in hospital until the danger period is over.

YOUR QUESTIONS

Q My four-year-old son has had a sore throat for days on end without really seeming at all poorly. Do you think it is worth troubling the doctor with it?

A Yes. You should always consult your doctor if a child has a sore throat that does not get better quickly. Throat infections can easily travel up into the middle ear via the tube in the throat known as the Eustachian tube. Children are particularly prone to middle ear infections, which can cause complications.

■ THRUSH

Thrush is a fungal infection which can affect various parts of the body. Little babies often suffer from thrush in the mouth, especially when bottle-fed, and it can also affect their bottoms.

SYMPTOMS

A baby with thrush may have a very sore mouth and this will cause her to seem uncomfortable and unhappy. If you look inside her mouth you should be able to see a white, blobby rash on her tongue and gums and inside the cheeks. In some cases the roof of the baby's mouth may also be covered with the rash. Some babies also get thrush around their anus (back passage), where it shows as a

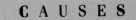
When a baby has a sore throat he will cry a lot and may seem to be off his food.

red rash that looks rather like nappy rash, but which is usually confined to the area of skin immediately around the anus.

CAUSES

The infection is caused by a fungus similar to yeast and known as *Candida albicans*. It is quite normal for *C. albicans* to be present in the mouth and in the intestines, where it is usually kept under control by other bacteria; sometimes, however this balance is not maintained and thrush is caused as the *C. albicans* multiply.

The infection is the same as the

YOUR QUESTIONS

Q Is there anything I can do myself to treat my child for oral thrush?

A It is always best to take your child to the doctor if she develops thrush. If you are breastfeeding, bear in mind the fact that you could have thrush on your nipples (a cause of soreness), and you could be passing the condition between the two of you. You both need to be treated at the same time.

Q My sister's baby is bottle fed and seems to have had quite a bit of oral thrush. Is there thought to be any connection between thrush and bottle feeding?

A Babies who are bottle fed do seem to suffer slightly more from thrush than breast-fed babies. Feeding bottles and teats should always be carefully sterilized before use to help prevent a variety of infections. This may reduce the chance of the child's getting thrush, but all babies are prone to getting it, however careful the mother is.

Q My baby has just been treated for thrush on his bottom. Is there anything I can do to make sure that he won't get it again?

A You cannot protect your child completely, but you can make sure that you give him a clean nappy frequently, so that bacteria in the nappy have less time to multiply. You should also let the baby go without a nappy in the fresh air whenever possible, as this seems to help prevent thrush in babies just as wearing stockings and loose-fitting pants helps to stop their mothers from getting the infection.

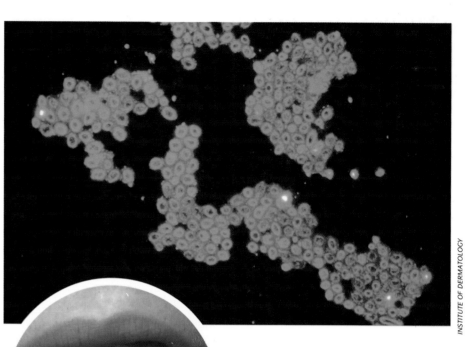

Thrush often affects the mouth causing white blobs to appear on the tongue (left) and inside the mouth. It is caused by a fungus known as Candida albicans shown here (above) as seen under the microscope.

INSTITUTE OF DERMATOLOGY

one that affects women's vaginas and also occasionally men's penises. In babies, it usually causes thrush to break out as described and it rarely affects older children, although they may occasionally have oral thrush, especially at times when their resistance is low through illness, or when they have been taking a course of antibiotics. (Antibiotics are linked to attacks of thrush because in suppressing the harmful bacteria responsible for the infection for which the child is being treated they also suppress the beneficial ones which were keeping *C. albicans* in check.) Little girls may also occasionally suffer from attacks of vaginal thrush.

TREATMENT

Treatment is usually simple and effective. You should take your child to the doctor, who will probably prescribe drops for the baby's mouth or cream for her bottom. Older children may be given lozenges to suck for oral thrush. The drops and ointment are antifungal in their action and usually contain nystatin as their active ingredient.

Make sure, if your doctor gives you a prescription for your child's thrush, that the whole course of treatment is completed, even if the symptoms disappear straight away. If your child's mouth is sore do not give her hot foods (in temperature or taste) — bland foods that have been cooled to luke-warm temperature are best. Also avoid giving anything acid, such as tomatoes, oranges or drinks based on citrus fruits, as these will sting the child's mouth. If your baby has thrush and is bottle-fed, make sure that you sterilize all her feeding equipment very carefully to keep it germ-free. If anal thrush is present, change her nappy frequently.

■ THYROID PROBLEMS

Situated in the neck, the thyroid is a gland which manufactures a hormone known as thyroxine. This hormone is released directly into the blood and travels round the body, playing a part in the way in which energy is produced. Thyroxine is produced when 'messages' are sent from the pituitary gland, a function of which is to monitor the level of the hormone in the blood.

HORMONE FUNCTION

The correct amount of thyroxine makes a person active, physically and mentally, keeps the rate of breathing and blood circulation up, and, in children, ensures proper growth. As in adults, if a child does not produce enough thyroxine for any reason, mental and physical activitiy slow down, as do the rate of breathing and blood circulation, and the body's temperature is lowered. In children, insufficient thyroxine also affects the child's growth in height, which almost completely stops.

At the other extreme, if too much thyroxine is produced, these body functions are all speeded up, and other worrying symptoms (described below) develop.

A second hormone, known as calcitonin, is also produced by the thyroid. Together with another hormone known as parathyroid hormone, which is secreted by four tiny glands known as the parathyroid glands situated next to the thyroid, this helps to control the way in which the body metabolizes calcium, the essential ingredient of bones.

PROBLEMS

Overactivity of the thyroid gland occurs only very rarely in children, sometimes accompanied by goitre (toxic goitre). However, an **underactive thyroid** gland (known as hypothyroidism) is slightly more common, causing serious problems if not identified and treated.

Other thyroid problems occasionally experienced in children are enlarged thyroid (**non-toxic goitre**), and (but this is very rare) thyroid nodules or **growths**. Occasionally also, the closely related parathyroid glands can fail to produce enough of the parathyroid hormone (**underactive parathyroids**).

SYMPTOMS

If the **thyroid gland is overactive**, the child will suffer from the overproduction of energy, with high body temperature, rapid pulse and loss of

The drawing (below) shows the position of the thyroid gland, which lies at the centre of the throat, in front of the trachea (windpipe). The inset drawing shows a section through the thyroid, with the cells that produce and store thyroxine.

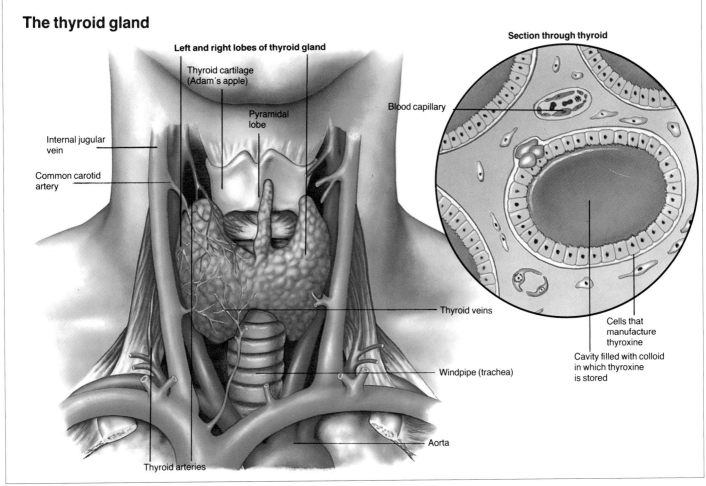

The thyroid gland

Left and right lobes of thyroid gland

Thyroid cartilage (Adam's apple)

Pyramidal lobe

Internal jugular vein

Common carotid artery

Blood capillary

Section through thyroid

Thyroid veins

Windpipe (trachea)

Aorta

Thyroid arteries

Cells that manufacture thyroxine

Cavity filled with colloid in which thyroxine is stored

FRANK KENNARD

weight, despite having an increase in appetite. The child's thyroid gland becomes enlarged, causing a goitre in the neck. In very serious cases there is also tremor in the hands, accompanied by nervousness, restlessness and sometimes protruding eyes.

If a child has an **underactive thyroid gland** he becomes sluggish and lacking in energy and always feels cold. Even though he may eat very little, he becomes overweight, while failing to grow in height. His skin and hair in particular show signs of the condition, with the skin being dry and the face looking puffy, while the hair is thin and dry.

Babies may be born with underactive thyroid glands, or occasionally with no gland at all. This can make them extremely lethargic, and their tongues usually loll. Such babies are also often pot-bellied. If this is not quickly detected and treated, the child may develop persistent jaundice and may fail to develop properly. Hypothyroidism itself develops when the child is six months to a year old, with stunted growth and impaired hearing, protruding tongue and flat face, thick hands and fingers, and coarse, dry skin, accompanied by extremely low intelligence.

SWELLINGS

An enlarged thyroid gland is visible as a pronounced swelling in the neck and can be found in association with underactive thyroid (non-toxic goitre) or overactive thyroid (toxic goitre). Thyroid growths or nodules, however, can develop into different kinds, all of which are rarely found in children – they are felt as little swellings or nodules in the throat.

PARATHYROID PROBLEMS

Children with **underactive parathyroids**, whose parathyroid glands produce insufficient parathyroid hormone, again have dry skin and hair. They may also suffer from cramps which affect the throat, hands and feet, and from numbness or tingling in the hands. All these symptoms are due to failure to metabolize calcium.

If the condition is not diagnosed and treated this can lead to the child having tetany, severe vomiting or convulsions; the teeth may fail to grow properly, the child may develop cataracts, and there is a danger of stunted growth.

On the other hand, **overactive parathyroid glands** in babies cause constipation, thirst, excessive passing of urine and even convulsions. In older children, there are bone pains, deformities and fractures, and renal stones. This condition can run in families.

CAUSES

Why the thyroid gland should sometimes fail to function properly is not fully understood. Many forms of goitre and altered function of the gland are related to genetic (prebirth) defects, or, it is thought, to antibodies formed in the body against its own thyroid tissue. What is certain is that without an adequate supply of iodine in the diet the thyroid hormone is not produced in sufficient quantities. This makes the pituitary gland stimulate the thyroid in an attempt to make it produce more hormone, and causes the gland to become enlarged. This is quite prevalent in areas where there is little or no iodine in the water or soil, and is known as 'endemic goitre'.

Nodules can vary from a harmless cyst to a malignant growth, and can usually be treated successfully. Why they form is again not really known, but in any case they are extremely rare in children.

TREATMENT

All thyroid problems are fairly rare, and they can nearly always be simply and successfully treated, especially if they are diagnosed early enough. Babies are usually examined soon after birth for problems of the thyroid gland, although of course in many cases these develop later and in some cases they cannot be detected in young babies.

Hyperactive thyroid glands may be removed and the necessary amount of thyroxine given instead in synthetic form. The treatment of underactive thyroid is to give synthetic thyroxine to make up for the deficiency, and as long as the condition is detected and treatment begun early enough, it is likely that the child will develop normally and developmental delays will be avoided.

Enlarged thyroid or non-toxic goitre is easily cured by adding iodine to the child's diet. This may be done through prescribed supplements or you may be advised to give the child fish and sea salt.

Hyperactive thyroid glands, growths, or any kind of thyroid enlargement may be surgically removed, involving a short stay in hospital. If the growth is a cyst it may be drained, more for appearance's sake than because it is harmful.

Failure to absorb sufficient calcium, caused by underactivity of the parathyroids is easily treated by giving the child supplements of vitamin D, which encourages the body to use the calcium in the diet. If the condition is severe the child may also be given injections of calcium at the start of the treatment.

In some cases the child may need to have life-long treatment and regular check-ups, but this should not stop him from developing normally and having normal ability.

YOUR QUESTIONS

Q Why is enlarged thyroid found more in some countries than others?

A This is because the condition is associated with lack of iodine in the diet. This is common when the soil and drinking water have very little (or no) iodine and the areas affected are known as 'goitre belts'. In recent years this condition has been much reduced in many 'goitre belts' by the addition of traces of iodine to the water supply and by the use of iodized table salt.

■ TICS
See also STRESS

A tic is a nervous habit which can be very irritating for other people but over which the child concerned seems to have no conscious control.

It is not particularly rare for a child to develop a tic, and these usually develop in children over the age of two, although some specialists also see head banging in younger children as a type of tic, and in most cases the child soon outgrows them. Typical tics are nervous twitching of the eyelid or the corner of the mouth — the kind of movement which is in any case beyond most people's control. But many other behavioural gestures that we normally make deliberately also qualify as tics — such as sniffing or coughing, pushing back the hair or

wrinkling the nose — if they become meaningless habits.

CAUSES

Children usually develop tics if they are insecure or anxious and having to adjust to new situations in their lives. You may notice that your child 'tics' more when he is tired or excited.

TREATMENT

In most cases no treatment is needed. If you notice that your child only has the tics when she is tired you can make sure that she is not allowed to get overtired as well as getting to recognize her tics as a sign that she needs more rest. If excitement seems to bring on the tics then these are unimportant, as long as the child

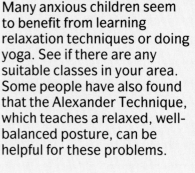

NON-MEDICAL HELP

Many anxious children seem to benefit from learning relaxation techniques or doing yoga. See if there are any suitable classes in your area. Some people have also found that the Alexander Technique, which teaches a relaxed, well-balanced posture, can be helpful for these problems.

seems otherwise all right — different children will respond to excitement in different ways and this is nothing to worry about.

STRESS

If, however, you think that your child is nervous or anxious and that the tics are a result of stress (see STRESS) you may be able to help by sorting out the problem or helping your child to come to terms with it. For example, if something at school is putting the child under pressure it may help to talk to the head teacher, who may be able to help in a practical way (by putting the child in a different group for example) or may be able to refer you to an educational psychologist if this seems necessary. You may also be able to help your child to feel less under pressure, for example by listening to her worries and taking them seriously, by having more time with her in the morning so

WATCHPOINTS

• However irritating your child's tics may be it will not be helpful for you to keep on pointing them out to her. She isn't doing it to annoy you. Concentrate on helping to make her feel secure and more self-confident.

A child can be quite unaware of twitches of the eyelid or at the corner of the mouth.

that she doesn't feel rushed, and by making sure that she has a relaxing bed-time routine with time for lots of love and cuddles.

Only if there are other worrying symptoms (*see* STRESS), if the tics seem to be a problem or if they last continually for over a year do you need to ask your doctor's advice. In extreme cases your child may be referred to a child psychologist or psychiatrist, but in most cases your doctor will assure you that there is no treatment needed.

YOUR QUESTIONS

Q My little girl has an irritating habit of pulling her fringe. Is this a tic, and what can I do about it?

A Yes, this sort of habit could be classed as a tic. If your child seems otherwise well and happy, the best thing to do is to ignore it. She will soon grow out of this irritating habit. Meanwhile, you could encourage her to have a different hairstyle, with the hair off her face!

■ TOADSTOOL POISONING

People tend to speak as though all mushrooms were edible and 'toadstools' were all poisonous. However, one of the most poisonous of all plants is a mushroom and the distinction between mushrooms and toadstools is a difficult one to make for someone who is not a botanist. It therefore makes better sense to speak of 'fungus' poisoning, as all mushrooms and toadstools are different kinds of fungi.

POISONOUS FUNGI

Many fungi are poisonous to different degrees. Some of them merely give tummy ache, while others cause prolonged diarrhoea and sickness. The most dangerous fungi can cause damage to the heart, liver and kid-

neys and to the blood cells and nervous system. In the case of a few species this can even cause death.

Although many poisonous fungi are unpleasant tasting, this is not always the case. And although some are very distinctive, this is not always so either. A toadstool which can cause death is *Amanita Muscari*, and this is like the toadstools in children's fairy stories, with a bright red cap sprinkled with white spots; but *Amanita Phalloides*, the death cap mushroom, looks quite similar to edible field mushrooms, yet is frequently fatal.

SEEKING ADVICE

The moral is to make it a strict rule never to allow children to eat wild fungi of any kind when out in the country, and not to pick mushrooms yourself unless you really know what you are doing. There are only a very few that are good to eat, compared with the huge numbers that are tasteless, inedible or poisonous, and even these can be dangerous if rotting.

In Britain there is not a strong tradition of fungus eating, but in most other parts of Europe many local people can readily identify those fungi that are worth eating. Local pharmacists often provide an excellent identification service and will give advice. In Britain, field rangers and other people working on national parks and nature reserves can often identify fungi. But you should never take advice from anyone unless you are quite sure they know what they are talking about.

SYMPTOMS

It takes a varying amount of time for symptoms to appear. With the fungus *Amanita Muscari* symptoms appear within one and a half to two hours, but with other fungi it usually takes longer. In some cases symptoms can disappear, only to return. A child who has eaten poisonous fungi may complain of tummy ache. She may be pale, cold and sweating, and may have diarrhoea and vomiting. In the worst cases these symptoms are followed by collapse.

*The innocent-looking death cap mushroom (*Amanita phalloides).

BRIAN HAWKES NATURAL HISTORY PHOTOGRAPHIC AGENCY

CAUSES

There are several toxins that may be present in fungi, but the two most dangerous of these are known as muscarine and phallin. Muscarine affects the activity of the nerve cells, and phallin behaves like snake poison, affecting the nerves to cause

YOUR QUESTIONS

Q I thought all mushrooms were safe to eat after cooking. Is this not right?

A No. There are a very few fungi that are safe to eat when cooked although they are mildly poisonous when raw, but the vast majority of poisonous fungi are equally dangerous raw or cooked.

Q My grandmother used to say that as long as mushrooms turned a silver spoon black when cooking they were not poisonous. Is this true?

A No. This is just an old wives' tale. The golden rule is to avoid eating wild mushrooms unless you are sure you know what they are.

paralysis and acting destructively on the body's cells. The death cap (which contains phallin) eventually kills by destroying the liver and causing general weakening of the whole body, and young children are particularly susceptible to these effects.

TREATMENT

If you know or suspect that your child has fungus poisoning, get her to hospital without delay. If you know what she has been eating, take a sample for identification, and keep a sample of her faeces and vomit, which may also help medical staff to identify the poison.

Hospital treatment will depend on the poison and the severity of the symptoms. In some cases an antidote can be given and sometimes a gastric pump will be given to remove the contents of the stomach. In some cases the child may merely be kept under observation, but in severe cases the child may have to be put on a life support machine and given intensive medical care.

■ TOENAILS

Toenails, like fingernails, are made of keratin (a type of protein that also forms the outer layer of skin and the hair). They grow from a tuck in the skin, which is in turn covered by a small patch of skin. This area is called the matrix. If the matrix is seriously damaged, your child may lose her whole nail but if the rest of the nail-bed (the part you can see under the nail) is damaged the effects will be less serious.

The growth and appearance of the nails is affected by a person's health. If your child is ill, her nails will not grow well. This is especially true if she is malnourished in any way. Iron deficiency in particular makes the nails become soft and concave rather than convex.

COMMON PROBLEMS

Many children suffer from split toenails. There is no obvious cause for this but keeping the child's

---

TOENAIL CARE

- Use small, blunt-ended baby scissors to cut your baby or young child's toenails.
- Always cut your child's toenails straight across and not too short.
- Cut your child's toenails regularly and don't let them get too long. It is often easiest to get into the habit of doing this once a week after a bath.
- Check shoes, tights and socks regularly to make sure they are not too tight.

---

toenails short and cutting them regularly may help prevent them splitting.

The skin at the side of the nails is easily damaged, especially if your child picks at her toenails. As a result the skin may become infected and pus can build up round the nail, causing a throbbing pain. If the infection gets between the nail and the nail-bed a small abscess may form, and unless this is treated fairly quickly it may spread so that part of the nail may have to be removed.

TREATMENT

It is not advisable to try to drain away pus yourself as you can easily dam-

If toenails are not regularly cut, they can sometimes dig into the skin causing bleeding.

IAN WEST/BUBBLES

---

age the nail-bed. If your child complains of a throbbing pain and you can see pus under the skin, apply a warm compress to help bring the pus to a head.

The pus may then drain away by itself, but if this does not happen take your child to the doctor who will probably lance the swelling under local anaesthetic to drain away the pus. Protect your child's toe with a thick pad of cotton wool and a plaster. If the infection is severe, your doctor may prescribe a course of

INGROWING TOENAILS

Ingrowing toenails occur most commonly in the big toe when the nail fails to grow straight out from the nail-bed but instead curves over into the side of the toe. This is more likely to happen if your child's toes are broad and plump, if her toenails are cut down at the sides rather than straight across, if her toenails are small or if her socks or shoes are too tight. If an ingrowing toenail is left untreated, the nail will dig into the skin at the side of the toe which will become inflamed and infected and there may be a discharge of pus round the edges.

If your child develops an ingrowing toenail which has not yet penetrated the skin, consult a chiropodist who may cut a tiny v-shape in the top edge of the nail to relieve pressure on the sides and apply an antiseptic cream to the sides to prevent infection. If you notice any signs of redness or pus, consult your doctor who may prescribe antibiotics to clear up the infection and antiseptic cream for the skin.

If the problem keeps on recurring your child may need a minor operation to remove the ingrowing edge of the toenail.

antibiotics and if it keeps recurring he may refer your child to a dermatologist who will check to see whether she has a fungal infection.

BRUISES

At some stage in her life your child may bruise the skin under her toenails, perhaps by dropping a heavy object on her foot. This can be extremely painful as the toes are richly supplied with nerves. If she bruises the skin under her nail badly enough to make it bleed it will hurt a lot as the bruised area swells up against the immovable nail. You can help by putting her toe under the cold water tap as fast as possible and keeping it there for about ten minutes. This will help to keep the small blood vessels closed and let as little blood as possible seep under the injured nail.

If there is still a lot of blood under the nail and your child is in a lot of pain, take her to your doctor or the nearest hospital accident and emergency department. The doctor may make a small hole to release the blood and relieve the pressure, which is effective only if it is done within about an hour of the injury.

YOUR QUESTIONS

Q My son dropped a heavy box on his foot which bruised the skin under his toe. I took him to the doctor, who said that it would be painful for a while but the bruise would eventually fade away. Is there any chance that my son might lose his toenail?

A If the matrix (the tuck in the skin where the nail grows from) is damaged, there is always a possibility of losing the toenail which is why it is always best to consult your doctor if your child injures a toenail or fingernail. However, as your doctor has been able to reassure you that the injury is not too serious you need not worry in your son's case.

■ TONSILLITIS

Tonsillitis is an inflammation and swelling of the tonsils. It is not usually serious, but it can lead to complications, especially if it occurs frequently. It generally makes the child feel ill enough to spend time in bed.

SYMPTOMS

The main symptom of tonsillitis is a sudden very sore throat, which can cause the child to have a high temperature and to vomit. Within a few hours, the child is very listless and is usually in considerable pain. There may also be difficulty in swallowing food if the child still feels like eating.

If you feel the child's neck you will probably find that the glands are swollen at the sides of the neck and around the chin. You may be able to feel hard little nodules and the whole area around the ears and jaw-line may feel tender to the touch.

Inside the throat the child's tonsils will be enlarged and inflamed, and may be covered in yellow spots. The adenoids (see ADENOIDS), although they are less easily visible, will also be inflamed. (You will be able to see the throat more clearly if you get the child to say 'ah' while you hold her tongue down with the handle of a small spoon and shine a torch into the throat.)

CAUSES

Tonsillitis is caused by an infection. This may be viral or bacterial and can be very contagious, so that a child with tonsillitis should be kept away from other children to avoid spreading the infection.

TREATMENT

Call your doctor if your child shows symptoms of tonsillitis with high fever. Meanwhile, give her plenty of fluids to drink and keep her temperature down by giving her paracetamol and by sponging with tepid water. She will probably feel like going to bed, but if she does not, she should be kept warm and stay indoors.

The doctor will examine her throat and check to make sure that the infection has not spread to the ears. He or she may also take a swab from the child's throat to be sent for analysis to find out exactly what the infection is.

You will probably be advised to give the child paracetamol in the appropriate form and dose for her age to keep the fever under control, and the doctor may prescribe antibiotics for the infection if it is caused by bacteria. If the child has no appetite there is no need to worry about her not eating so long as she has plenty of fluids, but she may find that yoghurt and ice cream are soothing to her throat. As her appetite returns she will find it easier to swallow puréed foods at first.

If your child is beset with attacks of tonsillitis over a couple of years your doctor may advise you that she should have her tonsils removed (tonsillectomy). This involves a stay of two or three days in hospital and a recovery period of about two weeks. The operation is quite straightforward, although the child's throat will be raw for a while afterwards. Even though this operation is now performed much less commonly than it once was, it is still considered the best solution to repeated attacks of tonsillitis. The body functions perfectly well without tonsils.

YOUR QUESTIONS

Q Why does the doctor examine a child's ears when she has the symptoms of tonsillitis?

A This is because infection can easily spread from the throat, via the Eustachian tube, into the cavity of the middle ear to cause middle ear infection (otitis media). If untreated, infections of the middle ear can be troublesome at a later date and it is therefore important for the doctor to check for it.

■ TONSILS

See also TONSILLITIS

The tonsils are glandular tissues at each side of the back of the throat. They are one of the first stages in the body's fight against infection, as they trap harmful organisms before they can pass into the airways.

Sore throats are often caused by inflamed tonsils, but when the tonsils are badly inflamed this is known as 'tonsillitis' – something which young children are likely to suffer from (*see* separate entry).

The tonsils reach their largest size in life when a child is six or seven years old, and after this they gradually become slightly smaller.

■ TOOTHACHE
See DENTAL CARE, DENTIST

■ TOXOCARIASIS

Many doctors now think that toxocariasis (an infection caught from the roundworm that lives in the intestines of some dogs and cats) is more common than was previously assumed. Some believe that as many as one in fifty people either is or has been infected with the worm. *Toxocara canis* (the dog roundworm) and *Toxocara cati* (cat roundworm) have been implicated in causing or aggravating asthma, epilepsy, liver damage, polio and eye diseases.

SYMPTOMS

Children suffering from toxocariasis rarely show any specific symptoms of the infection. The illness is usually mild, with symptoms such as loss of appetite, a slight temperature, recurrent abdominal pains or unexplained skin rashes. However, toxocariasis occasionally causes eye disease leading to loss of sight.

CAUSES

Toxocariasis is caused by the toxocara worm (roundworm) that lives in the intestine of some dogs and cats. The worm's eggs are passed out in the animal's faeces (stools), take two weeks to mature and can remain alive in soil or grass for up to two years. These eggs are very sticky and can attach themselves to your child's fingers, shoes, toys or clothes. If he then puts his fingers or another contaminated item into his mouth he may then swallow the eggs. Children who play in public parks are particularly at risk and toxocariasis is most likely to affect babies and toddlers because of their habit of putting things in their mouths.

The swallowed eggs hatch out and the worms burrow through the intestinal wall into the body, to be carried in the bloodstream to the lungs and other parts of the body. Your child will then cough them up from his lungs and may swallow them again when they will develop in the intestine leading to recurrent infestation.

TREATMENT

If your child shows any of the symptoms listed above or if he seems off-colour and has been playing on land where animals exercise regularly or has been playing with your pet, consult your doctor. He or she will examine your child and take a blood sample for laboratory analysis. If there is evidence of toxocariasis, your doctor may prescribe an antiparasitic drug and advise you to keep your child away from animals and infected areas. Your vet can help you keep your pets worm-free.

PREVENTING TOXOCARIASIS

You can help protect your child by:

• making sure he always washes his hands before meals and after playing with animals. (Carry a supply of moist wipes when you are out)

• making sure your toddler does not swallow soil or grass

• worming your dog or cat regularly and training it to use a special toilet area away from where your child plays. If an animal has defecated where your child plays, disinfect the area thoroughly

• using the areas in public parks where dogs are not allowed and keeping your child away from heavily fouled verges

• keeping sandpits covered when your child is not playing there.

Most puppies have roundworms. Make sure yours is treated before bringing it into your home.

CAMILLA JESSEL

YOUR QUESTIONS

Q I have heard that toxocariasis can cause blindness in children and I'm worried about letting my daughter play in the park as so many dogs roam and are exercised there. Can you tell me if she is really at risk?

A Toxocariasis can in very rare cases cause blindness when a worm lodges in the eye but the chances of this happening are so remote that it would be a shame to stop your child enjoying herself in the park. Perhaps you could compromise by keeping to the area where dogs are not allowed, and making sure she washes her hands after she touches an animal. You could also petition your local authority for more dog-free areas.

■ TOXOPLASMOSIS

Toxoplasmosis is a parasitic infection passed from animals to humans, most commonly via kittens. Your child is especially likely to catch it if she is given a new kitten to play with and does not observe the normal rules of hygiene.

Many people have toxoplasmosis without realizing it and the disease is not dangerous for a normal healthy adult or child but it can have very serious effects on an unborn child if a woman catches it while she is pregnant. Once a person has had the disease he or she is protected for life; however, if the immune system is damaged, as for instance in AIDS, toxoplasmosis can become fatal.

SYMPTOMS

These are usually very slight and include: swollen glands; excessive tiredness; headache; sore throat; aching muscles; and fever. In a few cases toxoplasmosis causes an illness like glandular fever.

TOXOPLASMOSIS IN PREGNANCY

In some countries pregnant women are given a routine blood test for toxoplasmosis either once or several times during pregnancy but in many other countries including Britain, such tests are not normally carried out unless there is a strong reason to suspect you may have the disease.

Toxoplasmosis is dangerous if caught during pregnancy because if so it can lead to miscarriage or stillbirth, or to a baby being born with severe handicaps including hydrocephalus (excess fluid in the brain), brain lesions (scarring of the brain tissue) – both of which can lead to severe mental retardation – epilepsy and chorioretinitis (damage to the retina at the back of the eye which causes blindness). If a woman is infected with toxoplasmosis before pregnancy there is no danger.

If you are diagnosed as having caught toxoplasmosis during pregnancy it does not necessarily follow that your baby will also be affected. But approximately 40 per cent of foetuses of recently infected mothers are infected, and with infections occurring early in pregnancy ten per cent of babies may be seriously damaged. However, if you conceive long after infection your baby will not be affected.

If you are at the beginning of an infection when you conceive you will be given an antibiotic which helps to prevent infection passing to the unborn baby. You may suffer side effects including rashes, nausea and/or vomiting and you will have to carry on taking the drug until your baby is born. This antibiotic reduces the risk of the baby becoming

infected by two-thirds and also significantly reduces the chances of severe damage should your baby be one of those to be infected. You may also be offered the option of terminating the pregnancy as there can be no guarantee that your baby will not be affected. Discuss all the options fully with your family doctor.

If you decide to continue with your pregnancy you will be offered an amniocentesis and umbilical cord sampling test at between 20 and 22 weeks of pregnancy to find out whether the baby is affected. The doctor will also carry out an ultrasound scan to see whether the baby has any visible abnormalities, in particular hydrocephalus.

If the tests do not show that the baby is affected, you will carry on taking the antibiotics and will be offered further tests later in your pregnancy. If the baby is affected you will be given a further mixture of drugs in the second half of your pregnancy which have been proved to reduce damage to the baby. These drugs do have side-effects for the majority of mothers and babies. The main one is to slow down the production of white cells in the bone marrow so that your baby may be born more prone to infection. The drugs are not given in the first three months of pregnancy as they can affect the development of the foetus but are generally taken together with other drugs to counteract the side effects in the second half of pregnancy.

After your baby is born her blood will be tested to discover if she is infected. If so she will have to take drugs for a year and will then be completely cured.

A KNAPP-BUBBLES

If you have a pet dog it is easy to train him as a puppy not to lick the faces of your children.

■ TRAVEL SICKNESS

Many people – adults and children alike – will be sick on a rough sea crossing, but it is common for young children to be so badly affected by travel sickness that any journey whether by bus, boat, train, car or coach, becomes an almost intolerable trial for the whole family.

CAUSES

Doctors do not know exactly why travel sickness happens, but it is thought to be a consequence of upsetting the delicate balance mechanism in the inner ear. This balance may be more sensitive in young children, and certainly most do grow out of travel sickness as they get older. Travel sickness may start when your child is very young, possibly before the age of six months, or it may not become apparent until she is older, perhaps nearer two years old. However, once your child starts to feel, or be, sick on most journeys, the sickness will probably continue until she reaches puberty and then will probably start to decrease.

The type of motion can have an effect on the severity of the sickness. Rough choppy movements often make a child less sick than smooth rolling ones, which is why more people are sick on boats than trains.

PREVENTION

Folk remedies abound for the prevention of travel sickness, including hanging a chain from the back of the car and sitting your child on brown paper. It is probably worth giving these a try as they certainly won't do any harm, but don't be too surprised if they do not work for your child. Some people also swear by special wrist bands that are supposed to act on acupuncture pressure points to prevent sickness. Again, these may work for your child.

You can buy various over-the-

CAUSES

Toxoplasmosis is caused by *Toxoplasma gondii*, a parasite that normally lives in the intestines of dogs, cats and other animals. It is caught by touching infected animals or their droppings, or by eating infected meat that has not been cooked properly. For safety, beef should reach a temperature of 70°C (160°F) throughout, lamb 80°C (175°F) and pork 85°C (180°F).

TREATMENT

Your doctor will prescribe drugs.

PREVENTION

Good hygiene is the best form of prevention. Teach your child always to wash her hands before eating and after touching pets and other animals. Make sure you do the same, and also before and after handling food. Do not handle raw meat without washing your hands immediately afterwards, and keep raw meat out of contact with other foods. Keep pet bowls and utensils separate from those used by humans, and use a separate brush or cloth to wash them.

Don't let your children play with your pets' food or drink or in areas where animals are fed or defecate. While you don't need to stop your children stroking their pets, don't let them kiss them or touch their rear ends, and make sure they always wash their hands after stroking any animal.

YOUR QUESTIONS

Q I was diagnosed as having toxoplasmosis in my last pregnancy and an ultrasound scan showed that my baby had hydrocephalus (excess fluid on the brain) so I reluctantly decided to have a termination. My doctor tells me that it is safe to try for another baby, but will the same thing happen again?

A If you have lost a baby through toxoplasmosis or have given birth to an infected baby, it is extremely unlikely to happen again in a future pregnancy as your high level of antibodies will protect you and a future baby from a further, fresh infection. However, many doctors recommend waiting about a year before becoming pregnant again. Discuss the subject again with your doctor to set your mind at rest.

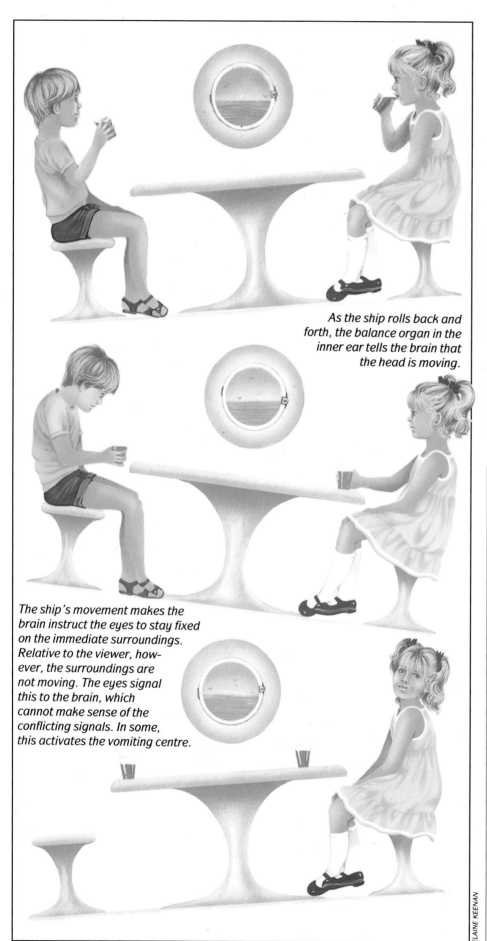

As the ship rolls back and forth, the balance organ in the inner ear tells the brain that the head is moving.

The ship's movement makes the brain instruct the eyes to stay fixed on the immediate surroundings. Relative to the viewer, however, the surroundings are not moving. The eyes signal this to the brain, which cannot make sense of the conflicting signals. In some, this activates the vomiting centre.

ELAINE KEENAN

counter medicines to take to prevent travel sickness, but it is advisable to consult your doctor first as some may have unpleasant side-effects such as a very dry mouth and overwhelming drowsiness. If you do give your child medicines, always follow the instructions carefully and make sure you give them at the recommended time in advance of the journey.

If you know that one form of travel, for example a boat journey, is more likely to make your child sick, try to choose an alternative, perhaps a combination of train and air. If you are driving, your child may be less sick if you can avoid routes and times when there will be a lot of stopping and starting. Driving at night on motorways may be best.

Eating a large greasy meal before a journey increases the likelihood of travel sickness, as does travelling on an empty stomach, so aim to have a light non-greasy meal beforehand and take a plentiful supply of plain

WATCHPOINTS

• Sadly there have been tragic cases of children leaping out of their car in order to avoid vomiting in it and being killed because their own car was moving fast or they leapt into the stream of oncoming traffic. If your child can undo her own seat belt, have childproof locks fitted to the rear doors and make sure she always has a supply of plastic bags or a bowl to throw up in. Keep an eye on your child while she is being sick and remember that plastic bags can suffocate.

• Never show annoyance when your child is sick — she cannot help it.

• After she has been sick encourage your child to sip some water slowly and offer her a mint sweet to suck to take away the taste.

• Keep a supply of damp flannels and cloths to clean up.

DISTRACTION

Although travel sickness is not all in the mind, it can be made worse by the emotions. Once your child has started to feel sick it will be almost impossible to take her mind off it, but you may be able to prevent an attack by distracting her with games, a walk on deck if you are on a ship or simply by maintaining an interesting conversation.

water, plain biscuits and glucose sweets for the journey. Avoid fizzy drinks as these can make sickness worse.

Try to keep your child as still as possible as her own motion may make her sickness worse. Make sure a younger child is always securely fastened in her own car seat and an older one firmly strapped in her seat belt so that she does not roll with the movement of the car on corners. Leaning her head against a cushion may also help as it has been found that travelling with the head tilted back, as if in a dentist's chair, disturbs the balance of the ears least. Try to keep her mind off being sick as dwelling on it is more likely to make her sick and don't keep asking her if she feels all right.

Reading in cars can make even the best traveller feel sick, so provide

YOUR QUESTIONS

Q My four-year-old son suffers from car sickness. Our car has very soft suspension and I've heard that this can make travel sickness worse. Would changing cars help?

A Soft suspension has been blamed for travel sickness, but before you take the drastic step of changing your car, try a journey in a harder sprung car to see if it does make a difference.

your child with alternative entertainment, for example story cassettes and games the whole family can play. Similarly squabbling and fighting among children in the back seat can make sufferers feel worse, as can active play, so it is worth making an effort to keep children quietly occupied on all journeys.

■ TUBERCULOSIS

Tuberculosis, commonly known as TB, was on the decline in the more prosperous parts of the world until recently when cases started increasing again all over the world. For this reason it is now standard practice in many countries to have children immunized. Although tuberculosis can be fatal if untreated, attacks can also be very mild and easy to recover from.

SYMPTOMS

The most common form of tuberculosis begins with what is known as a 'primary focus'. This is a mild attack that has no symptoms at all. The site of infection is usually the lungs, and the primary focus leaves a scar which can be detected by X-ray.

The primary focus gives the child immunity to the infection, but in a few cases, months or even years later a second attack can occur. As the infection runs its course the child can become seriously ill, with loss of weight, and having a fever and nighttime sweats, with coughing and, in more serious cases, spitting of blood. Also in a few cases the primary infection can spread rapidly, giving rise to the same symptoms, in the form that used to be known as 'galloping consumption'.

TYPES OF TUBERCULOSIS

Although tuberculosis usually attacks the lungs (pulmonary tuberculosis), it can also travel round the body in the bloodstream and may affect other organs or may cause little abscesses to form all over the body (miliary tuberculosis). In some forms of the disease the skin of the face is affected and becomes inflamed. The

lymph nodes are often infected and this may cause the lymph nodes in the neck to swell, while with abdominal tuberculosis there are usually few specific symptoms at first — just a general feeling of being unwell and loss of weight. Finally a complication known as tuberculous meningitis can occasionally develop, and this causes symptoms of meningitis with violent headache and fever leading to coma.

CAUSES

Tuberculosis is caused by a bacterium known as *Mycobacterium tuberculosis*. These bacteria thrive in dark, damp, unventilated places and it is partly because of improved housing conditions and improved diet that the disease has become less serious in the developed world.

The bacteria are spread by coughing. A variant form of the bacterium affects cattle and for this reason milk is pasteurized and dairy cattle are tuberculin tested, as drinking milk from cows which have been infected can also cause the disease.

Tests show that many people seem to have been infected with the disease during childhood and to have built up a resistance to it without showing symptoms, or just appearing to have mild flu at the time of the first attack. It seems that the infection develops to become serious only in certain conditions. Typically, bad housing, overcrowded, damp and poorly ventilated accommodation may play a part, perhaps because the germs multiply so much in these conditions. The general health of the child also makes a difference to the incident rate. However, it is usually not possible to find out how a child catches tuberculosis; and even very healthy and well-nourished children might catch it.

PREVENTION

Babies may be given the BCG vaccine (to prevent TB) as newborns or within the first six weeks. All children are tested at school at 11-13 years of age, and those with no resistance to TB are given the BCG vaccination

The progress of pulmonary tuberculosis

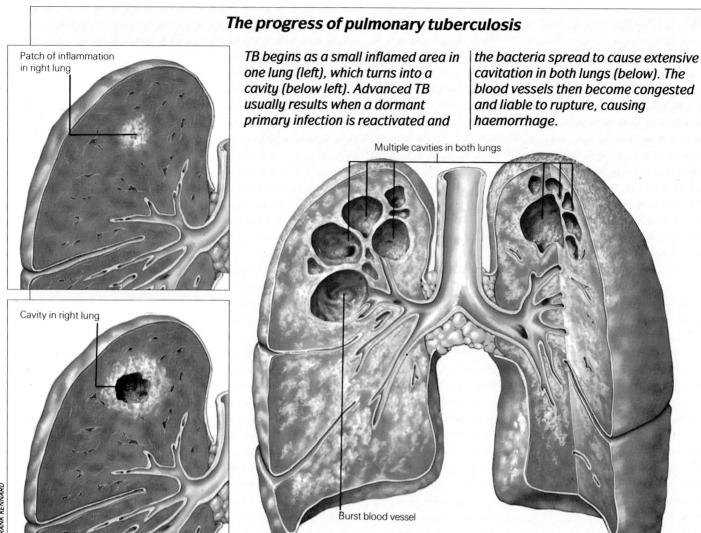

Patch of inflammation in right lung

Cavity in right lung

FRANK KENNARD

TB begins as a small inflamed area in one lung (left), which turns into a cavity (below left). Advanced TB usually results when a dormant primary infection is reactivated and the bacteria spread to cause extensive cavitation in both lungs (below). The blood vessels then become congested and liable to rupture, causing haemorrhage.

Multiple cavities in both lungs

Burst blood vessel

which gives a high level of immunity. There are no harmful side effects, and as the level of immunity given is the same as the natural immunity found in anyone who has had the disease, there will be little risk of the child developing a serious form of illness. Children thought to be at special risk may be tested and vaccinated when younger. The main source of prevention is through providing good housing and making sure that children are healthy and well fed. Parents must also make sure that they report to the doctor immediately if their child has been in contact with anyone suffering from the disease.

TREATMENT

Although tuberculosis often used to be fatal it is now nearly always successfully treated by modern drugs, despite the fact that some forms are quite serious.

If your doctor suspects that your child has tuberculosis he or she will send her for a series of tests, starting with a skin test to see whether the disease is present, and including X-rays and other tests to see where the disease has settled. In most cases, however, it should be possible for the child to be treated and cared for at home.

Before antibiotics were introduced, the only hope for a cure was rest, good air and a healthy diet, and even now these continue to play an important part. However the main treatment is by antibiotics, of which there are several types available. It will be two to three weeks before the child is well enough to return to school, so it may be a good idea to get in plenty of books and videos to amuse her. She will be allowed to have her friends to visit her as she will not be infectious 72 hours after being treated, and she will appreciate being able to have visitors of her own age.

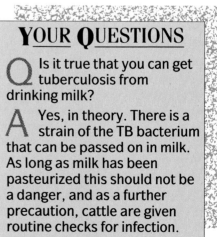

YOUR QUESTIONS

Q Is it true that you can get tuberculosis from drinking milk?

A Yes, in theory. There is a strain of the TB bacterium that can be passed on in milk. As long as milk has been pasteurized this should not be a danger, and as a further precaution, cattle are given routine checks for infection.

■ TUMMY ACHE

See also COLIC, GASTRO-ENTERITIS, WIND

Tummy ache is a very common complaint among children. Most of the time there is nothing seriously wrong, and the pain goes away quite quickly without treatment.

C A U S E S

There are many possible causes of tummy ache, which may occur on its own or together with other symptoms.

'WIND'

When it comes on its own the pain is usually caused by straightforward indigestion or 'wind'. Some doctors think this happens when the child has been eating too quickly and has swallowed air with his food. The child

JACQUI FARROW/BUBBLES

may also have eaten something to cause 'wind': certain foods create a lot of gas as they are broken down in the intestines and can cause 'wind' or tummy ache. Beans are notorious for this, and cabbage, broccoli, sprouts and leeks can also have the same effect. Anxiety or stress can also cause tummy aches, which may account for tummy aches experienced when the child goes to a new school, changes class or is anxious about real or apparent instabilities at home, or even when he has been over-excited — perhaps about Christmas or about his own or a friend's birthday party.

GASTROENTERITIS

Tummy ache in children may also be accompanied by vomiting or diarrhoea — usually both. This is generally a sign of gastroenteritis — an infection of the digestive tract caused by a virus or by bacteria. Although gastroenteritis is rarely very serious in adults, the younger the child, the more it is potentially dangerous in children. Babies in particular can soon become seriously dehydrated through gastroenteritis.

RECURRENT TUMMY ACHE

Some children suffer from what is sometimes known as 'abdominal

When your child has a tummy upset, hygiene is of prime importance. Teach him to wash his hands every time he uses his potty and wash his bottom, then ensure that the potty is thoroughly cleaned out after each use.

migraine'. Every few weeks the child complains of a pain right in the middle of the tummy and may even need to lie down. There is no known medical cause for this (although of course tests will be made to eliminate other causes) and the child usually eventually grows out of it.

WHEN TO CALL THE DOCTOR

Although parents should always be guided by their own knowledge of the child, the following are indications that medical help is needed when the child has tummy ache:

- acute abdominal pain which persists or becomes worse during a period of two to three hours
- acute abdominal pain with vomiting, diarrhoea or fever
- blood in the stools or in the urine
- weight loss with recurrent pains
- rashes, fever, stiff neck or inability to stand bright lights accompanied by abdominal pain
- dry cough or breathing problems accompanied by abdominal pain
- pain accompanying any problems with passing water.

BABIES AND TUMMY ACHE

It is hard to tell whether a baby has tummy ache, but if the child is crying and upset and you cannot see what is wrong, then this is a likely explanation. If there are no other symptoms, the problem may be wind or colic (see separate entries). But if the baby is vomiting or has diarrhoea, medical help should be sought if the symptoms have not passed within a few hours.

SERIOUS ILLNESSES

Several serious illnesses can cause tummy ache, although in this case the pain will usually be severe and will recur or persist over several hours. If a child has a bad pain for six hours or so the situation needs medical attention urgently.

Possible causes include **appendicitis** (the pain will probably move from the navel to low down at the right side of the abdomen; it will probably be accompanied by slight fever, loss of appetite and either constipation or diarrhoea); **strangulated inguinal hernia** (there will probably be tenderness and swelling in the groin — this affects mainly boys); **blockage in the intestines** (this is usually accompanied by vomiting of greenish or yellowish matter). In babies and very young children pain in the tummy can be a sign of **intussusception** (when the child will probably pass red, jelly-like motions). **Kidney disorders** and even **urinary infections** also cause tummy pain (often with fever and vomiting).

Other illnesses, not related to the bowels, can cause abdominal pain. These include **pneumonia, meningitis** and **diabetes.** In these illnesses the pain will often be incapacitating and there will be other symptoms which you are not likely to overlook.

T R E A T M E N T

Although in most cases a child's tummy ache is not a sign of anything serious, you should always seek your

WATCHPOINTS

Severe tummy ache can be caused by food poisoning. Make sure that you always prepare children's food in hygienic conditions, always keep food and milk in the fridge, and above all, always sterilize babies' teats and feeding bottles carefully before use.

doctor's advice if you are in doubt. The box (p.293) gives guidelines as to when medical attention may be needed, but if your child's symptoms worry you, speak to your doctor. Remember that the younger the child, the more swiftly symptoms can become serious.

If the doctor finds anything amiss he or she may send the child to hospital for further tests, and if the child is found to have a condition that needs hospital treatment then this will be given. If the child has gastroenteritis the doctor will advise you on how to nurse him in bed, and may prescribe oral rehydration powders to prevent the child from becoming dehydrated.

HOME TREATMENT

Tummy ache due to one of the minor causes, responds quickly to home treatment. First get the child to go to the lavatory, as passing a motion often brings relief. Sipping hot water and holding a warm, wrapped hot-water bottle against the tummy also help in the case of minor tummy aches, and such cases should be better in two to three hours. Do not give a child a hot-water bottle if the pain is severe, as the treatment is not to be recommended for more serious conditions such as appendicitis.

■ TYPHOID FEVER

This infectious disease (not to be confused with typhus) is still prevalent in most tropical countries. When travelling abroad with your child, you should always check with your doctor in good time (at least six weeks before you travel) to see whether the typhoid prophylaxis vaccination is needed.

S Y M P T O M S

For the first week or two after contracting the disease the person affected shows no symptoms. The disease then breaks out in the form of a severe fever and general illness, the precise nature of which depends on which parts of the body are being

PARATYPHOID FEVER

There are several forms of paratyphoid fever, all of which are caused by strains of *Salmonella* bacteria. In some cases the symptoms are like those of typhoid fever, but less severe, and in others there is intense diarrhoea. One type, known as paratyphoid B is quite common in Western Europe, but the types known as paratyphoid A and paratyphoid C are tropical diseases. Paratyphoid comes half way between food poisoning and typhoid fever proper in severity.

attacked by the bacteria responsible.

The small intestine is always affected, and this causes digestive upsets, which are more likely to be in the form of constipation but which sometimes cause diarrhoea. Within a week of the fever breaking out the child will come out in a rash of pink spots.

If the disease is not treated it usually attacks the spleen and the bones, but the bacteria can attack anywhere in the body, and any organ can become infected. Severe damage can be done to the blood vessels in the intestine, and peritonitis can result from perforation of the wall of the intestine. Typhoid fever can be fatal if not treated.

C A U S E S

Typhoid fever is caused by one of the many types of *Salmonella* bacteria — a strain known as *Salmonella typhi.* The bacteria only live on human beings, but they can also survive on food or in water. The disease can be contracted by direct contact with people who already have it, but it can also be caught from infected food or water. Food and water can be contaminated through the excrement of someone carrying typhoid and also by flies which have picked up the bacteria from human excrement. In

The typhoid organism is carried in human faeces, which in unsanitary surroundings, like this street market in Bangladesh, can contaminate food and water. There are far fewer typhoid epidemics in the west because of higher standards of hygiene and sanitation.

HUTCHISON LIBRARY

germs can be found. The source of the infection is then located.

TREATMENT

You should always consult your doctor if your child develops a high fever (39°C/102.4°F) that does not go down after tepid sponging, or if the child has a lower fever that does not go down within two or three days. If you have recently returned from a trip abroad, typhoid fever may be suspected and the doctor will have tests done.

If the child is found to be suffering from typhoid fever she will be kept in isolation in hospital and treated with antibiotics. As long as the illness has been detected in time there should be a full recovery, but the younger the child the greater the dangers. Prevention, and prompt action if there is any reason to suspect that the child has contracted the disease, are essential.

YOUR QUESTIONS

Q Is typhoid fever the same as typhus?

A No. Although typhus, like typhoid fever, causes a high fever it is caused by completely different bacteria known as *Rickettsiae* which are passed to human beings by lice, fleas, ticks or mites. Sometimes called spotted fever or epidemic fever, typhus mostly occurs in epidemics during times of war or famine, or following on from natural disasters such as earthquakes due to breakdown of proper sanitation.

many hot countries poor sanitation and heat provide the ideal conditions in which the bacteria can spread and multiply.

The bacteria first settle and multiply in the small intestine, and at this stage they cause no symptoms. When the fever and other symptoms occur, this is a sign that *Salmonella typhi* have entered the bloodstream and are circulating round the body.

PREVENTION

In countries where typhoid fever is prevalent, people can often carry the disease without showing any symp-toms. However visitors from other countries who have not previously been exposed to the disease will usually be severely affected if they come into contact with it, and children are particularly vulnerable both to catching the disease and to showing severe and life-threatening symptoms. Protection can easily be given by vaccination.

DIAGNOSIS

The symptoms of typhoid fever are similar to those of most other fevers. Typhoid fever is identified through laboratory analysis of a blood sample, in which *Salmonella typhi*

■ TYPHUS

Typhus, or epidemic typhus (not to be confused with typhoid fever) is a lice-borne disease which can spread rapidly in certain circumstances, giving rise to epidemics.

SYMPTOMS

The main symptom of the disease is a high fever which comes on very suddenly. The patient feels very ill and has muscular aches and pains and a headache. Three to four days after the fever begins there is a rash of small, flat spots, which after a week begin to darken and look like little bruises. At this point the patient can sink into a stupor, a cough develops, the kidneys may fail and the rash may become haemorrhagic. If no treatment is available the patient may die.

There are other, less severe, forms of typhus. These include murine typhus and scrub typhus, and the closely related tick fevers and Rocky Mountain spotted fever, all of which also cause a high fever.

CAUSES

Epidemic typhus is caused by bacteria (*Rickettsia prowazekii*) which are transmitted by human lice. In other forms of typhus the bacteria responsible are carried by tics, fleas or mites that live on rats and other rodents. Lice-borne typhus is only found when people have to live in close proximity and without facilities for hygiene — usually during times of disaster. It can break out anywhere in the world during the right circumstances, while the other forms usually break out in hot countries or localized areas and do not cause epidemics.

PREVENTION

It is possible to some extent to control the pests that carry typhus. However to protect yourself and family, if you are travelling to an area where typhus may occur it is possible to have a vaccination against the disease before going.

API/GAMMA/FRANK SPOONER PICTURES

TREATMENT

There are several drugs that successfully treat typhus, among them tetracycline and chloramphenicol.

YOUR QUESTIONS

Q How do lice spread typhus?

A Lice become infected by biting people who already have typhus and the typhus bacteria are then found in the lice's faeces, which are often deposited on the skin when the louse bites. Scratching the itch can rub the bacteria into the skin. Symptoms break out about ten days later.

■ UNCONSCIOUSNESS

See also CONVULSIONS, DIABETES, FAINTING

People made homeless by earthquake or war have to live in temporary camps without proper sanitation — ideal conditions for epidemic typhus.

Unconsciousness ranges in severity from a fleeting faint to a life-threatening coma. A child who is unconscious shows no awareness of his surroundings and cannot be roused. The condition arises because of changes in the brain caused by any of a variety of reasons.

The brain's activity can be measured as electrical impulses on a machine called an electroencephalograph (EEG). The impulses are presented as wave patterns, which vary considerably according to the degree of consciousness or unconsciousness. When someone is unconscious there are about three large waves a second, and as consciousness returns the waves increase in frequency until the pattern is a rapidly changing ten waves per second for a fully conscious person.

SYMPTOMS

A child who is unconscious may simply be in a light faint from which she quickly recovers. If more deeply unconscious, she cannot be roused, and when she eventually does come round she may be confused and

If the child is not breathing after an accident, artificial respiration should be given without delay.

dazed, with no memory of where she is or what has happened. The state is medically known as a coma and in a deep coma all the normal reflexes are suppressed, so that, for example, the child would not automatically cough to clear her throat to stop her from swallowing blood or vomit after an accident.

We have all heard of cases where a child has been in a coma for days or weeks or longer after a bad accident. In most cases the child will recover within minutes. But unconsciousness is always serious and should be reported to the family doctor.

CAUSES

There are many possible causes of unconsciousness. It can be caused by a head injury or by shock due to blood loss as the result of an injury or to loss of body fluids during an illness or in extreme heat. Pressure on the brain caused by infections, bleeding or an abscess or tumour can cause unconsciousness, as can poisoning or lack of sugar in the blood.

Children who are hypoglycaemic (suffer from low blood sugar level) may fall into a coma during attacks,

WATCHPOINTS

If the child has been injured in an accident do not move her unless you are sure of what you are doing. It is dangerous to move anyone with internal or spinal injury.

as do children suffering from diabetes if given too much insulin. Children who have epileptic convulsions often have a brief period of unconsciousness after an attack and, strictly speaking they are unconscious while having convulsions, even though they are moving.

Fainting is a very light form of unconsciousness brought on by reduction in the blood supply to the brain (*see* separate entry).

TREATMENT

All cases of unconsciousness, apart from passing faints, need medical attention. If you find a child in a state of unconsciousness, the first thing to do is to remove any danger, and check for breathing and heartbeat.

EMERGENCY ACTION

If the child has been poisoned by gas, remove him to the fresh air if possible, or at least turn off the gas and open doors and windows. If he has been strangled, remove whatever is round his neck, if possible by cutting it away. If he is suffocating with his head inside a plastic bag, of course remove the bag (this is best done by tearing or cutting open the bag), and if he is having an electric shock, separate him from, or turn off, the appliance.

FIRST AID

Next clear the child's airway of any blockage, such as food or vomit, by drawing your finger quickly round the inside of the mouth, and staunch any bleeding. Check for breathing by putting your face to the child's mouth to listen and feel for breathing and by watching to see if his chest is rising and falling. If he is not breathing, check the pulse.

If the child is not breathing, give artificial respiration (see p.17) and if in addition his heart is not beating, give cardiac massage (p.39).

If he does not need this treatment, put the child in the recovery position (p.115). Meanwhile, if possible get someone to call an ambulance while you take care of the child. If there is no-one else there, wait until the

heartbeat and breathing are restored before putting the child in the recovery position and calling help. Keep the child warm and be ready to reassure him if he comes round before professional help arrives.

If your child suffers from epilepsy you will get to know what the normal pattern of attacks is, and if it is usual for the child to remain unconscious for a while after an attack there is no need to call your doctor when this happens. However medical attention

YOUR QUESTIONS

Q I have heard that it is possible to have an injury which does not make you unconscious at the time but which 'knocks you out' later. Is this true?

A Yes. A blow to the head can cause haemorrhages within the skull that result in unconsciousness some time later. This will often be preceded by sickness and headaches. If your child ever complains of feeling unwell after being hit on the head or after hitting his head in a fall, you should call your doctor. If the child lapses into unconsciousness get him to hospital as soon as possible.

Q My little girl has terrible tempers and then usually passes out. What could this be?

A This sounds like 'breath holding' following a temper tantrum and is not uncommon in children between the ages of one and four. The child usually turns blue in the face and passes out during a fit of crying or rage.

Although these attacks are frightening for parents they are not serious and the child grows out of them. However, you should talk to your family doctor about this and have the condition properly diagnosed.

is needed if the child begins to have further convulsions without regaining consciousness. Place the child in the recovery position during an attack so that her tongue will not roll back and block the airway.

■ UNDESCENDED TESTICLE

A man or boy's testicles are located inside the scrotum (the bag of skin behind the penis). They need to be outside his body in order to develop normally at adolescence and to be able to produce sperm. Sperm can only be produced at a temperature slightly lower than that inside the body. If the testicles, or as more often happens, one testicle, are not in the scrotum but rather in the abdomen (tummy), sperm will not be produced normally and nor will the hormone testosterone which produces the male characteristics such as a beard and a deeper voice.

DEVELOPMENT OF TESTICLES

Before a boy is born his testicles grow and develop inside his abdomen, near the kidneys. They generally move down into their normal position in the scrotum before birth but occasionally this does not happen to one or both of them. This is particularly likely if your baby is born preterm (before his expected date of delivery).

ROUTINE CHECKS

If your son's testicles have not moved down into his scrotum — or if one has but the other has not — this is always

RETRACTILE TESTICLES

A baby boy's testicles are frequently 'retractile' – the doctor can 'milk' them down into the scrotum when examining your baby, but they disappear back into the abdomen of their own accord. They will soon descend of their own accord and remain in the scrotum.

YOUR QUESTIONS

Q When my son was born the doctor who examined him in the hospital said that one of his testicles had not come down into his scrotum. He said that this was nothing to worry about and that my own doctor would keep an eye on my son's development. However, I am concerned that my son may not be able to father children when he grows up. Is this possible?

A The doctor was correct in saying that your son's testicle would probably descend of its own accord. You can check to see if this has happened by feeling his scrotum occasionally. The descended testicle will feel rather like a pea, so see if you can feel the same on the other side. Warm your hands before checking as, if your hands are cold, the testicles may temporarily retract back into his abdomen. If the testicle does not descend by the time your son is a year old, your doctor will probably recommend an operation to bring it down. You need have no worries that this will affect your son in adulthood as both his testicles will develop normally after the operation.

picked up during the routine doctor's examination after your baby's birth. It is nothing to worry about as in the majority of cases the testicle moves down of its own accord within a few months. Undescended testicles do

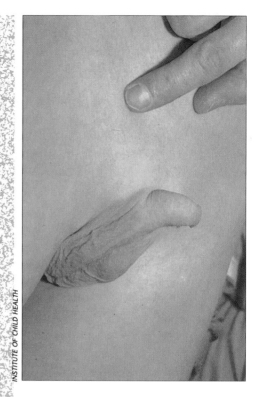

Undescended testicles are operated on to place them in position when the child is a year old.

INSTITUTE OF CHILD HEALTH

not cause problems in childhood but if they have not moved down by the time your son is a year old, he may then need a simple operation to lower them.

MISSING TESTICLE

Very occasionally a boy is born with one testicle completely undeveloped. Your doctor will notice this during routine checks and will probably suggest a false implant when your son gets older to make him look normal. False testicles are not usually implanted in young boys as they would need repeat operations to increase the size as they grow and develop. If your son does need a false testicle the appearance will be exactly as if he had two testicles of his own and the other testicle will produce sperm and testosterone normally.

■ URINARY TRACT INFECTIONS

See also KIDNEYS

The urinary tract consists of the kidneys, which filter waste products out of the blood to form urine, the ureters, through which urine is passed to the bladder, the bladder, where the urine is stored, and the urethra, through which urine is passed out of the body.

In children infections of the urinary tract usually affect the bladder and/or kidneys. Girls are more prone to infections of the urinary tract than are boys, since a girl's urethra is very much shorter than a boy's, and is situated much closer to the anus, so that there can be cross-infection from the bowels.

Even though these infections are usually a minor nuisance rather than a serious illness, they have to be treated promptly as there is a danger of them passing up the urinary tract and affecting the kidneys. If a child suffers repeatedly from infections of the urinary tract this could mean that there is some abnormality which predisposes her to infection and the cause needs to be investigated. The most common childhood urinary tract infection is cystitis which affects the bladder.

SYMPTOMS

Symptoms of infection may show up in the urine itself, which may be cloudy or may have an unpleasant, 'fishy' smell. The child may complain that it hurts to pass water, may want to pass water frequently, or may feel that she needs to empty her bladder

The bacterium E. coli *(below), shown magnified, can cause cystitis.*

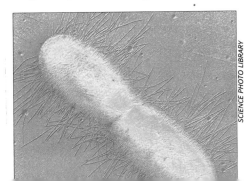

SCIENCE PHOTO LIBRARY

and then find it difficult to do so. She may complain of pain in her tummy or low in the back, and in some cases she may even have a slight fever, feel nauseous or be sick. If a child who has previously been dry suddenly starts to wet the bed, this too could be a sign that there is something wrong. Most commonly the infection will just cause a stinging pain on passing water and the need to do so frequently, but often without producing very much urine.

CAUSES

Infections of the urinary tract are usually caused by bacteria which are perfectly harmless in the bowels, but which cause irritation in the urethra and bladder. These bacteria can be easily transferred to the kidneys. In girls this can happen when the girl wipes her bottom, and in boys it can happen for no apparent reason. Some children have reflux – urine going from the bladder to the kidneys when urine is passed.

TREATMENT

If your child shows any of the symptoms of urinary tract infection she should see the family doctor, as prompt treatment will ensure that the infection does not spread and become more serious. The doctor will probably ask you to collect a sample of the child's urine, which is taken in

YOUR QUESTIONS

Q My little girl has a bladder infection which is causing her to have a pain in her tummy. What can I do?

A Take your daughter to the doctor for treatment if you have not already done so. The doctor may advise you to give the child paracetamol in the appropriate dose for her age to stop the pain for a day or two, but you must be careful not to exceed the recommended dose.

WATCHPOINTS

• To minimize the chance of your child getting an infection of the urinary tract:

• Teach girls to wipe their bottoms from front to back, and teach children of both sexes to wash their hands after defecating.

• Make sure that children do not become constipated as this can interfere with the emptying of the bladder. Give them plenty of fresh fruit and vegetables and other forms of dietary fibre.

• Encourage your child to drink plenty of fluids – particularly plain water, so that the bladder is flushed out regularly and the urine does not become concentrated.

the morning when it is at its most concentrated.

Laboratory tests will show whether there is infection present, and if this is so the doctor will probably prescribe antibiotics to cure it. He or she will also advise you to make sure that the child drinks plenty of fluids to dilute the urine and cause the child to pass water more frequently. This discourages the bacteria from breeding and helps to cure the infection quickly.

If a child frequently has problems with urinary infections, the doctor may refer her to hospital to make sure that there is nothing else wrong.

■ URTICARIA
See HIVES

V

■ VACCINATION
See IMMUNIZATION

■ VERRUCA

Very few children manage to grow up without getting a verruca — a harmless but sometimes painful wart-like growth on the sole of the foot — at some time or other. Eventually the body manages to build up defences against them.

SYMPTOMS

A verruca is a hard, horny wart growing on the sole of the foot, where it is under pressure from standing and walking so that the sensitive nerve-endings under the skin are irritated. For some reason verrucas are usually to be found on the underneath of the heel and on the ball of the foot rather than on the instep. Verrucas are fairly rare in young children but begin to occur when children go to school.

CAUSES

Verrucas, like all warts, are caused by a virus, and the virus finds it particularly easy to enter the skin when it is wet and soft. It is also infectious, and

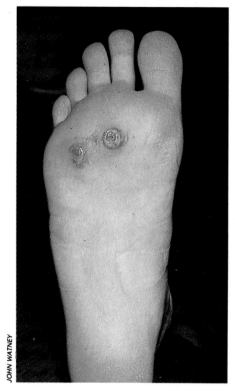

JOHN WATNEY

Verrucas develop on the soles of children's feet, and cause discomfort or even pain.

this is why children tend to pick up verrucas at swimming pools. There are several strains of the virus that causes warts, and verrucas are due to one of these, although the child can have warts from other strains on different parts of the body at the same time.

TREATMENT

Although the body eventually becomes resistant to the viruses that cause verrucas and other warts this can take a long time. This is because they cause so little harm and affect such a small area that they do not provoke the immune system into action in the same way that viruses such as the chickenpox virus, which rapidly affect the whole body, do. When the body finally 'notices' the verruca it shrivels up and disappears as if by magic. But this can be months or even years.

Various treatments are available from the chemist's, all of which involve applying a chemical to the spot and rubbing away the surface as it

gradually dries up and flakes away. The surface of the verruca has to be rubbed down before the treatment (usually containing salicylic acid) is applied, and care has to be taken not to apply the treatment to unaffected skin. The verruca should be covered with a dressing in between treatments, and an emery board is used to sand it down. As deeper layers of the verruca are attacked small, black dots begin to show on what remains of the growth, and when all this abnormal tissue has eventually dried up and been sanded off, the treatment is complete.

MEDICAL TREATMENT

If you are in doubt about whether the growth on your child's foot is a verruca or about how to treat it you should take the child to the family doctor, who may prescribe home treatment and advise you how to apply it. However the doctor may also send your child to an outpatients' department to have the verruca removed surgically under local anaesthetic. This is quite painless once the anaesthetic has been administered, but it can cause a lot of blood loss, and can be quite frightening for a child. With a painful verruca, or one that is resistant to home treatment, however, this may be the

WATCHPOINTS

• Verrucas are infectious. If your child has one make sure that he cannot pass the virus on at the swimming pool by getting him special socks (available from sports shops) to wear when swimming.

• Make sure that your child understands why it is important to use the foot-bath when going to the swimming pool, because if he has a verruca, it will make sure that he doesn't pass the virus on to other children, and if everybody uses it properly there is much less risk of the infection being spread.

YOUR QUESTIONS

Q Is there any way I can prevent my little boy from catching the verruca virus from his big sister?

A Yes. Make sure that your daughter keeps her verruca covered, and that she has her own foot towel which no-one else uses. Also encourage your son to dry his feet thoroughly as soon as he gets out of the bath or finishes washing them as wet skin is more susceptible to the infection. Children should always dry their feet immediately after swimming for this reason.

best solution for the child.

An alternative solution is to take your child to a qualified chiropodist. He or she will probably remove the verruca by applying a gel or lotion to burn it away. The advantage of professional treatment is that you have no fears of the healthy skin surrounding the verruca being damaged.

If the child does not find the verruca painful, there really is no need for treatment at all. It will eventually disappear of its own accord, but you should keep an eye on it to make sure that it is not getting any worse.

■ VITAMINS

Nutritionists are still finding out about vitamins and the role they play in health. Most vitamins are provided by food and cannot be manufactured by the body but we all need the full range of vitamins for our bodies to function properly. The key to making sure that your child has an ample vitamin supply is to provide a varied diet with plenty of fresh fruit, vegetables and fish. If you are making sure that your child has the right diet and are still worried about her health,

WATCHPOINTS

Remember that fruit and vegetables must be fresh. Store in a cool, dark place (eg fridge) and eat soon after buying or picking. Do not overcook. Vitamins are lost in storage and long cooking.

don't dish out vitamin supplements but, instead, take her to the doctor for advice. The government now

VITAMIN	WHAT IT DOES	SOURCE
A (retinol)	Helps with growth and normal vision	Liver, oily fish, dairy products
B complex: **B1** (thiamine)	Helps brain, nerves and muscles to function	Wholemeal cereals and flours, pork, peas, beans
B2 (riboflavin)	Aids production of energy from broken down food	Milk, liver, kidneys, eggs, cheese, green vegetables
B6 (pyridoxine)	Aids production of energy from broken down food	Most foods
B12 (cyano-cobalamin)	Involved in production of red blood cells; keeps nerves healthy	Meat (especially liver), eggs, milk and cheese
Bc (folic acid)	Involved in production of red blood cells	Green, leafy vegetables, liver, kidneys, pulses, oranges, bananas
PP (nicotinic acid)	Helps break down food to provide energy	Wholemeal cereal and bread, fish, meat
C (ascorbic acid)	Aids growth, protects capillaries from haemorrhaging	Fresh fruit (especially oranges, tomatoes, blackcurrants) and vegetables (especially potatoes)
D (calciferol)	Essential for bone development and maintenance	Oily fish, butter, eggs, sunlight
E (tocopherol)	Helps cells remain healthy	Most foods, especially wholegrain cereals, eggs, nuts and vegetable oils
K (phytomena-dione)	Required for blood to clot	Green, leafy vegetables, liver (also produced by the action of bacteria in the gut)

recommends vitamin supplements for breastfeeding mothers and young children up to the age of five. Again, consult your doctor or health visitor for the recommended dose.

REQUIREMENTS

Vitamins are given letters of the alphabet and are known as A, B complex, C, D, E and K. Vitamins D, E and K are soluble only in fat, so fat is

VITAMIN DEFICIENCIES

Although vitamin deficiencies are very rare in developed countries children may suffer from slight deficiencies when illness or the wrong diet prevents them from having enough vitamins. The list below outlines some of the better known symptoms of deficiency:

• Night blindness, rough, dry skin
caused by lack of vitamin A. Severe lack can retard growth.

• Corner of mouth cracks and sores
caused by lack of vitamin B2. Severe lack can cause eye problems and retarded growth.

• Pernicious anaemia
caused by severe lack of vitamin B12 (can be result of vegan diet)

• Growth problems, megaloblastic anaemia
caused by severe lack of folic acid

• Pellagra (dark, scaly skin)
caused by severe lack of nicotinic acid

• Scurvy
caused by severe lack of vitamin C

• Rickets
caused by lack of vitamin D

• Poor blood clotting
caused by lack of vitamin K (can be due to malfunctioning of the intestine)

ALUN DUNS

Fresh fruit and vegetables provide many of the vitamins that are essential for good health.

an important part of your child's diet. The body can produce its own vitamin D through the action of sunlight on the skin, and vitamin K is produced in the intestines, but all the others come from food only. Vitamins A and D are readily stored in the fat tissue of the body, but the other vitamins need to be supplied frequently as they are either not stored at all or stored inefficiently.

It is quite possible to have too much vitamin A and D, but impossible to have too much vitamin C, as excess is excreted. Vegan diets, which avoid dairy products as well as meat, supply little or no vitamin B12, but otherwise a mixed diet supplies all the vitamins.

For a guide to which vitamins are to be found in which types of food, and the role they play see the box on page 301.

■ VOMITING

Being sick seems to be a necessary part of childhood from babyhood onwards and although it is often unpleasant and upsetting for the child it is rarely due to anything seriously wrong. However, depending on the way in which the child is

vomiting and whether there are other symptoms, vomiting can also be a sign of serious illness.

Parents learn to distinguish when their child needs to see the doctor and when the proper care at home is all that's needed. But it is always important to remember that the younger the child the greater the danger from symptoms such as vomiting, diarrhoea and fever unless they clear up straight away.

SYMPTOMS

Babies often dribble back a little milk during and after feeds and this is not true vomiting, but is known as 'possetting'. In true vomiting the contents of the stomach are regurgitated quite forcefully. The child may be unusually pale and quiet for a while beforehand, but often in children, vomiting occurs with very little warning.

CAUSES

The most usual cause of vomiting is irritation of the lining of the stomach, but this can be brought on by a number of different conditions, ranging from gastroenteritis and viral infections to serious conditions such as appendicitis. Overeating and eating contaminated food can also cause stomach irritation and vomiting. But many children also suffer from motion (travel) sickness, with acute vomiting, thought to be caused by confusing messages reaching the brain from the eyes and the centres of balance in the ears. A blow to the head can also cause vomiting, and this is a danger sign that the brain has been injured in some way. Migraines can stimulate vomiting by causing changes in the brain.

TREATMENT

If possible, provide a bucket or bowl for the child to be sick into. If your child is being sick she will find it soothing and reassuring if you hold her forehead as she vomits, and afterwards she needs to be freshened up by having her face wiped with a cool flannel. If she is well enough she should clean her teeth to take away the unpleasant taste, and if she is in bed you can give her a glass of water to rinse her mouth with. Children are often sick quite suddenly, and the child's clothes and bedclothes may need to be changed. Make sure you keep the child well wrapped so that she does not get cold while she is out of bed if this happens. Put a child to bed when she has been sick and give her a bowl to be sick into in case it happens again.

FOOD AND LIQUID

The most important thing, when a child is sick, is to make sure that her fluid intake is high to make up for the fluids lost in vomiting. Give her plenty of water and diluted fruit juice or squash, and if she has been very sick or sick several times add a pinch of salt and a teaspoonful of glucose to plain water and get her to sip this, to make up for the loss of salts and sugars this has caused.

Do not try to make the child eat, but gradually offer her easily digested foods such as thin soups with bits of plain bread floating in them, puréed fruit or vegetables, and yoghurt until her appetite gradually returns. Reintroduce fats, red meats and strongly flavoured foods cautiously as the child gradually gets back to normal again.

CALLING THE DOCTOR

Sickness from minor causes usually passes within about six hours. If the child is sick for longer than this, and the sickness is not coming under control, you should call your family doctor. With babies it is wise to seek advice sooner, because of the greater danger of dehydration.

Call your doctor immediately if

A child often feels better if she cleans her teeth after being sick.

there are any other symptoms that worry you and particularly if the child shows any of the symptoms mentioned in the WATCHPOINTS box.

The doctor will need to know how long the vomiting has been going on, whether there has been diarrhoea, fever or any other symptoms and what the child has eaten. He or she will check to see whether the child has a fever and will advise you on how to care for the child at home. Oral rehydration powders may be prescribed (these are a properly balanced mixture of salts and sugars, which are added to water to provide a drink that makes sure that the body's lost salts, sugars and fluids are replaced.)

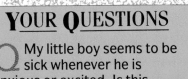

If the doctor suspects that the cause of the vomiting is something other than a gastric infection the child may be taken to hospital for tests and possibly treatment.

■ WARTS

Warts are very common, and usually quite harmless growths that are particularly likely to affect pre-teenage children.

SYMPTOMS

The most common kind of wart is a small, round growth on the skin surface, which has a rough, pitted surface. A wart is called a verruca (*see* separate entry) when it grows on the sole of the foot, and in this case it is usually a hard little knot more or less flush with the surface of the skin. The same is true of warts growing on the palms of the hands.

So-called plane warts, which are less common, but which usually occur only in children, are brown in colour and do not have a rough texture like the more common types of wart. Children are also prone to attacks of little white lumps known as *molluscum contagiosum*, which are closely related to warts.

Warts commonly grow on hands, knees and elbows, but can also occur on the child's face and ears.

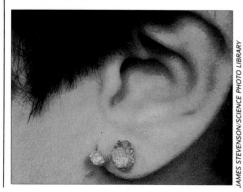

JAMES STEVENSON/SCIENCE PHOTO LIBRARY

CAUSES

Warts are the result of a viral infection which is spread by contact. The virus causes the skin cells to multiply in a disordered fashion so that a wart is effectively a benign tumour. Warts are the only type of growth known definitely to be caused by a virus. It is thought that a break in the skin makes it easier for the infection causing warts to enter the skin.

The child eventually develops immunity to the virus causing the wart, and the wart disappears. This can happen within a few weeks or months, but it may take a matter of years. On the whole, once immunity has been developed the child stops getting warts, and people rarely get warts when they are older simply because they developed immunity as children. However there are many varieties of the virus causing warts, so the child may have various types of wart before eventually becoming immune to all types.

TREATMENT

Many magical cures have been suggested for warts over the centuries but there really is no evidence that any of them works. Since all warts do eventually drop off as immunity develops, many apparent cures are simply the result of the infection having run its course.

There is no effective antibiotic against the virus causing warts, but various kinds of treatment are available. Although it is possible to get, without a prescription, paints and gels that are applied to warts, it is advisable to take your child to the family doctor if he develops warts.

Unless the warts are causing the child distress the doctor will probably suggest that you wait for a time as they may disappear spontaneously quite quickly. Otherwise, he or she will prescribe the most suitable preparation for your child's skin and advise you how to apply it. The treatment has to be applied carefully, only to the wart and not to the surrounding skin, and between applications the hard skin is rubbed off with an emery board or pumice stone as it loosens.

Occasionally the doctor may decide that the wart should be removed by burning, scraping or freezing if it resists other treatments.

YOUR QUESTIONS

Q Can warts be spread from person to person?

A Yes, warts can be spread by direct contact (for example, when children hold hands), or indirectly, from objects, such as a towel, that the child with warts has handled. A child can also spread his own warts by contact. So although warts are quite harmless, it is best to advise your children not to hold hands with children who have warts and if they have warts to try to avoid spreading them to other children, or to other parts of their own bodies, through contact.

Q Which parts of a child's body are most likely to be affected by warts?

A Although warts can appear on any part of the body, they are most common on the fingers and knees.

Q How long do warts last if they are not treated?

A This varies very much. In some cases warts disappear spontaneously within weeks, but sometimes they may last for up to three years.

■ WASP STINGS

Only female wasps sting, but most wasps are females. Although wasp stings usually do little harm they are certainly alarming and unpleasant and wasps can make quite a nuisance of themselves in late summer. Very occasionally a child may be extra-sensitive to wasp stings, and may develop an allergic reaction with the signs of shock, which needs medical treatment; and stings in the mouth are also potentially dangerous.

SYMPTOMS

Wasps generally do not leave their sting behind them, but if you look carefully you will see a small puncture mark on the child's skin where the wasp bit. The area round the mark will be red and sore and slightly swollen.

If your child is one of the very few who develop a serious allergic reaction to wasp stings or if he has been stung by many wasps there may be severe swelling. The child may become pale and clammy, with rapid, shallow breathing. He will probably feel dizzy and may swoon or lapse completely into unconsciousness. These are signs that immediate medical help is needed.

PREVENTION

If you are going to be outside when there are a lot of wasps or other biting insects about it may be a good idea to protect your child with an

When it is shown enlarged, a wasp looks pretty alarming. But in most cases wasp stings are not very serious and are easily treated by cooling the skin.

insect repellant. These are available as creams, lotions and sprays from any chemist's shop. Try the repellant on a small area of skin first, in case the child's skin is oversensitive to it.

Perhaps more importantly, teach your child not to panic and flap his arms about at the sight of a wasp. Wasps are much less likely to sting if not provoked. Try to make sure also that the child pays attention when eating outside, to avoid the dangers of being stung in the mouth.

TREATMENT

Many people believe that vinegar should be applied to wasps' stings, but this is just an old wives' tale, and the only effect the vinegar has is to cool the skin. This can be done better with an ice cube or a cold compress held over the sting.

A little antihistamine spray will soothe the sting and prevent it from flaring up. If the sting is obviously painful it is safe to give the appropriate dose of paracetamol.

SHOCK

If the child shows signs of shock, call an ambulance. If the child is conscious, keep him warm with his legs raised and supported so that they are above the level of his heart. If he is unconscious, put him in the recovery position (see p.115), keep him warm, and be prepared to give artificial respiration (see p.17) if he stops breathing while you are waiting for medical help to arrive.

STINGS IN THE MOUTH

If the sting is in the mouth, severe swelling may occur and this can affect breathing. Give the child ice cubes to suck, but if there is any sign of swelling or other worrying effects call your doctor or seek emergency help immediately.

YOUR QUESTIONS

Q I thought that wasps left their stings behind them. Is this not true?

A This only happens very rarely. But if any insect does leave its sting behind, you should remove the sting with tweezers or work it out with a needle. Tweezers or needle should be sterilized first, of course.

■ WATER ON THE BRAIN
See HYDROCEPHALUS

■ WEIGHT
See also GROWTH

Babies and children differ in body type just as much as adults do and two children of the same age may have completely different sizes and weights. For children of any age there is quite a wide range of weights and heights that are considered to be normal, and it is only if the child's weight falls above or below this range that you need to worry.

WEIGHT AND AGE

During the first few days of their lives, babies usually lose weight, and after

YOUR QUESTIONS

Q My four-year-old seems to have shot up in height but doesn't seem to have filled out at all. Is this normal?

A Children do noticeably change shape at about this age, and begin to look much less infant-like. This is because their proportions change, as their heads become less large in proportion to their bodies. The limbs also become longer in relation to the body as a whole. Your child probably has actually gained weight, while changing shape in this way. However, do consult your doctor if you have any reason to be worried about your child's growth and weight.

The charts on the right show the normal height and weight for boys (girls vary only slightly) from the ages of 1 to 12. Because children's growth rates vary, the charts show an acceptable range for each year of growth. You can assume that your son's growth is normal if his height and weight fall within the shaded areas for his age.

NUTRITION FOR CHILDREN

Children have much higher nutritional requirements, relative to their weight, than adults. This is because all the tissues in their bodies are increasing in size during the process of growth.

Children need large quantities of the right sort of food, not only to provide the building blocks for the new tissues but also to fuel the thousands of chemical reactions involved in the growth process – quite apart from the energy needed for their physical activity.

Calories and energy
The energy derived from food is measured in calories (more precisely, Kcal) and is normally used up at a fairly constant rate per day. The main sources are from carbohydrates and fats. Carbohydrates come from foods such as bread, cereals and pulses, and fats are found in milk, cheese, butter, vegetable spreads and oils. As they grow, children need very nearly as many calories per day as adults.

Carbohydrates provide about 4.2 Kcal of energy per gram weight and fats are more than twice as energy-intensive, providing about 9.3 Kcal per gram. Therefore the less fat your child eats the more carbohydrates he needs to make up the calories. The importance of energy-rich food is not always appreciated by parents, as so many adults keep putting themselves on weight-reducing diets. You should avoid giving your child too much sugar but you should not otherwise try to limit his intake of carbohydrates. Only grossly over-fed children normally become obese.

Protein requirements
The growing body also needs plenty of protein, the raw material from which the body's cells are built. Again, a child needs much more protein, relative to his size, than an adult. The best sources of protein are meat, fish and cheese, but peas, beans, pulses, nuts and cereals also provide protein, and are an excellent source when they are given in various combinations.

that there should be a steady overall weight gain, although at any particular time there may be short periods of little or no weight gain. Babies grow particularly fast, and put on a lot of weight, during the first four months, during which time they usually double their original birth weight. The child continues to increase quite fast in weight (and size) until the age of two, and you can expect him to have an appetite to match. But the increase in the second year is less dramatic than in the first — about 3.17kg (7lb) for the average child in the second year as

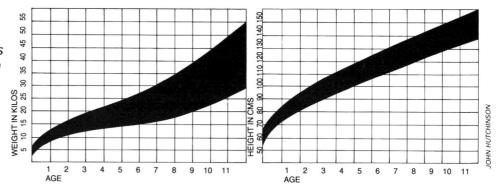

JOHN HUTCHINSON

COLLECTIONS/ANTHEA SIEVEKING

Children need a mixed diet which includes plenty of fresh vegetables. Eating together as a family helps to encourage healthy eating.

opposed to an average of 6.34kg (14lb) in the first year – and after this, weight gain levels out even more until the growth spurt of early adolescence.

Although it is interesting to see how your baby's weight changes, and an exciting milestone when he doubles and then trebles his birth-weight, weight gain is not the only guide to the child's development. If your child normally seems well, happy and alert there is almost certainly nothing to worry about, whatever his weight in comparison to that of other children of the same age. It is, however, unusual for children to lose weight, except for a short while during an illness, and if your child is losing weight, or if he is failing to put on weight and grow and seems un-well in any way at the same time you should consult your family doctor.

■ WEIGHT PROBLEMS

Weight problems can be due to digestive disorders or other under-lying (and rare) medical problems, but they are more often linked to poor nutrition. This can mean not eating enough (*see* WEIGHT) as well as eating too much of the wrong food, that is food that is filling but not nourishing.

UNDERWEIGHT BABIES

In babies, failure to put on weight may be a sign that the baby is ill or simply that she is not getting enough to eat. Consult your doctor or your health visitor for advice if your baby does not seem to be gaining weight as she should. If you are breastfeed-ing, you may need some advice on positioning, to make sure your baby is able to get a good feed and so stimulate a good milk supply. Feed-ing more often will build up a better supply. It's not recommended to start a baby on solids until the age of four months.

Some rare medical conditions can cause failure to gain weight. Your doctor will refer your child for tests if necessary to establish what the na-ture of the problem is.

POOR WEIGHT GAIN – CHILDREN

If an older child does not seem to be gaining weight as she should, first bear in mind that children do go through short periods from time to time when they put on little or no weight. For example, you do not

need to worry if a child who has recently been ill does not immediate-ly start gaining weight on recovery. It may be a month or so before she begins to gain weight again and there is nothing wrong as long as she is now eating well and seeming well. Whenever a child seems fit and well there is unlikely to be anything wrong, but you should always consult your doctor if you are worried. Nor-mally, if there is anything medically wrong there will be other symptoms apart from failing to gain weight.

ANOREXIA

Children sometimes suffer from the condition known as *anorexia nervo-sa*. This is more likely to affect teen-age girls, but younger children, in-cluding boys, can sometimes be affected.

Anorexia is thought to have emo-tional or psychological causes and the condition needs expert medical help. It causes the child to see herself as being overweight and to diet obsessively until she is pathetically thin, while at the same time thinking that she is too fat.

WATCHPOINTS

● Too much sugar is often one of the main culprits when a child is overweight. Never add sugar to drinks or food, and try to make sure that your child does not consume too many sweet, sugary drinks such as fizzy drinks and squashes. Natural fruit juice is naturally sweet and it is a good idea to dilute this. Water really makes the best thirst-quencher of all!

● If you are bottle-feeding your baby make sure you use the correct formula milk for the child's age, and do not dilute the milk more than recommended, so that the baby gets the right nourishment from the feeds. Always let your baby feed for as long as she wants, whether breast feeding or bottle feeding.

OVERWEIGHT

Overweight leads to obesity, which causes health problems. The problem often starts with the wrong eating habits in childhood.

There is a fairly wide range of acceptable weights in relation to height, and a child is in danger of becoming obese if she weighs more than the highest of these weights (*see* WEIGHT). Children are considered to be obese if they are 20 per cent or more overweight. Although most babies and toddlers tend to be pleasantly chubby, with well rounded tummies, if a baby or young child has rolls of fat on her arms, legs and tummy she may be overweight. Overweight babies and toddlers tend to be lethargic and less active physically than other children of their age.

If your child seems fatter than other children of her age consult your doctor or health visitor. It is unusual for medical problems to cause over-

SALLY & RICHARD GREENHILL

SALLY & RICHARD GREENHILL

Being overweight is a condition that often affects the whole family, and over-eating is generally involved. Parents and their children can be overweight without realizing it, just as anorexics (left) often wrongly see themselves as being fat.

weight, although it is possible that a glandular disorder may be suspected and investigated. It is much more likely that the child's diet is to blame.

DIET

If your child is bottle-fed, continue sticking to a recognized baby formula for drinks until your baby is at least a year old, though small amounts of cow's milk are fine for mixing with solid food from six months. Your baby may not always need milk to drink — try giving water occasionally to satisfy thirst, particularly in hot weather. For babies under six months, the water should be boiled. Your doctor will also probably advise you to avoid giving your child foods high in sugar, such as sweet rusks, biscuits or cake.

As the child gets older, try to make

YOUR QUESTIONS

Q Is it a good idea to make children eat what they are given or should they be allowed to eat what they like?

A This is a difficult question. It is certainly not a good idea to make children eat everything you put on their plates, as their appetite is usually a good guide to what they need and you do not want to get them into the habit of eating too much, to be 'good'. On the other hand, a child who has been allowed to eat too much between meals will not feel hungry at mealtimes.

It is certainly unwise to let your child fill up on fattening foods that are relatively low in nutritional content, such as biscuits and cakes, and much better to be flexible with mealtimes than allow your child to get into the habit of eating snacks. Encourage your child to eat pieces of fresh fruit and vegetables as snacks and keep sugary, processed foods to a minimum.

sure that she does not develop the habit of filling herself up on sugary snacks between meals, rather than eating nutritious food at mealtimes. As a rule, snacks between meals should be limited. Lollies, ice cream, sweets, chocolate, biscuits and cakes should be occasional, rare treats and not daily fill-me-ups. It may be necessary to look at the whole family's eating habits, and make a few changes in your own diet too. Bear in mind that the most important factor in obesity is eating too much of all foods. Do not be afraid to ask your doctor's advice in planning a healthier way of eating.

Exercise is important too. If your child is overweight she will feel less active. Try to encourage your child to enjoy being lively and active from an early age – this will be good for her mentally as well as physically.

■ WEIL'S DISEASE

This is an unusual, but serious disease that occasionally hits the headlines. It is caught from water that has been contaminated by rats.

SYMPTOMS

The symptoms are similar to those of severe flu, and break out three days to two weeks after the child was exposed to the infection. In some cases the symptoms die away after a week to ten days, but in others the liver, heart and kidneys are infected and this can cause jaundice and heart or kidney failure, which can result in death if not treated. Some forms of the disease can also cause meningitis (*see* separate entry).

CAUSES

The disease is usually caused by a strain of bacterium called *Leptospira*, which is carried in the kidneys of rats without apparently making the rats ill. It is transmitted to people from the rats' urine, usually when people swim in canals, rivers or pools that are infested with rats. (The danger is greater if the water is stagnant.) The bacteria enter the body through

Canals and slow-moving rivers can be a host to rats, which may infect the water with the bacteria that causes a rare infection known as Weil's disease.

breaks in the skin (cuts or grazes) or through water being swallowed.

Dogs and farm animals can also carry strains of the *leptospira* bacterium, and can pass on infection to people. This type of Weil's disease often causes meningitis.

TREATMENT

Treatment is with penicillin, and for it to stand the best chance of being successful it has to be given early. However, since the first symptoms are just like those of flu, the disease is not always recognized at first. Once it has begun to develop it is less responsive to penicillin, and complications can develop. These are given the appropriate treatment in hospital, where the child may have to be put on a kidney machine or be given other intensive treatment to save his life.

Because the disease is so dangerous, it is very unwise to allow children to run the risk of catching it. Do not allow your children to swim in rivers, canals and pools, especially if the water is stagnant; and if your child develops flu-like symptoms after coming into contact with water (perhaps, for example, by falling in while boating), consult your doctor straight away.

■ WHEEZING
See also ASTHMA, BRONCHITIS

Wheezing occurs when the flow of air in and out of the lungs is made difficult because of a narrowing of the child's airways.

SYMPTOMS

When children find breathing difficult and begin to wheeze, the characteristic sound this makes is worse during breathing out. Wheezing attacks can sometimes come on very suddenly and cause the child to panic, which is very alarming for parents too. Some children seem to be prone to suffer from conditions that cause wheezing.

CAUSES

Wheezing is caused by conditions which narrow the bronchi (the main airways into the lungs). This can be brought on by a spasm in the muscular lining of the bronchi, as in asthma, or by excessive swelling and inflammation of the bronchial wall, as in

bronchitis. Both these conditions are fairly common in young children.

Other, more unusual causes are oedema, or fluid, produced in the throat or lungs by inflammation or heart failure; an obstruction of the airways; or something constricting the throat.

TREATMENT

If your child repeatedly suffers from wheezing you should make an early appointment with your family doctor, who will listen to the child's chest and check his breathing using instruments known as a flow meter (which measures the speed at which air can be blown out of the lungs) and a spirometer (which measures the volume of air breathed out).

Treatment, which depends on the cause of the wheezing, is usually very successful. If the child has oedema of the throat or an obstruction in the airways hospital treatment will be given, but asthma and bronchitis (see separate entries) can usually be treated at home.

Consult your doctor if your child has wheezing attacks. You may find that inhaling steam from a jug of hot water eases the symptoms.

JOHN WATNEY

■ WHITLOW

A whitlow, medically known as a paronychia, is an inflamed swelling at the side of a toe or finger nail. These can be quite painful and often need medical treatment, but they are nevertheless a minor problem.

SYMPTOMS

Whitlows usually come on suddenly. The nail fold at the side and base of the nail becomes red and feels hot and painful. The finger soon begins to throb and the area round the nail becomes swollen as pus builds up. If this does not die down, or is not treated, pus will begin to collect under the nail and the whole finger-tip can become infected.

Whitlows known as herpetic whitlows also start suddenly, but in this case with one or more blisters appearing near the nail fold. These blisters grow and multiply and are filled with a clear fluid which gradually becomes more cloudy. Herpetic

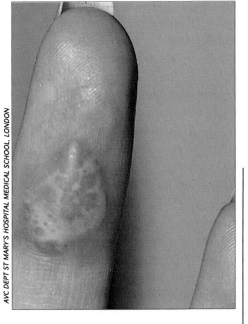

AVC DEPT ST MARY'S HOSPITAL MEDICAL SCHOOL, LONDON

Whitlows usually develop round the sides of the nails, but they are caused by infections that can also affect the fingers.

whitlows can also appear on other parts of the fingers as well as round the nails.

CAUSES

The infection enters through a damaged cuticle or an ingrowing toenail. It can be due to common bacteria or more rarely to fungi. The skin is more vulnerable when it is wet and this is why babies and toddlers who suck their thumbs and fingers and people who do a lot of washing up tend to get whitlows. Nailbiting also makes the skin more susceptible to infection. The herpes virus can be transferred from the mouth to the fingers when a child with cold sores bites her nails or sucks her fingers.

TREATMENT

If a whitlow flares up, you should see your family doctor as soon as possible as there is always a risk of the infection spreading. The doctor may prescribe antibiotic or antifungal ointment to be applied to the infected area and in some cases will also prescribe antibiotic tablets to be taken by mouth.

If the whitlow is full of pus it may

need to be lanced under local anaesthetic. This allows pus to escape; it usually brings almost immediate relief and the whitlow will be completely healed within a few days.

There are specific ointments or paints for whitlows caused by the herpes virus.

■ WHOOPING COUGH

See also ENCEPHALITIS, IMMUNIZATION, PNEUMONIA

This disease, medically known as pertussis, is still fairly common in childhood, although it is easily prevented by immunization. In very young babies it can, very rarely, be fatal, and it is frightening and unpleasant for children of any age, even though full recovery is the norm.

SYMPTOMS

Whooping cough develops slowly, and for the first week or so the symptoms are merely those of the common cold. You are unlikely to suspect that the illness is whooping cough at this stage unless the child has been in contact with someone known to have the disease.

The full symptoms will probably not begin to develop until a week or more later, when the cough gets worse and the 'whoop' develops. The 'whooping' cough attacks in violent, prolonged bouts which leave the child almost suffocating, as it is impossible to draw breath during the cough. The cough produces phlegm at the end of an attack, when the child gasps for breath in a characteristic, 'whooping' way, and then will often retch or vomit. In many cases the child feels quite well once she has recovered from the coughing attack, and until the next attack comes on.

As with many illnesses, the symptoms are not equally violent in all children. Some children have mild attacks of whooping cough which can be mistaken for a cold at every stage, but, unlike those of a cold, the symptoms last and last. In many cases, it is ten or twelve weeks

---

YOUR QUESTIONS

Q Would a child with a whitlow ever have to have a nail removed, and if so, would the nail grow back again?

A Very occasionally, if treatment is not given in time, the nail has to be removed. A new nail will grow again within about three months, but occasionally there will have been some damage to the nailbed and the new nail may be flatter and more grooved than the original nail.

Q My two-week old baby had a whitlow on his toe. Is this unusual?

A No. Babies seem to be quite prone to developing whitlows on fingers and toes. Usually these respond very quickly to antibiotics given in the form of drops.

MIKE ABRAHAMS/NETWORK

Unless your doctor advises against it you should have your child immunized against whooping cough as soon as possible.

before the child recovers from a bad case of whooping cough, and even mild cases take several weeks.

DANGERS

A serious case of whooping cough is in any case alarming and debilitating for a child. But in some unusual cases, especially in babies, or if the child has a weakness, complications may develop.

The chief complication is that of secondary chest infection, which may lead to pneumonia and cause permanent lung damage; but whooping cough can, in up to two per cent of cases, also cause encephalitis (inflammation of the brain), and the coughing fits can cause a burst blood vessel in the brain and, in susceptible children, epileptic fits. These complications are less likely to result if

the child receives good medical care, and it is important to call your doctor as soon as you suspect that your child has whooping cough.

CAUSES

Whooping cough is caused by bacteria, which are passed from child to child during coughing fits. Because the early symptoms are so similar to those of the common cold, parents may not realize that a child is infectious until it is too late and other children have been infected. If your child seems to have a cold and has in the previous ten days or so been in contact with someone who has whooping cough, it is best to assume that she has contracted the disease and keep her away from other children. She will be infectious for at least three weeks after the first attack.

The cause of the 'whoop' lies in the fact that, because the coughing fits attack so suddenly, the child has no chance to draw breath before an

attack. During the coughing it is impossible to breathe, because the glottis at the opening of the windpipe closes spontaneously, and at the end of a bout of coughing the child is almost suffocating. She quickly learns to breathe in against the resistance of the glottis, and this makes the characteristic noise.

Small babies sometimes fail to acquire this knack, which is partly why the disease is more dangerous for them, and it is also possible for a child with whooping cough not to make the 'whooping' noise.

PREVENTION

There is a vaccine for whooping cough, and although this is not absolutely effective in preventing the disease, any child who has had the vaccine will suffer from only a mild form of the disease if she subsequently contracts it.

However, there are some problems connected with the vaccine. The first is that it cannot be given to babies before they are two months old, so that very small babies most at risk cannot be protected.

The second problem is that there

YOUR QUESTIONS

Q My little girl had whooping cough badly nearly a year ago but she still seems to get whooping attacks. Is this normal?

A Yes. The illness itself can take two to three months to clear up, and afterwards it is quite normal for children to have attacks of whooping for a year or so whenever they get a cold. This is a habit rather than a recurrence of the disease, which leaves the child with permanent immunity. You can reassure yourself and your little girl that this will soon be over now, but if the attacks do go on for much longer it would be wise for you to let your doctor know.

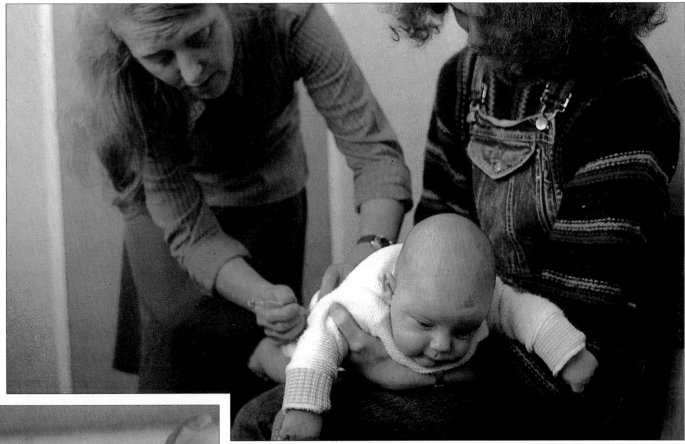

MIKE ABRAHAMS/NETWORK

has been some controversy connected with the vaccine itself, with some reports having linked the vaccine with brain damage in young children (see IMMUNIZATION). It now appears the risks of this happening are much less than was previously thought, though research still continues. Ask your doctor if you are in any doubt. Children with a family history of convulsions or epilepsy, for example, should receive the vaccine, contrary to previous belief. The evidence is that epidemics can occur if widespread immunization isn't carried out, and most children are at more risk from the illness and its complications than from the vaccine.

Most family doctors will be sympathetic with parents who are worried about whether to have their children vaccinated and will explain the pros and cons to them, so do not be afraid to consult your doctor.

T R E A T M E N T

Although whooping cough is caused by bacteria, it is not simple and straightforward and there is no real cure for it. Your doctor should be called as soon as you realize that there is something wrong, even if your child is not making a 'whooping' sound when coughing. The doctor may decide to take a throat swab in these cases to establish whether the illness really is whooping cough.

Antibiotics will probably be prescribed to prevent secondary infections and limit the period during which the child is infectious. In the case of a baby, the doctor may decide that she should be taken to hospital to make sure that she does not suffer from any complications,

Immunization against whooping cough is usually given when the child is three, five and nine months old. The serum used (left) is a triple vaccine and also protects against diphtheria and tetanus.

and otherwise he or she will advise on the care of the child. You will be able to help the child during coughing fits by supporting her in a sitting position, and reassuring her to keep her calm.

You may find that a moist atmosphere, provided by bowls of steaming hot water, helps during an attack, and you should not expose the child to cigarette smoke. You will need to make sure that bowls are available for the child to vomit into. Giving her frequent small meals may help her to keep food down, and, as always when a child is ill, she should be given plenty of fluids to help prevent dehydration.

If the child feels quite well between attacks, she need not spend the time in bed, but she must be kept away from school and should not be allowed to do anything strenuous until she is better. Especially at night she will probably feel very ill and frightened during coughing fits, and will need a great deal of comforting. If possible, she should not be left alone, so ensure that someone is there to reassure her when she has night-time attacks.

■ WIND

See also COLIC, INDIGESTION

'Wind' is not a medical term, but to most mothers it has a perfectly clear meaning.

SYMPTOMS

When parents speak of the baby having 'wind', they mean that he is unhappy and irritable after a feed and becomes cheerful again after 'breaking wind'. This is different from colic, which can make the baby cry for hours on end. A baby with colic cannot be soothed or comforted and has regular attacks, whereas a baby will just get 'wind' occasionally, or for only brief periods.

CAUSES

Paediatricians disagree over what

causes 'wind' and they do not all accept the theory that it is gas in the stomach, caused by the baby having swallowed too much air. However, many mothers find that the baby seems to suffer from the condition if he has been gulping air during a feed. Certainly babies often seem to suffer from 'wind' if they have gulped down their milk. 'Wind' might also be a sign of milk allergy.

PREVENTION

Feeding the baby when he first feels hungry, before he is screaming with hunger, and feeding him in a calm, relaxed atmosphere often seems to help to prevent 'wind'. With bottle-fed babies, using a teat with larger holes may help for babies prone to attacks of 'wind'. Holding the bottle obliquely as the baby feeds will help to ensure that he does not suck in air. Or you can buy a special design to overcome the problem.

TREATMENT

Patting the baby rhythmically on the back until he burps usually gives relief. In more persistent cases gripe water can be given, strictly in accord-

ance with the recommended dose. Some parents find that fennel water, a traditional old remedy, solves the 'wind' problem.

■ WORMS

See also TOXOCARIASIS, TOXOPLASMOSIS

There are several kinds of worm that can live in the human intestines — usually doing little harm. Children seem particularly vulnerable to threadworms, which are extremely infectious and can affect everyone in the family. In some parts of the world, particularly where the weather is hot and sanitation is poor, worms can be a great problem, causing debilitating diseases. The technical term for worms that are parasites of human beings is 'helminths'. These are divided into three main types: roundworms or nemataodes; tape-worms or cestodes; and flatworms or trematodes.

A lot of babies feel uncomfortable after a feed — particularly if they have been gulping and swallowing air. A few firm pats on the back will usually put things right.

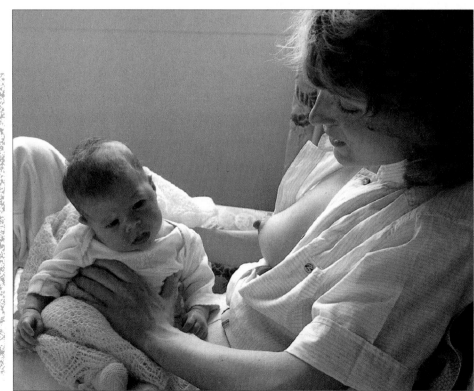

The ascaris, shown in its larva form (right) and as an adult (below), and the whip-worm (bottom) are both roundworms.

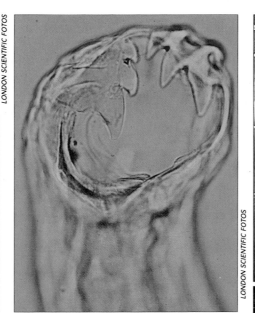

LONDON SCIENTIFIC FOTOS

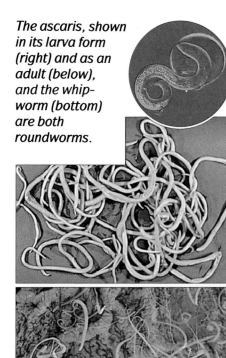

C. JAMES WEBB

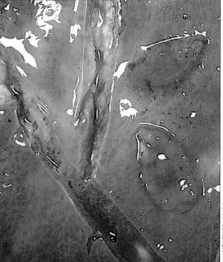

HEATHER ANGEL

The hookworm (enlarged above) is rare in developed countries.

LONDON SCIENTIFIC FOTOS

C. JAMES WEBB

The tapeworm (above) can be up to 11 feet (3.3 metres) long and comes from undercooked infected meat.

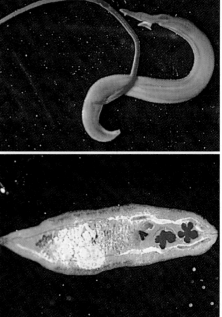

LONDON SCIENTIFIC FOTOS

Liver fluke (top) infests cattle; Bilharzia fluke (centre) affects people, and Opisthrocus viverna (bottom) lives on fish.

SYMPTOMS

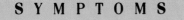

Threadworms, the most common worm, cause anal itching, and as the worms are active at night this causes the child's sleep to be disturbed. Although they usually affect the child's anus (back passage) they can also sometimes get into a girl's urethra (front passage) and vagina. This can cause pain on passing water, and there may also be a vaginal discharge. Some of the worms are passed out of the body in the faeces (stools), and are visible as tiny white threads.

Roundworms usually cause no symptoms, but are visible as white worms of the size of an earthworm when they are passed out of the body in the faeces. A child who is badly affected may look thin and feel slightly 'unwell'.

Tapeworms have been linked to various kinds of digestive upset, but again there are no specific symptoms until the worm is expelled from the body. These worms, as their name implies, are like a length of tape or ribbon and can be alarmingly long.

CAUSES

Threadworms can be passed from person to person as eggs can get on to the child's hands when he scratches. If the child puts his fingers into his own mouth this causes reinfection, and when he touches other people he can transfer the eggs to them. Eggs also drop off into the general household dust and linger in bedding and on towels. The eggs can also contaminate food.

The eggs that enter the digestive tract hatch out in the intestines, and when the female is fully developed she makes her way out of the child's body via the anus and lays more eggs there, which causes the itching.

Most roundworms are only found in conjunction with tropical climates and poor sanitation, where their eggs can contaminate food. Some types of roundworm are normally parasites of dogs and cats and can be transferred to the child from an infected animal. Again they hatch out in the intestines, where they then lay their eggs. Eggs may be excreted before they hatch and are passed on through poor hygiene.

The eggs of tapeworms can infect both pork and beef. They are killed

YOUR QUESTIONS

Q Is it true that there is a worm you can catch from eating watercress?

A You are thinking of the liver fluke – a flatworm that can sometimes be found on watercress that has grown where sheep graze. You are perfectly safe as long as you buy watercress that comes from a recognized source, but it is not advisable to pick and eat wild watercress.

Liver fluke can also be found in fish and it is a fairly common human parasite in South-East Asia, where fish is eaten raw.

Q What is hookworm?

A This is a type of worm that rarely causes problems in the developed countries. It is prevalent in underdeveloped countries and is caught by walking barefoot in places where sanitation is poor and the ground is contaminated by excrement. The worms cause a mild form of anaemia and can only be treated by strong drugs.

by thorough cooking, but can enter the digestive system if meat that has not been thoroughly cooked is eaten. In most countries meat is checked by inspectors before it is allowed to be put on sale and is very rarely contaminated by tapeworms.

TREATMENT

Fortunately, once they have been identified, worms are easily treated, and although the very thought of them makes people feel squeamish there is no reason to feel embarrassed if you suspect that your child has worms. Take her straight to the doctor, who will prescribe a drug known as piperazine (for threadworms or roundworms) or niclosamide (for tapeworms). Make sure that you follow the instructions carefully when giving the drug, so that the right amount is taken at the right time.

PRECAUTIONS

Since threadworms' eggs can so easily be passed from person to person, the doctor may well advise you to treat everyone else in the family (including yourself) as well as the child, and this is a sensible precaution. It is also important to observe the strictest standards of hygiene, washing your hands and scrubbing under the nails after going to the lavatory, before eating, and when about to handle food. Don't let children share towels and sheets if anyone in the family has worms, keep the infected child's fingernails short so that they cannot harbour eggs, and make sure that boys and girls alike wear pyjamas in bed so that their fingers are less likely to come into contact with the eggs.

■ WOUNDS
See BANDAGES, BLEEDING, DRESSINGS, FIRST AID, SCARS

■ WRY NECK

The medical term for wry neck is 'torticollis'. A child can wake up one morning with wry neck, and it may be found in young babies.

Treatment by an osteopath can cure wry neck if it does not get better on its own, and can be given to adults and children.

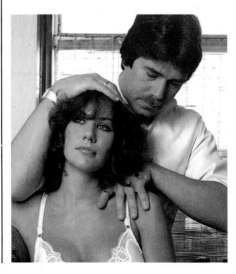

SYMPTOMS

The child's head is twisted to one side and he is unable to move his neck and head properly. This can be painful as well as feeling stiff.

CAUSES

The condition is caused by a spasm in one of the two main muscles of the neck (known as the sternocleidomastoideus muscle). It may happen when the child has been sleeping in an awkward position and it is sometimes a minor complication of tonsillitis. Babies can be born with wry neck, as a result of a difficult birth.

TREATMENT

Generally no medical treatment is needed for wry neck in children and the condition wears off within a few days. Ointments that ease muscular pain can be rubbed in and it is best to keep the child's neck warm by wrapping it in a scarf. A well wrapped, half-filled (to make it flexible) hot-water bottle or warm pad held against the neck can be soothing and help the muscle to relax, and if the child is in pain she may need to take paracetamol (in the appropriate dose for her age), especially at bed-time.

This is the kind of condition that can often be successfully treated by osteopathy (*see* separate entry), and if the neck has not put itself right within a few days you may wish to consult an osteopath if you know of one who is well recommended. Very occasionally if a baby is born with a wry neck surgery may be recommended to put it right, but more often gentle manipulation will right the condition.

INDEX

Index compiled by INDEXING SPECIALISTS, Hove